WESTERN VOICES IN CANADIAN ART

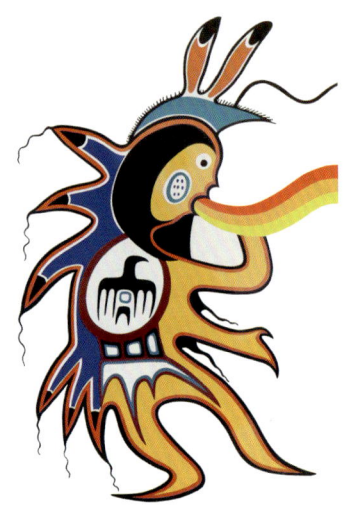

WESTERN
VOICES
IN CANADIAN
ART

PATRICIA BOVEY

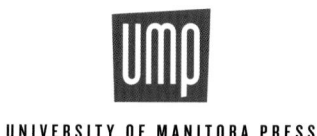

UNIVERSITY OF MANITOBA PRESS

PUBLISHED IN COLLABORATION WITH ST. JOHN'S COLLEGE PRESS

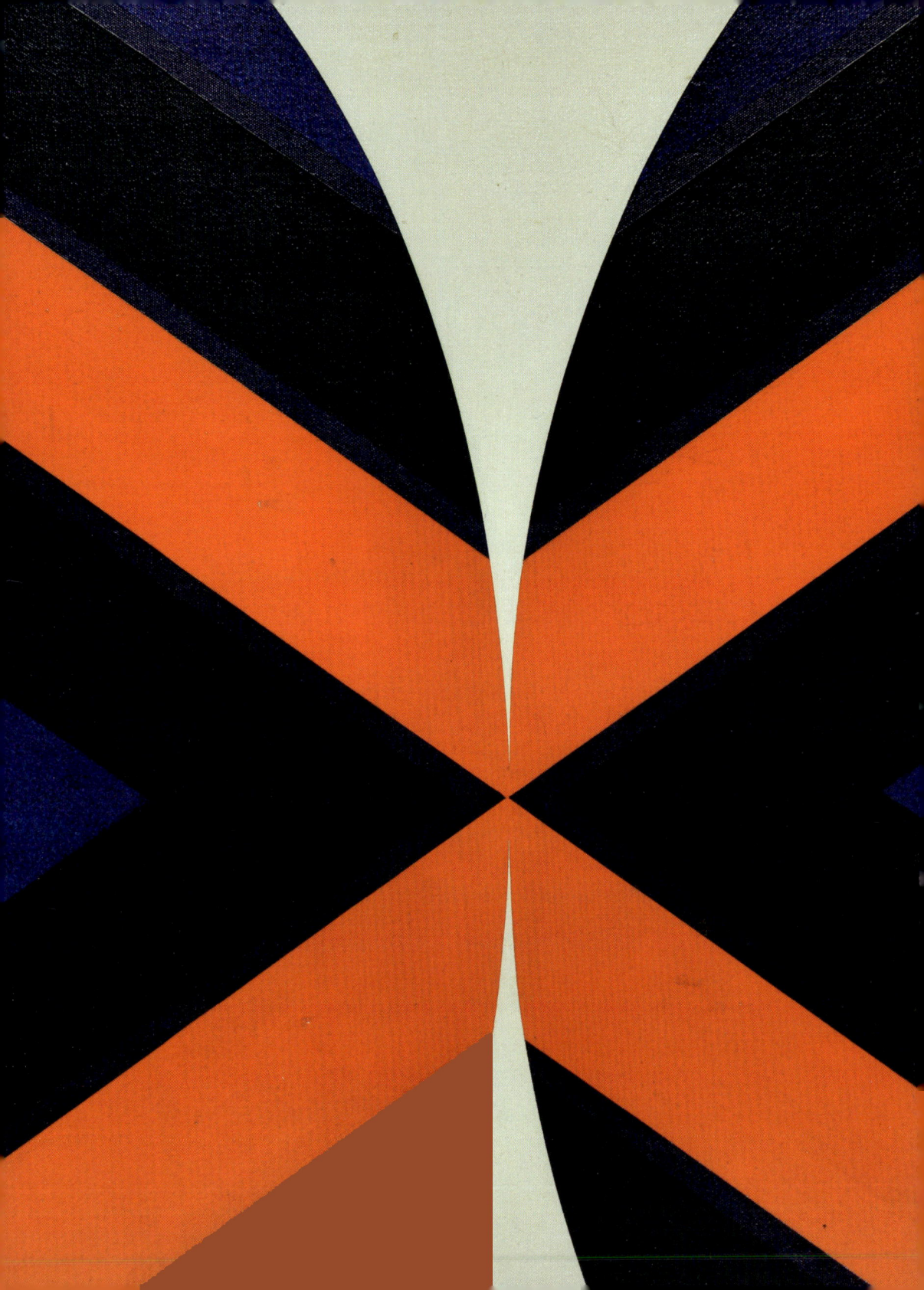

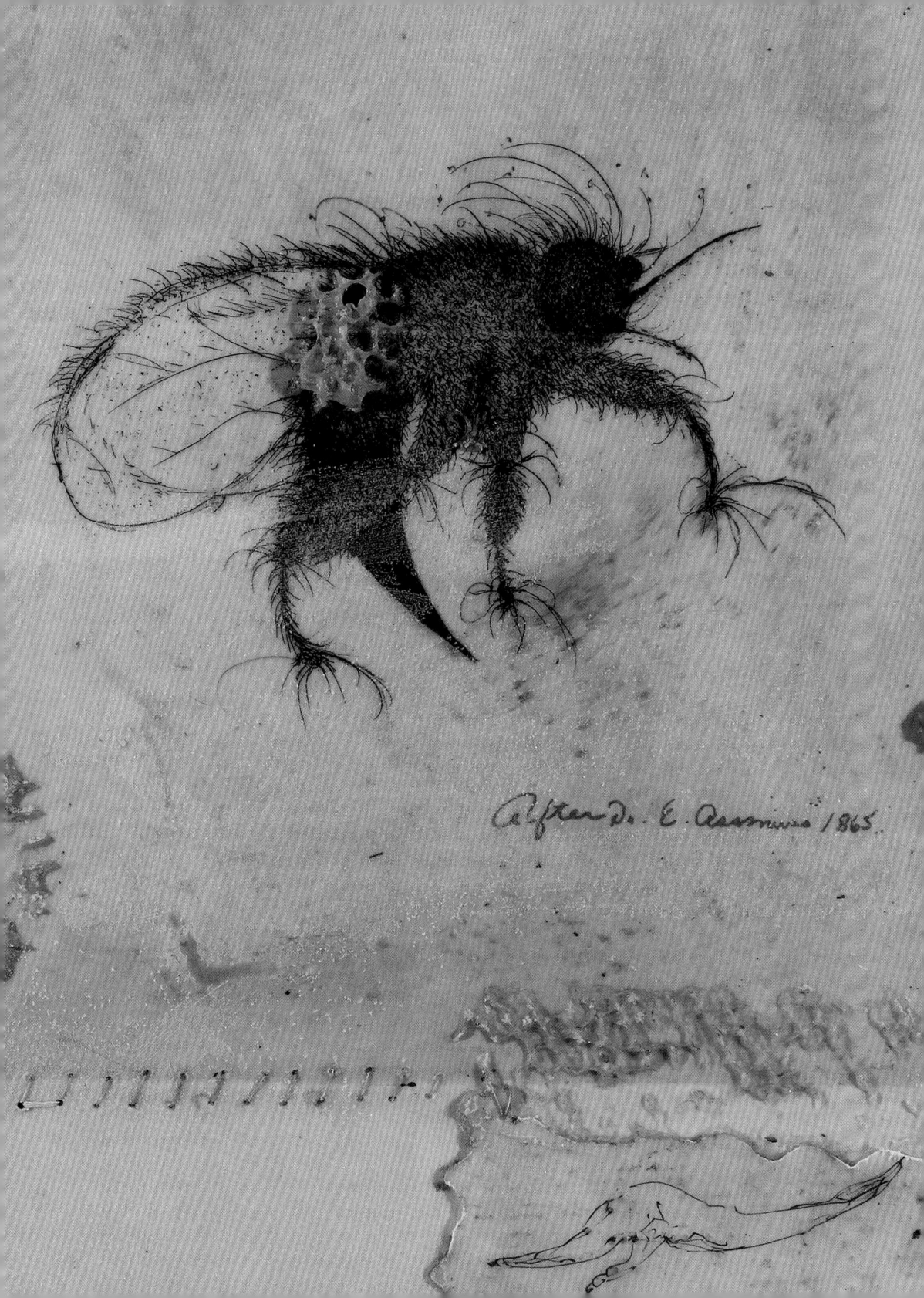

After do. E. Assmuss 1865.

. . . .

This volume is dedicated to Western Canadian artists who have,
and have had, the visual acuity to inspire and enrich society by allowing
us to see, think, and engage.

and with special thanks to

The Hunt family of Fort Rupert of the Kwakwaka'wakw Nation, who
adopted me as an honorary member in April 1994 in a special ceremony
during which I was honoured to dance in a headdress and Chilkat blanket
of celebrated Chief and artist Mungo Martin.

and to

Manitoba artist and Knowledge Keeper Val Vint, for hosting my
First Nations Prairie Focus Group in February 2005, which accorded me
permission to write about the work of Prairie Indigenous artists.

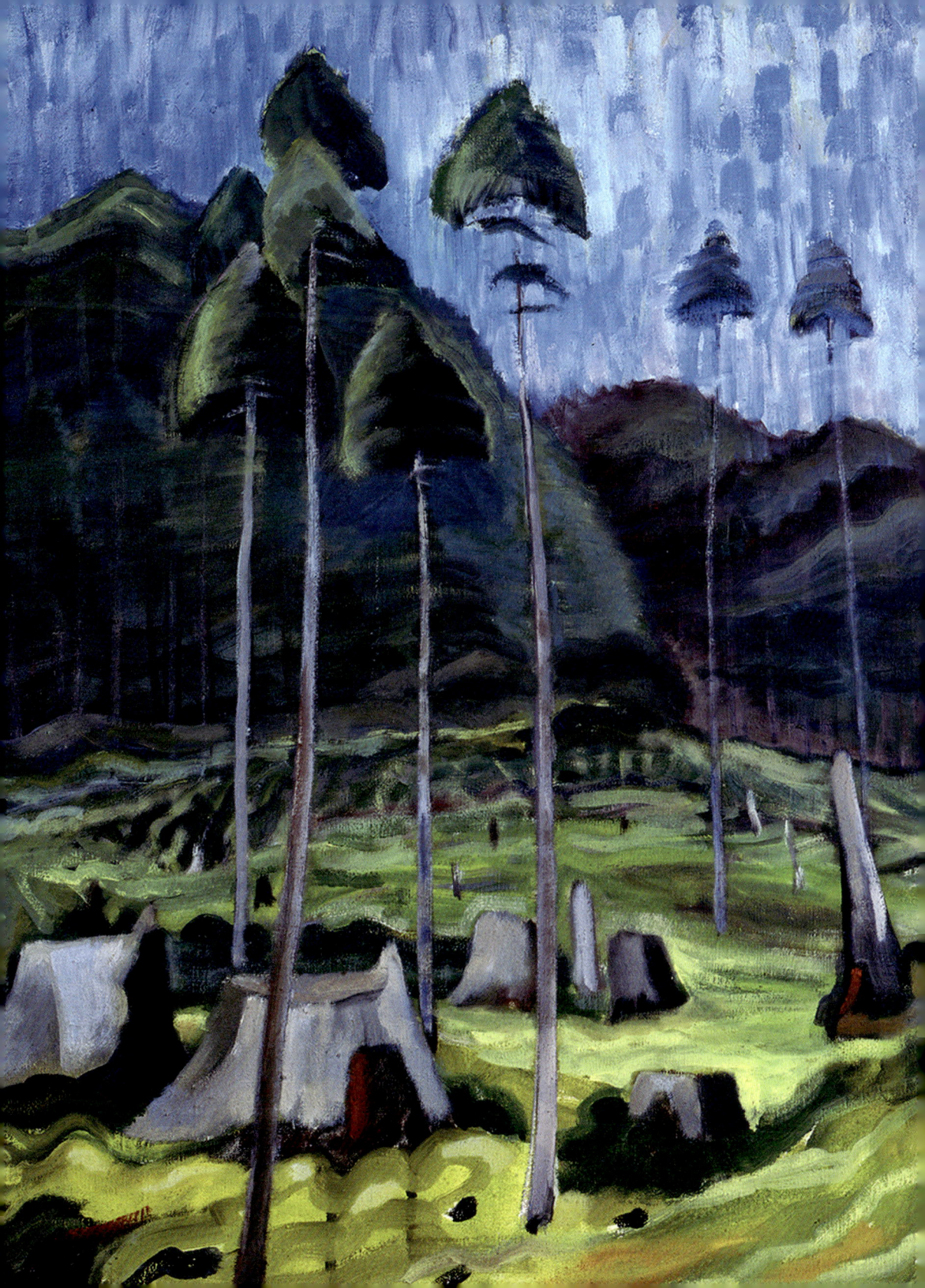

University of Manitoba Press
Winnipeg, Manitoba, Canada
Treaty 1 Territory
uofmpress.ca

Cataloguing data available from Library and Archives Canada
ISBN 978-0-88755-047-8 (bound)
ISBN 978-0-88755-069-0 (PDF)
ISBN 978-0-88755-083-6 (EPUB)

Cover and interior design by Frank Reimer

Printed in Canada by Friesens

The University of Manitoba Press acknowledges the support of the Canada Council for the Arts.

The University of Manitoba Press acknowledges the financial support for its publication program provided by the Government of Canada through the Canada Book Fund, the Canada Council for the Arts, the Manitoba Department of Sport, Culture, and Heritage, the Manitoba Arts Council, and the Manitoba Book Publishing Tax Credit.

Publication of this book has been made possible by the generous support of Margaret Berry, Danny Bubis and Jennifer Blumenthal, Chris and Gerry Couture, Bryce and Nicki Douglas, Susan Glass and Arni Thorsteinson, Diane and Dave Johnston, Julia Berry Melnyk, Ted Ramsby, Rob and Penny Richards, Hartley and Heather Richardson, Tanis Richardson, Lewis Rosenberg, and Eleanor and J. Timothy Samson.

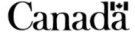

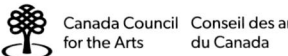

FRONT COVER

Robert Houle, *Muhnedobe uhyahyuk* [Where the gods are present], 1989.

BACK COVER AND SPINE DETAILS FROM LEFT TO RIGHT

Steve Gouthro, *Green Rider*, 2012.

Winston Leathers, *#17 Cosmic Order/in a line plane*, from the series *Cosmic Variations*, 1972.

Linus Woods, *Buffalo Runner*, 2011.

Norval Morrisseau, *Power of the Spirit of Manitou*, 1978.

William Kurelek, *Portrait of the Artist as a Young Man*, 1950.

Lita Fontaine, *The Pagan*, 1996.

FRONT SECTION DETAILS

PAGE II **Jackson Beardy**, *Thunder Dancer*, 1981.

PAGE IV **Roy Kiyooka**, *Untitled— Geometric Abstract*, 1963–1964.

PAGE V **Aganetha Dyck and Honeybees**, *after Dr. Eduard Assmuss 1865*, 2009.

PAGE VII **Emily Carr**, *Odds and Ends*, 1939.

PAGE IX **Tim Paul**, *Nas-Win-Is (When Night and Day Cross)*, 1997.

PAGE XII **William Pura**, *The Suburbs*, 2000.

PAGE XIII **Kent Monkman**, *The Chase*, 2014.

PAGE XIV **Ted Harrison**, *Northern Sun*, 1989.

PAGE XVII **Pat Martin Bates**, *The Angel of the Blue Sky is Crying Parallax Tears*, 1998.

PAGE 454

Terrance Houle, *liniiwahkiimah*, 2012.

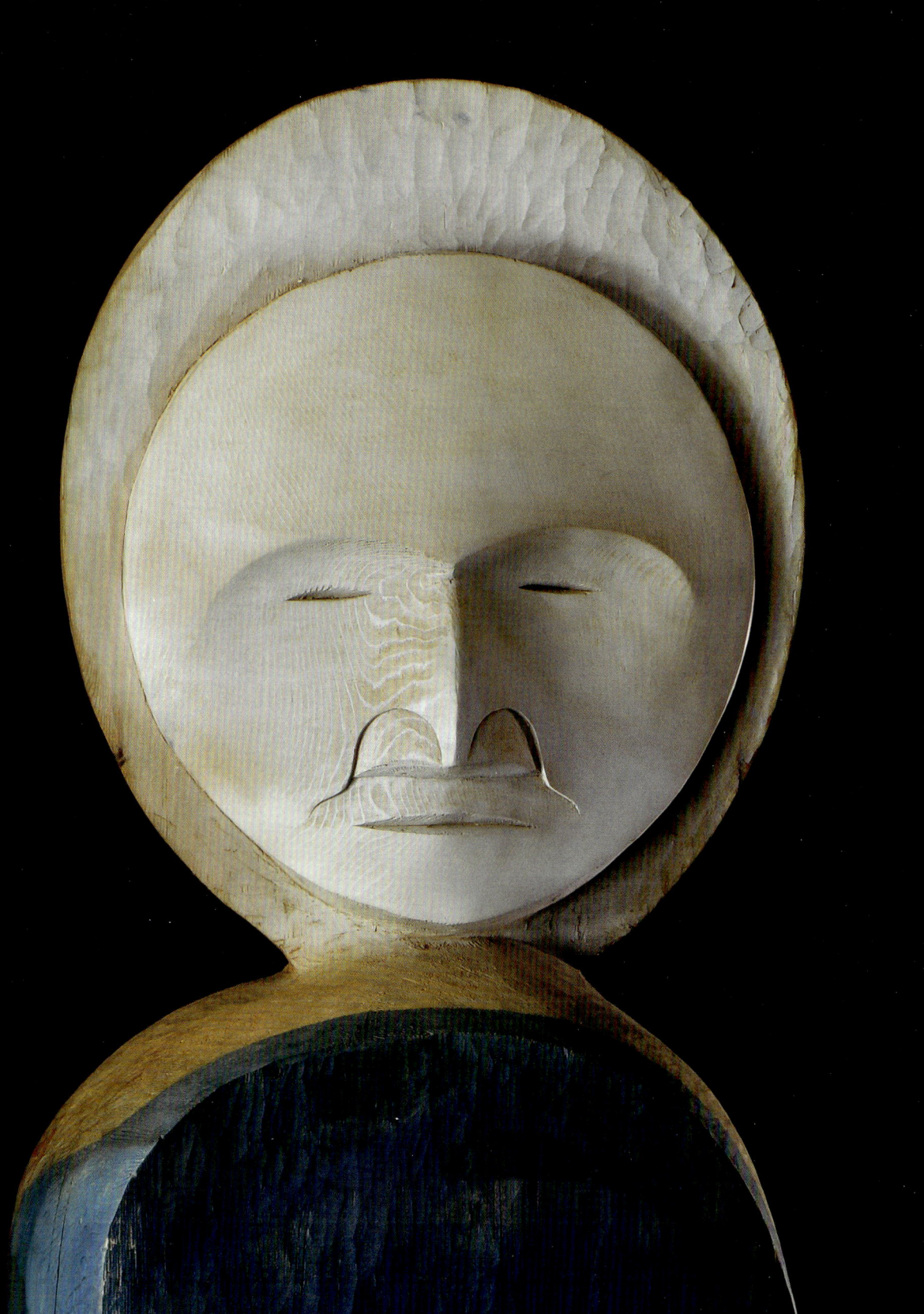

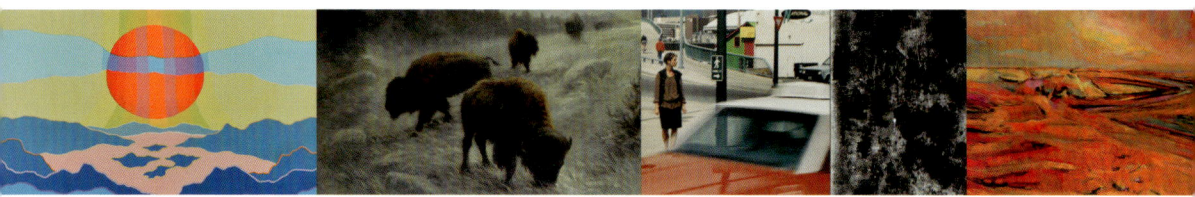

CONTENTS

Preface   xv

Part One – An Evolving History

I. New Departures: Developing Artistic Voices in Canada's West   3

Context and Overviews: The Birth of Distinctive Visual Expressions   4

1821–1870: Itinerant and Resident—Experiences and Expressions   13

1870–1930: Supports and Opportunities—Coming of Age   20

1930–1960: Frameworks and Artists' Recognition   29

1960–1990: Breaking Norms   44

Into the Twenty-First Century: Leading-Edge Innovations   55

II. Expanding Techniques: Creating a New Visual Language   59

Two-Dimensional Twists   61

Investigations in the Third Dimension   91

New Media and Engagements   102

Part Two – Prevailing Themes in Western Canadian Art

III. Landscape as Culture   119

Landscape as History   122

Landscape as Place   128

Landscape as Spirit   160

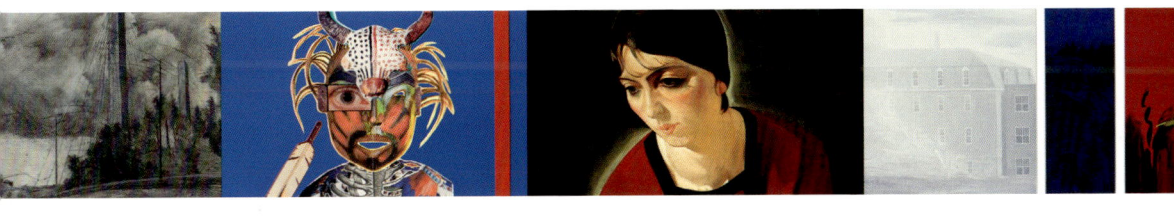

IV. Urbanization and New Meanings   171

        Changing Dynamics: The Rise of Cities   172
        Neighbourhoods: Streetscapes and Back Lanes   192
        Lifestyles: Industrialization, Work, and Leisure   202

V.   Abstraction into the Spiritual   221

        Abstracted Realities   223
        Religious Philosophies and the Spirit Abstracted   250
        Abstracting through Sculpture   270

VI. People: Portraits and Inscapes   285

        Portraits: Commissioned and Not   287
        Psychological Inscapes   314
        Perspectives of Human Form: The Figure and the Abstract   330

VII. Visual Voices and Societal Concerns   341

        The Environment and Climate Change   343
        Health and Human Rights   354
        Self-Rule and Post-Colonialism   372
        Residential Schools and Reconciliation   382
        War and Conflict   392

        Epilogue   406
        Acknowledgements   407
        Appendix: Western Canadian Art Milestones   409
        Illustrations   420
        Notes   429
        Selected Bibliography   440
        Index   444

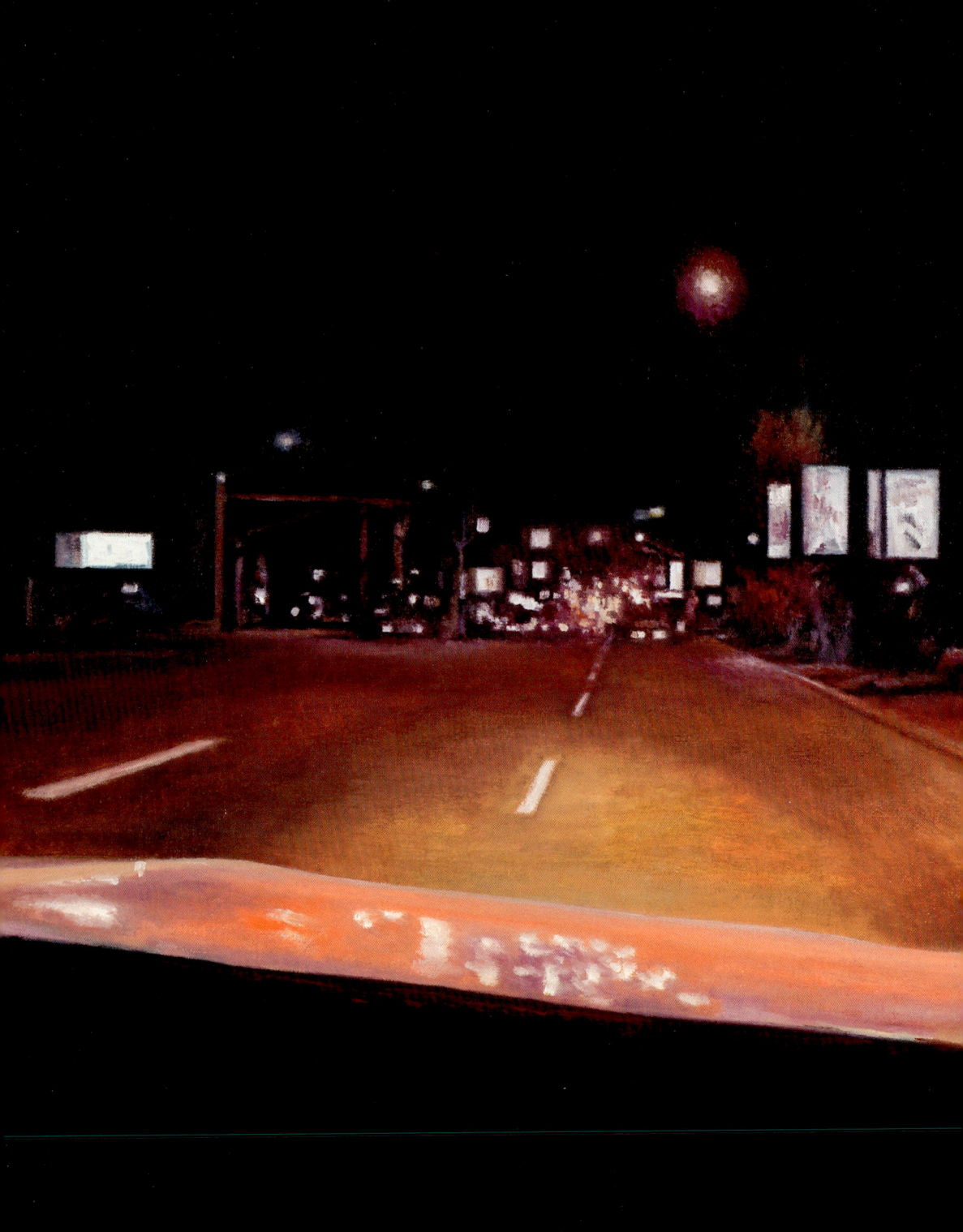

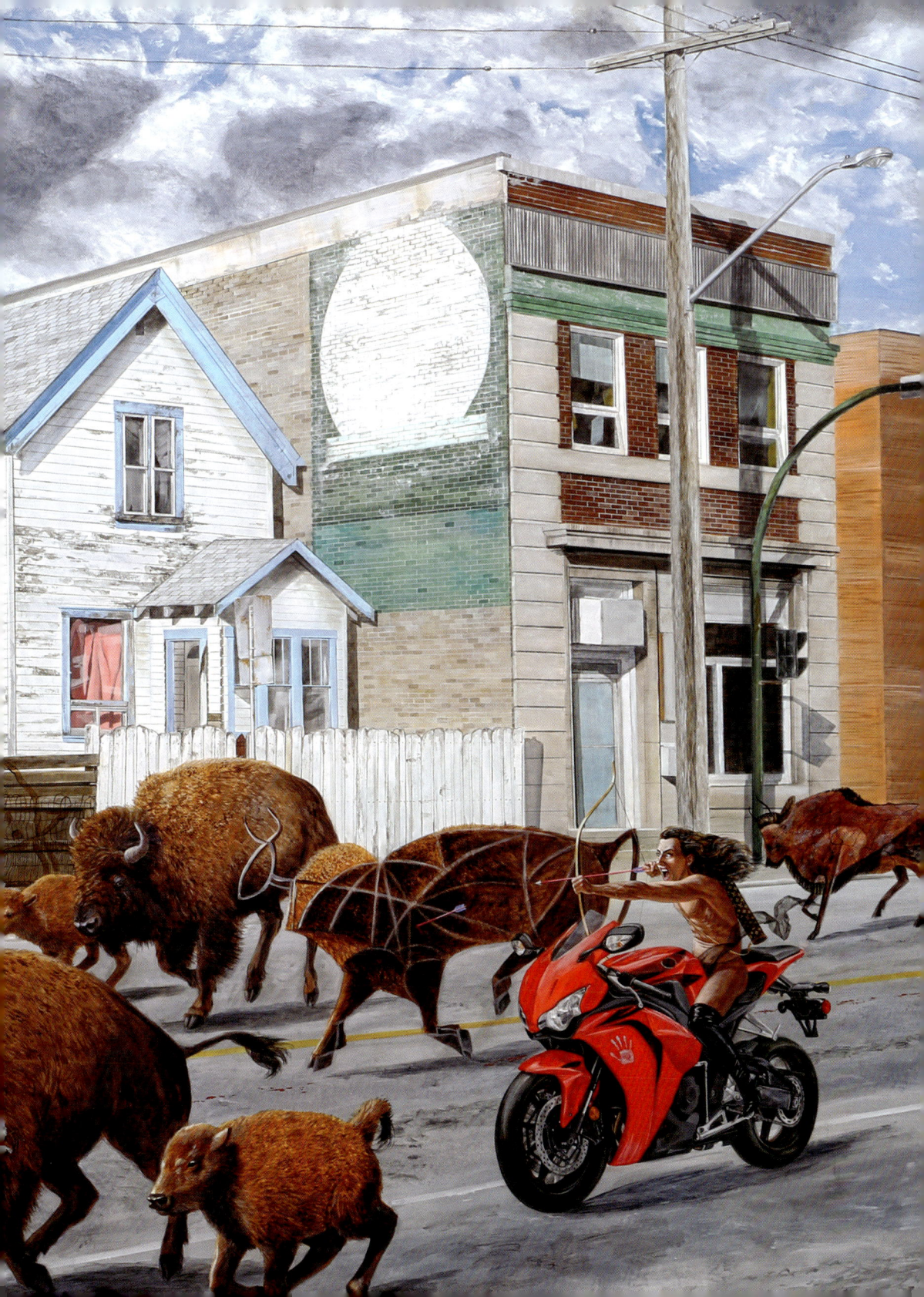

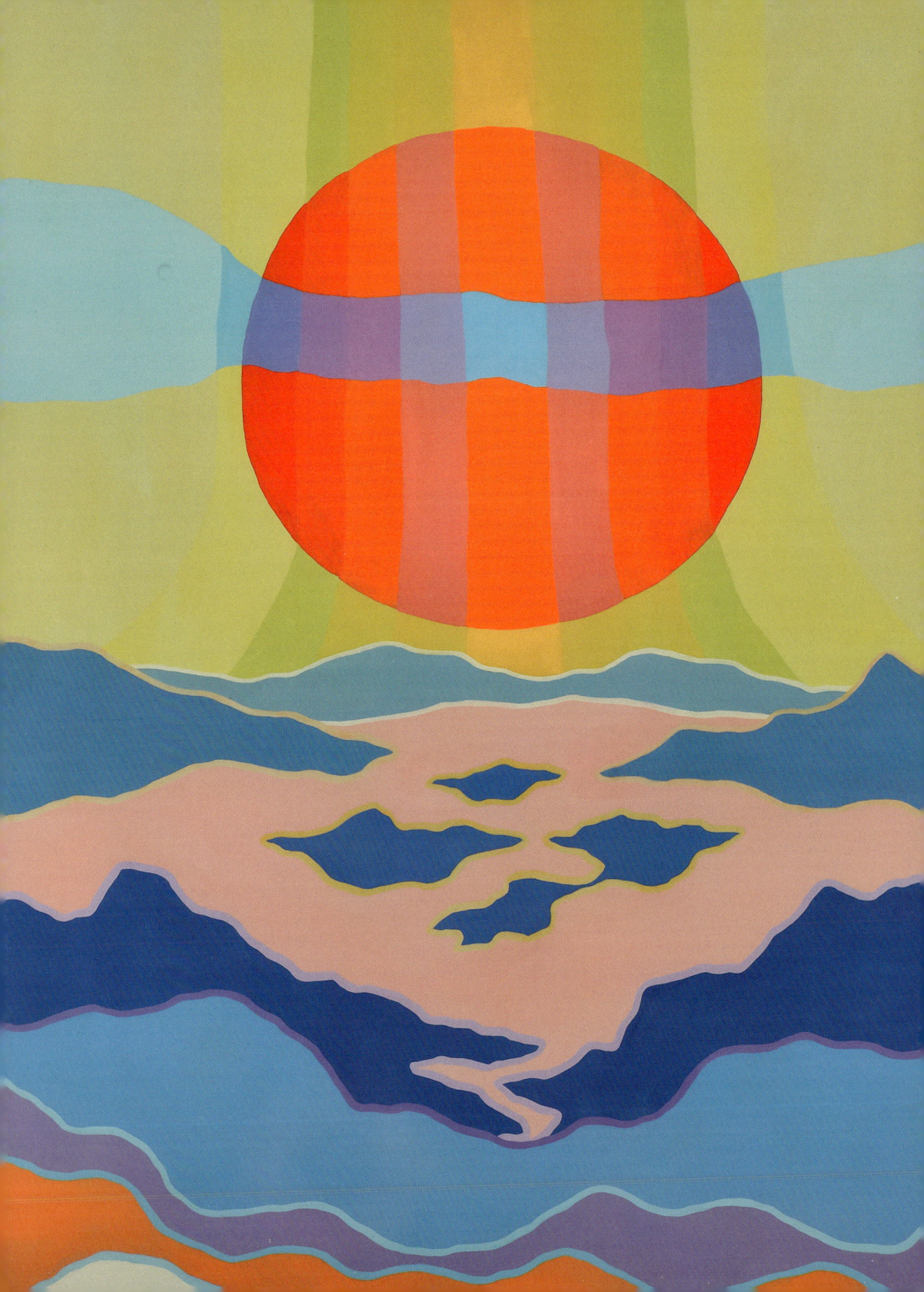

PREFACE

IT HAS BEEN A REAL PRIVILEGE to write this book. I admit it has been in the making for decades, during which time I have gathered material, interviewed artists, curated exhibitions, and written about work in various books, catalogues, and articles. My goal in these pages is to bring the depth, scope, and importance of the creativity of Western Canadian artists to the fore. Much groundbreaking art in all media has been created in our four western provinces, spelling new directions for Canadian art as a whole. In reality the excellence of art from the region is far too vast to cover in one volume. Nonetheless, I felt it was important to address some of the key ideas, themes, and significant milestones in Canadian art that have emanated from Manitoba, Saskatchewan, Alberta, and British Columbia.

Excellent exhibition catalogues, monographs, and volumes dedicated to art in individual provinces abound, but the literature on Canadian art has been missing an overview of the West as a whole. I hope *Western Voices in Canadian Art* fills that gap, and meets my commitment fifty years ago to author and art historian Russell Harper, who, in 1970, challenged me to write about the work of Western Canadian artists.

In a volume such as this many artists and much strong and substantive work cannot be included. For that I am sorry, and I am all too aware of omissions. Space was limited and selections were difficult. In the end decisions were based on my years working with Western Canadian art. My curatorial career began as Manitoba was celebrating its Centennial year and has been spent in the West since. It therefore seems fitting that this manuscript was submitted to the University of Manitoba Press fifty years later, in Manitoba's 150th anniversary year, and on the eve of British Columbia's 150th in 2021.

The diversity in Western Canadian art includes the richness of the visual perceptions of First Nations and Métis artists—the Blackfoot, Cree, Anishinaabe, Oji-Cree, Haida, Kwakwaka'wakw, Coast Salish, to name but some. Pre– and post–Second World War immigrants from many parts of the globe—including the United Kingdom, western and eastern Europe, Asia, Africa, South America, Mexico, and the United States—have added immeasurably, too. First- to fifth-generation Canadians are core to our visual story, as are the contributions of artists who left to travel, study, and live elsewhere, and returned with new perspectives.

My focus is on the pioneering visual directions from the Canadian West that became significant turning points in Canadian art. Examining past and present insights and approaches, I have woven innovations by themes rather than delineate work according to provincial borders. This means there will be recurring references to some artists as their work addresses different themes of this volume. As Alberta Indigenous artist Terrance Houle aptly said, "We don't have geographical boundaries."[1] Neither do the ideas and impacts of the work of the artists of the West.

Part 1, "An Evolving History," is an introductory chronological overview from the 1780s to the present, contextualizing major events, issues, and the wider environment within which artists worked as well as various technical developments in the visual arts. Part 2, "Prevailing Themes in Western Canadian Art," examines specific themes from multiple perspectives, each crossing geographical boundaries and multiple decades. A comparative international, national, and Western Canadian chronology of major arts events and their contexts concludes the volume in the appendix.

"Seminal," "contribution," and "influence" are three important concepts in this discussion. "Seminal" is defined as "having possibilities of future development, or highly original and influencing the development of future events";[2] "contribution" is defined as "adding to or augmenting the field"; and "influence" is defined as "to flow into." "Influence," an astrological term in the fourteenth century, referred to the "streaming ethereal power from the stars acting upon character or destiny." That essence of flowing, or streaming ethereal power, is especially relevant to artists' influences. No serious discussion of developing schools of painting, styles, or visual approaches can be had without acknowledging the manifold conscious and unconscious inspirations for artists' works and thoughts. The seminal contributions of Western Canadian artists have resulted from myriad "influences," those from elsewhere, artists' own personal experiences and places, their times, contemporary and past art practices, and the defining aspects of culture, politics, and ideas.

My views have developed from years of looking at artists' visual expressions and the many conversations I have had with artists in all disciplines. Studio visits have been an important ballast for me throughout my professional career, and I thank all those who have so generously welcomed me and shared their viewpoints and perspectives. Visual and verbal insights, past and present, are grounding and inspirational.

Maxwell Bates wrote in 1962:

I am an artist, who, for forty years
Has stood at the lake edge
Throwing stones in the lake.
Sometimes, very faintly,
I hear a splash.[3]

His "splash" was far greater than he realized. It is my hope that this volume may at least be a "faint splash" in celebrating Western Canadian artists. May these pages open readers to the rich extent of pioneering work from the West, and encourage artists to continue breaking barriers of visual expression and others to write about that which space has precluded here.

If I have any overriding message at all, it is to listen to the visual voices of artists. They tell us so poignantly who we are, what we must cherish, and what we must address as a society.

Patricia Bovey

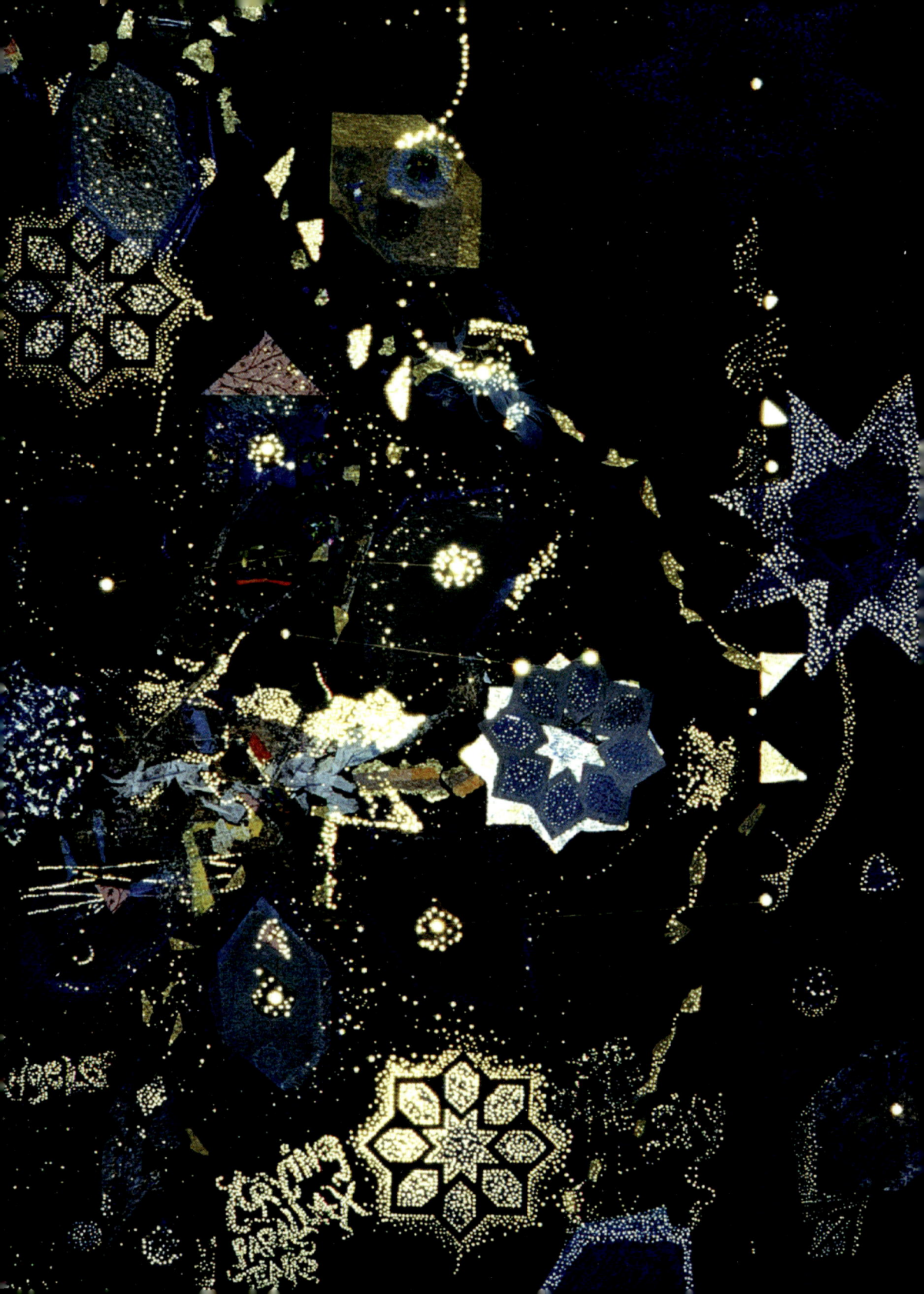

PART ONE

An
Evolving
History

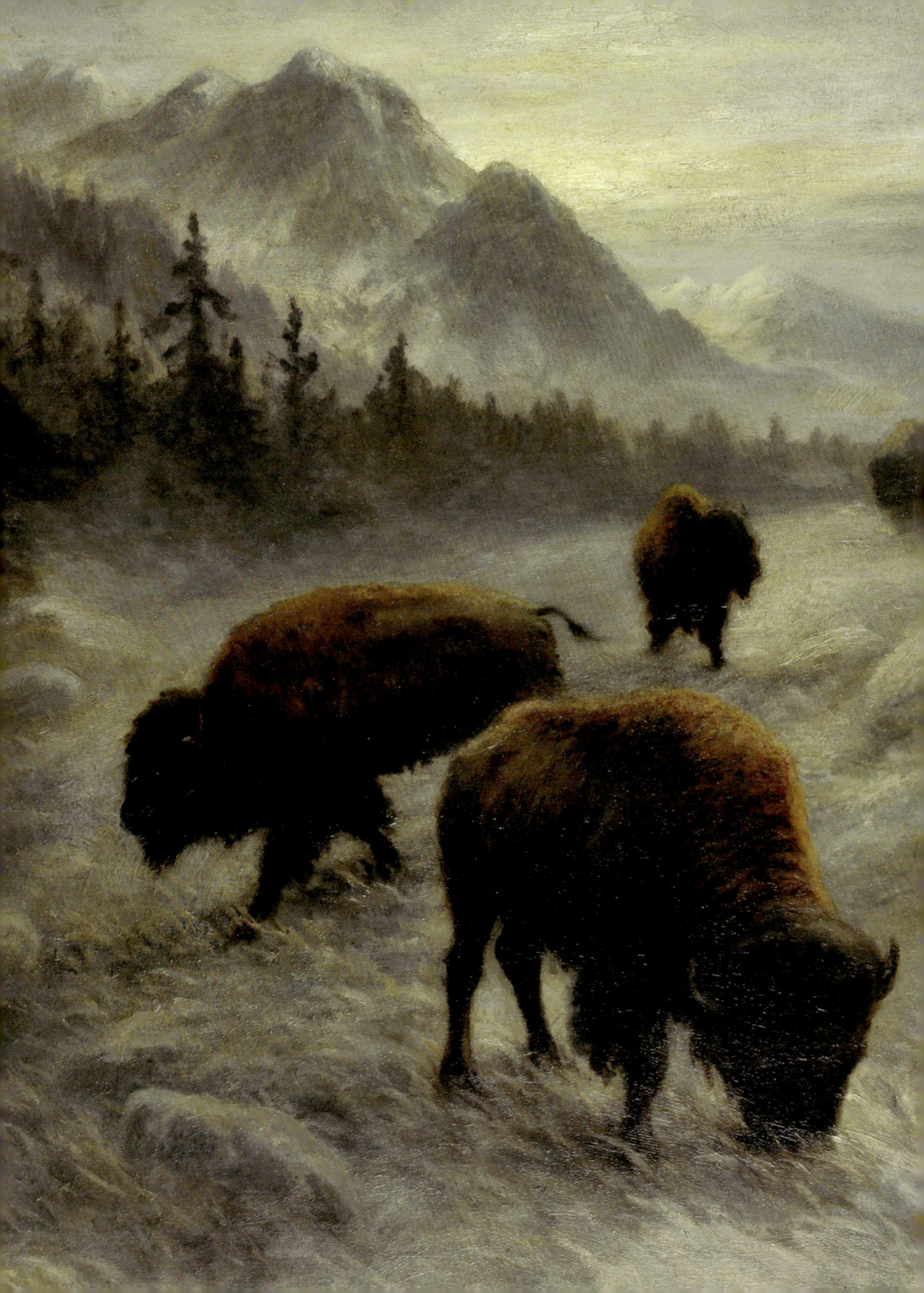

I New Departures: Developing Artistic Voices in Canada's West

"Art validates cultures." [1]

Europeans and North Americans from 1650 to 1850 alike often used the words "barren," "cold," "desolate," and "inhospitable" to describe Canada's West, as R. Douglas Francis does in his discussion of early Western Canadian art.[2] The art that has come out of Western Canada, however, actually dispels that description of this vast and inspiring part of our country. "Honest," "light," "skies," and "space" are more applicable words. Portraying its diversity of place, people, and customs, Western Canadian art has had a substantial impact from the outset and, as former Senator Murray Sinclair opined in the epigraph above, clearly validates the many cultures across the West, Indigenous and non-Indigenous.

Western Canadian art is rich and multifaceted. Visual expression, essential to Indigenous cultures in Canada for millennia, has been integral to their spiritual beliefs, thought, and life. In more recent times, drawing from diverse sources and influences, varying cultural and artistic backgrounds, differing landscapes, and multiple spiritual dimensions and personal circumstances, Western Canadian artists have been particularly vibrant contributors to Canadian art and culture. Their many seminal visual explorations and experimental creative dimensions comprise distinctive aspects in Canadian art. As Russell Harper wrote in the 1960s, "The country's art . . . takes on more meaning when examined as an integral part of the life of an expanding nation."[3]

Frederick Verner, *Buffalo in the Foothills*, 1914 (detail).

Context and Overviews:
The Birth of Distinctive Visual Expressions

The story of Western Canadian art began with the millennia of visual expressions by Indigenous people, their carvings, quill work, birchbark biting, and early pictographs. The colonial era commenced when European artists first travelled in the Canadian West on land and sea exploration expeditions in the late eighteenth century. The first professionally trained artists to settle in the western territories came to Red River in 1821. Uncharted by Europeans, this western territory was the centre of the fur trade, and many of the artworks were done for the Hudson's Bay Company in London. By the latter part of the nineteenth century, artists were hired by the railway and engineering firms to encourage settlement in the new land, where they met unexpected hardships of mosquitoes, floods, snow, and heat. These drawings and paintings from the early forays are compelling first-hand depictions and perceptions of places, exotic flora and fauna, Indigenous peoples and lifestyles, and ceremonial events and treaty signings.

The appreciation of Canadian art on the international scene was slow; that of Western Canada was even slower. In 1946 John Davis Hatch Jr. of the Albany Institute of History and Art in New York made truly interesting observations about Canadian art: "The study of Canadian Art History [is] still in its infancy. . . . The span of Canadian art is far greater than that in our country. . . . Painters in our country have been far more numerous, probably because of the larger number of inhabitants in the United States. One suspects, however, that in the proportion of artists to the population, Canada might be found to lead. Certainly the quality of the work produced . . . merits Canadian artists more serious consideration and study by the people in the United States than they have received in the past."[4] Four major international exhibitions of Canadian art were held in the first half of the twentieth century: the *Wembley Exhibition* in London in two parts in 1924 and 1925; one in 1937 at the Musée du Jeu de Paume in Paris; *A Century of Canadian Art* in 1938 at London's Tate Gallery; and the 1946 exhibition in Albany. Unfortunately, few Western Canadian artists were included in any of these milestone exhibitions. The work in the 1924–25 controversial *Wembley Exhibition* of Canadian art in Britain included the Group of Seven, Montreal's Beaver Hall Group, and Western Canadian artists James Henderson, Emily Carr, and Lionel LeMoine FitzGerald (with *Summer Afternoon, The Prairie*, 1921). That exhibition, according to Anne Clendinning, who wrote about the exhibition in *Social History*, was "divided into roughly two groups: the scenic and the industrial. The main corridor consisted of panoramic murals of the Canadian landscape including cornfields, homesteads, prairies, mountains and forests."[5] The 1938 Tate exhibition, *A Century of Canadian Art*, was from the National Gallery of Canada (NGC) during Eric Brown's directorship included 263 works aimed to strengthen Canada–United Kingdom

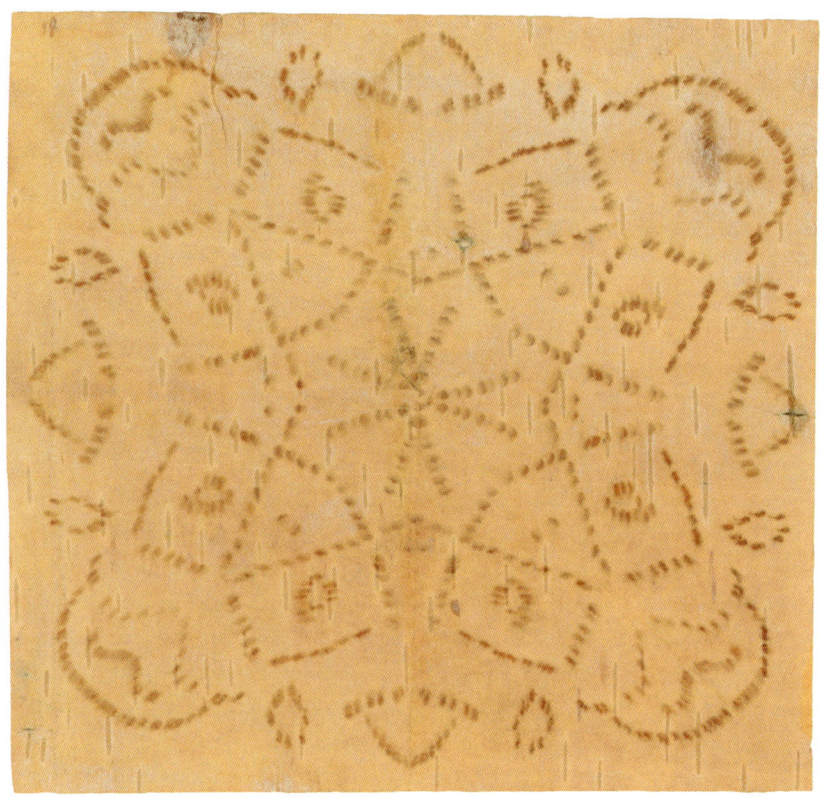

relationships. It was broad in scope, with portraits, landscapes and religious works, and it received good reviews in the British press. West Coast First Nations artists and Emily Carr were included alongside Paul Kane, Cornelius Krieghoff, Robert Harris, Tom Thomson, and members of the Group of Seven.

The 1946 Albany exhibition presented seventy-five works, five by artists who had travelled to or worked in the West: Paul Kane (with a work done in the State of Washington); *British Columbia Coast* by Constant Auguste L'Aubinière (who studied with Corot and Daubigny in France); *Blunden Harbour* by British Columbia's Emily Carr; *Doc Snider's House* by Manitoba's Lionel LeMoine FitzGerald (1890–1956); and *Tulips* by Cavin Atkins (who had studied at the Winnipeg School of Art). Only work from Eastern Canada, however, was discussed in the exhibition catalogue.

FIGURE 1.1. **Angelique Merasty**, *Birchbark Biting*, 20th century.

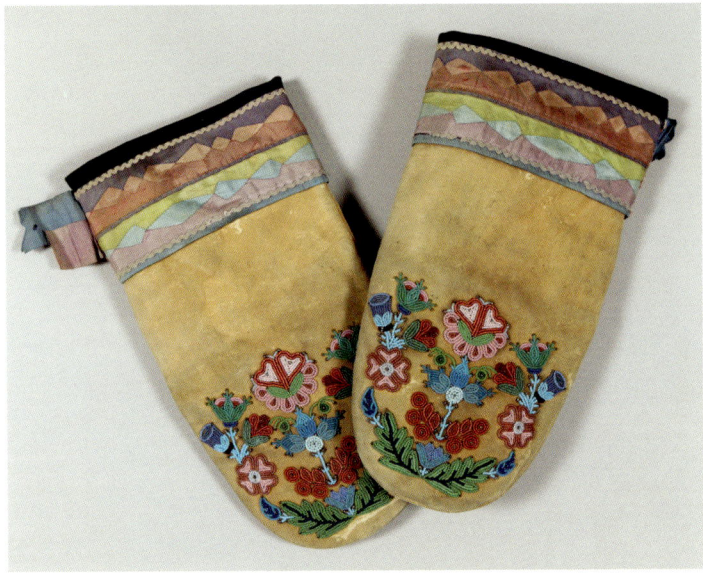

FIGURE 1.2.
Unknown artist,
Mittens, 1870–1880.

Burgeoning Talents: Inspirations and Firsts

Many artistic "firsts" originated in each of Canada's four western provinces. Home to the first European artist to settle in the West, Peter Rindisbacher (1806–1834) in 1821, Manitoba has consistently been a hotbed of leading-edge work in almost every decade, from realism, abstraction, and innovations in installation and performance art, to new media and computer-generated art. From 1950 forward, individual artists, organizations, the Winnipeg School of Art, arts collectives, and artists' groups together created the phenomenon dubbed the "Winnipeg Effect," an impact felt across Canada. The development in Winnipeg of one of two of Canada's first artist-run spaces, Plug In, the other being Open Space in Victoria, pushed the boundaries further for the presentation of new art. Artists organized and ran these non-collecting spaces and determined the exhibition programs with much fewer bureaucratic structures and considerably shorter timelines than established public galleries. By the late 1960s artists felt art galleries were not reacting fast enough to new contemporary expressions or considering cutting-edge art.

Further west, groundbreaking work was likewise substantial. Emerging in the 1960s, Saskatchewan's Regina Five and the Emma Lake Artists Workshops have been inspirational for

FIGURE 1.3. **Emily Carr**, *Blunden Harbour*, c. 1930.

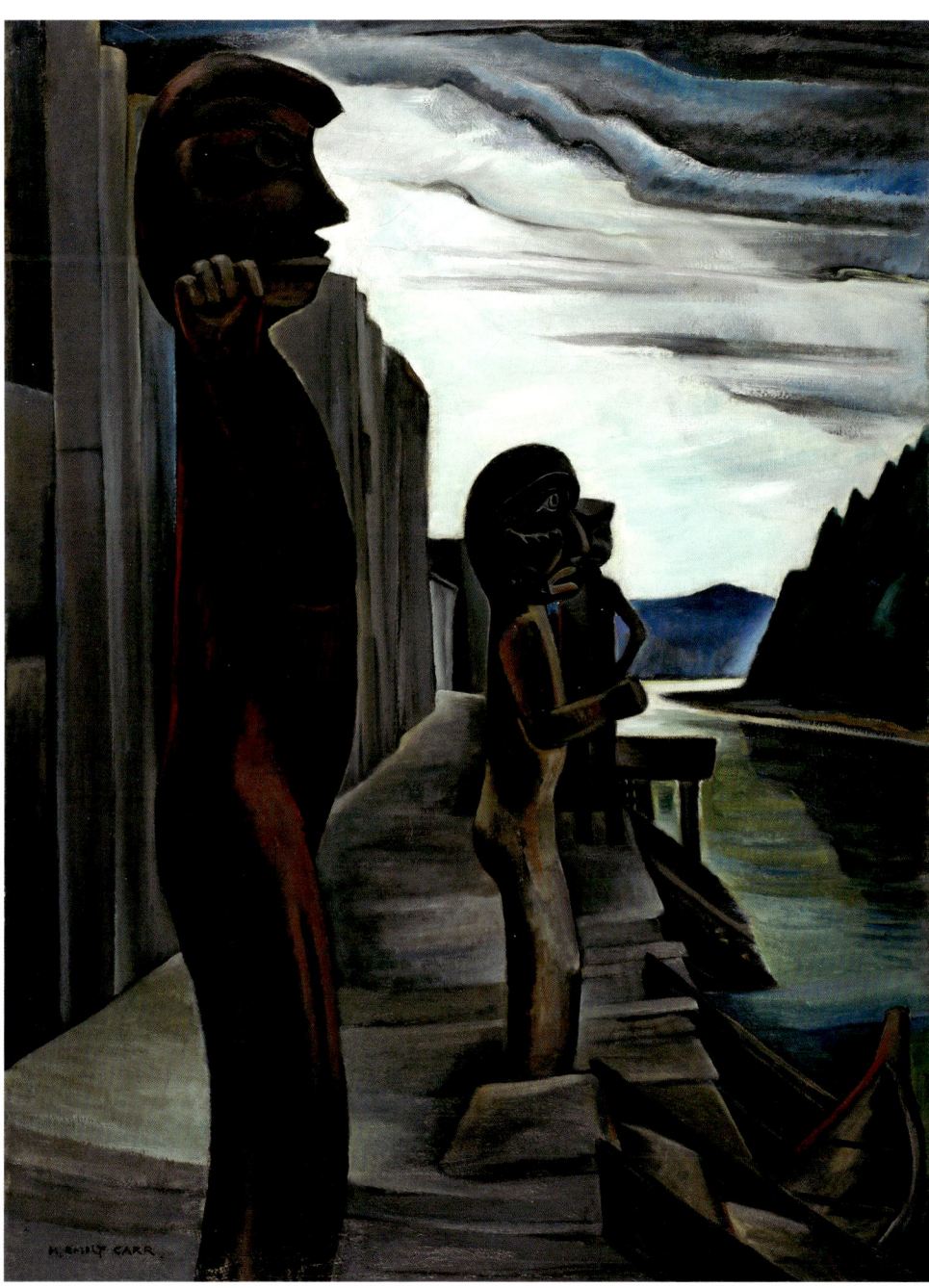

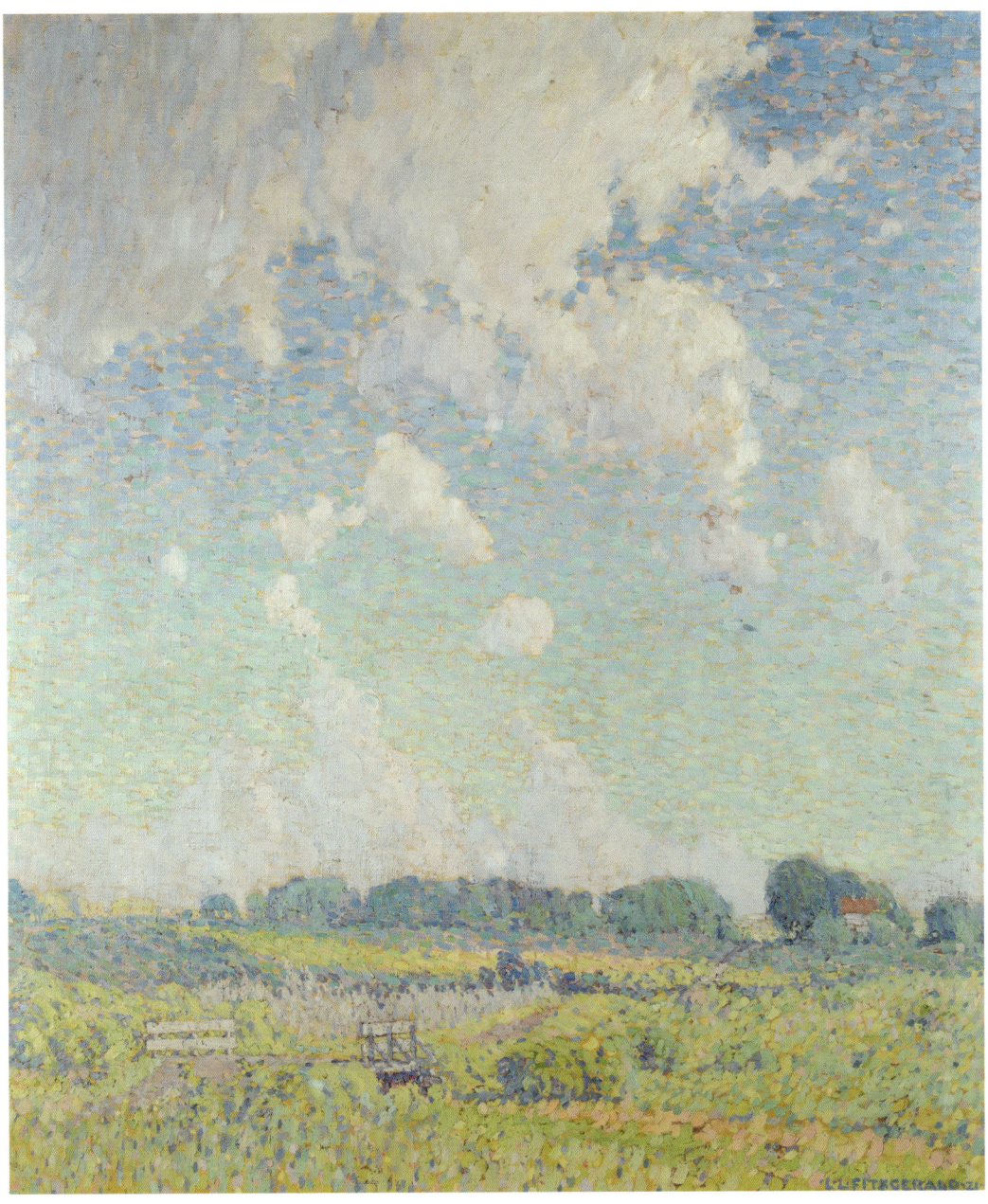

generations of artists across Canada. In Saskatoon the constructivists, led by artist Eli Bornstein (b. 1922), took art in new directions. In Alberta the impacts of artists such as John Snow, Marion Nicoll, and Maxwell Bates have been particularly broad. The Banff School of Fine Arts, the Alberta College of Art, and the prairie university fine arts departments all certainly contributed to artistic expression across Canada, while British Columbia's Vancouver School of Art, now Emily Carr University, also trained many nationally and internationally recognized artists since its 1926 founding. Emily Carr, Jack Shadbolt, Pat Martin Bates, Gathie Falk, Jeff Wall, Rodney Graham, and Ian Wallace are only some British Columbia artists whose art has consistently added challenging avant-garde elements to Canadian art.

Indigenous artists across the West have likewise made impressive and distinctive contributions to Canadian art. The Professional Native Indian Artists Incorporated, now known as the Indigenous Group of Seven, was founded in 1972 by Jackson Beardy, Daphne Odjig, Norval Morrisseau, Eddy Cobiness, Alex Janvier, Carl Ray, and Joseph Sanchez. They exhibited nationally and internationally and were a groundbreaking force in contemporary art. In the Pacific Northwest, Mungo Martin, Bill Reid, Robert Davidson, Roy Vickers, Arthur Vickers, Tony Hunt, Richard Hunt, and Eugene Hunt all transformed the Canadian art scene. So, too, have Saskatchewan's Robert (Bob) Boyer (1948–2004) and Ruth Cuthand; Alberta's Joane Cardinal-Schubert, Jane Ash Poitras, and Terrance Houle; and Manitoba's Robert Houle (b. 1947) and Colleen Cutschall (b. 1951), to name but a few internationally acclaimed Indigenous artists from the West.

Western Canadian artists, with their diversity of birth, training, cultures, and languages, have not been indiscriminate followers of international trends. In some aspects of subject matter, especially landscape painting and the depiction of social life, Canada was ahead of the international "creative curve." By Canada's Confederation in 1867, for example, seven years before the landmark first impressionist exhibition in Paris, landscape painting had been a primary subject in Canada for almost a century. In France it was only in the 1850s, at Barbizon outside Paris, that artists who painted the landscape outdoors propelled the genre to the status of acceptable subject. Until then landscape was primarily a backdrop for portraits or history or allegory paintings. In England, on the other hand, landscape painting gained its gravitas earlier, in the 1820s to 1840s, with the work of John Constable and J.M. William Turner. However, in Canada itinerant artists understood the landscape early on and they captured the essence of the spaces and light decades before the European academies actually "sanctioned" landscape as subject.

Depictions of daily life in the 1820s in Western Canada also predated similar subjects in Europe. Rindisbacher's portrayals of treaty agreements and, in the 1860s, William Hind's

FIGURE 1.4. **Lionel LeMoine FitzGerald**, *Summer Afternoon, The Prairie*, 1921.

depictions of life in his *Overlander Journal* are just several examples. Sociological interests in France were first seen in the work of Gustave Courbet, Honoré Daumier, and Jean-François Millet in the late 1850s and early 1860s. On the other hand, depictions of social life and social commentary were part of Canadian art from the arrival of the first European artists in the late eighteenth and early nineteenth centuries.

Canada's artistic path, therefore, differs from countries with longer traditions, and transformational approaches in subject, technique, and composition characterized creativity in Western Canada. In 1940, however, Alexander J. Musgrove, the Scottish immigrant head of the Winnipeg School of Art, said in a radio broadcast, "People have not kept up with the artists; the leaders of thought. Many, and they include educators and well-meaning people, still think of art as the making of pictures. Art is much greater than that. It is the barometer of a people's intelligence."[6]

Training: Abroad and at Home

Over the several hundred years since European contact in Canada, most immigrant artists received their basic artistic training from British, European, and American art schools. That training, especially in the United Kingdom and Europe, raises several questions: What was the scope of the curriculum that artists studied? Did the Canadian landscape change and shape the work of immigrant artists or did artists continue to make art as they had been taught? What were the responses of early artists in the West to the visual impulses of their new landscape with its different light and colours, the long prairie horizon, and the majestic mountains and oceans? Interestingly, between 1860 and 1940, the curriculum at London's Slade School of Art shows no evidence of courses in landscape painting. Some artists arriving in Canada continued to work with their own traditions. For other artists, though, their approaches to visual expression were transformed by their new home. Their groundbreaking visionary experiments helped build Canadian art with new ideas and experiences.

The earlier training of early artists who came to Western Canada, therefore, was varied, and many artists had no art training at all. One example is the British army-trained Sir Henry James Warre, a military officer and talented watercolour artist. Travelling as part of a military reconnaissance related to the Oregon Boundary Dispute in 1858, and earlier to Red River, he completed a particularly accomplished watercolour of Lower Fort Garry in 1848. Other artists had studied privately before coming to North America. Peter Rindisbacher, for instance, took instruction in Switzerland from landscape painter Jakob Weibel.

From the 1890s forward, Canadian-born artists travelled elsewhere to study and were thus exposed to major international movements. British Columbia's Emily Carr, for example, studied at the San Francisco Art Institute from 1890 to 1892, at the Westminster School of Art

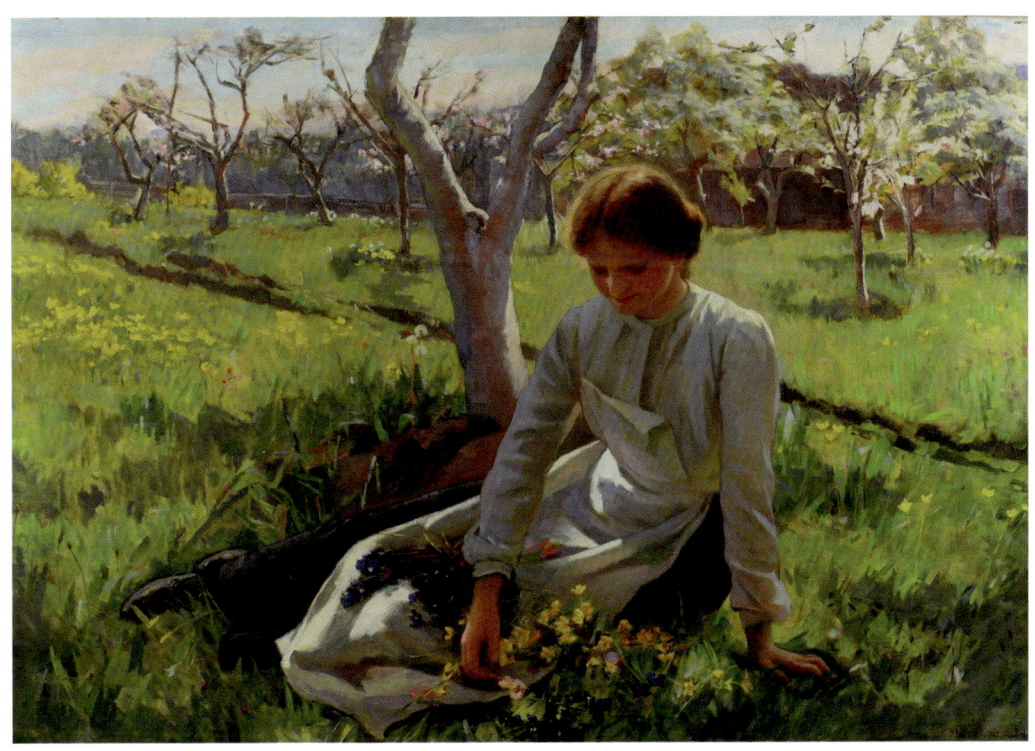

in Britain in 1899, and in 1910 at the Académie Colarossi in Paris. The strong, rich colours and the treatment of form of the post-impressionists and Fauve painters she saw are evident in Carr's painting. Sophie Pemberton (1869–1969) was also from British Columbia and studied overseas, first at London's Slade School of Art and the Westminster School of Art from 1892 to 1896, and, in 1897, at the Académie Julian in Paris. These studies were contrary to the will of her father, who felt such study abroad defied proper social conventions for women. His pride, however, was evident when in 1897 she became the first British Columbia woman to receive international acclaim in a Royal Academy exhibition in London for her 1897 work *Little Boy Blue,* and then, in 1899 in Paris she became the first woman to win the coveted Prix Julian. The Académie Julian, a progressive school open to women, offered a wide-ranging training and was at its heyday when Pemberton was there. Their students in the 1880s and 1890s included some of Europe's best-known artists, including Henri Matisse, Pierre Bonnard, Édouard Vuillard, and

FIGURE 1.5. **Sophie Pemberton**, *Spring,* 1902.

John Singer Sargent. Pemberton saw their works, met some of them, and studied with some of the same teachers. The impact of the impressionists and post-impressionists in subject matter and colour is evident in Pemberton's paintings. She was both a studio artist and a plein air painter, and her subjects include landscapes and portraits. In *Spring,* 1902, she depicts a young woman at leisure outdoors, capturing a particular moment. Her brushwork for the grasses is loose; the long and rhythmic parallel strokes enhance the tranquility of the scene, and the diagonal path lengthens the sense of space. *Un Livre Ouvert,* 1900, an assured interior painting, conveys the depth of relationship and personal feelings of a precise moment. The light from the fire in the background, the sole light source in the work, highlights the faces of two young Victoria society women: Ethel Vantreight and Ellie Paddon.

Throughout the late nineteenth and early twentieth centuries, Manitoba artists also studied internationally. Some members of the Winnipeg chapter of the Women's Art Association of Canada, for instance, studied with James Abbott McNeill Whistler in Paris and William Merritt Chase in New York. New influences were also felt from Britain in the nineteenth century through the work and writings of John Ruskin and William Morris. The result was an increasing sense of internationalism in Western Canadian arts.

At home, artists learned in various ways. Lionel LeMoine FitzGerald, for example, as a youngster was a frequent user of Winnipeg's newly built Carnegie Library, which opened near his home in 1904. An avid reader of the latest art magazines, including *Studio International*, he accessed all he could to keep abreast of newly breaking aspects of visual expression. He first visited Chicago in 1910, and then studied at the Art Students League in New York in the winter of 1921–22. His New York training was transformational, especially regarding his understanding of organic growth in nature and his sense of line and form.

In Western Canada formal art training began at home with the 1913 founding of the Winnipeg School of Art, followed by the 1926 establishment of the Vancouver School of Art and the Alberta College of Art. These schools opened new opportunities for artists in their home communities. Until then local training had been given by individual artists in their own studios. Ontario-born, Paris-trained Frank Armington, for instance, ran his Winnipeg teaching studio from 1900 to 1905. In 1909 FitzGerald studied privately with Polish immigrant artist Alexander S. Keszthelyi, who had learned his craft in Warsaw and Vienna and also taught in the United States. That year Keszthelyi posed insightful questions about the artistic potential of the West in Winnipeg's *Town Topics* newspaper: "Who shall estimate the artistic development that is possible in this magnificent country of Western Canada? . . . An incalculable amount of work remains to be done by future generations of artists . . . and beyond doubt, many of them will be sons of this city of Winnipeg, the capital of the West."[7] Lionel LeMoine FitzGerald proved that prophetic comment, as did other Mantioba artists, including Bertram Brooker, who moved to Toronto in 1921, where he worked with the *Globe* newspaper and at *Marketing*, the trade journal of the Canadian advertising industry. Charles Comfort (1900–1994) eventually moved east, too, in 1925, where he taught painting at the University of Toronto before becoming director of the National Gallery of Canada. For his part, Walter J. Phillips moved further west as head of the Banff School of Fine Arts after being a central figure in the Winnipeg art scene. The future careers of these and others of their colleagues proved art historian Angela Davis's conclusion that "in just over a decade a milieu had been established within which artists of great future importance in Canadian history could live and work."[8]

Over many decades, international artistic interests, training, and travel have affected all artistic media—painting, sculpture, ceramics, and printmaking—in Western Canadian art. For example, since the Second World War, British ceramist Bernard Leach linked ceramic artists from Britain, Canada, and Japan, all inspiring connections for Victoria ceramist Robin Hopper. British sculptor Barbara Hepworth had an exhibition at the Montreal Museum of Fine Arts in 1955–56, and her home city of St. Ives, Cornwall, became a dynamic centre for artists from Western Canada from the 1950s on, as did Paris, Glasgow, London, and Berlin. As opportunities to study and work abroad expanded, Western Canadian artists availed themselves of travels, residencies, workshops, and sabbaticals in many parts of the world. Manitoba's Don Reichert (1932–2013) went to St. Ives for a year in the early 1960s; British Columbia's Pat Martin Bates studied in both Belgium and Paris in the late 1950s; and Victoria's Jim Gordaneer (1933–2016) and Winnipeg's Bruce Head (1931–2009) and Don Reichert were among those who frequently went to Mexico to work.

Through myriad formal, informal, and general life's experiences, the visual expression in the West expanded. Western artists' sensibilities, techniques, and approaches have continued to evolve through innovation and experimentation, and their work is substantive. The support garnered from the twentieth-century development of art galleries, exhibitions, art associations, and funding arts councils was essential for that evolution, and collectively created the platform for sustained development.

1821–1870: Itinerant and Resident— Experiences and Expressions

"The maps, sections, plans, water-colour drawings and photographs, contributed by Professor Hind, results of his exploring expeditions in the western country, were exceedingly interesting. By them we were able to realize, far better than from written description, the scenery of the regions which is now rapidly rising into importance."[9]

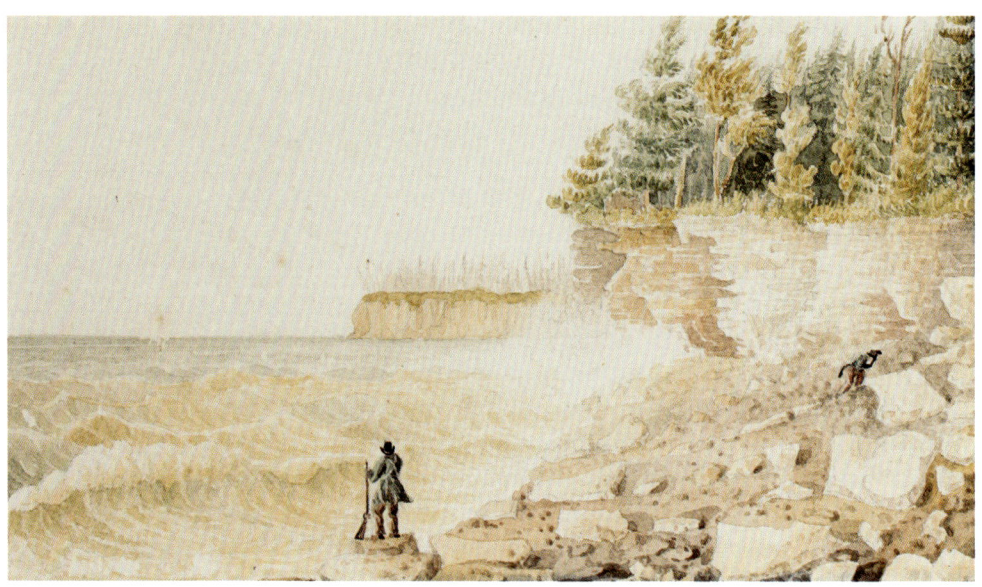

New experiences and new forms of expression for Europeans abounded from what they saw as a distant and unknown vast territory with a challenging climate. Faced with new and, to them, exotic subject matter, these artists had to embrace new means of survival, modes of travel, and ways of living. Canada's First Peoples were their guides, providing the much-needed survival lessons.

Western Canadian post-contact art history begins with the "Itinerant Era," at the time of the Hudson's Bay Company and the North West Company and the establishment of permanent settlements in the West. Early extant depictions by European artists include an engraving after a sketch by Samuel Hearne of Fort Prince of Wales, circa 1769; a watercolour sketch by H.J. Robertson of Fort Gibraltar dated 1804; and an 1817 engraving after a sketch by Lord Selkirk of Fort Douglas. Most early itinerant artists passed through the region as members of various exploration parties. Sir George Back (1796–1878), for instance, accompanied John Franklin on two Arctic expeditions and did some particularly interesting detailed topographical sketches. Back's *Limestone Rocks, Lake Winnipeg*, 1825, shows the magnitude of that particular site with its detailed striations of limestone formations and the turbulence of the water. Like others of the period, his are small works, done in watercolour and ink. On the Pacific coast artists travelled on

FIGURE 1.6. **Sir George Back**, *Limestone Rocks, Lake Winnipeg*, 1825.

expeditions such as those led by Captain Cook and Captain Vancouver, and on several Spanish expeditions, such as the 1792 voyage of Galiano and Valdés.

Peter Rindisbacher, who arrived in Hudson Bay with a group of Swiss immigrants, became the West's first resident artist, staying in Red River from 1821 to 1826. His art training as a boy from landscape painter and miniaturist Jakob Samuel Weibel is evident in his works of Red River.[10] Art historian Gilbert Gignac points out his compositional debt to his teacher in some of his works, the differences being that the people, dress, and ceremonies of Red River substituted for those of the Old World. However, Rindisbacher's new surroundings and its fauna fascinated him, and his work changed in response to what he saw. He painted many portraits of Indigenous peoples engaged in daily traditional activities and ceremonial treaty signings, and the interior of the Hudson's Bay buildings, and he also recorded Europeans in the region. The respect, the sensitivity, and the ability with which he portrayed his subjects are captivating. His landscapes of the region are fresh depictions that capture the light and vast spaces of Manitoba. Many were later made into prints for the European market.

William Hind (1833–1889) painted small oil paintings on board in Red River. His *Horse Drinking at an Ice Hole* and *Breaking a Road in Manitoba—Sioux Indians in the Background* have become landmarks in Canadian art; these works are considered to be the first oil paintings done outdoors in Canada, twelve years before the first impressionist exhibition in Paris. They are also revolutionary in technique. Rather than using the accepted academic method of first priming the canvas with heavily dark tones and building light from that dark base, Hind commenced with a light prime. With fewer layers of paint he achieved the evocative light of the prairie skies in his oils as he did in his watercolours on white paper. The directness and crispness of these winter scenes suggest they were done on the spot and not translated later from a sketch in his studio. Hind's oil paintings, the same size as his watercolours, were easily accommodated in his specially fitted paintbox when they were wet. In contrast, for instance, Paul Kane did his large oil paintings in his Toronto studio from the sketches and watercolours he did in the West. He built from the dark base, and his oil paintings are much heavier in feel than his works on paper done on-site.

Artists lost many works and materials in the accidents and challenges they faced on their constantly moving explorations. As they travelled overland on foot and in carts, and in canoes and over rugged portages, supplies had to be light, small, and portable. Quick, fast-drying techniques were essential, and thus watercolour and pencil predominated. Art was done after the camp was set up or during travel breaks. The artists' rich visual legacy of many "firsts" is coupled with their diary recordings of daily routines, travels, methods of painting, and trials of transporting art supplies. William Hind, who portrayed Red River, British Columbia's gold rush, and aspects of Victoria, wrote to his brother of these challenges:

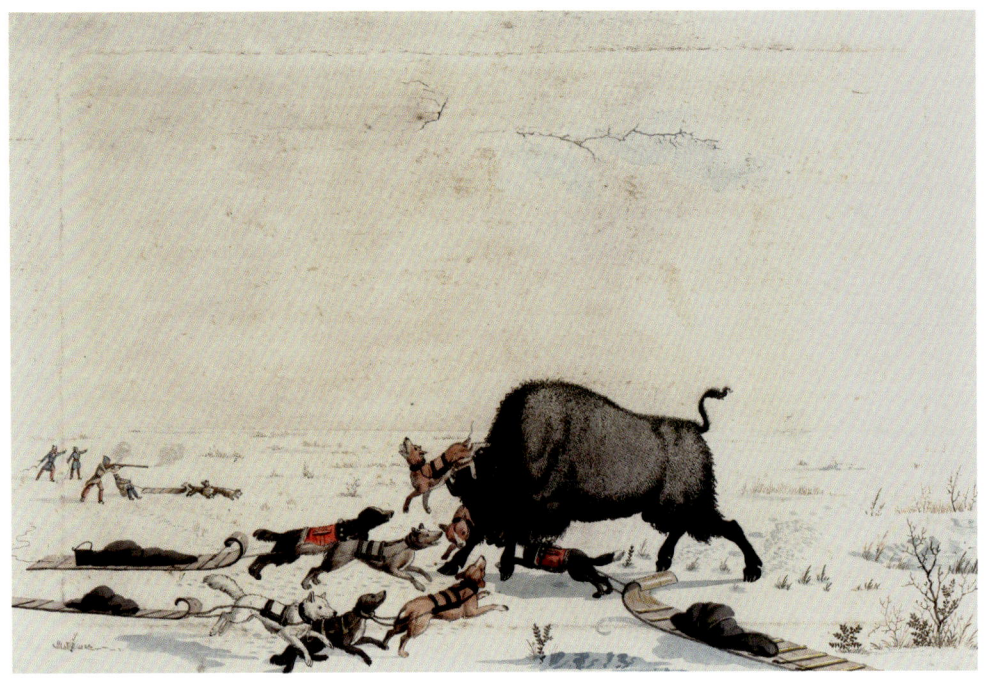

We had a jolly time coming over the Plains, but when we approached the Rocky Mountains difficulties began to appear in the way of large pine and bog swamps, and small lakes of water through which we had to lead our oxen, packing is not such easy work as driving a cart. Redgrave and I with another were three days in advance of our party when we first struck the perpendicular wall of the Rocky Mountains, opposite which we camped on Tundra, and were in a state not to be envied as we fancied we were surrounded by Grizzly bears during the day and night, mistaking the note of the mourning owl, for the grunt of a Grizzly. Down the Fraser was the worst part of the journey, as it is full of rapids and caverns etc. living on dried ox meat alone during the time. Pemmican is infinitely better food.[11]

Humphrey Hime (1833–1903) recorded the 1858 expedition led by Henry Youle Hind. An early photographer, he also made significant breakthroughs with his art. Overcoming many hazards and problems to take the significant number of landscape and portrait photographs he

FIGURE 1.7. **Peter Rindisbacher**, *Sled Dogs Attacking a Bison*, c. 1822–1824.

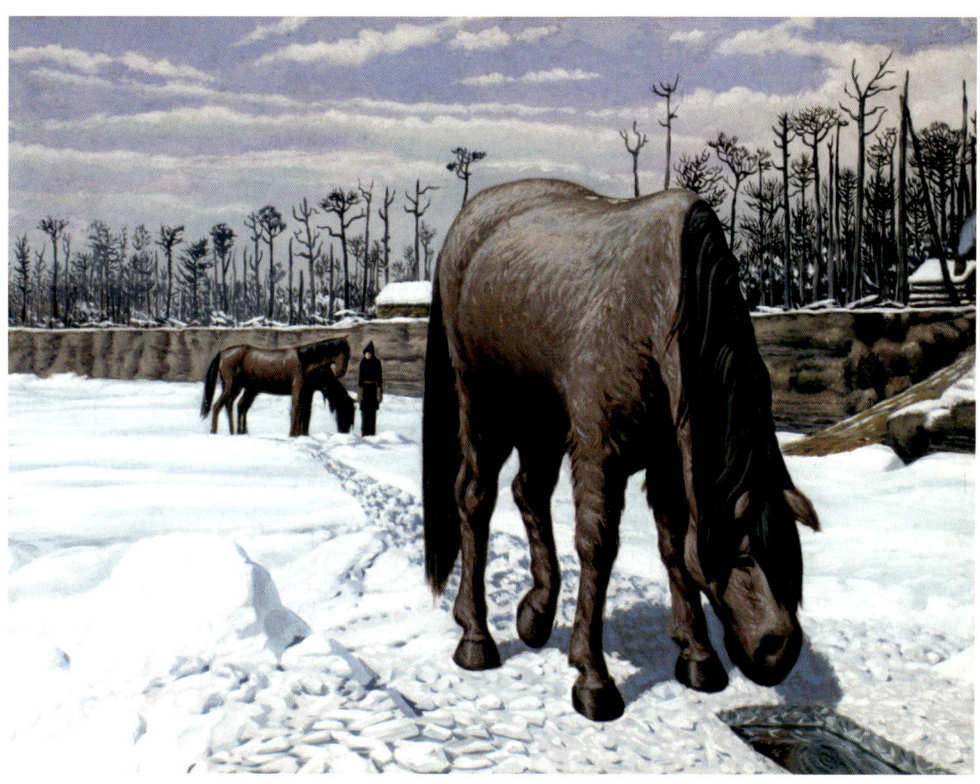

did was a challenge. Setting up his photographic equipment alone was particularly complex: the glass plates were fragile, the chemicals were dangerous, and the apparatus was bulky and heavy. The exposures were long and the elements of nature were a challenge. His early photographs, however, breathe of the artist's individuality, and his compositions and subjects, the Cree and the Red River Settlement, are handled in a personal and sensitive manner. While capturing the personality of the sitter, Hime simultaneously portrayed the specific setting, which provided a focal point.

Paul Kane and Frederick Verner are perhaps the best-known itinerant artists in the West. Kane first went west in 1846–47 and returned to Red River a second time in 1849. He was, in fact, the first professionally trained artist to work in Alberta, where he spent time at Fort Edmonton. His subjects included Indigenous people and their customs, ceremonies, and

FIGURE 1.8. **William Hind**, *Horse Drinking at an Ice Hole*, c. 1863.

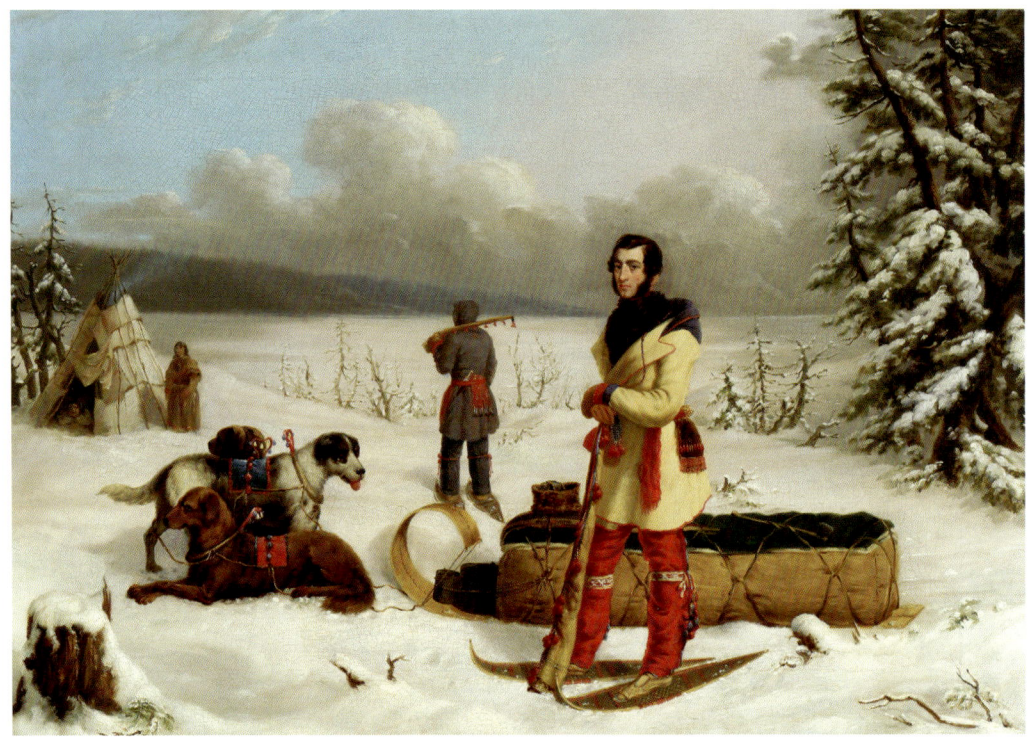

artifacts. *Assiniboine Hunting Buffalo* and *Winter Travelling with Dog Sled* are two well-known works of that time. Verner, whose friend and idol, according to some accounts, was Paul Kane, did not travel as extensively. Yet Verner did accompany Alexander Morris to the Lake of the Woods in 1873 for the signing of Treaty 3, the North-West Angle Treaty. The drawings and watercolours by both Kane and Verner are fresh and confident, evoking the feeling of the vastness, light, and skies of the prairies. These are the basis for their larger oil paintings done later in their Toronto studios, where they were painted indoors in candlelight. Their canvases, primed with the traditional dark ground, are heavier and more laboured in feeling than the sketches. With the dark underpainting, they lose some of the freedom and sensitivity of their watercolours.

In his book *Wanderings of an Artist,* Paul Kane chronicled his travels across Manitoba, the Northwest Territories, the interior of British Columbia, Washington, Oregon, and up the Pacific

FIGURE 1.9. **Paul Kane**, *Scene in the Northwest—Portrait*, c. 1845–1846.

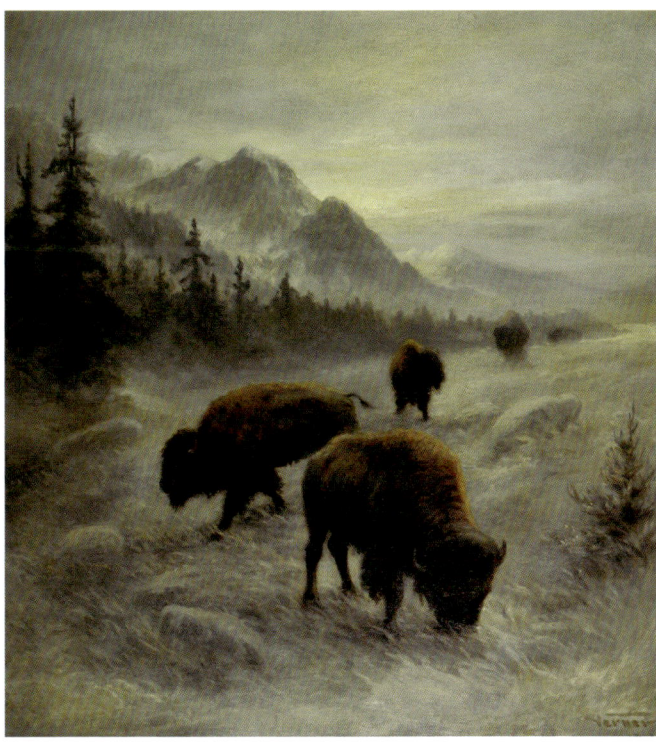

FIGURE 1.10.
Frederick Verner,
*Buffalo in the
Foothills*, 1914.

Coast to Vancouver Island. His written descriptions are evocative. He describes a storm at sea off Vancouver Island:

> At 3 o'clock A.M. we embarked [into their canoe] and proceeded to make a travers of thirty-two miles in an open sea. When we had been out for about a couple of hours the wind increased to a perfect gale, and blowing against an ebb tide caused a heavy swell. . . . It was with the greatest anxiety that I watched each coming wave as it came thundering down, and I must confess that I felt considerable fear. However, we arrived safely at the fort at 2 P.M., without further damage than what we suffered from intense fatigue, as might be expected, from eleven hours' hard work, thoroughly soaked and without food; but even this soon passed away before the cheerful fire and "hearty" dinner with which we were welcomed at Fort Victoria.[12]

Frances Anne Hopkins was the first female immigrant artist to do significant work in the region. Her husband worked for the Hudson's Bay Company and she travelled with them on their voyages across the West. Her watercolours and oils show various aspects of the expeditions on which she accompanied her husband in the early 1870s. She demonstrates a good handling of colour and composition, conveying the light and moods of the skies with aplomb.

1870–1930: Supports and Opportunities—Coming of Age

"The increasing prosperity of western Canada has, during the past few years, caused increasing attention to be paid to the refining and elevating influence of the arts. . . . With the lightening of the pressure of pioneering life and the progress of the people towards competence and wealth, comes a corresponding recognition and appreciation of the place and part that beauty plays in the plan of life."[13]

Artistic hubs require a number of factors to succeed, including political leadership, economic stability, a population of sufficient size, and artists who are keen to push boundaries. Manitoba had these convergences. From the time the province joined Confederation in 1870 to the 1930s, the boom in the arts was significant, and opportunities to learn, show work, and engage audiences expanded rapidly across the West. With Winnipeg's 1873 incorporation and the first city council assuming office in January 1874, Red River officially became the City of Winnipeg and Manitoba's provincial capital. The city witnessed a rapid population growth, from 241 people in 1871 to 34,954 in 1894, to become Canada's eighth-largest city. Community expectations and needs grew as the population increased; agriculture and business flourished; the cultural scene blossomed; organizations were founded; visual arts exhibitions were presented; and art classes were started. The city's main street burgeoned with major buildings designed by leading American architects. Meanwhile, in 1885 the railway connected the country. The first passenger train from Montreal to Vancouver ran in 1886.

The influential Winnipeg branch of the Women's Art Association of Canada was founded in 1894 by a group of determined and dedicated women, inspired by Mary Dignam and Mary Hiester Reid, the Toronto branch leaders. The Winnipeg Women's Art Association and the Virden Fair both contributed substantially to the young province's flowering art scene, and their leadership spawned a number of organizations in Winnipeg and across the province.

The 1893 Virden Agricultural Fair's Fine Art Section was so successful that subsequent agricultural fairs in Manitoba became the visual arts' major exhibition venues. Their exhibitions were regularly reviewed in the press and accompanying catalogues listing artists and entries were produced. Meanwhile, the Winnipeg Women's Art Association also developed a number of programs for artists—exhibitions, sales, lectures, and advancements in art education curricula. By 1908 their confirmed aims, as historian Virginia Berry says, were: "To direct and encourage public interest in the study of art in Western Canada and to maintain a permanent collection of art objects."[14]

In 1876, according to Berry, the *Manitoba Free Press* had "dismissed local art as being in its infancy."[15] By the turn of the twentieth century, however, Western Canadian artists felt the need to address a perceived eastern domination of the arts, and the Manitoba Society of Artists was founded in December 1903. The *Manitoba Free Press* reported, "Western artists have long felt that the limitation of eastern standards hampered the development of western initiative and the formation of the Society of Artists is a step towards the establishment of western ideals of artistic excellence."[16] The West's first provincial art association, the Manitoba Society of Artists, articulated their objective in their 1903 constitution and bylaws as being "the encouragement and fostering of original and native art in the Province of Manitoba."[17]

Winnipeg aspired to be the "Chicago of the North." As the city became an important railway centre, shipping exhibitions from Chicago and Toronto became possible, and these were often set up at the Winnipeg station like pop-up exhibitions. The arts were significantly enhanced with the new 1904 Winnipeg Carnegie Library, two new technical high schools, and the 1919 completion and 1920 opening of the Manitoba Legislature building. These civic additions increased access to arts information, artists' training, and exhibition spaces. The growth of commercial galleries around 1899 created change, too. Berry writes that with the efforts of George Cranston, Winnipeg's chief art dealer from 1901 to 1905, "because of its prosperity and modest art initiatives, Winnipeg had become a potential market for eastern dealers."[18] Through the first years of the twentieth century, the Women's Art Association and the Manitoba Society of Artists together actively sought the establishment of an art gallery and school of art. However, when their request first reached Winnipeg City Council, it was turned down. The art community seems to have been of two minds. While all wanted a building devoted to art, there was no consensus whether it should be a gallery or a school. Some indeed envisioned a combination of both, like Chicago's Art Institute or Pittsburgh's Carnegie Institute.[19]

A similar request in Victoria would also be denied. In the 1930s that city's mayor replied to Emily Carr's passionate plea for an art gallery: "That is very interesting Miss Carr, but Victoria already has Beacon Hill Park, the ducks and Kermode the bear. What more could Victoria want?"[20] In Victoria it took until 1951 for the formal establishment of a civic gallery through the gift of property by Sara Spencer, daughter of the founder of the lucrative Spencer Stores. In the case of Winnipeg, fortunately, City Council's rebuke was not as long-lasting. The city's business leaders founded the Winnipeg Art Gallery in 1912 and provided it with some annual funding. Established in Winnipeg's Industrial Bureau on Main Street, it thus became Canada's first civic art gallery.

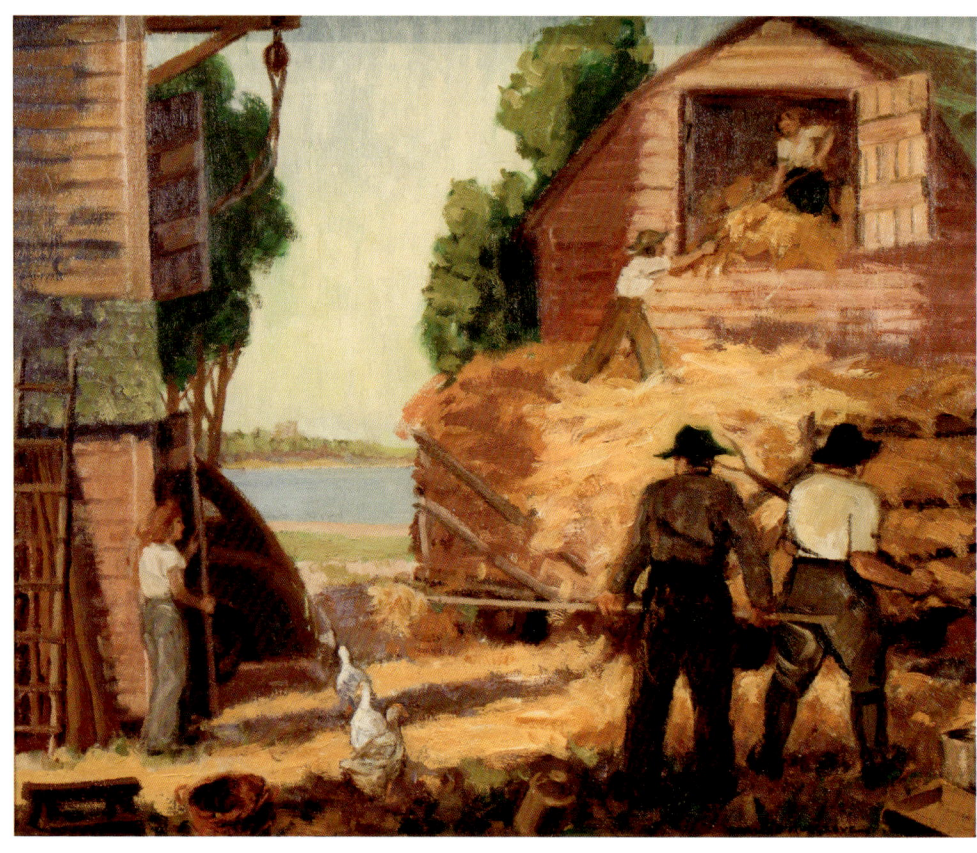

The Winnipeg School of Art opened a year later, in 1913, headed by experienced Scottish artist Dr. Alexander Musgrove (1882–1952). In his letter of offer to Musgrove, Jas. MacDiarmid, chairman of the art section of the Industrial Bureau, underlined the challenges, given the newness of the community: "Briefly the school is a new venture and the details must be worked out by the Principal himself and to do so he ought to be here to see the needs of the city and outline his plan of work. . . . In this new country it may be uphill work at the start and quite likely the principal may feel his efforts scarcely meet with the appreciation or with the success his work merits but to a capable man with his heart in the work and his work the first thing in life success and appreciation must come."[21] The chairman noted the annual remuneration

FIGURE 1.11. **Alexander J. Musgrove**, *Manitoba Farm*, n.d.

for this landmark job would be 500 pounds. Musgrove accepted on 10 April 1913. He left Liverpool on 30 May, and visited the Liverpool School of Art for ideas en route.

Shortly after arriving, Musgrove gave a talk about the "recently opened Winnipeg School of Art" in which he commented on the rising importance of art and art education in the city with the art gallery's opening the prior December. He noted the good equipment for the fledgling school's studio-based programs and its growing numbers of students. He correctly prophesized that Winnipeg would become a "city of culture" with a prominent gallery and art school, and observed:

> In the past those seeking education of an aesthetic nature were compelled to go to the States, or abroad to require it, but this School obviates such a necessity by providing here at hand a place where one may study along the best lines and in accordance with modern and practical ideas, while the best of the traditions of art are retained. We must not think that because it is near that it cannot provide what is best. That environment and tradition which belong to the old established art centres will soon become a part of the artistic life of this City. . . .
>
> Canada, so far, has not a distinct school of painting but there is no reason why a set of artists, properly trained should not evolve such a school, which would possibly obtain its inspiration from the clear skies, the great plains, and the mountains of the west.[22]

Musgrove was equally as definite about the importance of art galleries as he was about art education: "It is a strange fact that art has almost to apologise for its existence. Yet we can no more live without Art than we can without bread. . . . The main purpose of an Art Gallery is of education—education in the best sense of the word . . . a refinement of the intellect."[23]

Though it was the "gateway to the West," Winnipeg's perennial problem of isolation from other parts of Canada was evident from the outset of the city's establishment. Weather challenges added to those of geography. With the founding of the Winnipeg Art Gallery and Winnipeg School of Art, however, Winnipeg was at the forefront as a major Canadian artistic metropolis. By 1910 Winnipeg was imbued with internationalism, earlier than other Western Canadian cities. Virginia Berry rightly opined: "The legacy of [the Winnipeg Women's Art Association] was an enhanced appreciation of the visual arts in Manitoba. Without them it would have been slower in coming; after the club disbanded, the capacity remained."[24] It should be noted, too, that the Winnipeg Women's Art Association had also been visionary in including Indigenous art in their exhibition and education programs.

Winnipeg also demonstrated early connections between commercial art and studio artists. W. Frank Lynn (1835–1906), both a commercial and well-trained studio artist, like his

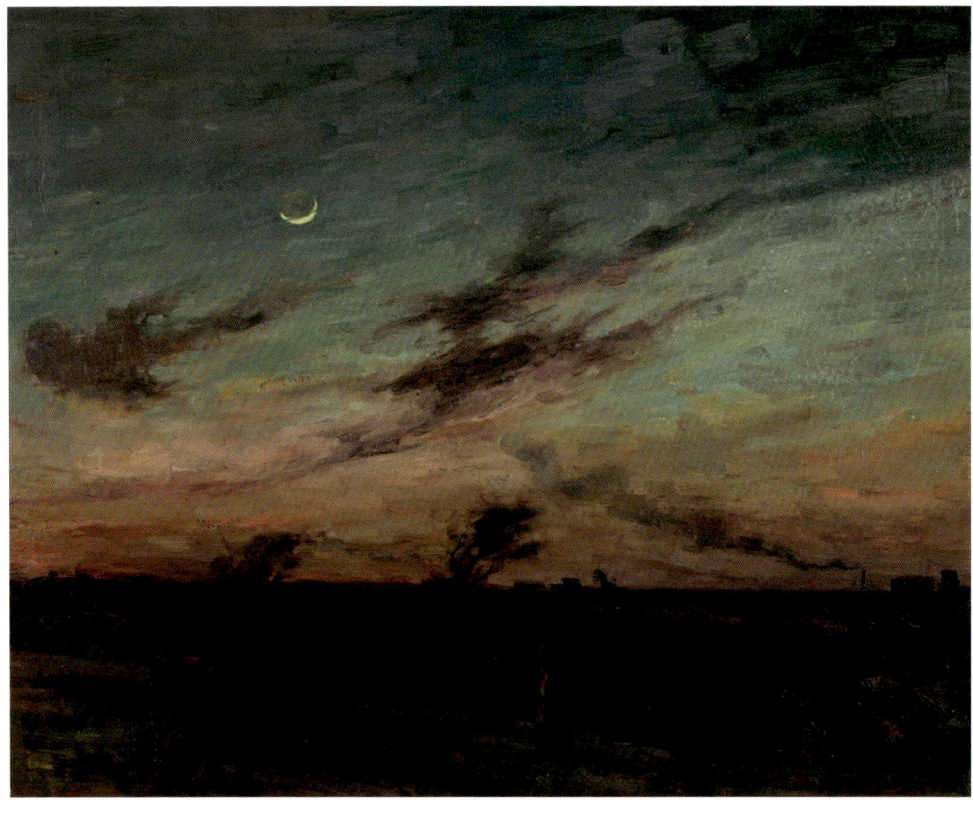

predecessors, painted places and contemporary activities, particularly at the Forks and the Hudson's Bay's Upper Fort. *The Dakota Boat*, circa 1875, proves his capability in the treatment of composition and handling of colour. The tonal shading in the sunset and the group in the foreground combine to lead the eye through space, from the central group, across the river to the Fort, on to the evening sky. Several of Lynn's paintings can be traced back to having been hung in Winnipeg hotels, and a number of versions of his more typical scenes are in existence. Attesting to their contemporary popularity, like Rindisbacher, Lynn received commissions, enabling him to earn a living as a commercial artist.

The expansion of Winnipeg's visual arts and international connections continued into the twentieth century. Artist Mary Riter Hamilton (1873–1954), for instance, involved in the

FIGURE 1.12. **Donald MacQuarrie**, *Landscape with Crescent Moon*, 1913.

Winnipeg Women's Art Association, went to France immediately following the First World War. As a woman, she had not been eligible to be an official Canadian war artist in the First World War. That did not lessen her determination to paint the battlefields. Her series of French battle sites is particularly poignant, and she was awarded l'Ordre des Palmes académiques by the French government and was the first Canadian to be made an officer of the Académie française.

The collective impact of these initiatives transformed the community. The expanded activity and growing interest enticed others to come. Artists, teachers, and architects arrived from England, Scotland, and Eastern Canada, including Valentine Fanshaw (1878–1940), the first art teacher at Winnipeg's Kelvin High School. Walter Phillips arrived in 1913. Arnold Brigden came from Toronto in 1914 to found Brigdens of Winnipeg Limited, the commercial engraving and advertising firm that produced the Eaton's mail-order catalogue for Western Canada. Brigdens was the largest employer of artists in Winnipeg for years. Eric Bergman (1893–1958), who came to Winnipeg from Germany via Toronto, joined the western branch of Brigdens Limited in 1914. Charles Comfort arrived in the city with his family in 1912 and also worked at Brigdens before moving to Toronto. The core artists at Brigdens became national leading figures in the visual arts. Keen to expand exhibition and joint studio opportunities, they and members of the Manitoba Society of Artists were among the founders of the Winnipeg Sketch Club in 1914.

Manitoba and Winnipeg, however, were not the only vibrant hubs of visual arts. British Columbia followed Manitoba into Confederation in 1871, and Alberta and Saskatchewan joined in 1905. During these years the first generation of Canadian-born artists began their visual practice, including Victoria's Emily Carr, born in 1871, and Winnipeg's Lionel LeMoine FitzGerald, born in 1890. At the same time growth on the national scene was exponential. The National Gallery and the Royal Canadian Academy were founded in 1880, both to be catalysts for the developing art scene across the country. By the end of the First World War, Canada was feeling its nationhood. The West was integral to the whole, and the visual arts were no exception.

Opportunities and support for the visual arts continued to grow as new art schools, artists' associations, and art galleries were founded across the West through the 1920s and 1930s. On 3 February 1921, the first meeting of the British Columbia Art League was held, its goals being, according to scholar W. W. Thom: "To promote and encourage education in arts and crafts, to cause to be founded and maintained a central and branch schools of fine arts and industrial arts and crafts, and permanent art galleries and museums, to hold arts and crafts exhibitions, to improve civic art, town and home planning, architecture and landscape gardening."[25] The Edmonton Museum of Art was founded in 1923, and the Provincial Institute of Technology and Art in Calgary and the Vancouver School of Art both followed in 1926. In Calgary, the first instructor was Lars Haukaness, succeeded by Alfred C. Leighton in 1929. Leighton had

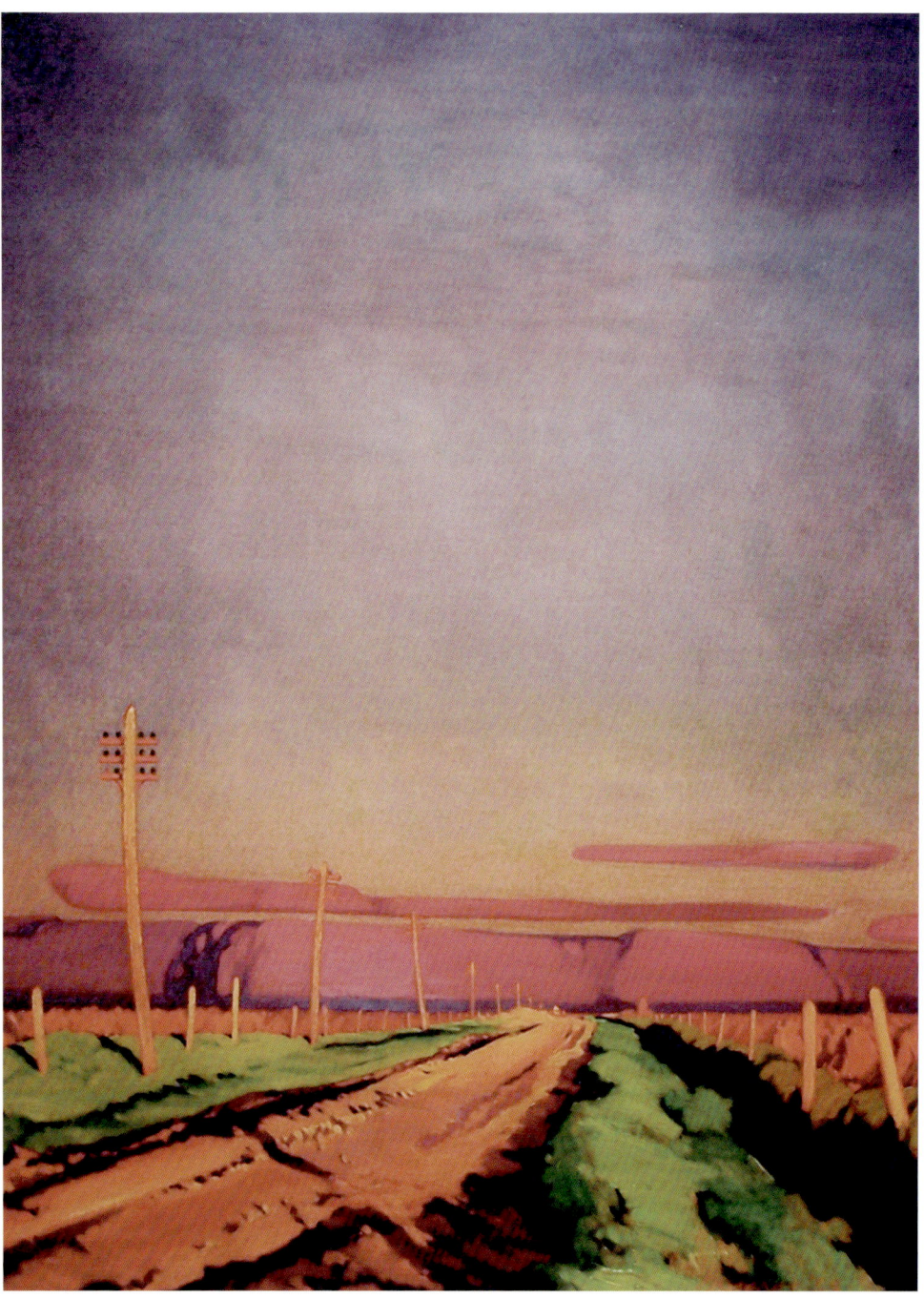

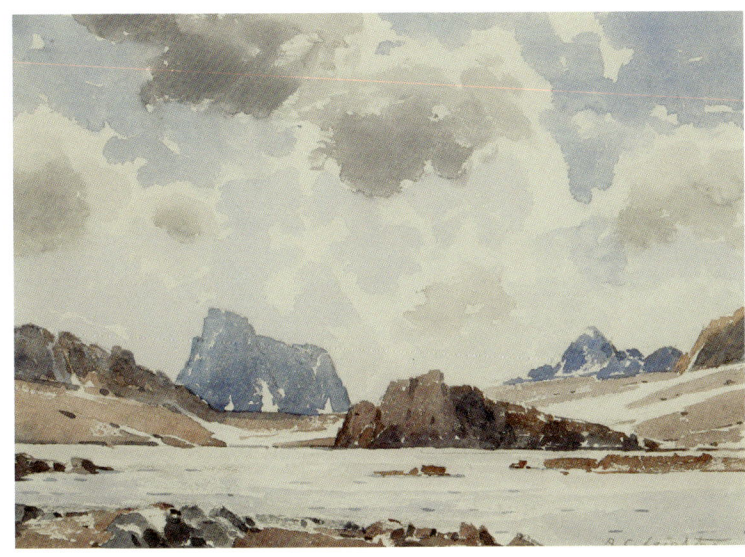

FIGURE 1.14.
A.C. Leighton,
Molar Pass, c. 1950.

arrived in Calgary in 1927. Taken by the landscape, he founded the Alberta Society of Artists in 1931 and the Banff Summer School in 1933. The impact was lasting; so, too, was that of the Vancouver School of Art. Charles H. Scott, a graduate of the Glasgow School of Art, became its director, and a talented group of artists joined its faculty, including Fred Varley (1881–1969) from Toronto and Jock Macdonald from England. They brought Grace Melvin from Scotland to teach with them, creating, as curator Lorna Farrell-Ward describes, "a fresh perception of the British Columbian landscape, [and] a new generation of painters began a domination of Vancouver painting that was to last the next two decades."[26]

Group of Seven member Fred Varley was particularly influential in Vancouver's art scene after moving there in 1926. His interest in Buddhism and the occult grew during this period, expanding the spiritual and philosophical aspect in Canadian visual arts. Those interests influenced his palette. The blues and greens he often used were considered to be colours of the highest state of spirituality.

Jock Macdonald and Jack Shadbolt (1909–1998) were the first art-class teachers at the Art Gallery of Greater Victoria in 1951. Macdonald was another great artistic influencer at the time; his work in abstraction was leading edge. Unfortunately, like Varley, Macdonald was affected by the 1930s Depression and the financial woes of the School of Art. Disillusioned, they left teaching for a time.

FIGURE 1.13. **Charles Fraser Comfort**, *Prairie Road*, 1925.

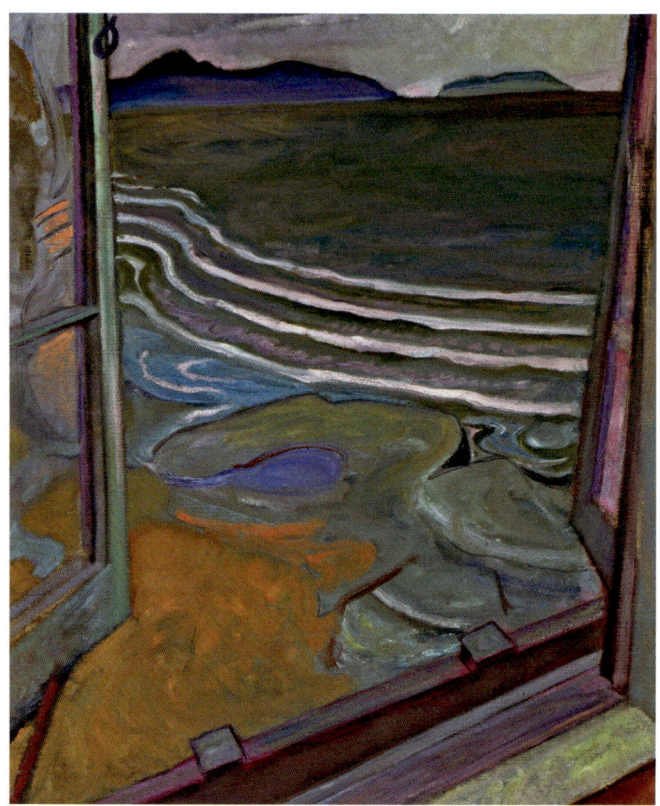

FIGURE 1.15.
Frederick Horsman Varley,
*View from the Artist's
Bedroom Window, Jericho
Beach*, 1929.

In the late 1920s and early 1930s, Western Canadian artists continued to create unique work that transformed Canadian visual expression. In 1927 and 1928 Bertram Brooker, for instance, painted Canada's first abstractions. By then he had relocated to Toronto. However, it was in 1905, while he was in Neepawa, Manitoba, that he is reported to have said, "If ever I paint, I want to paint music." In 1928 Emily Carr (1871–1945) made her second trip to visit British Columbia First Nations communities and created seminal works of the west-coast forests, seascapes, and First Nations people. Some of these works were purchased by the National Gallery of Canada as early as 1928. Eric Brown, the National Gallery's director, invited Carr to exhibit with and meet members of the Group of Seven. Lawren Harris (1885–1970) became a good friend after he moved to Vancouver. American Buddhist and spiritual artist Mark Tobey came to Victoria on various occasions at this time, too, and Carr took a workshop with him.

Interest in spiritualism and internationalism was high on Vancouver Island at the time among artists and writers. Victoria College teacher Gwladys Downes was part of that early 1930s group, led by artist Max Maynard. Downes said Maynard referred to Victoria as "a desert for any aspiring artist or interested amateur . . . there were no visible, visual stimuli to broaden experience, feed the curiosity, or train the vision of young people growing up."[27] For Downes,

his [Maynard's] stimulus, like Jack Shadbolt's came first from within himself, from a spontaneous delight in the appearances of things which transformed itself into a desire to seize the essence of a particular scene, to record, to recreate, to make it new by arranging seeming chaos into coherent form. . . .

He talked—all the time—forcing his listener or listeners into agreeing or disagreeing, asking questions, opening new areas of perception or thought, referring to music or poetry. . . . His mentors at this time were Clive Bell and Roger Fry in art criticism, and Bertrand Russell, . . . the atheist of that seminal essay for the pre-war young "A Free Man's Worship." . . . It is tempting to characterize the people who washed in and out of Max and Evelyn's household between 1932 and 1942 as the far western reflection of the Bloomsbury Group. They were intellectually lively, highly talented and they stimulated each other.[28]

In the midst of these intense philosophical discussions on Vancouver Island in the 1930s, Western Canadian artists were receiving national acclaim. By the time Emily Carr died in 1945, she had received the Governor General's Award for Literature, as had Bertram Brooker (1888–1955) before her. In 1931 Lionel LeMoine FitzGerald became the first western member of the Group of Seven. Many artists were making significant marks in the field. FitzGerald and Carr had become two particularly vocal visual solo voices, and each, with their own unique visual language, helped transform Canadian art.

1930–1960: New Frameworks and Artists' Recognition

"It was fortunate that last summer I was able to take a trip out west. During the course of that trip I came to realize that by knowing people in Alberta, by meeting people in British Columbia, you came to appreciate their work more."

—André Biéler, at the opening of the Kingston Conference, 1941[29]

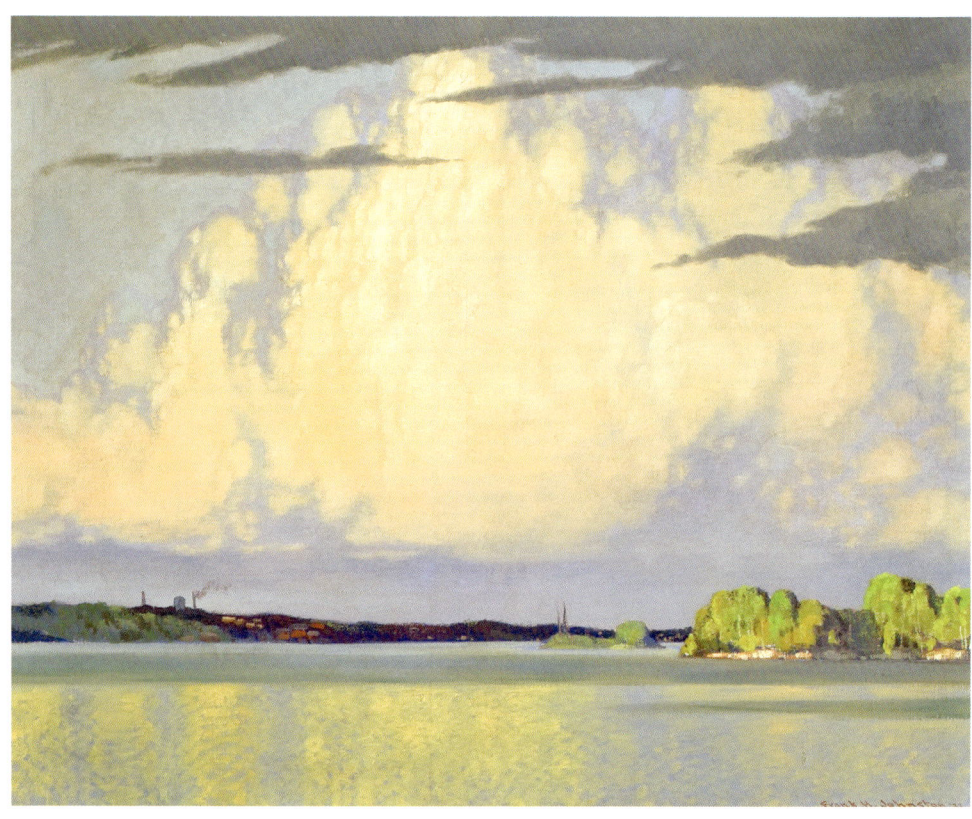

Tensions among nationalism, pluralism, and regional feeling were evident in the art and writings of Western Canada. Between 1930 and 1990 regionalism in artistic expression grew and the sophistication and depth of the visual artists in the West exploded across all four provinces. The artistic energy, increasingly contagious in the West, was aided by the development of public galleries, art schools, and artists' associations and societies.

In October 1931, the new Vancouver Art Gallery, founded by Henry Stone, opened with a memorial exhibition to British Columbia artist Thomas W. Fripp. After that inaugural opening its galleries were available for rent by art societies and clubs. In 1931 young Jack Shadbolt, aged twenty-two, came to Vancouver to teach at Kitsilano High School. The next year, 1932, the major Arts and Crafts Exhibition was held in Victoria, organized by artists Ina Uhthoff and

FIGURE 1.16. **Frank H. Johnston**, *Serenity, Lake of the Woods*, 1922.

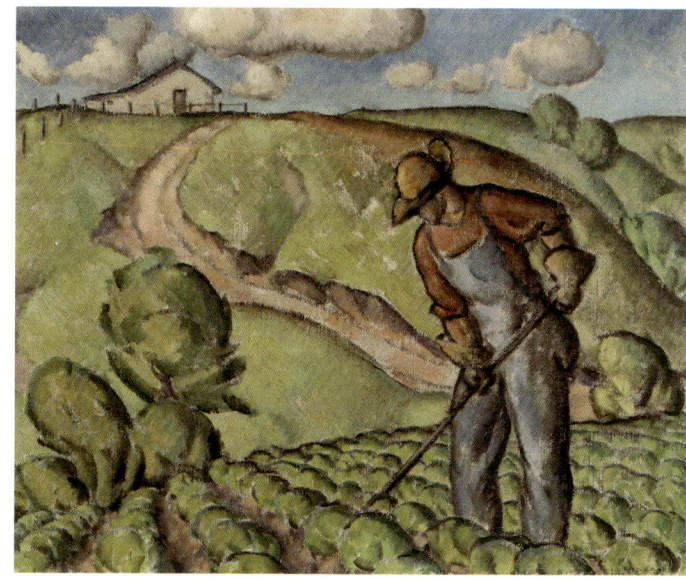

FIGURE 1.17.
Lionel LeMoine FitzGerald, *Potato Patch, Snowflake*, 1925.

Emily Carr. This exhibition met with tremendous interest and became the foremost precursor for the 1951 founding of the Art Gallery of Greater Victoria. In the meantime, artistic growth in Alberta and Saskatchewan was also fast-paced. The Edmonton Museum of Arts Gallery presented its first exhibition in 1924, and 1931 witnessed the founding of Regina's Norman MacKenzie Art Gallery, and, in 1933, Saskatoon's Mendel Art Gallery. The Mendel Art Gallery became the Remai Modern in 2017 and the Regina gallery is now the MacKenzie Art Gallery. Originally part of the University of Regina, the MacKenzie gained its independence in 1953 though continues a vibrant partnership with the university.

In the 1920s and 1930s Canadians were finally being hired in increasing numbers to teach in, and head, fine arts departments in all the western provinces. The Winnipeg School of Art's first Canadian head was Group of Seven Member painter Franz Johnston, who was appointed in 1921 and held the post until 1924. Lionel LeMoine FitzGerald succeeded him to become the first locally born artist to head the school, a post he held from 1924 until 1949. After FitzGerald's 1949 retirement, the Winnipeg School of Art joined the University of Manitoba in 1951, and its programs reached new heights with new energies, new approaches, and exciting results. In Saskatchewan, the University of Saskatoon's fine arts program was also strong, and Group of Seven member Arthur Lismer taught painting in summer schools early in the 1930s. In 1936 Augustus (Gus) Kenderdine (1870–1947) began the University of Saskatchewan Art Camp at Emma Lake, the precursor to the Emma Lake Kenderdine Campus and the Emma Lake Artists'

Workshops. The Banff School of Fine Arts, originally founded in 1933 by the University of Alberta with a grant from the U.S.-based Carnegie Foundation, became an active independent centre in 1935. Support from the Carnegie Foundation and the Carnegie Corporation to the arts in Canada was significant. Their contributions included the building of libraries across the country in the early years of the twentieth century; the support for the Banff Centre; and, in 1941, funding for artists to travel from all parts of Canada to attend the Kingston Conference, a seminal national meeting of artists that called for a national funding body for the arts.

A truly prominent figure in Saskatchewan's artistic milieu at the time was Ernest Lindner, who emigrated from his native Austria after serving in their military in the First World War. In addition to his art making and teaching, he was actively involved in organizing artists in order to improve exhibition opportunities. Lindner successfully reorganized the Saskatoon Art Association in 1932, and, as art writer and curator Terrence Heath says, it "began a program which made Saskatoon the most active community in art in Canada. They mounted exhibitions in rented store windows, organized sketching trips, portrait and model painting, evening art classes, travelling exhibitions, technical demonstrations, small bursaries for needy students, and wrote illustrated booklets, on such subjects as lino-cut printing and glass etching, for distribution to the schools. All these activities, including the printing of the booklets were carried on at the members' expense."[30]

In 1940 they were given a room in Saskatoon's Hudson's Bay Company building, and the Saskatoon Art Association initiated the first Western Canadian art exhibition with art from all four provinces. That show inaugurated a regular exchange between artists in Manitoba and Saskatchewan. Not everyone, however, was supportive of Lindner's proposed initiative for a Saskatchewan Society of Artists and lecture programs. According to Heath, the concept of "an art association exclusively for artists seems to have annoyed Regina lawyer Norman MacKenzie, who dominated the cultural affairs of the province." MacKenzie felt the "art affairs in the province were being taken care of," and further that "Ernie's second scheme, a public lecture program on Saskatchewan artists," caused even more trouble. Its most objectionable feature was an implicit rejection of European art as a standard by which to measure and judge painting in Canada.[31]

Western artists were, however, beginning to make waves in Eastern Canada. In 1941 the *Windsor Star* published an article titled "Western Art Is Winning Fame." It opened with the statement: "Eastern artists and art lovers are naturally less informed about cultural developments in Western Canada than in their own part of the country. However, there is an important group of western painters winning Dominion-wide recognition, among them A.J. Musgrove, A.S.G.A. of Winnipeg."[32] In that same *Windsor Star* article, Valerie Conde acknowledged that Alexander

FIGURE 1.18. **Ernest Lindner**, *Skeleton of the Forest*, 1966.

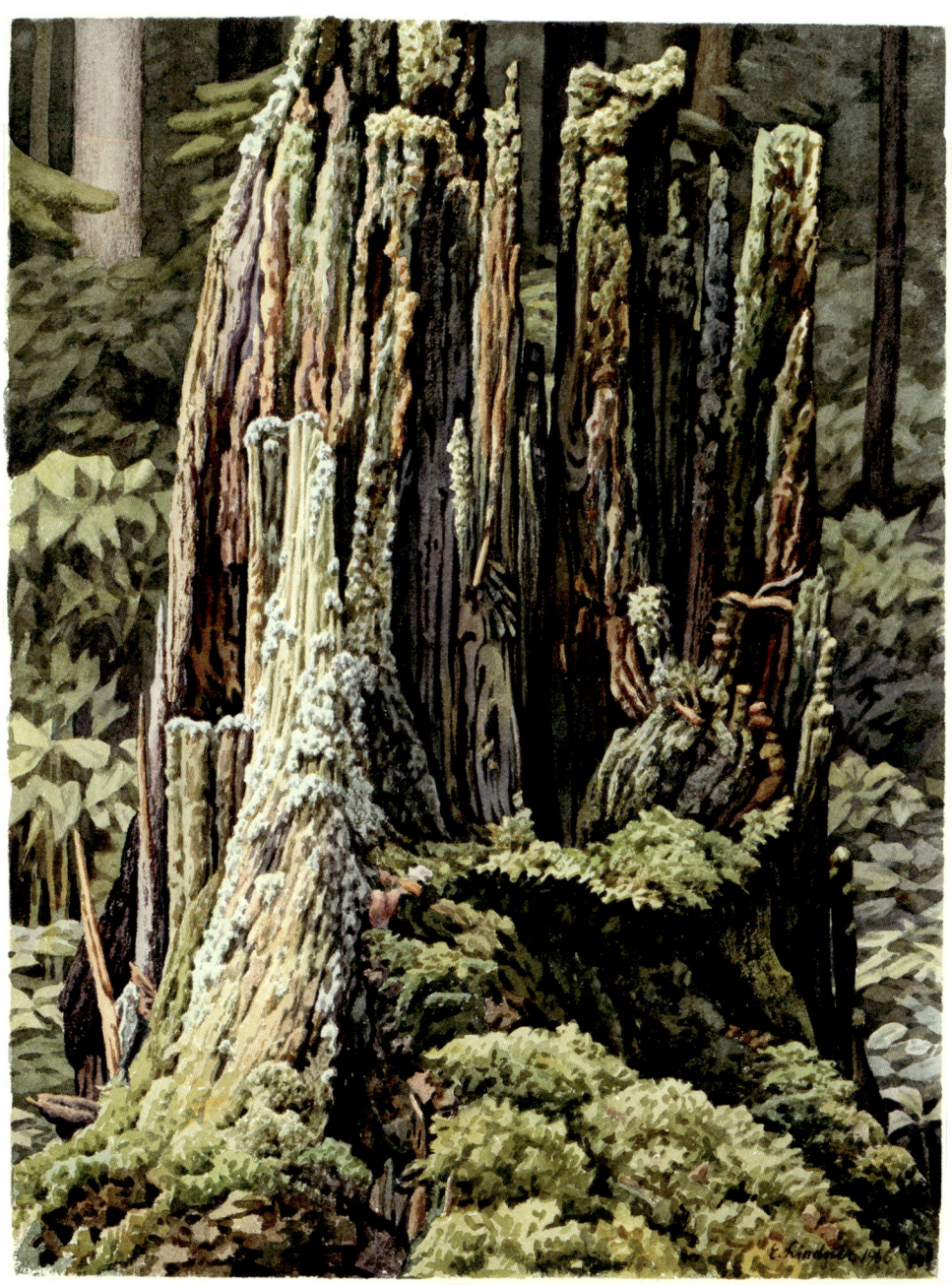

Musgrove felt more needed to be done in art education, despite the advancements made: "In his opinion, they [Canadian artists] are on the whole too much influenced by outside sources, particularly by the French Post-Impressionists, though he thinks they are on the right track in seeking to express Canadian life and depict the Canadian scene. Undoubtedly Canadian art will change and make great advances, in Mr. Musgrove's opinion. However, he thinks Canadian artists need much more education, not only to understand what is really great in art, but to learn their craft thoroughly. When they have mastered their media to a greater extent . . . an art truly expressive of Canada will come into being."[33]

In his February 1940 CKY−CKX Radio Talk, titled "An Appraisal of Canadian Painting," Musgrove told listeners:

> It is evident that much knowledge of life and nature along with a mastery of the art of painting, are the factors which count, and so it seems that three requirements to a great Canadian painting are apparent. First, our artists must master the means of expressing themselves. A deeper knowledge of the art of painting—for there is an art, a craft, if you will, of painting—is clearly needed. Along with this our artists must acquire a greater knowledge of life; a knowledge intensified by a deep appreciation of what has already been done by the great in the arts and in the field of learning. Secondly, the Canadian public must become more appreciative, more conscious of what art means in a design for a fuller enjoyable democratic living, and so more sympathetic, that art may grow and artists be encouraged to express themselves. Thirdly, more art galleries with their vital programmes of educational activities, more opportunities to study exhibitions of the art of the world, must be provided. Art appreciation, with its inestimable value to mankind, taught by trained and truly understanding teachers, must be given to the rising generations in public schools and elsewhere.[34]

The year of Musgrove's broadcast coincided with the revelatory summer that André Biéler, Queen's University's professor of fine art, spent at the Banff Centre. Biéler returned to Kingston having met Western Canadian artists and seen work previously unknown to him. He felt it was essential for Canadian artists to meet. The result was the 1941 Kingston Conference, which Queen's University Principal Robert Charles Wallace offered to host on hearing Biéler's story. Held in the summer of 1941, funding from the United States' Carnegie Corporation enabled artists to travel to Kingston from every part of the country. Those three days of discussion and presentations were pivotal and the result for Canadian art was tremendous. Western attendees came from each of the four provinces and included Jack Shadbolt, Ernest Lindner, Lawren Harris, Gus Kenderdine, Jock Macdonald, Alexander Musgrove, Bart Pragnell, William Weston,

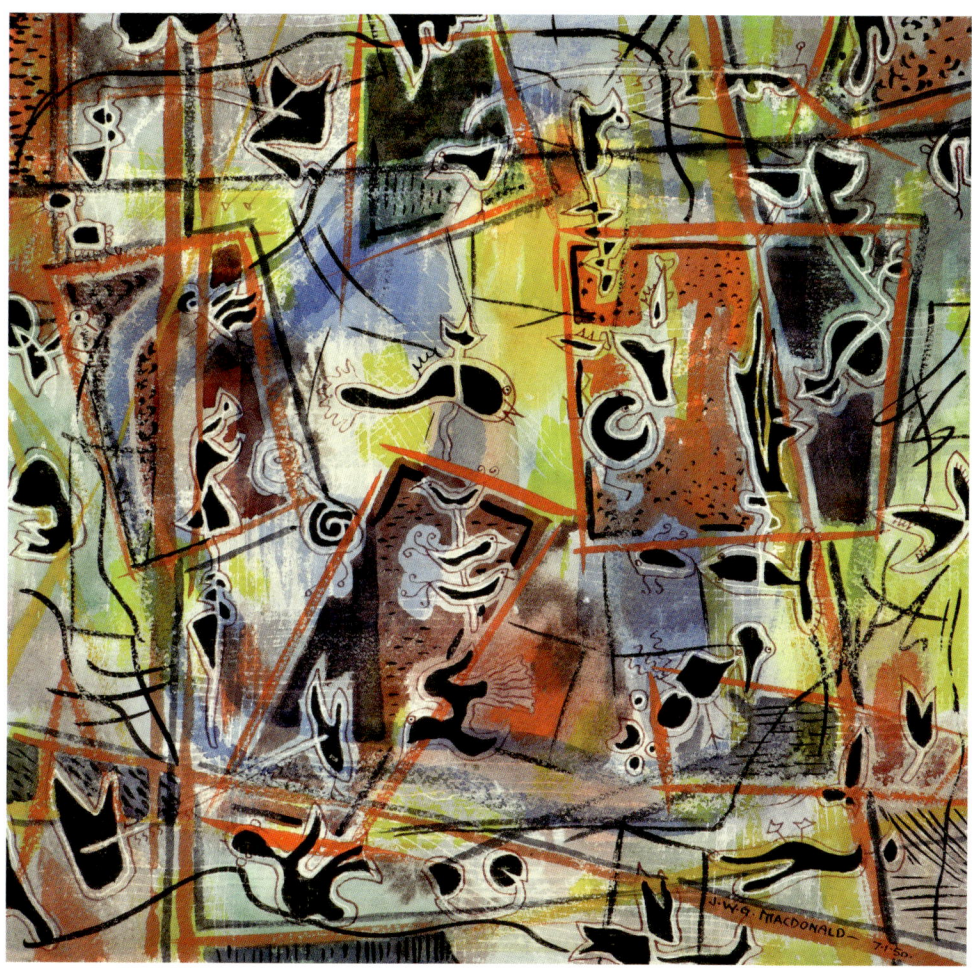

Dorothy Willis, Gertrude Snider, and Charles Scott. Of the event, Shadbolt said: "It was the first time that Canadian artists right across the country achieved any sense of social identity. . . . Community . . . local involvement, political involvement, the workers' cause and the domestic scene in general; this was becoming a necessity—I think something had emerged in Canada."[35] Art historian and Biéler's biographer, Frances Smith, further commented: "This was the first

FIGURE 1.19. **Jock Macdonald**, *Revolving Shapes*, 1950.

time any meeting of artists from east and west in Canada had been conceived and organized. That it happened during a war, when cultural values tend to be distorted or ignored, gave greater significance to one of the main concerns of the conference—to examine the role of the artist in Canadian society in a free and open discussion."[36]

The Kingston Conference followed the Depression and people began to look to artists to assume social responsibilities. Some, like Jack Shadbolt, were interested in social realism. The conference was a critical catalyst in providing Canadian artists starved of the opportunity to travel to see the work of others while enabling audiences to see original art. Smith reports that the attendees agreed the Canadian Federation of Artists should be formed "to unite all Canadian artists, related art workers and interested laymen for mutual support in promoting common aims; the chief of which is to make the arts a creative factor in the national life of Canada and the artist an integral part of society."[37] According to Frances Smith, the Kingston Conference had "served to sharpen the awareness of the artist in Canadian society and the federation had been set in motion, concerned with something bigger than the tenets or any particular creed—concerned with the welfare of art in Canada."[38] At its conclusion, pressure was put on the unreceptive Prime Minister William Lyon Mackenzie King to establish an arts council for Canada. He showed no interest in meeting with the representatives. According to Smith, aides said he was "too occupied with affairs of state and personal matters to meet with any artists' groups in 1946."[39] Not surprisingly, frustration mounted.

On the formation of the Federation of Canadian Artists in 1941 following the conference, Ernest Lindner and Lawren Harris were the national representatives for Saskatchewan and British Columbia, respectively. Lindner knew exhibition opportunities had to be expanded for Western Canadian artists to take their places in Canadian art. He advocated for practical changes such as reducing shipping costs and bringing art exhibition judges to the West as well as having Western Canadian artists on juries in the East as well as the West. He felt that would encourage "more flow of ideas between East and West and, assessment of western art on its own terms, not by its correspondence to eastern fashions."[40]

The Second World War was still going on when the Kingston Conference took place and Western Canadian artists served in the war, including Vancouver's Jack Shadbolt and Molly Lamb Bobak (1922–2014). Their impact on artistic developments was significant, as had been the case with Canada's First World War artists. Women artists, however, could not serve in the First World War and could not go to the Front in the Second. Thus Bobak depicted the scenes and people in the overseas army camps. Her painting *VE Day Celebrations* depicts the joyous mood at the end of the war with the fireworks, lights, and crowds around a community fire. Charles Comfort, also appointed as a Second World War artist, served in the Italian Campaign and painted front-line action. Though he was living in Toronto by the outbreak of the Second World War, his Western Canadian connections from his early career at Brigdens in Winnipeg

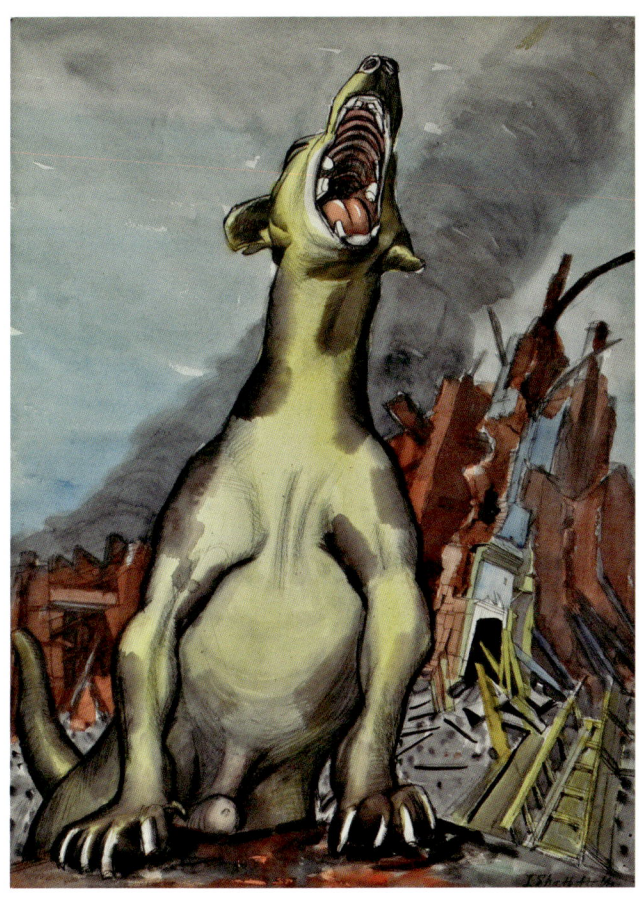

FIGURE 1.20.
Jack Leonard Shadbolt, *Dog Among the Ruins*, 1947.

were strong, his first solo exhibition having been held at the Winnipeg Art Gallery in 1922. Looking back, one wonders about the artistic relationships between Canadian and British artists, and resulting influences and ideas. Jack Shadbolt's postwar work, for instance, shows interesting connections to several leading contemporary British war artists, especially Graham Sutherland and John Piper. Through the 1950s Shadbolt's approach to form and colour was unique, with artwork that juxtaposed the devastation of warfare with signs of natural rejuvenation.

The political events in Europe of the 1930s and 1940s led a number of artists to immigrate to Canada's West. George Swinton (1917–2002) and Richard Ciccimarra, like Lindner, were from Austria. Hungarian-born Eva Stubbs (1925–2017) arrived in Canada as a refugee in 1944. She had been separated from her family in childhood during the 1929 international economic crisis and lived with her uncle and aunt until she was ten. Later, with the rise of Franco and the Spanish political revolution, she was reunited with her family in Tangiers, where they secured passage to North America to escape from that situation and the Nazis. These politically forced situations had a lasting impact on Stubbs and she later talked of these separations as the reason for her artistic concentration on the family, particularly her mother-and-child themes.[41] Also, as a young mother in 1946 she contracted tuberculosis and once again had to leave her family. After that recovery, and the breakdown of her marriage, she was once again alone, this time with a son to raise. She came to Winnipeg and attended the Winnipeg School of Art, a revolutionary step in the 1950s for a single mother, especially one pursuing sculpture.

The 1944 inauguration of the Western Canadian Art Circuit and the touring of art exhibitions throughout Western Canada marked another seminal step in the growth in the West's professionalism of the visual arts. As a result of the mounting pressure from artists across Canada following the 1941 Kingston Conference, the federal government finally formed the Massey Commission in 1949. Headed by future Governor General of Canada Vincent Massey, the commission undertook cross-country hearings on all issues pertaining to the arts in Canada. Hilda Neatby, a distinguished historian from the University of Saskatoon, and Norman MacKenzie, president of the University of British Columbia, were the western members. The commission's scope was broad and included all the arts and sciences within federal jurisdictions. The commission's mandate stated: "Our concern throughout was with the needs and desires of the citizen in relation to science, literature, art, music, drama, film, broadcasting."[42]

The Massey Commission delivered its comprehensive, milestone report in 1951, stating: "The arts and letters lie at the roots of our life as a nation. . . . Culture is what can make Canada great and what can make it one."[43] As Frances Smith commented, the commission "urged that Canadians must have the will to proceed to develop their own culture, even at a time when the nation is preoccupied with defence."[44] The commission's insights were clear, and the key recommendation was the establishment of a national body that would encourage and support the arts, both at home and internationally, promoting international exchanges and "increase Canada's knowledge in and with other countries . . . giving arts workers a wide export market . . . and enrich the cultural presentations from abroad."[45] This body, to be comprised of fifteen members, including its chair and vice-chair, would be "known as the Canada Council for the Encouragement of the Arts, Letters, Humanities and Social Sciences to stimulate and to help voluntary organizations within these fields, to foster Canada's Cultural Relations abroad, and to perform the functions of a national commission for UNESCO, and to devise and administer a system of scholarships."[46]

The Saskatchewan Arts Board, founded in 1948, a year before the Massey Commission was established, was the first arts council in Canada. That province's role nationally in the postwar era was visionary and remarkable for all its advancements in and for the arts. The Emma

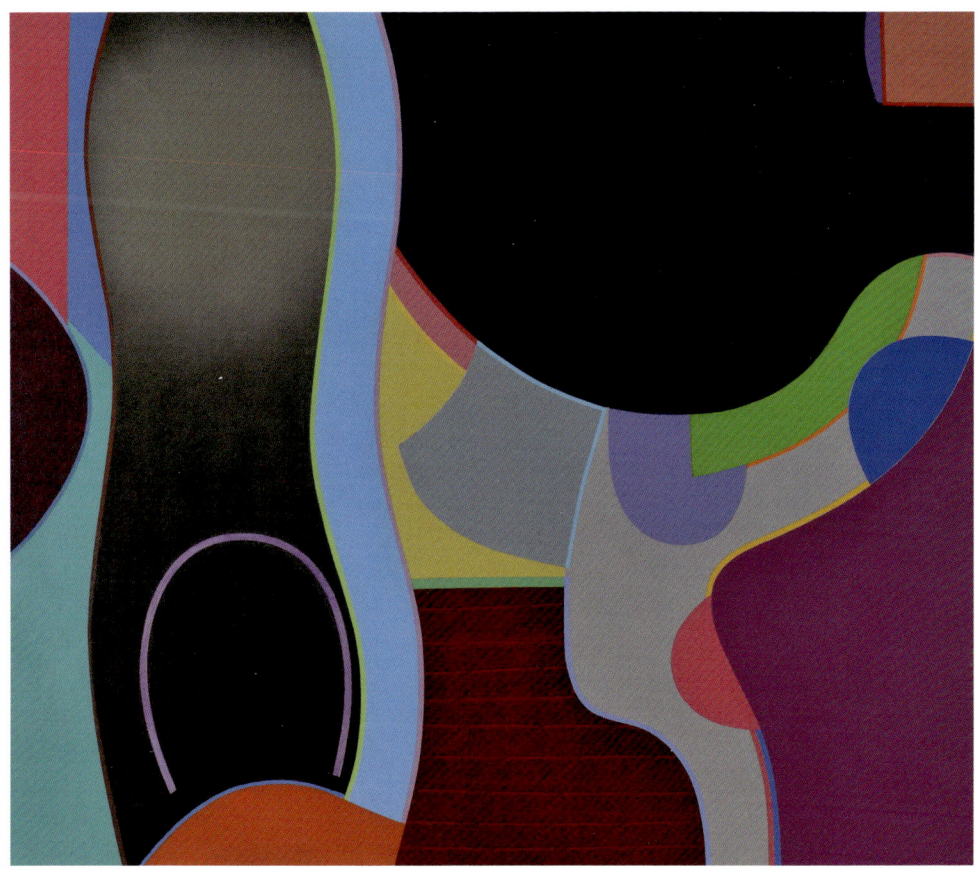

Lake Artists' Workshops and its leaders were especially influential. Terrence Heath observed: "After the war, painting changed rapidly and strong, young painters were emerging. The tradition of impressionistic watercolours, which had in its time pushed out academic painters like Kenderdine, was suddenly old-fashioned. The art school in Regina College, under the directorship of Ken Lochhead [1926–2006], was beginning to function as the most dynamic art centre in the province. The Regina painters were riding on a new wave of experimentation, looking to international movements for direction and inspiration. . . . The [Emma Lake] workshops did drastically change the practice of art on the prairies, and indeed in Canada."[47]

FIGURE 1.21. **Doug Morton**, *Ida Grey*, 1975.

There is no question that artists who were repeat attendees at the workshops, like Ernest Lindner, experienced different dimensions and stimulating expressions each year. Jack Shadbolt was the leader at the first Emma Lake workshop in 1955, organized by Ken Lochhead. Lindner wrote Lochhead: "I do not think that I have ever learned so much in such a short time and that I have ever received so much for so little. Mr. Shadbolt's lucid and broad expounding of the creative process in painting, both in the present and in the past, in theory and in practical demonstration, has opened new vistas to me. It will take time and much work before I will be able to digest properly all that I have taken in, but I know that I can never be the same again."[48] Lindner wrote similarly to Donald Buchanan, editor of *Canadian Art*: "I feel this summer's Workshop will in future be considered as the most important single event in the Art development in this province."[49] His comments about the 1957 workshop, led by American Will Barnet, were equally positive: "Mr. Barnet's understanding help has done more for me than I ever dared hope for. I believe he has helped me to a definite breakthrough in my work and I hope, no, I am convinced that my contact with Barnet will prove a definite turning point in the quality of my work."[50]

During this period art schools across Canada's West took new strides. The Winnipeg School of Art, for instance, joined the University of Manitoba in 1951, and individual teachers made memorable and transformative impacts on their students. William McCloy (1913–2000), from the United States, headed the School of Art from 1950 to 1954 and was revered by a number of students. The instructors McCloy hired from Britain and the United States introduced contemporary international movements. The colour theories of New York artist Hans Hofmann (1880–1966) were taught and revolutionized students' thinking. Dianne Scoles wrote insightfully of these directions: "The new American director accepted what could be called a missionary role of bringing the concept of 'modern art' to Winnipeg."[51] McCloy, Bruce Head's major and early influence, counselled students that, as Head said, "all you need is desire. . . . He was a God-send and one of the first intellectuals I had met."[52] Other artists in those first classes of the 1950s—Tony Tascona, Ivan Eyre, Winston Leathers, and Eva Stubbs—all commented to me about McCloy's being an inspiration. For Tascona, McCloy's gift was making "students aware of the function of the anatomical structure."[53] To Eyre, McCloy was an "intellectual"; and he told Stubbs "to take sculpture seriously."[54] Cecil Richards, professor and mentor, then became her "greatest encouragement and supporter."[55] The art school thus became a Mecca, giving this first generation of trained professional prairie-born artists an excellent grounding. Many were to become major Canadian art figures, and their expressive innovations broke traditional norms.

The mid-1950s also witnessed two independent, yet particularly definitive, national juried exhibitions: the *Winnipeg Show*, run by the Winnipeg Art Gallery; and the *Montreal Spring Show*, organized by the Montreal Museum of Fine Arts. The first *Winnipeg Show*, 1955, was an inspiration of artist and University of Manitoba fine arts professor George Swinton and gallery

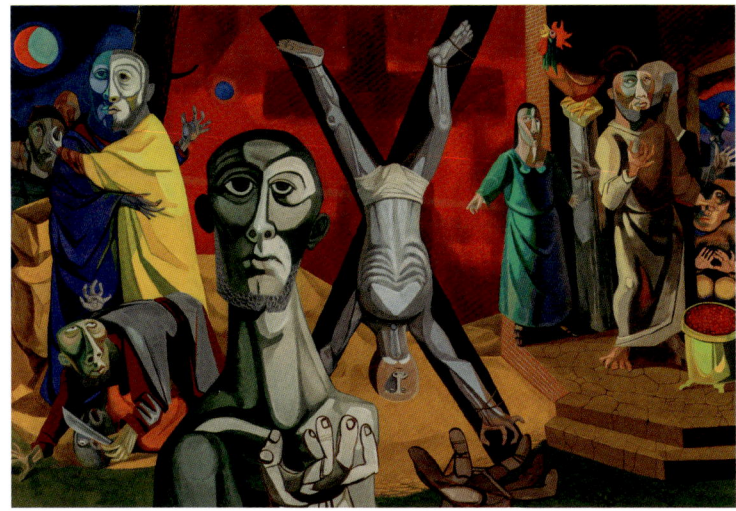

FIGURE 1.22.
**William Ashby
McCloy**, *And Peter
Followed Afar Off*,
1951.

director Ferdinand Eckhardt. Welcoming submissions of recent artwork from artists across Canada, it encouraged and celebrated experimental work. Over the years leading Canadian and American curators and artists served as jurors for the *Winnipeg Show*, extending artists' national exposure and ensuring Winnipeg's reputation as a vibrant centre of Canadian contemporary art. Acceptance in the *Winnipeg Show* made the careers of many Canadian artists. With the amount and scope of Canadian contemporary art it brought to Winnipeg, Bruce Head, who spent his entire career in the city, never felt isolated: "Here you can find out what's happening in the art world; you can get really active. But you can also be left alone if you want."[56]

Both faculty and this gifted group of students were encouraged by McCloy to submit work to the *Montreal Spring Show*. Interestingly, all the students' work was accepted but none of the faculty's.[57] Buoyed by this inclusion and subsequent exhibition invitations across the country so early in their careers, Bruce Head, Kelly Clark, Don Reichert, and Frank Mikuska drove to Montreal, their car filled with art, and they met up with Tony Tascona (1926–2006) in Montreal, as he was working at Trans Canada Airlines there. The artists recounted to me that when they opened the back of their station wagon art poured over Montreal's Sherbrooke Street and Montreal Museum of Fine Arts director, Evan Turner, helped pick it up. Turner subsequently bought work from Head and perhaps from some of the others for the museum.[58] These annual exhibitions were important for Ivan Eyre (1935–2022), too, as the 1957 *Winnipeg Show* introduced Eyre's work to Ferdinand Eckhardt, which led to Eyre's career breakthrough with his 1969 solo exhibition in Germany.

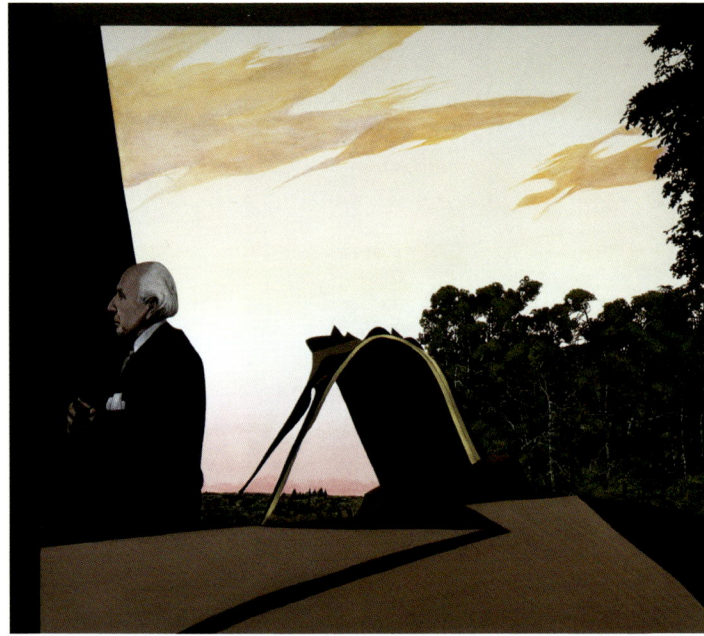

FIGURE 1.23.
Ivan Eyre,
Director, 1974.

During this artistically explosive period, and before the 1957 establishment of the Canada Council, Western Canadian art gallery directors—Ferdinand Eckhardt of the Winnipeg Art Gallery, Archie Key of the Allied Arts Centre in Calgary, and Colin Graham of the Art Gallery of Greater Victoria—formed the Western Canadian Art Circuit, expanding Lindner's earlier Saskatoon program. The *Massey Report* noted the impact of this exhibition circuit for artists, audiences, and collectors as it brought art to small and large communities. The Carnegie Corporation in New York gave generous financial support and helped the development of gallery and museum education programs.

Ferdinand Eckhardt and Colin Graham were two particularly influential and visionary gallery leaders and provided opportunities for artists and audiences in the West and across Canada. Graham had assumed the directorship of the Art Gallery of Greater Victoria in 1951, a post he held until his retirement in 1973. Eckhardt was the Winnipeg Art Gallery's director from 1953 until his retirement in 1974. Both arrived at their posts with international gallery experience in art education: the Austrian-born Eckhardt in Vienna, Berlin, and Washington, DC; and Victoria-born Graham in California. Both their academic backgrounds were in medieval art: Graham as an undergraduate at the United Kingdom's Cambridge University, and Eckhardt with his PhD on the Utrecht Psalter. Their museological approaches were likewise

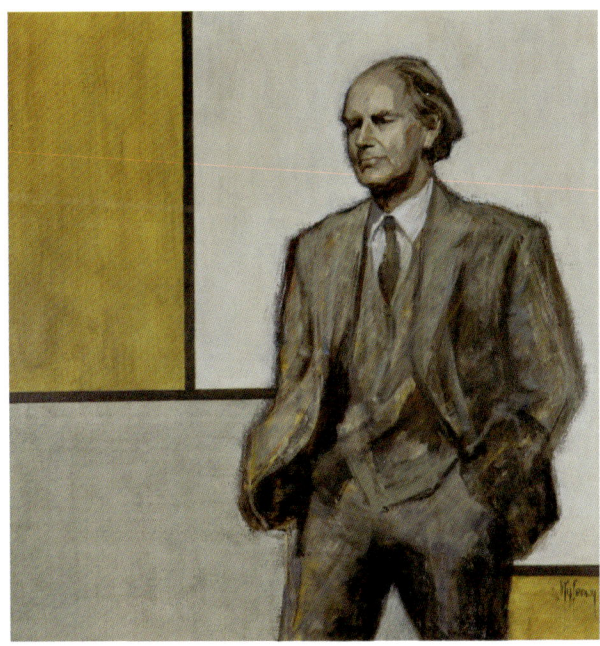

FIGURE 1.24.
Myfanwy Spencer Pavelic,
Colin Graham, Director
1951–1973, 1973.

similar as each sought historical and contemporary art of the highest calibre by local, national, and international artists. Thus, when the Canada Council finally became a reality, Canadian art in the West was ready for the ensuing revolution. Gaining Royal Assent on 28 March 1957, the Canada Council and the arts in general were guaranteed a measure of independence with financial awards decided by peer juries of artists. George Woodcock noted that this

> created an entirely new situation for the arts in Canada . . . the arts have since flourished and interest grown. . . . The Canada Council was not established to attempt the impossible task of creating art, but to support artistic endeavours when they had taken on an identity and proved their seriousness. . . . During the early years of the Canada Council the revival of the arts and the emergence of public support seemed to parallel each other with little sign of trouble ahead. . . . The fact is that patronage in itself never creates an upsurge in the arts or inspires artists in the sense of stimulating them to achievements beyond their evident powers.[59]

The artists' voices from the 1941 Kingston Conference and the Massey Commission were heard at last. With travel grants, Western Canadian artists became connected to colleagues across the country. They met artists and saw work from other parts of the country, and art galleries received monies to present, publish, and tour exhibitions of contemporary art.

While the first half of the twentieth century was a time of quantum shifts in the visual arts in Canada and the West, by the end of the Second World War the centre of the art world had moved from Europe to New York City. In the 1950s interest in the visual arts deepened with increasing numbers of art journals, new colour reproduction technologies, more public and commercial galleries, and new, stronger, and expanded art schools. Milestone exhibitions received national attention, and a new generation of gallery directors were making their mark. In 1955, Richard Simmins, newly appointed curator at Regina's Norman MacKenzie Art Gallery, brought new insights, modes of expressions, and a generational shift in artists to the fore with the exhibition *Ten Artists of Saskatchewan 1955*. Ernie Lindner, for years considered to be the leader of Saskatchewan's artistic community, was not included. The work of ten younger artists was. They were Ken Lochhead, Nonie Mulcaster, Dorothy Knowles, Art McKay, MacGregor Hone, Doug Morton, Clara Samuels, Anthony Thorn, Henry Bonli, and Reta Cowley. As Terrence Heath wrote, "It was as if a new generation of painters had replaced the old."[60]

1960–1990: Breaking Norms

"Native-born and resident populations faced an art world in the post-1970 period that was as complex, as divisive, and as multi-layered as anything ever seen before."[61]

The 1960s brought even more change. Canada's 1967 Centennial celebrations, Manitoba's Centennial in 1970, and British Columbia's in 1971 provided further impetus for the visual arts. The University of Regina continued to be a national hotbed of contemporary art. Five young faculty members—abstract artists Ron Bloore, Ken Lochhead, Doug Morton, Ted Godwin, and Art McKay—made national history with their 1961 exhibition, *The Regina Five*. By the time it was shown at the National Gallery of Canada, Richard Simmins had left Regina and was the National Gallery's coordinator of extension services responsible for that Ottawa presentation. Unquestionably connected to leading-edge international art, these artists collectively and individually made landmark contributions to abstraction in Canada and drew international attention to Saskatchewan's visual arts. In addition, the artists and critics Lochhead brought to Emma Lake as presenters in the early 1960s, before he moved to Winnipeg, were impressive. One was New York art critic Clement Greenberg. So, too, was colour field painter Barnett Newman, whose painting *Voice of Fire* is in the collection of the National Gallery of Canada.

FIGURE 1.25. **Kenneth Campbell Lochhead**, *Sky Location*, from the *L Series*, 1967.

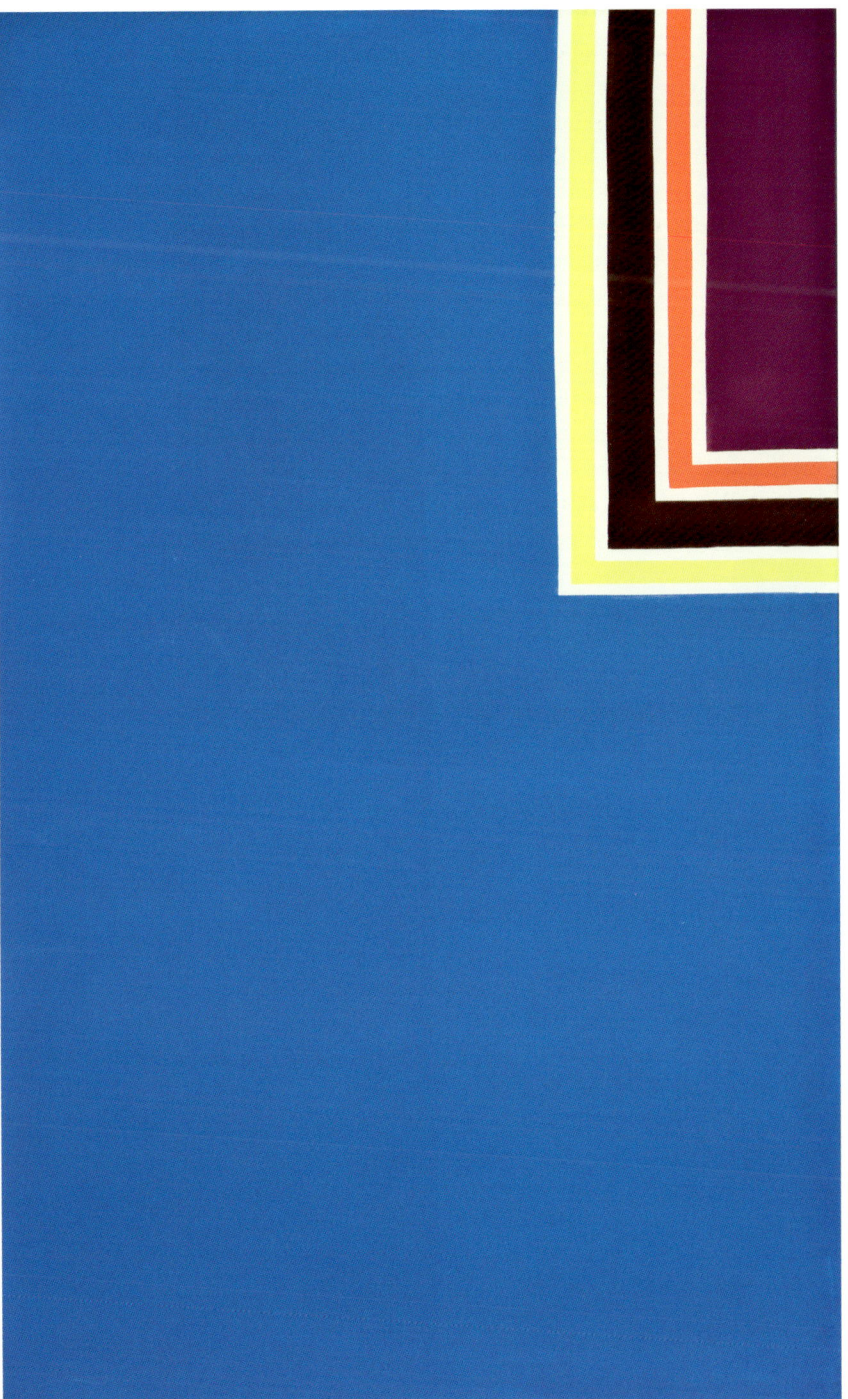

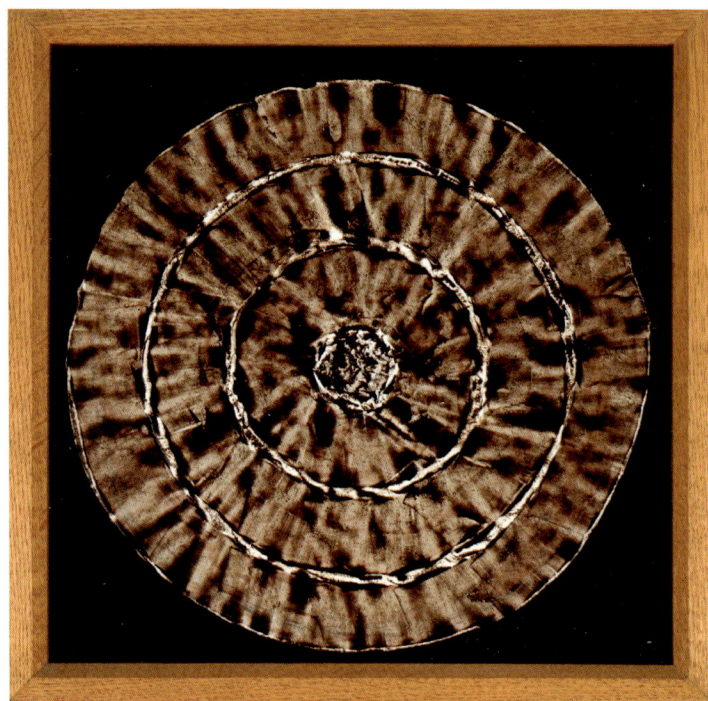

FIGURE 1.26.
Arthur McKay,
*Untitled (Concentric
Circles),* 1970.

Manitoba's Bruce Head was also producing work that was being seen across the country. At only age thirty-five, he had become one of Winnipeg's leading abstract artists. His rich, pure colours and strength of line were his trademarks. He achieved complex textures by tearing and then stitching his canvases. He also created three-dimensional paintings by stretching the canvases over discarded film canisters or plastic containers. Critic Ralph Watkins wrote in 1966 that "he wants the viewer to look at his manipulation of colour and lines without being distracted by the subject of the painting. . . . They are, essentially, elegant compositions in colour, texture, mass and line."[62]

Ivan Eyre, originally from Saskatchewan, graduated with the famous Winnipeg School of Art class of 1956. His 1969 solo exhibition at Germany's Frankfurter Kunstkabinett, organized by Ferdinand Eckhardt, garnered him a solid and lasting international reputation. His art was unique, different from that seen internationally or nationally, with its surrealistic combination of unlike objects on prairie landscapes and his floating figures and periodic use of acrid colour. He incorporated overlapping imaginative mythologies and personal metaphors. Eyre knew international art history yet eschewed any one style, group, or painterly school. He

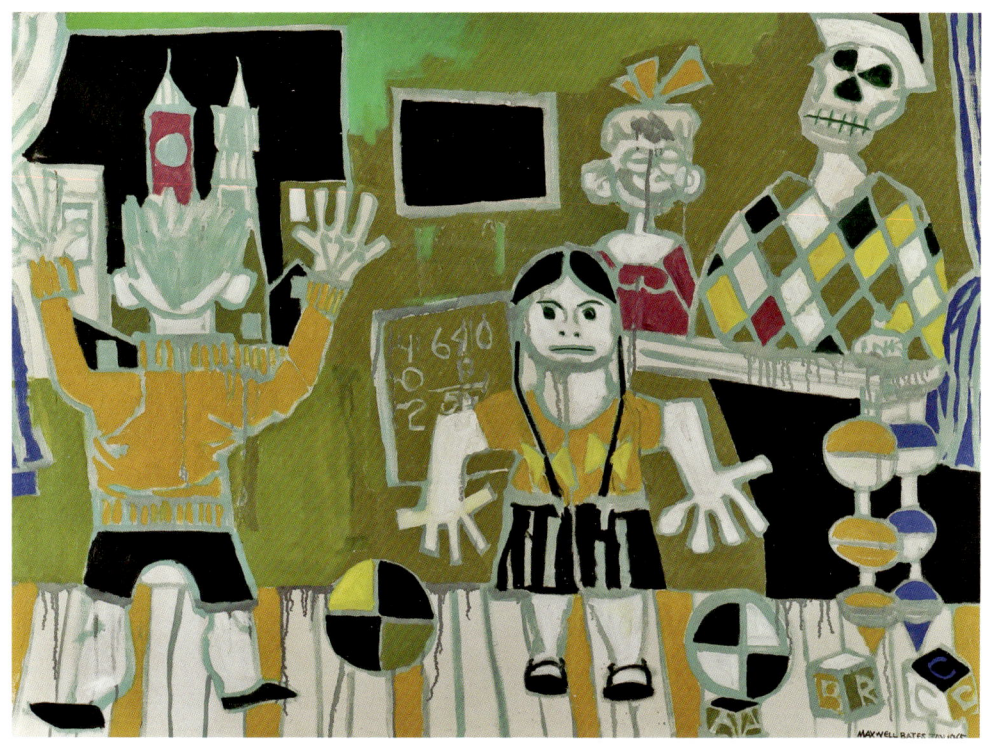

reminisced: "I was attracted to Botticelli and Mantegna, not to the Renaissance. I was taken by Pissaro and Seurat, not by the so-called Impressionists. I like Max Beckmann, not the German Expressionists. I think any painter who works according to the dictums of the group is foolish and probably not an artist. It is a mistake to paint according to theory as opposed to perception. Bosch and Ensor did see all these things. . . . It is important to work in isolation. It is a great advantage to be out of the mainstream."[63]

During the 1960s Calgary artist Maxwell Bates brought social issues into the mainstream through his expressionistic paintings detailing the hardships of farming on the prairies and with his *Cocktail Series* and *Worker Series*.[64] Drawing attention to the economic and social plight of many people, his visual commentaries about social issues and foibles increased following his 1963 move to Victoria. The impact of the horrors of his war imprisonment by the Nazis never left him.

FIGURE 1.27. **Maxwell Bates**, *Kindergarten*, 1965.

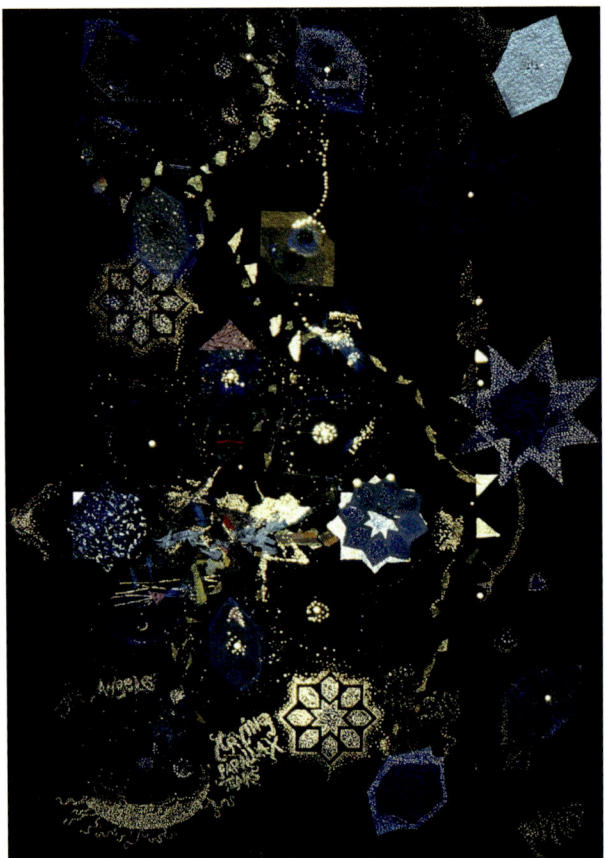

FIGURE 1.28.
Pat Martin Bates,
*The Angel of the Blue Sky is
Crying Parallax Tears*, 1998.

    The year 1964 also witnessed the initiation of visual art programs at the new University of Victoria, where acclaimed artist Pat Martin Bates (b. 1927) inaugurated their printmaking program. Canada's position in the art world internationally increased, too. In 1964 Victoria sculptor Elza Mayhew (1916–2004) represented Canada at the Venice Biennale, along with Ontario painter Harold Town. Prior to Mayhew's participation in the Biennale, Western Canadian participation had included Emily Carr (posthumously in 1952), Bertram Binning (1954), and Jack Shadbolt (1956). Canada's participation in this prestigious exhibition dates from 1952, though the exhibition began in 1895. Since Mayhew's involvement Western Canadian artists selected as Canadian representatives have been General Idea (1980), Ian Carr-Harris and Liz Magor (1984), Roland Brenner (1988), Rodney Graham (1997), Janet Cardiff and George

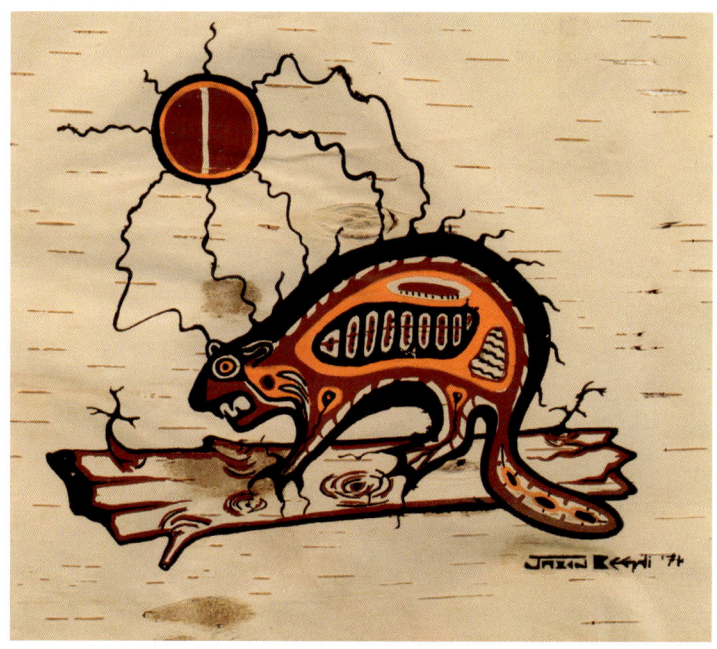

FIGURE 1.29.
Jackson Beardy,
Untitled, 1971.

Bures Miller (2001), Indigenous artists Edward Poitras (1995) and Rebecca Belmore (2005), and Vancouver's Stan Douglas in 2022.

In addition to the new universities, new fine arts programs, and expanding art galleries and museums across Canada, the 1960s also saw the growth of commercial galleries and the network of provincial arts councils. All these positively affected artists and audiences. Legislation to establish the Manitoba Arts Council was passed in 1964, though its first board was not appointed until 1968, and only in 1969 were the first grants awarded to visual artists. The Alberta Arts Foundation came into being in 1972, and that in British Columbia in 1995, but both those governments had awarded funding to organizations prior to the establishment of their respective arts councils.

Exhibitions of Indigenous artists' art unfortunately were slow in coming. For Canada's 1967 Centennial celebrations, the National Gallery of Canada presented an exhibition of the work of First Nations artists—the first presentation of First Nations' work in a Canadian art gallery, though Inuit art had been shown in the Winnipeg Art Gallery since 1952 and already formed a significant part of that gallery's collection. The 1967 National Gallery exhibition included the work of many Northwest Coast artists, and it became clear that more exhibitions were warranted and wanted.

The Indigenous Group of Seven, founded in Winnipeg in 1972 as the Professional Native Indian Artists Incorporated, through Daphne Odjig's gallery, was another important milestone. Including Jackson Beardy, Eddy Cobiness, Alex Janvier, Norval Morrisseau, Daphne Odjig, Carl Ray, and Joseph Sanchez, the Indigenous Group of Seven had a major exhibition at the Winnipeg Art Gallery in that year of their founding. Some of this group subsequently represented Canada in exhibitions in Paris in the 1970s. These were important events, but only marked the beginning of long overdue recognition.

Artist-initiated programs and spaces were other new markers in the visual arts in the late 1960s and early 1970s. A paradigm shift for printmaking occurred in 1968 with artist Bill Lobchuk's founding of the Grand Western Canadian Screen Shop in Winnipeg. With Len Anthony as its much heralded technician, it became a transformative catalyst in contemporary printmaking in Canada, just as Walter J. Phillips and Eric Bergman had been for colour woodblock prints and black and white wood engraving in earlier decades. Not only did leading Western Canadian artists such as David Thauberger (b. 1948) and Joe Fafard (1942–2019) come to Winnipeg to do their prints, but the Screen Shop also undertook exchanges with St. Michael's Printshop in Newfoundland and Pierre Ayot's studio in Quebec.

At the same time, in 1971, artists across the country, led by those in the West, inaugurated a strong and groundbreaking network of artist-run spaces. Winnipeg's Plug In and Open Space in Victoria were among the first. They showed new experimental work, and their approaches in presentation, discussions, and performances defied the traditional processes of established collecting art galleries. The impact of these artists' collaboratives was significant. Performance artist and curator Shawna Dempsey noted: "With the rise of the artist-run-centre movement, alternative community spaces, and an expanded art discourse, performance art came indoors."[65] The beginnings of performance art as an artform had been presented primarily outdoors as major galleries declined to host them. Installation art grew as well during these years, and there were seemingly no boundaries for creation or presentation.

Canadian Artists' Representation/Le Front des artistes canadiens (CARFAC), the union of artists, was also formed in 1972. It successfully lobbied for public art galleries to pay exhibition fees to artists and later forced galleries to pay fees when presenting works under copyright in their collections. That year also saw the beginning of the Museums Assistance Program, now under the Department of Canadian Heritage, created to support the circulation of exhibitions of historical art, in the manner that the Canada Council supported contemporary art exhibitions. In 1972 the National Museums of Canada Corporation also developed a number of exhibition centres across the country, enabling the presentation of art in smaller communities. The teaching of fine arts expanded as well, with universities and colleges introducing a number of new media, including printmaking and video, to a greater extent than before. In the early 1970s, for instance, acclaimed printmakers Walter Jule, Lyndal Osborne, and Liz Ingram founded the printmaking program

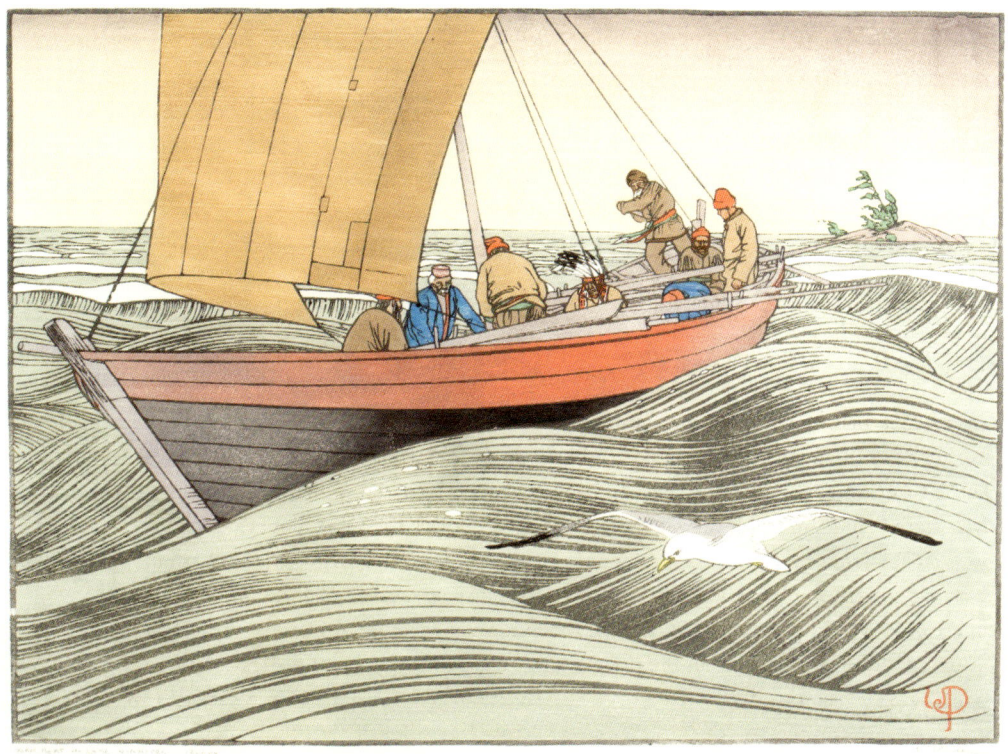

at the University of Alberta in Edmonton, and in 1977 Bill Laing was hired by the University of Calgary to establish its printmaking studio. These Alberta initiatives inspired the Print and Drawing Council of Canada to move their head offices to Calgary in 1978, and two years later to Edmonton. This leadership spawned many printmakers and new dimensions in the art form.

This visual arts explosion of new media and technologies, which revolutionized the way artists made art, continued apace through the 1980s, in part due to the influence of magazines like award-winning *Border Crossings, Artmagazine, Galleries West,* and *Canadian Art.* They brought work and visual ideas to wider national and international audiences.

Government programs expanded to the end of the century. While corporate and private collections of contemporary art grew increasingly substantive during the 1970s, 1980s, and 1990s, the federal Department of Foreign Affairs enabled significant internationally touring

FIGURE 1.30. **Walter J. Phillips**, *York Boat on Lake Winnipeg*, 1930.

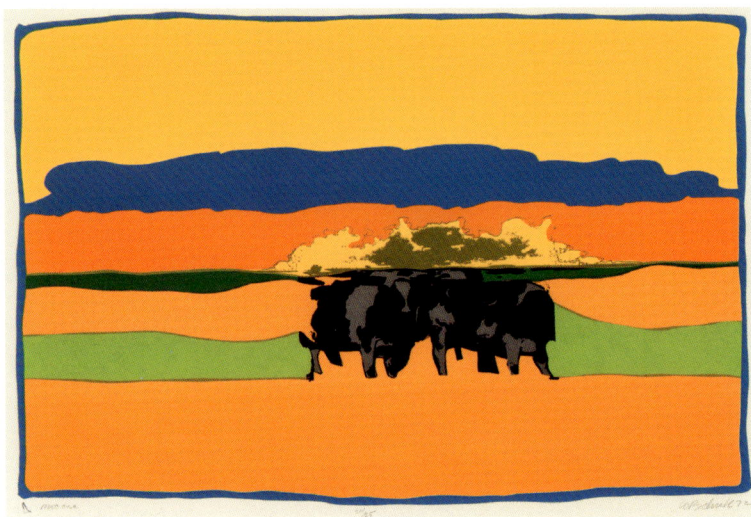

exhibitions of Canadian art and supported Canadian artists' international residencies. In the 1980s and 1990s a number of Canadian artists lived and worked overseas for various periods of time, some for years. These collective results appreciably contributed to audiences' engagement with new artistic concepts, and the place of Canadian art abroad grew. Victoria's Michael Morris (1942–2022), a Governor General's Award in the Visual Arts recipient and well-known abstract painter, filmmaker, and artistic collaborator, for instance, lived and worked in Berlin for eighteen years from 1980 to 1998; and Winnipeg's Eleanor Bond and others shared a studio for a number of years in Holland.

At the same time other new pieces of federal and provincial legislation supporting creative endeavours were introduced. Canada's new Copyright Act was proclaimed in June 1988, the first since 1925. Status of the Artist legislation was adopted in several parts of the country, and the new National Gallery of Canada and the Canadian Museum of Civilization (now the Museum of Canadian History) were opened in 1988 and 1989, respectively. These, and the building of, and new additions to, other major galleries, such as the Montreal Museum of Fine Arts and the Art Gallery of Ontario, gave the visual arts increasing national and international presence.

By the 1980s Indigenous art, both traditional and avant-garde, was increasingly shown, published, and widely celebrated for its excellence. Through their paintings, sculptures, videos, installation works, and performance pieces, Indigenous artists have raised multiple social and political issues. The honest and painful visual revelations, especially regarding colonialism, the

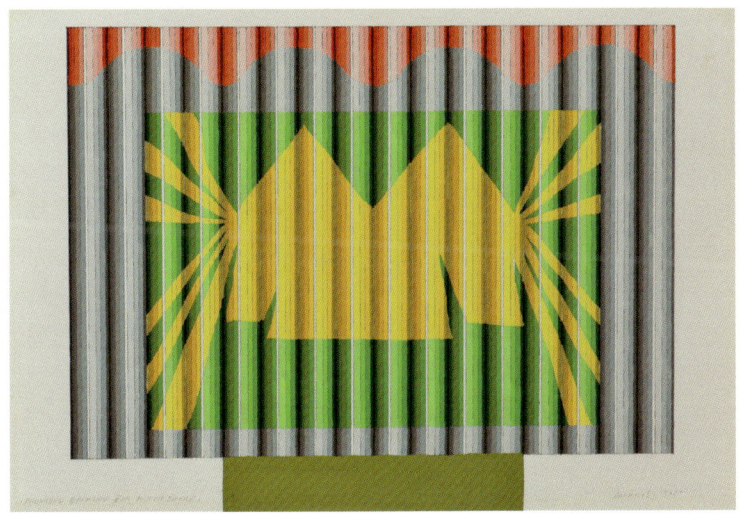

FIGURE 1.32.
Michael Morris,
*Proposed Backdrop
for North Shore*, 1965.

horrors of residential schools, and the crises of missing and murdered women and girls, have been transformative for Canadian society. Joane Cardinal-Schubert, Jane Ash Poitras, Robert Boyer, and Robert Houle were particularly resolute in the expression of their perspicacity.

World events in the latter part of the twentieth century and early twenty-first century also brought new dimensions to Canadian art and that of Western Canadian artists. The Tiananmen Square massacre of 1989 has had a lasting impact on British Columbia, and multimedia artist Gu Xiong visually brought those consequences to light. After graduating with his Bachelor and Master of Fine Arts degree in 1985 from the Sichuan Fine Arts Institute, he attended a residency at the Banff Centre for Fine Arts in 1986, the first artist from the People's Republic of China to do so. On returning to China, he was part of the 1989 *China Avant-Garde* exhibition closed by police mere hours after opening. The Tiananmen protests took place four months later. Xiong was in the square that day and emigrated to Vancouver immediately after the revolution. His subsequent multimedia installations, such as *The River,* 1998, portray streams of cultural connections, politics, and ways of life. In his work he addresses the question of cultural identity. As he said in his artist's statement:

> All cultures are complex, of course, but the one into which you are born is the one you come to understand most profoundly. Thus, this influence is what finds its way into the work of an artist, and I believe it is expressed almost instinctively. If a person should move to another culture, he or she must make both a conscious and instinctive adjustment in seeking to understand what at first is a strange new world.

It is within this dynamic milieu that I currently find myself. . . . This conflict of cultures in my work is in a state of constant evolution. It is a continuous generation of "artistic electricity" that fuels change in both my personal life and my work as a contemporary artist and instructor.[66]

The opening of the Berlin Wall and the fall of the Soviet Union in December 1989 precipitated other subjects in Western art, including the past memories and cultures within which artists lived before emigrating to Canada. Czechoslovakian-born Vancouver artist John Koerner (1913–2014) was perhaps among the first to depict the very personal dimensions of this political change in eastern Europe. Koerner left Prague in 1922 to study law at the Sorbonne in Paris, where he settled until the rise of the Nazis triggered his emigration to Vancouver to work as a lawyer in the lumber industry. In 1951 he turned to art full time and taught at the Vancouver School of Art. His paintings celebrate cross-cultural connections, and his *Slavonic Dance 7, Opus 9030,* 1990, draws from his Czech roots and shows the family home complete with the broken window from his soccer-playing youth. Author Ted Lindberg wrote of Koerner's 1990 return to Czechoslovakia after being away for fifty-two years: "He is swept back, in almost hypnotic, psychic regression, to the sensations of his boyhood mind and body. In *Slavonic Dance 7, Opus 9030,* . . . a discontinuous array of sensations; interior/exterior scenes, [float] in a pastel ambience that characterizes the colour of Czech architecture and folk art. . . . The reference to Slavonic Dance and Antonin Dvorak's utilization of Czech folk music is one of the uniting threads that links past and present Czechoslovakia for Koerner, as well as the folk designs and motifs. . . . What is lost in the linear narrative is more than gained in monolithic impression."[67]

Many other international events have also had huge impacts on art, culture, and the importance of the visual within society as a whole. The release of Nelson Mandela in 1990, for instance, brought serious issues of human rights to the fore at home and afar. Numerous comparisons have been made between the situation in South Africa and that with First Nations in Canada. The AIDS epidemic, 9/11, and water safety issues in Indigenous communities are only some of the other key precipitators of visual commentary and reflection. Artists projected those issues in dire need of political and social resolution and change, calling for societal norms to shift.

During these same years the economy boomed and some of the corporations that developed major collections of contemporary art commissioned works directly from artists. Others bought from dealers. The spinoff for artists was significant, enabling many to focus solely on their art making without the need for parallel careers. They continued to explore revolutionary art-making possibilities and to challenge society.

Into the Twenty-First Century: Leading-Edge Innovations

"I am more interested in ideas than medium."[68]

Art in the twenty-first century began the same way as it closed the twentieth century, with new media and developing technologies inspiring and probing new ideas and realities. Computer-generated work, digital imaging, and sound and interdisciplinary creation proliferated. Reva Stone, a recipient of the Governor General's Award in Visual Arts, pushed those technological boundaries substantially. *Carnevale,* 2000–2002, a life-sized, double aluminum cut-out of a girl, is a complex, groundbreaking work using new technologies to engage viewers. On a moving platform, this robotic silhouette carries a video camera and moves through the gallery space. She is clad in a dress with puffy sleeves, baggy shorts, and bobby socks, and the video projector she carries has wireless technology with playback and storage capabilities. The robot interacts with gallery visitors as she turns and moves towards them. The Winnipeg Art Gallery documents: "At random intervals, the visitors' images and movements are captured onto video. These images are combined and overlaid with previously stored images and projected outward sometimes in focus and sometimes not. After several playbacks the computer either adds the new video record to memory or discards it."[69]

Stone's *Imaginal Expression,* 2004–2006, is another viewer-responsive computer-generated installation, building on her earlier interactive computer-generated works. These three-dimensional moving projections of wrapped and scanned protein molecules reference the flesh, hair, blood vessels, and bruising and scarring of the living body. Stone said that her research and artwork of the 2010s explore artificial intelligence, surveillance studies, and privacy concerns.[70]

In addition to the incorporation of new technologies in contemporary art, new places and spaces for presentation of creative work have expanded opportunities for audience engagement. Many of the artist-run centres of the 1970s and 1980s, like Winnipeg's Plug In, have formally shifted to become institutes of contemporary art. While still non-collecting, they are no longer as focused on local artists' presentations as they once were but increasingly on national and international leading-edge work, giving access to that dimension of creative expression to their viewers. Also, at the cusp of the new century, the presentation of art in public spaces accelerated with public art across Canada having blossomed to become a significant aspect of the visual arts scene. Civic policies in many Western Canadian cities enable and support creation of work for public spaces, enriching urban centres, increasing safety and citizen pride, and enhancing tourism. The Winnipeg public art program states: "A vibrant public art program reflects the identity of a city, gives voice to community and builds relationships between diverse groups.

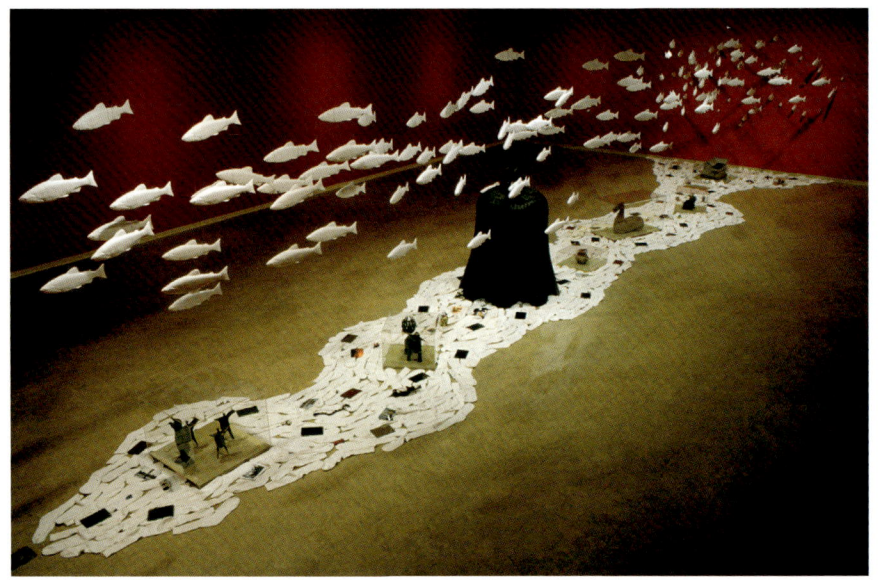

Public art enhances the urban environment by increasing the use and enjoyment of public space and building social cohesion. The exploration, through art, of the social, historical, cultural and natural environment gives meaning to place and celebrates the unique character of Winnipeg."[71]

Competitive calls for public art submissions across the West have included sculptors, painters, light artists, and multidisciplinary artists. Some installations are created in collaboration with other artists; some are created by individual artists only. All are done with site developers, city administrations, and civic planning departments. Projects are selected by juries of artists, architects, planners, and, at times, police officers, as the positive impact of public art in crime prevention and the reduction of crime in communities. Val Vint's *Education is the New Bison,* and KC Adams's *Tanisi keke totamak—Ka cis teneme toyak*, meaning "What can we do, to respect each other," are but two poignant recent Indigenous public art pieces unveiled at the Forks in Winnipeg. Both were commissioned to assist in seeking truth and understanding as the country moves towards constructive reconciliation.

Art, like society as a whole, is on the verge of significant change, pointing to paradigm shifts in means of expression, messages parlayed, and engagements with audiences in person and online, and consciously and subconsciously. At the same time art depicts significant society shifts, and comments on the impacts and consequences of those shifts. Contemporary artists continue

FIGURE 1.33. **Gu Xiong**, *The River*, 1998.

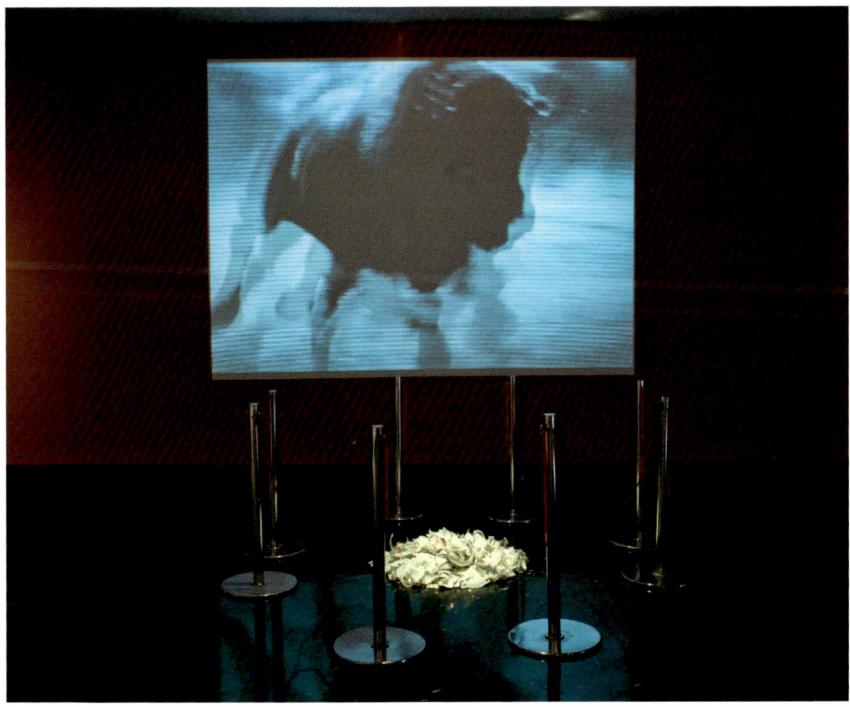

to reflect regionalism as they do nationalism and globalism, consistently and simultaneously penetrating core community concerns and personal interests. These approaches are seen, too, in the recent years of Canada's Governor General's Awards in the Visual and Media Arts awarded to artists engaged in all visual fields and regions of the country for their lifelong achievements and contributions to new directions. The diversity of the many Western Canadian recipients underlines the continued impact of the Western voice in Canadian art.

Visual art, as the Honourable Murray Sinclair, former chair of the Truth and Reconciliation Commission of Canada, has said, validates cultures and communities. Artist Pat Martin Bates further underlines the personal connection between art and philosophy: "One's own philosophy is a growing thing—it's mutable. The thing in mankind comes from seeing things and feeling things and wondering what they mean—honing the skill in us to see and perceive, the 'umbrication of the eyes and the umbrication of the soul'—shedding layers and shedding the veils beyond veils."[72]

FIGURE 1.34. **Dana Claxton**, *Buffalo Bone China*, 1997.

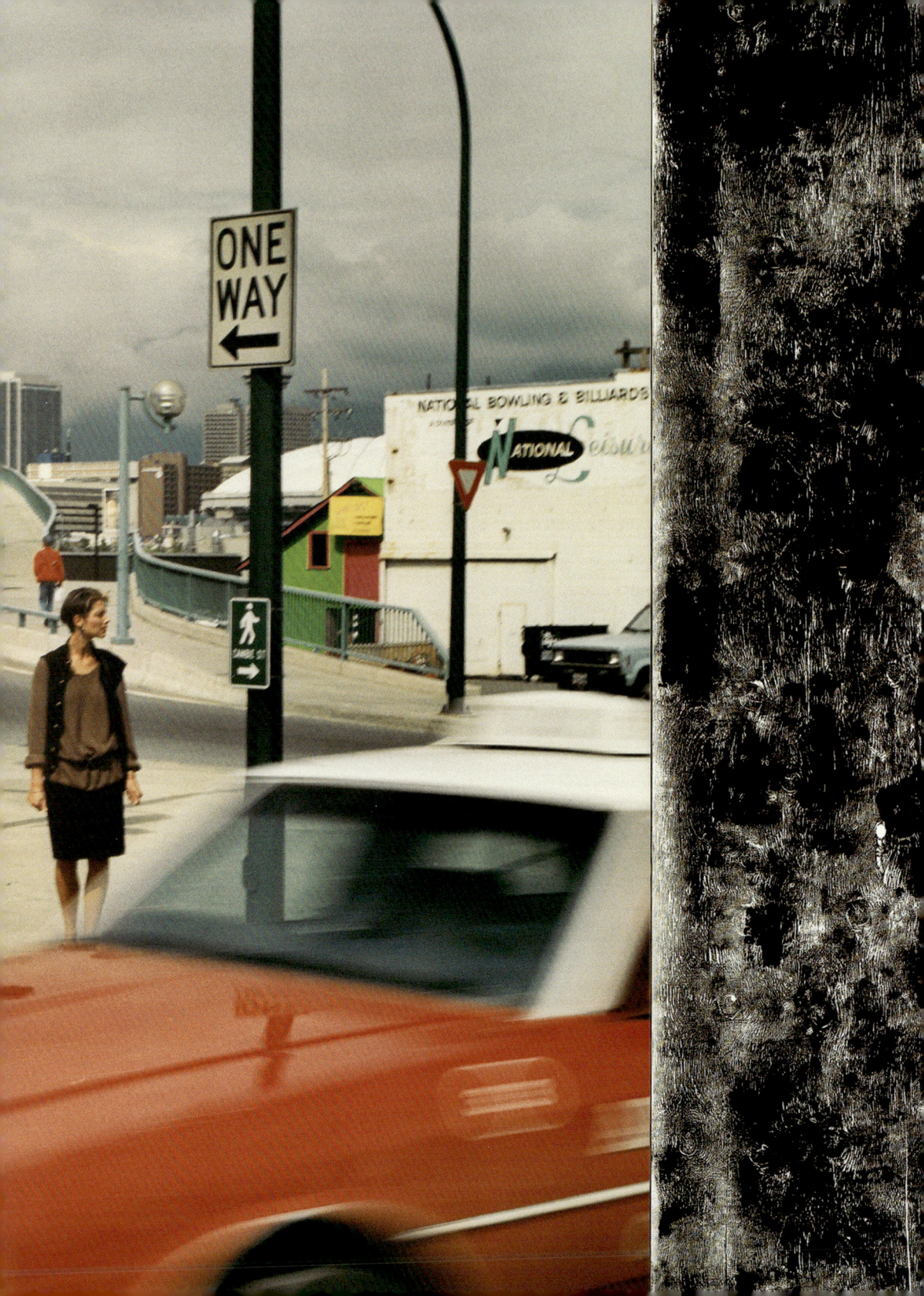

II Expanding Techniques: Creating a New Visual Language

"Bringing image and process together provides the challenge I relish." [1]

Adeptness with techniques and a thorough knowledge of materials are critical for artists to be able to convey their messages succinctly, with insight and meaning. Line, form, colour, and light are the elements of any composition, in all media and throughout all historical periods. Modes of artistic expression have certainly changed over time, as has the multiplicity of media and the infinite and persistent experimentation with materials. The methods and manner with which artists use their tools become the grammar of an artist's individual visual language—traditional, novel, or a combination of both. Artists' iconographies, symbols, and forms are their nouns, adjectives, verbs, and adverbs. In the post-contact era artists' visual vocabularies are evident in all visual media: painting, drawing, printmaking, sculpture, ceramics, textiles, photography, wood, metal, glass, and new technologies. Throughout the pre-contact millennia, porcupine quill work, bark biting, rock painting, carving of stone and wood, and use of natural dyes from plants were key means of expression.

Continuing experimentation has resulted in new ways of presenting ideas that have transformed Canadian art, shifting its impacts on and for society. Definitions and concepts of aesthetic excellence in art have evolved from early British and European sensibilities to those of a North American perspective. In the latter part of the twentieth century and in the twenty-first century, aesthetic shifts have increasingly included the poignant iconographies and visual vocabularies of Indigenous traditions and of diverse cultures. These evolving creative

Ian Wallace, *Untitled (In The Street I) (Lyse)*, 1988 (detail).

platforms have brought new criteria into the visual arena, some resulting from societal changes and conventions and others emanating from technological advances and the introduction of performance art, installations, and video and multimedia expressions.

In the 1960s two Western Canadian fine arts professors in particular, George Swinton and Ken Lochhead, underlined the value of art to society as a whole. The shifts in creation and the contemporary dialogue proffered considerable wisdom about the philosophy, meaning, and methods of art. Contrasting Canadian philosopher Marshall McLuhan's pronouncement that "the medium is the message," many artists emphasized that an artist's message is far greater than the materials or media used. In 1968, for instance, University of Manitoba professor George Swinton, described by students and colleagues alike as "the most brilliant person on faculty,"[2] opined about the power and purpose of visual language: "Both line and language convey ideas. In this regard they are means not ends. They are means for carrying ideas. They are media conveying messages. They are not messages."[3] Regina Five member Ken Lochhead, self-dubbed "a performer—an evangelist in the visual arts who wanted to spread the word about the value of the arts,"[4] consistently stressed the importance of visual language to convey multiple messages.

Works of art are ideas, visual viewpoints to engage a viewer, an engagement that is vital for a work to have currency. Art is not created for the artist alone. The artist starts a dialogue; the viewer continues that dialogue, both when the work is new and for the years to follow. As Max Bates said: "I want to express my own individual view, but on the other hand I also want to be universal so that everyone can understand me. . . . Good painting must offer something meaningful to the spectator, but it may be enigmatic. To convey emotional states of mind is not necessarily enough. Painter and spectator collaborate unconsciously."[5] For Emily Carr, "The idea must run through the whole, the story that arrested you and urged the desire to express it."[6] She also said: "In the studio your imagination steps in, your sense of design, what you want. That is why the first sketch done on the spot smacks of something bigger and more vital than the fixed-up product of the studio."[7]

Space unfortunately precludes a discussion of the many new departures in techniques and materials, so in the following chapters I have highlighted some of those artists with whom I have worked closely and who, in my view, have added distinctive twists to visual language.

Two-Dimensional Twists

"Simplicity, directness and intensity; these are the things I am after."[8]

Primarily executed on flat surfaces such as canvas, wood, paper, or vellum, two-dimensional art includes painting, drawing, photography, digital images, printmaking, and textile assemblages. Each artist has their preferred media and they select specific ones depending on their message, often using a variety of media and materials within a single work.

Drawing is seen by many as essential for art making in all media. Winnipeg wood engraver Eric Bergman expressed that view to the secretary treasurer of the Society of Canadian Painters and Engravers in the 1940s, writing that "good draftsmanship is the fundamental essential when producing a print. We could reach a number of fine artists by giving the drawing its proper place in the Graphic Arts and at the same time it would add interest to our shows."[9] Eighty years later, Alberta's Bill Laing, who established the University of Calgary printmaking program in 1977, expressed it even more succinctly: "Drawing is the skeleton for printmaking."[10] He always encouraged students to take courses in all media, as one built on the other. He, for instance, like Winnipeg printmaker E.J. (Ted) Howorth (b. 1943), started in sculpture.

George Swinton often talked about the process of creating itself: "The desire to create—that is to think, to dream, to fantasize and then give shape to ideas and thoughts and to vision—takes many forms . . . my perceptions and fantasies and discoveries relate to my interests in art and life."[11] He clearly articulated his thoughts on drawing in his 1968 poem:

> Drawing is thinking—a process of feeling one's way.
> Drawings are thought. I like to think and so I draw.
> I always draw. My drawings are thoughts, my thoughts.
> I draw in series which are developments of themes and
> ideas: probing depths,
> exploring possibilities,
> discovering relations,
> finding the unexpected.
> Drawing is my road to freedom:
> leaping from the unknown to the idea,
> from the sensed to the formed,
> from the imagined to the image.
> Drawing is visualization: through drawing I bring my vision and myself into focus.[12]

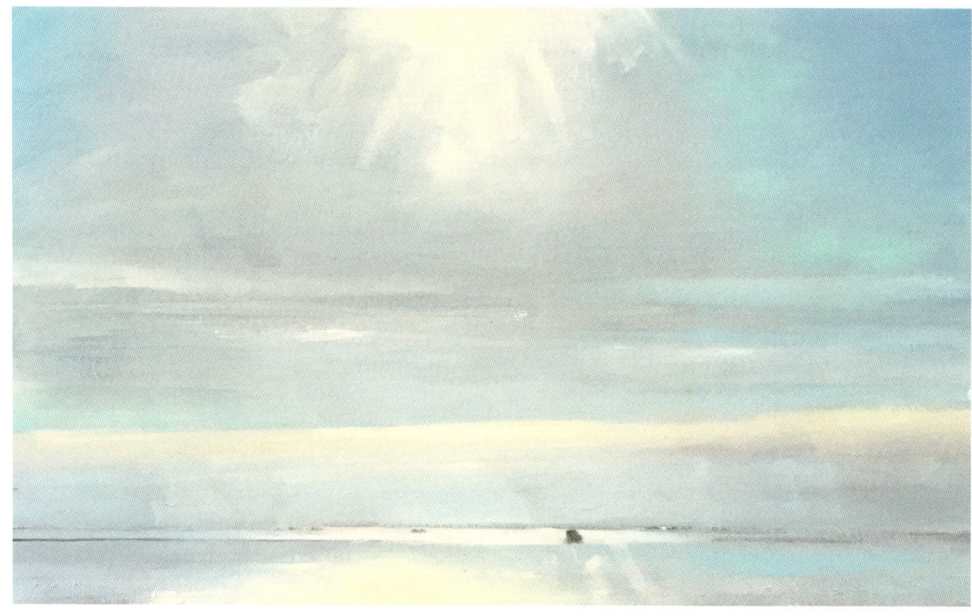

Drawings can be both sketches for preliminary explorations of an idea and finished works in themselves. They are executed in a number of media using pen, pencil, pastel, or brush, and the choice of materials is fundamental. Eva Stubbs, for instance, used oxides to draw on clay. Arnold Saper (1933–2019) etched into metal, drawing with acids. Emily Carr often sketched on paper in oil paint she thinned with gasoline, being, as she said, inexpensive and light to carry. Don Proch (b. 1942) actually forsook painting in 1964, drawing being what he likes most.[13] He draws with meticulous precision in silverpoint, pencil, and coloured pencil on the surfaces of the three-dimensional masks and sculptures he constructs with fibreglass.

Watercolour has been used by artists for centuries, the colours originally having been made from plants and minerals. Until the middle of the twentieth century, in Canada watercolour was primarily used in traditional ways on dry or wet paper. For the early itinerant artists in Western Canada, watercolour was most convenient when they were on their travels, being light to carry, quick to dry, and easy to set up. Some of these were preliminary works for later oil paintings; others were stand-alone works. Watercolour is also versatile for multiple modes of expression, allowing Lionel LeMoine FitzGerald, for instance, the freedom of brushwork for his evocative self-portraits, precision for his abstractions, and detail in his pointillist still lifes.

FIGURE 2.1. **Terry Fenton**, *GLARE, Saskatchewan*, 2016–2021.

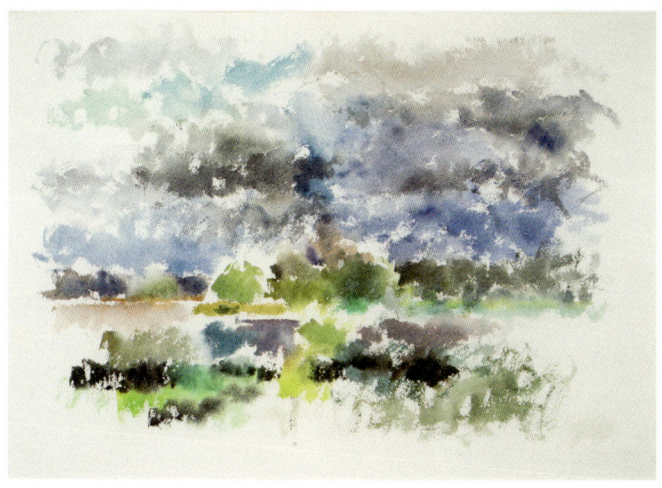

FIGURE 2.2.
Reta Cowley, *Emma Lake #2*, 1963.

During the second half of the century, watercolour took on yet other dimensions at the hands of a few artists. Gallery director and art writer Terry Fenton opined: "Since the death of David Milne in 1953, three Canadian artists have brought something new to the medium: Toni Onley, Ernest Lindner and Reta Cowley, all from the Canadian West."[14] Toni Onley (1928–2004) employed watercolour to depict places, space, and light of many parts of the world, especially parts of British Columbia, where he lived and painted after immigrating from the Isle of Man. In these entrancing works he combined watercolour washes and drawing with the tip of his brush, thus capturing multiple sensibilities. Saskatchewan's Reta Cowley (1910–2004), on the other hand, used the white spaces between her brush strokes particularly effectively to give voice to the expanse of the prairie and its special quality of light.

Line in every medium is the essence of many artists' work. Swinton was clear about his own reliance on line:

Although I cannot forsake colour, I like to rely on line. Line inevitably sacrifices such magnificently physical qualities as actual motion, actual substance, actual mass, actual volume, actual colour, in favour of qualities which actually do not exist in nature. Thus, however sensuous or descriptive it may appear, line is essentially intellectual and abstract; yet for this very reason line seems to me to contain more humanness and more subtlety than other visual media.

In spite of its abstractness, line has become to civilized man an intrinsic reality, a second nature. In its power to communicate, line is very much like speech but in its imagistic potential, line is more universal than language.[15]

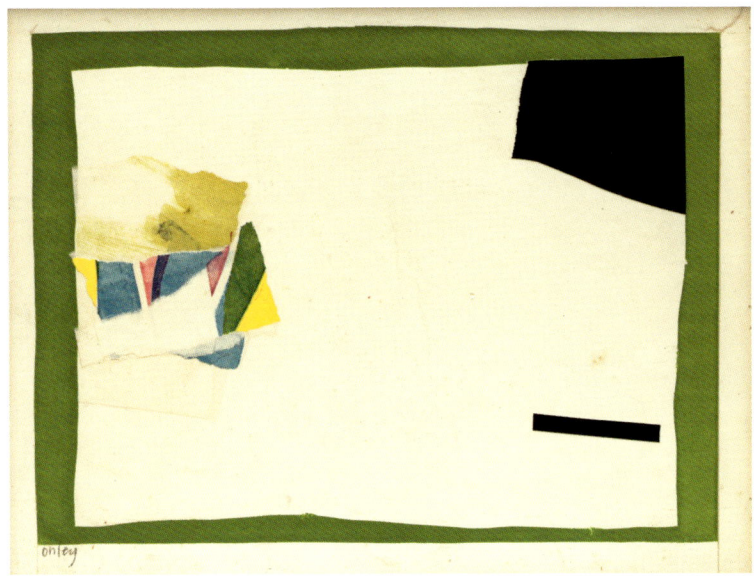

FIGURE 2.3.
Toni Onley,
Untitled Collage 1B,
c. 1963–1964.

Energetic, linear movement is the signature of the drawings of British Columbia's Ann Kipling. Held in high esteem over many years for her landscape drawings, portraits, and her *Goat Series,* she works in watercolour, aquarelle, pencil, ink, and coloured ink, capturing the light and shifting skies, clouds, and space in all her drawings. Her quick, short, syncopated lines are compelling, each essential and each perfectly placed to convey her message. She draws what she sees and is confident in her visual translations of what is seen from her studio window. She reflected: "I am incapable of working from conscious memory, or of drawing artificially constructed images . . . the need for a direct and constant outside stimulus is absolute."[16] She never erases or changes a line, her pencil marks being as deliberate as Reta Cowley's brush strokes. Art writer Robin Laurence commented about Kipling's results: "With its sensitive register of time and movement through sometimes concentric, sometimes radiating lines, her art appears to vibrate with life, to quiver or shimmer on the page. What makes her style so distinctive is the way its formal language—a dynamic network of nervous lines, dots, dashes, curls, zigzags, tendrils, and cross-hatching-hatches; often identified as 'calligraphic'—captures the essence of her living subject. Her art is a direct unmediated, almost electrical response to the plants, animals, and people that share her environment."[17] Colour moves fluidly across Kipling's watercolour and aquarelle washes, creating an expanding sense of space.

Colour is critical in conveying mood and message. Wanda Koop's painting *Reflect: Deep Magenta-Luminous Yellow,* 2008, and Bev Pike's *Caressing Room,* 1990, for instance, with similar

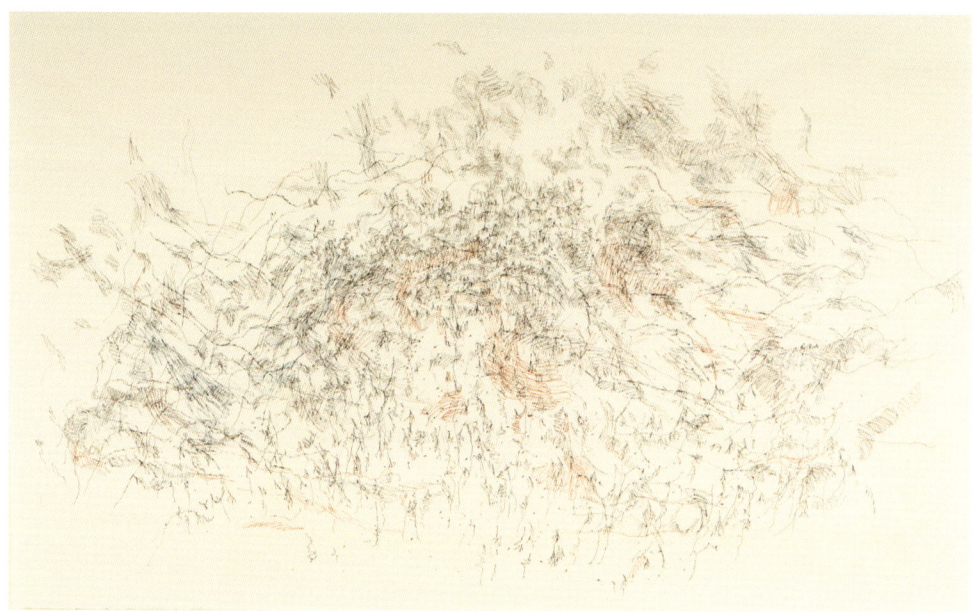

colour tones, achieve completely different sensibilities. Koop's abstraction with its clearly defined shapes and forms penetrates light, evoking philosophical aspects of reflection. With smooth brushwork, Koop builds her layers of colour allowing preliminary layers of blues and reds to show through. The luminous yellow stripes and her use of black, some precise in form, others fluid, link the painting's vertical space. Contrasting the magenta tones of the whole, these additions enhance the sense of distance and reflections. What is reflecting what? Is it the reflection of forms and colours in the work itself, or the viewer's reflections the work evokes? Bev Pike, on the other hand, with a freer brushwork, yet the same colours, reds, purples and blues with highlights of yellow in the patterns, uses oil glazes and metallics to convey the intimacy of the setting. Forms, fabrics, patterns, quilts, cushions, and the rug flow one over another, all conveying energy and motion. The bed, the door, the floor, and the figure straightening the bedding are abruptly cut by the picture plane, leaving one to ask what is going on, or has gone on. What is caressing what—sleep, relationship, the connection of cultures depicted in her chosen patterns?

Oil, acrylic, and watercolour are the major media used by painters. Not surprisingly, however, artists often add other materials. Victoria Limners Society artist Herbert Siebner,

FIGURE 2.4. **Ann Kipling**, *July. 31/2008,* from the series *Sky Mountain,* 2008.

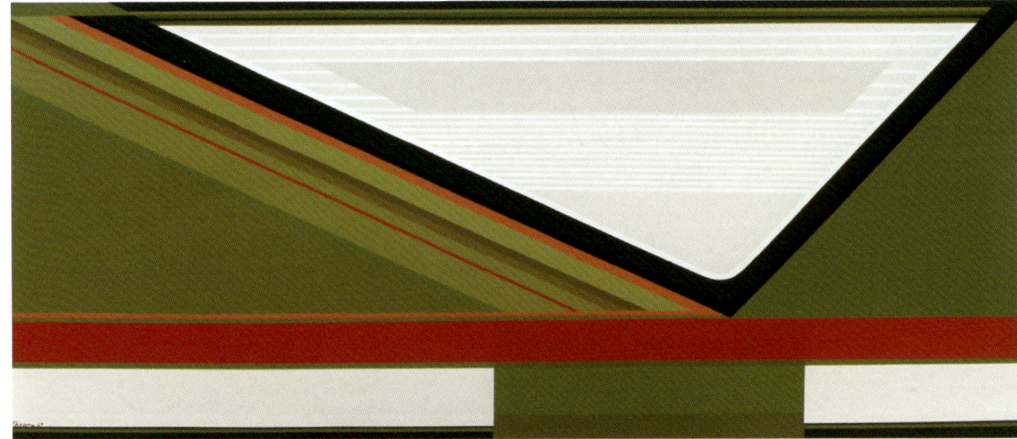

for instance, added sand to his paint to achieve his desired rough texture.[18] Manitoba's Tim Schouten (b. 1953) painted with encaustic on vellum, and British Columbia's Jane Everett (b. 1958) used chalk, fixative, and erasers for many of her vellum works.

While working as a metal plating technician at Trans Canada Airlines in the 1960s and 1970s, Winnipeg artist Tony Tascona began experimenting with aeronautical materials and resins early in the 1960s: "I can't stop doing the resin pieces. They are like poetry to me; I can't write but these are like poetry."[19] Heeding William McCloy's advice to "be aware of anatomical structure and to understand structure,"[20] Tascona layered airline materials of resins, lacquers, epoxies, and aluminum to build his artworks. Writer Alison Gillmor commented in 1997 that Tony Tascona's art

> is an unblinking commitment to the power of pure form and colour that has ranged through experimental media such as aluminum and epoxy resin, expressed itself in intimate prints and public murals, touched on the geometry of the machine as well as the organic cycle of the Prairie seasons. . . . Allusions to this high-tech labour come out in many of his works—in his use of lacquer on aluminum as a medium, in his often cool colours (running from silver to gun-metal grey to blues and violets with smooth sheen of industry), and in the occasional suggestions of crisply delineated nuts-and-bolts machine parts in his subject matter . . . other works contain grids, mathematical forms, cross-sectioned shapes or lines that suggest the undulations of sound waves.[21]

FIGURE 2.5. **Tony Tascona**, *Inverted Apex*, 1969.

Tascona himself reflected: "My work is about structure. My compositions work because I understand structure, . . . one cannot just put one colour over another, I overlayer in segments so the whole becomes one. I need to know everything is in its place. I was also made aware of colour, which now comes to me instinctively, but I had to go through a cycle of learning."[22]

Winnipeg's Esther Warkov (b. 1941) developed her own unique techniques of expression throughout her career. Her subject matter is inspired by people around her, those on the bus or walking. In her early paintings and in her characteristic paper works, she invented stories about people's fictitious lives. In her early works she applied the paint smoothly, and her surrealistic, seeming unrelated objects interested Ferdinand Eckhardt:

> What do all these figures mean, these houses, bulls and birds, vases with flowers, horses, tables and chairs, flying angels, winged busts, even once a nude or a staircase, part of a brick wall or a bicycle, put in a strange order or no order at all, scattered over the plain sheet? They are kept together by a system of lines which give a feeling of depth and space. Doubtless everything is the output of a deep-thinking person with lots of fantasy but also with thoughts. . . . In her pictures we find feeling for space, colour, composition and particularly for the human.[23]

The importance of drawing and the experimentation and evolution in painting is clear. Printmaking, however, as a stand-alone medium, warrants a deeper discussion, given its many innovations in techniques and materials. Western Canadian printmakers have had a far-reaching impact across the country with a number of techniques and the various ways they have combined printmaking modes of expression. These include coloured woodblock, wood engraving, linocuts, etching, drypoint, lithograph, embossed prints, collographs, photography, computer-generated images, monotypes, and silkscreens. Some artists print on stone; others, on wood, metal, or glass. Some put their work through the press once; others, multiple times. Sand is added to give texture at times, and some artists make their own papers to achieve their desired textures.

Curator Shirley Madill wrote in 1981, "The print has proven to be the most democratic medium in the history of art. . . . The versatility of prints seems inexhaustible. The print can be molded to the social and aesthetic needs of a given society and to the individual expression of a particular artist. . . . The print medium has been and still is in a constant state of evolution."[24] In summarizing the development of Western Canadian printmaking, printmaker and print archivist Ted Howorth commented: "The 1940s were the 'woodblock era'; the 1950s, with the arrival of faculty to the University of Manitoba from Iowa, marked the introduction of etching in a major way; and the 1960s was the era of printmaking opening up, becoming more collaborative."[25] It was then that group printmaking studios were developed. In 1967, for instance, Signal Hill

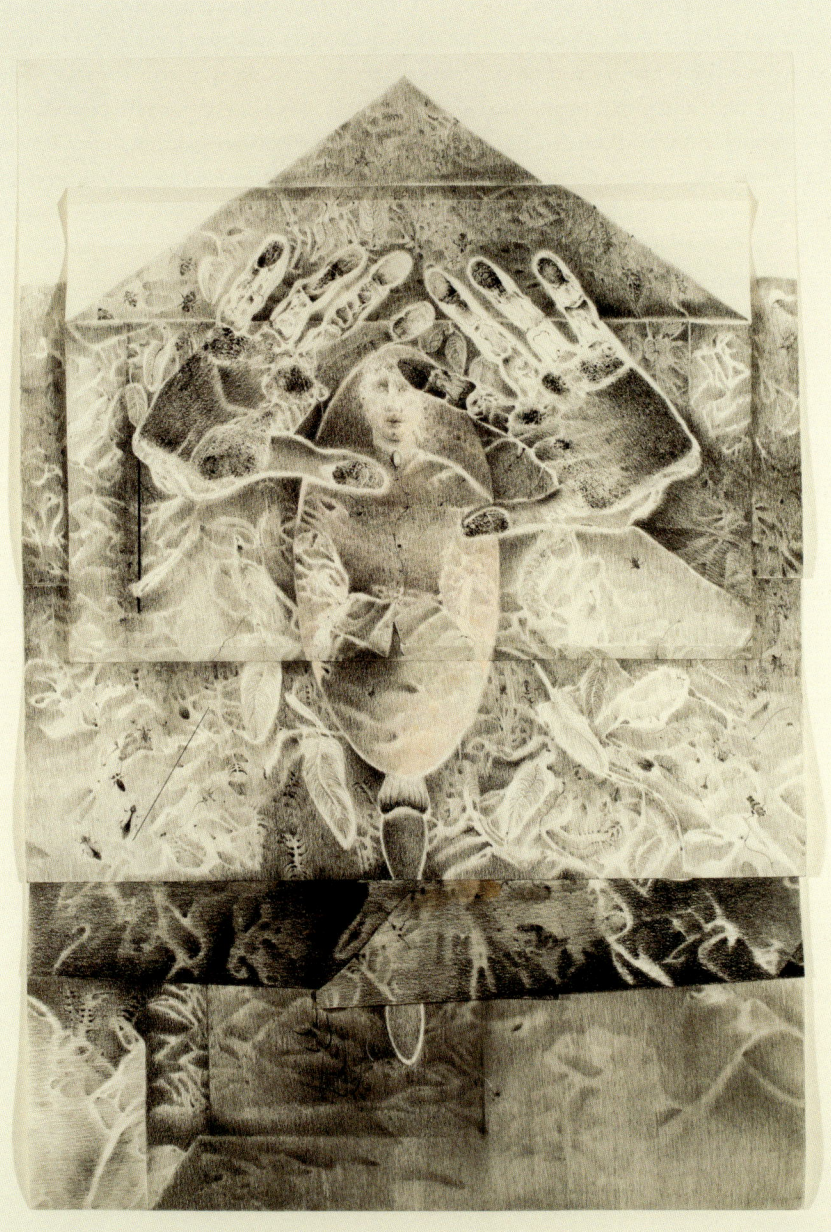

cooperative on Vancouver Island was founded. It became X-Changes in 1979. Bill Lobchuk's 1968 founding of the Grand Western Canadian Screen Shop was a seminal event in the country's printmaking history. Manitoba Printmakers Association was formally founded in 1984, joining other Canadian print studios in the 1980s such as St. Michael's Printshop in Newfoundland, Open Studio in Toronto, Moosehead Press in Winnipeg, and the 1985 New Leaf Editions on Vancouver's Granville Island established by Peter Braune. In addition, a number of universities opened printmaking departments, such as those in Victoria, Edmonton, and Calgary.

These organizations and artists' cooperatives did significant work making the West the hub of Canadian printmaking in the late 1970s. Each added different perspectives and dimensions as the printmaking rose from craft to major fine art medium. New work, new ideas, and much experimentation were the hallmark of the printmaking field with both Alberta's universities playing influential roles in printmaking experiments and developing creative opportunities for emerging artists. The leadership of the Print and Drawing Council of Canada moved from Ontario to Alberta during those years, first to Calgary under the leadership of Bill Laing, and then to Edmonton under Walter Jule. Meanwhile in Winnipeg, at the Grand Western Canadian Screen Shop, Ted Howorth, its lead printer, and master printer Len Anthony collaborated with Indigenous artists Jackson Beardy, Alex Janvier, and Carl Ray in addition to printing for artists including Tony Tascona, David Thauberger, Joe Fafard, and Russell Yuristy. Bill Lobchuk also organized artists' exchanges, and the Screen Shop printed for many artists from across Canada, including General Idea and Pierre Ayot from Montreal. Through these connections Lobchuk, Howorth, and Anthony were challenged to incorporate new technologies into screen printing, such as printing on velvet, using unconventional materials, including photographic images, and working at large scale. They succeeded. That spirit of 1970s Western Canadian experimentation has carried into the twenty-first century, and printmaking studios like Martha Street in Winnipeg have grown to include not only studio facilities but sales and gallery operations.

During this explosion of new materials and experiments, including the use of photography in printmaking, Madill noted:

> Contemporary developments have stimulated a more expansive view of the meaning of printmaking and what the processes themselves can do. . . . Many artists have moved away from the two-dimensional paper print to investigate new materials such as canvas, aluminum and plastic. Three-dimensionality, introduced through collage, assemblage, moulds and the dye transfer, techniques usually associated with painting and sculpture, have given rise to a new type of limited-edition print, the multiple.

FIGURE 2.6. **Esther Warkov**, *House of Tea,* 1999.

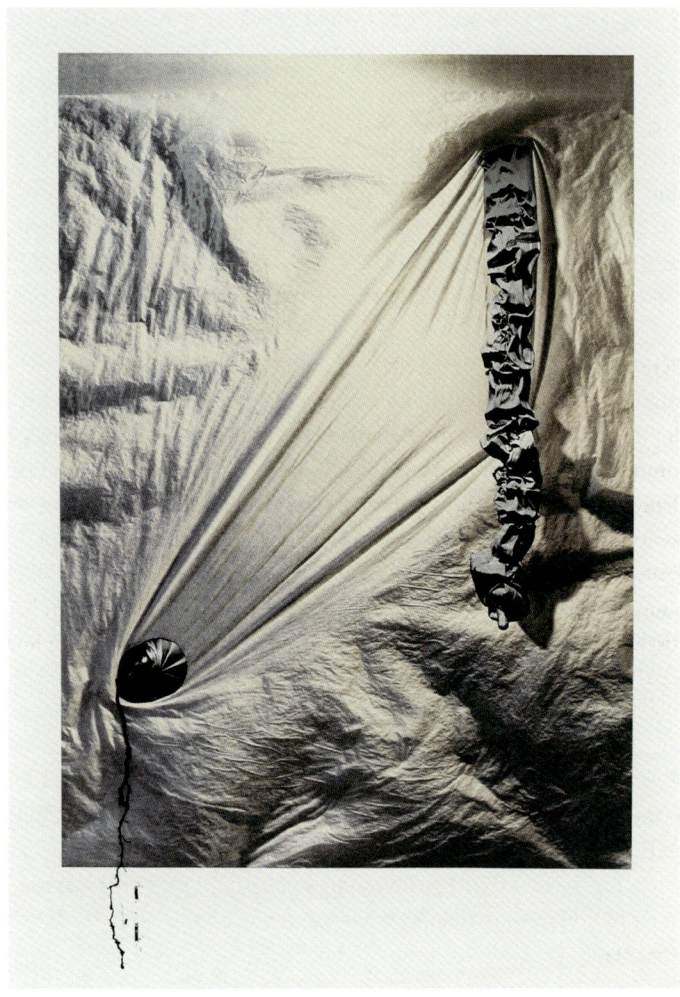

FIGURE 2.7.
Walter Jule, *Neither Dusk nor Dawn*, 2008.

Some prints, such as the object print, are actually freestanding three-dimensional pieces. . . . Combination prints, where more than one technique or process is used, are becoming more and more popular.[26]

To delve into new departures in printmaking, it is instructive to look at major catalysts. One was the work of commercial firms like Brigdens Limited. In the early years of the twentieth century, printmaking became a means of creating art for art's sake. Walter J. Phillips emigrated from the United Kingdom to Winnipeg in 1913, and Eric Bergman, who hailed from Germany in 1913, arrived in Winnipeg in 1914 to work at Brigdens. The former brought the coloured woodblock technique to Canada; the latter introduced the technique of black and white wood engraving. Their joint contributions were seminal in the development of Canadian printmaking. Linocut also assumed a new voice and substance. Vancouver Island's Sybil Andrews (1898–1992), originally trained in the United Kingdom, arrived in Campbell River, British Columbia, in 1947 and the next year she had a solo exhibition at the Vancouver Art Gallery. She took linocut to a new level with her strong colours, definite lines, and rhythms. Eschewing all but absolutely necessary details, Andrew's compelling portrayals of daily life were filled with movement and strength.

Lionel LeMoine FitzGerald began printmaking after returning from his 1922 winter at New York's Art Students League. He did drypoints, engravings, and linocuts. The connection to drawing for him is evident. Helen Coy, long-time curator of the University of Manitoba's FitzGerald Study Centre, commented of his drypoints: "This venture into a new medium was closely tied to a dramatic change in his approach to drawing. . . . FitzGerald started making small drypoints and the occasional engraving, at the same time embarking on a tradition of making his own original prints for Christmas cards, mostly linocuts."[27] Coy further observed that "FitzGerald's elegantly austere approach to drawing is nowhere more apparent than in his prints, which mirror the artist's preoccupation with the meaning and grace of his drawing line and the form which it evoked."[28] In his prints he depicted similar subjects as in his drawings and paintings: trees, the landscape, and rooftops.

It should be pointed out that in the 1920s, 1930s, and 1940s, when Phillips, Bergman, FitzGerald, and Andrews were leading the printmaking field, there was a relative paucity of printmaking in Canada. Winnipeg became the printmaking centre. Coy underlined Winnipeg's importance: "Even though serious printmaking had not the place in Canada it has now, a small, but active group of printmakers had been working in Winnipeg since the early part of the century. Some of these were employed in the art department of the T. Eaton Company, the CPR, or Brigdens, while others taught at the technical school."[29]

From the 1950s to 1970s, John Snow and Maxwell Bates (1906–1980) dominated printmaking in Alberta. Snow was considered to be Alberta's premier lithographer, and Bates's expressionistic prints and paintings were known across Canada. Bates encouraged Snow to use lithography, feeling it would suit Snow's characteristic blocks of colour. When Snow learned that Calgary's Western Printing and Lithography had discarded their lithography equipment behind the shop in the back lane, he took immediate action: "I woke up with a real urge to go down to Western Printing and Lithography . . . so I took my long legs and ran . . . and there they were, the end of March, in the snow and ice in the back alley. Got a truck and picked up every bit and piece that I could . . . and I got a book from the Public Library and read about it. . . . And I taught myself to do these lithographs."[30]

Still lifes were Snow's primary subject, and his interest in geometry is evident in his compositions filled with large planes of solid colour, which give depth and movement. His sense of form and the relationship of form, space, colour, and light were masterful. Never employing studio assistants, Snow was adamant that only his hand was to be in his work. He was a perfectionist in colour and registration, saying about his way of working:

> About my "method"—the usual way is to take 5 stones and put a design on one to be printed—in say yellow—one for blue and so on. A margin is left of about an inch and a register is made with needles through the paper to the stone to make sure the blue goes where it is supposed to. I wanted to use all the stone and didn't like the somewhat sterile procedure of a stone for each, so I use one stone and put a quite abstract design on, and print it in yellow on 20 sheets of paper—using a corner of a frame to achieve registration. Then I grind the stone clean and put a second design to be printed in another colour on the same 20 sheets of paper. This process continues until I have completed the edition of 20 sheets (probably end up with 18 good ones).[31]

American critic Clement Greenberg had made it clear on his 1963 tour of prairie studios that he "didn't want to see any prints because I know what I will see,"[32] effectively dismissing printmaking, a fact not forgotten by many artists. On the other hand, Will Barnet, leader of the 1957 Emma Lake Artists' Workshops, had been very interested in printmaking and encouraged artists to explore its opportunities for expression. Ken Lochhead recalled that Barnet "was considered to be one of the best printmakers in the U.S., and was a friend of George Swinton. He came with spats and a black fedora. I picked him up and drove him to the cabin. He had never lit a fire or a coal lamp. He wanted still life materials and a model; inks and linoleum for the participants, and large paper. It was a renaissance!"[33]

Printmaking had another important impetus—the appointment of Kathleen Fenwick as the National Gallery of Canada's first curator of prints and drawings, a position she held from 1928 until 1968. Knowledgeable and influential, she was especially supportive to printmakers and was credited, during her induction as an Officer of the Order of Canada, for being "largely responsible for developing the collection into one of the finest of its kind."[34] Fenwick not only purchased work, but she organized exhibitions of Canada's printmakers for international tours, including the 1963 Primera Biennale Americana de Grabado, Chile, at which the Canadian artists, including Pat Martin Bates, received the Grand Award of Honour for pushing the boundaries of the medium.

In Winnipeg in the 1960s, printmaking experimenter Winston Leathers (1932–2004) and John Kenneth (Ken) Esler together invented the collograph technique. Leathers proudly noted that "Ken Esler and I were given credit by Stanley Hayter, a noted American Printmaker, for the invention of collographs."[35] Ken Esler, for his part, recalled:

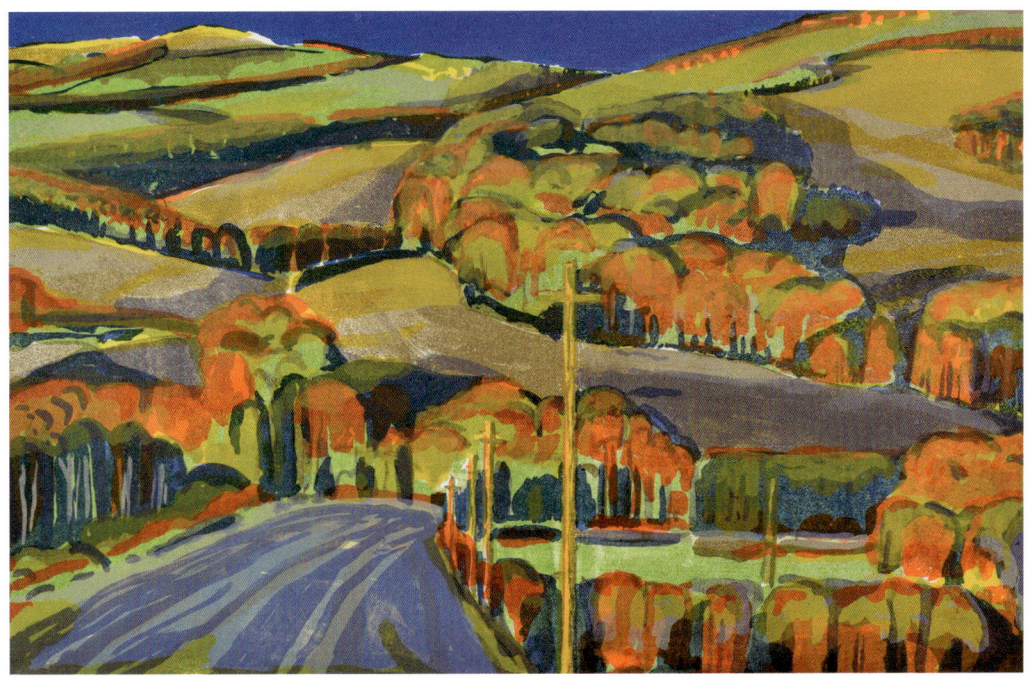

I wanted maximum textural effect in my prints and would work with bits and pieces of cardboard, materials and paper as a collage before fixing them with glue, whereas in etching, redesigning or correcting a plate was hard work and time-consuming . . . I did not refer to this work as a collograph. I called it a "fabricate print," referring to the fact that the plate was constructed or fabricated. I switched to the word "collograph" after learning more about two Americans. . . . The breakthrough . . . was that the collograph technique led me to bold abstract imagery with full rich textural effects which were created by the very material I was using . . . I carried a lot of collograph experience into my later work in coloured etching.[36]

Years later, Bill Laing, Esler's teaching colleague at the University of Calgary, echoed that praise. New materials were a mark of 1960s printmaking, too. Leathers experimented with printing on wax paper and Pat Martin Bates was the first to print on plexiglass. Later in the decade Leathers started using the new Day-Glo paints, and IAIN BAXTER& pressed images into plastic.

FIGURE 2.8. **John Snow**, *September Landscape*, 1978.

In the 1960s and 1970s when these print studios were flourishing, Canada was entering an era of renewed feminism, political debate, and exponential growth of galleries, artist-run spaces, cooperatives, and funding programs. It was, as art historian Angela Davis wrote, "a period of experimentation and social encounter, both in art and everyday life," and print studios were "where art, technology and communication could meet."[37] Davis aptly concluded that this was when "printmaking became the 'rebellious' technique in a socially rebellious time."[38] Recognizing the democracy of prints, Davis continued: "The print is uniquely capable of becoming . . . an inexpensive bridge to an understanding of the wealth of visual expression in Canadian art. . . . This was the aspect of printmaking that would make the new art form so important."[39] The artists involved collectively succeeded in breaking the traditional barriers of the hierarchy of art-making media. By the late 1960s printmaking was recognized as a legitimate art form in contemporary Canadian art.

A 1966 graduate of the University of Manitoba's School of Art, Bill Lobchuk, founder of the Grand Western Canadian Screen Shop, focused on the landscape, details in nature, and the immediacy of colour in his vibrant work. His clear, direct compositions respond to the prairie rhythms and patterns, and his interest in light and the saturation of colour is evident. Evoking stage sets, he sets trees against the background with colours in the foreground often mirroring those of the sky. Omitting unnecessary details and heightening his colour, he projects his passion with boldness, as in *Trees,* 1976. In *Northwest Triptych,* 1982, he conveys the vast expanse of distances by extending their sense beyond the image. Lobchuk also often gives a sense of monumentality to the small, as in his *Ladyslipper Series,* 2002–2005. His flowers, birds, and endangered species are imbued with dynamism, personality, and beauty. His attention also encompassed prairie towns as in *Neepawa Noon I* and *II,* 1977. In many ways his patterning and use of colour are reminiscent of the early twentieth-century French Fauve painters Henri Matisse and André Derain, and his distinct forms recall the structure of stained-glass windows, enhancing a spiritual element in his subject. Lobchuk's knowledge and long experience in printmaking certainly informed the deliberate compositions and colour placement of his later painting.

Artists' experiments and trial processes frequently tested traditional printmaking boundaries. Saskatchewan's David Thauberger, for instance, who printed at the Grand Western Canadian Screen Shop, liked the texture, bold, distinct colours, and crisp linear definitions of silkscreen. A consummate explorer of innovative materials, he used velvet, flocking, antique marbleized papers, Letraset, and enamels. He frequently overpainted his printed image in his 1990s etchings and aquatints, and over a number of years incorporated computer or photographic images into the print itself. His 1970s quest to print on velvet posed specific conundrums in achieving his mutually incompatible goals of flatness and texture. Despite Lobchuk's view that printing on velvet was "a crazy idea,"[40] Thauberger was steadfast: "I was

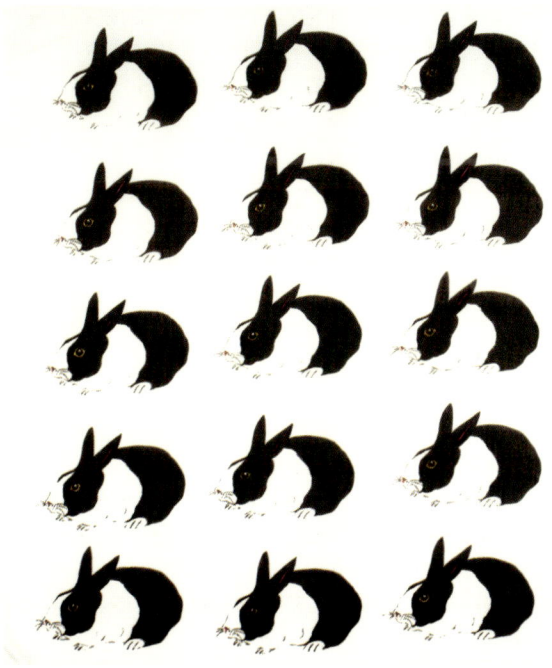

FIGURE 2.9.
David Thauberger,
Velvet Bunnies, 1977.

interested in what it was that so many people found so attractive in the 'black velvet' aesthetic and wanted to see if there wasn't something positive to take from these commonly disparaged (in art circles) paintings that were everywhere."[41] *Velvet Bunnies* was done both in black on white velvet and in white on black velvet. The first attempts at the velvet prints were deemed "unsuccessful" because the inks, when printed on velvet, were "too crumbly and unable to achieve the desired flatness, impossible because the nap changed direction with the light. The velvet moved and stretched as it was being printed. We could not print multiple colours and finally resorted to hand colouring! . . . It was a steep learning curve!"[42]

After much finessing the black version of the image was described as "magic." Thauberger then undertook the challenge of flocking in *Dolly and Bill*, in *Icon*, and in *Double Feature*, noting "it was the age of popular flocked wallpapers." Len Anthony was the master behind meeting these challenging requests. He recalled that flocking, not generally associated with printing, was "simple. . . . We bought flocking in bulk, sprinkled it on the wet paint, and shook loose bits off to use another time."[43]

Thauberger stretched the medium to achieve shadow effects. He applied colours and flocking over ground layers of enamel, giving the sensibility of the siding on farm buildings.

In *Double Feature*, 1982, for instance, the thicker paints attained his desired shadows. He "did the lawn by dragging a comb through the wet paint for the striations of the grass."[44] Other inventive approaches included bronzing varnish, metallic powders, and the use of Letraset as the trees in *Little Christmas*, 1984, and *Bungalow*, 1989. Letraset, Thauberger said, provided a "warmer imagery than present day clip art. That from the U.S. was better than the French variety."[45]

Don Proch also experimented with innovative technical aspects of printmaking, extending the properties and boundaries of the medium. Two of Proch's prints in particular challenged the Screen Shop much as Thauberger had—*Firefly* and *Horizon Detail*. Proch wanted the feeling of an original drawing in some of his prints. To achieve the pencil-like subtle gradations of grey in the black and white version of *Horizon Detail*, 1974, for instance, he used roller-bearing graphite, which he got from a local automotive machine shop, and mixed it with bronzing varnish. He called it "a liquid drawing,"[46] and it yielded a quality almost indistinguishable from his drawings. Proch also wanted his work to be large, a scale beyond the capacity of commercial printers.

A master in balancing black and white with colour, Proch achieved maximum psychological effects of serenity and drama. The only area of colour in *Firefly*, 1978, is the electrifying neon rainbow. Dramatic in impact, the rainbow depicted in the lightning storm is the source of the natural electrical charges striking the ground. That sparks the lightning, which in turn ignites the trees. Experimenting with new technology in this work, Proch had Ernest Mayer photograph three-dimensional neon tubes, and with assistance from Len Anthony and Ted Howorth, Proch transported the photographs directly into the print, thus achieving another technical advance—the introduction of three-dimensional objects into a two-dimensional print. Proch credits Anthony's technical knowledge and skill for meeting his printmaking ambitions.

Not surprisingly, Ted Howorth continues to push the boundaries of printmaking. A student of Alberta's acclaimed woodblock artist Noboru Sawai, Howorth bridges the worlds of contemporary digital printmaking with the traditional, successfully combining previously deemed "incompatible" techniques. His open-ended narrative themes are suggestive of the told and the untold and the public and private, simultaneously revealing the real and the imaginary. His goal was that his "implied narrative will spark the viewer's own memories and imagination."[47]

Howorth's late 1960s and early 1970s "bubble prints" are filled with images and references to everyday activities. By the mid-1970s flat shapes of bright, solid, psychedelic colours with heavy black outlines became his trademark. *The Double Crossing*, 1979, heralding the flight of the human-powered aircraft *Gossamer Albatross* across the English Channel, includes the aircraft, a black and white image of a Manitoba blizzard projected onto a drive-in movie screen, and a photo of fellow artist Don Proch. Howorth's interest in human-powered vehicles is seen again in *The Passion of Coquille St. Jacques*, 1985, an early example of his counterpoints of side-by-

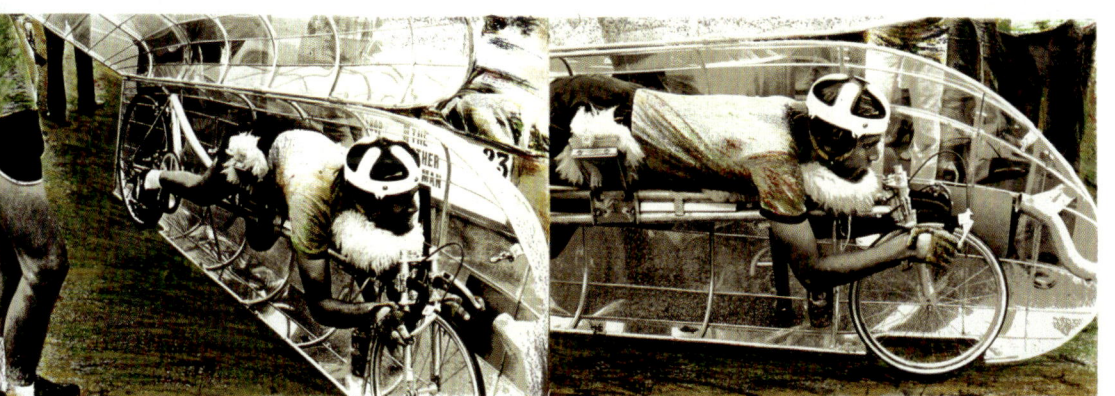

side double images. By the 2000s he was developing digital images to which he added screen printing thus creating technical counterpoints paralleling his counterpoints of imagery. Using digital techniques, he breaks down details to give his work fine resolution. Superimposing screen printing allows him to add multiple layers of deep and evocative colour and to achieve a continuous tone throughout a work. Each technique affords unique qualities: lithography gives breadth of tonality; screen printing enables colour control. Howorth has also screen printed with wallpaper paste and watercolours; he has sprayed, scraped, sandpapered, and stenciled images; and he has used stains and frottage with caulking compound, first doing a rubbing when dry and then burning it into the silkscreen. Howorth's method is physical: "For me, the secret to making prints is to physically begin. The physicality of making a print requires time. Process, busy work, also offers a time for reflection, evaluation and evolution of my ideas. This is an important part of the ongoing build that will take a print through to completion."[48] A further major contribution of his to printmakers is his 1970s and 1980s extensive research on water-based printing inks. His findings revolutionized print studios, garnering consequential positive health impacts for artists and for the environment.

Technique provides the platform for visual expression for all printmakers, as Pat Martin Bates said: "You need the platform to jump off into space. You must have it."[49] Constantly testing, inventing, and expanding their media, many printmakers fuse printmaking with painting and sculpture. Bill Laing's 2020 works, *Walking #1* and *Walking #9,* for instance, are created with plaster, wood etching, silkscreen, a plastic mirror and found objects. The artist told me that he "likes intimate works hence working in small scale,"[50] and his resulting level of detail is akin

FIGURE 2.10. **E.J. (Ted) Howorth**, *The Passion of Coquille St. Jacques*, 1985.

to that in Eric Bergman's prints and Don Proch's meticulous drawings. Laing magnifies details, such as the structure of the leaf, revealing his interest in nature. The view through lace curtains onto bare winter trees inspired many of his works, with the lace evoking the veins of the leaves and vice versa. The relationships between the interior and exterior throughout his oeuvre are both physical and psychological. Laing states that

> collections of objects, memories and ideas have manifested into drawings, prints and sculptures, that describe the isolation of the figure or objects in space. They are about contemplation and stillness. I refer to the sculptures as assemblage, because they are layered in objects that together describe a narrative. Referencing domestic environment, many works have shelves that support cameo shapes, lace, leaves, mirrors and various objects evoking associations from the past. Objects from the natural world such as leaves and twigs, are often a part of my work, as well as printed images and cut out shapes of leaves, and trees.[51]

These sensibilities were evident in his work of the 1970s, like his mixed-media construction, *Bradford Still Life #2*, 1979, and his 1973 cast resin pieces, *Queue* and *Within the Landscape*. Details of the leaves are seen in the former; in the latter figures foreshadow his work of 2020.

Walter Jule, Laing's counterpart in the printmaking department at Edmonton's University of Alberta, has exhibited globally, and his ties with Japan and Japanese printmaking and spiritual roots are strong. He has organized many artists' residencies and exchanges between Edmonton and Japan. His practice of meditation is ever present in his imagery and in the overall aura of his works themselves. He joins Japanese-born and -trained printmaker Noboru Sawai in having a profound effect on Canadian printmaking. Sawai carried on centuries of woodcut traditions in his work and teaching in Calgary and Vancouver.

Pat Martin Bates, whom both Laing and Jule celebrate, was also influenced by Japanese printmakers, and, like Jule, has participated in, and received accolades from, international print biennales for decades. Martin Bates, Laing, and Jule encouraged other Canadian printmakers to join them and, like Laing, Martin Bates also links printmaking to multiple techniques of art making and sculpture. She said, "Printmakers were always painters as well as sculptors. I take things and scrape them away."[52] Her 1972 three-dimensional cubes, lit from within, had pierced prints on every face with a technique about which Richard Simmins said: "Her technique is so varied, the forms so varying in scale and juxtaposition that each work is a new experience. She is a master of her media . . . you can feel the monumentality and the ease with which her forms could be integrated into an architectural environment. And the cubes belong to the world of sculpture though each facet is an intaglio print. The possibilities for an enriched vision using new materials, light sources, texture are limitless."[53]

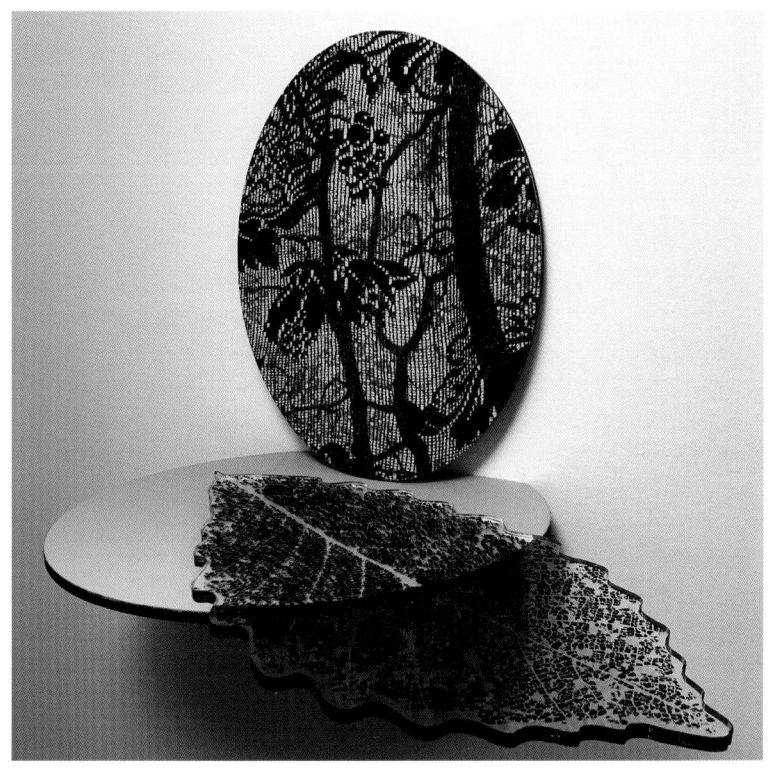

FIGURE 2.11.
William Laing,
Walking #1, 2020.

The balance of inking and choices of papers are decisions printmakers must make, and the thickness and textures of the papers become part of the essence of the work itself. Handmade papers have particular qualities. Papers with a good tooth take the inks: for lithography one needs stiff inks and for etching warm inks are needed. Sometimes for highly textured paper sand is added to wet paper, thereby achieving a Braille-like appearance. For smooth, parchment-like papers, artists soak the paper in water and dry it out like a skin.

Winnipeg artist Karen Cornelius's choice of medium and technique is very clear, too: "Within my art practice, printmaking has been my discipline of choice. The transfer of image and texture from one surface to another as well as the repetition and layering of image attracts me to the medium." Her *Fabric of Belonging* series includes images of the front and the back of a child's dress, and her varying patterns are executed in various colour combinations. Process is as important to her as the final outcome is. This inveterate experimenter explains, "Although trained in traditional printmaking methods, I have progressively pushed the traditional boundaries exploring non-traditional materials and methods."[54] She, like Howorth, uses water-based inks and environmentally sound materials throughout her art.

British Columbia First Nations artist Arthur Vickers has pushed the printmaking medium into new forays as well with his incorporation of hidden or ghost images within his prints. These, usually the traditionally symbolic images of the eagle, salmon, or moon, reveal themselves only in particular lights and from certain angles, as seen in works like *Legacy,* 1997, or *Mount Baker,* 1999. In *Legacy,* a salmon is in the sky. Vickers wrote of these interconnections and transcendent meanings:

> The image I have created is where the salmon gather on their final journey to give birth to a new generation. It is also where all of the clans gather to give thanks and to selectively harvest the salmon for their nourishment. The female salmon carries humanity on her back, as does she carry the Eagle, Raven, Wolf, Bear and the Orca. She also is the carrier of her future generations.
>
> There is a delicate balance of harvest and preservation in this circle that our ancestors left to all of us . . . passed on from one generation to the next. . . .
>
> If this delicate balance is broken the Eagle and the Raven no longer fly, and the Wolf, Bear and Orca perish as does humanity and all future generations.
>
> This circle must not be broken by any of us lest our legacy be the final sunset.
>
> We as humanity are required to pay serious attention to this sunset, now.
>
> We as mankind hold in our hands our future as well as the future of all living things.[55]

While profound in message, these serigraphs are technically challenging, and, like Ted Howorth, Vickers used layer upon layer of inks, carefully balancing tones.

Many Indigenous artists have made prints, the members of the Indigenous Group of Seven being among the first. Those working on the West Coast likewise have a long tradition of printmaking and draw images from their centuries of traditional cultural roots. Richard Hunt, for instance, portrays tradition and family, rich in symbolism, past and present. In *Parliament Buildings,* 2018, for example, he depicts the British Columbia Legislative Building with totem poles and crests on the lawns in front of the building and animals in the sky. The crests belong to the Kwakwaka'wakw people of northern Vancouver Island, rightly making the point that his people were the first on the site. The work is personal, strong, and colourful. Hunt comments:

> This design is about my memories of living in Victoria, the traditional Territory of the Songhees people. I grew up around the Parliament Buildings because my dad,

FIGURE 2.12. **Arthur Vickers**, *Intangible Heritage*, 2011.

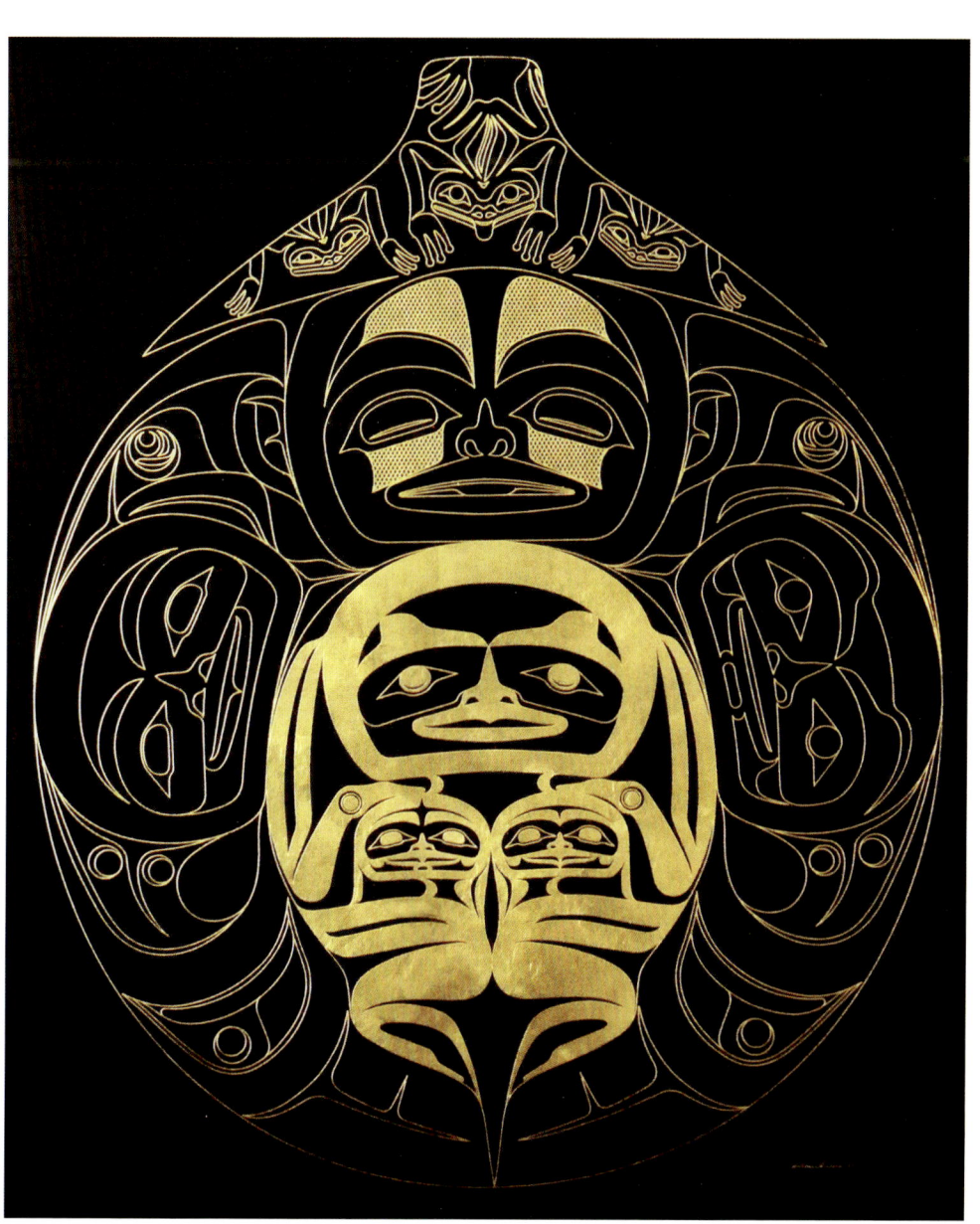

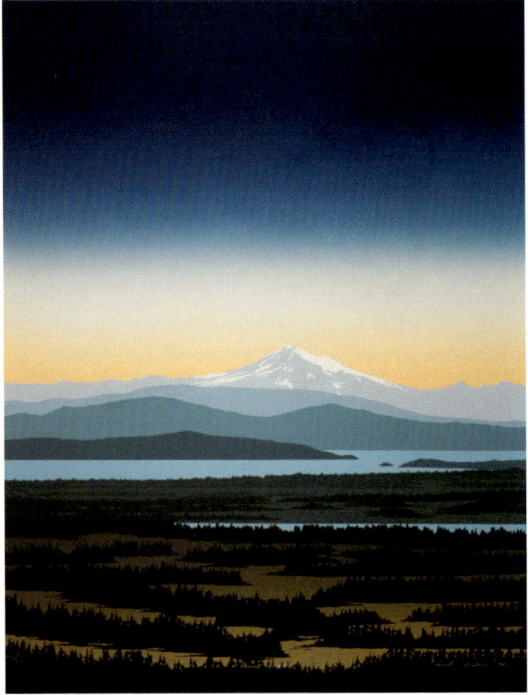

FIGURE 2.13.
Arthur Vickers,
Mount Baker, 1999.

Henry Hunt, worked at Thunderbird Park with Mungo Martin. I was 2 when my family moved here from Fort Rupert, B.C. At the top of the design is a raven, a bear, an eagle and a wolf. They are all crests of the Kwakwaka'wakw people of Northern Vancouver Island. The Moon is illuminated. The tree on the right is a big redwood tree. The raven in the middle is displaying our wealth which is our culture. On the left, is my Mom and my Dad singing because they are happy. There are two of my family members on each side of the box with the raven on the top. The box holds our families' wealth. The brother on the right holds the Chief's Wild Woman and the other holds the copper, a symbol of wealth for my family.[56]

Hunt's 2018 serigraph *Komokwa,* the Chief of the Sea, shows Komokwa's family, the sea eagle, the sea bear, Komokwa holding a copper, the sea wolf, and sea raven. Hunt has depicted an eagle design on the face of the copper, the traditional symbol of wealth.

Photography as an art form, like printmaking, has also long provided artists the opportunity to experiment and effectively create new dimensions in their work. Photography is an excellent medium for the exploration of light and space, and its early innovations are witnessed in the work of Humphrey Hime and Hannah Maynard (1834–1918) in the nineteenth century. In recent years, photography has had a number of consequential transformations: first, the introduction of colour, followed by the Polaroid camera, and in recent years, digital and computer-generated and -manipulated images. The subjects of photographers are usually a person, social activity, or a physical environment, reflecting both reality and realism. Photography takes advantage of mass media, consumerism, and pop culture, the latter portrayed through objects. The work of Winnipeg's Bill Eakin (b. 1952) includes bottle caps and decorative cake tin lids. Some in both series are executed in black-and-white, others in colour. His *Light Garden Series* conveys the detail, shadows, and depth in these common objects. David Firman (b. 1954), on the other hand, portrays the panoramic landscape, parlaying a psychological aspect while providing the viewer with a full and total surround experience of space, light, and atmosphere.

Acclaimed photographer and artist John Taylor (b. 1946), of Victoria, earned an international reputation with his architectural photographs exploring space and details in heritage and modern buildings by architects of the past and the present. Interestingly, while he depicts spaces for people and human interaction, his architectural images are mostly devoid of human action. Some of the buildings he photographs are still in use. Others are in various states of desolation or demolition or periods of transformation. His series *The Great Domes of Italy* concentrates on the splendour, geometric purity, and symbolism of their architecture. To Taylor, "Architecture is mankind's highest artform in the sense that the built environment embodies our thoughts and aspirations . . . an ascendance of thought that involves the physical as well as the mental, emotional and spiritual realms. These domed spaces are sanctuaries of human transcendence."[57]

Taylor's concern for the loss or transformation of community icons is evident in his pre-demolition series of Victoria's Blue Bridge and in the series recording the process of the demolition of the Memorial Arena. A number of critical questions abound in his work: How and where does the human being "fit"? What is the relationship of the human to the cultural philosophies and religious spirituality represented in the architecture he portrays? Or, are we just voyeurs into times and places past? These questions form Taylor's extensive preliminary research, which fuses space, light, form, texture, and perception. His two-dimensional images read as three-dimensional forms. Depths are conveyed through rich blacks and his setting of one black tone against another. Each image portrays detail, mystery, and surrealistic sensibilities.

Vancouver's highly acclaimed Rodney Graham (b. 1949), painter, photographer, and filmmaker, also depicted interiors. His 2007 *The Gifted Amateur, Nov. 10th, 1962*, is comprised of three transmounted, chromogenic transparencies in painted aluminum light boxes. He examines what it is to be an artist, depicting himself pouring paint on an abstract work with colours

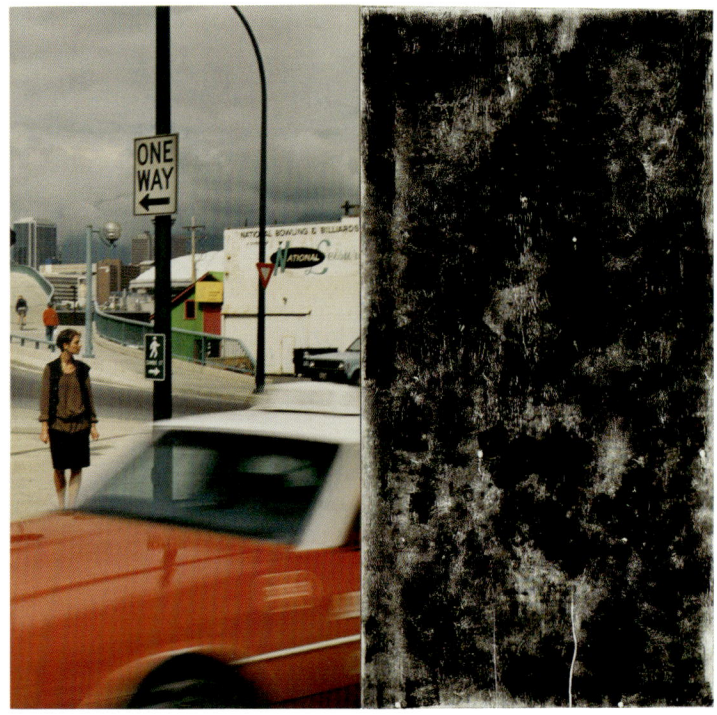

FIGURE 2.14.
Ian Wallace, *Untitled
(In The Street I) (Lyse)*,
1988.

dripping down the canvas. The floor of this mid-century living room is covered with newspaper and paint, and the period teak table is filled with books. Winner of many awards and a finalist in the 2014 Scotiabank Photography Award, Graham is a writer, musician, painter, filmmaker, and photographer, and a performance, sound, and installation artist. He came to the fore in the late 1970s with a group of young Vancouver artists including Jeff Wall (b. 1946), Ken Lum, and Ian Wallace, which became known internationally as the Vancouver School. Rodney's nomination for the Scotiabank Award noted: "His earliest works, in which he utilized historical processes such as the pinhole camera and the camera obscura, were based on a deep understanding of the essential science and technology behind photographic image-making, and this understanding has continued to inform his entire artistic output. Created with an exceptional degree of technical mastery, his photographs are most often presented in large-scale light boxes—a formal innovation which brought the artist and his contemporaries broad recognition."[58]

Throughout his career Ian Wallace, a Vancouver conceptual artist, has examined the multiple aspects of modernism in his installations, videos, paintings, and photographs. Over the years he has focused on street life, especially intersections and crosswalks, as in his 1988

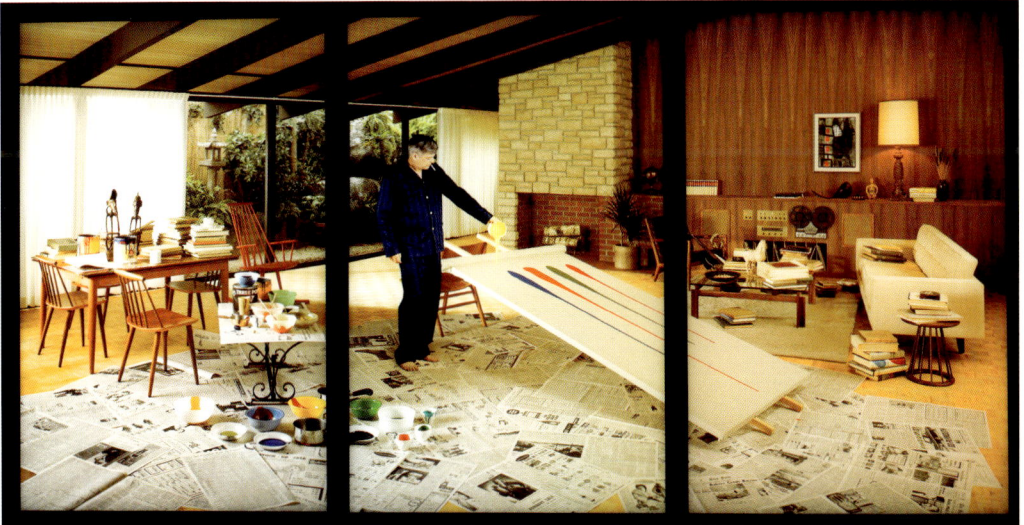

photograph *Untitled (In the Street I) (Lyse)*. A photolaminate with acrylic and ink monoprint, the left half of this work shows the busyness of the city. The taxi in the foreground is moving; a woman waits to cross the intersection; arrows point in different directions and downtown buildings are in the background with the bridge diagonally cutting part of the image. The right-hand portion of the work, a monoprint, represents the pavement. He thus draws the viewer into the known, yet the contrast of the vertical abstract element of the monoprint forces us to question place, texture, and societal directions.

African Canadian and Vancouver-born Stan Douglas (b. 1960) is Canada's 2022 Venice Biennale artist, and is also recognized as part of the Vancouver school of photoconceptualists. His social conscience and social inquiry permeate his art in film, photography, and theatre as he combines a view of past pivotal social and political times with a forward-looking lens. His 2008 work, *Abbott & Cordova, 7 August 1971*, for instance, depicts a re-enactment of the Gastown Riots. This double-sided photo mural hangs in the Woodward Building, near where the police broke up the 1971 pro-cannabis smoke-in.

Painters also include photography in their work, an approach adopted often by Indigenous artists Robert Houle and Jane Ash Poitras, to highlight past realities, family, and/or historical events. Poitras, for instance, has included a personal picture in the middle of a number of her paintings, increasing the poignancy and heightening the depth of meaning, as seen in *Assiniboine*

FIGURE 2.15. **Rodney Graham**, *The Gifted Amateur, Nov. 10th 1962*, 2007.

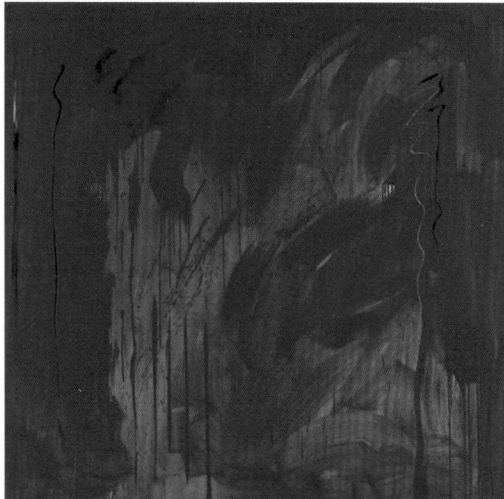

Treaty No. 1.... ARTICLES OF A TREATY made and concluded this third day of August in the year of Our Lord one thousand eight hundred and seventy-one, between Her Most Gracious Majesty the Queen of Great Britain and Ireland by Her Commissioner, Wemyss M. Simpson, Esquire, of the one part, and the Chippewa and Swam[py] [In]dians, inhabitants of the count[ry] hereinafter defined and descr[ibed] chosen and named as herei[n] other part....Whereas all the India[ns] [of the c]ountry....have been notified and i[nformed by] said Commissioner that it is the desire of Her Majesty to open up to settlement and immigration a tract of country bounded and described as hereinafter mentioned, and to obtain the consent thereto of her Indian subjects inhabiting the said tract, and to make a treaty and arrangements with them so that there may be peace and good will between them and Her Majesty....The Chippewa and Swampy Cree Tribes of Indians and all other the Indians inhabiting the district hereinafter described and defined do hereby cede, release, surrender and yield up to Her Majesty the Queen and Successors forever all the lands included within the following limits, that is to say:-Beginning at the internatio

Fool Society. Robert Houle included historical photographs as part of each work in his series of *Premises For Self-Rule* and in *Sandy Bay*, anchoring past times and agreements that have negatively affected Indigenous lives.

Textile likewise affords artists considerable opportunities for expression in both two- and three-dimensional forms. Some artists use textile to bridge modes of expression, sometimes comprising full-scale installations. Calgary-based installation artist Laura Vickerson (b.1959), for instance, uses discarded objects and materials in her work, such as her installation *Rose Red Curtain,* 1999. Created from rose petals, organza, and pins, it hangs on the wall and flows into the room along the floor. For her, as with the work of Aganetha Dyck (b. 1937) and Vic Cicansky, the things of ordinary everyday life are their objects for art making. Vickerson says: "I am interested in the stuff of life. I often work with discarded objects and materials that were, at one time, a part of everyday experiences. Through changing trends and a general desire to consume these things outlive their usefulness or become obsolete. At times, the materials I employ are ephemeral such as flowers and rose petals. Once they have passed their prime in the garden or at the florists they are transformed into large-scale installations."[59]

Alberta's Shelley Ouellet (b. 1964) also bridges two- and three-dimensional approaches with her 2011 work *Johnston Falls.* Made of strings of plastic beads that cascade down the wall, it pours out onto the floor. The work, based on the tourist destination of Johnston Falls, conveys the sparkle and movement of the waterfall itself.

FIGURE 2.16. **Robert Houle**, *Premises for Self-Rule: Treaty No. 1,* 1994.

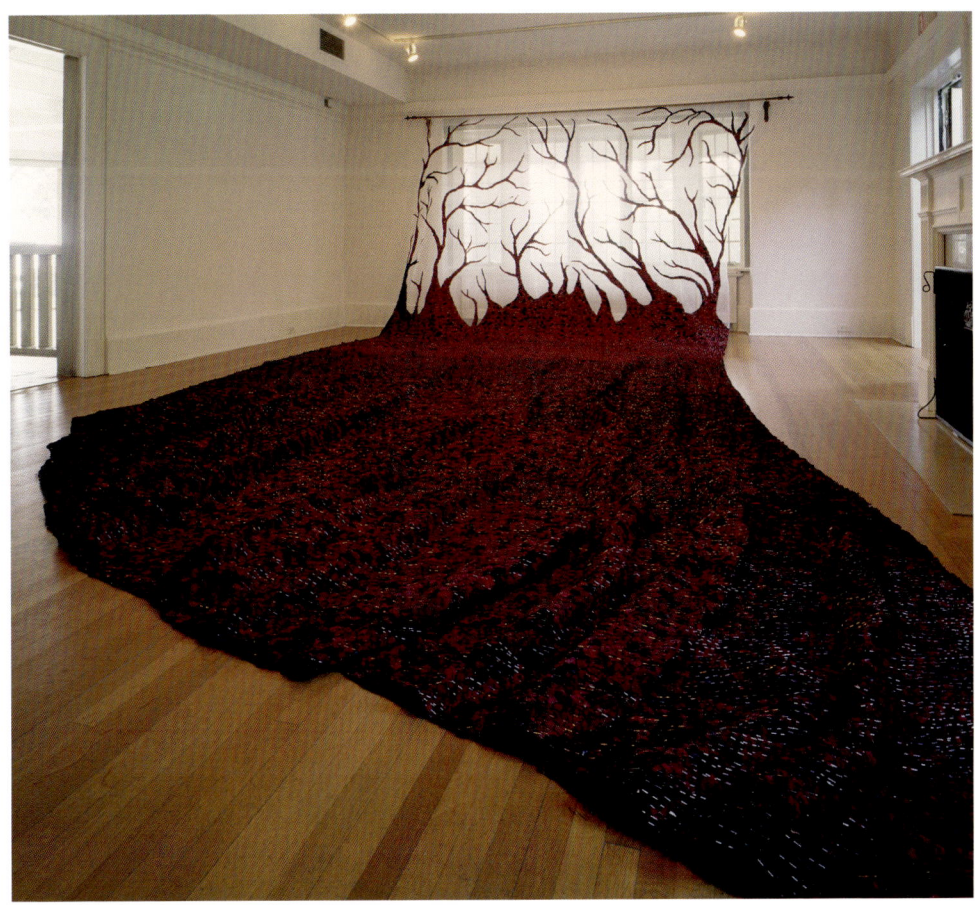

British Columbia's Carole Sabiston (b. 1939) takes her flat textile assemblages into the third dimension. She, too, uses found objects, labels, scarves, gloves, collars, lace, and myriad other components, each carefully selected for symbolic or biographical reasons, or both. These multiple layers add multiple meanings. Keen that her process, the "workings" of her art, be transparent, she wants viewers to understand what and she has done and how she has done it: "I have always left my structure visible; I don't try to hide it. I suppose it's like contemporary architecture, like the Pompidou Museum in Paris. The structure is visible; all the conduits are outside."[60]

FIGURE 2.17. **Laura Vickerson**, *Rose Red Curtain*, 1999.

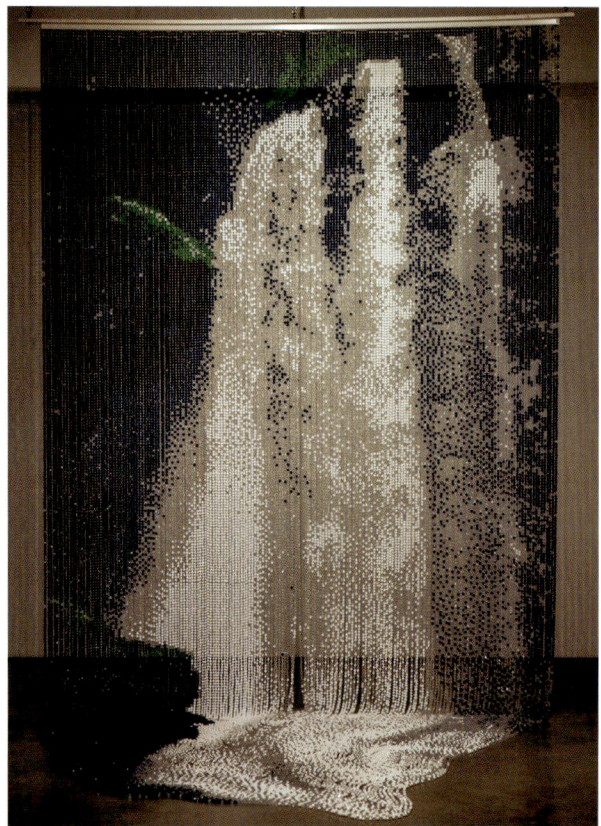

FIGURE 2.18.
Shelley Ouellet,
Johnston Falls, 2012.

Writer Barbara Lee Smith describes Sabiston's processes:

Once the work is laid out, all the pieces and the overlaying net are pinned with glass-headed pins. Those first positioning lines are now covered by the bits of fabric, so it is necessary to remark the placement by laying string over them. . . . Using the string as a guide, she cuts out the sections. Each section is machine sewn with a wide zigzag stitch, which holds the fabric and net to the Pellon ground. Smaller strips are now cut from these wider sections, which ultimately will form the diagonal bands seen in most of her work. . . . Once cut, they are either reversed in place or worked into another panel of the same piece. . . . Technically, the matching and seam-making must be exact. With 4 inches lost every time a strip or section is cut and re-sewn, Sabiston must consider how this will affect the design.[61]

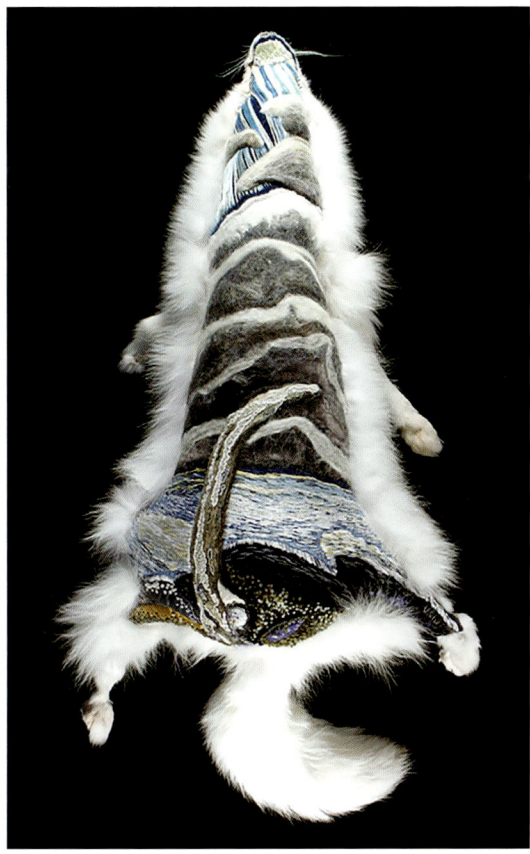

FIGURE 2.19.
Willow Rector, *The Singing Bone* (rear view), from the series *TRAPPED*, 2013.

Sabiston has always been insistent that her method of creating is visible, whether for her environmental works or her portrait pieces.

Willow Rector, an artist working in Manitoba, also uses materials in new ways. Her *TRAPPED Series: The Singing Bone*, 2013, is hand-embroidered on Arctic fox pelt. Her rhythmic imagery of the land, water, and sky, coupled with traditional techniques of embroidery, explore intersections of settler and Indigenous cultures.

The many aspects of line, colour, and space in artists' two-dimensional paintings, drawings, prints, photographs, and textile works often extend across media and into expansive spaces. In order to convey their messages and create meaningful engagement with audiences, artists must be accomplished in their techniques and be willing to experiment with them and challenge the possibilities with new approaches and materials.

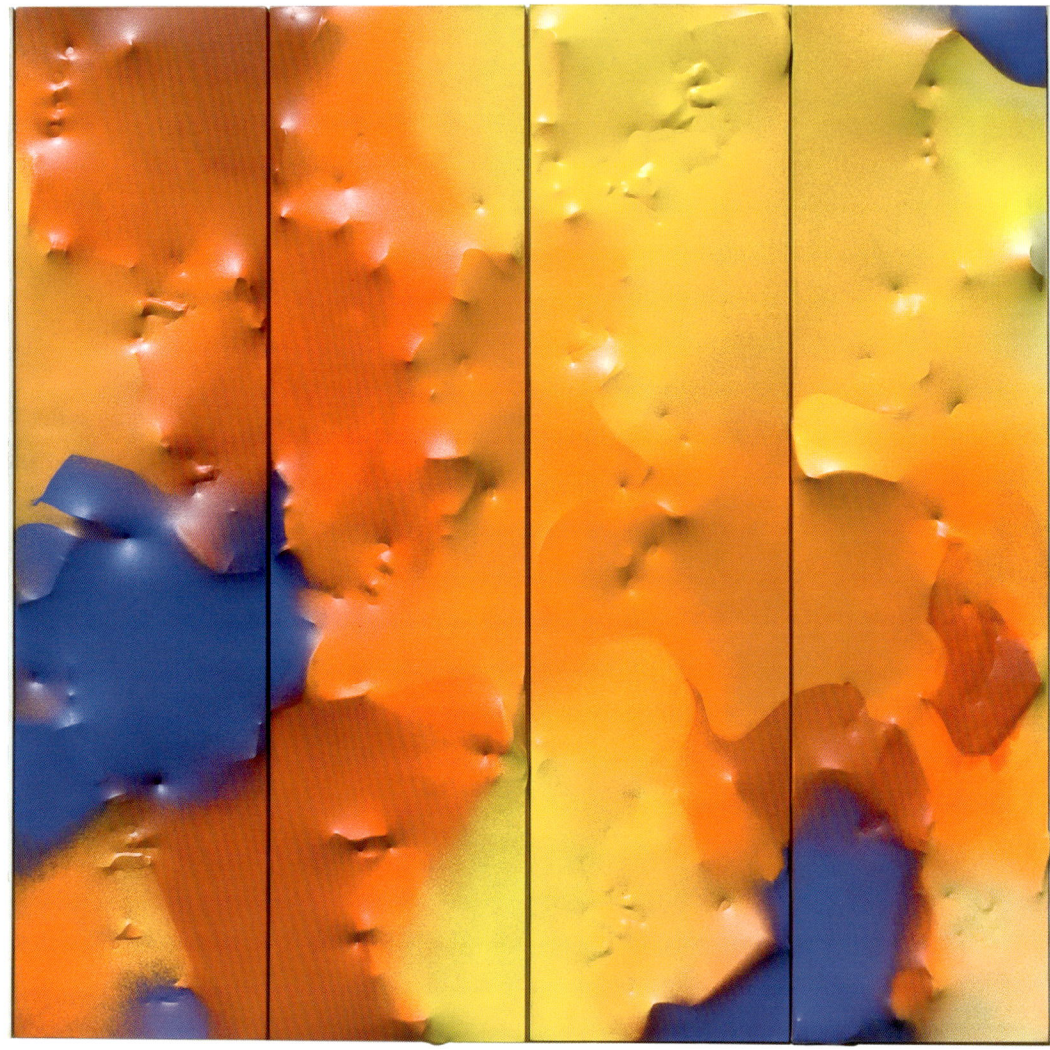

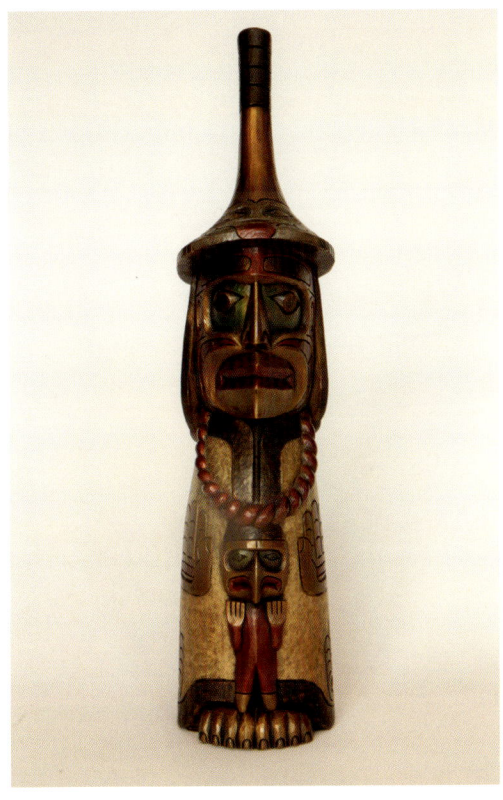

Investigations in the Third Dimension

"95% of creativity is curiosity and discovering, essential in an artist's work."[62]

Sculpture as a creative endeavour has also evolved in its modes of presentation, materials, and execution, frequently breaking with tradition. Sculpture is essentially made in one of two methods: modelling and building by adding to a basic form, or carving or cutting to create a form. Since the middle of the twentieth century, many sculptural works have moved off pedestals to sit directly on the floor, to hang on the wall or from the ceiling, or even to be situated into the middle of a field or outdoor setting. Works like the abstract sculptures of Robert Murray (b. 1936) or John Nugent (1921–2014) are examples of outdoor, public,

FIGURE 2.20. **Bruce Head**, *Quartet*, 1978.

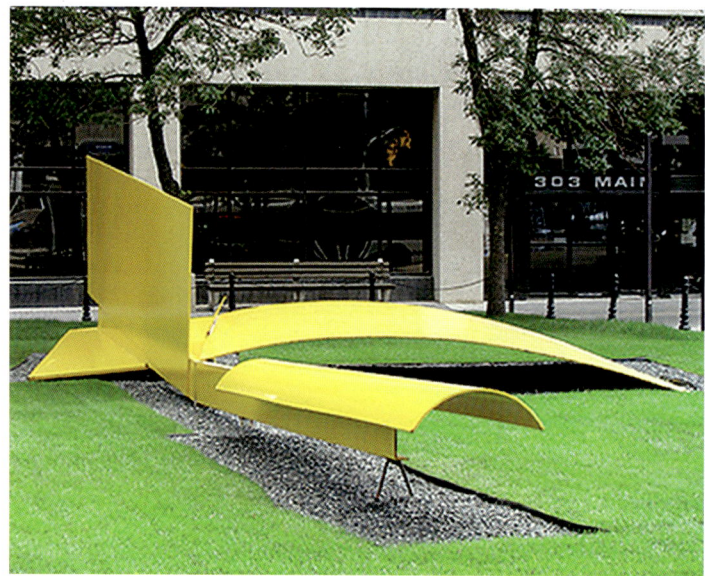

FIGURE 2.22.
John Nugent, *No. 1 Northern*, 1976.

colourful pieces representing space and place. Presentation and siting have increasingly become part of a work's conception. At the same time the focus of artists working in the discipline has shifted. Some artists concentrate primarily on the surface; some, on the subject; and others, on viewer engagement. For many the engagement with architecture has been paramount as public art commissions have expanded. Sculptors' materials also shifted after the middle of the twentieth century, expanding from the traditional wood, bronze, and stone works to include found materials from scrapyards, lumberyards, and building sites, or repurposing household items. Artists like Aganetha Dyck, for example, started using household objects and clothes purchased at thrift shops. For others, plexiglass, sisal, fibreglass, mesh, wire, rubber, rope, and myriad other found objects became common creative materials. The introduction of these many new materials meant that the methods of creating three-dimensional art had to change. Sandblasting, enamelling, laser cutting, and rusting became more common sculptural techniques in addition to traditional polishing and cutting.

Alberta's Peter Hide (b. 1944) was a student of internationally acclaimed sculptor Anthony Caro and, like Caro, pursued a career in sculpture to become one of Canada's pre-eminent artists of abstract, large, welded works created from rusted industrial scrap metal. Douglas Bentham (b.1947), working in Saskatchewan, was also a master of welded steel sculpture, and he created abstracted constructivist works. These two leading artists investigated the intersections between architecture and sculpture.

Saskatchewan's Joe Fafard used both modelling and carving methods in creating his three-dimensional art. Redolent of prairie farms, his art in each of his many media—prints, paintings, bronze, steel, and ceramics—conveys his deep sense of place. Fafard's persistent exploration of form and materials led him to create large laser cut-out works, some of single animals and others of groups of animals. *Running Horses,* 2017, a major work depicting a herd of galloping horses with manes flying, made of steel and bronze, is installed outside the National Gallery of Canada. For it, Fafard first drew and cut the forms in Styrofoam, and then cast them in bronze. To add richness and realism to this work, he wanted various textures and realistic modulations of colour. He experimented with a number of surfaces to finish the bronze, disliking the shiny traditional patinas, because, he said, "they remind me of plastic"[63] and because they require ongoing regular care and waxing. He told me that he was really pleased to discover the new material of powder-coating. Applying the coloured powdered polyesters and then baking the work, he obtained his desired surface effects and colours. Powder-coating stands up better than traditional patinas to Canada's climate extremes of heat, cold, sun, and snow. Always environmentally conscious, Fafard never wasted anything, so he repurposed the cut-aways, the by-products from the laser pieces, the retaillés, to create his built sculptures. He welded leftover bits to make new works and used leftover cut-outs from his laser sculptures to create embossed prints, tangibly linking printmaking and sculpture.

Fafard also reflected on current and cultural events in his work. *My First Pony,* 2008, and *Everything Is Under Control,* 2014, both exuding energy and personality, are but two examples. In *Everything Is Under Control,* a minotaur rides a horse on wheels and tries to rein in its speed. It is Fafard's direct response to economic events, especially oil extraction and oil prices.[64] His art in all media poses serious questions about many environmental concerns, which extend to food production. Does contemporary society really understand the cycles of food production? Are we aware of the demise of critical species as a result of the use of pesticides? Are we cognizant of the cost to society with the loss of small farms? Throughout his prolific body of work, Fafard constantly returned to the theme of the balances required in nature and for the protection of the environment. He said, "Unless we care for those things we are not going to save anything. Too many people are isolated from the production of food; we need the variety of plants, insects, birds and animals, wild and cultivated. We must work in cooperation with nature—we learned that growing up on the farm."[65]

British Columbia Indigenous artist Brian Jungen (b. 1970) builds his sculptures from everyday objects. His powers of innovation are evident in his creations of whale skeletons made from plastic chairs and the totem poles and masks he made from sports equipment. Pop culture and consumerism form the basis for much of his work, highlighted by the fact that his materials include Nike shoes, Air Jordans, and sports bags. Fashioned into Northwest Coast Indigenous cultural icons, his *Prototype for New Understanding #7* is a twenty-three-part series of soft

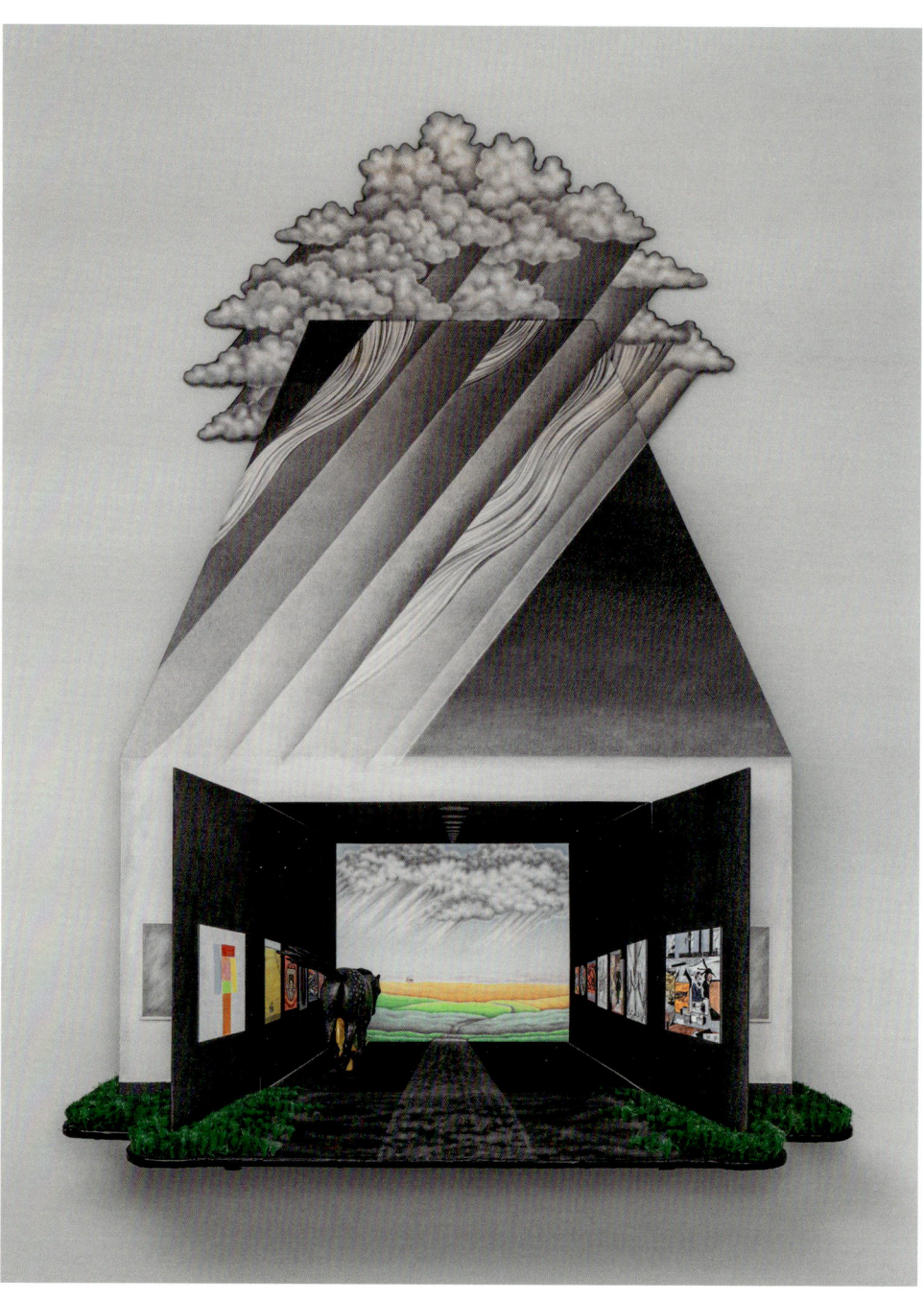

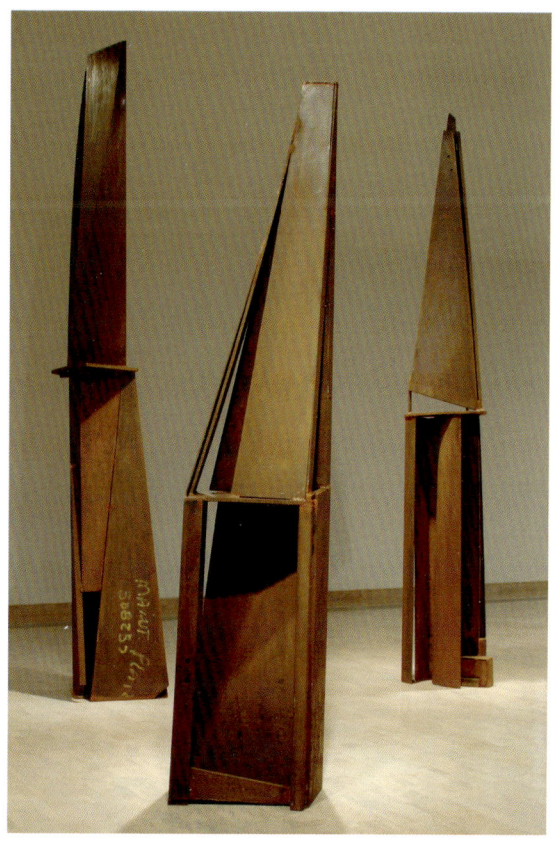

FIGURE 2.24.
Douglas Bentham,
Pinnacle I: Marking Time;
Pinnacle II: Relic of Memory;
Pinnacle III: Ray of Light, 2003.

sculptures created between 1998 and 2005. They are made from commonplace objects stacked, sewn, and interwoven together. His meticulous craftsmanship is obvious. By using objects everyone owns, he places his Indigenous culture at the centre of today's lifestyles, challenging societal preconceptions. His art carries a bite. *The People's Flag,* 2006, for example, was inspired both by the workers' anthem, "The Red Flag," a poem written by Irish political activist Jim Connell, and by Greenpeace banners, an organization that interests him. Assembled and stitched together on-site at Tate Modern in London, this large, red, floor-to-ceiling textile installation is made from mass-produced red articles of clothing, including coats, hats, shirts, scarves, and dresses as well as ordinary objects like umbrellas.

FIGURE 2.23. **Don Proch**, *Colville's Horse Races Through the Prairie Drive-Thru Gallery, Brushing Past John Nugent's "No. 1 Hard," Heading West to Haida Gwaii*, 2016.

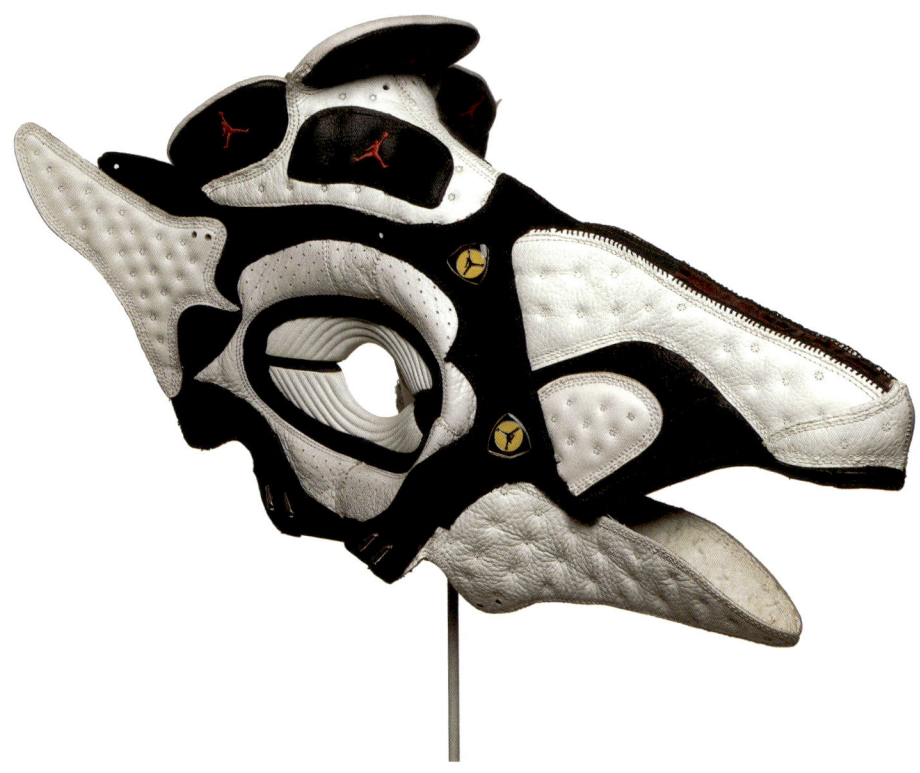

A number of Western Canadian artists have used glass innovatively to express multiple ideas and experiences, taking that material to new artistic directions in quite different ways from other art forms. Warren Carther, for instance, creates large-scale architectural installations. His works, like *Prairie Boy's Dream,* 1994, at One Canada Centre, Winnipeg, as well as his 1999 *Chronos Trilogy,* in Lincoln House, Hong Kong, *Euphony,* 2004, at Alaska's Anchorage International Airport, and *Aperture,* 2011, at Winnipeg's Richardson International Airport, all engage the viewer with symbols relevant to the business or building. They evoke the geology, space, and light of the particular place. Throughout his art Carther employs various techniques—stacked, blown, and etched—and various kinds of glass.

Manitoba's Ione Thorkelsson, recipient of the Governor General's Award in the Visual Arts/Saidye Bronfman Award, has worked both in blown glass and cast glass throughout her

FIGURE 2.25. **Brian Jungen**, *Prototype for New Understanding #7,* 1999.

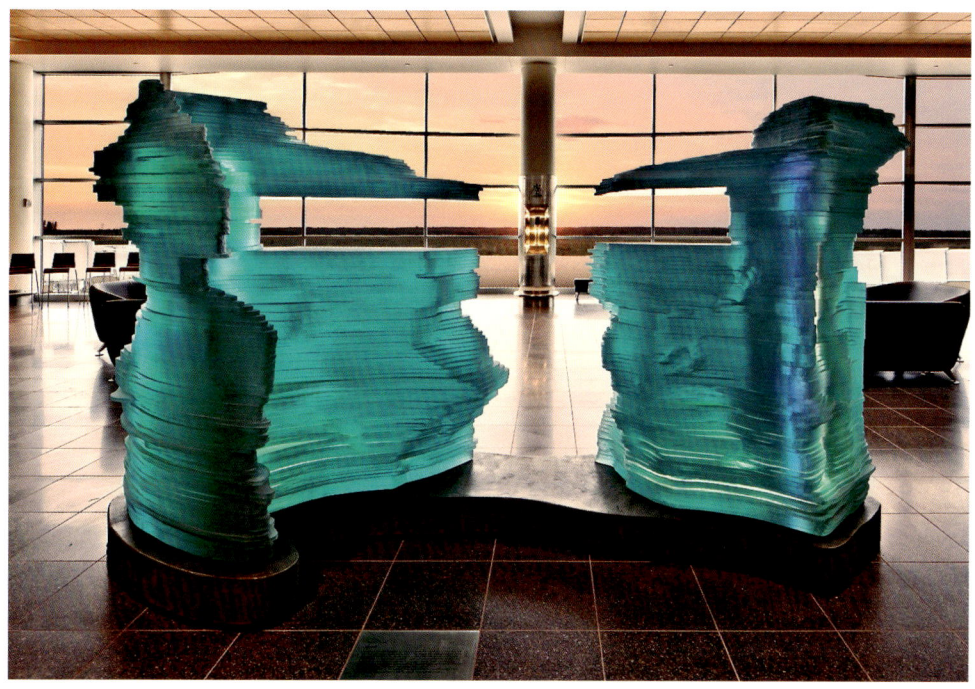

career. As she says, "Glass has an effect that is like nothing else. You can make it translucent, transparent or opaque. I'm working with emotion and mood as well as with ideas and glass can do that for you."[66] Working with blown glass from the 1970s until 2006, she experimented with colour and always achieved fascinating layered effects. She commented that "for almost 25 years I have worked as a glass blower… I tend to want to jump to something new as soon as a piece is successful. I have developed work that allows me the freedom to work with colour in layers and on the surface."[67] Her move to working in cast glass has allowed her to delve into archaeologically based forms in her installations. She admits she is a craftsperson first, and "as an object maker I am always on the look-out for things to cast and there are always lots of bones hanging around the studio. … Bones are always such a nice shape, all those complex curves."[68] Her Winnipeg airport work, *Incoming*, 2012, her first architectural commission, is a flock of cast-glass bird wings, evoking flight. It is uplifting and soaring, and has been described by art critic William Ganis as "simultaneously gorgeous and nightmarish. Each pair of colorless wings is disembodied, with the rest of the bird replaced by a steel armature."[69]

FIGURE 2.26. **Warren Carther**, *Aperture*, 2011.

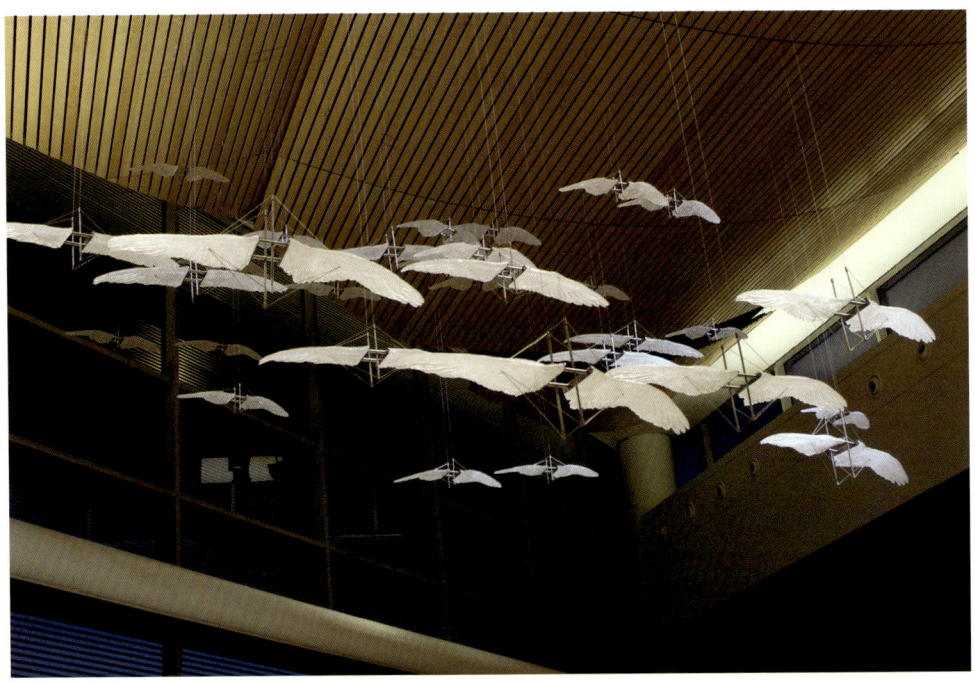

On Vancouver Island Waine Ryzak sandblasts glass to create archetypal three-dimensional works that emanate a prehistoric sense and spirituality, and some recall classical forms and ideas of the Greeks and Romans. In Vancouver Mary Filer's large-scale floor-to-ceiling blown and fused colour-filled glass abstractions have been installed at Simon Fraser University and a number of public buildings.

Clay is another material that has been the chosen medium for many artists across the West. Some have deservedly earned international recognition. Ceramic artists create functional works, small and large one-of-a-kind pieces, and significant installations. Individual in concept, inspiration, and execution, contemporary ceramic artists have built on centuries of international advances in form, colour, and glazes. Robin Hopper in Victoria, for example, explored many historical ideas and methods over the years, such as his agate wares of layered blue and white clays. Some of his forms, for instance, are derived from those of ancient Greece and Rome, and while a number of his glazes recall early ceramics from the Middle East, his work is definitely at the front edge of contemporary ceramics.

FIGURE 2.27. **Ione Thorkelsson**, *Incoming*, 2012.

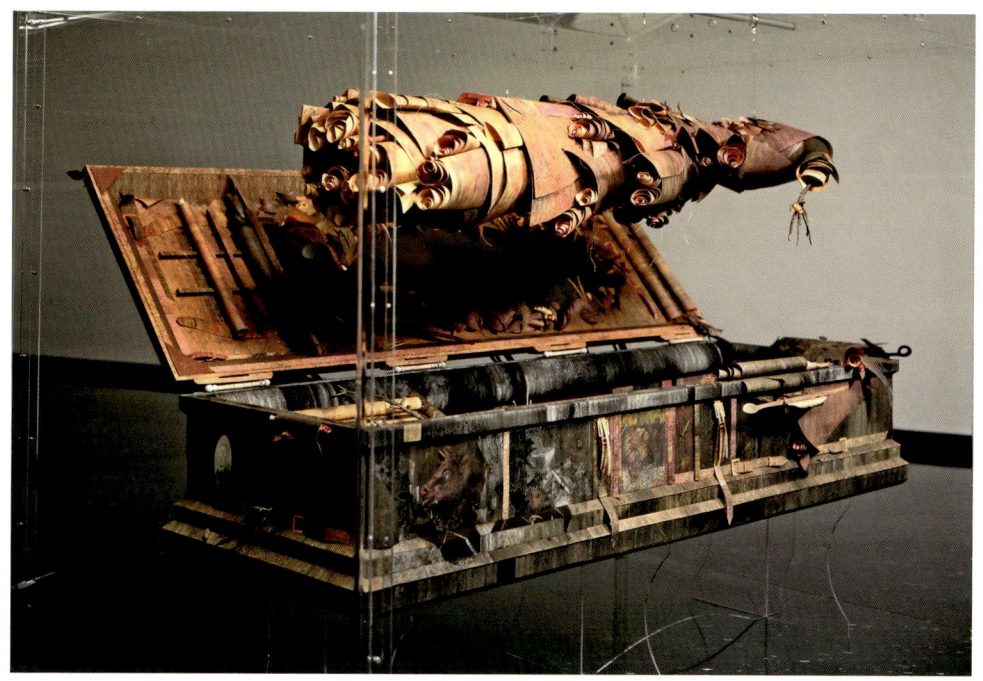

Alberta ceramic artist Jeannie Mah, who works in porcelain, is also inspired by the history of ceramics. Author Jill Sawyer wrote: "Much of Jeannie Mah's inspiration during the past 20 years can be traced to a trip to Crete in 1983. There, in a museum, she came across a Minoan cup made in the 14th century BC which has become an apocryphal part of her own development as an artist."[70]

Master ceramist Walter Dexter was particularly interested in the surface of his pots for decorating and his depth of knowledge of calligraphy is evident. He never ceased experimenting with glazes and colour and the deep red glazes he developed are characteristically his own. Late in his career, on the opening of his kiln, he showed me with delight a new pink glaze and an orange one, both having been goals of his for some time. He also transformed his pots into unique sculptures by exaggerating the bottles' necks and bodies into those of human dimensions. Dexter had studied at the Alberta College of Art and later at the Swedish School of Art. Encouraged by painter Luke Lindoe, he never left ceramics once he

FIGURE 2.28. **Esther Warkov**, *House of Tea*, 1997–1998.

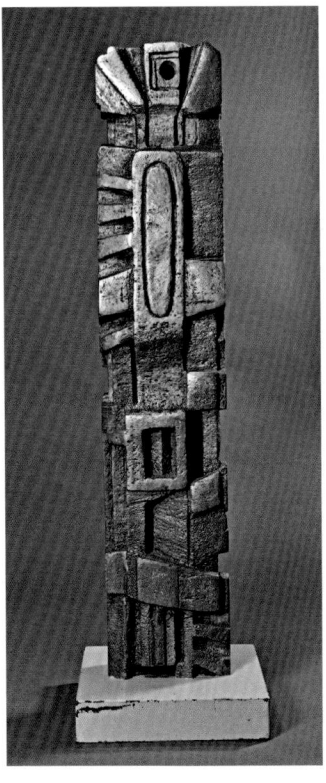

FIGURE 2.29.
Elza Mayhew,
Princess, 1963.

found the medium when he was a student. Throughout his long career he always used Medicine Hat clay; he told me, "I rather like the Medicine Hat clay which I have always used."[71]

The forms, colours, and combinations of works by Alberta's Greg Payce are fascinating. He often installs his large-scale pieces of specific shapes, often with striped patterns, together as one installation. Of different sizes, they stand like a crowd of people. While the positive shape of the individual works stand out, so, too, do the negative spaces in-between them, these, like the pots themselves, taking on figure-like appearances and scale. As such, Payce's work is mathematical in its presentation.

Many acclaimed Western Canadian ceramic artists have represented Canada in the international sphere. They are installation artists such as Grace Nickel; landscape and portrait artists such as Les Manning, Mel Malkin, and Joe Fafard; and sculptors such as Eva Stubbs. Each has depicted place, time, and issues of contemporary concern. Artists including Tam Irving, John Chalke, Jack Sures, and Robert Archambeau are all giants in the field as artists, as teachers, and as international workshop leaders.

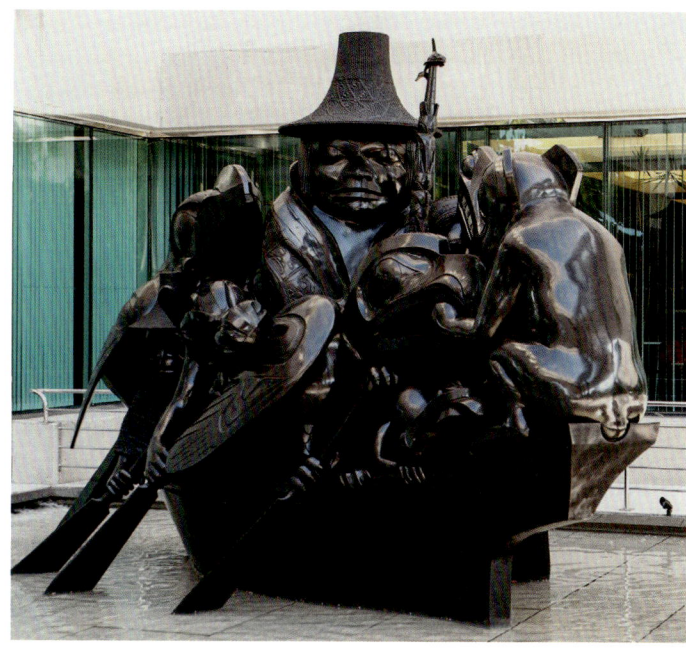

FIGURE 2.30.
Bill Reid,
*The Spirit of Haida
Gwaii: The Black
Canoe,* 1991.

Varying clays have varying interests for artists: porcelain is finer, translucent, and more fragile; stoneware is more dense and heavier and affords greater surface textures. Firing temperatures affect the resulting glazes, as does the type of kiln: electric, wood, or gas. The sources of influence are infinite, including the land, light, and function. The field of Western Canadian ceramics is rich and much has been published on the legacies of the artists involved. As professor Mary Ann Steggles wrote: "Just as the legacy provided by the members of the counter culture continues in aspects of mainstream culture, so too does the legacy of masters of Canadian studio pottery. . . . Indeed, these masters have practiced their art in excess of four decades creating functional pottery as well as specialty objects for exhibitions. They have won the highest awards possible for any artist in our country and their work is now recognized beyond our borders."[72]

Esther Warkov uses the traditional materials of paper and pastel to construct significant sculptural pieces and installations, resulting in a unique three-dimensional approach. A true innovator in technique and message, she reflected in a 2000 interview: "I think the medium of three-dimensional drawings will be my contribution if anyone ever knows what I do."[73] In creating her paper drawings, and sculptures, like *House of Tea,* she tears, folds, and rolls paper, into which she has worked layer upon layer of pastel and graphite. She blends her colours by smudging the pastel with Kleenex and never uses fixatives. At the National Gallery of Canada in 2000, Warkov said: "The reason I work with the materials that I use is that they are more flexible in a way that I can actually create a third dimension to my work. I started drawing in the 1980s and I haven't painted for twenty years."[74]

New Media and Engagements

"Performance art is a visual art that plays fast and loose with the traditions of everything from opera to architecture. . . . It is changing, fugitive. . . . Performance art produces nothing more (or less) than an experience."[75]

New media and new technologies allowed an exponential explosion in the means of creating art with film, video, and computer-generated work, all of which enabled the visual arts to be more democratic, more widely accessible, and simultaneously considerably more complex. At the same time, installation art, conceptual art, public art, and performance art have increasingly provided audiences with means of creative engagement in their everyday life activities—on their computers, in the street, in parks, and in planned gallery or community settings. Op art and pop art were at the forefront in the 1960s, bringing the everyday, such as soup cans and Brillo boxes, not only into the realm of artists' subject matter but also into major galleries in Canada. These international ideas infused Canadian art, and are linked to artists' groups like General Idea, N.E. Thing Co., and Western Front, the latter co-founded by Victoria artist Michael Morris with seven others in 1973. The 1970s provided a sea change in art making.

Installation, public art, and performance art embody the ephemeral and the permanent through powerful aspects of visual creative endeavours. Collaborations with creators in different disciplines—architects, actors, musicians, poets, filmmakers, and set designers—were exciting and frequent. Installation art, created for a specific space and a specific time span, was done so the viewer was included, or implicated, in the space. Conceptual art was image-based—IAIN BAXTER& and N.E. Thing Co. was an early leader. Drawing from contemporary pop culture, it challenged accepted ideas, forcing deeper analyses of what had been taken for granted in society. Performance art was an event. It was interdisciplinary and usually presented as a story or a social situation.

Métis Saskatchewan artist Edward Poitras's 2012 exhibition *Thirteen Coyotes* and his *Ground and Tree,* for instance, bring multiple realities of identity to the fore. Poitras (b. 1953) engages his viewers, interweaving shared histories and ongoing change. Coyotes frequent much of Poitras's art, as image and as self. As curator Michelle Lavalle noted:

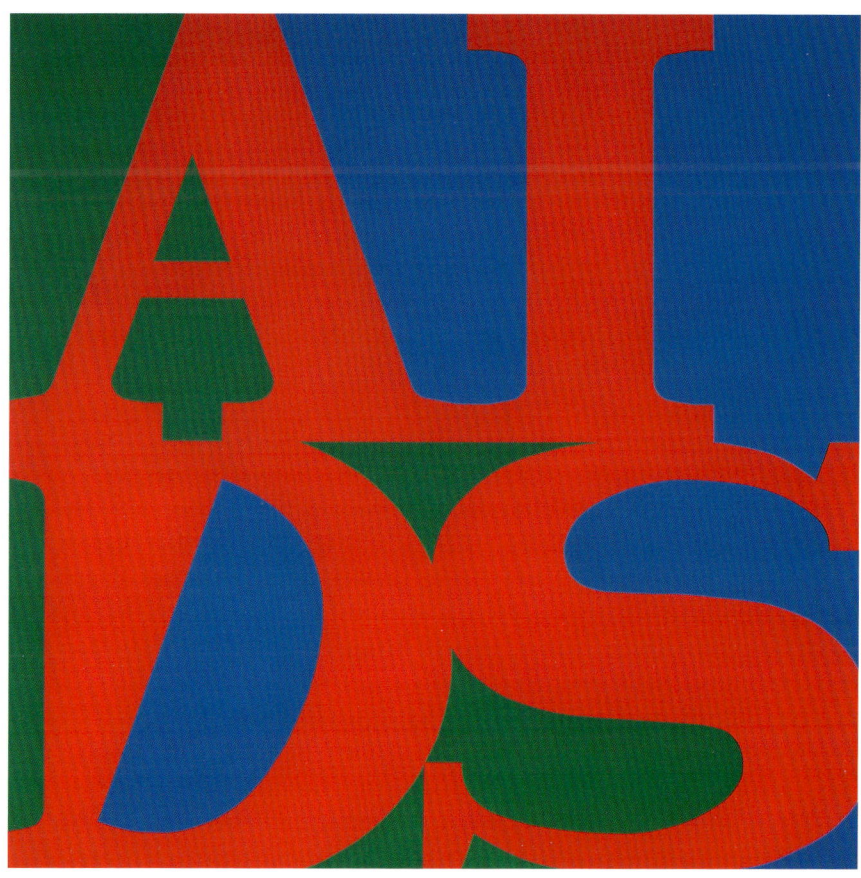

[his] multi-dimensional artistic practice explores imaginative territories that extend
beyond the borders of identity and location to consider the self in global terms . . . and
explore imaginative territories, themes, issues and concepts . . . a reworking of imagery
and meanings that address a whole range of themes and issues which have evolved and
proliferated throughout Poitras' life on Turtle Island. . . . Individual coyotes and coyotes
in transformation spring to life from bones and other materials. Their mutating forms
mimic the endless transformation that we ourselves experience as we pass through
various planes of existence. The coyotes' transformation is also connected to Poitras'

FIGURE 2.31. **General Idea**, *AIDS*, 1988 (detail).

contemplation of time . . . takes into consideration ancient cultures and their "long count" calendars (one in particular which indicates December 21, 2012 as a key moment of transition and period of change). The work is about time and space, or rather the illusion of time and space.[76]

Performance art, an experience-based art form for artists and for audiences, is presented outside traditional exhibition formats and often challenges the status quo. It has the aura of the performative, yet involves objects, frequently those at hand and/or made by the artists themselves. Though momentary, it is a critical part of contemporary visual expression and one of the more visceral means of engaging the public in contemporary issues. In early years it drew attention to feminism; later, it addressed the lack of democracy accorded to the gay community, concerns for the environment, and missing and murdered Indigenous women and girls. While pushing society to greater justice, performance art can also embody empathy, kindness, and positive societal change. Performance artist and curator Shawna Dempsey wrote: "Unlike traditional artforms that suspend time by immersing the viewer in an alternate reality/narrative, performance often draws attention to the passing of time and the discomfort that entails. The living, breathing performer also flagrantly displays idiosyncrasy. . . . when we take the time to attentively watch another person (as happens in the performance setting), we are confronted with an individual. This personal complexity is all the more layered if a performer is enacting his or her beliefs, experiences, or concerns. . . . It is a situation that threatens our assumptions."[77]

Taking hold in the 1960s, at first in alternate spaces, performance art often was presented in conjunction with other art forms, like music, dance, or theatre. Much of the early performance art on the prairies was done outdoors. As Dempsey said, "By definition, the artform requires performer(s), an audience, and space, and Winnipeg's geography offers infinite amounts of the latter. To merely stand up on the prairies is to take a performative position, such is the extreme flatness of our landscape. The early performance community positioned itself on the vast horizontal plane and interacted with any audience who joined them there."[78]

A number of performance artists advanced the medium, including Winnipeg's Doug Melnyk, who also works in drawing, photo-collage, and installation. Alex Poruchnyk and Sharon Alward, professors at the School of Art at the University of Manitoba, have continued to stretch and expand the medium, as have their students, Daniel Barrow, Ken Gregory, Sandee Moore, and Nicole Shimonek. The cross-pollination of many media, especially that with music, is an important element of performance art. Dempsey opines: "Hybridity is the essence of performance art, and cross-pollination continues to expand its very definition."[79]

Winnipeg-born Vancouver artist Gathie Falk defined performance art in her 1981 article in *artscanada*:

From my perspective, to make a performance piece is to put together, or choreograph, or compose a work of art that has a beginning, an end, and a middle, with preferably, but not necessarily, a climax or several climaxes. Sometimes a piece works in a linear way with one event following another . . . ; sometimes the choreography is worked out like a fugue in music, with one event beginning close upon the heels of another, and a third event intertwining with the first two. The analogy of music is apt. One of my works, *Red Angel* (1972), is like a rondo, with theme A followed by theme B, followed by theme A.[80]

Falk continues about her own work:

The events, or themes, I like to use are, guess what, activities of ordinary everyday living: eating an egg, reading a book, washing clothes, putting on makeup, cutting hair, together with slightly exotic events such as shining someone's shoes while he is walking backwards, singing an operatic aria, sewing cabbage leaves together, smashing eggs with a ruler as in playing croquet, making a painting out of lipstick, powder, and perfume. . . .

To some spectators it seemed that all this effort was made with a view to toppling the usual order of things or that the aim was outrageous. Not so. The activities that I used belonged together in that mysterious way that all things in every strong work of art belong together, with neither too much nor too little of anything. . . . I wasn't fighting any battles: just doing, creating, with different material, the things I also made with more traditional materials.

This new material was people, used not in the conscious way of dance nor the narrative way of theatre, but in a way that only a visual artist would find natural.[81]

Falk refers to the onset of performance art, conceptual art, and video art as a "cultural revolution": "The result of this cultural revolution was that painters kept on painting, sculptors kept on doing what they do, and some of us flamboyant Performance artists went our own naughty ways."[82]

Shawna Dempsey and Lorri Millan are two of Canada's best-known performance artists and they have presented their work across Canada and internationally, from Frankfurt to Sydney, Australia. Their work primarily addresses social, feminist, and lesbian issues. Tragically, they lost all their material in a large studio building fire in Winnipeg in 2019, a devastating event for many of the city's leading artists. The only works by Dempsey and Millan that remain are those in public collections or those that were on tour. However, through her strong career Dempsey revealed her own sense of audiences and herself as artist: "The audience's ambivalence

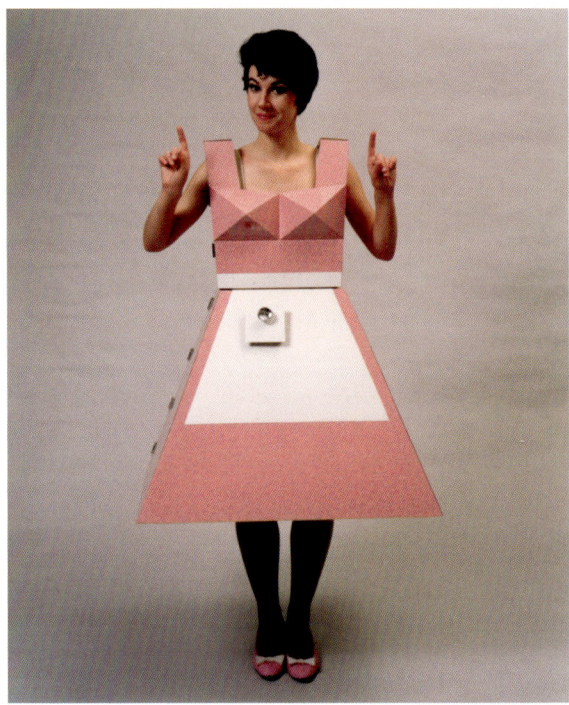

FIGURE 2.32.
Shawna Dempsey and Lorri Millan, *Arborite Housedress,* from *The Dress Series*, 1993.

(or outright hostility) toward performance is shared by performers themselves. I can personally attest to no greater fear than standing before an audience armed only with my body and my ideas. Mortality looms large. Vanquishing dread becomes a heroic feat."[83] In their *Dress Series,* 1989–1996, Millan and Dempsey examined female societal stereotypes and female dress by fabricating contemporary dresses in unlikely materials, such as their 1995 *Arborite Housedress*:

> This is about a domestic love-affair between myself and advanced interior decorating technique. This is about the in-between of my placement, of my desire. Me, in-between: wallpaper valances, contrasting trim, kitchen islands, ferns.
>
> This is about me, trying to make the look work; me, wanting it to all hang together; me, giving it that je ne sais pas; and me, getting the details right, the little things, the finishing touches.
>
> > Oh, oh and that feels so . . . hard.
> > Oh, oh, oh, and I'm so very . . . pointed.
> > Oh and yes and oh . . . I think I'll . . . clean up a bit.[84]

Humour coupled with their sincerity and concern for community underlines all their work, as do aspects of democracy, in works like *Big Wig,* 2017, and their *Disembodied Head,* which explore democracy for women. This is especially relevant during the time of COVID, which has particularly affected women's place in the workforce. The concept of embodiment and disembodiment of person and society as a whole is layered in these videos and performances, and, as with their earlier work, their goal is to address central societal ideas and change the world.

In March 2022 it was announced that Shawna Dempsey and Lorri Millan, part of the Winnipeg design team that won the major public art commission for the new LGBTQ2+ National Monument in Ottawa. Their proposal will continue their work in engaging audiences and encouraging greater human understanding. Entitled *Thunderhead*, the design draws on the symbolism of the cloud to embody "strength, activism and hope," and as Michelle Douglas, executive director of the LGBT Purge Fund, said, it was "powerful, captivating and extraordinary. . . . It will stand as both a beacon of inspiration and a reminder of the pain of discrimination."[85]

Winnipeg musician and composer Christine Fellows has created performance art with visual artist Shary Boyle, who represented Canada at the 2013 Venice Biennale. Their collaborative work ties into Falk's perceptions, building on the older artist's concepts of choreography and the analogy of a fugue in music. This was particularly apparent in Fellows's 2009 *Reliquary/Reliquaire*, presented in the original St. Boniface Museum chapel with Shary Boyle and several colleague musicians. That work resulted from her Winnipeg Arts Council's six-month residency at Le Musée de Saint-Boniface Museum. Fellows had full access to their early francophone and Métis collections, archives, and photographs. Combining music, film, and visual art, she wove a story of St. Boniface history laced with contemporary overlays. The Winnipeg Arts Council's press release said, "The result was a hauntingly beautiful performance at times both melancholy and playful. The chapel provided a deeply evocative space and wonderful acoustics for this outstanding and moving performance."[86] Productions like this help realize Shawna Dempsey's vision for performance art. As Dempsey writes, "Performance art is difficult to pin down. While it may resemble theatre, music, and dance in its use of live bodies in space, it is not nearly so comprehensible, familiar, and safe. And not consequentially, in a capitalist society, it refutes the notion of commodity."[87]

Conceptual art is also difficult to pin down, as is some video art. These art forms, too, are integrally tied into the creative explosions of the 1960s and 1970s, which excited and challenged audiences as artists took their art beyond the traditional gallery and museum spaces. Winnipeg's AA Bronson, Felix Partz, and Jorge Zontal of General Idea were early conceptual art pioneers, and they took their ideas and activities nationally. They printed *File Magazine*, had Mr. Peanut run for Vancouver mayor in 1974, and founded Art Metropole in Toronto in 1987. Their issues came from popular culture, mass media, and the work of Marshall McLuhan. The HIV/ AIDS epidemic and its related issues were critical foci of this group from 1987 to 1994. Their public performances, like other performance art, galvanized communities to contemporary issues, and though the issues were serious societal ones, they addressed them with a spirit of fun and humour.

Video art also emerged as an art form in the mid-1960s and it, too, overlapped with film, performance art, music, theatre, and photography. Video artists presented images as narrative, perceptual, and documentary. The new, easy to use Sony portable cameras enabled video and the electronic moving image to become widespread, bringing television-like production into the creative hands of artists. Vancouver artists Eric Metcalfe, Hank Bull, and Paul Wong documented fictions that examined human behaviour, and they had both sets and actors. Curator Shirley Madill reflected: "With a growing theatricalization of video and performance in the mid-1970s and an increasing tendency to narcissistic estheticization, it is understandable that the focus of the video activities of politically and socially committed artists returned to television. But, where television is concerned with programs which deliver the audience to the advertiser, video hopes to establish a two-way communication between creator and viewer. . . . Where television pretends to be objective and impersonal, video art is subjective and personal. . . . Their intention is not merely to represent an existing world but as artists to bring a new world into being."[88]

York University's art historian Joyce Zemans saw the importance of video art and its many extensions when she wrote in 1973 of N.E. Thing Co.'s use of video to "explore another aspect of perception . . . and the manifest repercussions for the contemporary artist involved with video. . . . One of the most important aspects of the medium lies in its ability to reach a large number of people and as long as artists are content to use the medium with a gallery setting or a fine art context, its value is limited chiefly to the initiated. How to go beyond the security of the traditional gallery setting and explore avenues for reaching a broader audience are quests few video artists have explored."[89]

Alberta's Janet Cardiff (b. 1957), who works with her husband, George Bures Miller, has explored many issues in her videos and sound works, her *Audio Walks* and *Forty Part Motet* being but a few key examples. Cardiff, whose work is experiential and incorporates sound in a manner to create psychological tension, recalled her 1991 residency at the Banff Centre:

> I was out recording things—wearing a pair of headphones, making sure I was getting good sound—and at one point I was reading the names of grave sites out loud . . .
> I pressed rewind, then pressed play—losing track of where I was—and I heard my voice describing what I was seeing in front of me. It was such a strange and particular feeling—one of those serendipitous moments, I guess. Over the next few weeks, I made my first walk, but only about a dozen people tried it. I wasn't even sure what it was at the time—is this thing even art?[90]

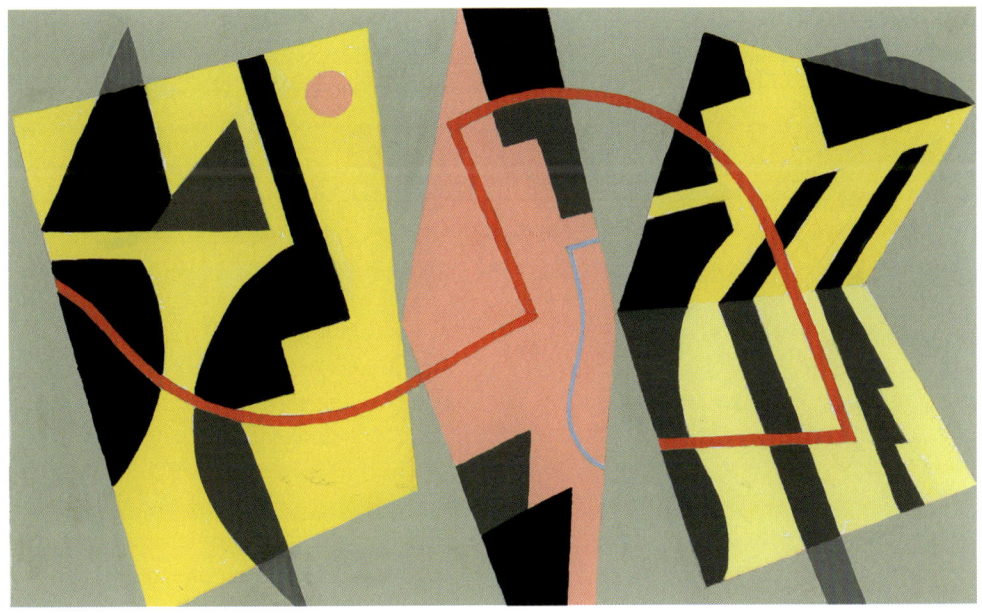

These works are captivating and mysterious. They often compel a participant to question one's safety, some when walking and others in a theatre, like her 2001 Venice Biennale piece, *The Paradise Institute*. Through the headphones, voices or heaving breaths come from all directions, beside, behind, or in front of one, creating a sense of vulnerability. Her *Forty Part Motet,* the installation of forty speakers set in a circle playing a choral motet by sixteenth-century composer Thomas Tallis, is spellbinding. Installed in the Rideau Chapel at the National Gallery of Canada, the work has also been shown globally. The sound comes from forty different speakers at different times. Surreal and sublime, it is simple yet complex.

IAIN BAXTER& is a giant in the development of conceptual art conveying environmental and social concerns. With his wife, Ingrid, he founded N.E. Thing Co. in 1966 and incorporated it in 1969 to become a catalyst in the Vancouver photo-conceptualist movement. While photography and the Polaroid camera were some of his key tools, his work took many forms and dealt with ideas from consumerism to the environment. He reminisced of the time that "conceptual art swept us all into its flow."[91] He noted the influence of press coverage on how his work was received, given the scandalous nature of much of his art: "It made people question whether or not what they were looking at was really art. I considered art as information and

FIGURE 2.33. **Eric Metcalfe**, *Furthermore*, 2011.

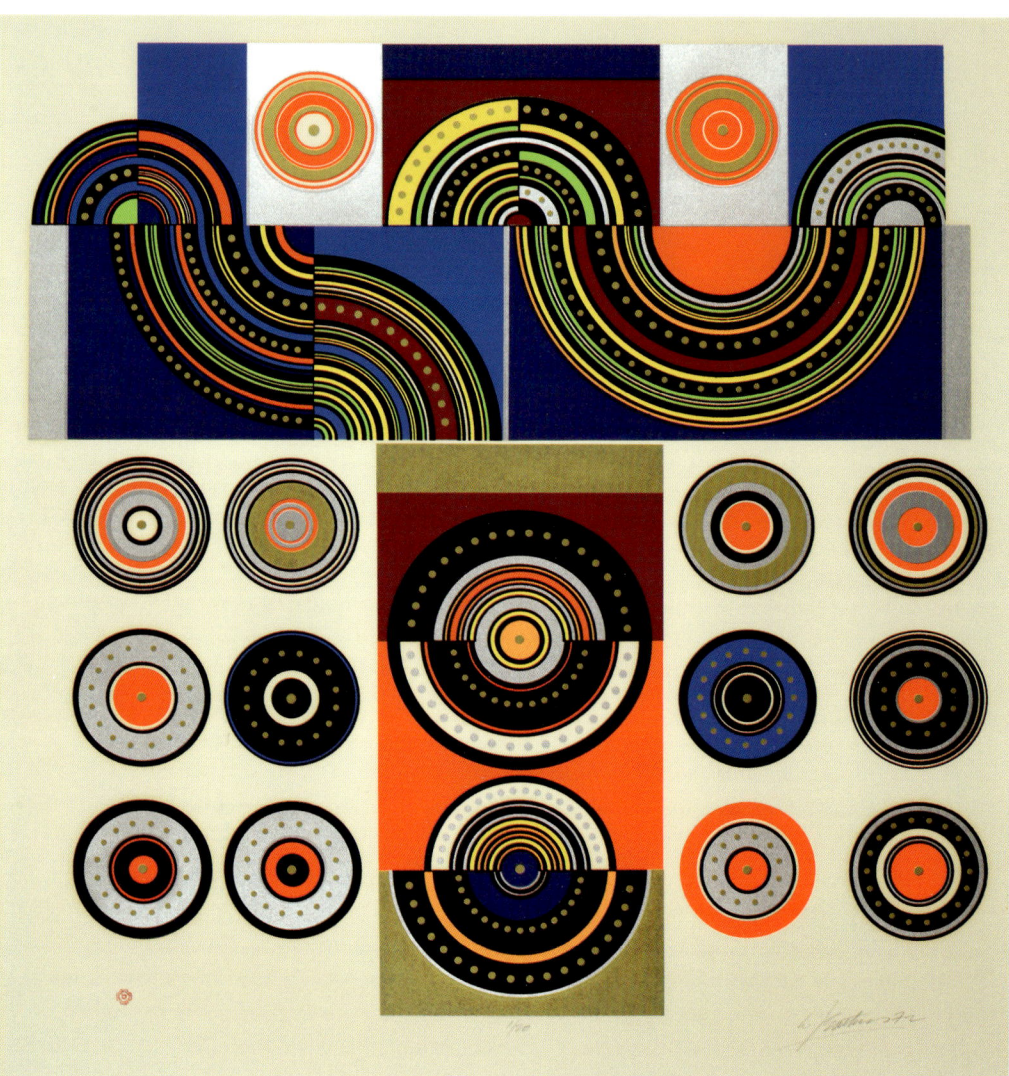

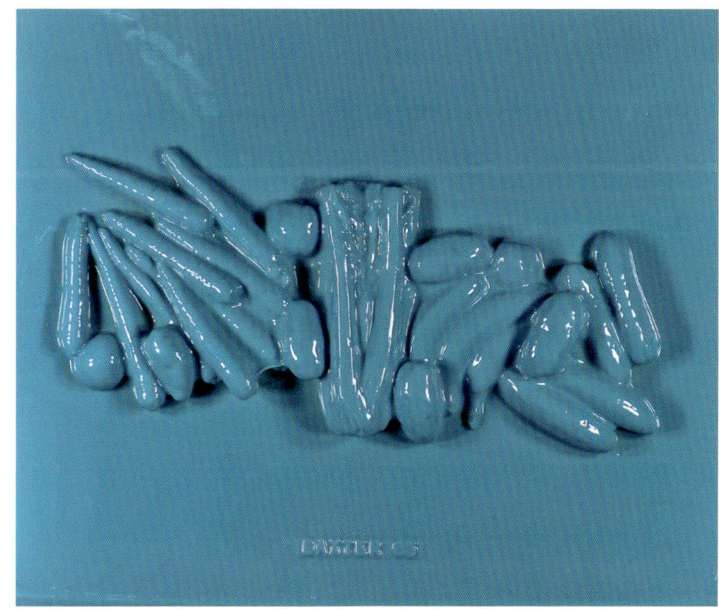

FIGURE 2.35.
IAIN BAXTER&,
Still Life, n.d.

created a new definition for art. . . . A lot of my work pushes boundaries of what's accepted as art; it picks at the art world in the way that the work of someone like Duchamp did. So a lot of press thought my work was a put-on."[92]

BAXTER& explored many aspects of contemporary society around him, including the amount of plastics in local dumps, feeling that "plastic bottles were the common pottery of his period."[93] He revealed his own preoccupation with plastic in an interview with Joan Lowndes: "I'd always gone to dumps and I noticed all kinds of plastic throwaways. It became real to me that we lived in a plastic world, that everything we see, touch, drink from, the artificial ventricle for the heart, is plastic. It was a revelation of the plastic coating that goes on around the electronic revolution. And I wanted to make these things."[94]

His 1965 vacuum-formed works, such as *Still Life with Carrot, Landscape with One Tree and Three Clouds,* and *Still Life with Eight Bottles,* strongly carry his message about the amount of plastic consumed in contemporary life and about the import of the environment. Minimal details of imagery and his use of vacuum-formed plastics, some with acrylic paint and others with rigid Styrofoam, together with his *Bagged Series,* underlined the precipice he felt society was on with regard to the sustainability of the environment.

FIGURE 2.34. **Winston Leathers**, *#17 Cosmic Order/in a line plane,* from the series *Cosmic Variations,* 1972.

BAXTER& also explored the possibilities of new technologies, especially Telex and photocopiers. Joan Lowndes noted: "So we have Iain Baxter working not at an easel in a studio but sitting in front of his Telex in an incredibly cluttered little room that is the head office of the N.E. Thing Co. And he is using this machine as a whole new art form, as intellectual play and potential for group play, not to place orders or transact business but for Trans–S.I., Transmitted Sensitivity Information."[95] His goal was to present the connections between nature and how we look at it and consume it, the tourist implications, and, as early as the 1960s and 1970s, the concern for its protection.

There is no question that the 1969 exhibition of the N.E. Thing Co. at the National Gallery of Canada was a seminal time for Canadian art, with the opening of its doors to the conceptual and pop consumerism of the era. The Honourable Ron Basford, federal Minister of Consumer and Corporate Affairs, opened the exhibition, and he drew new public liaisons between the art world and the rest of the world: "Many of my responsibilities involve the relationship between the corporation and the consumer, and it seems to me that Mr. Baxter and the N.E. Thing Co. are exploring this relationship with humour and imagination. The fact that he has incorporated himself to do this simply underlines the fact that Iain Baxter is determined to take the artist out of isolation and put him right in the thick of our present everyday environment."[96]

The connection between artist and consumer was also evident in many of Don Proch's works, particularly his 1972 exhibition *The Legend of Asessippi* at the Winnipeg Art Gallery. To achieve the complexity of that installation, he, too, formed a company, the Opthamalia Company, which included people with the technical and mechanical skills necessary for the presentation of his vision. As he said: "It was rugged and stark and it wasn't the kind of imagery that art critics or people at the Art Gallery were used to. I really didn't care. That's the way the work came out. The concepts came from a rural, environmental situation that most people in Winnipeg weren't familiar with. . . . The camaraderie [of the Ophthalmia Company] made it a support group . . . the entire company worked with a remarkable kind of intensity."[97]

Large, complicated, farm-related, and multi-layered, the exhibition was groundbreaking, challenging the usual notions about the making of art, the definition of what an exhibition was, and how audiences interacted with art. As there had never been a show like it at the Winnipeg Art Gallery before, critics could not write as they had about earlier exhibitions. Proch had catapulted the art world into new arenas. Reviewer John Graham wrote:

> it is an investigation into the nature of an environment and the interaction of
> the agencies which operate within it . . . they have attempted, by translation into
> expressive images in new contexts, to give more universality of meaning to what they
> have recorded. . . . Much of the inner meaning of the work depends for its clarity

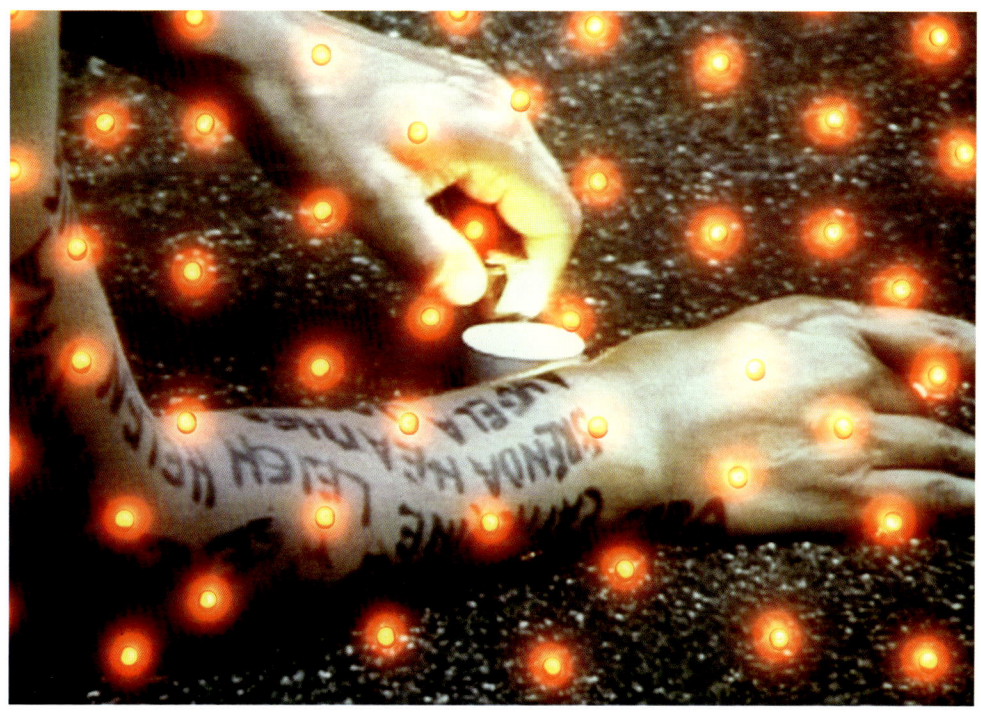

upon the ability of the observer to identify with the rural scene in the prairie context, with its ambiguous confrontation of earth and sky, and the elemental struggle to wrest a living against the will or spirit of the land. For the true urbanite, this may be a difficult experience to appreciate, just as it must also be for the conventional gallery goer who expects to see "fine art."[98]

Proch's use of materials and farm equipment in this work elicited great interest, as it related not only to the cycle of growth but also to the changing ways of how human beings have used and impacted that cycle. The *Winnipeg Free Press* review of his 1975 exhibition *Asessippi Clouds* at the Winnipeg Art Gallery noted:

In his sculpture, he takes recognizable objects and modifies and transforms them into new configurations . . . the motorcycle crowd and the farmer—and represents

FIGURE 2.36. **Rebecca Belmore**, *The Named and the Unnamed* (still), 2002.

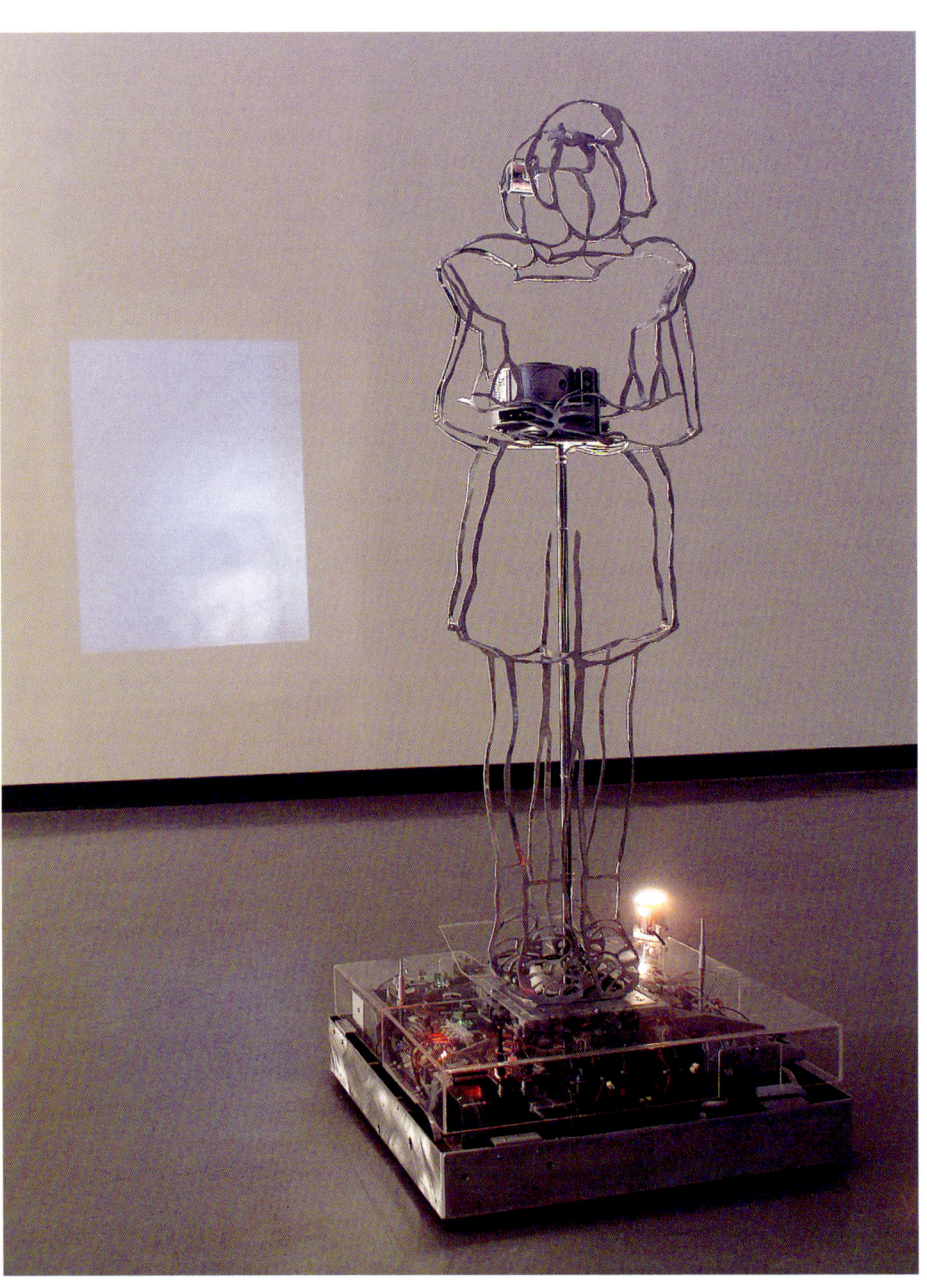

the difficulty of those living an essentially closed way of life in adapting to the complexities of rural life . . . first colour since 1967 . . . adds yet another dimension to this latest series. . . . Opthamalia Company "dedicated to the expression of the prairie farmer's experience of the land." The Company had adopted an essentially collective and social view where its creations are the result of the collaboration of all its members.

Rather than trying to represent the prairies, the works in the exhibition present basic prairie values—what it is like to live on the prairies—and explore themes based on the reciprocal opposition of man and the land.[99]

Exploring the interconnections between art and social discourse, artists who use video, performance art, and outdoor and non-gallery settings as well as public and private spaces for their work encourage ideas to converge. Artists continue to bring social dialogue into new settings, as KC Adams did with her *Perception Series,* and Rebecca Belmore did with *The Named and the Unnamed.* These are two of many initiatives across Western Canada that made a substantial mark in the development of art and artists' roles across the country. The search for new ways of engaging the public with and through new technologies is ongoing. Reva Stone's pursuit, for instance, of artificial intelligence leads to her conceiving new works that will explore how and why we use artificial intelligence and its inherent dangers. Both in and out of galleries and museums, artists effectively have taken their art onto bus shelters, billboards, and banners; into the street and other public spaces; and into our virtual world.

FIGURE 2.37. **Reva Stone**, *Carnevale 3.0*, 2000–2002 (detail).

PART TWO

Prevailing Themes in Western Canadian Art

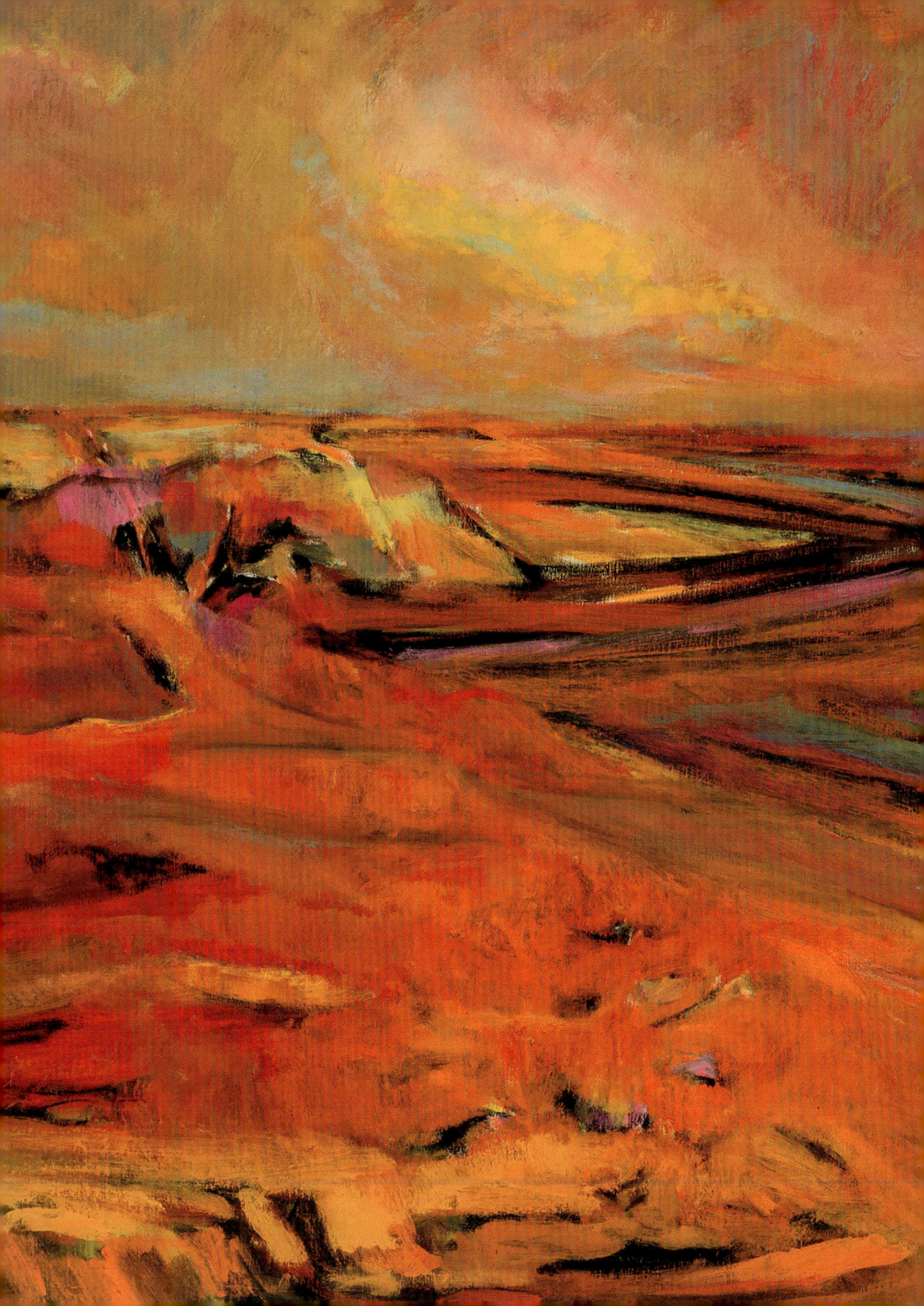

III Landscape as Culture

"Art is not the most important undertaking in my life. That priority
goes to the maintaining of my relationship with the natural world."[1]

Landscape, a major theme for many Western Canadian artists, itinerant, resident, historical, and contemporary, has been treated in myriad ways, from multiple perspectives, and in various media over several centuries. Art depicting the Western Canadian landscape documents place, captures the particular, explores the ephemeral, and defines human relationships with the land. Artists have embodied both its micro and macro aspects. Some have been daunted by its magnitude; others, challenged by its magnificence.

The word "landscape," Middle Dutch in origin, dates from about 1600, and means "region," from "land," and principally refers to paintings representing natural scenery. Landscape became an acceptable subject in itself in most of continental Europe only in the late 1840s, prior to then being primarily a backdrop for portraits, history, and religious paintings. In Canada, the story is different. Landscape was a primary subject for artists from the earliest explorations in the eighteenth century. Artists' journals and letters contain visual and verbal descriptions of this new land. By the late eighteenth and early nineteenth centuries, trained and untrained artists were hired specifically to render the landscape both for charting the terrain and to augment the verbal descriptions of the places. Later, during the construction of the Canadian railway, artists were hired to paint the land for the marketing campaigns aimed to entice people from Britain and Europe to settle the West.

George H. Swinton, *Birth of a Prairie River*, 1959–1960 (detail).

119

"Landscape" evokes the picturesque, diverse natural environments of Canada's expanses, dramatic mountains, coastlines, skies, rivers, and national parks. Iconic natural wonders of Western Canada feature in many canvases, sketchbooks, and prints. However, landscape is much more than the depiction of the picturesque. Embodying culture, landscape defines who and where we are, our communities, regional characters, and local histories. Depicting the spirit and life of Canada as a whole, landscape encompasses our essence, past and present; rural, urban, and uninhabited places; and our dreams, realities, needs, and peoples.

Portrayals of the land as culture and as the basket of civilizations are multidimensional and at times filled with dichotomies. "Culture" suggests growth and diversity. Its Latin root *cultivare*, "to cultivate," relates to agriculture and the psychological and intellectual growing of individuals, organizations, and groups of people. The provider of shelter and food, the land also proffers difficulties and often insurmountable challenges. Both these sensibilities, provider and challenger, are embodied in artists' renderings of the land.

The art of Western Canada demonstrates deep respect for the prairies, mountains, and coast. The landscape that confronted early immigrant artists was unlike any they had seen before in Europe or the United Kingdom. The light, land formations, climates, and peoples were new to them, and challenging to depict. Some early immigrant artists had attended art school or received limited training prior to reaching the "new land," but most had had no art training at all. Little, if any, curriculum in British art schools in the late nineteenth and early twentieth centuries included landscape as a subject, which is not surprising, given the relatively low ranking of landscape in the subject hierarchy prior to the mid-1800s.[2] Early Canadian painting, dependent at first on European traditions, burgeoned in response to what the artists saw. Over the decades, artists brought many "new departures" to their subjects, including the use of new materials and techniques, innovative approaches to composition and imagery, and changing understandings of the spiritual in relation to the land.

In the 1840s Paul Kane captured the places and people in his watercolours as he crossed the West. His writings and his sketches skilfully illuminate the prairies, the mountains, and the coast with freshness. Once he was back in his Toronto studio, a number of the works from his travels became the basis for his celebrated canvases. In my view, these lack the directness and sensitivity of his works on paper, as they are heavier and darker in feel and tone.

The light, atmosphere, spaces, and geology of the West continue to inspire artists. One hundred and fifty years after Kane explored the region, Don Reichert was inspired by the geology around his studio at Bissett, Manitoba, as evident in *Folds,* 1979. Reichert placed the unstretched canvas directly on the rocks so it assumed the natural indentations of the striations and crevasses. He poured wet paint on the surface, and then folded and crushed the whole canvas into a ball while still wet. Lichens, leaves, and sticks stuck to the wet paint, creating a natural collage. The result was a truly visually active pattern. For some works he experimented by soaking heavy paper until it was wet and, wanting it to take an impression, placed it on the

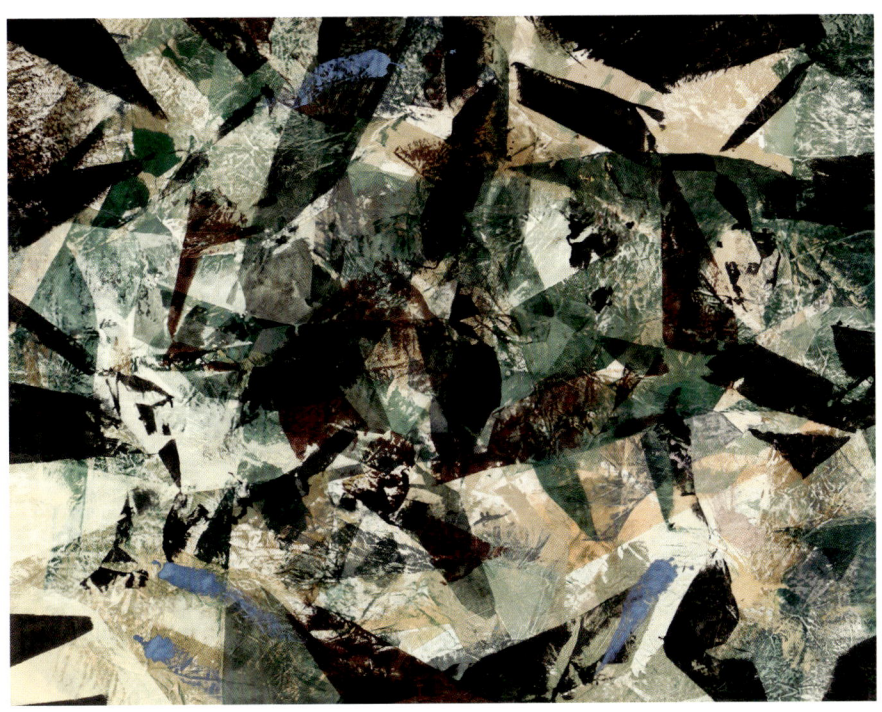

rocks and walked on it with bare feet. When it was dry he painted on it with acrylic washes. Another artist inspired by geology, Alberta ceramic artist Les Manning, taken with the Rocky Mountains, created his striated, geological-coloured clay sculptures and pots.

Though Western Canadian artists have delineated the beauty and magnitude of the land over many decades, they have increasingly exposed environmental dangers and devastation from clear-cuts, oil extraction, forces of nature, or contemporary lifestyles. Emily Carr was perhaps one of the first artists to be visually vocal against clear-cut logging, evident in *Odds and Ends,* 1939, and other paintings from the early 1940s. Carr's abhorrence to clear-cuts was also apparent in her journal, *Hundreds and Thousands.* Her concern for clear-cutting continued in the work of other artists through the twentieth century. Doug Morton, Don Harvey, Toni Onley, and Jim Willer, for instance, were all actively involved in the 1980s protests against the clear-cutting in British Columbia's Carmanah Valley old-growth forest.

The importance of landscape art cannot be underestimated, in both its gentle and strident forms. As the landscape has inspired artists, how do their depictions of the land inspire audiences?

FIGURE 3.1. **Don Reichert**, *Folds*, 1979.

Landscape as History

> "Western history and western landscape are bound inexplicably. The land is part and parcel of our history and our history has to do absolutely with the land. For me the land is our basic metaphor."[3]

The earliest depictions of Western Canada are important visual historical documents. Executed with varying degrees of skill, many of the earliest renditions were actually done to fill long hours, and making art was rarely a primary responsibility. Works were done in watercolour and pencil and some later became engravings for publication. On returning home some artists redid their watercolours and drawings in oil in their studios. Historian R. Douglas Francis noted the importance of these endeavours:

> Throughout its history, the Canadian West has evoked strong images in the minds of those who visited, settled in, or sometimes simply wrote about the region. These people saw in the West what they wanted, or were conditioned by their cultural milieu, to see. At different times, they perceived a West that was a wasteland, a pristine wilderness, a source of national greatness and imperial grandeur, a utopia, a harsh and cruel land, or a mythical region shaped by the attitudes and beliefs of its people. Each of these images held sway for a period of time and then gave way to new images, resulting in changing images of the Canadian West.[4]

Considerable evidence of work done forty years or more before artists were resident in the West is extant. One is an engraving circa 1769 after a sketch by explorer Samuel Hearne, who had left Churchill 6 March 1769 to go to Fort Prince of Wales, in what is now northern Manitoba. Surviving drawings also include one done off Haida Gwaii by George Dixon in 1785; Reverend H.J. Robertson's watercolour sketch of Fort Gibraltar, 1804; and an engraving after an 1817 sketch by Lord Selkirk of Fort Douglas.

Both professional and amateur artists accompanied explorations to Red River, to the north and west, and as part of the Pacific coastal voyages. James Cook, for instance, had skilled professional artists as part of his crews in the 1770s. Though Captain George Vancouver had no one with official responsibility for artistic documentation, he was certainly aware of the importance of visual recording, noting that he fortunately "was able to persuade the Admiralty to include a supply of drawing materials."[5] As Vancouver wrote, "It was with infinite satisfaction that I saw, amongst the officers and young gentlemen of the quarterdeck, some who, with little instruction, would soon be enabled to … draw landscapes, make faithful portraits of the several headlands, coasts, and countries which we might discover [sic] . . . without the assistance of professional persons."[6]

Spanish, French, Russian, and American vessels collectively made at least 200 voyages to northwest North America between 1785 and 1805. Art made on these trips is found in both published and unpublished journals.

The more expertly drawn works were most often done by those who had had art training with the British Navy. A drawing school, established in 1693 at the sixteenth-century Christ's Hospital in Sussex, England, as part of the Royal Mathematical School, was meant to augment the program founded twenty years earlier. It trained students to sketch sea views and coastal profiles, which did raise the standard of artistic renderings of their travels. Other countries, too, provided art training to mariners. In 1785, for instance, the French explorer La Pérouse was instructed to have his draughtsmen sketch "all the views of the land, and the remarkable situations, portraits of the natives of the different countries, their manner of dress, their ceremonies, their pastimes, their edifices, their vessels, and all the production of the earth and of the sea."[7] First-hand observation was key, and the standard instructions given to all the artists on expeditions to the New World were to ensure accuracy, with no embellishments. Works were not to be done from memory.

John Webber (1751–1793), a highly regarded artist in his era, had been encouraged to submit three works to the 1775 Royal Academy's annual exhibition. These were noticed by Captain Cook's former crew member Daniel Carl Solander, and led to Webber's appointment as draughtsman on Cook's third voyage. His charge read:

Whereas we have engaged Mr John Webber Draughtsman and Landskip Painter . . . in order to make Drawings and Paintings of such places in the Countries you touch at in the course of the said Voyage as may be proper to give a more perfect Idea thereof than can be formed by written descriptions only . . . taking care that he does diligently employ himself in making Drawings or Paintings of such places . . . as may be worthy of notice . . . also of such other objects and things as may fall within the compass of His abilities.[8]

Webber's results were well received. Writer John Frazier Henry said that "no voyage undertaken in the days before photography ever returned so well documented with pictorial illustrations, or had so great an area of the earth's surface come under one artist's observation."[9] Webber was granted permission to use 200 of his drawings personally, and he made and sold copies of them, garnering ongoing income. He was elected to the Royal Academy as associate member in 1785 and full member in 1791. Historian Douglas Cole commented that Webber was "an excellent landscapist . . . his draughtsmanship is good, he possessed a fine sense of composition and his choice of subjects was interesting and appropriate . . . although he gives a characteristic but inappropriate elongation to all his figures."[10]

Other well-known artists also made important works. George Back created significant works of Sir John Franklin's trips, and his watercolour and ink drawings are filled with detail and precision. Zachary Mudge (1770–1852), after whom British Columbia's Cape Mudge on Quadra Island was named, served in senior roles on a number of voyages, including Captain Vancouver's to Puget Sound. The description of that voyage is vivid: as quoted by John Frazier Henry, Vancouver said, "The fog had no sooner dispersed, than we found ourselves in the channel for which I had intended to steer, interspersed with numerous rocky islets and rocks, extending above [a] clutter of islands towards the shore of the continent. . . . it would engage our utmost attention, even in fair weather, to preserve us from latent dangers."[11] The ship became grounded and Vancouver commented that their escape was "a very providential circumstance"; the ocean was calm, the tide high, all preventing "immediate and inevitable destruction."[12] The engraving from Mudge's 1792 drawing depicts that calm, the sky, Haida Gwaii, Vancouver's ships, and the Indigenous people's canoes.

Several years earlier, George Dixon had executed a particularly detailed work, showing with precision the vegetation, scale of the site, and the English and Indigenous peoples. Dixon's accounts, complete with his drawings and maps, were published in his volume, *A Voyage Round the World: But More Particularly To The North-West Coast of America*. Of the event shown in his drawing, he recorded the following in his journal:

> About two o'clock in the afternoon, being close in shore, we saw several canoes putting off, on which we shortened sail, and lay to for them, as the wind blew pretty fresh. The place these people came from had a very singular appearance, and on examining it narrowly, we plainly perceived that they lived in a very large hut, built on a small island, and well fortified after the manner of a hippah, on which account we distinguished this place by the name of *Hippah Island*.
>
> The tribe who inhabit this hippah, seem well defended by nature from any sudden assault of their enemies; for the ascent to it from the beach is steep, and difficult of access; and the other sides are well barricadoed with pines and brush-wood; notwithstanding which, they have been at infinite pains in raising additional fences of rails and boards; so that I should think they cannot fail to repel any tribe that should dare to attack their fortification.[13]

John Bartlett's 1791 *Haida Totem Pole* is another particularly interesting drawing. Wilson Duff, scholar and archaeologist, wrote that this is the earliest known drawing of a Haida Pole. It was a frontal pole about forty feet high, located in the village of Dadens on Langara Island in the Queen Charlotte Islands.[14] In his journal, *Remarks on Board the Ship, Massachusetts,* the artist had commented: "The Dore of it is made like a man[s] head the Passage in to the House is in Betwen his teath and Boult be fore they nkowd the youse of Iron [sic]."[15]

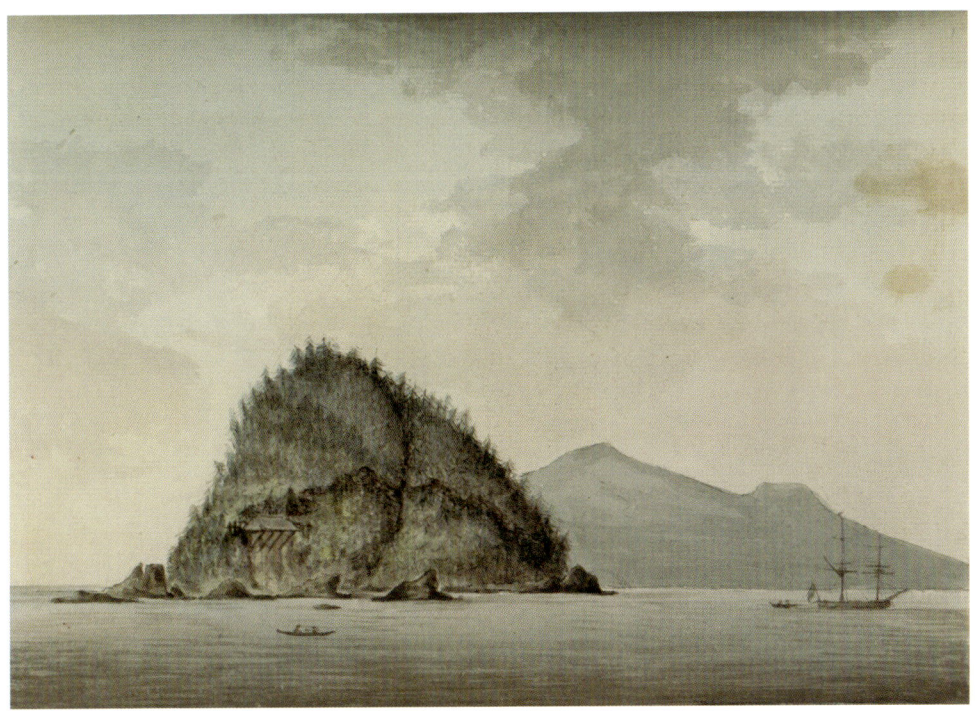

Peter Rindisbacher's arrival in Red River in 1821, where he stayed until 1826, marked the next stage in Western Canadian painting, that of professionally trained resident artists. As we have seen, in 1818 Rindisbacher received training in Switzerland from Jakob Samuel Weibel. It is clear from the scope of his subject matter and the stature he gives his subjects that he was trusted by both settlers and Indigenous leaders. According to the *Winnipeg Free Press*, "Rindisbacher saw and knew Indians well. His style depicts nobility and mobility. It is well suited to the scenes of ceremony, action and violence which he witnessed and recreated."[16]

An early professionally trained resident artist in British Columbia was Grafton Tyler Brown (1841–1918), an African American artist who lived on Vancouver Island from 1882 to 1884, sixty years after Rindisbacher had settled in Red River, and only a few years after William Hind had settled in British Columbia. Brown moved north from Sacramento, where he had worked in a hotel for several years. His paintings in California drew local acclaim early, in a November 1859 local paper: "We noticed last evening some very excellent painting done by Grafton

FIGURE 3.2. **George Dixon**, *A View of Hippa Island, Queen Charlotte's Isles*, c. 1788.

T. Brown, a servant boy in the St George Hotel. . . . The lad has never taken lessons but his execution will compare favourably with that of acknowledged artists."[17]

The newspaper report continues, noting that in British Columbia

Brown accompanied [Amos Bowman] on the [Canadian Geological] survey as a draughtsman, giving himself the opportunity to travel and sketch the scenic grandeur of this "almost unknown territory" . . . by September 1882 as they travelled from Kamloops, south through the Okanagan Valley, west up the Similkameen River, and back to the Fraser River at Hope by late October. By November Brown had established himself in a studio in the Occidental Hotel at the corner of Store and Johnson Streets in Victoria. The British Colonist newspaper directed clients to him, describing him as "an artist of more than local celebrity in California and elsewhere."[18]

Brown's works of the area are painted with a high level of competence in his handling of paint and composition. His 1883 painting *Esquimalt Harbour* shows in detail the activity of the harbour with the mountains in the distance. Art historian Mary Jo Hughes noted that Victoria had "few professional artists at the time."[19]

Brown held an exhibition in June 1883 of the paintings he made from his sketches of the survey, and added those of Victoria scenes. The exhibition drew the following comments from the *British Colonist*: "Yesterday was the opening day of the exhibition at The Colonist's new building of oil paintings from the brush of our local artist, Mr. G.T. Brown. Viewed in the light of artistic productions they were excellent, but when inspected by those with whom the scenes represented were familiar, their fidelity elicited an extra meed of praise."[20]

Depictions of the North and of what was to become Saskatchewan and Alberta are also extant from the nineteenth century. William Armstrong was prolific and, working as both engineer and artist, he travelled across the West with the Grand Trunk Railway. A drawing master, he sketched and painted in watercolour wherever he went. In Red River, circa 1870, as chief engineer to Colonel Garnet Wolseley's expedition, he travelled the Dawson Road, with its particularly difficult terrain and which seemingly was more a water than land route. His interpretations are sympathetic and skillful. His use of colour, his strong compositions, and his scrupulous attention to detail render them significant historical records.

Paul Kane's sensibilities of place, light, and natural details, and his feeling of landscape as history, continued into the twentieth century. One hundred and thirty years later, in the 1970s, Norman Yates also saw that, "Western history and western landscape are bound inextricably. The land is part and parcel of our history and our history has to do absolutely with the land. For me the land is our basic metaphor."[21] It is in that sense that the land becomes culture. Historian R. Douglas Francis wrote that Kane's images of the West "have been more than passing

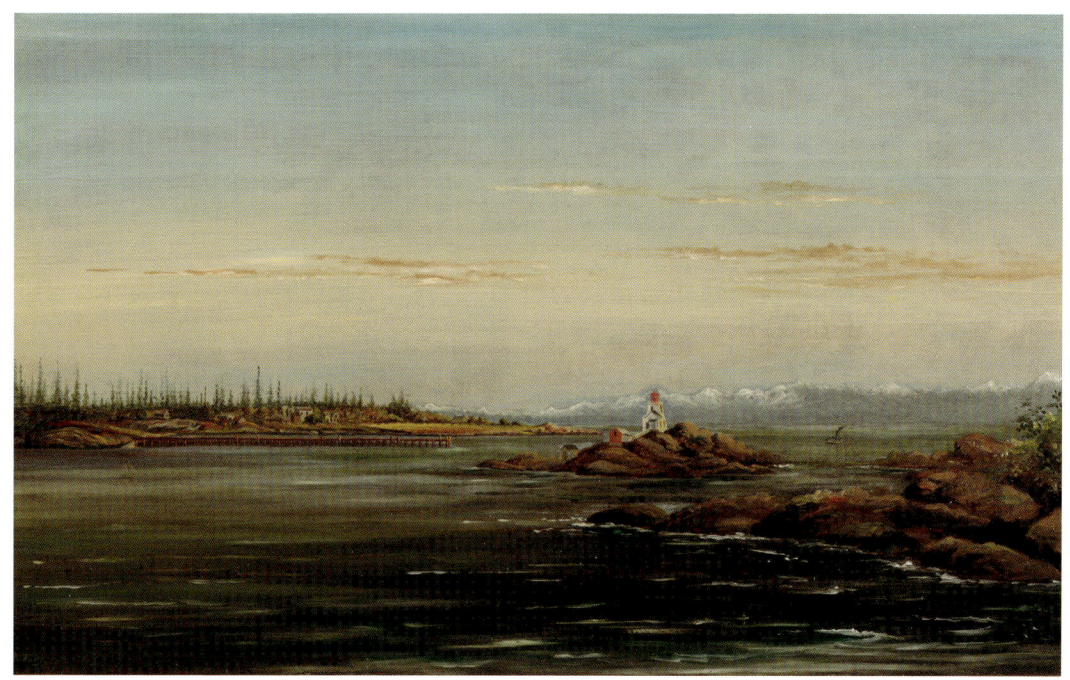

commentaries on the region; they have greatly influenced—and sometimes dictated—policies toward the area, and thus profoundly affected the historical evolution of the west."[22]

Jeanette Johns, early in her career at the outset of the 2000s, explored the threads of history in her series *Retreating Agassiz,* printed on cartographical paper. The series, drawing from history, maps the geological receding of Manitoba's Lake Agassiz. She documented its diminishing size over time by superimposing gold leaf on her silkscreen and etched prints, marking the scale of the lake at specific moments. Her interest in mapping from history is also seen clearly in her 2009 *Steady Drift Series*, in which she explored her long fascination with old maps and documents, and developed her sense of geographical place and her interest in biography. She commented:

> Printmaking, for me, is repetition and layering. In looking at an old map of the Arctic I noticed these two little islands named Jeanette and Henrietta, which are the names of my two grandmothers. The ship Jeanette had been destined for the North Pole in the late 1800s, but they [the explorers] got themselves wedged in the ice floes just

FIGURE 3.3. **Grafton Tyler Brown**, *Entrance to the Harbor*, 1883.

north of Siberia. . . . They finally floated past these two tiny islands—really, just two piles of rock. . . . The Captain had kept a journal . . . and all [my] titles are quotes from his journals. It's a parallel of my personal journey, and a collective "trying to understand" what goes on in the world and trying to observe and discover, and take in information.[23]

Landscape as Place

"To me the landscape is something living. A landscape has personality, is capable of community, is capable of letting me share in her experiences and in turn shares mine. What I am trying to paint is this relationship. My landscapes are not naturalistic, nor what I generally called distorted. They are changed into form and colour in order to tell what the landscape told me, made me feel—not what I saw at any particular moment."[24]

These words are those of George Swinton, whose landscapes are about both place and the spiritual. In October 1960 he said: "I have found my roots in the Prairies and in the North. . . . And I declare my sensuous, spiritual love for the Prairies and the North as well as for the human figure in repose and for the Passion of Christ. They are not merely subject matter for me, they are my life."[25] Distances, skies, horizon lines, trees, and geology have been compelling subjects for artists from the earliest forays into the West—whether on the prairies, in the mountains, or looking over the Pacific coastlines. For some, upon their arrival in the West, these spaces and majestic places have been all but overwhelming. By the early twentieth century, landscape was increasingly being painted primarily for its own sense and less for the recording aspect of documentary evidence. Most twentieth-century artists who immigrated had had art training, and a generation of artists had been born and trained in Canada.

In discussions of landscape as place, Humphrey Hime (1833–1903) is unique. An early photographer, he captured the power and evocative nature of the horizon line across the infinite prairie spaces with particular poignancy. The simplicity of his abstracted horizon line in his 1858 sepia photograph, *The Prairie on the Banks of the Red River Looking South,* is strong, definite, and uninterrupted. The sky is empty and his perception of the never-ending space was keen. Approximately 110 years later, Ken Lochhead's *August Path,* 1964, similarly evokes the stretching horizon. A narrow long work, only 22.9 by 363 centimetres, its shape emphasizes the reality of the horizon. The background yellow is reminiscent of the golden wheat fields

FIGURE 3.4. **Jeanette Johns**, *11,500 BP, 11,100 BP, 9,900 BP,* and *9,400 BP,* from the series *Retreating Agassiz,* 2009.

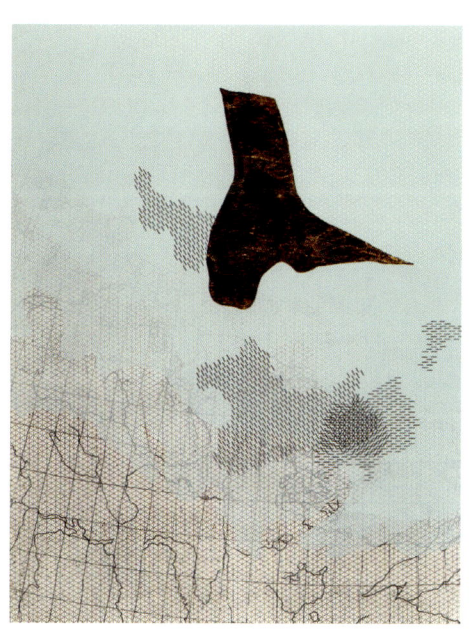
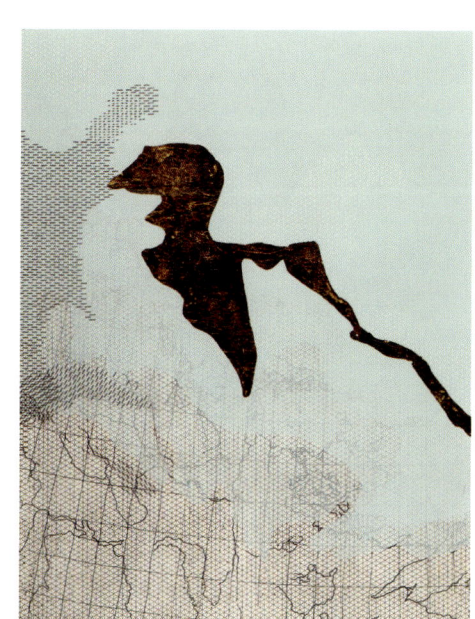
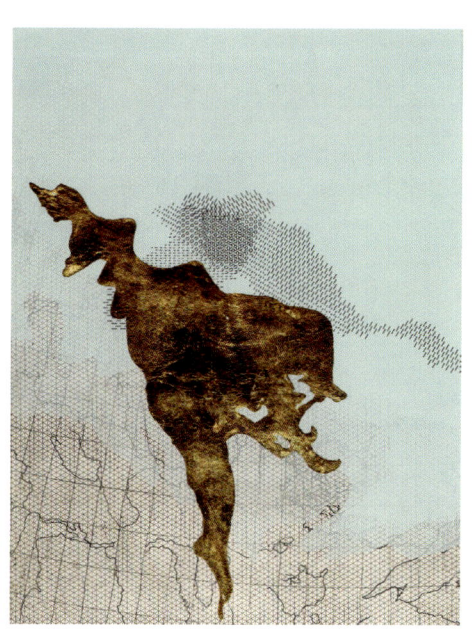
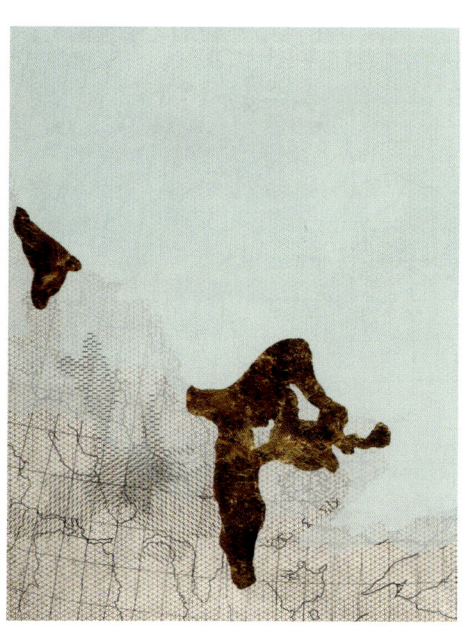

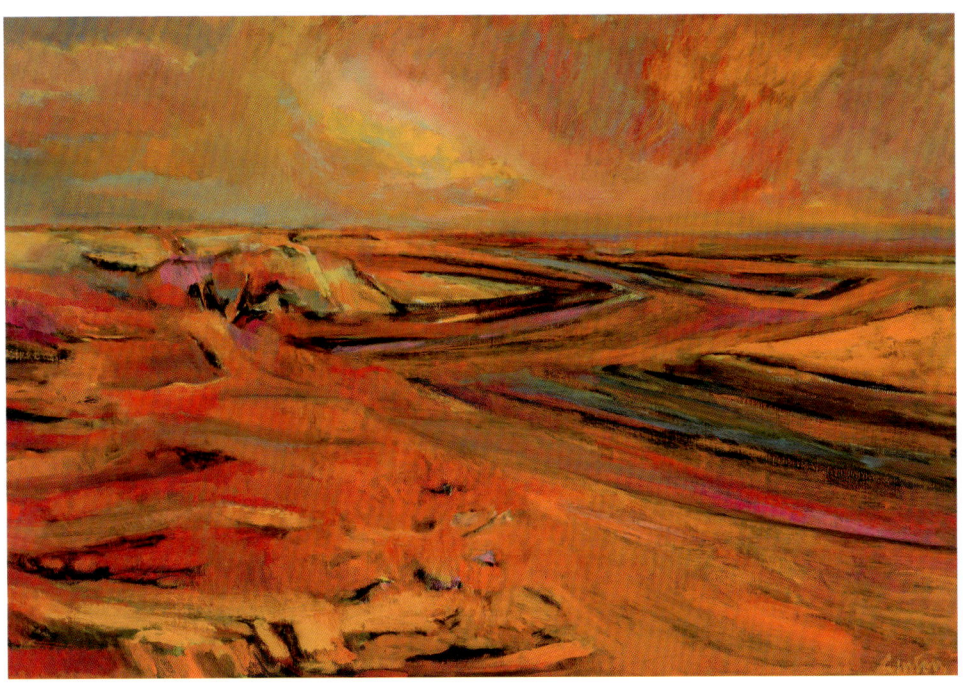

of the prairie. A pale blue line, one of the work's four stripes that goes across almost the entire work, is suggestive of the sky. The other three colours, the green, red, and pink horizontal lines, relate to the seasons and the richness of the prairie fields in spring, summer, and fall. The parallel overlapping placements of these thin lines give the work its continuum, movement, and energy. Lochhead's seemingly simple composition and colour use underline his sensitivity and understanding of the part of the country where he spent so many years, first teaching in Regina and then in Winnipeg. The connections between these two abstracted works, Lochhead's and Hime's, separated by a century, exemplify the ongoing preoccupation with the limitless sense of space.

With the dawn of the twentieth century, the purpose of art had shifted in the West. No longer primarily for documentary or marketing purposes, art became a mode of expression for the personal interests and views of individual artists. It became more subjective in its creation and public engagement. Manitoba-born Lionel LeMoine FitzGerald's early major impressionistic painting *Summer East Kildonan,* 1921, for instance, shows his interest in light,

FIGURE 3.5. **George H. Swinton**, *Birth of a Prairie River,* 1959–1960.

space, and the ephemeral character of the clouds and skies, an interest that carried throughout his entire career. A prime example of FitzGerald's use of impressionistic techniques, it nevertheless exudes a sense of solidity, as do his other impressionistic landscapes. While his application of colour consists of impressionistic dabs of bright hues, he mixed them on his palette, not relying on the viewer's eye to do the mixing. Perceiving that the shadow of an object is contained in the object's complementary colour, he used colour in rendering his shadows, especially the blue from the sky reflected in the snow. Robert Ayre, an art critic and a contemporary of FitzGerald's, noted that the artist adapted the "dab" technique as it was "quick and easy" and because it suited his subject matter.[26] In all his work FitzGerald balanced technique and subject.

Several years later, in the *Potato Patch, Snowflake,* 1925, FitzGerald shifted his technique and built his subject in a manner that shows his interest in Paul Cézanne's artistic philosophies emphasizing the cylinder, cone, and sphere. He consistently built his compositions with considered colour and deliberate brushwork, making form of equal importance to light. Ayre recorded the importance of form and volume for FitzGerald in 1925: "Now he searched for volume, he began to focus his attention more intensively on nature to feel it from within rather than be cheated by haphazard appearances."[27] FitzGerald, a serious and deliberate gallery-goer whenever he had the opportunity, wrote of his 1930 visit to New York's Metropolitan Museum, underlining his interest in Cézanne:

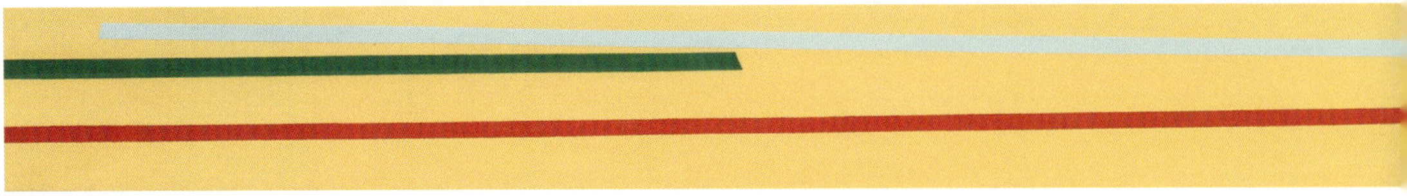

Off to the Metropolitan . . . to the Cezannes particularly, five in all. . . . All the
landscapes contain many things that are most useful thoughts. Always the edges of
the canvas is [*sic*] treated in a most careful manner, never any paint overdone but
enough variety to keep the eye within. . . . The outstanding quality in all these big
things which is being more and more impressed on me, is the terrific sense of unity,
everything being thought of to keep the eye within the picture and still it remains
a thing of apparent ease. And always a sense of reality no matter how abstract the
thing may be.[28]

That feeling of unity was evident in the *Potato Patch, Snowflake*. Childhood summers at his
grandparents' farm in Snowflake, Manitoba, gave him a profound understanding and respect
for the vastness and subtleties of the prairiescape, and he returned frequently in adulthood.
Potato Patch, Snowflake, with its rhythmic flow of colours and shapes, conveys that deep feeling
for the land. The high horizon line, punctuated by the building and tree, coupled with the
gently rolling clouds suggests the expanse of the prairie sky. The meticulous brushwork is the
"trademark" of his mature style. An indirect influence on this work was that of French painter
Jean-François Millet, whose subjects and approaches resonated with FitzGerald. Like Millet's
painting *The Angelus,* FitzGerald showed the figure's full height, creating a monumentality
extending through three-quarters of the height of the canvas. By repeating the colours of
the fields in the figure itself, and using a rough technique throughout, he successfully fuses
the farmer with the land. The impact of the figure is also heightened by the strong emphasis
FitzGerald gives the hands. The roughness of the fields is intentionally enhanced by the bits of
raw canvas showing through the paint.

Manitoba places, urban and rural, fill FitzGerald's art, earning him the label of the "Artist of
the Prairie" and the reputation as a trailblazer. His sense of space and the rhythms of Manitoba's
fields and skies in his drawings, watercolours, and oils, as manifested in *Manitoba Landscape*, 1941,
and *Doc Snider's House* and *Abstract in Green and Gold* is unparalleled.

In a CBC broadcast in 1954, FitzGerald reflected on the horizon of the prairie:

FIGURE 3.7. **Kenneth Campbell Lochhead**, *August Path*, 1964.

Recently I had to go to Regina and went by train, during the day, so I could look at the country again for a longer period than is possible on a short motor trip. The day was especially lovely, with a fine sky and plenty of lights and shadows to break up the visible expanse of land seen through the car windows. I was more than ever impressed with the wide variations in the contours from the flatness outside Winnipeg to the gradually increasing roll of the ground as we went westward. A marked blue in the distance gave the feeling of low lying hills and, sometimes, close up a higher mound, topped with trees, broke the long line of the horizon in a most pleasant way. Even where the flatness dominated and the horizon seemed one long straight line, bluffs of poplar, farm buildings and the wide variety in the fields from the light of the stubble to the dark of the freshly ploughed land, relieved the possible monotony and kept the interest.[29]

On British Columbia's west coast, Emily Carr also painted skies in the 1930s, and the sea featured in many of her works. Her art met the goal she expressed in her journal, *Hundreds and Thousands: The Journals of Emily Carr* on 19 March 1931: "I want to paint some skies so that they look roomy and moving and mysterious and to make them overhang the earth, to have a different quality in their distant horizon and their overhanging nearness."[30]

While Indigenous art had abounded in the West long before contact, it was around 1905 when Saskatchewan and Alberta joined Confederation that immigrant artists from Europe brought their classical training and assumed professional careers in the visual arts, many as teachers. Increasingly, however, artists were also hired as graphic designers and commercial artists. Landscape painters Augustus Kenderdine, Inglis Sheldon-Williams (1870–1940), Illingworth Kerr (1905–1989), James Henderson (1871–1951), and Viennese-born Ernest Lindner (1897–1988) all made significant impacts in Saskatchewan as teachers and painters. Their influences are obvious in the work of several subsequent generations.

Primitive folk artist Jan Wyers (1888–1973), working in Windhorst, east of Regina, depicted the narrative of his community. In the 1930s Saskatchewan's Ernest Lindner and Stanley Brunst (1894–1962) worked in realistic yet abstracted formats. Art critic and writer Terrence Heath says Brunst employed "a flat, vaguely cubist manner, with a strong decorative sense and an awareness of the total canvas area."[31] Saskatchewan's art scene developed quickly,

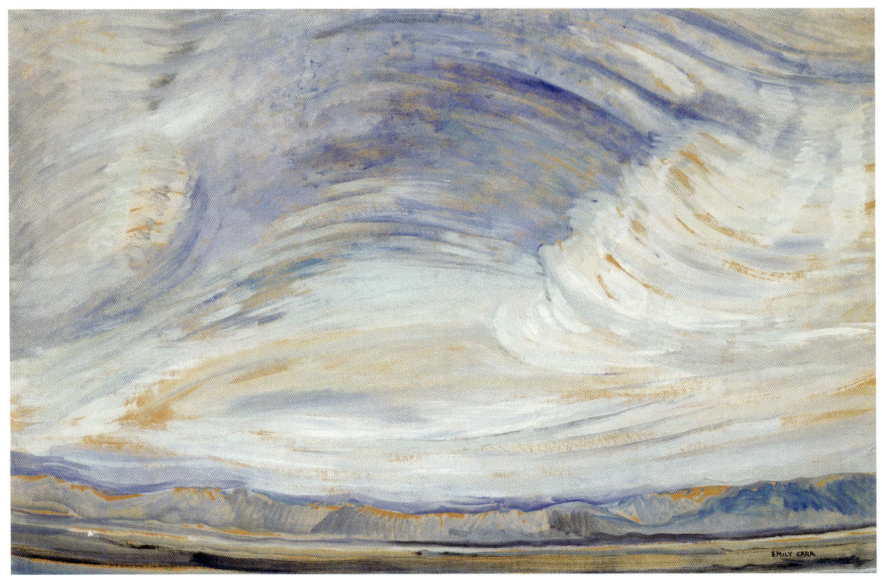

in part due to two major benefactors who enabled its quick flourishing by facilitating the construction of new, purpose-designed gallery buildings for their ongoing work. Norman MacKenzie, a lawyer and art collector in Regina, spearheaded the building of Regina's Norman MacKenzie Art Gallery in 1953, and Fred Mendel, with his largesse and personal art collection, built Saskatoon's Mendel Art Gallery in 1964.

Ernest Lindner's role as artist and arts leader was of prime importance for Saskatchewan and Canada. He preferred interior landscape subjects and enclosed scenes of forest growth and underbrush, and worked in subdued colours. Lindner arrived in Saskatchewan in 1926 and worked on a farm to escape his overly religious upbringing and overbearing father. His biographer, Terrence Heath, observed that "even at 85, Ernie is aware of the sense of confinement he experienced as a child and has tried all his life to shake off. Incidents from childhood became for him symbols of his need to escape restraints."[32] Heath comments further:

> Ernie has always been a person of enthusiasm and life on the prairies became a
> marvellous adventure which he never tired of describing to family and friends in
> Austria. He wrote of the complete democracy, unspoiled nature and unlimited
> opportunities of the country. . . . Even living and working on the unspoiled prairie,
> however, was not totally satisfying and Ernie at one point fantasized a more complete

FIGURE 3.8. **Emily Carr**, *Overhead*, 1935–1936.

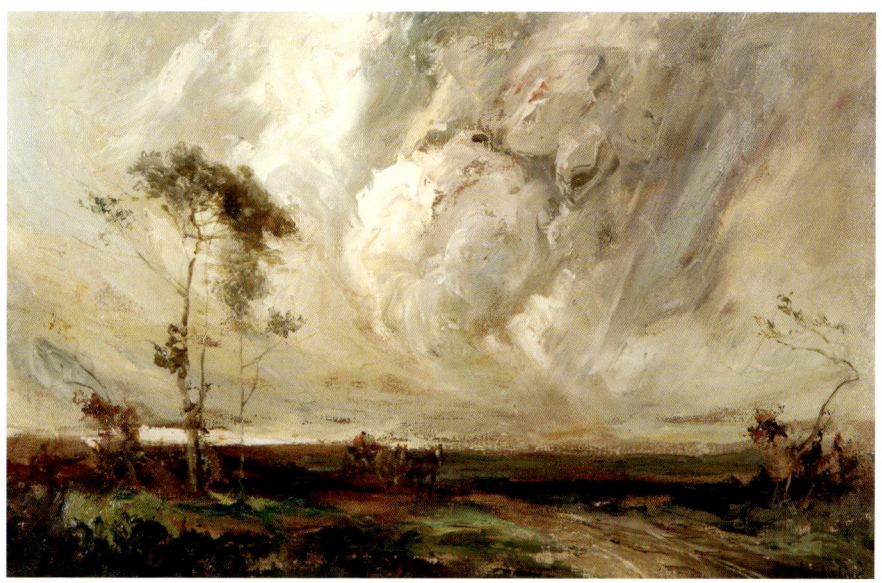

union with nature. . . . Right from the time of his arrival in Canada, Ernie found that his drawing and painting was a way of bridging the gap he felt between himself and the people he met.[33]

Lindner studied art at the University of Saskatoon with Gus Kenderdine, whom he first met in 1927, and who, on seeing his student's technical facility, suggested he take art classes. Heath concluded: "What he had learned came from library books and his infrequent contact with a few artists, such as Kenderdine, Lismer and Illingworth Kerr. When Lismer visited his studio in 1932, Ernie told him of his ambitions to go to art school and make art his lifetime work. Lismer told him he didn't need to go to school, he had the skills, all he had to do was start some art work."[34]

Lindner's creative sensibilities were sparked by his arrival in northern Saskatchewan's boreal forest and Emma Lake in 1935, being "the fulfillment of his dream."[35] Heath noted: "He began to paint the forest growth with an all-absorbing enthusiasm. . . . He felt totally in harmony with his new environment and, for the first time in Canada, perhaps for the first time in his life, Ernie felt 'at home.'"[36] Heath continued: "Much later, in the 1960s, when Ernie began to focus on the minutiae of forest growth, his tightly constructed watercolour technique worked superbly."[37]

FIGURE 3.9. **Augustus Kenderdine**, *Homeward Bound*, 1925.

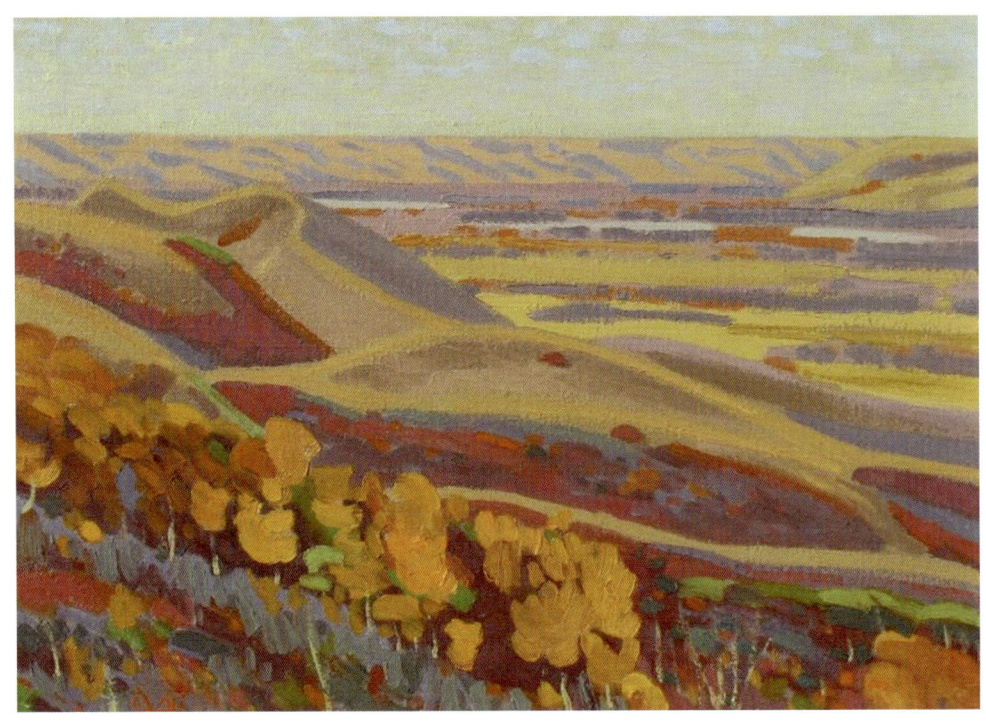

Three other quiet but truly prolific and important prairie artists whose landscapes reflect different approaches, with strikingly unique results, are Luke Lindoe (1913–2000), Norman Yates (1923–2014), and Dorothy Knowles (b. 1927). Lindoe worked in both clay and paint; the other two were painters. Lindoe, an early modernist, developed his painting style in direct response to the austere yet rich-toned landscape of southeastern Alberta. He embraced the strong, simple, linear forms of the land in both his ceramics and paintings. Artist Les Graff observed that Lindoe's aesthetic in clay "is an appreciation of the inherent qualities of clay: limited colour—like the prairie, compact form, natural textures."[38] Lindoe taught at the Alberta Institute of Technology and Arts (now Alberta College of Art and Design) and was a key mentor to a number of Canada's leading ceramic artists. British Columbia artist Walter Dexter (1931–2015), for instance, a Governor General's Award in the Visual Arts/Saidye Bronfman Award recipient, recalled to gallerist Jonathon Bancroft-Snell that Lindoe "took me to an area of the college where somebody was working the [potter's] wheel. . . . He told me the first time he put his hands in clay, it was magic."[39]

FIGURE 3.10. **Illingworth Kerr**, *Boggy Creek Autumn, [near the Qu'Appelle Valley]*, 1970.

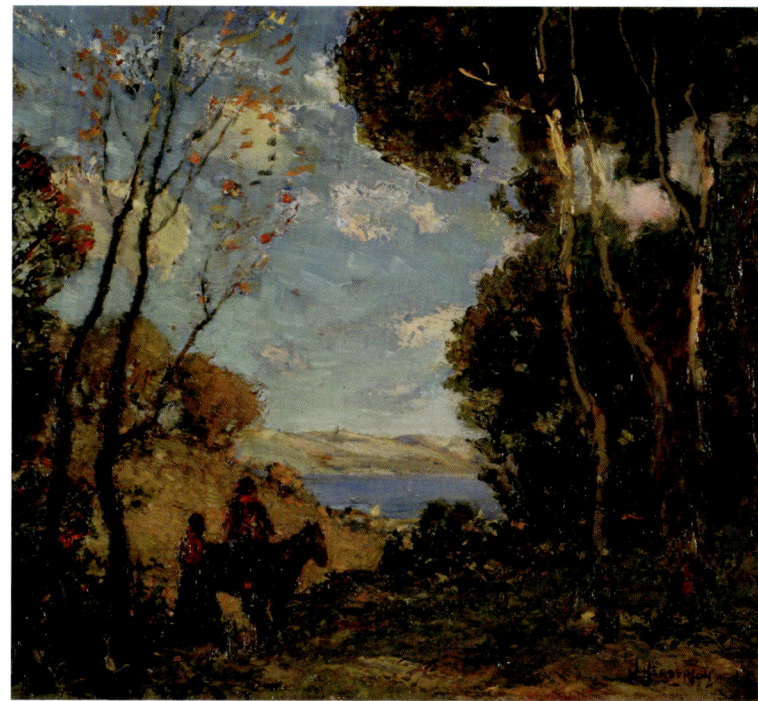

FIGURE 3.11.
James Henderson,
Qu'appelle Valley,
1932.

Lindoe's primary inspiration for his own paintings was without doubt the land. He saw its shapes and colours. Using strong repetition of lines and colours, he built planes and movement in his work, as seen in his 1947 oil on masonite, *Alkali Basin*. The rhythmic flowing curved lines in the foreground swirl up into the sky forming dramatic, foreboding clouds. The turbulent sky opens to the horizon and light beyond. Buildings are in the far distance. His use of the colour teal in the basin itself is carried into the sky and the touches of orange in the basin are enhanced in the background. Writer Mary-Beth Laviolette comments on Lindoe's achieving "an almost prismatic effect . . . [to] suggest the spiritual and purifying power of the environment."[40]

The prairie landscape was especially evocative for Norman Yates, and the movement and energy of its light and the limitless space became the subject of his free and spontaneous paintings. Yates painted what he called "landspaces" and worked with modular panels, as he wanted to "erase" the sense of a window frame. By adding panels to form three-, four-, or five-panelled works, he was able to expand his images to capture the sensibilities of limitless space. The results are series of works from differing perspectives depicting different states of light and weather. Yates's paintings are flowing, evocative, ephemeral, and always changing,

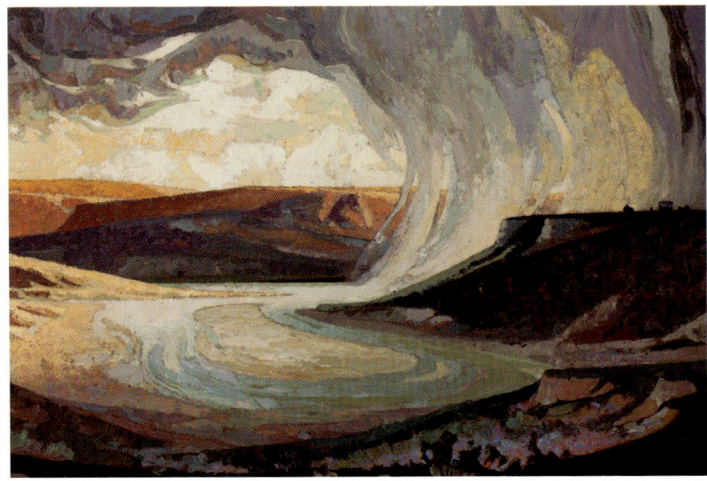

FIGURE 3.12.
Luke Lindoe,
Alkali Basin, 1947.

reflecting the intangibility of the light, skies, and atmospheric effects. In 1954, when he was still living in Ontario, he made a trip to the prairies that had a lasting impact on him: "[It struck me how much] the Group of Seven were completely concerned with the 'surface' of things; light reflecting off facets of rock, the shapes of leaves. Even the clouds were solid forms modeled in a painted sky. Crossing the Prairies (in a car called Mayflower), I was struck by the ambience; not the surfaces but the space."[41]

Writer Brian Brennan paid tribute to Yates's insights, inspirations, and ways of working:

While Yates didn't have an opportunity to view art as a child, he had plenty of opportunity to make art, first sketching with crayons and pencils in the five-cent newsprint scribblers bought for him by his parents, and later doing cartoons for his high school newspaper at Regina's Scott Collegiate Institute. He recalled sitting and sketching in fields on the outskirts of Regina as a child, and being "overwhelmed by the beauty of it all." . . . Abandoning the city in 1972, he and Whynona [Yates's wife] bought a quarter section ("natural boreal mixed forest, with wild fruit and wildlife") near Tomahawk, 96 kilometres west of Edmonton, and that precipitated a turning point in his development as an artist. "I had a real breakthrough there. I had been working—so to speak—through the window, painting what was in front of me. And one day I realized there was as much space behind me as in front."

Yates's realization that the horizon around him was endless, not cut off by the edge of a canvas, led him toward creating a series of panoramic abstract and semi-abstract paintings that he called "landspaces." A landscape was a prospect of scenery seen from one point of view. A "landspace" created a feeling of continuous and unbounded

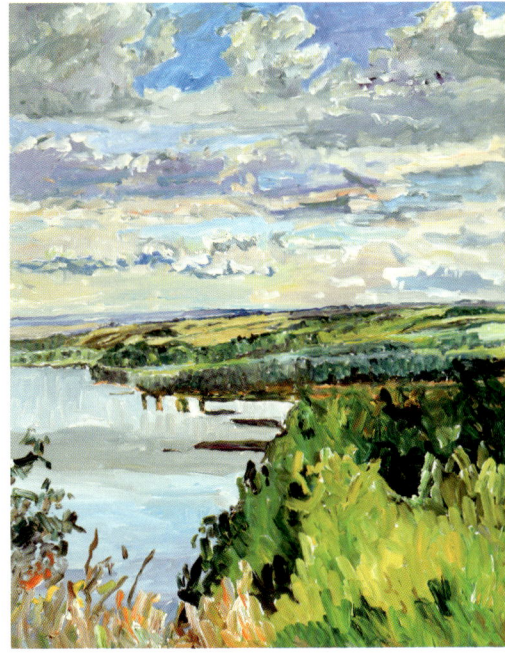

FIGURE 3.13.
Dorothy Knowles,
North Saskatchewan River, 1989.

extension in every direction, with an abiding sense that the painting would never stop. Using nature, weather, light and space as his elemental raw materials, Yates found himself following in the footsteps of the great English romantic painter J.M.W. Turner, whose visionary interpretations of landscape eventually became less about subject matter and more about space, change, movement and colour.[42]

In 1987 Yates moved to Victoria after retiring from teaching at the University of Alberta. The light and spaces of the coast then became his subject and, Brennan says, he "continued to draw his inspiration from the experience of walking out into the actual landscape and absorbing the changing colours and light 'like a big sponge.' The coastal environment provided him with new sources and possibilities. 'When I was in Alberta, it was all space and stillness and light because of the big skies. When I moved to the coast it became more colour and movement because of the sea, but the space is the continuing force throughout.'"[43]

Yates's landspaces are significant works in the annals of Western Canadian art for their colour and movement portraying the natural forces of nature, their rhythm and vision. Those portrayals are enhanced by the manner in which Yates "grew" his canvases to capture the breadth and power of the vastness of the spaces. Yet, he achieved it with his own personal sense of the intimacy of those spaces. *Landspace 241* (2011), for instance, is filled with colour,

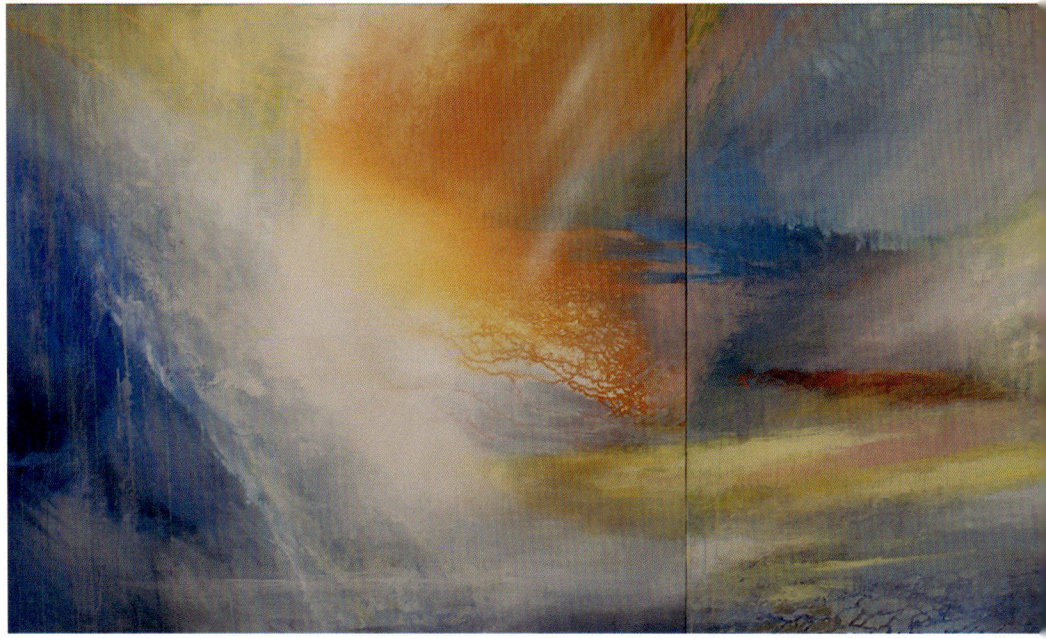

movement and positive energy. A video by Two Rivers Gallery describes his method: "[Yates] begins the painting with movement; applies the paint in a very spontaneous way and works on the wet surface of the canvas. Acrylics offer movement because you can use them in a very liquid form . . . if you make them (acrylics) thin enough they can be transparent and act as glazes. He starts with thick paint to set up the relationships between colours and as the painting develops works with thin paint. The magical part—something begins to emerge in the sense of an image."[44]

Reta Cowley, who moved from the United Kingdom to Saskatoon in 1947, was a student of Gus Kenderdine. She, too, painted the Saskatchewan prairie landscape, and was a teacher and mentor to Dorothy Knowles. Kenderdine commented of Cowley that she "is a beautiful watercolourist and her mastery of the medium is sublime."[45] Following the 1963 Emma Lake Artists' Workshop led by Kenneth Noland, Cowley had a freshness and freedom in her brushwork, and she began using India ink to highlight specific forms. As she herself said: "I work directly from my subject matter, which is the landscape in the Saskatoon area. I find in the landscape, which is always fluid, the colours, shapes and lines that I need to construct my paintings. Colour, shape, line, size, texture must work together to make an entity."[46]

FIGURE 3.14. **Norman Yates**, *Landscape 241*, 2011.

140

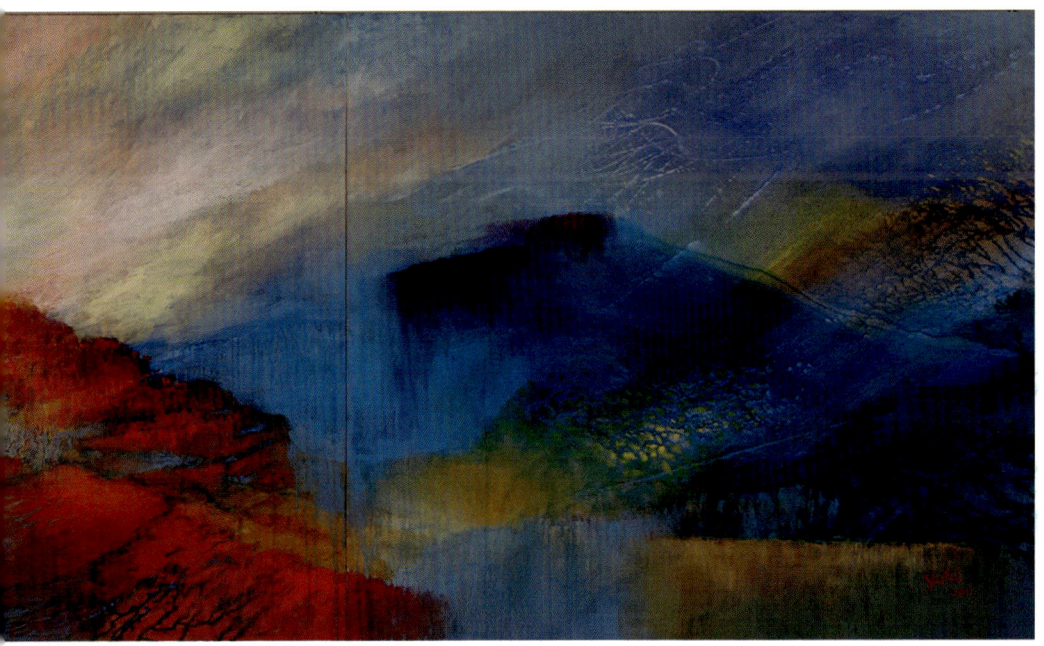

Eminent Saskatchewan artist Dorothy Knowles has her own particular approach to the prairie landscape, its beauty being her inspiration. Growing up as the youngest child on a prairie farm, Knowles was always inspired by the Saskatchewan landscape and fascinated by nature and growth. Knowles discovered that she really could paint when she was at Emma Lake. As happened with many artists, the annual Emma Lake workshop leaders were significant for Knowles's artistic development, particularly the sessions led by Joseph (Joe) Plaskett (1918–2014), Will Barnet, Barnett Newman, and Clement Greenberg. As Knowles recalled in an interview with artist, curator, and author Terry Fenton, Greenberg was "very generous and there for everybody—[he] looked at your work and lectured. It was a dream workshop."[47] Knowles told journalist Mandy Higgins that the New York critic gave her a worthwhile piece of advice: "At that time, I was painting in a much more abstract style. He told me to look closer at the motif and paint that—in other words, if you see a tree, paint the tree. I took those words to heart and started painting more realistically."[48]

When Knowles attended Kenneth Noland's workshop in 1963, he encouraged her to increase the size and scale of her work. Her response was that it was "natural; I relate to it very well. When I was doing a lot of oils outside I could fit a 4 by 4 quite nicely into my van. In the afternoons would do a medium size; and little ones in the evenings; Large ones in the morning! Finished in a morning, about 3 hours."[49] She did move to the larger format for some works.

Forging her own visual language with her personal style of punctuation in her colour and brushwork, her interest in foregrounds and garden details was genuine. Knowles begins with charcoal drawings and then highlights them with colour, either acrylic or oil. Of her subject, she commented, "I have to really want to paint a certain thing" and "trust [the] intuitive self. . . . We grew up with it, the ditches were full of flowers and it was enchanting."[50] The power of the sky and spaces is evident in *North Saskatchewan River,* 1989. She was dedicated to working outdoors whenever she could and used a van as her portable studio—much the way Emily Carr had used her caravan, the Elephant, those years before. Friends had towed Carr's Elephant and parked in the spot of the artist's choice each summer. Knowles, who emphasized that "I work in the field," however, was not dependent on others to tow a van.

In her nineties, she said: "Different materials do affect my approach. Working in my studio, I usually use acrylics rather than oils or watercolours and paint larger—although at 90 I'm working on smaller pieces now. . . . I often use charcoals with acrylics; it's very adaptable—you can rub it, erase it and I just like the feel of it. The works done in my studio tend to be more layered and contemplative, sometimes moodier. In a way they touch a deeper place, and it's a different way to connect."[51]

If Lindoe, Yates, and Knowles represent the second generation of prairie landscape painters, Gus Kenderdine, James Henderson, and Inglis Sheldon-Williams had represented the first. Each had immigrated from Britain and they approached the landscape quite differently from Yates, Lindoe, and Knowles. As Fenton observed, they focused on the valleys rather than the open prairie, rarely painting the open, limitless expanse. Illingworth Kerr was one of the first generation of Saskatchewan-born painters, and the first to become a professional artist.

In Winnipeg, artist and long-time teacher and mentor Diane Whitehouse (b. 1940), who immigrated from the United Kingdom, is clear about the impact of the landscape on her thinking. While the landscape is evident in and the basis of many of her works, she does not paint the land. She lives in the land. Admitting she is affected by the vastness of the Canadian landscape, she said, "I use the landscape as a vehicle for my ideas."[52] She talks of her paintings as being a "transition timeframe" and as "threads of ideas from life." This can be seen her mixed media work *Beaches . . . Dieppe,* 2017, which recalls the war, the memories of her family who served, and the changes to society thereafter. Her painting *Not Quite Dark* refers to her husband's Alzheimer disease and the changes that made to her life, his life, and those close to them both. The colour in the latter is strong. The light in the sky is white in the middle and breathes into yellows to the left and the right. In the lower left is an empty frame, denoting that something is missing. A mother, grandmother, artist, professor, who has lived in the United Kingdom, Alberta, and Manitoba, Whitehouse notes that her world is "fragmented," especially with the illness of her husband. While she tends to the narrative in her art, it is not literal: it is symbolic. She often adds objects to her paintings, in this case a small piece of wood,

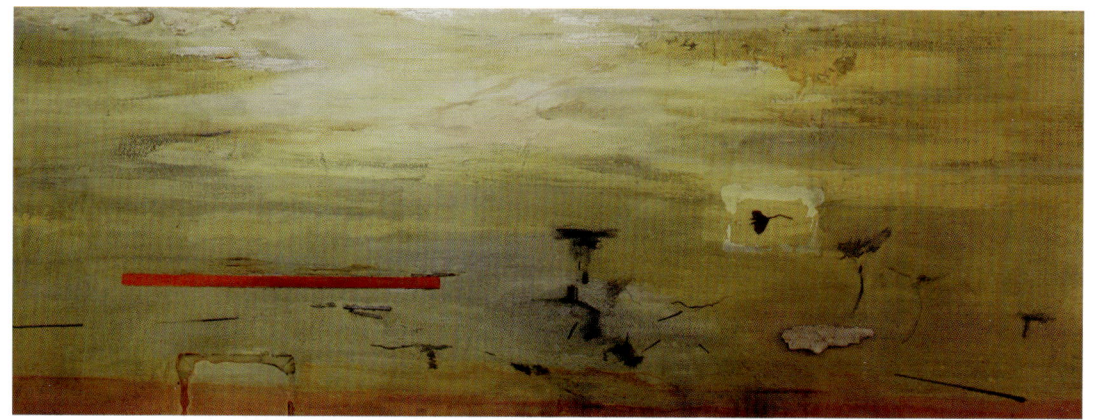

which enhance the texture she achieves with her distinctive brushwork. Her sense of rhythm permeates all her work as she links a sense of realism of the land with her unique abstracted approach to her subject. She sums up her approach: "I paint to sort out ideas that are best expressed visually. . . . The constant dialogue of building an idea and taking it apart has had an impact on my own artistic process. . . . I am comfortable and enjoy working this way—a slow visiting and revisiting a thought in a visual act. I am often referred to as an abstract painter but I think in many ways I am a painter of the visual who paints abstractly. A constant source for the painting is the landscape, mountains, water, rooms, and intimate spaces."[53]

Not surprisingly, many other mid-prairie artists have become far-reaching with their ideas and modes of expression, too. This group includes painters Robert Sinclair of Saskatoon, and Jeffrey Spalding, Barbara Milne, and ceramist Les Manning from Alberta. Another, now living in Victoria and formerly of Edmonton and Saskatoon, is curator, writer, and artist Terry Fenton (b. 1940), who paints light and space of both the prairies and the coastal waters. His fluid, rhythmic works are compelling. Independent curator Wayne Morgan shares my view of Fenton as being one "who understands light. . . . Unlike so many others he has an ability to deliver the nuanced light of the prairie."[54]

In Falkland, British Columbia, Ann Kipling's landscape drawings of views from her second-floor studio window are powerful and sensitive, yet delicately intricate. She is acutely attentive to her environment, and her observations and working method are intense. As she says, "Being intrigued by natural phenomena—a leaf, a bird, a tree, etc.—I have put drawing to an intense concentration on these things . . . they are by-products of intense observation."[55] Short, expressive, powerful lines convey depth and movement, depicting all that is before her and her

FIGURE 3.15. **Diane Whitehouse**, *Untitled*, from the series *Not Quite Dark*, 2017.

143

truly personal relationship with her subject. The elements of nature around her—the wind, trees, mountains, and the light—are in constant motion, presenting her with constantly shifting panoramic views, both at close and long distances. As she works in the 360-degree landscape, Kipling's drawings, depictions of time and place, are about both what she sees and what she feels, rather like a portrait, capturing a mood or sensibility of a specific moment. The manner in which Kipling portrays the evocative skies, wind, and clouds creates movement throughout each work, setting up her characteristic syncopated rhythms. That strong sense of rhythm is enhanced by the way she carefully places spaces between the intense areas of interlocking and parallel lines. Her use of spaces contrasts the intensity of her quick strokes. As she has said: "I have found drawing the most immediate, probing and exploratory way to come to terms with my personal vision. My drawings are very disciplined. There is no room for the wrong mark. . . . The mark cannot be made in the wrong place. . . . It cannot be made darker than it is; it cannot be lighter. It has to be right."[56]

Pat Martin Bates was certainly captivated by the prairie light and space, and later that of the ocean in Victoria. On reaching Alberta from Ottawa, in September 1962, she was quickly aware of, and impressed with, the power of the landscape. Its impact on her work was immediate: "I love the feel of openness. I was enchanted by the prairie and the stubble through the snow—gold at night when the sun went down."[57] That sensibility inspired her white-on-white works, drawing her to alchemy and all turning to gold. Sound also permeated her work at the time as she was fascinated with how it projected across the flat snows. She incorporated patterns of sound into her work through her poetic titles such as *Night Growing Sounds,* and she did a number of works in the 1960s to honour the prairie silence using the circle form to portray sound, evoking its travel across the empty spaces.

Of Alberta's impact on Pat Martin Bates's art, writer Alma de Chantal commented: "Little by little new forms of inspiration arose, marking the beginning of an important stage in the artist's pilgrimage. The first white circles encrusted on a white background appear, the Tantric mandalas and mandorlas which are major elements in Bates' work."[58] That inspiration was long-lasting, informing much of Bates's future work and its technique, her symbolism, and her alchemical quest that is apparent in many of her lightboxes in which aspects of the image turn to gold when the box is lit. Bates's colleague Mary Kerr, artist and theatre designer, and recipient of the 2020 Molson Prize, wrote: "Later, in the boundless snowscape of northern Alberta, she felt driven to find new ways 'to see the other side' and subsequently created new techniques of art beyond the traditional definitions of printmaking, painting and sculpture."[59]

Pat Martin Bates developed her own multilayered techniques for her unique paperworks. First she printed them, putting them through the press several times. Then she painted them, pierced, collaged, and grommetted them, and finally wrote on them. All incorporate her own iconography and symbolism. Using heavy leather-like papers, thread, reflective materials, and light boxes, she achieved her goal of alchemy by transforming her images with light. *Sky*

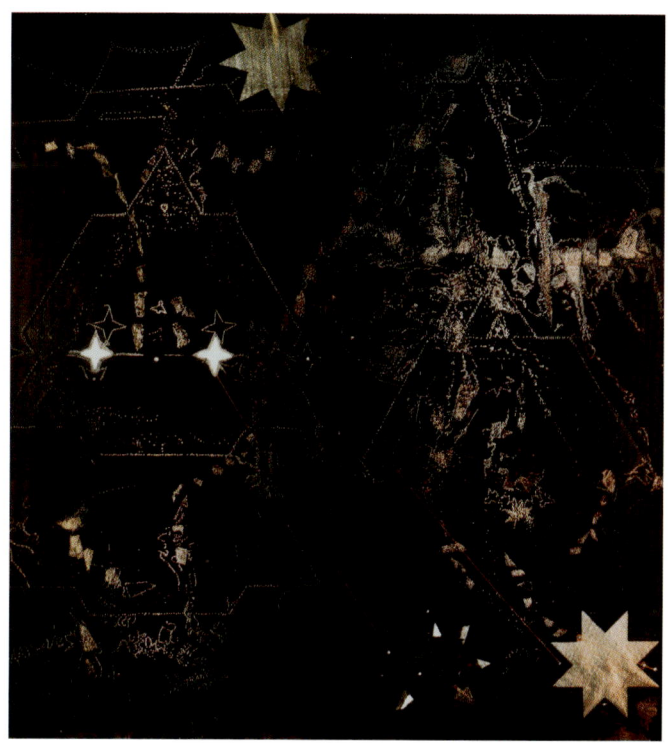

in Skye—the 9th Island—Darwin Night Watch on the Barque Marques, 1985, a light box with a collaged, pierced, embossed screen print, chine collé, gold threads, foils, and leaf and oil pastels, evokes the night skies filled with stars. The repeated points of direction in the work underline the importance of the stars for navigation. The constellations of the night skies, forming many pathways through the works, are joined together by gold threads. The brightness of the stars and reflections of the collaged gold reflective papers give the work light, rhythm, and constant motion. The artist has pierced flowing streams of light across the surface. The title, with its words weaving among the piercings and collaged gold papers, becomes part of the overall imagery. The work presents in two ways. When lit from the front, the texture and subtle blues and reds provide depth and richness enhanced by the reflections from the gold paper. When lit from behind, the sparkle of the light through the interlaced linear perforations gives a tremendous sense of movement.

Manitoba colleagues and kindred spirits Winston Leathers and Bruce Head shared her never-ending interest in light, reflections, and space, and the diverse moods of the skies. Both 1950s graduates of the early years of the Winnipeg School of Art at the University of Manitoba,

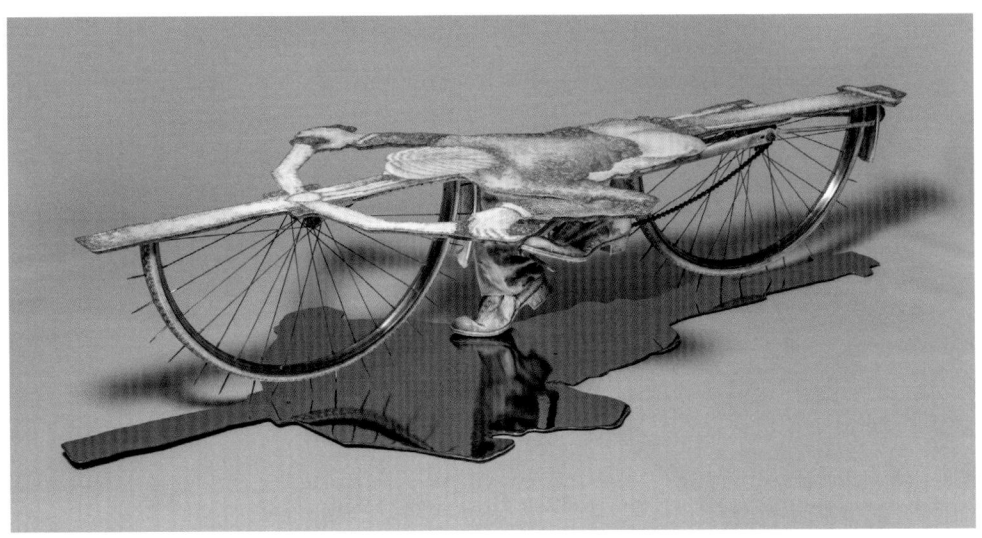

they were students of George Swinton, and his attitudes and sincerity in his art impacted them both. They were certainly in tune with Swinton's relation with the land, which itself was noted by Ferdinand Eckhardt: "He loves to paint the great excitement of nature, the landscape, the unexplored North as well as the not yet fully recognized prairie. He tries to express it in shapes, outlines, structure, light and colour."[60] Friend and colleague Arthur Adamson talked of an almost ethereal aspect to Swinton's art: "We notice first the colour . . . his paintings sing with a memorable resonance. . . . For Swinton space has an almost mystical quality. . . . The paintings are regional in the sense that they emerge from direct sensual experience and an individual viewpoint."[61] This is particularly evident in *Birth of a Prairie River,* 1959–1960. This work conveys the artist's infectious love of the prairie. It shows his particular strength of colour, line, and brushwork with its multiple rhythms moving within and across the painting, and extending a boundless horizon beyond the picture plane. His intersecting series of parallel diagonal lines zigzagging across the right side of the painting are juxtaposed with the sweeping, freer brush strokes on the left. The sky, comprising one-third of the composition, is executed with impressionistic brushwork. Swinton's visual vocabulary includes many means of "mark making," which enable him to convey a forceful, often spiritual message enhanced by a consistent palette. In this rich work the strong yellows and reds are punctuated by black and teal strokes, reflecting the prairie heat. As he said: "The act of creating art was spiritual, evoking meaning and integrity."[62]

FIGURE 3.17. **Don Proch**, *Asessippi Tread,* 1970.

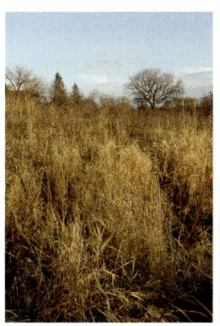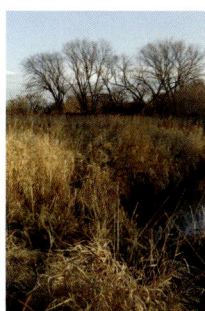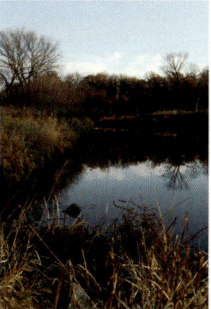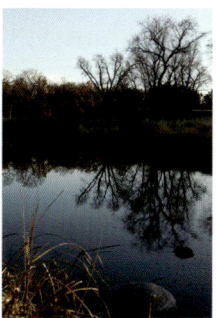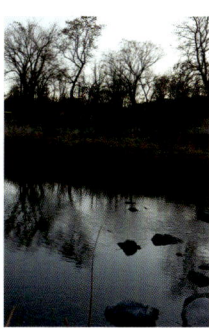

Meaning and the act of creating for Head and Leathers came through their depictions of light and its reflections, movement, and colours. The two frequently drove across the prairie together, and although they said they did not discuss their respective art, one has to question their attestations.[63] Head said, "We stopped when the space or light was of particular interest and would agree on what we should see again."[64] When swimming, Leathers often had his eyes at water level so he could not only see the horizon and its reflections on the water but, in his words, "feel it." In Leathers's works like *Evening Calm* or *Light Over the Island,* one sees his combination of reflective metallic paint and sumi ink. Leathers had a long and great interest in Japanese calligraphy, and that too is ever present in his later work.

For his part, Bruce Head commented: "I am unconsciously a landscape painter. My work is always related to the land. I called the round sculpted canvases 'sky pies.' With the sculpted canvases they were the flow of the landscape and the grain fields."[65] Head, like Leathers and Bates, used reflective paints, which give energy and movement to his portrayal of the subliminal sensibilities of nature. He strove for a "total environment' in his work, recalling the strip farms of the Red River plots, which he achieved by stitching strips of torn canvas to make the whole.

Don Proch took another approach to the landscape as place by suggesting its presence in his breakthrough sculpture *Asessippi Tread,* in the 1970 national juried *Winnipeg Show.* Something new, imaginative, and ground-breaking happened with *Asessippi Tread.* It changed the viewer's perception of and engagement with art. Its subject, the speeding bicycle down the Asessippi Valley, its materials, a bicycle with extruding spokes, its flat surface with its compelling drawing of a crouched rider, and its presentation on the floor forcing viewers to look down on it were all new ideas.

The specificity of the prairie landscape has been part of many artists' work, both consciously as subject and subconsciously as their work evolved. Many, as we have seen, have

FIGURE 3.18. **Sheila Spence**, *The Creek*, 2008.

painted the land, and Ivan Eyre is no exception, though his works are not of specific sites. He told me "place is very important in my work; it affects the work through the subconscious—on reflections—the reflecting part of working would bring forth the dreamy memory of places."[66] His large-scale landscapes like *Sand Bank,* 1996, are compelling. Yet, of no specific place, they are always a compendium of seasons, places, and times of day. As he said, "Using more than one season in a landscape work offers more variety and contrast in the painting process. . . . Any combination of trees, land, water, and sky are possible, and when all seasons are thrown into the mix the possibilities for expression are endless. . . . I realize that *Sand Bank* only remotely relates to the world around Roseisle in mid-autumn."[67] In doing these landscapes, he said: "It had to be a different approach [from his other subjects] because the subject demanded it and I worked at a stroke with the brush and paint, not geometric, and by repeating it arrived at a surface with simulated leaves and trees. Therefore it is not pointillist, but what I found with a brush."[68]

Manitoba's Sheila Spence (b. 1952) portrays the extensive horizons of her native prairie landscape with her camera, not a brush. She does so with multiples, her photographs often being two, three, and sometimes five panels. They convey the never-ending space much as Norman Yates did with his paintings. Photographic memory underlies many of Spence's portraits and landscapes, recalling a personal past, including memories of a specific place. She captures the moment, the detail, colour, the changing atmosphere, and many textures of her subject. Her collective body of work becomes an emotional mapping of the subject and of the viewer, as she said, a "form of journaling, an interiorized psychological mapping."[69] *The Creek,* 2008, near her Winnipeg home, for instance, becomes a personal nostalgic record. This five-panelled photograph simultaneously captivates both the particular and the universal of that landscape, the texture and movement of the grasses, and the moods and colours of the water, while reflecting the patterns and personality of the sky.

On the West Coast Carole Sabiston has had a long and successful career as a textile assemblage artist who also created large multi-panelled works like *Flying into Delos.* For her, the horizon line over the water is as important as it is for the artists depicting the prairies. So, too, is the reflection of light on the water and the liveliness of the sky. In all her work she focuses on movement, particularly sailing and flying. She said, "From the window looking out to space or from space looking back to earth, I like to examine the concept of movement between near and far. I am compelled to look at ways we travel around and through our environment in reality and in our imaginations."[70]

The horizon line coupled with the continually changing skies and waters, the reflections, moods, and colours are the essence of Sabiston's art. Her self-devised technique of fabric assemblage involves layers of opaque, transparent, and reflective materials, including floating gauze and voile, to create the multiple effects of light and movement and constantly shifting patterns and personalities of the sky. Changes of perception, perspective, distance, and space, so central to Sabiston's work, are accentuated by her fusing the macro and micro, the far and near,

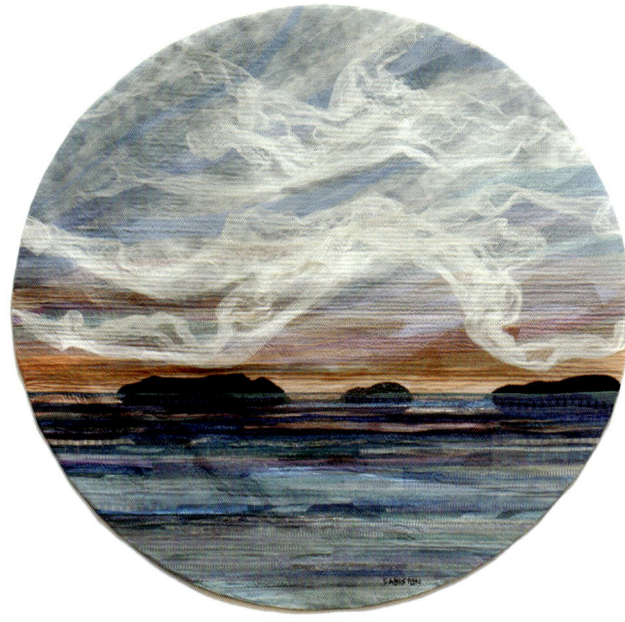

FIGURE 3.19.
Carole Sabiston, *Flying Rondels at Dawn*, 1987.

in every work. The sensibilities of Sabiston's textile assemblages echo those of Yates's paintings after he moved to Vancouver Island. In comparing the prairie with the sea, as Brian Brennan reported, he had commented that "space is the continuing force throughout" his art; for Sabiston, it is light.

The sky with its distances and the personalities of clouds is of real interest to Carole Sabiston, too, as seen in her major installation work, *Take Off: Point of Departure and Mode of Travel*. The land and sky portions of this large piece depict a seascape and skyscape through which she travelled frequently, by boat and air. Sabiston states of the inspiration the sky affords her imagination regarding flight:

> This is a particular flight that I take very often as do many people who live in this region where we are either plowing across the water or flying above it. I chose this particular area because it is a direct area of transport. There is a carpet itself embedded into the surface of the earth. I have always had a great fascination with Kilims or rugs from the Orient, in the random patterns, each pattern peculiar to the weaver or region it has come from. I like to think this is a modern, contemporary carpet made of extraordinary and exotic fabrics far out of reality. The carpet itself is at the same time the earth and a carpet. It's an aerial view between Victoria on Vancouver Island, and Vancouver on the Mainland, flying over the Gulf Islands.[71]

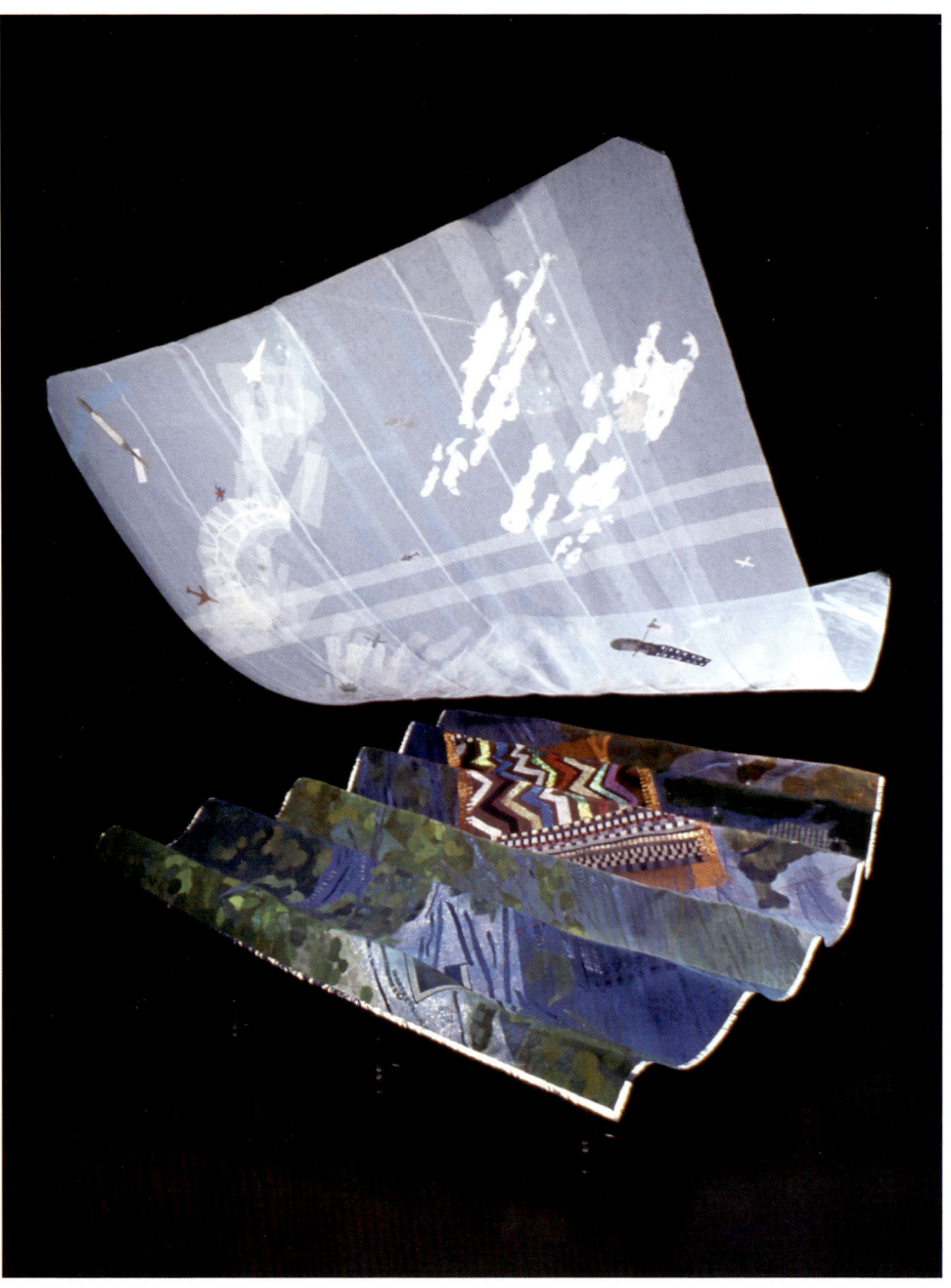

In the original installation of this large work, the earth, the floor piece, was supported by Plexiglas rods of graduated heights, suggesting the natural undulations in the land and the sense of the earth's carpet lifting off into space. The sky canopy, suspended from the ceiling, was made of layers of netting and gauze into which the artist incorporated a number of real and fantasy objects among the clouds:

> Some of the details in the sky or in the atmosphere allude to things that are flying in present-day reality or imaginary. For instance, we have satellites, all kinds of planes, from helicopters to twin Otters, to the Concorde. We have Superman, of course, and we have two gloves almost touching. This, perhaps, is a reference to Michelangelo's The Creation of Man. It's always that illusion [as we] look up at the sky and the clouds, and I always see gaps or dinosaurs, or a soup plate or whatever you want. It's all these illusions of things that fly up in the sky, and they are there.[72]

Her use of netting as the sky gives its translucency, and the elements such as gloves and various fabrics become the clouds. These flying and floating objects are weightless figures drifting above the sea and the Gulf Islands.

Takao Tanabe (b. 1926) and Gordon Smith (1919–2020) are both giants in the Canadian painting scene and masters of painting the land. Each captures the moods, spaces, and horizons in works done over many years. Their surfaces enhance the space, and their judicious use of colour and line extends both space and light.

Winnipeg's John King expresses joy in the freedom and lyricism of his calligraphic brushwork. His acrylic on canvas *Churchill Night,* 2013, shows the power of his response to the prairie landscape with its inherent moods. The balance of line, colour, and movement, the repetition of individual elements, and the energy of his gestural marks underline this lyrical abstraction, the automatic action of his brush having become an extension of his arm. One sees the horizon, activity in the night sky, birds, and clouds, with the fluid yellow/white line providing a window, light, movement—all with one stroke. The brush held varying amounts of paint and the artist shifted the position of the brush to give different kinds of energy to the strength and force of the line. One has to ask if the structure, which takes up most of the work, refers to the fact that Churchill, Manitoba, is often referred to as the "Gateway to the Arctic," and if the birds are reminiscent of the Canada and snow geese flocking in the fall.

Skies are obviously a key aspect of landscape as place, defining the momentary sensibilities. Roger LaFrenière, for instance, for whom landscape is a key subject, often talks of the sky in his work, as seen in his series of the prairie skies, including his acrylic on canvas *The Zone,* 2015. LaFrenière is inextricably rooted in the Manitoba prairie; its light, space, colour, rhythms, and life are the substance of all his work, evident in each of his realistic portrayals and abstractions, whether large or small in scale. Movement and light have become his signature. LaFrenière frequently talks of his love of the prairie sky expanse in *The Zone*: "The sky's expanse is, in its immense depth and soothing calm, the launch pad for the release of the thoughts that soar above this expansive landscape. The marks hovering in this space are like trails to follow in these ephemeral treks. I love the prairies—the openness of the sky, the softness of the light, the intensity in the winter."[73] His depiction of the prairie sky, with its wisps of clouds and vapour trails, draws the viewer's eye through and beyond the work, reflecting LaFrenière's simultaneous interest in reality and abstraction. His smooth application of paint, applied layer on layer, stretches the infinite sense of the prairie sky.

As he has said:

My work has grown and changed over the years as I have, but not necessarily at the same rate. It floats in and out of flirtations with semi-realism and abstraction. Both of these genres are important to my opus because they permit me, as well as the viewer, to input their feelings into the work. My work is an outpouring of love that I have with the light, the texture and the movements of this beautiful living, breathing land that we are so fortunate to live on. The Canadian Prairies offer us clean air, pristine skies and an ever-changing panorama. Each season is a beautiful force in itself and brings about a constant renewal of energy, of hope, and for the visual artist, a palette of new colours. We are truly fortunate to share the subtleties of such a powerful source.[74]

What turns an artist's attention to the sky from the landscape itself? Is it the draw of the horizon, or the unknown and the lure of going where few have been? Is it a continuation of interest in light? Or is it because the sky is very much part of the overall landscape? Gathie Falk's *Night Sky Celebration No. 23,* 1980, and Barbara Milne's *Nocturne Blue and Gray,* 2011, both explore sky, Milne's being above the clouds and Falk's looking up to the clouds. Milne's evocative use of colour adds to the atmosphere and the adventure seemingly from space. She did this work as a result of her 2009 summer two-week residency in Iceland at a place that has been called the Golden Circle. She reflects:

No amount of research prepared me for the sensorial experience of this raw, elegant and epic landscape. Geothermal pools, pure water, geysers, glaciers, waterfalls and black volcanic terrain combine in a place of mystery and wonder. The midnight sun is described as a permanent dusk or glare in the northern skies in midsummer. This light persisted in ways that both softened and sharpened the depth of field. . . . Since that time my paintings are reflections on the elemental quality of the open spaces and the remembered Icelandic palette. The works are about the void and a response to the

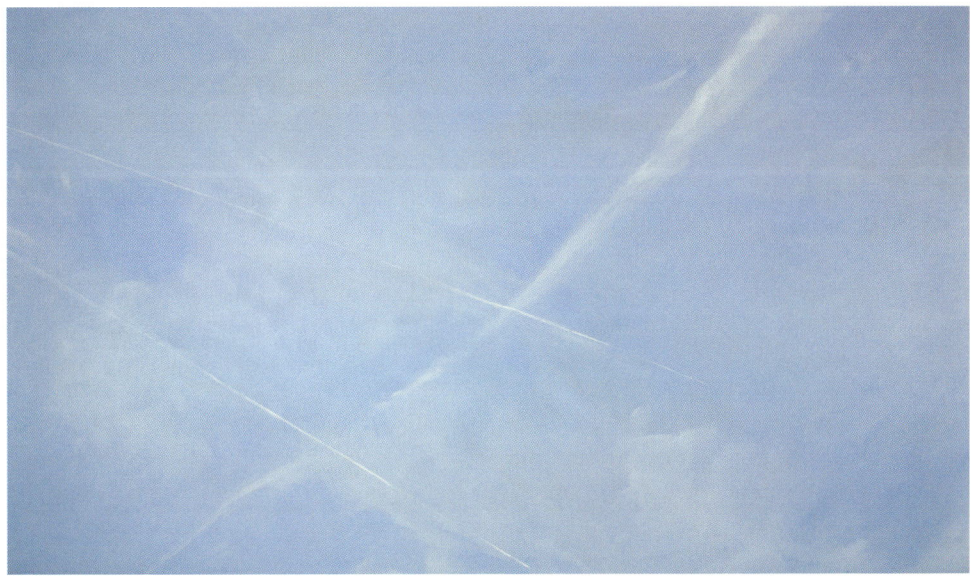

atmospheric effects of light, fog, temperature and moisture . . . pared down in subject matter, these works are emblematic, reduced and distilled.[75]

Milne's 2020 *Nocturne Island,* inspired by a trip to Salt Spring Island, continues her interest in landscape and atmosphere, and, as she told me, her paintings are about the interior and exterior aspects of space and thought, or metaphors of the internal and external sense of place.[76] She clearly remains inspired by place, as she had been with the grandiosity of the land and skyscape when she moved to Calgary from Toronto in 1979:

> I had not anticipated the powerful draw of the foothills and mountains. Nor did I then see how such vastness would bring about an enhanced appreciation of the minutiae from which such vistas are formed. As I began to contemplate the idea of working within the theme of landscape I was inspired by the works of Georgia O'Keefe, Arthur Dove, and Emily Carr, artists who ventured into abstraction and whose works I regard as meditations on the essence of place, both external and internal. . . . Direct observation, sketching and photography . . . and collage as a creative lens enables me to subvert the logic and order of what I experience. Through editing and amplification

FIGURE 3.21. **Roger LaFrenière**, *The Zone*, 2015.

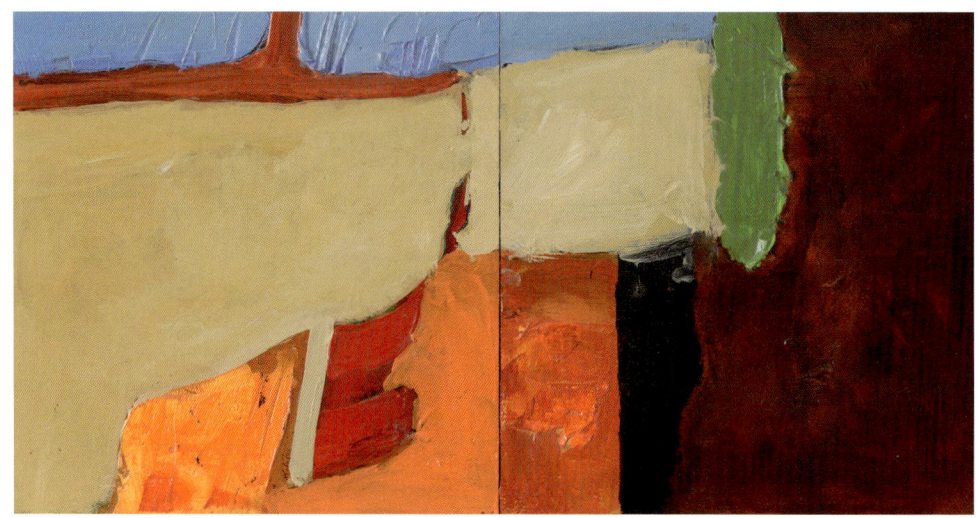

of details, I am looking at our fragile relationship to the land, both the micro and macro, pondering ideas of stewardship, vulnerability and even loneliness. I am ever reminded of temporality—of presence and absence—nature as we encounter it and as we remember it.[77]

Jane Everett, a Winnipeg native with vivid memories of sitting under the birch trees at the family cottage at Minaki, Ontario, is a convert to the landscape of British Columbia's interior, where she has lived and worked for more than twenty-five years. Its majesty and details are her primary subject matter, and she wants to share her feeling and her sense of being in her landscapes. Light is enhanced through her use of vellum, giving both transparency and a reflective quality. Her forms seemingly dissolve into her portrayals of light, space, and reflection. Everett works quickly with an innate sense of line and movement. Her initially realistic renderings, whether of tree canopies, water, or bird themes, highlighting the micro and macro in nature, become increasingly gestural as she works, to convey an impressionistic, at times abstracted, feeling. Everett's intrigue with the effect of water on light permeates many of her subjects, and in some works their abstracted qualities have nothing but colour and texture left.[78] She is working on a new series inspired by the waterlilies and plants in the water at her Shuswap cottage as well as the waterways on her daily walk in the city. One, a large oil on canvas from 2021, titled, *And drifted, one ear tuned to the dip of your paddle,*

FIGURE 3.22. **Roger LaFrenière**, *By the Lake*, 2007.

154

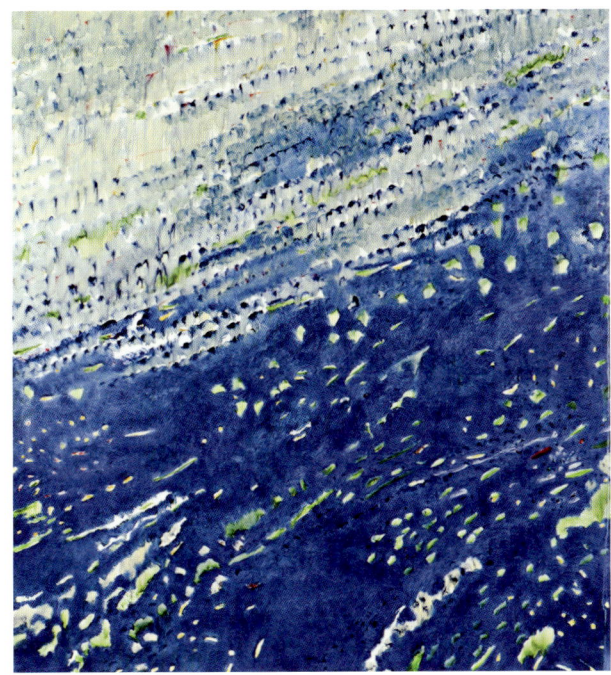

FIGURE 3.23.
Gathie Falk, *Pieces of Water #10—El Salvador*, 1982.

was also influenced by the work of Helen Frankenthaler. Everett told me that "with narrative titles, this painting distills the memory of a place and time into line and colour. The scale of this piece, at 5 by 8 feet, makes a presence nearly large enough to walk into. It is descriptive of a specific, quotidian event. The work is loosely based on a location, the North Shuswap, in particular, the mouth of Onyx Creek. As the lake rises, the water invades the bushes and reeds that grow at the edge of the forest. The effect of the morning sun is therefore profoundly altered, reflecting up and drenching the landscape in light from all directions. While the painting is about longing to hold onto those transient moments, the titles address the subtext of the relationship between the paddlers."[79]

For Everett, reflection has taken several forms over the years, physical, impressionistic, and those of word play: reflections on information, reflections of memory and stories, reflecting on possible narratives, and the reflections on water and of light. As artist and writer Lubos Culen says, "Her exploration in capturing light together with the fragmented landscape forms reflected on the surface of water bodies results in images that are ephemeral and invoke a feeling of a peaceful sensual experience."[80] She often used vellum rather than canvas in her earlier works and the "slidey surface," of vellum, on which she used pastel, fixative, and, at times, oil, imbued

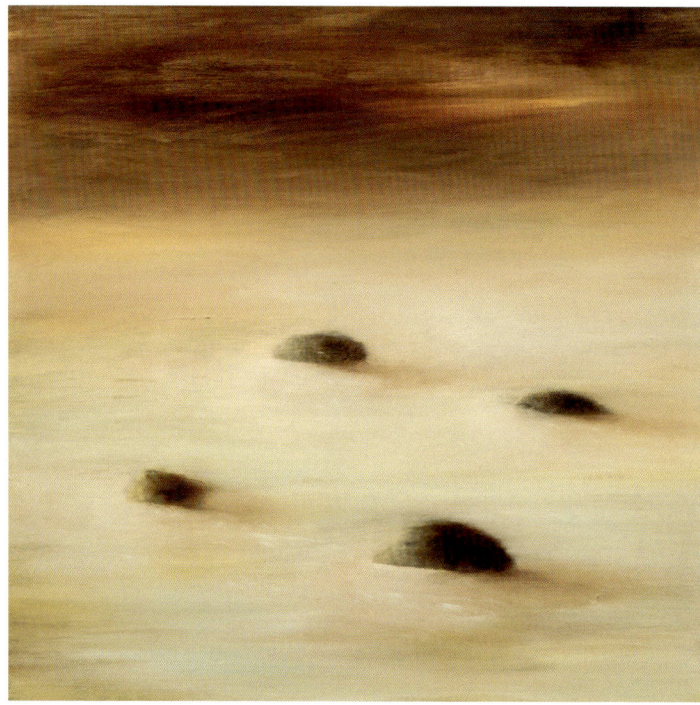

FIGURE 3.24.
Barbara Milne,
*Nocturne Blue
and Gray*, 2011.

her art with immediacy, depth, rhythm, strength, and energy, particularly in her tree canopies. Lines of force made by strong slashes with an eraser to make marks add lines across the surface of a work, rather than taking them away, thus enhancing the motion and feel of the wind between the trees. Drips of fixative are coupled with her use of pastel with layers of colour.

Geology is another critical interest of Western Canadian artists and has found its way into the inventive work of artists, painters, ceramists, and sculptors. It is material for the work of ceramic artist and Governor General Award in Visual Arts recipient Robert (Bob) Archambeau with his sensibility to the surface of his pots. Don Proch also incorporates layers of geological formations in his masks and unique sculptures. In *Typeface Mask,* 2017, the tiny pieces of bone, rendered in a detailed, soft-hued palette that reflects the subtlety and intricacy of his coloured pencil drawings, are stacked like building blocks to represent the layers of geological history. Some pieces of bone are placed with the porous side showing; others, with the smooth edges facing outwards. Together they portray the geological striations of the Asessippi Hills where he

FIGURE 3.25. **Jane Everett**, *Birch on Birch I*, 2014.

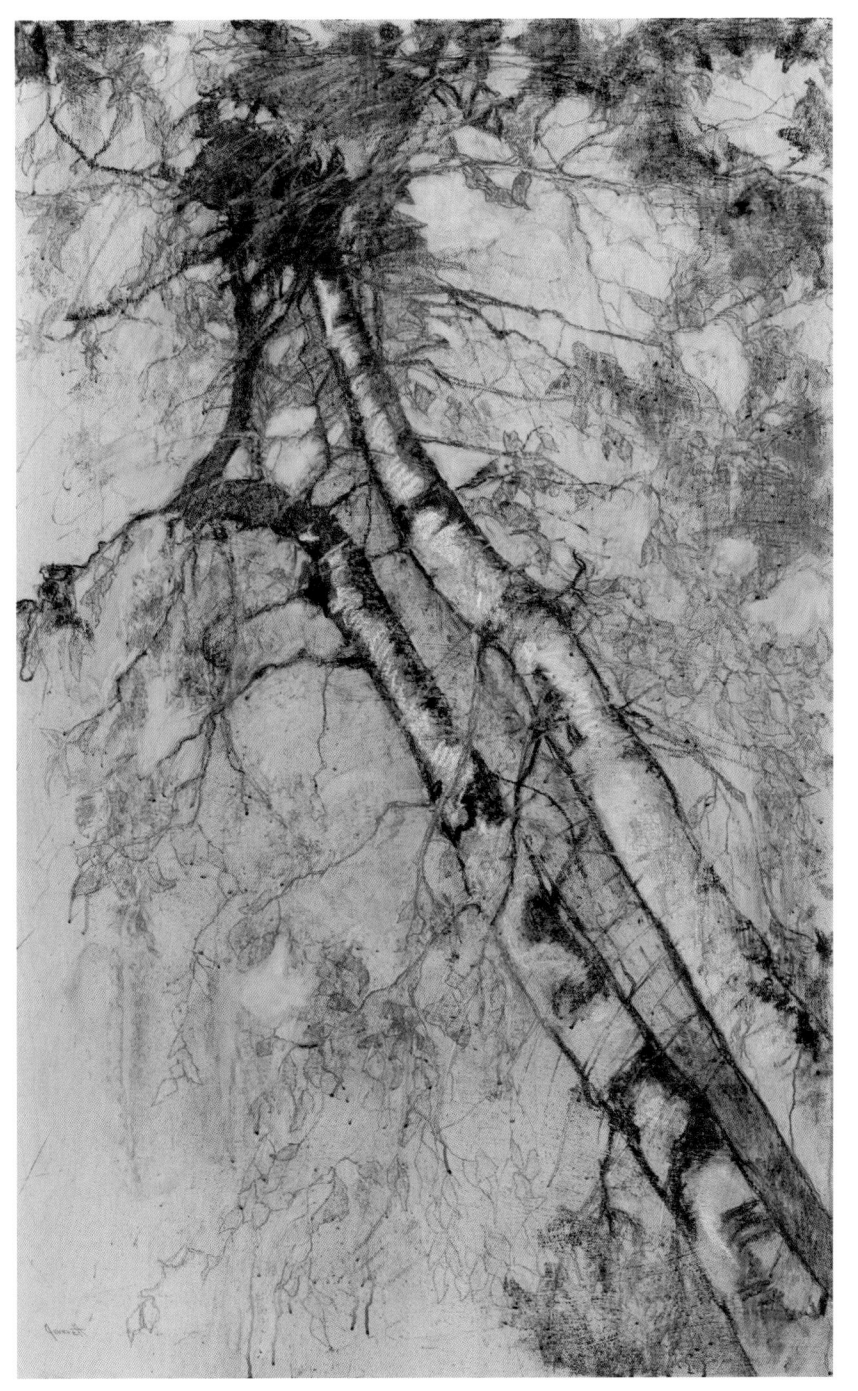

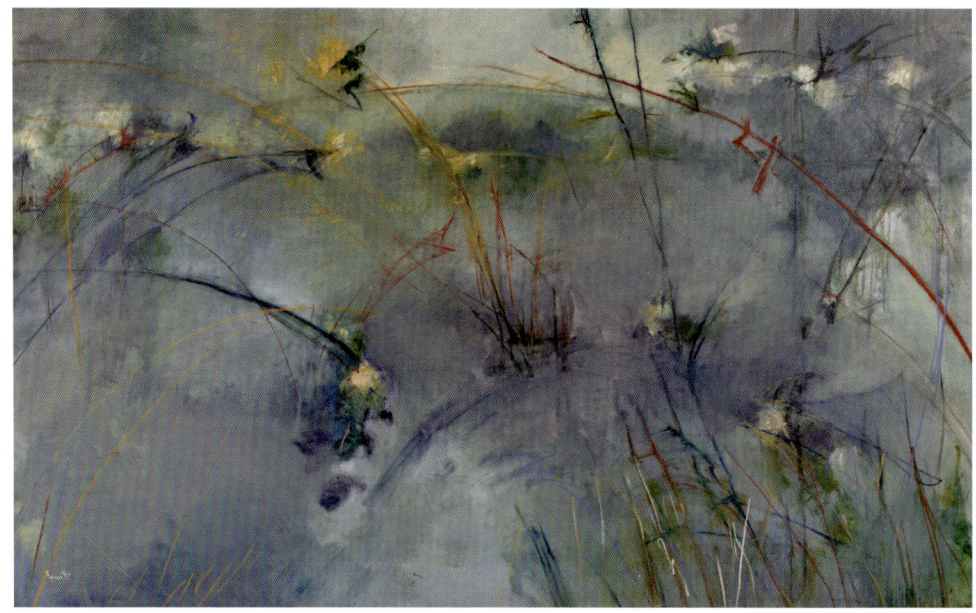

grew up. In this piece Proch juxtaposes various materials, ideas, and images, each of particular relevance to his past and his present and to his environmental concerns for the future. The past, defined by the incorporation of the stacked bones on one side of the face, is enhanced with the typeface, once used by a rural newspaper, on the other side. The letters, infixed at different lengths, create the work's outer form, contours, and shadows. An old Selectric typewriter ball forms the cheek. His exquisite drawing of the lyrical landscape of prairie hills of western Manitoba depicts the present. The future is foreshadowed by a tear, the waterfall in one eye, alluding to the harmful effects of acid rain on nature and farming. The tiny, white, wooden grain elevator, placed in one eye in front of the full moon in a midnight blue sky, references the farming roots and preoccupations of the West. Proch's iconography is rich and deepens the complex layers of meaning that link his Winnipeg studio to his prairie life. Emphasizing physical realities and contemporary psychological quandaries, his deliberate ordering of materials and textures reflects the dichotomies of one's inner and outer selves, and those of the inner and outer sensibilities of community.

Clay is another material that artists employ to depict Western Canada's geology. Inspired by that sense of place, for instance, Puck Janes's textured art is in large part inspired by the prairie

FIGURE 3.26. **Jane Everett**, *And drifted, one ear tuned to the dip of your paddle*, 2021.

landscape, our imprint on it and the land below the surface. Her hand-built explorations of Saskatchewan's geology are particularly evident in a small three-sectioned wall ceramic. Each section is about four inches high and no more than six inches long. She effectively conveys the expanding distances of the prairie horizon in the three sections, rather like the multiple sections of the work of Norman Yates and Sheila Spence. The work has its own dichotomies and hearkens back to her Iranian ancestry, the blue of the sky having the intensity of lapis lazuli rather than the lighter, softer tones of a prairie sky.

We have seen the striations of layered coloured clays in the pots and sculptures of Alberta's Les Manning. The sense of space and expansive natural history is also caught by British Columbia's Robin Hopper in many of his ceramic pieces, especially his slab bottles, which are like canvases for him. In my interview with him, he described them: "They are rolled on canvas so the surface has a canvas texture which picks up the glaze in a very interesting way and is much the same sort of quality as painting on canvas, except that one uses materials which change in the firing. What you put into the kiln has little visible resemblance to what comes out of the kiln."[81] He knew what those changes would be and often talked of the interaction of ceramics with geology, chemistry, and physics. In the same interview he said, "Physics is the firing process; chemistry is all the materials we use; yet we have to realize that those materials come from a geological base. . . . there's a marvellous fascination with colour, surface, texture, patterns, crystallization and all the things that have come through nature. . . . I've always tended to turn that interaction to a relationship with the landscape."[82] His slab bottles, part of his *Mocha Diffusion Series* depicting landscape abstractions, are thrown and hand-built black-stained porcelain, with white and iron slips and mocha diffusions in manganese brown, and reduction fired in a gas kiln at cone ten. Visiting his studio was akin to entering a science laboratory filled with an artist's creative energy, work in every stage of creation, and a pervasive spirit of excitement about his current experiments with glazes, forms, and sources for ideas. His love of land and nature was paramount.

Saskatchewan artist Melvyn Malkin's ceramic plates are likewise landscape-inspired. His edges, initially the surfaces for painting landscape, evolved into larger, flat, plate-like square surfaces on which he created aerial depictions of the prairie. The foregrounds of geometrically composed fields lead to a high horizon line above which is a pure blue prairie sky. These landscape works later became fully abstracted works evoking the patterns of prairie grain fields. Like painters Bruce Head and Winston Leathers, Malkin uses metallic glazes to allow for the reflection of light.

Glass artist Warren Carther, whose work includes large-scale architectural installations worldwide, pays particular attention to the geology of Manitoba. The Winnipeg airport commission, *Aperture,* 2011, created from stacked carved and sandblasted glass, is situated for travellers leaving the security area to see the prairie horizon through the sculpture's centre. The stacking of the layers of glass suggests the geology below ground. The shifting light sources, including natural light from the windows, airport lighting, and that which the artist installed within the sculpture, collectively and deliberately enhance the spiritual in the work. Carther's smaller glass sculpture, *Serendipity Tree,* 2018, made from stacked, sandblasted, coloured, and etched glass, also incorporates dichroic glass, which changes colour with different times of day and lights. When reflecting light, the dichroic glass reveals multiple shades of pinks and yellows. The image in this piece is taken from the view from a ninth-floor window onto trees below. It incorporates the light and landscape beyond, and the shapes and forms blasted onto the surface of the work evoke the natural forms within the landscape itself.

Landscape as Spirit

"Art exposes the basic residues of cultural myths, it reaches into the unknown layers of spiritual being."[83]

Never failing to provide artists with multiple realistic inspirations, the landscape also penetrates the spiritual. The concept of culture and the spirit being embodied in and on the land is frequently expressed by Canada's Indigenous and non-Indigenous artists. Portrayals of the land also embrace histories of exploration and land treaties. As we have seen in the work of Swinton, the spiritual permeates art both consciously and subconsciously. One has to question why; what draws an artist to explore the spiritual in their work? Is it reflective of their formal religious beliefs or the power of the landscape itself? In my view, it is both and is evident in realistic and abstracted renditions. As John Koerner expressed in the epigraph above, it "reaches into the unknown layers of spiritual being."

Spiritual aspects in the landscape are particularly important in the work of Indigenous artists. Alex Janvier's *Manitoba*, for instance, evokes the rich water systems of Manitoba, depicted with his many-coloured rhythmic lines through the vertical centre of the work. He underlines not only the importance of the water for life and culture of the region but, more importantly, its spiritual interconnections. The artist's rhythmic use of line and colour conveys the depth of history in the region over millennia and the paths of life and spirit it embraces. His colours are drawn from the Indigenous spiritual colour wheel, and his fluid lines have a sense of ongoing continuity. His 2018 major solo exhibition at the National Gallery of Canada revealed the substance of the strength of the artist's oeuvre. The exhibition overview noted that these "unique paintings, with their vivid colours and calligraphic lines, combine Denesuline iconography with Western art styles and techniques, such as automatic painting and modernist abstraction. Exploring the geocultural landscape of Janvier's northern Alberta home, his works on paper, canvas and linen reference Indigenous culture and history, including his own experience of the effects of colonization and residential schools, within a personal aesthetic that is universal in its appeal."[84] They certainly provide a summary for many of the sections in this volume, the artist's viewpoint being that "art truly is a universal language that can communicate any idea, any feeling, of anyone, regardless of their social standing, their religious beliefs or the language they speak."[85]

Indigenous artist Robert Houle also intrinsically ties the spirituality of the land and Indigenous culture into his paintings, as keenly apparent in his abstract, four-panelled work *Muhnedobe uhyahyuk* [Where the gods are present] *(Matthew, Philip, Bartholowmew, Thomas)*, 1989. The place that inspired him "was the object of a pilgrimage for the Native people of the area. The painting refers to a specific spot on a narrow stretch of a lake where the current ebbs and flows. As the water hits the porous limestone of the shore it makes a muffled drone resembling the far away sound of drums."[86] His use of colour—one panel being red, one green, one blue, and the last, ochre—is symbolic of the sacred place the work represents and the four directions. The brushwork is deliberate, and the horizon lines throughout the four panels are consistent. Shirley Madill notes that "*Muhnedobe uhyahyuk* is a work of re-appropriating and reclaiming Manitoba."[87]

Manitoba Indigenous artist Linus Woods has evoked the spiritual within and on the land and nature in a number of prairie landscapes, at times with abstracted eagle forms in the sky, or a horse on an abstracted blanket protecting the earth itself. In *Buffalo Runner,* 2011, his colours are primarily the traditional ones based on the spirit wheel, making the symbolism of the blanket particularly strong. Mother Earth, the source of life, is the physical manifestation and embodiment of creation. In depicting the land as a blanket protecting the earth, Woods visually talks about the need for environmental stewardship as well as honouring the Great Spirit. The patterns of the blanket refer to prairie fields and city buildings, showing the interdependency between the rural and urban, perhaps alluding to the complex contemporary issues as people leave reserves and move to the city. The work has further historical and symbolic depth, the horse having been essential to the life, history, and culture of Indigenous peoples. Woods's horses are personal as well as symbolic, as those he paints belong to his uncle, who lives next door to his Long Plains home. The abstracted eagle, like Mother Earth, is sacred and a direct connection to the Creator. Symbolizing grace, power, wisdom, and intellect, the eagle flies over the blanket, protecting the earth, and its wings cover the full width of the sky. Woods's inclusion of these abstracted, powerful spiritual meanings adds a depth of perception and a consciousness of the importance of the land to the physical and spiritual lives of Indigenous peoples.

The spiritual in the landscape also resounds in the work of non-Indigenous artists. The impact of Group of Seven member Lawren Harris's move to Vancouver's North Shore, in 1940, was especially significant to the place of the spiritual in landscape painting. He quickly became a leader in the Vancouver scene, galvanizing ideas and organizing exhibitions and wider community engagement with the visual arts. For years he hosted Sunday-evening gatherings of artists and musicians. They discussed art, culture, and other topics, and listened to Harris's extensive collection of music recordings. These evenings became weekly fixtures

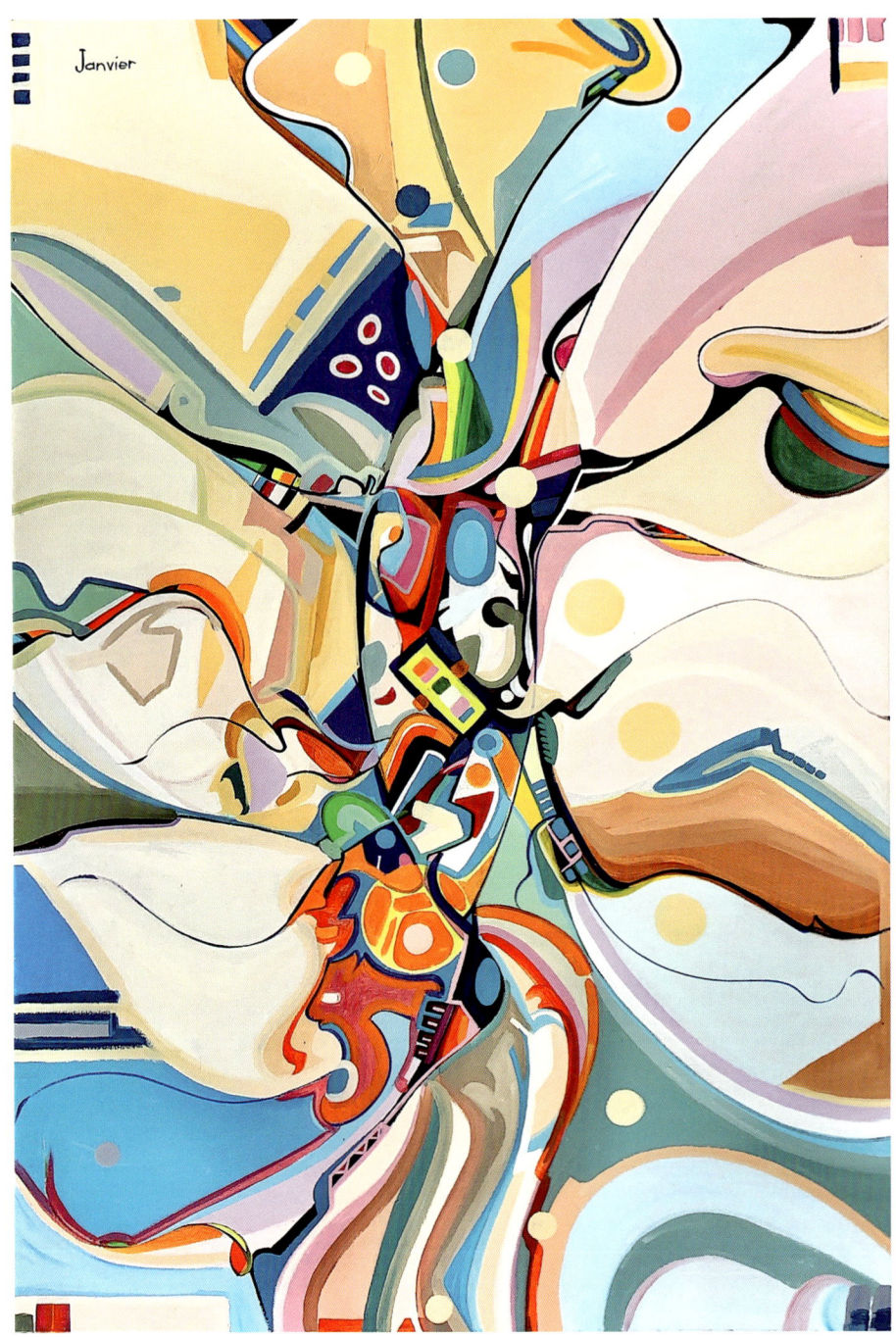

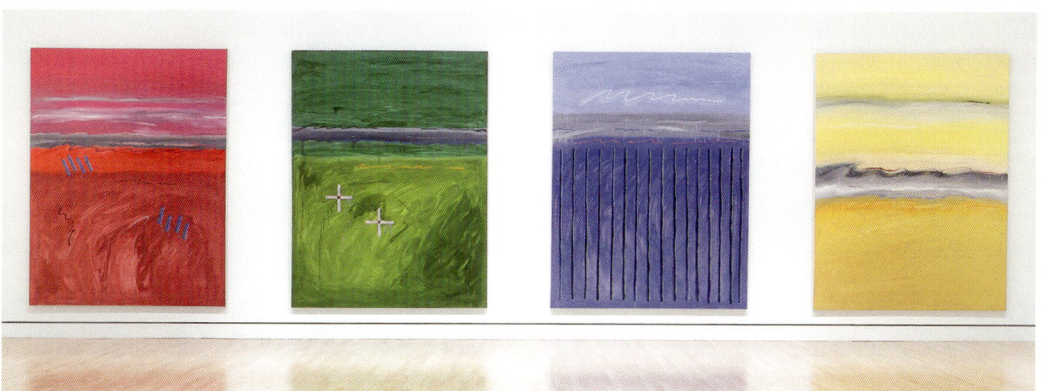

for those involved, including artists Jack Shadbolt, John Koerner, Bertram (BC) Binning (1909–1976), Joseph Plaskett, Takao Tanabe, and Gordon Smith; architect Arthur Erickson; musicians Frances and Harry Adaskin; and Emily Carr's executor, Ira Dilworth. The evenings, however, ended abruptly when the Harris music collection was stolen.[88] I asked several of the attendees if theosophy was a frequent topic and received differing responses. Shadbolt, for instance, said "yes"; Koerner, "no." I therefore cannot attest with any certainty as to whether theosophy was discussed or not.[89] Nonetheless, it was a pervasive aspect in much of British Columbia art at the time.

Harris's deep involvement with theosophy in the 1920s and 1930s, and with the Transcendental Painting Group in New Mexico, inspired his growing interest in abstraction. He admitted to Koerner that his interest in theosophy waned after he moved to British Columbia from New Mexico. In Vancouver his art became fully non-representational. Rooted in many ways in the mountain landscape, it achieved unity between experience and expression, and underlined the core element of the human psyche that reaches into unknown layers of consciousness and spirituality. Koerner quoted Harris that "perhaps the arts may help us realize the creative life in us and informing spirit, which sustains the universe, are one and the same."[90]

Lionel LeMoine FitzGerald, whose landscape works also often evoke a sense of spirituality, enjoyed his visits with Harris when he was in British Columbia. He, too, commented on the power of Harris's art: "A visit to Lawren Harris is always a memorable one. . . . To see a number of Harris paintings together and to talk about them with him, is to appreciate more fully what

FIGURE 3.27. **Alex Janvier**, *Manitoba*, 2008.

FIGURE 3.28. **Robert Houle**, *Muhnedobe uhyahyuk* [Where the gods are present], 1989.

163

he is working for and better understand them. They are serious productions from a serious mind. They are also the natural outcome of all his previous painting. His fine sense of design, beautiful restrained colour and exquisite craftsmanship, contained in the older pictures, comes [sic] to greater fruition in these more recent abstractions."[91]

It was clear for many that Harris's art brought thought, the spiritual, and the craft of painting to new levels, and a number of artists joined in those soul-searching philosophical pursuits. John Koerner himself had grappled with the definition of "spirit," noting that "artistic expression is deeply rooted in the spiritual sphere . . . the spiritual world is a reality just as the physical world is a reality and both worlds permeate each other. Spirit is the most delicate substance, at the other end of the scale from the substance of matter."[92] Koerner's thoughts on theosophy in the published version of his diary are interesting:

> Theosophy can be divided in two parts. One part was described by the Russian painter Wassily Kandinsky. He believed that human emotion consists of "vibrations of the soul." He wrote, "Words, musical notes, and colours possess the psychic power of calling forth some vibrations . . . ultimately bringing about the attainment of knowledge. In theosophy, the vibrations are the formative agent behind all material shapes." . . . The other side of theosophy carried the idea of mysticism further. Based on the writings of Helena Blavatsky, it led back to the art of alchemy as practiced in the Middle Ages and to astrology.[93]

Lawren Harris suggested to Emily Carr that she, too, should explore theosophical ideas, while also encouraging her to paint British Columbia skies and landscapes. She forsook theosophy, but her paintings certainly convey the spiritual. Carr and Harris met through National Gallery director Eric Brown when she travelled to Ottawa in 1927 for the Group of Seven exhibition, which, though she was not a member, included her work. Carr found artistic kinship with several members, especially Harris. However, her art remained unique in approach, execution, and spirit, and the spiritual was especially strong in her paintings of trees and forests. From a religious family, Carr was very aware of the difference between "Church" and the spiritual in nature. She wrote: "I longed to get out of church and crisp up in the open air. God got so stuffy squeezed up in church. Only out in the open was there room for Him. He was like a great breathing among the trees. In church he was static, a bearded image in petticoats. In the open He had no form; He just *was*, and filled all the universe."[94]

Doris Shadbolt articulated Carr's goal aptly and succinctly: "ultimate philosophical equation was a triad that encompassed God, nature and art. . . . Understandably, Carr, whose spirituality was firmly rooted in her temperament and her upbringing, was unaware that the simple reaching-for-God which directed her art and her life might be part of such a larger strain."[95] Indeed, for Carr, movement was a critical element in a painting. As she said, "The

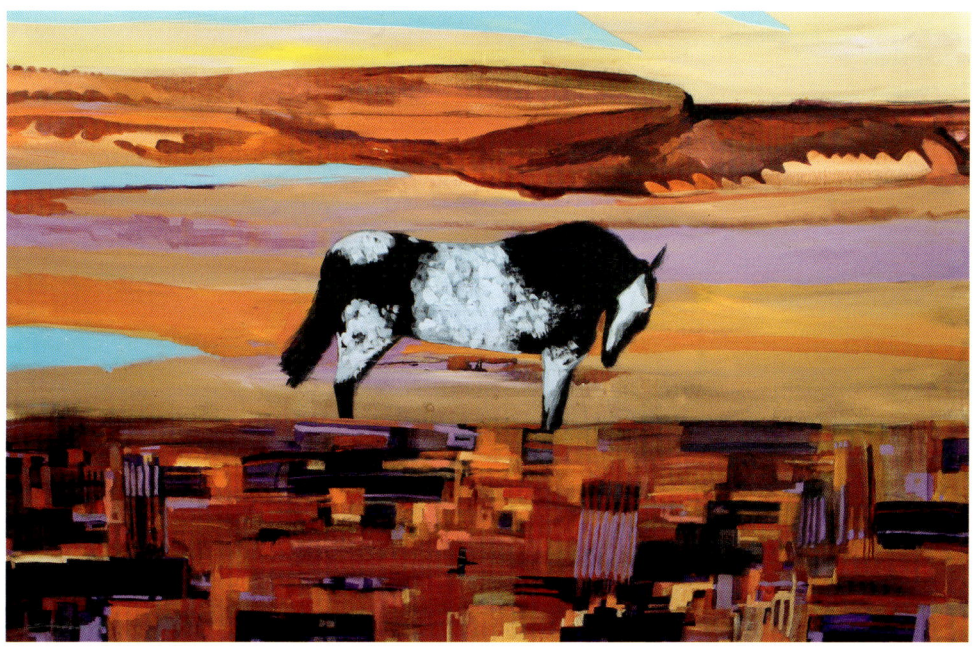

movement and direction of lines and planes shall express some attribute of God—power, peace, strength, serenity, joy. The movement shall be so great the picture will rock and sway together, carrying the artist and after him the looker with it, catching up the soul of the thing and marching on together."[96]

Lionel LeMoine FitzGerald joined the Group of Seven in 1931 and became their only Western Canadian member. His abstractions were primarily rooted in nature, the landscape, or still life. His December 1954 CBC broadcast underlined the importance of being in nature and observing it:

Naturally, this meant spending a long time on a single picture, requiring great patience to carry it through to the final brush stroke. However, all this concentrated effort did result in the accumulation of a greater knowledge of natural forms, and more sureness in drawing, making it easier to express ideas and emotional reactions.

I am now using this accumulated knowledge in some painting of an abstract nature where I can give more rein to the imagination freed from the insistence of objects seen, using colors and shapes without reference to natural forms.

FIGURE 3.29. **Linus Woods**, *Buffalo Runner*, 2011.

It calls for a very fine balance throughout the picture requiring many preliminary drawings and color schemes, before beginning the final design.[97]

In writing to critic Robert Ayre, FitzGerald noted of his own abstractions: "Subconsciously the prairie and the skies get into most things I do no matter how abstract they may be. Occasionally I get out on the prairie just to wander and look, without making any notes other than mental ones and always come back with an inner warmth from the familiar but always new feeling. Never a highly emotional reaction, just a sort of quiet contentment. And all this finally penetrates the drawings."[98] Not only did these feelings penetrate his lyrical and sensitive drawings, they also are evident in his paintings of the period, *Abstract in Green and Gold,* 1954, being a prime example. Its overlapping forms, shapes, and planes have an innate lyricism and flow rhythmically across the canvas, while the colour palette is that which had characterized much of his earlier work. Lawren Harris had written to FitzGerald in 1928 about his work in the Toronto Arts and Letters Club: "I particularly like the way you extricate a suggestion of celestial structure and spirit from objective nature in your drawings."[99]

That sensibility of celestial structure and the spirit from nature held through FitzGerald's art-making career. It should be noted, however, in discussing FitzGerald's abstractions, that nature, not the spiritual, was at their core. Colleague artist and Toronto sculptor Elizabeth Wylie said: "FitzGerald never chose Theosophy as a belief system and likely did not want to produce didactic art promoting it."[100] Philosophical spiritual discussions were frequent during the middle decades of the twentieth century, as was the great interest in Winnipeg in Walt Whitman and William Blake. With FitzGerald's friends such as Bertram Brooker and Eric Bergman, "he would have had numerous opportunities to discuss Theosophical ideas. Although he did not subscribe to Theosophy, nor to any organized religion, his thought was in harmony with certain Theosophical principles."[101] Nonetheless, this questioning and many of its principles made a mark on many artists' thought processes and their art, including that of FitzGerald.

The landscape was the basis for John Koerner's evolution into abstraction. Well versed in the work of many international artists, Koerner was especially inspired by the work and lyricism of Henri Matisse, the colour paintings of American painter Mark Rothko, and those of abstract expressionist Richard Diebenkorn. He found Rothko's work to be deeply spiritual. For Koerner, intellectual and philosophical thoughts and cultures merged, as he wrote in his diary: "Art exposes the basic residues of cultural myths, it reaches into the unknown layers of spiritual beings."[102] The merging and understanding of cultures, cultural diversities, and spiritual intelligence led to his multiple juxtapositions in his *Pacific Gateway Series,* which explores Canadian cultures and nature, with those across the Pacific Ocean. Koerner presented complex visual and philosophical ideas with apparent simplicity, reflecting his delight in Japanese aesthetics in art and poetry. However, it was the writings of the German philosopher Bô Yin Râ, as he told me, that gave him "insight into the objective structures of spiritual reality and

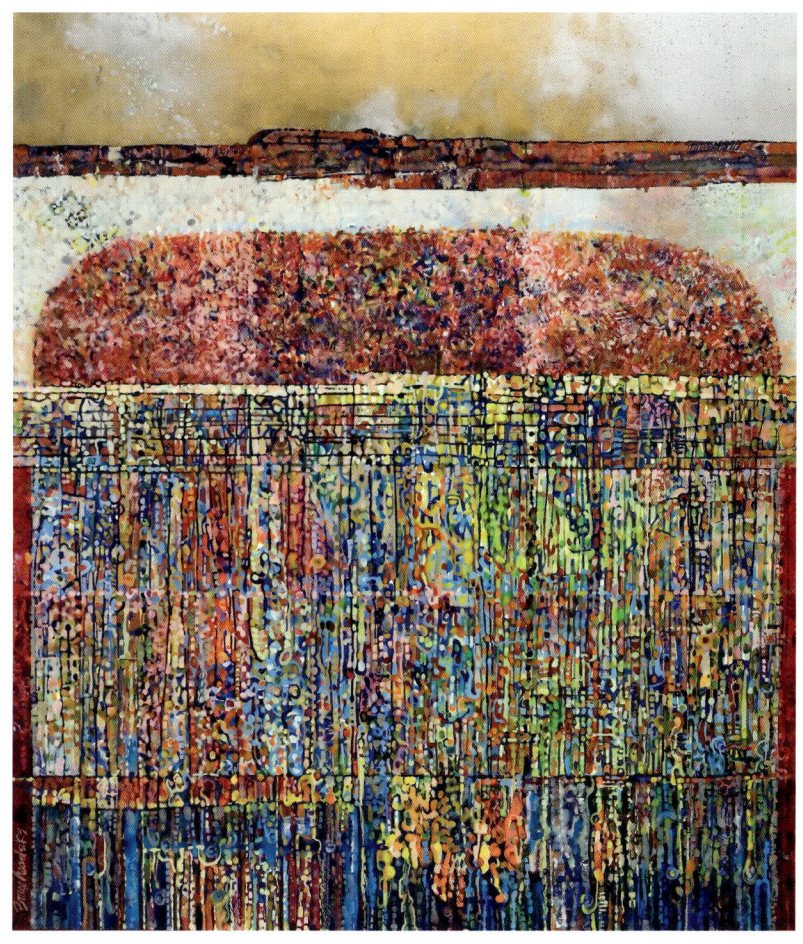

the illumination of the human condition and the connections with the spiritual sphere which permeate our lives."[103] He used landscape to express the connections between the human condition and the spiritual sphere, though he frequently emphasized to me that he "was not a landscape painter, but the landscape is often the vehicle I use."[104]

Koerner had left his career in corporate law in 1951 to become a full-time painter and teacher at the Vancouver School of Art. He felt his role as an artist was as one who transforms ideas, and it was the spiritual in the land that empowered his visual voice. He

FIGURE 3.30. **Bruce Head**, *Sleeping Giant*, 2003.

wrote: "Transforming colour into light from its natural opaqueness (luminosity). Transforming matter into 'changes' which emit the painterly 'message.' Transforming elements of the outside work into hints and inklings of the nature and structure (allusions) of the world of the spirit. Transforming the discovered form and the invented configuration or the fortuitous accident—the recognized form—into the intended main theme."[105]

Discussing abstraction in his published diary, Koerner wrote: "Abstraction is not an opposition to figuration but, rather, an enrichment of creative possibilities. Personally, I find that both figuration and abstraction can coexist in a work and reinforce it. Both offer innumerable ways of giving form to observation, experience and memory, feeling and intuitive invention."[106] This is evident throughout all of Koerner's art, his landscapes and pure abstractions, and every painting takes on a life of its own for Koerner, the unity of the physical and the non-material being paramount. His art is filled with lyricism, warmth, and peace, enhanced with his use of harmonizing colours. He described his process as one of:

> fermentation, a state of promise, and preparation. . . . When I do get to work there are no preconceived notions as [to] the final form the work should take. I only have a feeling about the direction it should take that cannot be verbalized but that has a great urgency to be given form. The work may begin with a very general idea and then each step relates to the next step in what seems an inevitable way. At that stage everything depends on full concentration and an alertness for discovery and instant reaction to what is happening on the surface. . . . One of the really exhilarating moments of the working process consists in experiencing what I call the "recognition of form." The work in progress changes constantly.[107]

He often talked of his full concentration as a mystery. In his *Pacific Gateway Series,* the term "pacific" means "peaceful," and the gateway is a symbol of transition from one place or culture to another, and of transition from this life to the next. The gateway might be a kimono, a torii, or Indigenous imagery, all connecting the spirit of the West Coast rainforest and beaches to the contemplative Japanese gardens, and engaging the viewer in multi layers of ephemeral or obvious meanings. Geometry is an essential element in his compositions, especially his *Balcony Series.* Koerner's philosophical symbols also include numbers: "2" and "5" are the symbolic links to nature and balance. He felt that numbers point toward an intellectually "almost unfathomable order in the universe."[108] The constants in Koerner's work, therefore, are the land, the spiritual, abstraction, memory, and cultural understanding. His deep belief was that "art exposes the basic residues of cultural myths, it reaches into the unknown layers of spiritual being."[109]

The silence of place and the landscape was Pat Martin Bates's entry to her spiritual abstractions, especially the winter snows in Alberta with its sharp and reflective light. The gold stalks of wheat piercing the snowy landscape were the pathway to alchemy in her art, and her

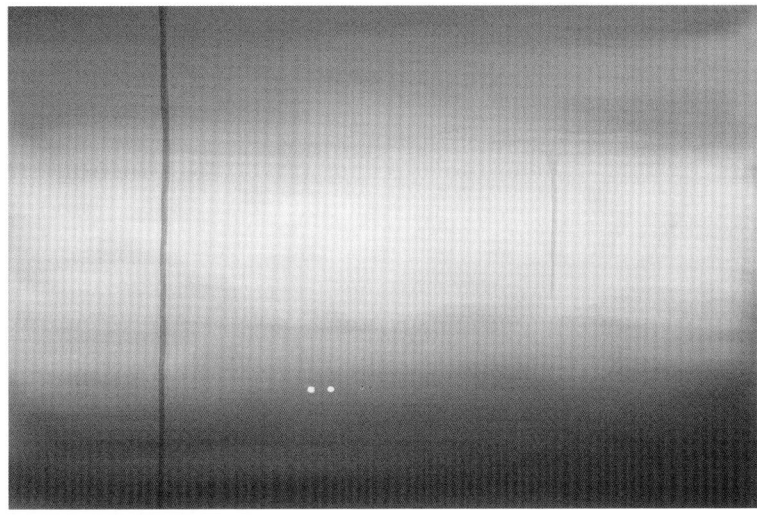

FIGURE 3.31.
Wanda Koop, *Road to Nowhere*, 2021.

alchemical investigations were philosophical, spiritual, and scientific, fusing chemistry, physics, metallurgy, mysticism, spiritualism, and astrology. Stars inspired her as a child, and certainly influenced her unique pierced prints and paper works, such as *China Night and the Star That Acts in the Stillness,* 1984. When not lit, this light box evokes a winter stillness in the blue-green shades of Chinese celadon porcelain, its pierced stars permeating the work as they are placed rhythmically throughout. When lit, the work becomes golden and the details within the stars' perforated forms radiate.

Lorne Roberts eloquently expressed the import of the landscape as spirit for Bruce Head when he wrote of *Sleeping Giant*: "The play of light and juxtaposition of the almost abstract with soft linear forms give energy and magnetism."[110] That statement could well be extrapolated to the work of many Western Canadian artists, given the many dimensions and qualities of the land in the West. For example, Winston Leathers saw both the water and skies as the places of spiritual connection. The majesty and power of the mountains and the many personalities of the sea are equally inspiring for artists' expressions of the spirit, mystery, and the metaphysical. It is clear in assessing the work of many artists working in many media that the spiritual in, and emanating from, the western landscape's many faces and facets permeates the art of Western Canada in myriad ways, and enriches the depth of expression in the nation's art. In addition to the essence of the spiritual in the land, contemporary depictions have expanded from the recording role of the early artists and, while continuing to draw from the reality of space, their work also brings the cultural roots of place to the fore.

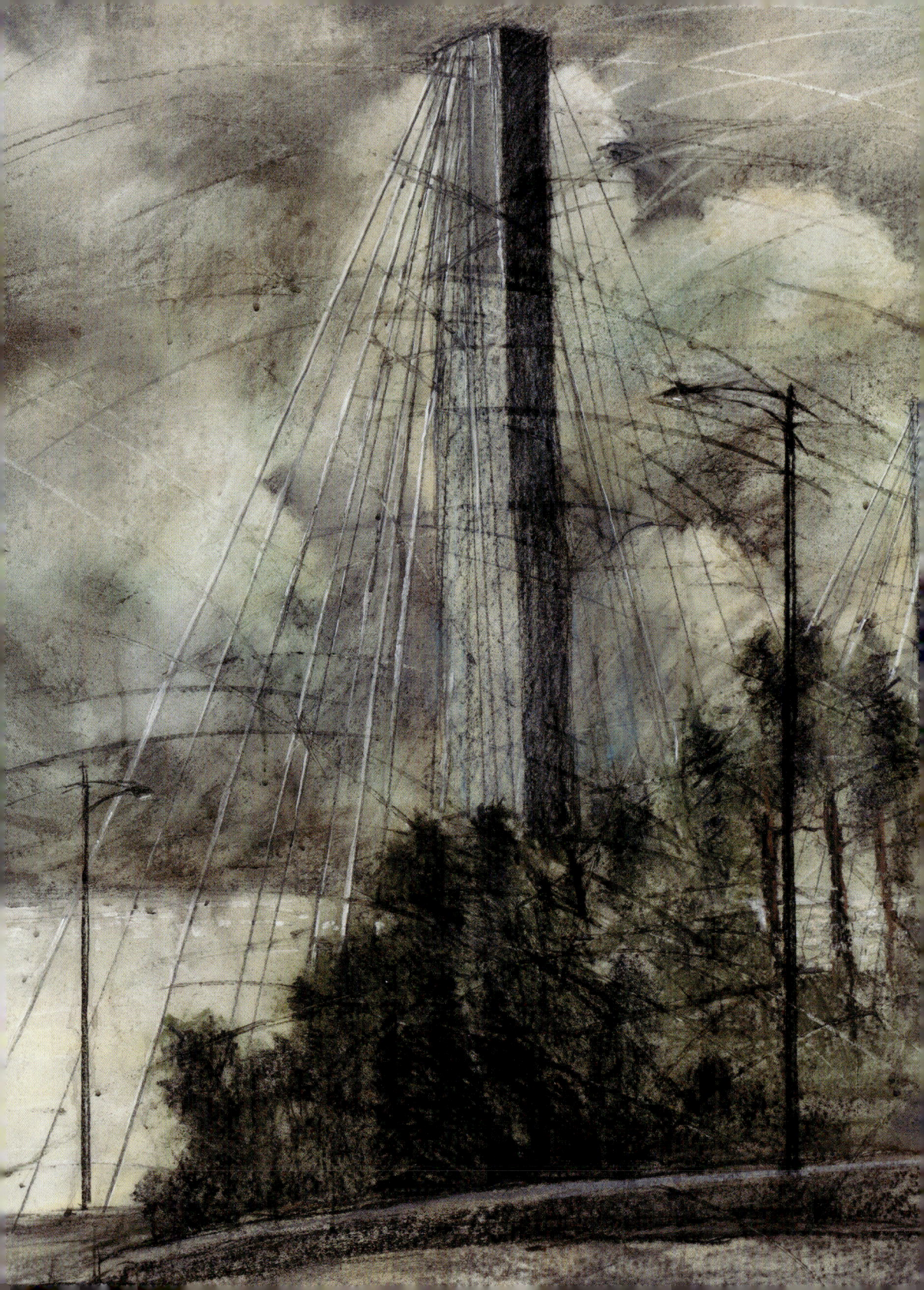

IV Urbanization and New Meanings

"Monumental buildings become castles in this new landscape of the late 1800s, designed and built with purity of form and honesty of materials, expressing the culture with power and dominance in the landscape. I respond to 'pure and/or original landscape' made manifest with human intervention. . . . Presence and memory link time and space." [1]

Human intervention in the developing, maturing, and flourishing of the West, its towns, cities, and industries, has changed many dimensions of this part of the country. Increasing urbanization in Western Canada in the latter years of the nineteenth century furnished artists with new subject matter: the depiction of urban centres and the resulting social shifts. Early portrayals of civic main streets, smaller prairie towns, and new legislative buildings and business centres became common in paintings, prints, and drawings as the western provinces joined Confederation: Manitoba in 1870, British Columbia in 1871, and Alberta and Saskatchewan in 1905. Early civic incorporations include New Westminster (1859), Victoria (1862), Winnipeg (1873), Calgary (1876), Regina (1882), Saskatoon (1883), Vancouver (1886), and Edmonton (1904). This growth resulted from the gold rush, the railway, and the growing economic importance of trade. The art of, and about, each was important. Washington Frank Lynn, for instance, detailed early economic exchanges between Indigenous people and the Hudson's Bay Company at the forks of the Red and Assiniboine rivers in *The Dakota Boat*, circa 1875, in which First Nations and Hudson's Bay Company leaders are shown in discussion in front of the teepee, with the Upper Fort on the far side of the river.

Jane Everett, *Race the Roaring Fraser I*, 2015 (detail).

Changing Dynamics: The Rise of Cities

"My work grows out of the city—I am an artist who is affected by my environment—I always reflect where I am immersed. The subject will dictate how I paint it."[2]

An artist remembered only as D. MacDonald, active between 1867 and 1897, painted his oil on canvas *Winnipeg Main Street* in 1882 when Winnipeg's dreams of becoming "Chicago of the North" prevailed. An early depiction of this Western Canadian capital city's business core shows its architecturally significant buildings and boardwalks on both sides of the street. The commercial activity of the city centre is clear, with the snowy road filled with horse-drawn hay wagons, sleds, and people of purpose. Three decades later, in 1914, British-born artist Cyril Barraud, employed by Brigdens of Winnipeg, executed two detailed etchings of important Winnipeg buildings: *CNR Station* and *The Industrial Bureau Doorway,* the latter being the first home to the Winnipeg Art Gallery, Canada's oldest civic art gallery, founded in 1912. These works illuminate the prominent architecture and business and social endeavours of the period. Depictions of city centres of large and small cities and prairie towns extended across Western Canada. Urbanization continues to be an important subject in contemporary expression.

Ina Uhthoff (1889–1971), a founder of the Art Gallery of Greater Victoria and friend and colleague of Emily Carr, depicted Victoria's downtown in *Street in Victoria* in 1945. She shows the wet pavements, the traffic and pedestrians, Victoria's characteristic street lights, buildings on the corner of Government Street, and indoor activity seen through shop windows. The block structures of the buildings fill the vertical height of the painting, and details of windows, rooflines, and corners underline their architectural significance. At the same time Dorothy G. Rice-Jones (1884–1970) painted *Government Street, Victoria, BC.* A night scene, her oil painting is redolent with reflected light and abstracted fluid shapes in blues, greens, and reds. The British Columbia Parliament Buildings in the background at the end of the street are the focal point.

Individual buildings feature in many urban landscapes, such as Maxwell Bates's pencil and watercolour *St. Mary's Cathedral, Calgary,* 1955. The building depicted was his design and shows his ability as both an architectural draughtsman and visual artist. The importance of the proposed building is emphasized with its steeple towering over the trees.

As cities grew, small towns remained key subjects for a number of Western Canadian artists, including Janet Mitchell, with *Cochrane,* 1942. Margaret Shelton also painted a number of Alberta hamlets, such as *Dogtown in July, Rosedale, Alberta,* 1949; as did Henry Glyde with works such as his watercolour *Prairie Town,* 1949. Glyde's RCA diploma piece, his oil and tempera on canvas *Miners' Cottages, Canmore, Alberta,* 1950, reveals the significant inspiration he gleaned from small regional communities. Each of these works shows clusters of buildings, fences, telephone

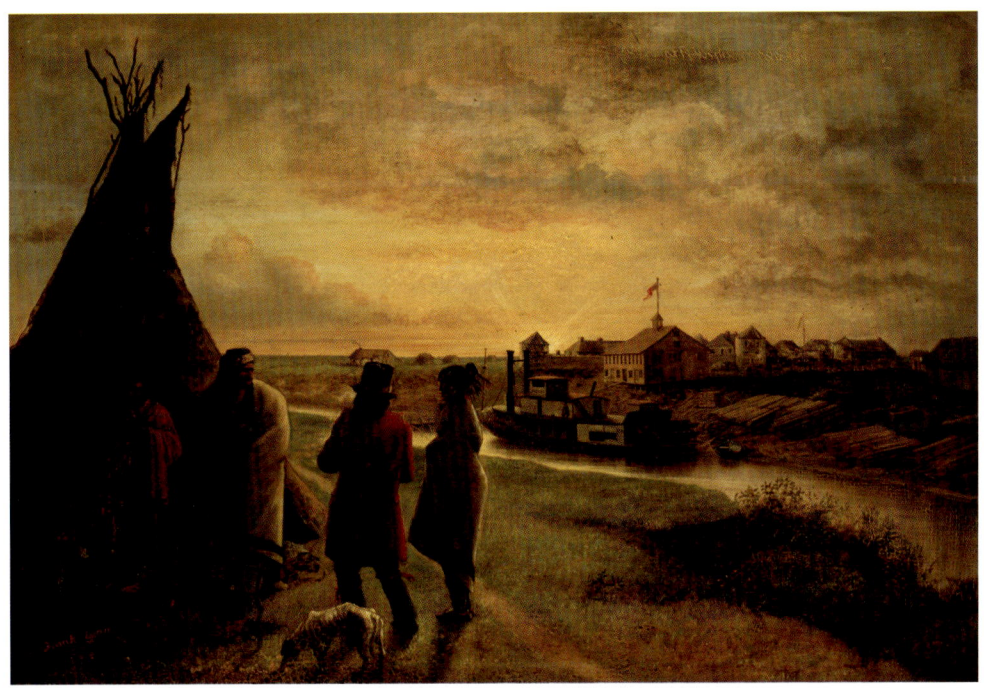

poles, and houses. Glyde included the general store as well. Glyde's colour tones—browns, greys, and greens, all from the land—convey Canmore's rural roots. His inclusion of farm-like buildings mixed between newer structures marks the progression of rural farm to town. In *Rosebud, Alberta,* 1946, for instance, we see figures walking along the town's boardwalks on either side of the wet muddy road. A grain elevator is prominent, set against the brown hills in the background. This watercolour evokes both the past and the changing present.

Renditions of small Saskatchewan towns by Bartley Pragnell (1907–1966) captured their unique sensibilities. Their houses and town centres were the subject of many of his untitled 1930s watercolours. Born in rural Saskatchewan, he studied with Lionel LeMoine FitzGerald at the Winnipeg School of Art and later lived in Edmonton, where he taught at the University of Alberta. The prairie sky, with which he was so familiar, is an important element in these works. So, too, is his knowledge of art history; his appreciation for cubism is evident in a number of his compositions. He frequently depicts buildings in geometric forms with overlapping placements. The industrial aspect of towns and cities was also addressed by artists at the time. In 1935, for

FIGURE 4.1. **W. Frank Lynn**, *The Dakota Boat*, c. 1875.

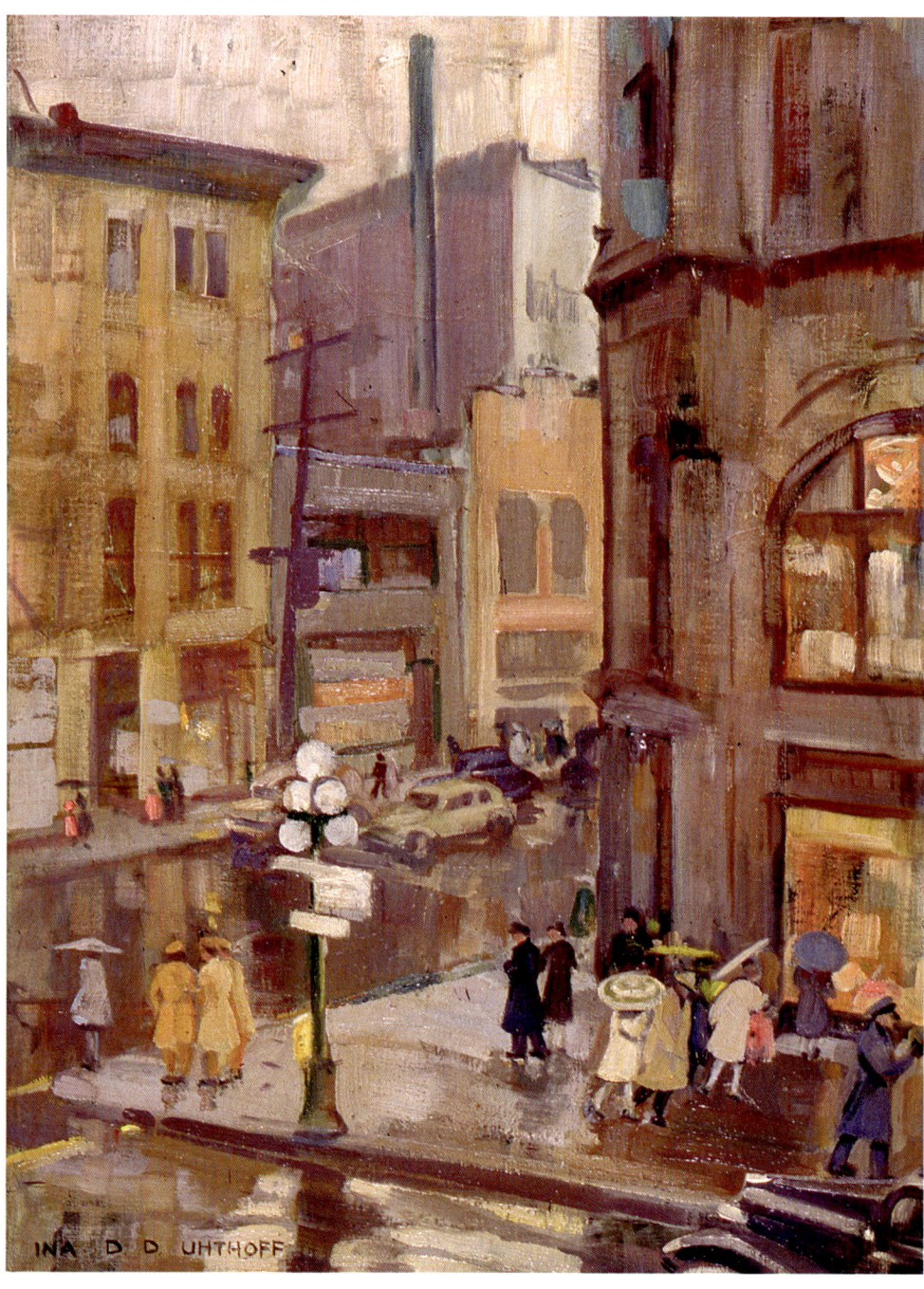

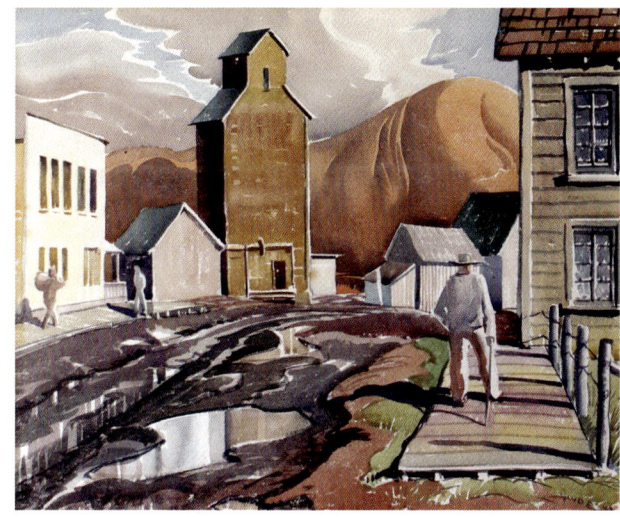

instance, Saskatchewan's Stanley Brunst did a compelling colourful industrial scene filled with buildings, a road, and multiple telephone and hydro poles. Robert Hurley (1894–1980) was also interested in the changing scenes, and in the early 1940s he painted Saskatoon's *A.L. Cole Power Plant*. That 1911 power plant is set on the side of the riverbank, and, occupying the centre of the watercolour, it is reflected in the river. A red line runs along the foundation of the building, underlining its importance to the community. Hurley continued to paint the rural aspects of the prairie in the ensuing years, as seen in his 1950 untitled watercolour of grain elevators and telephone poles in winter. The sky takes up almost 80 percent of the image. Artist and curator Terry Fenton speaks of Hurley's vibrant transparent washes as being important for the colour field painters who followed him.

Small towns were very much part of Bill Lobchuk's imagery, too, as seen in his pair of 1977 silkscreen prints, *Neepawa Noon I* and *Neepawa Noon II*. A dog lies at the foot of the gas pump, the central focus of both prints. The Neepawa scape is behind the pump. His 1988 print *Harvest at Sunset*, 1997, and his 1990 *Grain Elevator Sentinels* depict the national historic site of the five grain elevators in the Manitoba town of Inglis. The sweep of clouds in strong yellow and oranges in the former is vivid, and the scene is nostalgic with a horse-drawn wagon delivering grain to the elevator.

Changing perspectives of development in cities continue to be key subjects for artists. From his downtown Winnipeg studio window, Steve Gouthro (b. 1951) observed buildings

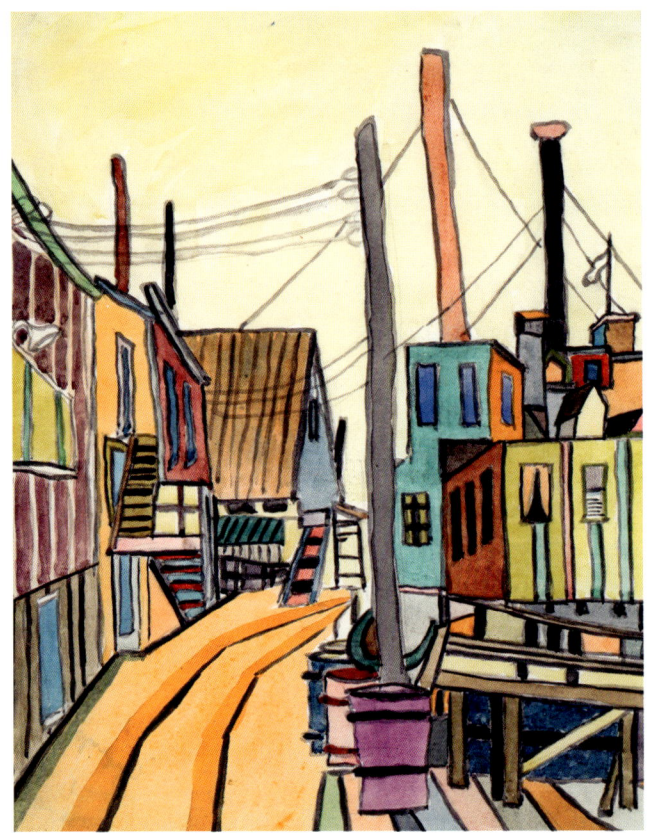

FIGURE 4.4.
Stanley Brunst, *Untitled (Bright Coloured Industrial Scene)*, 1935.

in the area and witnessed the demolition of the old and the construction of the new. In his monumental multi-panelled work, *Building,* 1990, he simultaneously documented the tear-down of the Child's Building (constructed in 1910) at the corner of Portage Avenue and Main Street in the heart of Winnipeg, and the construction of its replacement, the new Toronto-Dominion Centre, currently known as 201 Portage. Gouthro is intrigued with the human need to build and to build large. His complex work *Building* is comprised of thirty-five canvases and, when installed, it measures six metres high and nine metres wide. His use of multiple canvases evokes construction with bricks and cement building blocks, each panel and each brick carefully stacked to form the whole. While the work reflects on the importance of the building being demolished, it also looks forward to the significance of tall bank towers in contemporary society. It also portrays the noise, dust, and turmoil of construction in the present. Art critic Robert Epp wrote:

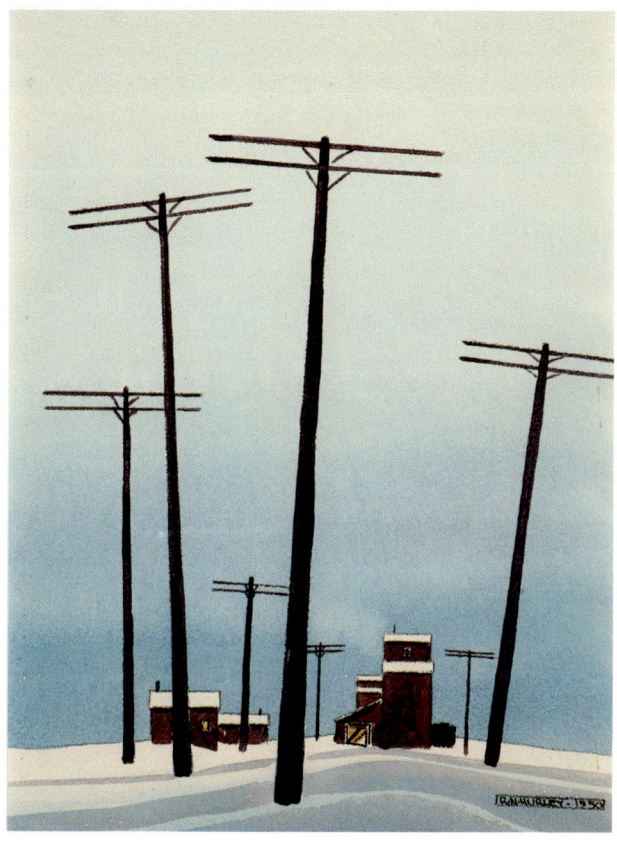

FIGURE 4.5.
Robert Newton Hurley,
Untitled, 1951.

Gouthro is also adept at rendering the many different forms and elements that make up the content of the painting: the architectural surfaces of brick and stone, cement trucks, cranes, clouds of dust, and the miniature men swarming around the construction site. He relies on a loose, painterly approach in which swatches of black, brown, and cream paint blend together to suggest visually the brick of the Child's Building.... The final form and content of *Building* point to the historical sources Gouthro used for the painting. The shape of the painting suggests a "ziggurat," a massive stepped pyramid which was the sacred edifice of the larger Sumerian cities of Mesopotamia, and the origin of the biblical Tower of Babel.[3]

Downtown studios afford many vistas, and Ivan Eyre painted *Winter Lot* in 1972 from his Winnipeg Donald Street studio, which he rented from 1969 to 1974. Of this work he wrote:

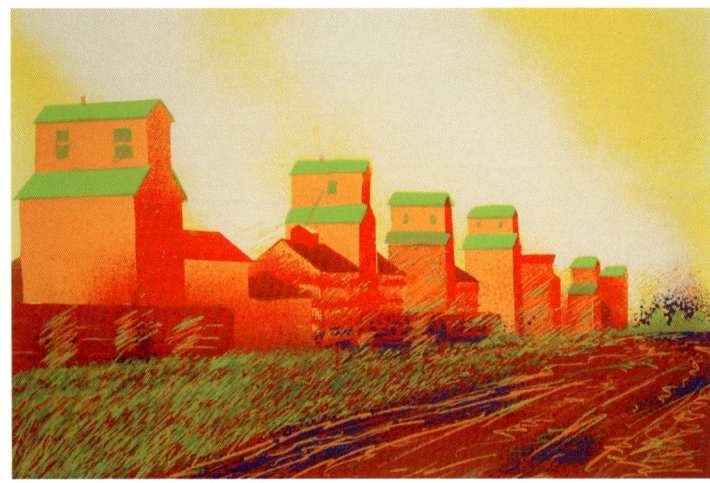

FIGURE 4.6.
Bill Lobchuk,
*Grain Elevator
Sentinels*, 1990.

"Directly behind the studio was a parking lot set between turn-of-the-century brick buildings. Hydro poles and wires and steel fire escapes lined the old alley. Storms blew the snow into piles along the lot fence and subsequent winds formed small drifts on the piles. I was drawn to these formations because of the similarity to some of the components of still lifes I had been working on."[4] This is one of his more realistic works, predating the mythical landscapes with financial towers in the backgrounds, a focus of his time in New York in the 1980s. *Flight Path,* 1987, for instance, is a complex work with masked figures in the foreground and towers in the background. Eyre describes that work's intent: "Stylized cloud patterns substitute for the helmeted figure's clothing then proceed to infiltrate the vest and shirt of the two of the front figures. This movement of clouds is the overriding feature in this work. Even the windowed building becomes part of the overall camouflage. . . . Any particular symbolism is lost in the abstract exchange of area with area, figure with figure, etc."[5]

These works evoke questions: Where are they? What do the individual components suggest for now and for the future? Eyre insightfully concludes with a comment that runs through a number of his paintings: "At best, I can suggest that the painting 'speaks' about our relationship with cities, with all their complexities."[6] This futuristic sense of place, combining a semblance of the known with the mysterious and surrealistic, fills Ivan Eyre's unique paintings. He says: "Place is very important in my work; it affects the work through the subconscious—on reflections—the reflecting part of working would bring forth the dreamy memory of places."[7] This approach is evident in many of his paintings, including those with tall corporate buildings in the background and menacing figures walking across the front or mid-ground of the composition, always juxtaposed with other related and unrelated objects strewn about,

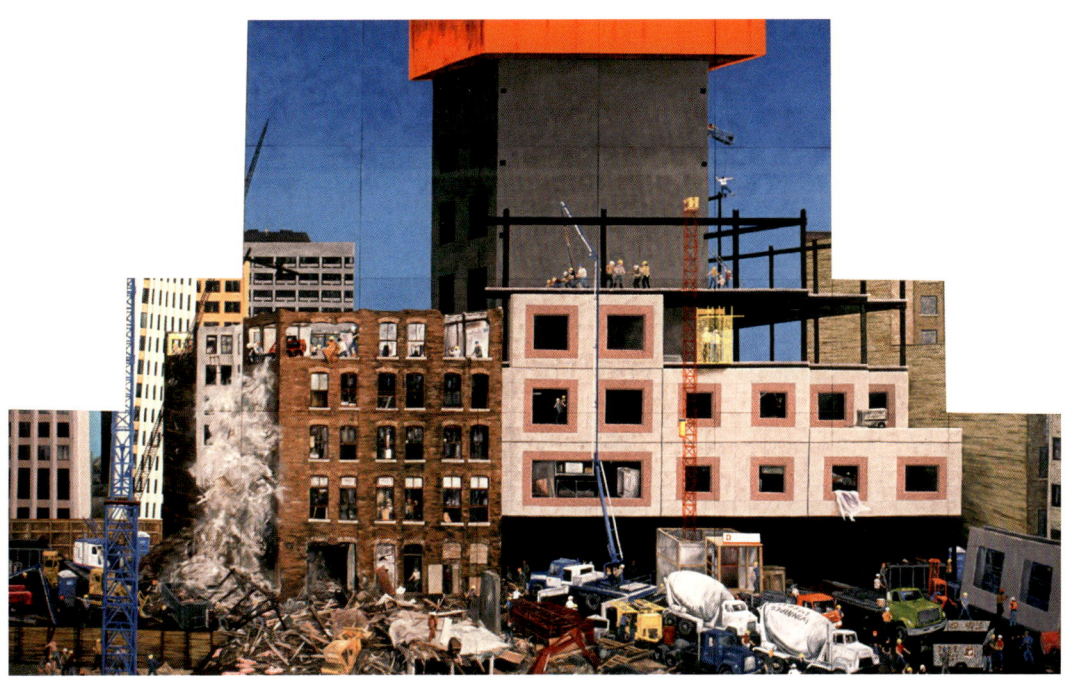

all included intentionally. Each points to the importance of cities, past, present, and future, economically, environmentally, and socially.

Aliana Au works in her downtown third-floor Winnipeg studio and paints the "stuff" and routines of life, the landscape, and, like Steve Gouthro, the vistas from her window. Canada is her chosen home. Born in Guangdong, China, she studied Chinese painting from 1967 to 1970 in Hong Kong with international calligraphy master Au Ho-nien. His teachings continue to resonate with her, and she often uses traditional Chinese painting techniques. She also uses the Western painting traditions she learned when she arrived in 1970 and became a student of Ivan Eyre, George Swinton, and Robert Bruce at the University of Manitoba's School of Art. At her hand, Eastern and Western traditions often meld in a single work.

Au's large acrylic on paper diptych *Bleeding Orchid I,* 2011, is the view from her studio, her Western place, painted in her Asian tradition. Her calligraphic paintings are structured and balanced, each bearing its own equilibrium. The sky in the left panel of *Bleeding Orchid I* is black; the sky in the right panel is blue. Immediately apparent is her use of wet paper, her varied

FIGURE 4.7. **Steve Gouthro**, *Building*, 1990.

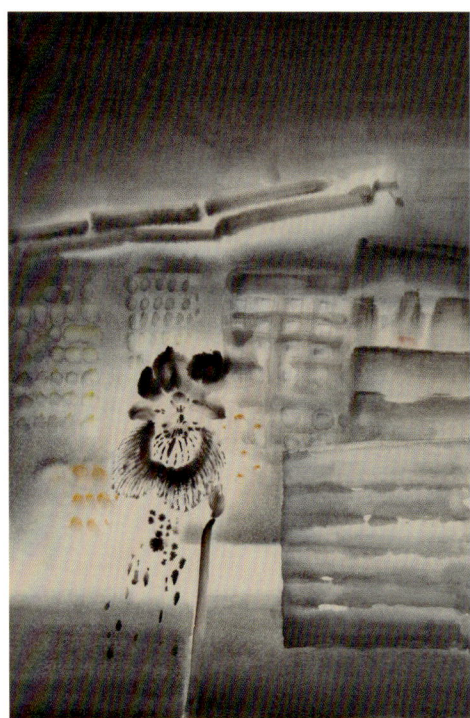
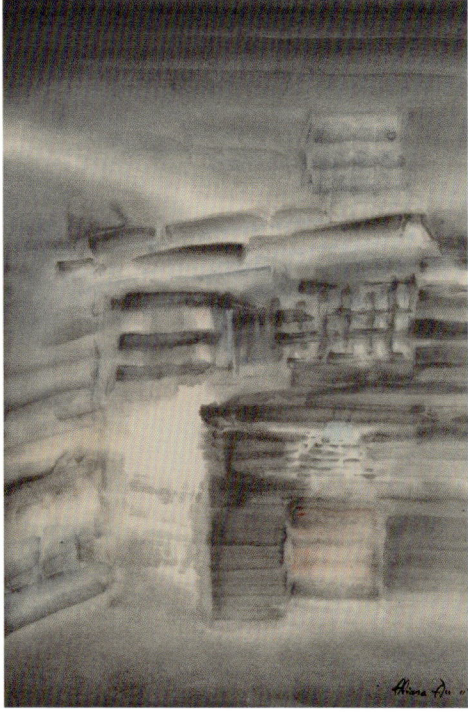

and carefully considered brushwork, and the detailed fine lines of the orchid. Every aspect relates closely to the elements and forces of nature, and links to the kinesthetic energies of the human body. By using both the tip and the side of the brush, she creates two- and three-dimensional effects in the work. Always in control, she balances restraint and the dynamism of her subject by varying the pressure and speed of her brushwork. Breathing of Winnipeg, *Bleeding Orchid I* has a dual meaning, being much more than a view from a window. Is she portraying clashes of cultures, or the lack of cross-cultural understandings? Why is the exotic flower bleeding? This painting reveals the depth of her personal and communal introspection of the external reflections of the realities she sees: "The world is forever changing. Events both near and far, large and small, are having a profound effect on me. Whether it is a conscious or subconscious force I am not certain, but I believe these occurrences affect my perceptions. Events such as the Gulf War; the tragic massacre of the women students in Montreal; the immense public interest and celebration of Van Gogh's life and work; and the startling

FIGURE 4.8. **Aliana Au**, *Bleeding Orchid 1*, 2011.

180

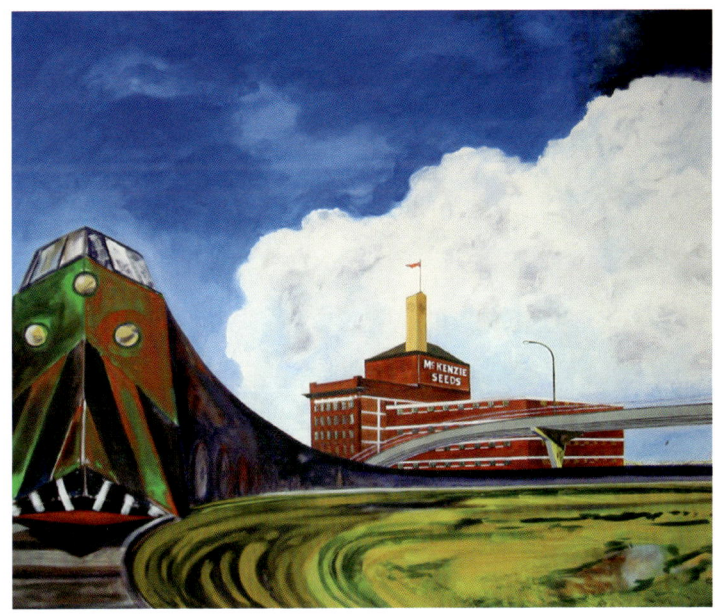

FIGURE 4.9.
David Owen Lucas,
*This Sideshow's
Leaving Town*, 2009.

realization of Tiananmen Square as a fight for freedom in China all challenge us to redefine our understanding and our humanity."[8]

Regina-born David Owen Lucas (b. 1944) also portrays aspects of the city, tying specific locales to a universal theme—the history and architecture of a place. "My work," says Lucas, "is about city/landscape experience with the human subject as viewer or interpreter but always implicit, never explicit."[9] He refers to "significant buildings and spaces as place-markers of time, territory and culture . . . reflecting the founders' vision and ethos, that is also woven into decay and regeneration as it adapts to a 21st century existence from a 19th century vision."[10] In his examining how buildings frame local and universal society, the city's underbelly, as he calls it, fascinated him. As he says: "I am in search of the incipient archaeology of the city—the urban underbelly. I look for the magic of the urban spatial experience—the theatre of the built form. The architecture is 'the set' which frames, conducts and contributes towards the drama of the performance and its evolving, morphing, physical manifestation. I am intensely interested in the perspectival and hyperbolic experience of space and the effect of the presence and power of the horizon line. It has a minimal/maximal ability to define and separate space and time."[11]

Scale is essential to Lucas's work; his monumental canvases underline the import and vulnerability of the built environment. For instance, as he describes, Brandon's McKenzie Seeds building "is all that is left in majestic monumental scale; it dominates, they have taken parts off but added very little."[12]

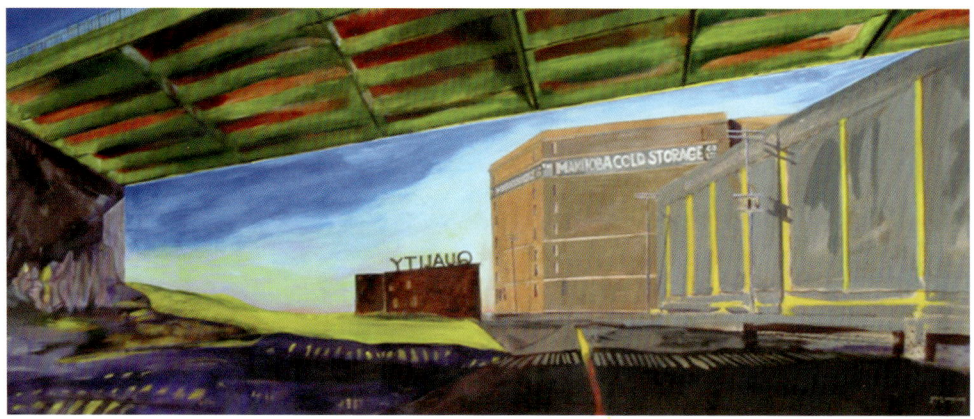

Bridges and lines of transportation, highways, roads, and rails linking western cities to the rest of Canada have also been the subject of artists' explorations. Roads are connections and divisions, and present both opportunities and dangers. Defining communities, they exude beauty and strength, as well as cities' ugly and less visible sides. Lucas's *This Side Show is Leaving Town,* for example, portrays a menacing train engine sweeping towards us. Filling the canvas, its size is symbolic, and envelops the viewer into the vortex of the city's history and present reality. Is the train a powerful malevolent force or the instrument of positive change?

Lucas's *Disraeli Undertow,* 2003, of Winnipeg's Disraeli overpass, shows an abstracted prairie landscape on the underside of the bridge. The ominous social aspect of life under the bridge is the artist's core message: "Under the bridge was a bit of protection from the elements and it was a gathering place for homeless who collected in companionship there and had a burning barrel with which to warm themselves. . . . It seemed as though the assembled souls were the undertow of society and discarded the way the very fine Manitoba Cold Storage buildings were."[13]

Calgary's Chris Flodberg is fascinated with what he calls "the banality, the beautiful and the ugly face of Calgary."[14] The everyday that fills his series of Calgary urban landscapes is about a city "commuting, its roads and freeways."[15] The specificity of place is evident in his 2017 oil on wood *Crowchild Trail and 17th Avenue.* The Southern Alberta Institute of Technology building is in the background. The pavement and turnoff comprise the major portion of the painting. The top of a lamppost is cut off, and the overpass and the landscape covered in snow set both place and time. There are no people or vehicles in this grey depiction. The dark shadows under the bridge add mystery and a sense of foreboding. Has society killed the natural?

FIGURE 4.10. **David Owen Lucas**, *Disraeli Undertow*, 2003.

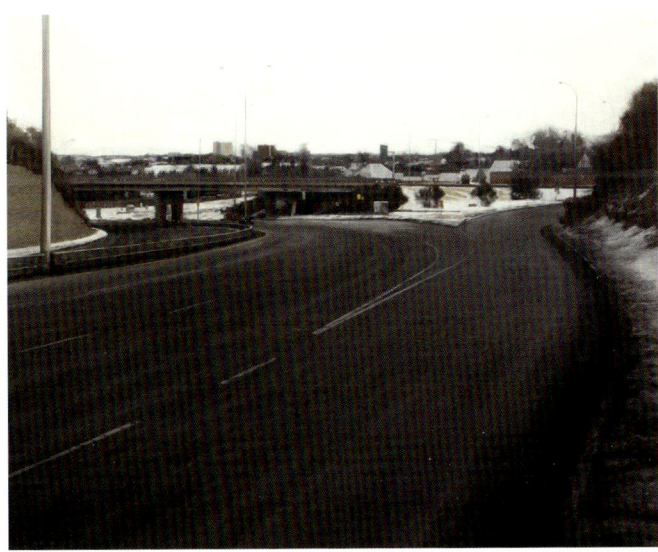

FIGURE 4.11.
Chris Flodberg,
*Crowchild Trail and 17th
Avenue,* from the series
Urban Landscapes, 2017.

Flodberg and Lucas are not alone in depicting bridges, the means of crossing rivers, gullies, and railroads. In his black and white wood engraving *Red River, Winnipeg,* 1933, Eric Bergman combined his interest in the city and in nature, but with none of the sense of anxiety Flodberg brings to his subjects seventy years later. The natural details Bergman depicted were as important as their urban setting. Rendering only the lower part of the tree trunks, with his characteristic short, crisp lines and dots, he captured the minutiae in the scene and in the texture of the bark. The light in the sky between the tree trunks illuminates the view of the bridge over the river, the print's primary focus. His judicious use of white attained a luminous quality of light and injected the work with the power of the spiritual, an aspect central in many of his works.

On the West Coast, Alistair Bell (1913–1997) in his 1947 black and white woodcut *Bridges,* depicts the view of False Creek in Vancouver, the two bridges being his primary subject. A boat passes under the bridge in the centre of the print, and an open swing bridge is in the distance. Vancouver's City Hall is in the far distance. Strong linear intersections in the water, the buildings, the land, and the sky create tension and movement.

More recently, Winnipeg's Don Reichert was fascinated by the reconstruction of the Redwood Bridge in his neighbourhood. He photographed its restoration in many phases of its reconstruction. He was a versatile artist, and his media spanned oil on canvas, acrylic, drawing, watercolour, and, from the 1980s onwards, photography. At times he painted over the photograph, rephotographed it, scanned and enlarged it. His later digital "computer paintings"

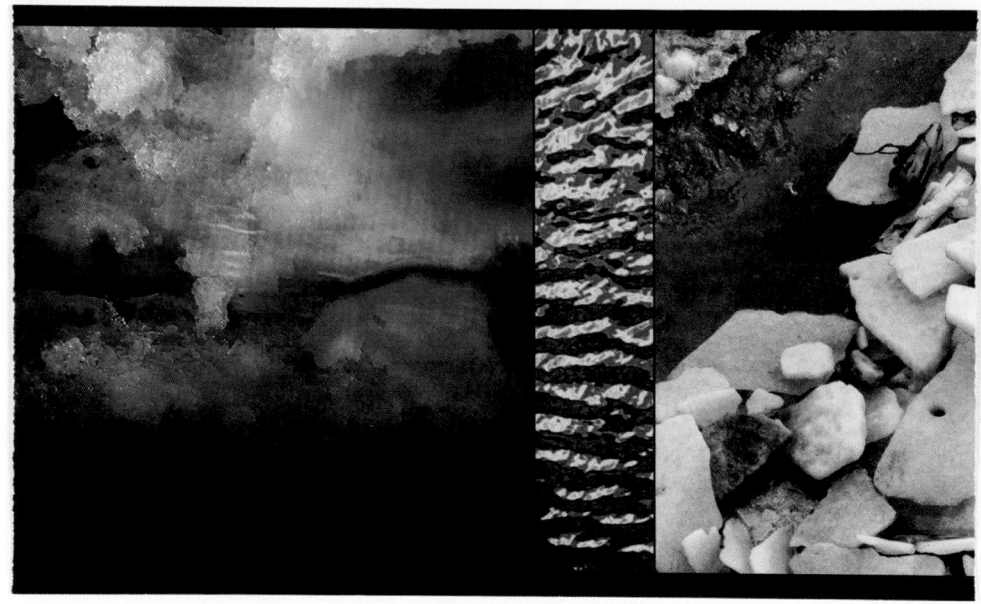

continued his preoccupation with his long-preferred subject matter: drawing our attention to the everyday. In his inkjet on photo rag paper *Redwood Bridge Reconstruction,* 2008, part of the *Redwood Bridge Series,* Reichert cuts and repeats, and then reverses, and manipulates the image of the bridge itself to achieve the rhythmic, geometric, mirrored reflections of the mechanical structure of the bridge in the water below. Patterns, colours, and light become the geometric triangles, squares, and polygons of the bridge. These complex, mirrored, intersecting patterns were foreshadowed in his late 1960s explorations in abstraction. Works like *Superimposition 1,* 1969, for example, were "not beholden to the hallowed surface of the canvas but beholden to the edges."[16] Forms thrust forward while others receded. Those thrusts are also dominant in the *Redwood Bridge* works decades later, evident in the intersections of the sky, water, and complex reflections through the structure of the bridge. The rich patterns delighted him and he stretched his technical possibilities as far as he could.[17] Winnipeg's Martha Street Studio 2008 Don Reichert solo exhibition statement read: "Reichert is able to take us into a dreamlike alternative where bits and pieces of the familiar are recomposed as an improvisation of the world as we know it and blur the line between reality and architectural fantasy."[18]

FIGURE 4.12. **E.J. (Ted) Howorth**, *Spring Breakup #1 & #2, 2008–2009.*

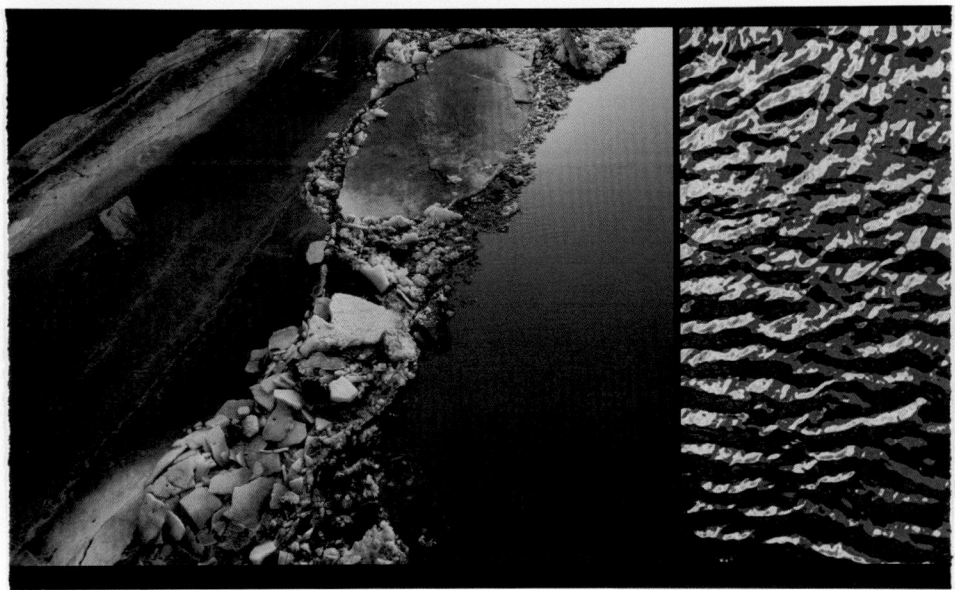

Printmaker Ted Howorth, Reichert's colleague, depicted the spring melt of the river under the Osborne Bridge in his Winnipeg neighbourhood in *Spring Breakup #1 & #2, 2008–2009.* Howorth states that he "explores the beauty and drama in everyday life. Print media assist in this drama. The changing of seasons, the breaking up of ice on the river and the solitude evoked by listening to the sounds of warm summer evening stimulate me."[19]

Combining his interest in the mysterious with the differing textures of the ice, water, mud, stones, and understructure of the bridge, Howorth uses digital images to which he adds screen printing. He deliberately mixes his printing techniques to achieve technical counterpoints that parallel his counterpoints of imagery. He achieves fine resolution in his art through the precision with which he uses Photoshop in breaking down details within his image. Screen printing on top allows him to continue to add layers of colours. Howorth commented: "The creation of my prints involves two independent processes. There is the creation of the idea and the printing element that manifests this idea. Both parts are equally important to achieving the finished piece."[20]

In Kelowna, prolific artist Jane Everett works quickly. Her surety and innate sense of line and movement are evident throughout her oeuvre. As discussed earlier, she often starts with a photograph of a place like the Port Mann Bridge, or a reflection, or specific light, and she is

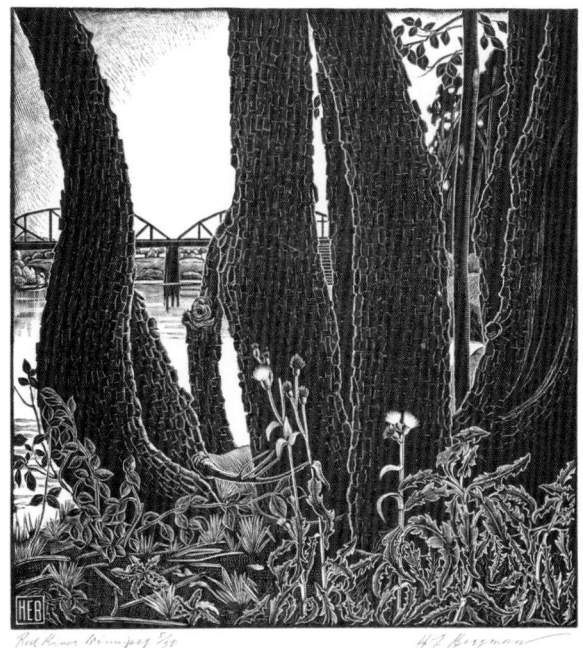

Red River Winnipeg 5/50

H.E. Bergman

selective about the details or sensitivities she pulls from her photographic image. She paints and draws on a variety of materials—canvas, linen, paper, and vellum—and achieves a particularly strong, individual voice with her technique of combining pastel and fixative on vellum. The way in which she layers colour on and into the paper or vellum, with the drips of fixative, enhances the overall mood of a work, and fills her subjects with immediacy, depth, rhythm, strength, and energy. In her statement entitled *Message and Meaning,* she wrote: "In my *Port Mann* series I believed my subject was the half-built bridge. The earlier drawings focus on the cranes and equipment, celebrating the hardscrabble mess of the construction site, but as the series progressed the rain forest began to assert itself."[21] The mood and power of the wind and rain are augmented by her use of an eraser to draw the fixative over the pastel, thus creating lines of force across the sky. The white diagonal lines of the structure of the bridge in the foreground fill the vertical height of the piece, further enhancing the movement in the composition and tying all the elements together. There is greater focus on the terrain under the bridge than on the actual bridge itself.

Everett's initial realistic renderings become increasingly gestural as she works, and result in truly impressionistic sensibilities. As curator Barbara Tyner writes: "[Everett's] tools are twilight greyscale—the subtraction of colour—and the erasure of complete narrative and resolved form.

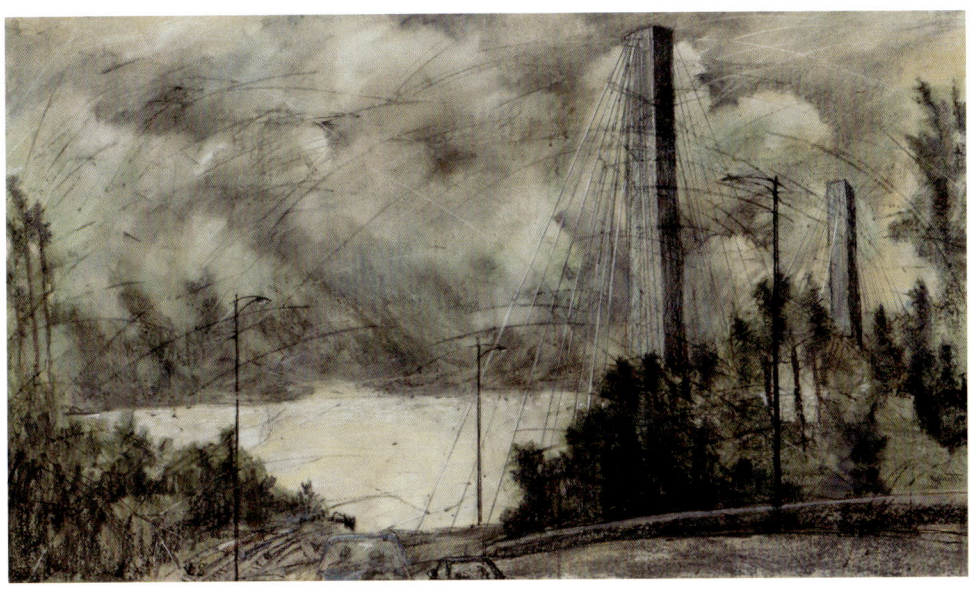

Erasure imbues the works with not just the physical tonal variations of her sooty media, but temporal gradations that speak to the unfixed-ness of memory and dreamtime. What is unseen gains psychological heft. Everett is deft with her eraser, motion-charging her works, carving lines in charcoal-stained surfaces, subtracting direct references."[22] For Everett, reflection of light and water is both physical and impressionistic. As she says: "Studies of light are very important to any practice. . . . Some paintings have nothing but colour and texture left."[23]

The feeling of wind was captured by Calgary-born Philip Surrey (1910–1990) in his charcoal and white chalk drawing from the 1930s, *Windy Day.* Like Everett's, the artist's use of white creates tension—white lines on the road come to a sharp angle in the lower right foreground, and crosswalk signs are the only other white in the work, giving contrast in an otherwise limited palette. The energy exerted by the pedestrians he depicts, leaning into the wind as they cross the road, their clothes swirling in the wind, underlines the wind as the subject of the work. In contrast, two stationary cars in the background are set off by the buildings, reminiscent of theatre sets. Both Everett and Surrey effectively use their restrained palettes to increase the dominant impact of the weather.

Changing civic landscapes and the demolition of the old are featured in much of John Taylor's art. His detail-filled photographs mark significant urban and industrial change. His

FIGURE 4.14. **Jane Everett**, *Race the Roaring Fraser I,* 2015.

187

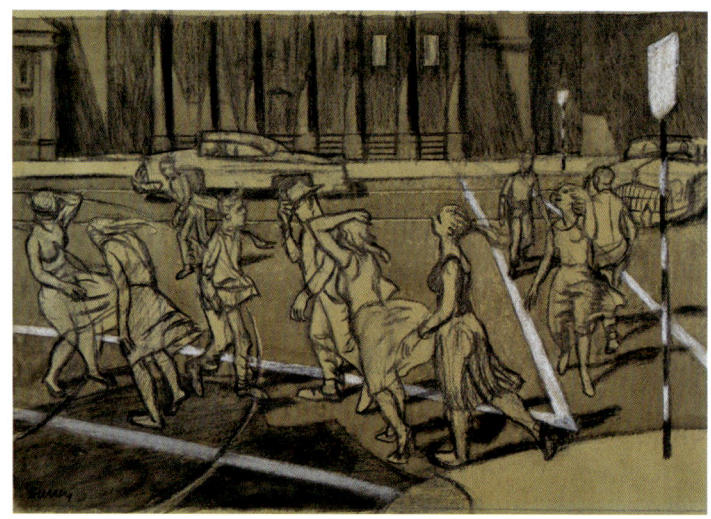

FIGURE 4.15.
Phillip Henry Surrey,
*Windy Day "Street
Scene,"* n.d.

Blue Bridge Series, for instance, documents the 2018 tear-down of Victoria's iconic, almost 100-year-old Blue Bridge. He expressed his goal in creating his photographic narrative of this historic structure: "I wanted to reflect on its sculptural form isolating the abstract overlay of beams, pattern and texture."[24] The series also gives insights into the bridge's technical workings, the kinetic functions of raising and lowering the deck that enable boats of all kinds to enter the Inner Harbour. He captures its texture, the rust, bolts, and myriad details, through his overlapping lines, angles, and forms. Taylor similarly depicted the demolition of Victoria's Memorial Arena: "My objective in witnessing the deconstruction of Victoria Memorial Arena was to observe the conceptual process of fragmentation and abstraction reverting order into chaos. These sequential borderless composite images reveal planes of intersection where memory and time seem to collide in an otherworldly landscape."[25] His triptych *Memorial Arena,* with each panel at a different height, evokes the staged process of its takedown. The view of the city beyond underlines its civic importance as a people place in British Columbia's capital city. Many works in this series depict the dust and noise of demolition and the wet of the rain. The near details, like the bleachers still in evidence, are juxtaposed with distant buildings. The textures and angles are multidimensional and complex, portraying many perspectives, especially in the works of three or five panels.

Scott Stephens Benesiinaabandan, a Manitoban-born Anishinabe artist, creates visual discussions of urban connections and meanings. His digital prints challenge issues of place, memory, and crossover cultures. He created his *interland:memories* series during his 2014 residency in Sydney, Australia. His artist's statement notes: "I was spending a lot of time

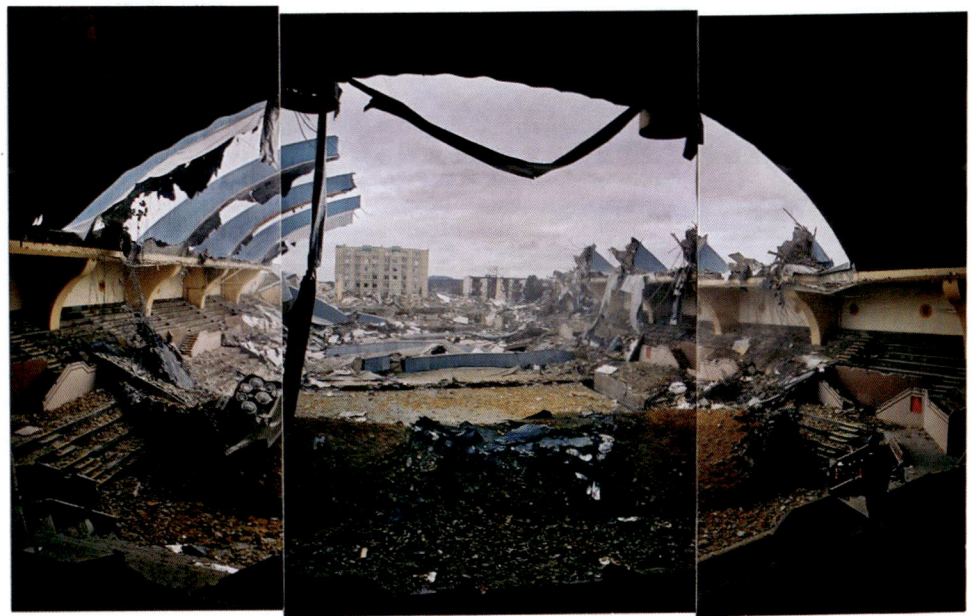

thinking of ideas of land, migration and translocation and how these inform and shape ideas of Indigeneity from a global perspective." In *interland:memories no3* Benesiinaabandan includes one of his earlier *Alien Landscapes,* 2010, in the middle of his portrayal of a park in Sydney. The juxtaposition of an aerial view of a snowy urban landscape, perhaps real, perhaps imaginary, on the lush vegetation of Sydney emphasizes the crossovers of Indigenous cultures through urban imagery. Throughout his work he examines key questions and understandings core to Canada's reconciliation actions the country must resolve.

The future for urban living does not escape artists' imagination and canvases, either. Winnipeg's Eleanor Bond (b. 1948) explored that future world in a number of her works, including her oil on canvas *Rotterdam Pioneers New Technologies for a Subterranean Eco-suburb, an Environment with Clean Air, Clean Water and Abundant Daily Sunshine,* from the series *Cosmoville,* 1995. Throughout her art she creates spaces that overlay reality, illusion, and metaphor. As the judges said when this work received the York Wilson Prize: "For over a decade she has been exploring the concept of a 'future world' in her paintings, presenting fictional narratives that cannot easily be separated from the harsh reality of living in a post-industrial, technological

FIGURE 4.16. **John Taylor**, *Victoria Memorial Arena Deconstruction*, from the series *Destruction of Memory*, n.d.

189

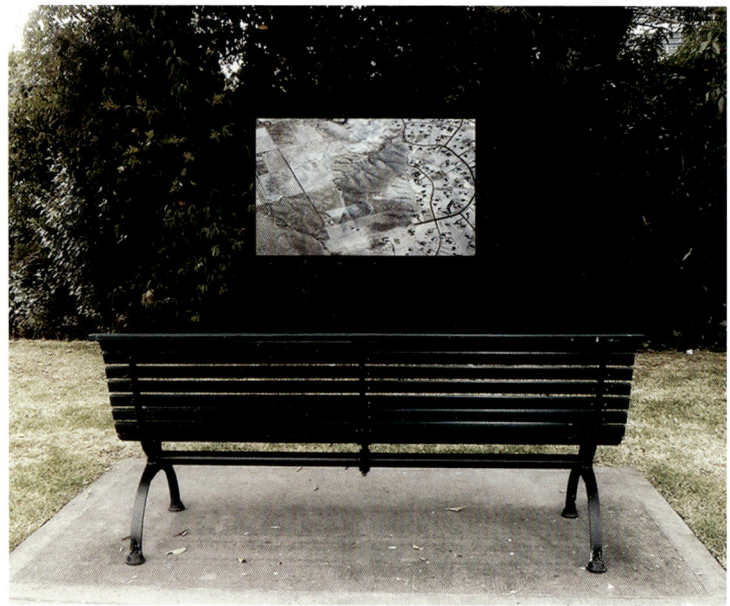

FIGURE 4.17.
Scott Benesiinaabandan, *interland:memories no3*, 2014.

world."[26] She depicts place and essence of community but does so in an illusionary manner, combining the known and the unknown, especially apparent in *Offshore Barge Draws the Beach and Sailing Communities*.

Bond reflects on contemporary concepts of community and place in her large unstretched canvases. She shares her interest in the sensibilities and connections among public and communal spaces, and personal thoughts and emotions. Futuristic in scope, her work explores the concept of space by using multiple perspectives, strong, fluid brushwork, movement, and her vibrant, pure colour. The viewer is faced with current societal workplace and living issues in these portrayals of her imagined future urban environments. These imaginary places are neither fact nor fiction. As metaphor, they occupy the space between reality and illusion. In the Winnipeg Art Gallery's *Future Cities and Virtual Cities Project,* Bond's 1997 oil on unstretched canvas *Shared Space in the Underground City* was described as

> representations of city spaces where chaos is blurred and transmuted. Using a bird's eye view, she destabilizes her subject and alters viewers' perceptions thereby creating a

FIGURE 4.18. **Eleanor Bond**, *Offshore Barge Draws the Beach and Sailing Communities*, 1989.

FIGURE 4.19. **Eleanor Bond**, *Departure of the Industrial Workers*, from the series *Work Station*, 1985.

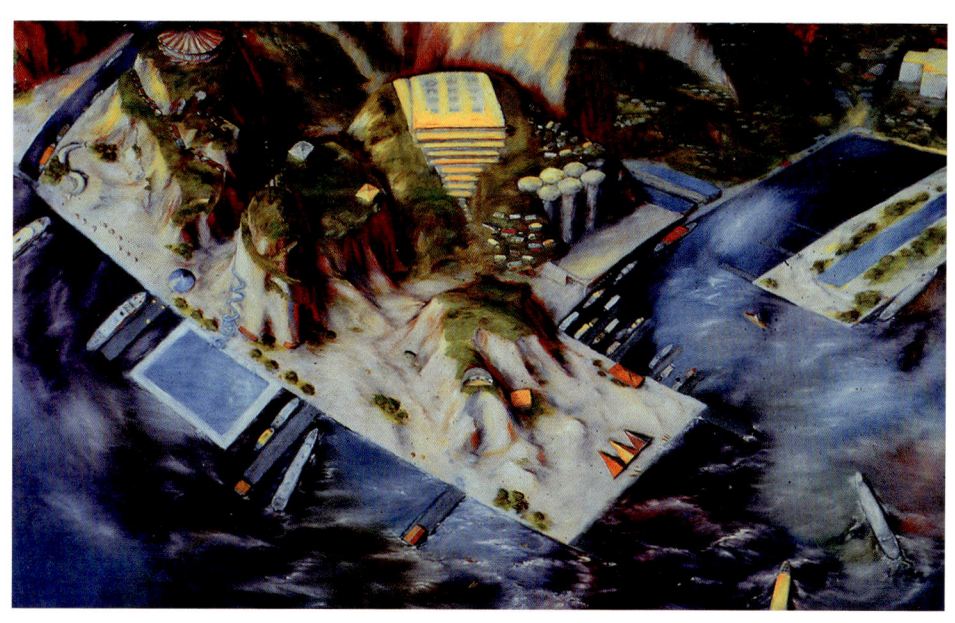

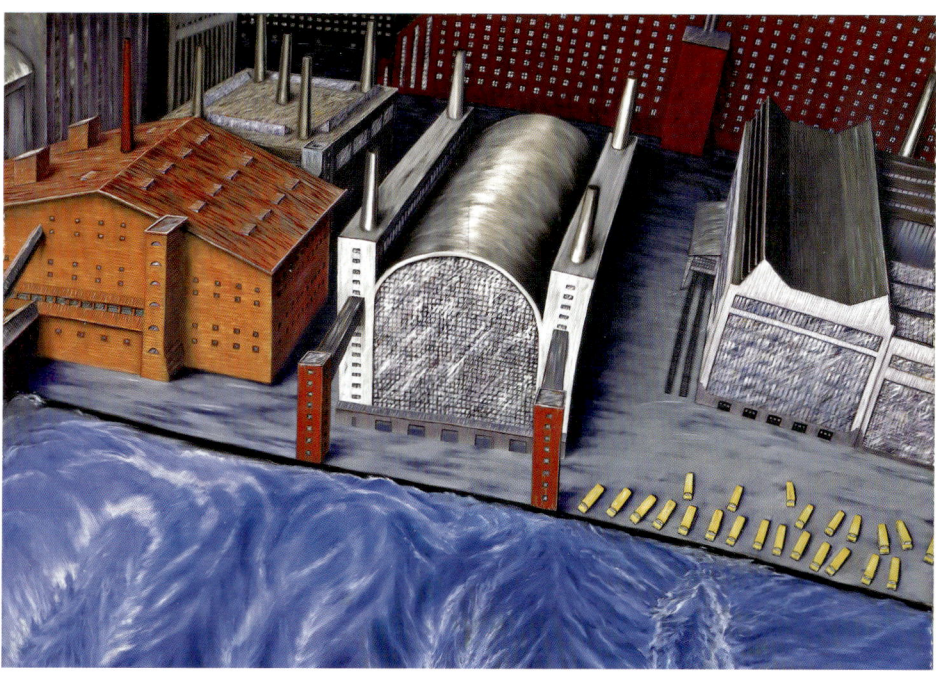

sense of vertigo. Her cities appear ambiguous, compressed, even anxious. Her paintings are distinguished by the precarious balance between the representation of the familiar universe, marked by the uncertainties of technological post-industrial society and the depiction of an unreal world, whose impact on the viewer belongs more to the realm of the imaginary. The futuristic aspect of her fictional sites holds our attention as she explores the ideas and contradictions in the contemporary city.[27]

Eleanor Bond's 1985 oil on canvas *Departure of the Industrial Workers,* from her *Work Station Series* is futuristic, showing the dehumanizing aspect of industry and much of urban life, almost a soullessness. She juxtaposes reality and unreality; the suggestion of the known with that of illusion, evoking questions as to the place of the human in work as the world is increasingly technological. Georgie Wilcox's 1939 *Western Industries, Steel Pour, Vulcan Iron Works* and Steve Gouthro's *Steel Mill Series* of the early 2000s, on the other hand, depict the reality of the heat and the physicality of the work.

Cities, realistically portrayed or futuristically imagined, force viewers to think about their own place and their contributions to the urbanscape and urban lifestyles. Regardless of the decade in which works were created, or what part of the West they depict, they collectively document the rapid changes of the built environment and resulting societal impacts.

Neighbourhoods: Streetscapes and Back Lanes

"Just living in Saskatchewan from 1950 to 1980—that's really what these paintings are about."[28]

The depiction of specific neighbourhoods comprises a particularly important aspect of Canadian art, recalling personal and communal nostalgia and linking past to present. Artists across Canada have presented intimate and distinctive portrayals of houses, interiors, gardens, and back lanes over many decades. In the four western provinces, neighbourhoods have been frequent subjects for more than a century. Perhaps the best known are by Lionel LeMoine FitzGerald in Winnipeg and, more recently, Wilf Perreault (b. 1947) in Regina. However, they are not alone.

The 1936 pencil drawing *A Backyard in Downtown Vancouver* by Edward J. Hughes (1913–2007) is a simple, intimate work showing a car in front of a wood-panelled house that boasts a small porch and chimney. The tracks of the car lead the viewer's eye to the automobile in the centre of the drawing. Debris and sundry objects are littered in the yard on either side of the car. A few years later, in 1939, Jack Shadbolt did a strong watercolour and graphite work entitled *Vining Street, Victoria,* proffering the view of the upper portion of houses against each other with

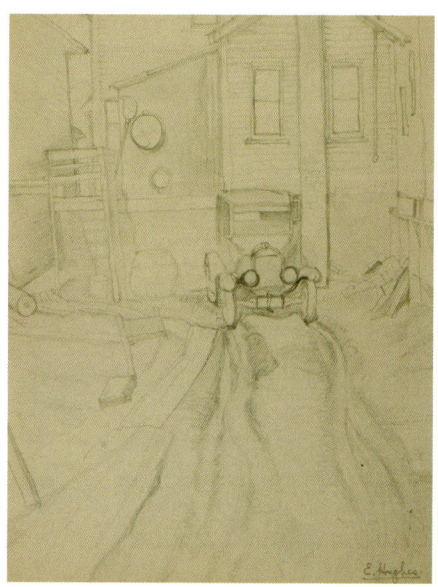
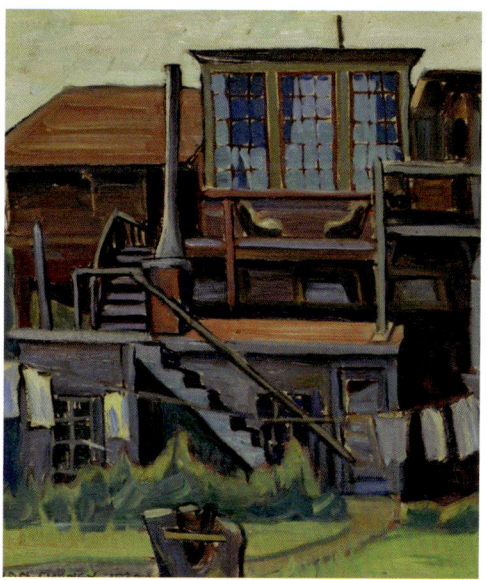

stylized trees and sky in both the background and the foreground. In Shadbolt's work, colour builds the composition of cubist shapes and forms.

Lionel LeMoine FitzGerald's neighbourhood houses, garages, and back lanes are well known, and include *Doc Snyder's House,* 1931, and *Williamson's Garage,* 1927. Both are winter scenes, and the multiple colours in the snow reflect the light from the sky. Trees link the foreground with the background and their trunks are depicted in his characteristic style with shading on the edges enhancing their three-dimensional volume. The branches reach beyond the upper edges of the painting. FitzGerald imbues the trees with the sense that they are actually growing, just as he was encouraged to do when he studied at the Art Students League in New York. Some of his trees take on almost human-like sensibilities. He started painting *Doc Snyder's House* at Christmas 1929, and he wrote Bertram Brooker about his process: "I put in some time each day, working on a larger canvas of some trees in the front yard with the buildings next door. This will keep me busy for the rest of the winter over the weekends. I am putting in every bit of spare time on some kind of work and hope that my winter will be generally profitable."[29]

Vancouver's Nan Cheney (1887–1985), Emily Carr's good friend and biographer, painted *The Back of the House of All Sorts,* Emily Carr's Victoria rooming house, in 1930. Laundry hangs

FIGURE 4.20. **Edward John Hughes**, *A Backyard in Downtown Vancouver,* c. 1936.

FIGURE 4.21. **Nan Lawson Cheney**, *The Back of the House of All Sorts,* 1930.

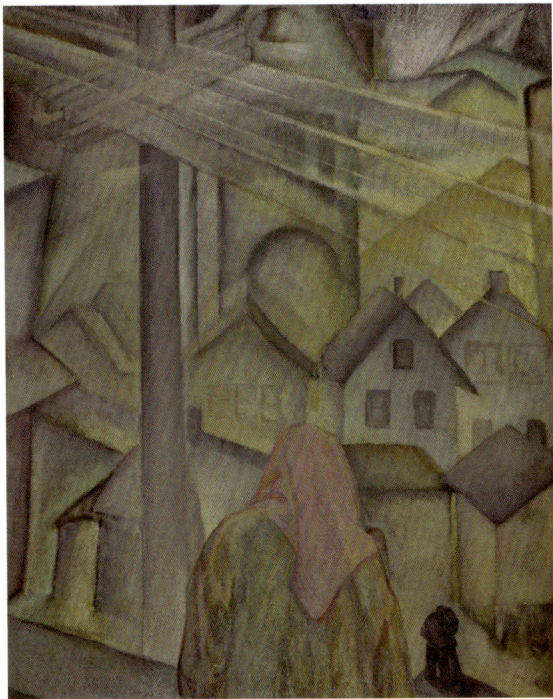

on the line, and the back steps and railing unite the lower and upper portions of this oil on canvas. The house itself, formed with geometric shapes of varying colours, comprises the whole canvas. The sky and the grass frame its upper and lower edges. This strongly executed work echoes the personality and art of Emily Carr.

Also working in the 1930s and focused on urban subjects is Vera Weatherbie, student and for ten years partner of Group of Seven artist Fred Varley. She brings an international futuristic element into her work *Night Time*. A lone figure walks into the painting. The back view of the figure's sloped shoulders sets the eerie tone, augmented by the work's restricted palette. The pink head scarf in the lower centre of the painting is the strongest colour and contrasts the muted greens and browns. Houses are cheek by jowl and a tower extends from the mid-ground through the balance of the vertical composition. Sharp, diagonal, parallel lines of force from the upper left to the upper right reflect the only apparent source of light: streetlights not depicted in the painting. This work evokes psychological overtones of loneliness and isolation.

The isolation, solitude, and desolation of small-town neighbourhoods captured the imagination of a number of Western Canadian artists, such as British Columbia's Sybil Andrews and her *Chinatown-Cumberland,* 1963, or Max Maynard and his drawing *Suburb in Winter,* 1942.

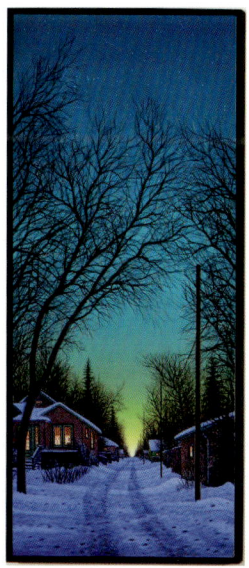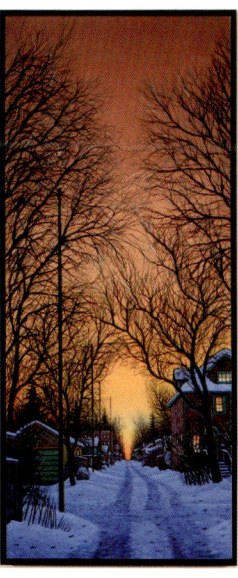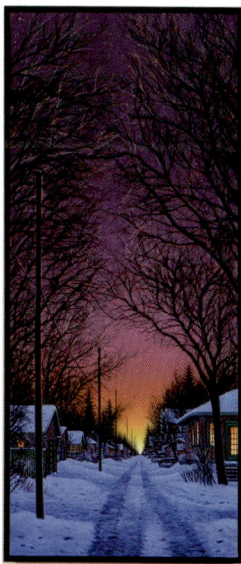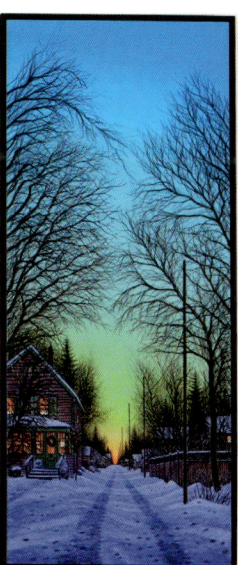

In the latter, the mood is built through line: the ruts in the road and the contrasting sharp, dark, intersecting lines of the sky. The tilted fence posts and telephone poles add to the feeling of loneliness. The ramshackle sense in Andrews's ink and chalk is conveyed with the depiction of the trees, the path up the hill, fences, and the three log and wood buildings positioned in front of each other. She worked quickly. Her pencil work in the landscape is free and sure; that for the buildings is more detailed.

Regina's Wilf Perreault's long focus on back alleys, their light and unique personalities, presents another aspect of the prairie urbanscape. Perreault was a student of Ernest Lindner and a "fan of the honesty of the feeling in Lionel LeMoine FitzGerald's art."[30] His early paintings were of landscapes, and then that interest shifted to back lanes. Curator Timothy Long wrote, "Wilf's vision of the back alley, I think, captures something about this city, about this region, which is unique and resonates with people from a wide variety of backgrounds."[31] Back lanes, characteristic of older sections of many prairie cities, evoke nostalgia. Perreault's innate knowledge and understanding of life and culture of prairie back lanes emanates throughout all his alley works. Exploring the spaces, garages, and the ruts in the snow, he paints the light— daylight, evening light, and the reflections of sunsets and sunrises on the snow and puddles. His colours are rich, recalling the impact of the prairie sunsets on the work of Paul Kane and

FIGURE 4.23. **Wilf Perreault**, *Rebecca's Alley, Christina's Alley, Catherine's Alley,* and *Ellen's Alley*, 2019.

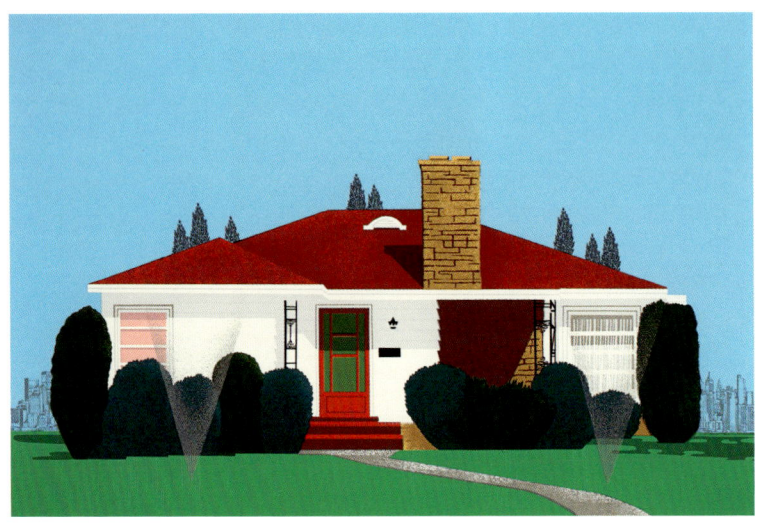

FIGURE 4.24.
David Thauberger,
Bungalow, 1989.

Frederick Verner. Perreault's 2019 private commission is comprised of four works that together form an impressive installation: *Rebecca's Alley, Christina's Alley, Catherine's Alley,* and *Ellen's Alley*. The unique starting point for this project were the favourite colours of each of daughters of the commissioner. Perreault found working from the perspective of colour exciting, and this new approach has inspired ideas for future large works.[32] Though reminiscent of Monet's *Waterlilies, Rouen Cathedral,* or *Hay Stack* series, which captured the haystacks at different times of day, Perreault's work has the unique inception of the arbitrariness of colours. The results are the differing respective dominant sunset colours at the end of each alley. In his 2019 private commission the sky fills 80 percent of the vertical seven-foot height in each panel and his characteristic ruts in the snow lead down their alleys which are framed on either side by the houses and garages. The fences and telephone poles provide further definitions of space. While the garages and houses differ in each panel, the horizons and vanishing points are consistent in each. Streetlights are non-existent. Interior light from the houses add to the light and aura of the setting sun.

The emergence of suburbs had captured Walter J. Phillips as well. He embraced suburbs as subjects early in his career with a number of coloured woodcuts. His 1927 coloured woodcut *Winnipeg Street, Snowbound* was a visually articulate depiction of the piles of snow against the backs of the houses. The line of houses runs horizontally across the work. A lone telephone pole defines the street. The foreground is white with snow, and the background is filled by the pale, watery blue sky. The focus, however, is the depiction of the back porches and sheds, which are almost submerged by the snow. The composition certainly points to human isolation in winter.

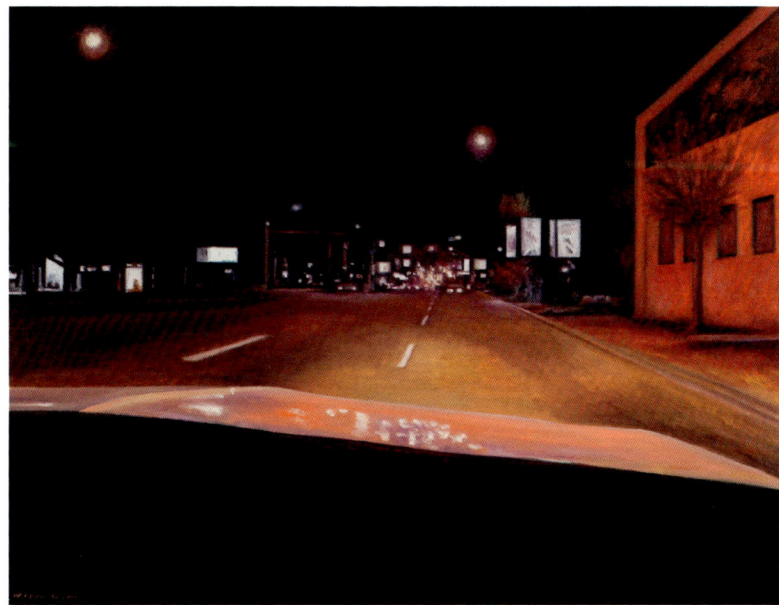

FIGURE 4.25.
William Pura,
The Suburbs,
2000.

More recently, artists such as David Thauberger and William (Bill) Pura (b. 1948) took the suburban subject into new directions. Both artists are precise in their technique and use of colour. The former gives a sense of domesticity and provides precise details of the houses and their setting. The latter adds a twist of mystery and foreboding in his eerie portrayals of the evening light.

David Thauberger, a Regina painter and printmaker, portrays the ordinary elements of life and everyday places close to home, urban and rural. Pop culture was an important source for both his imagery and his approach to making his images. While he uses a variety of media for his art, he feels that the "communal aspect of making prints enhances that human essence."[33] He liked silkscreen's bold, distinct colours and crisp linear definitions, which enhanced his iconic vernacular images and amplified the sense of reality in his images. Experimenting with inventive techniques in the 1970s, he added new dimensions to printmaking when he was working at Winnipeg's Grand Western Canadian Screen Shop. Texture was important to him as well, and in 1977 he explored the textural possibilities of velvet, flocking, and antique marbleized papers, and other means of applying and working with colour. He also used Letraset to depict the shrubs and trees in *Little Christmas,* 1984, and *Bungalow,* 1989. In his 1990s etchings and aquatints, he often overpainted the printed image, sometimes incorporating computer or photographic images into the print.

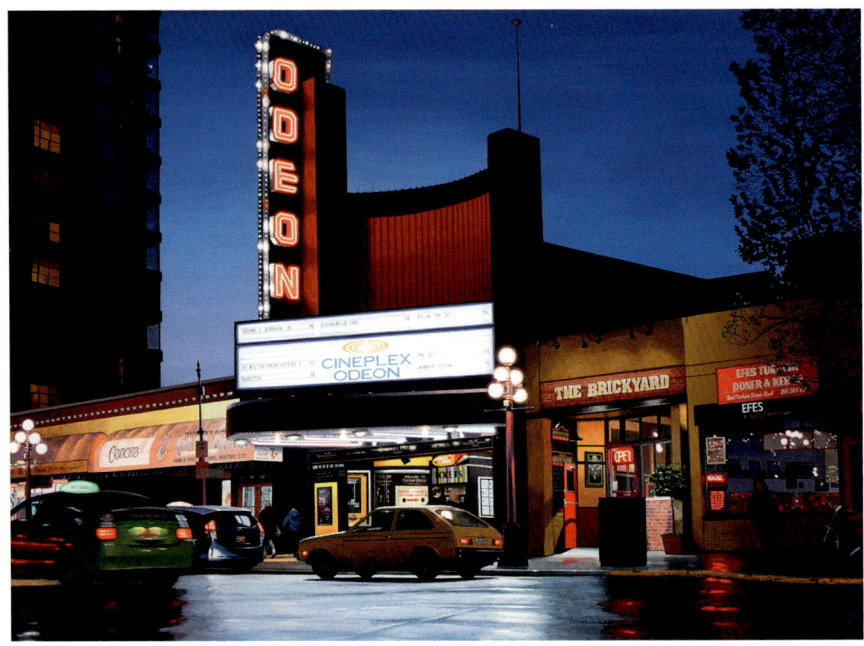

Thauberger's prints are stand-alone works of art, not preliminary or auxiliary to his paintings. However, his interest in postwar, suburban, middle-class, domestic residences carried into his painting. As responses to place, these paintings of homes became, as writer Peter White says, "portraits of the realization of the widely shared aspiration to enjoy a comfortable life in attractive surroundings. In one sense what is interesting about them is that there is nothing about them that is distinctive, something that is only amplified by the small variations in the decorative touches. At the same time, however, they reflect a society that under new economic circumstances continued to be structured more horizontally than vertically."[34]

Thauberger reflected on the technical links between his printmaking and painting:

I learned the importance of tightening up my painting—the image and registration. Prints had to consider the borders of the paper and accurate drawing is vital. That became important to my painting. Thinking the technical process through was completely different than with painting . . . thinking in terms of producing multiples . . . perhaps the biggest barrier of all was realizing that no matter how hard we tried, these were never going to look like paintings . . . I had to adjust my expectations. . . .

FIGURE 4.26. **Tad Suzuki**, *Odeon Theatre, Victoria*, 2016.

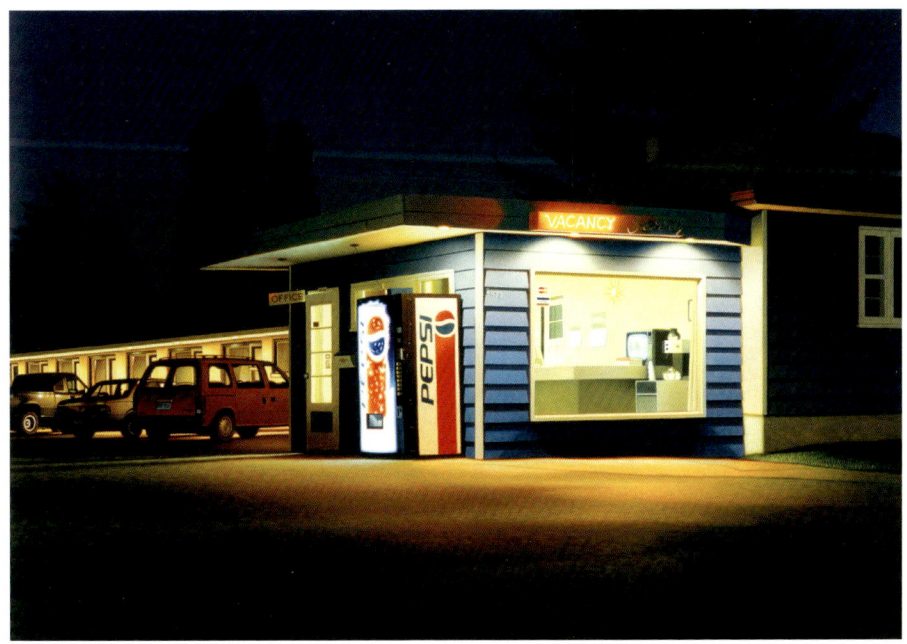

Eventually I came to appreciate the different aesthetic that the prints demanded and to work with them on their own terms . . . prints are just not paintings. . . . This, I realized was a positive thing and I like to think that I was able to adjust my approach when making prints . . . in fact, the adjustments have had a positive impact on my subsequent paintings . . . so the influence has been both ways.[35]

Comparing the solo painter's studio with the communal experimental print shop, he also opined, "While in his painting studio he, the artist, has the idea and realizes it; in the print shop, he the artist has the visual idea and image, and others realize it."[36]

Bill Pura, a Winnipeg artist, musician, composer, and writer, now living in the United States, has done several series of paintings depicting suburban neighbourhoods, their houses, streets, and corners. Lit with streetlamps, they are absolutely devoid of people. In some, one sees the hood of the car and the viewer seems to be driving. Works such as *The Suburbs,* 2000, evoke a chilling loneliness and sinister mysteriousness. In *The Suburbs*, the dark background has only two streetlights. In the dark foreground an eerie yellow light is at the centre of the street.

FIGURE 4.27. **Andrew Valko**, *Night Shift*, from the *Motel Series*, 1997.

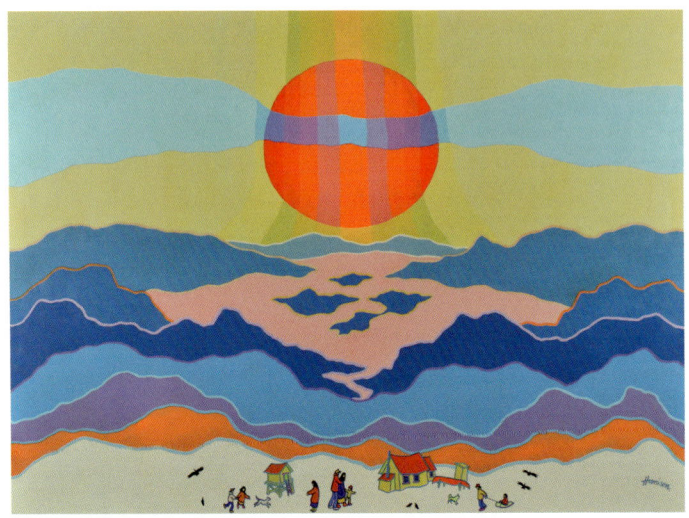

FIGURE 4.28.
Ted Harrison,
Northern Sun, 1989.

Buildings are on either side. The interior lights in the more distant buildings punctuate the composition. The large building on the right, however, shows only reflected light on its red/orange exterior, enhancing the mystery.

Pura uses photographs as a starting point for some works, and though he acknowledges that he "uses realism," he emphasizes that he is not a "realist painter."[37] His fascination with the mythical nineteenth-century German Romantic painter Caspar David Friedrich has been carried into these ominous, yet beautiful, mysterious suburban streetscapes. We feel we know the precise intersections, buildings, and roads he painted, but, as seen in *Stafford Street* or *Andy's Corner,* he transforms those local suburban places into a universal narrative. Pura's forms are clearly rendered, the works are precisely executed with smooth layerings of paint, and the sense of mystery is enhanced by his use of colour, magnifying mystery and emotion to enhance the viewer's discomfort. Pura's art is about light—direct light sources such as streetlights or headlights; interior lights; reflected light; and moonlight. Pura combines their complex effects to create a hypnotic quality. These paintings are at once personal and distant; known yet foreign.

Another approach to light, buildings, and civic life is expressed by Victoria's Japanese-born Tad Suzuki (b. 1963). He moved to Canada from Tokyo when he was in his early twenties, and noted that "as an immigrant artist, I am perhaps more sensitive to what appears to be ordinary."[38] The light of urban spaces, especially neon lights and signs and their multiple reflections, captured his interest. He said, "Initially I was drawn to illuminated signs because of the technical challenge of creating the illusion of lighting up on canvas. . . . I also like the lighthearted interplay of words in the urban environment."[39] Author and curator Mary Jo Hughes is insightful about Suzuki's fascination, particularly that in his 2018–19 *Honest Ed* series, done just before the historic Toronto building and social centre was demolished: "Within these paintings he has managed to distill his intensive and contemplative consideration into something that makes us aware of much more than we would have seen if simply walking through that cityscape."[40] In *Odeon Theatre, Victoria,* Suzuki's 2016 acrylic on canvas, we see the confluence of multiple light sources and the challenge the artist faced in capturing the different kinds and qualities of light: neon, street lights, interior light, and general reflected and mixed light. Suzuki commented: "Light is everything. Some artists are painting objects. Whether it is artificial light or natural light, I am painting the light activated, not the object. Light is the main character, the protagonist."[41]

This fascination of light is also the essence of Andrew Valko's *Motel Series.* They are a compelling contemporary social commentary, and as narratives they involve the viewer in their story. These postwar buildings captured Valko's imagination for the light they proffered, both as subject and the stage for the suggested, yet undefined, human activities within. Ordinary 1950s motels are everywhere across Canada, but the ones Valko liked to paint were in Vancouver's Kingsway district. The figures, painted with precision, are jarring. Partially attired, they appear nonchalant. The objects in the motel room, such as a gun, a camera, a television showing a movie, and a mirror enhance the non-connection between the figures. By construing his settings with such particularity, Valko draws the viewer into the drama as voyeur.

Portraying another aspect of community is the Yukon's Ted Harrison (1926–2015). Born in the United Kingdom, Harrison adopted the Yukon, where he taught high school art for decades before retiring to Victoria. Both the Yukon and British Columbia featured in his art; the works of the North are particularly compelling. Animated and cheerful, his colourful paintings evoke the energy and spirit of the people, their livelihoods, time, and place. His paintings, critiqued by some as "naïve," are both accessible and sophisticated in composition and message. In talking about his art-making approach, he commented that it was a "process of simplification, the cutting away of all that seemed superfluous to the main theme; that of creating a personal style which would enable me to interpret my new surroundings, not only with feeling and sensitivity, but with enjoyment."[42] Painted in simple forms, his anonymous subjects are children and adults engaged in everyday activities, in playgrounds, on walks, or shopping. The skies are prominent, and the rhythmic patterns and movements of the land and skies mirror each other, echoing the movement and dynamism of the northern lights. His colour, primarily primary colours, is arbitrary and bright, applied on the canvas directly without shading. Throughout, Harrison blends elements of reality and abstraction and, as he said, "I draw my idea directly on the canvas."[43]

While Harrison tells stories of daily activities, Valko, Pura, and Suzuki are social chroniclers foreshadowing aspects of the unknown. Light is core to the work of them all, natural and artificial, each conveying the energy of contemporary urban life and relationships between people, neighbourhoods, and their environment.

Lifestyles: Industrialization, Work, and Leisure

"I believe it's important to get very specific about your life. Then it becomes universal."[44]

Where do ordinary life and the inclusion of the everyday figure in the art of the West? Work, leisure, and aspects of personal daily life are all universal images in the art of Western Canada. The subjects of these images are frozen in their own time, and include interiors, lifestyles, still lifes, gardens, and play, documenting societal domestic, transportation, and occupational shifts. Artists engage audiences in these contemporary changes often as they are happening, raising questions about how and where we live and the impact of change on individuals and society. In their visual documenting of lifestyles, ceremonies, and events, artists play important roles in providing deeper understandings of evolving social patterns, work, and lifestyles.

This concentration on painting and drawing lifestyles began with the first European artists' arrivals in Western Canada. In the 1790s on the Pacific Coast, for instance, details of specific events witnessed by those on early explorations are shown in *A Dance at Friendly Cove,* 1791, by Tomás de Suria, and *Interior view of Maquinna's house at Tahsis,* 1792, by Atanasio Echeverría. Archibald Menzies recounted the actual event in his journal corroborating its contemporary visual depictions of the opening ceremonies, dancing, and dinner, and the reception they received: "Maquinna together with his Brother & Attendants received us on the Beach, & we were conducted to the Chief's House which was large & spacious. … During the dancing, Maquinna stole away . . . masked himself behind the group & entered the Area capering & dancing with great agility. . . . Vancouver responded by getting 'some of the Sailors to dance a Reel or two to the Fife.'"[45]

Peter Rindisbacher, when he was in Red River during the 1820s, portrayed official events with First Nations and Hudson's Bay Company leaders, in works like *Captain Bulger, Governor of Assiniboia, and the Chiefs and Warriors of the Chippewa Tribe of Red Lake, in Council in the Colony House in Fort Douglas,* 1823. Lifestyles of the Indigenous peoples of the area were frequent subjects of his, and many consider that this young Swiss artist's works are sensitive and respectful documentary images.

In the late 1850s and early 1860s, William Hind had also painted life as he witnessed it on his western travels, including British Columbia's gold rush. Works such as *Chinese Gold Washers on the Fraser River, BC,* 1862, showing the workers' focused engagement, are important historical visual documents. As writer and former curator Barry Lord opined, "it was Hind, not Kane, who extended the documentary approach to the Canadian figure that artists like Rindisbacher had begun, and most particularly directs our attention to the working people and their actual production processes of the land. Hind's little pictures are a major step forward toward a people's art."[46]

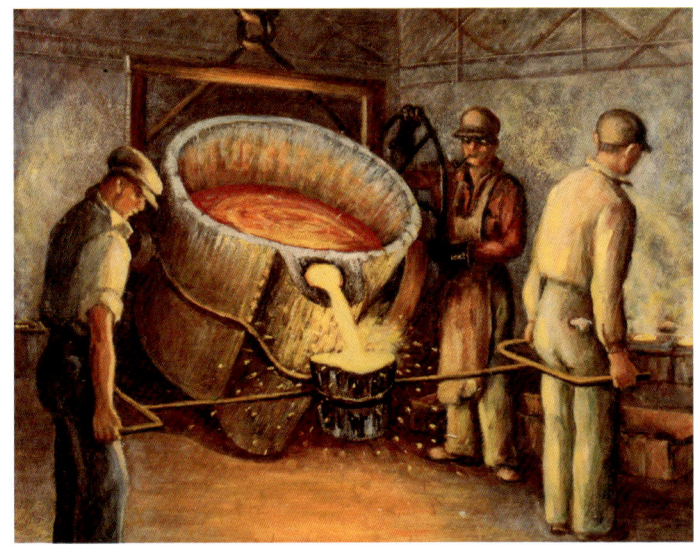

FIGURE 4.29.
Georgie Wilcox,
*Western Industries
(Steel Pour, Vulcan
Iron Works, Winnipeg)*,
c. 1939.

Through the twentieth century, too, Western Canadian artists painted people at work, on the farms, at socials, family events, and in urban industrial centres. This includes the figure work of Maxwell Bates, Joe Plaskett's dinner tables, William Kurelek's *Manitoba Party 1964,* Georgie Wilcox's 1939 *Western Industries (Steel Pour, Vulcan Iron Works—Winnipeg)*, and Allison Newton's *Onion Graders*. Steve Gouthro, artist and former Brandon University professor, is one whose work includes penetrating portrayals of individuals' lives: "My work over the last few years has focused on growth and decay in contrast to human aspirations for immortality and transcendence. An offshoot of this is an interest in how cultures work to ensure their continuity, and the parts played by individuals within those structures."[47]

Much of Gouthro's work is about ordinary things and daily activities, such as riding a bicycle to or from work as in *Green Rider,* 2012, but it is imbued with more than its surface story. The artist conveys an ethereal quality of the spiritual combined with a sense of duty, heightening the importance of an individual's role in society. The rider, the primary subject, framed on two sides by shadows, is shown moving out of the centre of the work. Gouthro explores human attitudes, commitments, and interests, drawing his inspiration from the commonplace. When undertaking series, like *Steel Mill Series,* or *Military Series* from Camp Shilo, Manitoba, Gouthro first takes many photographs, collecting and documenting ideas for potential works. He reworks the images on the computer to extract greater levels of detail and enlarges and lightens them to get more "information," especially in the dark areas and shadows of particular interest to him. The resulting photograph is but one source document for him, as

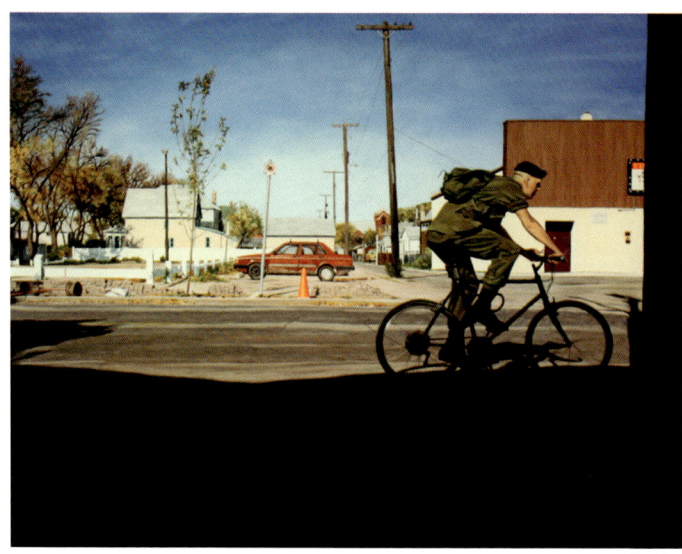

FIGURE 4.30.
Steve Gouthro,
Green Rider, 2012.

a single work often emanates from several or more photos: "While I am true to what is going on, I will also invent."[48] He seeks the "whole experience"—the colours, forms, light, smells, textures, and sounds. *Loading Zone,* part of the *Military Series,* exemplifies Gouthro's contrasts. The soft pink recycling bags used by the military to collect used materials add a softness, almost an ephemeral feminine element, providing contrast to the militaristic green, gold, and brown tones of the overall scene. He stated: "I came from working class roots and thus have a sense of practicality, wanting my art to be functional, by working in a somewhat documentary way, keeping ideas. More ideas are conveyed by being representational than by being abstracted."[49]

Maxwell Bates's *Cocktail Party Series,* 1965, and his *Workers Series,* also of the 1960s, are unquestionably seminal commentaries on life, the former perhaps dealing more with appearances than realities. The *Cocktail Party* paintings, done after Bates moved to Victoria, are of people he knew, including art collectors and many fellow artist members of the Victoria Limners Society (1971 to 2006), a group of seventeen artists dedicated to portraying the human condition. Writer Nancy Townshend commented: "Bates' bold and highly colourful cocktail party and reception paintings of the 1960s and 1970s in Victoria, also about bondage and freedom in the human condition, transcend the constraints of symbolic art of the earlier puppet/scarecrow works. In these meaningful transpositions of real-life scenes in Victoria, Bates often exposes humankind's inhumanity to humankind of varying degrees in socially charged settings, by inference freedom from this. In these socially engaging paintings Bates takes Expressionism to a new level."[50]

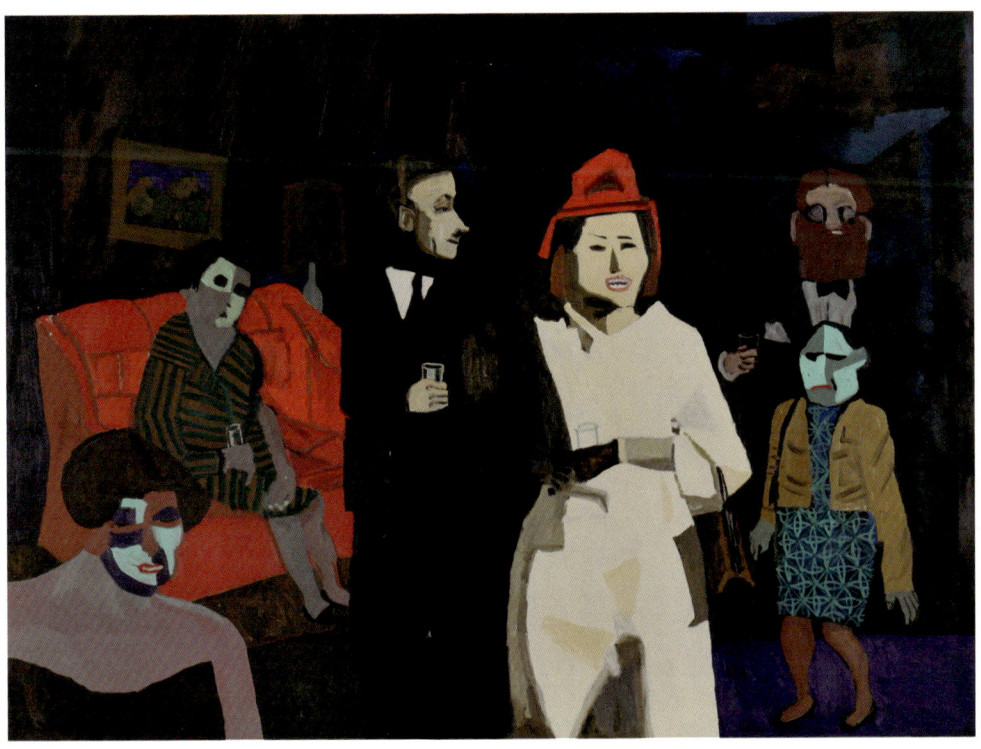

For his part, Bates wrote: "Experience gives me increased ability to transpose what I see. My intention is to transpose meaningfully. This amounts to expressionism. . . . Good painting must offer something meaningful to the spectator, but it may be enigmatic . . . the aim is to convey something on one's own terms to the spectator who can respond."[51]

Joe Plaskett, a major international artist, grew up in New Westminster, British Columbia. As a student he studied with international colourist Hans Hofmann, whom he counted as the best teacher he ever had. He praised Hofmann's discipline and attention to the whole image, the subject, and its resulting negative spaces, or to what he called "the Push and Pull, the dynamics that set the machinery of picture making at work, of feeling oppositions, of animating what was static, of colour as a force of its own."[52] Plaskett was the interim head of the Winnipeg School of Art from 1950 to 1952, after the retirement of Lionel LeMoine FitzGerald, and later of the Banff School of Fine Arts. A good and supportive teacher himself, Plaskett encouraged Tony

FIGURE 4.31. **Maxwell Bates**, *The Cocktail Party*, 1965.

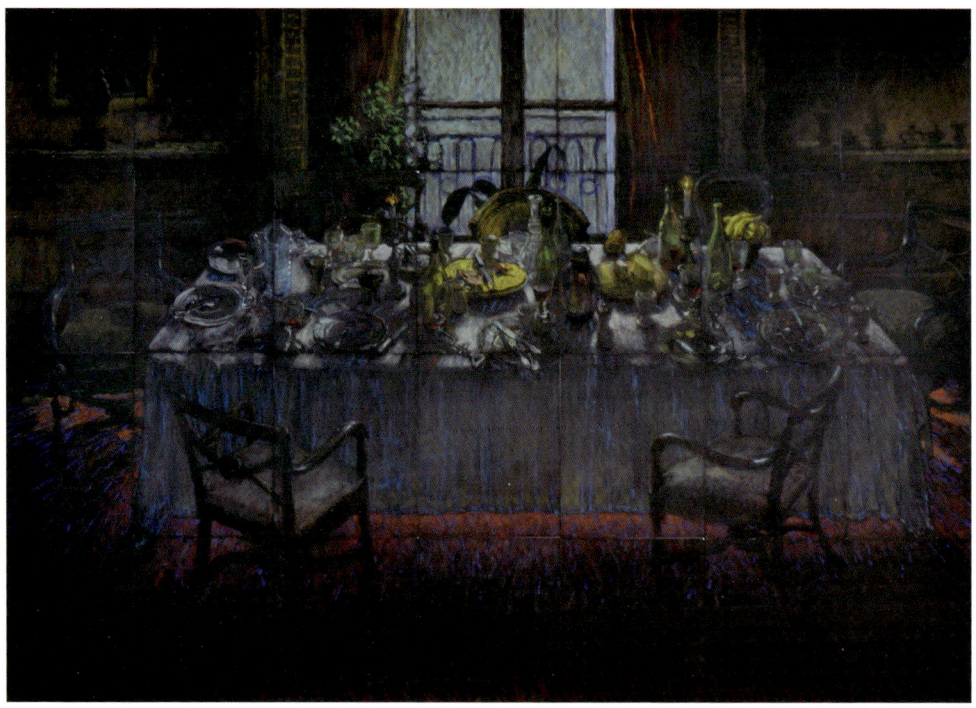

Tascona to enrol in the school and become an artist. Plaskett, however, spent a large part of his career in Paris and England.

Plaskett's art, his landscapes and his tablescapes, brings together a number of international art movements. Plaskett travelled widely, and his art reflects his interest in internationalism combined with the specificity of place. He worked primarily in pastel, on paper, and bought his pastels from the same shop where impressionist artist Edgar Degas had bought his. The focus of Plaskett's work was to portray life—how we eat, entertain, and live. He said in an undated speech to the Contemporary Art Society:

> In my forties I may have been contemporary. I was an experimenter, being successively surrealist, automatist, abstract and much else. As an artist, however, I was only an embryo.
>
> In 1949 I went to Paris and eventually stopped trying to be an abstract painter and gradually developed a personal figurative manner. . . .

FIGURE 4.32. **Joseph Plaskett**, *Easter Table*, 1989–1993.

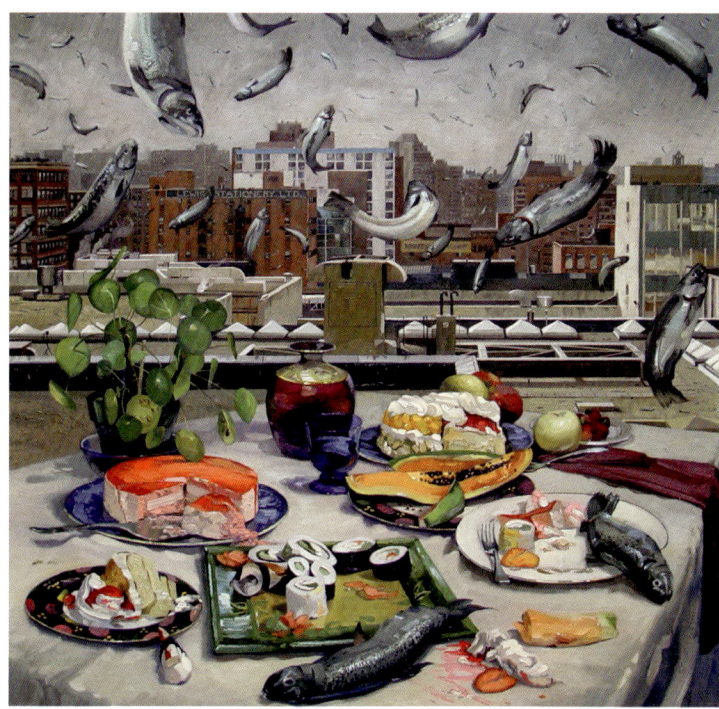

FIGURE 4.33.
Chris Flodberg,
*Freakish Acts of
Nature and Other
Distractions*, from
the series *Matters
of Denial*, 2004.

The world I create is intensely private, but it is part of a public world. . . . I need
hardly remind you it is an interior world, not only dealing with the physical space
of the indoors but also with the interior, the insides, of myself. My trademark is my
living room cum studio, with its mirrors and chandeliers, its chairs, its tables holding
fruit, flowers, the remains of meals or the trophies of my collections. Into this private
space the outside intrudes—shafts of sunlight remind me of the outside, the noises of
the streets or nature.[53]

About the meaning of his own art, Plaskett continued: "What is my art about? I like
to think it is about feeling, but it is also thinking—reason and logic, but it is above all about
feeling. The artist thinks through feeling. He gropes for a shape or a colour. Reason may tell
him it should be a certain tone or shade—hot or cold, light or dark, but Reason is usually
wrong. It gives the predictable answer. A creative decision must be instinctive. . . . We may
admire technique, which may dazzle by its virtuosity, but nothing new has been said."[54]

On the occasion of the exhibition honouring his eightieth birthday in 1998, Plaskett
reflected that he found sketching to be spontaneous, particularly when using pastel, his chosen

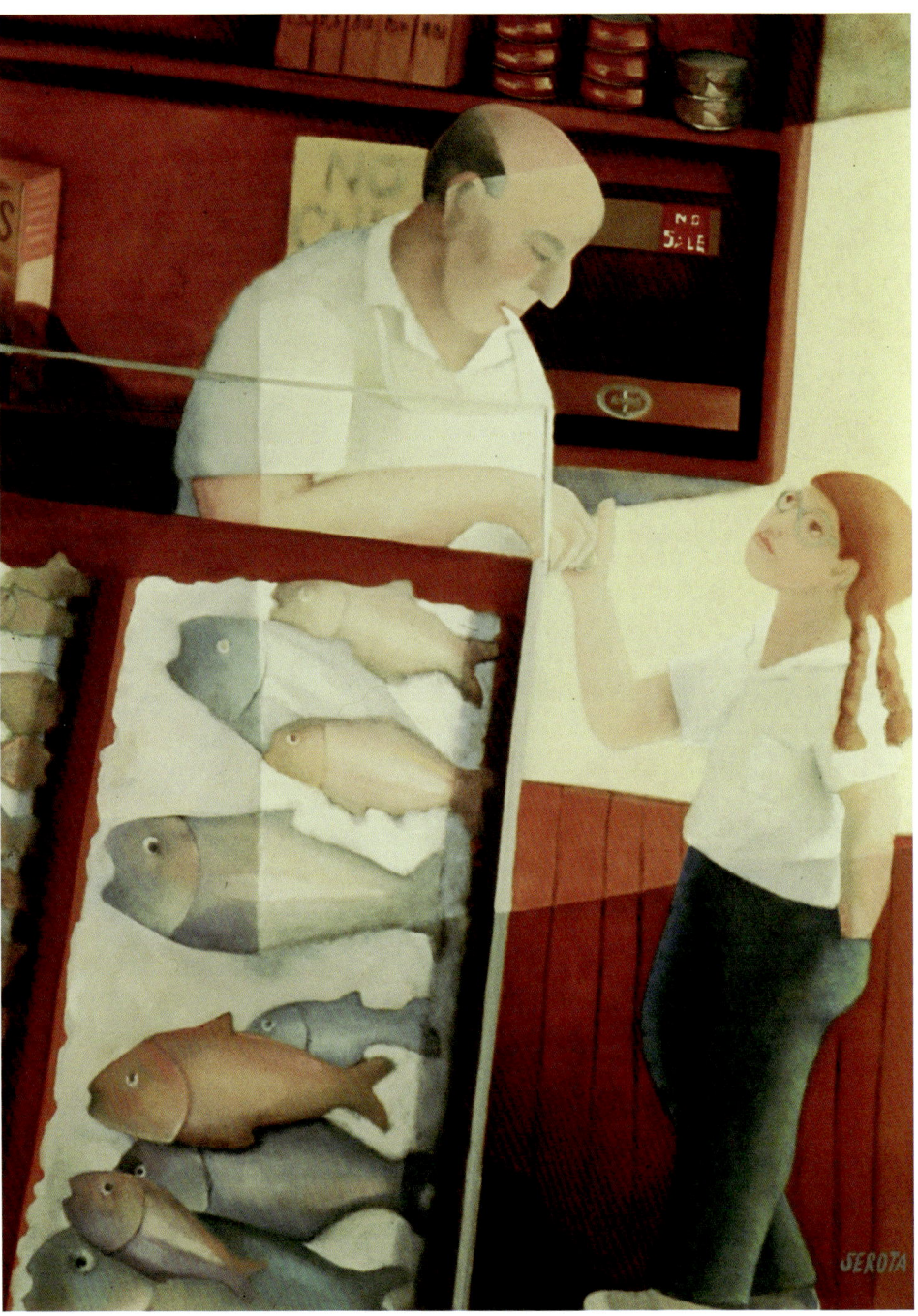

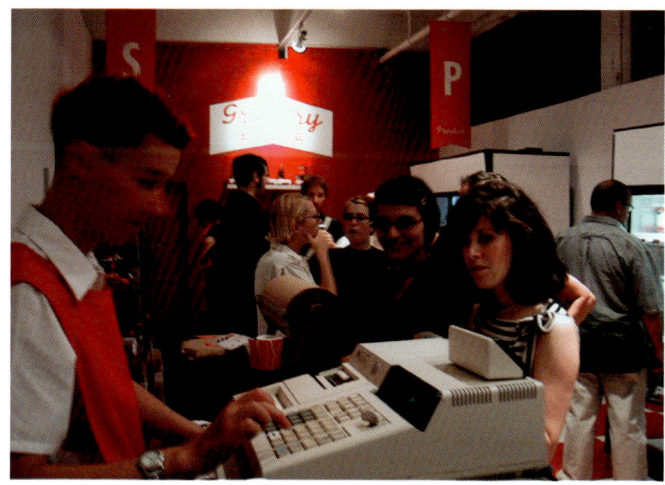

FIGURE 4.35.
Shawna Dempsey, Lorri Millan, jake moore, Zab, *Grocery Store,* 2002.

medium for *Easter Table,* 1989–1993, comprised of twenty-eight sheets of paper, unframed, and installed directly on the wall, four sheets high and seven sheets long, each sheet abutting the next. He said: "I found I could extend a pastel painting in any direction by adding another sheet of paper and more and more until the work grew to its full adult state, the largest of these was made on 36 sheets of paper. . . . I felt as if I had invented something. . . . In the end, my achievements may . . . come from something I have no control over—the spirit that lies behind the work—my own sensitivity."[55]

In *Easter Table*, the table is strewn with the remnants of the Easter meal, the chairs are pulled away from the table, and the guests have gone. The French doors in this room, his Paris apartment, open onto his balcony and provide the light on the scene, forming the backdrop in the centre of the piece. Plaskett worked the pastel well into the paper, and the various tones of pastel into each other, layer on layer. Using his colour this way gives a richness and depth to the elements in the work, including the intensity of the blues and reds in the carpet, the substance of the material in the tablecloth, and the strong yellow of the flowers that punctuate the composition. Plaskett told me when I was his guest for lunch that he was interested in the aftermath of a social happening, whether in Paris or England, and as he worked he recalled the conversations, the meal, and the energy of the time.[56] At another time, he noted: "My still life paintings are often scenes of intense activity, the table crowded with objects. . . . One area of still life I made my own—the remnants of meals. I christened them 'tablescapes.' They tell the story of daily living. The feeling is one of intimacy."[57]

FIGURE 4.34. **Phyllis Serota**, *Package of Philip Morris, Please,* 1985.

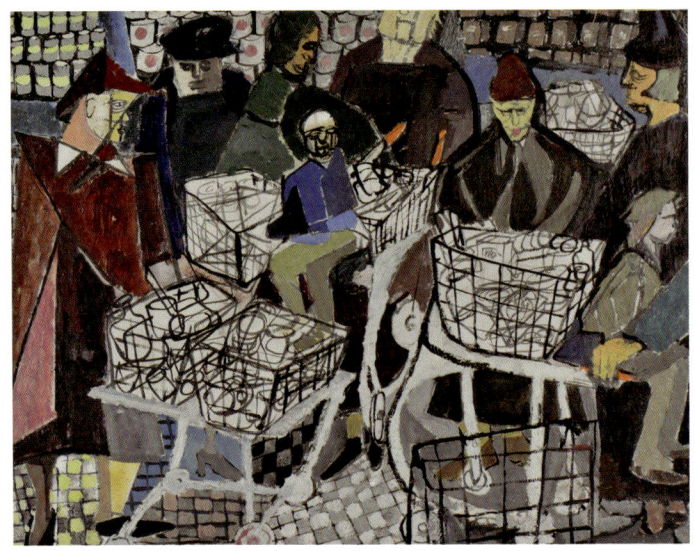

FIGURE 4.36.
Molly Lamb Bobak,
Supermarket, c. 1955.

Calgary's Chris Flodberg also portrayed the end of a meal, but in his case he questions what the end of society will look like, given the calamitous consequences of climate change. In *Freakish Acts of Nature and Other Distractions,* his oil on canvas painted in 2004, he talks of his anxiety about today's situation, and being "really concerned about the 'end of the party'—the end of art and the end of nature. This work portrays my anxiety—rotten food is on the table, fish are falling from the sky being the metaphor of nature gone awry and in the chaos it is raining fish."[58] Calgary is in the background, though, as he pointed out, its image is reversed. *Freakish Acts* is part of a larger series, of which each piece is steeped in the anxiety he feels. Others portray mythologized landscapes, some of which are drawn from art history. Are these paintings anticipatory for the end of civilization and the world as we know it? Is this the ultimate effect of unstemmed climate change? What, he also projects, is the future of art?

Victoria's Phyllis Serota (b. 1938) has produced many canvases depicting aspects of daily life, from dancing to shopping. Her oil on canvas *Package of Philip Morris, Please*, 1985, is autobiographical. Part of her larger *Family Series,* a group of twelve works, this painting shows the artist as a child buying cigarettes for her uncle. She said, "My Aunt Rosie and Uncle Jake lived just around the corner from our flat in Chicago. They had a beautiful apartment behind their fish store. I would go there often and stare at the fish. It was one of the only places in the world that I felt safe! Uncle Jake would occasionally send me to the store to get his cigarettes, package of Philip Morris, please."[59] The floor and display case are tilted forward, allowing us to

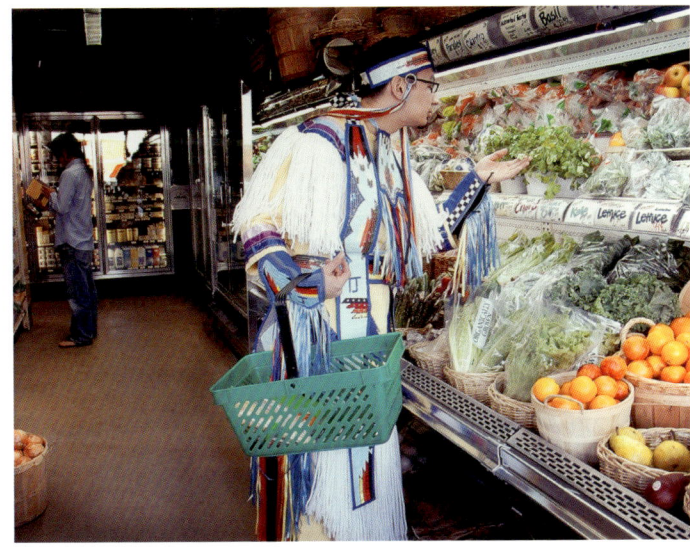

FIGURE 4.37.
Terrance Houle,
Urban Indian #7,
from the series
Urban Indian, 2007.

see the floorboards and rows of fish. The shelves are on another angle, which provides details of the shop. The eye contact between Phyllis and salesperson is direct. Her use of colour, like her composition, is controlled and enhances the notion of a business transaction.

Though Serota talks of the shop as being one of the only places in the world in which she felt safe, her oeuvre is filled with works of joy. Of *Gabriel's Dream,* 2005, she says: "My vision of a peaceful, joyous world. One in which all of us, no matter who we are, whom we choose to love, whether alone or together, will dance in love and celebration."[60] The palette in this work is pinks, blues, green, and yellow, and figures, dancing on the edge of the world under the star-filled sky, are joyous, and the movement throughout carries the eye of the viewer through the entire work.

Shawna Dempsey and Lorri Millan, Winnipeg performance artists, have presented many facets of contemporary life, particularly gaps in civil society, in works such as *Lesbian National Parks and Services* and *Grocery Store,* the latter which they created with jake moore and Zab. A number of their performance pieces are especially relevant to contemporary urban lifestyles. *Grocery Store,* 2002, was a site-specific work lasting three weeks in August. Set up at Winnipeg's Ace Art Gallery in the city's Exchange District, it underlined the area's changing character as it became increasingly gentrified, displacing artists' studios. They drew attention too to the reality that Winnipeg's downtown was without a grocery store. In the three weeks, they sold $5,000 worth of food, and other essentials. They ran radio ads and "a circular advertising sale prices, and a mail-in-coupon campaign to the mayor requesting real-life downtown services, and expanded the discussion about the direction of urban revitalization in our city."[61]

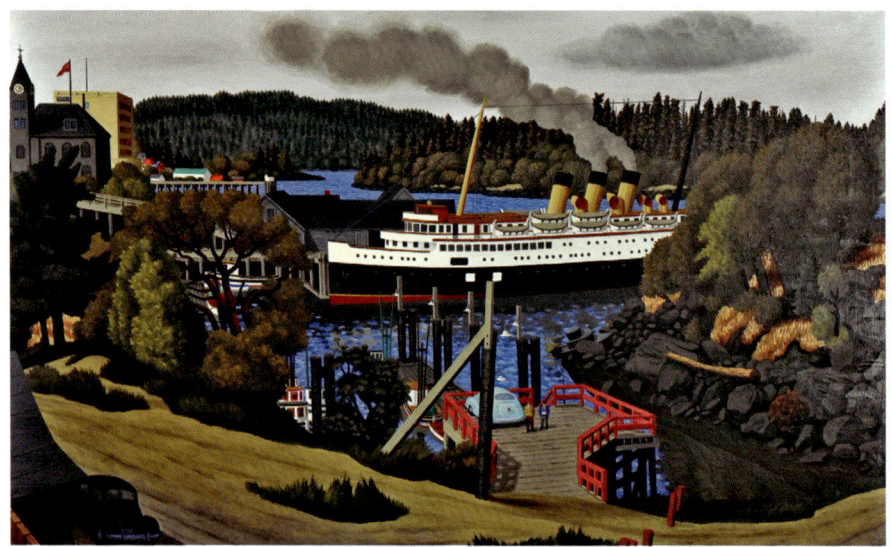

Ordinary people undertaking their ordinary daily routines were the centre of many of Molly Lamb Bobak's paintings. *Supermarket,* circa 1950s, and *North Vancouver Ferry*, 1950, are two examples. In both, using cubist forms, she fills the canvases and effectively expresses the bustle of the scene, with myriad shopping carts in *Supermarket* and the patience of waiting in *North Vancouver Ferry*. Her use of colour mirrors the overall mood. The human element was always central to her work, evident in her Second World War works like *Private Roy,* 1946, and in later years with her scenes filled with human activity—hockey, horse shows, fairs, street crowds, and beaches. Throughout her career she conveyed the energy of life, the specific scene, and her personal engagement with it all.

While Bobak's *Supermarket* was a commentary on ordinary shopping, Terrance Houle (b. 1975), a Blackfoot artist in Alberta, takes the ordinary into new directions. He visually overlays the perceived activities of society and the very real paradigm shifts they caused for the urban life of Indigenous peoples, those who moved in from the reserves and those who grew up in cities. The shift from country food and traditional means of finding food to supermarket experiences represented a quantum, and difficult, leap, forcing people to adopt new ways of living and surviving. Houle's photographic *Urban Indian Series* is compelling and thought-provoking, detailing his riding the buses, sitting at the desk in an office, greeting on the front doorstep, and going grocery shopping. In each work he wears his full powwow regalia. In his

FIGURE 4.38. **Edward John Hughes**, *Steamer at the Old Wharf, Nanaimo*, 1958.

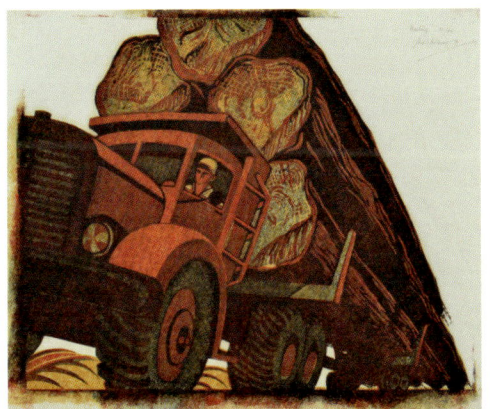
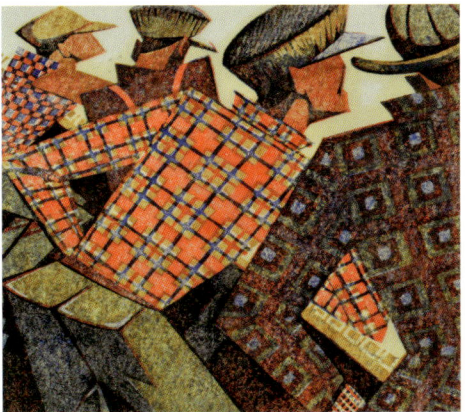

photograph of grocery shopping, he has the plastic shopping basket on his arm as he assesses the parsley. Challenging stereotypes, Houle draws attention to concerns and the depth of racism. Through his humour, he questions societal and cultural understandings and stigmas. It is clear his images are filled "with irony and stereotypical depictions of 'Indianness,' [and] juxtaposed within everyday scenes."[62] His humour pushes needed public debate and is aimed at dismantling long-held stereotypes. As he says in his artist's statement of the series:

> The *Urban Indian Series* is a comment on personal identity and cultural commodity in today's contemporary culture. Specifically, what is my culture as it compares to the mainstream understanding of Native Peoples? My regalia is both a catalyst in the image, breaking up the sea of mundane western garb, and a representation that is part of my everyday, much like my culture, thus challenging the suggestion that I am out of place in a world that only identifies with conformity. The work serves to question ideas of tradition, identity and culture that are often negated or replaced by Western cultural standards. Also, in capturing the image of the "Indian" in portraiture and regalia, the *Urban Indian Series* seeks to comment on the historical relationship between photography and aboriginal identity.[63]

By encouraging an ironic gaze, Houle asks us to be critical viewers of cultural stereotypes, and clearly calls for action on reconciliation. When juxtaposed with KC Adams's *Perception Series,* 2015, in which she points out, head-on, the extent and devastating impact of racism in urban life, that gaze is even more clearly honest and poignant.

FIGURE 4.39. **Sybil Andrews**, *Hauling*, 1952.   FIGURE 4.40. **Sybil Andrews**, *Coffee Bar*, 1952.

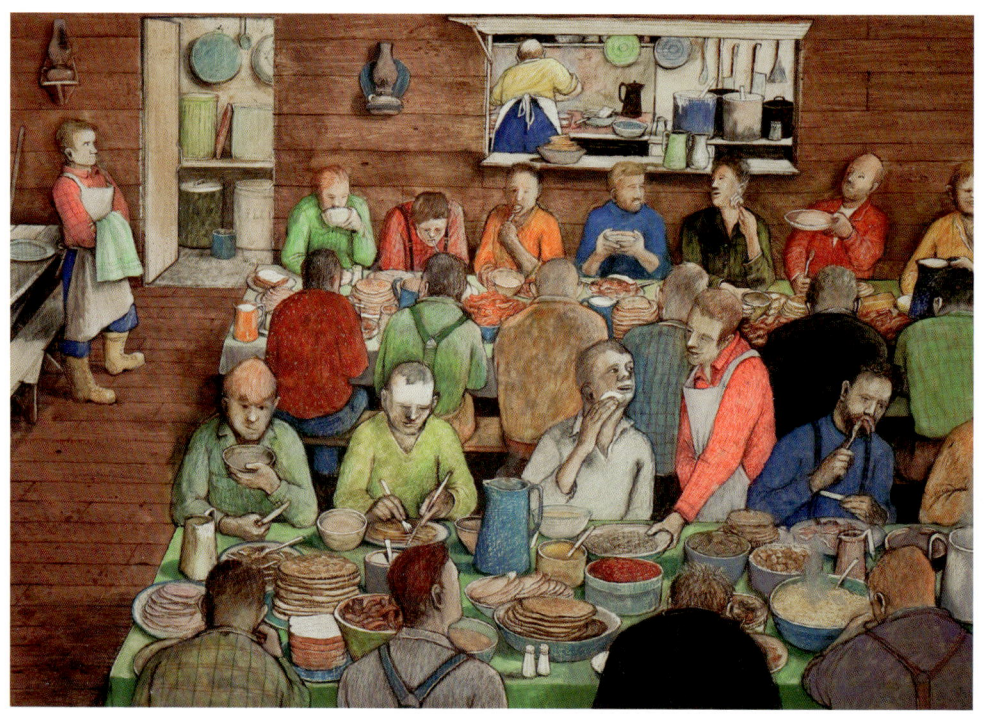

Place also defines lifestyles, especially for those living on an island, which E.J. Hughes portrayed in so many of his canvases. As he said, "I have painted in the Cowichan Valley for fifty years and it is the most beautiful place on earth."[64] His knowledge of place and painting enabled him to depict the life and landscape with precise detail and colour. Indeed, as writer Jacques Barbeau said, "Hughes's art IS British Columbia. The raw strength of his coastal scenes, the silent majesty of his ferries, the vigorous representations of the fishing and forest industries, and the tender rendering of his inland scenes provide a virtual encyclopedia of this magnificent province."[65] *Steamer at the Old Wharf, Nanaimo,* 1958, is one example of his paintings of the harbour and seascape. His use of colour, exactness, and obvious joy makes his work immediately accessible to viewers. He never adhered to current trends but kept the art of the real at the fore.

Vancouver Island British immigrant Sybil Andrews, whose art was influenced by futurism and vorticism, also conveyed through her art the communities and lives she witnessed in the places she lived. She arrived in Canada from Suffolk, England, and made her home on the shore in Campbell River, British Columbia. She had been a welder in the First World War, and her

FIGURE 4.41. **William Kurelek**, *Lumberjack's Breakfast*, 1973.

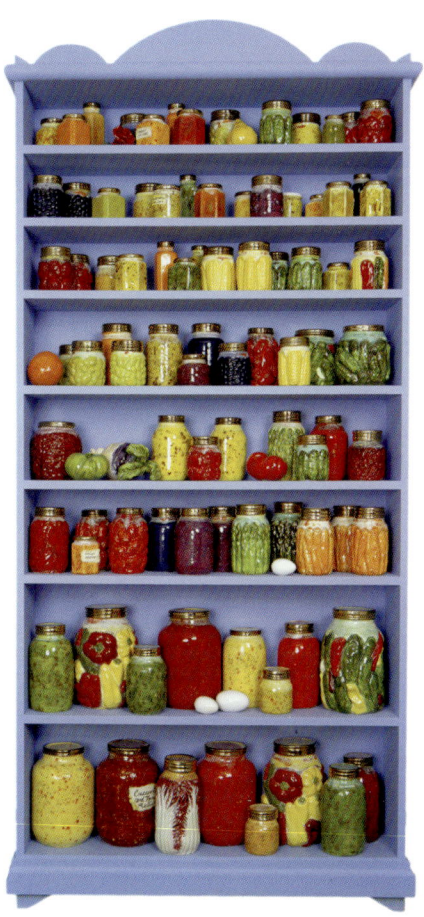

FIGURE 4.42.
Victor Cicansky,
Blue Pantry, 2003.

artistic subject became manual labour, a theme she continued throughout her career. Near the end of the war, in 1919, she secured a job teaching art and art history and then she set up her studio. A printmaker, she worked in linocut, where line and composition were paramount in expressing the figures and activities she depicted. Her oeuvre is extensive, and shapes, patterns, and rhythms preoccupied her. Andrews's many notes are full of colour notations, as well as notes about the levels of pressure she needed for the actual printing. Works like *Speedway,* 1934, *Hauling,* 1952, or *Coffee Bar,* 1952, all show her focus on colour, and the movement and repetition of shapes and patterns she built in her compositions imbued each with energy and strength. *Hauling,* for instance, shows a Vancouver Island logging truck coming around a curve; its power is enhanced by the immensity of its scale, the partial image of the truck filling the

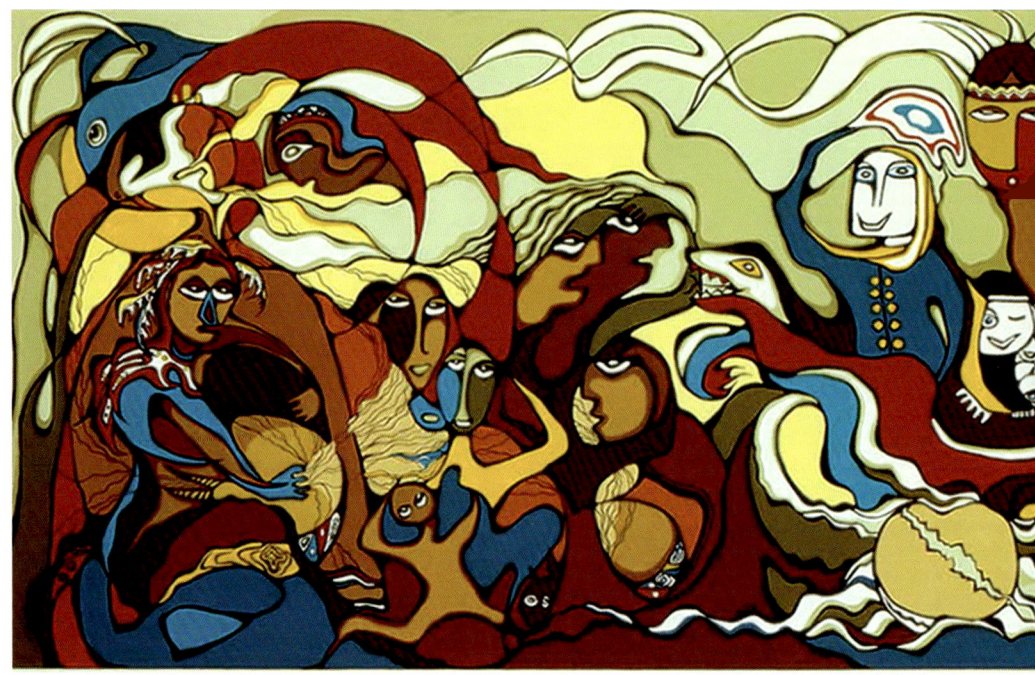

entire work. Her focus on workers throughout her art underlines her recognition of their importance to society. Andrews felt that it was the spiritual essence of a subject that gave a work its form and meaning. Expression of, and for, an individual came through her depiction of the person's body. Many of her figures are faceless; details of facial expressions were not of primary importance for her. In *Coffee Bar*, 1952, she portrays her friends and neighbours at the Esky Bar in Campbell River. Its crisp lines, the angles of the hats, and the colourful patterns of the plaid shirts define the energy and spirit of the gathering and the warmth of the individuals' personalities.

Artists' works often tell stories, and their visual narrative depicts the details of daily life, with keen first-hand knowledge. William Kurelek's *Prairie Boy in Winter, Prairie Boy in Summer,* well-known children's books, and *Lumberjack's Breakfast* are prime examples. So, too, are many of the works by Saskatchewan's Jan Wyers in which he describes place, people, and history.

Cree artist Allen Sapp (1928–2015) does likewise in his direct portrayals of his childhood, as seen in *Babysitting the Kids,* 1970, and *Bringing More Wood Into The House,* 1976.

FIGURE 4.43. **Daphne Odjig**, *The Indian in Translation*, 1978.

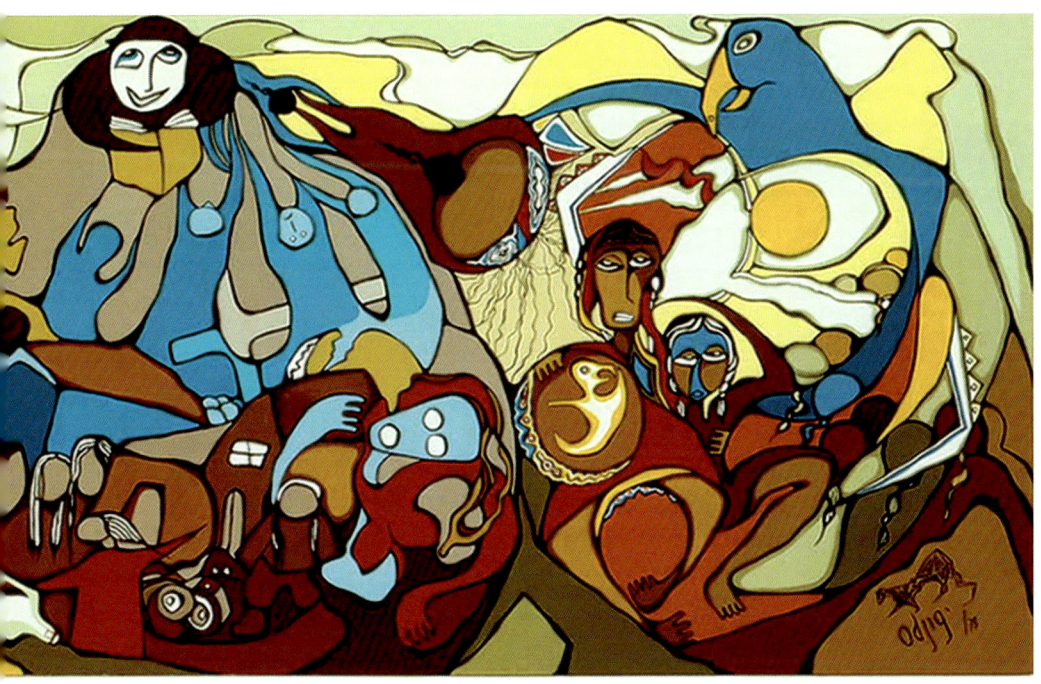

Indian Drums, 1972, is central to his Cree culture. He remembers that he first heard the drums when he was young, and rhythms and powwow circles were important in his youth. As curator Timothy Long commented, "For Sapp, canvas is a drum that pulses with memories; when we look at his paintings, we join the living circle of the drum."[66] These sensibilities are also reflected by writer Alison Mayes: "Sapp had an uncanny, photographic memory for scenes from his childhood. Soon memory paintings of the everyday, hard-working life on the reserve in the 1930s and '40s started to pour out of him: images of women cooking, digging for Seneca root or scraping hides, of men repairing fences, threshing hay or hauling water, or kids playing hockey or chasing gophers; and of the community sharing powwows, sundances, prayer, songs and games."[67]

Andrew Valko (b. 1957) portrays a darker aspect of contemporary life in his *Motel Series*. As well, his *Drive-in* paintings showing famous stars in ordinary places juxtaposes fame with the ordinary, connecting "us" and "them." Those in their cars watch the movie; so, too, do his viewers outside the painting. As he does in his motel works, he casts the viewer as voyeur. In his words, the movie is "like a reality in the sky."[68] Both series speak to an interest in the nostalgia of prairie life, in which he paints the prairie landscape and its unique light while exploring the psychological duality of the ordinary and the extraordinary in activities of daily life.

Contrasting these portrayals of the extraordinary activities of life in ordinary settings are the daily activities of leisure, fairgrounds, beaches, and sporting events, which are subjects Molly Lamb Bobak and Ken Lochhead have painted frequently. Bobak captured the movement and excitement at local equestrian gymkhanas and fairgrounds and in her winter skating scenes. She frequently painted large crowds, some in oil and many in watercolour. Her daughter's riding stable on Vancouver Island furnished her with opportunities to paint equestrian events, some of which I experienced as Bobak was collecting her ideas. Her small watercolour *Country Fair,* 1993, is colourful and its spontaneous brushwork conveys the carefree fun and engagement of the crowds. Detail is suggested, not precisely executed.

Ken Lochhead likewise painted sporting events—curling and hockey—both at the beginning of his career, and again later, after his long and influential abstraction period. His 1954 *Bonspiel* shows the players in discussion at the side of the ice under a typical prairie sky. The figures themselves have a monumentality and solidity of form, recalling Cézanne's emphasis on the cylinder, sphere, and cone, and that of Picasso's monumental works of the 1920s. His 1992 *Pressure* conveys the action of hockey in a quick and freely painted work; the action is at the goal end of the rink. These works contrast with *Journey into the Garden,* 1986, in which toys in a surrealistic composition are set in a garden under a clear blue sky, and all details are precisely constructed to become an outdoor still life.

Still lifes, the depictions of objects of daily life within our homes and personal spaces, have always had a currency in art. This is true in Western Canadian art, too, with Lionel LeMoine FitzGerald's still lifes, for example, like *Geranium and Bottle,* 1949, *From an Upstairs Window,* 1950–51, or *Two Apples,* circa 1940. He executed these paintings with precision. The objects are carefully set on a tabletop or window and the geometry of the setting is critical to the whole. FitzGerald examines the intersection of angles as acutely as the form, surface, and reality of the objects he depicts. In *Geranium and Bottle,* for instance, the glass and the distortion it gives the terracotta plant pot become the primary subject. The plant leaves set against the geometric placement of the background table surfaces add both softness and complexity to the work. *Two Apples,* painted with his exacting pointillism, focuses on the surfaces of the apples and the light falling on them.

Flower still lifes formed an important aspect of the oeuvre of Maxwell Bates as well. His *Still Life,* 1971, shows a vase of flowers off-centre on the left, balanced by a curtain in the background on the right. The vase, placed on a black-and-white-checkered tablecloth, contrasts the fluidity and the pinks and yellows of the flowers. The tabletop is tilted forward, as many of the tabletops in FitzGerald's still lifes were. Bates's checkered tablecloth pattern recalls the geometric diamond patterns in his abstractions and his paintings of harlequins and clowns.

Regina's Vic Cicansky is well known for his ceramic sculptures of vegetables, fruit, and pantries. Cicansky's fruits and vegetables, seated in chairs or on couches, are fun, mimicking people in their intimate settings. His pantries also hearken back to the long prairie custom of "putting away for the winter." Of works like *Blue Pantry,* 2003, he writes in his artist's statement:

I love colour. The pantry idea gives me shelves of opportunity to play with dazzling coloured glazes. I want the colours to be zany and aggressively exuberant. Wild. Once I decide on the colour for the pantry, I paint it. The shelves then become the field on which I can play with colour. I begin by filling each shelf with finished jars. Colours are set side by side in a random fashion.

Once the shelves are filled I begin to remove one here and there, and either leave a space or fill it with another colour. I am never really sure. This process can go on for weeks until I achieve a balance of colour and shape that settles over the whole.

This act of creation is in constant flux. Ideas are proposed, considered and discarded until I arrive at a complete work. The new work is not the end. It is only one of many searches for an image that represents a feeling, an emotion, a passion for colour.[69]

Fruit is also the subject of a number of paintings by Victoria's Phyllis Serota, in which she masterfully works with colour, light, and shadows. The depth of her dark tones—purples, greens, and blues—in her paintings of plums and pears is sensuous. *Pear Blues* depicts a round bowl of pears in the upper right of the image; the circular form of the bowl is reflected on the table, which in turn is enhanced by the round edge of the table beside the window, the light source in the work. She captures both the direct light reflected on the pears and the shadows it casts.

Artists' depictions of lifestyles and the varied aspects of our personal lives, public events, interiors, and exteriors are insightful portrayals of reality, memory, and narrative.

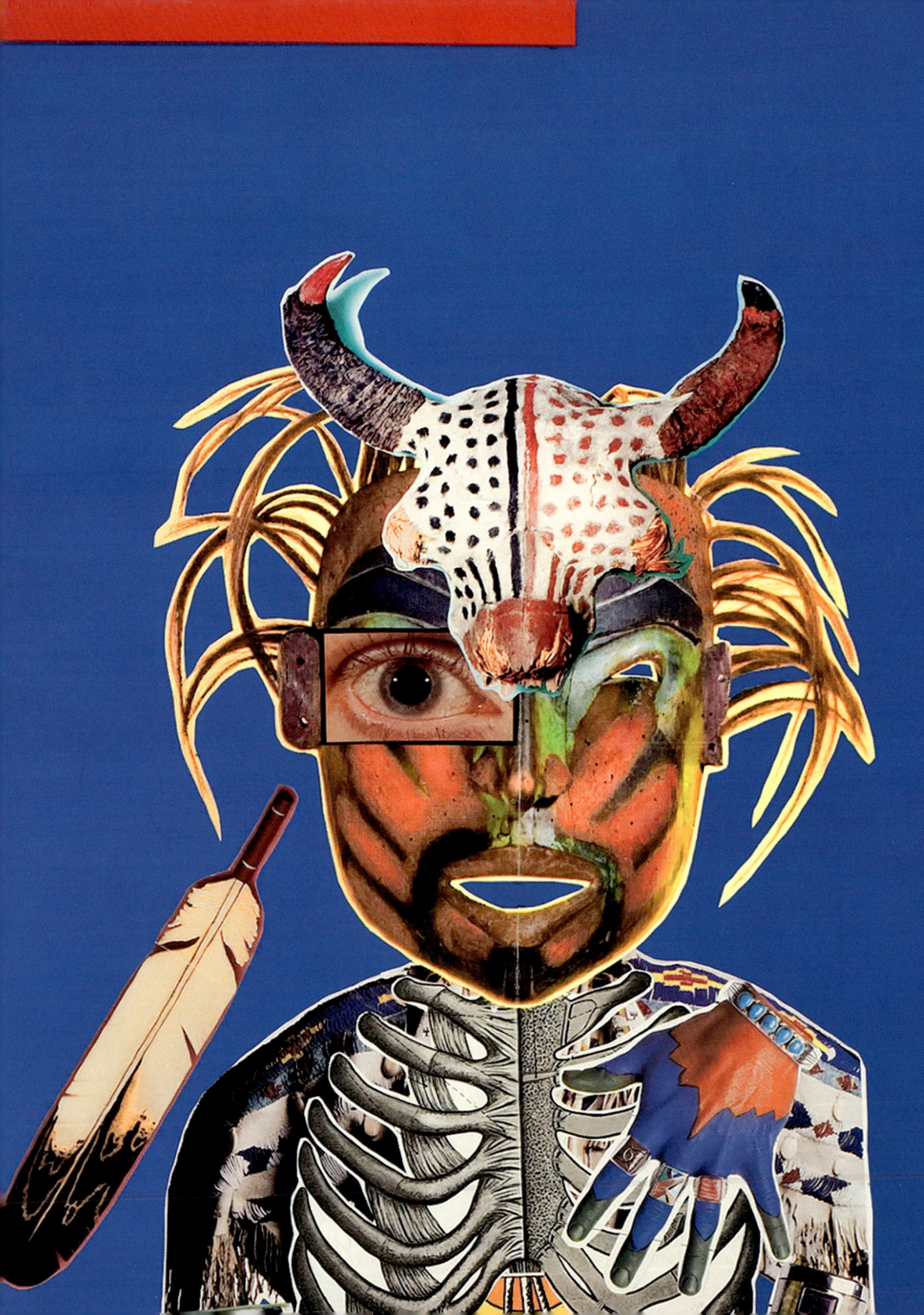

V Abstraction into the Spiritual

"For me it's to manifest a visual idea."[1]

Abstract art is without doubt an aspect of Canadian visual expression in which artists from the western regions of the country have made significant contributions. Abstraction in Canadian art drew its inspiration from many conscious and subconscious influences. Coincidental circumstances—including international art movements, and those in music, literature, and local realities—the landscape, still lifes, and specific sensibilities of light and colour were all important roots. In addition to these societal, cultural, and natural elements, converging aspects of global spiritual philosophies have likewise played meaningful roles in the various forms of abstraction.

Abstract art is generally considered a European artistic innovation from the early years of the twentieth century, born in part from its precursor, cubism, in the first two decades of the century and from the new visual departures in the immediate aftermath of the First World War. Canada was not far behind Europe in the beginning of abstraction, and Western Canada was at the forefront. Indeed, Bertram Brooker, the first abstract artist in Canada, started his career in Manitoba before his 1921 move to Toronto. Forty years later, a group of Saskatchewan artists, the Regina Five, fired the imagination of the country with an exhibition at the National Gallery of Canada in 1961. In-between these seminal works were many visual experiments and exciting landmarks in abstraction from each of Canada's four western provinces. Abstraction continues to be a significant mode of expression today. Abstract patterns in visual expression, however, long predate twentieth-century painting abstractions, with the geometric and log cabin patterns in textile art being prominent since the early nineteenth century.

Lita Fontaine, *The Pagan*, 1996 (detail).

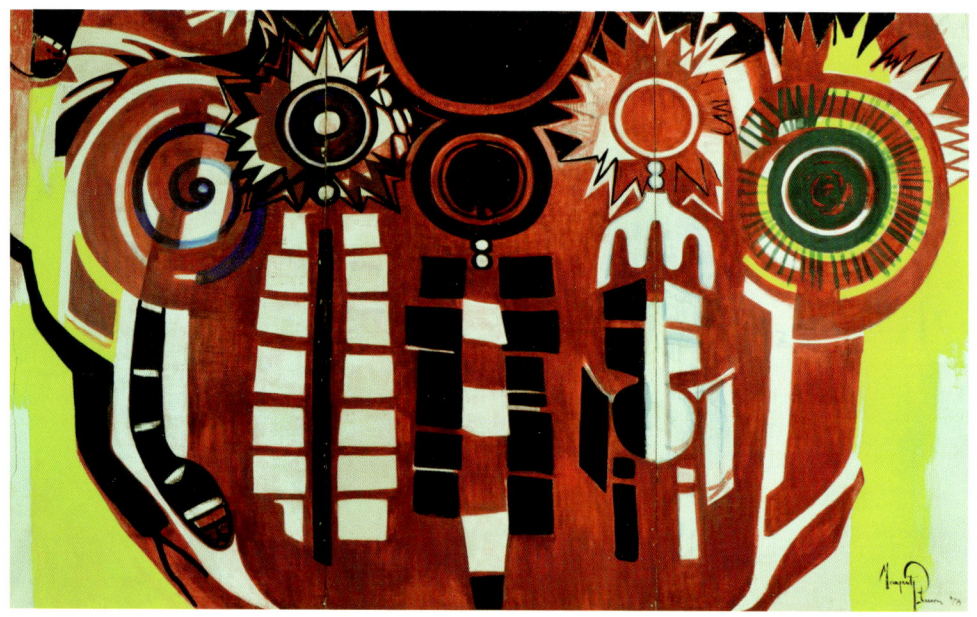

Artists across the Canadian West have explored all the concepts of abstraction, those linked with the land, objects, artistic theory, and spiritual philosophies. Their work and ideas were far-reaching, in many cases ahead of their time, and not surprisingly drew negative criticism and certainly public misunderstanding. The spiritual in abstraction was critical for those who painted pure abstractions and for those who included aspects of abstraction in their art. Emily Carr, who felt misunderstood by society, for instance, wrote in the 1930s about the power of movement and the spirit, sensibilities particularly evident in many of her expressive forest and sky paintings. Spiritual thought was very much part of the focus of Bertram Brooker's abstractions in the 1920s and Eric Bergman's in the 1930s. Both were interested in music and in the writings of William Blake. Group of Seven member Fred Varley, who lived in Vancouver from 1926 to 1937, explored Buddhism, as did Vancouver Island artist Jack Wise (1928–1996), from 1966 onwards. Working in North Vancouver after moving there in 1940, Group of Seven member Lawren Harris was interested in theosophy. Mexican native spiritual meanings permeated the work of Victoria's Margaret Peterson (1903–1997) from the 1950s until her death.

Art today continues to embrace abstraction in all media, two and three dimensional. Robert Murray's powerful, large metal sculptures evoke the landscape. Saskatchewan's Eli

FIGURE 5.1. **Margaret Peterson**, *Storm Gods*, n.d.

Bornstein created unique constructivist pieces over several decades. One of those was the major installation commissioned for the Winnipeg airport in 1964, and which is now installed outdoors at the University of Manitoba.

All these artists, however, garnered controversy; their work was not understood because their imagery was not easily recognized. Portraying esoteric thoughts and ideas in art was new, but, fortunately, artists were not deterred from their visual paths. Don Reichert was at the centre of a particularly venomous controversy over abstract art when he taught at the University of New Brunswick in 1962. A letter from a friend, after a strong community outburst over his abstractions that he had showed in a lecture, summarizes those sentiments: "May I say how much I enjoyed your exhibit and how sorry I am that you have been subjected to such personal attacks. That was really what I tried to prepare you for when we were speaking of the local attitude towards art in your studio one day. But if it is any comfort to you, I think that the controversy has really broadened many minds."[2]

Abstracted Realities

"The history of abstraction during the last century was that representation became more and more abstracted until it reached pure abstraction sometime around mid-century. What I am trying to do is to make my abstract work more representational."[3]

Questions as to how to define "abstract" are many: What makes abstract, abstract? Is it the lack of the recognizable or identifiable? One definition of "abstract" means "to take away," suggesting that in abstract painting the artist takes away, or does not include, details and elements he or she feels are unnecessary to convey the essence of the work. An early example of "abstracting" a subject is *Prairie Road,* painted in 1925 by Charles Comfort. In this large vertical canvas, the country road and landscape are fully recognizable, but the telephone wires and fence wires are "abstracted out," not being critical to the expression of the scene or mood of place. Annora Brown's *Foothills Village,* painted in the early 1950s, shows the mountains in the distance depicted geometrically with shafts of light emanating from the edges of the mountain forms crossing the fields. Some fields are rendered naturalistically, others in geometric shapes. The houses and grain elevators are depicted in their basic rectangular and triangular forms with few details save the rectangles as windows and doors. A road runs parallel to the shafts of light from the primary elevator to the mountains, linking the foreground to the background. In other cases, artists pare everything down to a few colours and one or two geometric shapes, as Ken Lochhead did in *Sky Location* of 1967. The large area of blue in this vertical painting was smoothly applied, only the upper right corner breaking the expanse of solid blue. A magenta

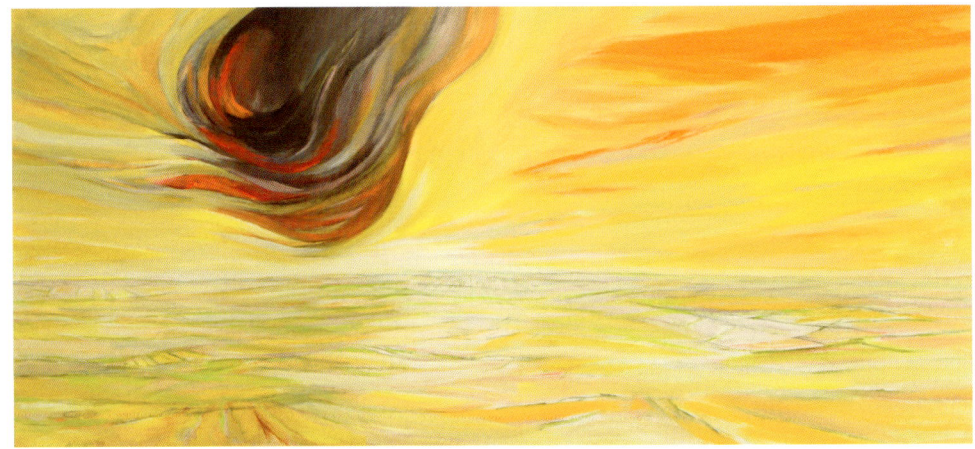

rectangle in that upper corner is bordered on two sides by red, black, yellow, and white lines; each of these colours is natural to the prairie landscape—the sky, soil, grains, and flax.

Chris Cran (b. 1949), working in Calgary, explores the intersection between the abstract and the representational in his 1991 seven-foot oil on canvas *Grey Green Crowd #2*, described by writer Katherine Ylitalo: "From various angles, a tug-of-war plays out between what you see and what you think you see. Approach from the side and you see a black–and–white photograph of a crowd of about 12 people. Head on, you see an abstraction constructed of two main elements: a screen of crisp, thin stripes and a photographic image (a fragment of a half-tone photograph, perhaps?) that seems to slip out of focus. Close up, the building blocks of the painting dominate: stripes, dots and swaths of black and white."[4]

His technique was low-tech, starting with a layer of gesso, then a pale green one. As Ylitalo commented, he placed "quarter-inch sign-painter's tape vertically with a system of weights, matte medium to seal the tape and another layer of white gesso over all. Cran used a macro lens to photograph a fragment of a newspaper ad showing a crowd of people, already out of focus, capturing a small section of the faces. Using a slide projector, he painted the projection on the canvas with black and dragged a wide brush lightly through the dots from top to bottom."[5] After he removed the tape, the green stripes were visible and disrupted the image.

Colour and form are the primary elements of abstraction. The mood or meaning of a work is enhanced by the manner in which the artist applies the paint. That application might be smooth, worked into the canvas layer on layer, or rolled on, or stained. It might be applied with strong, expressive brushwork and gestures filled with tremendous energy, or by using a

FIGURE 5.2. **George H. Swinton**, *Untitled*, 1964.

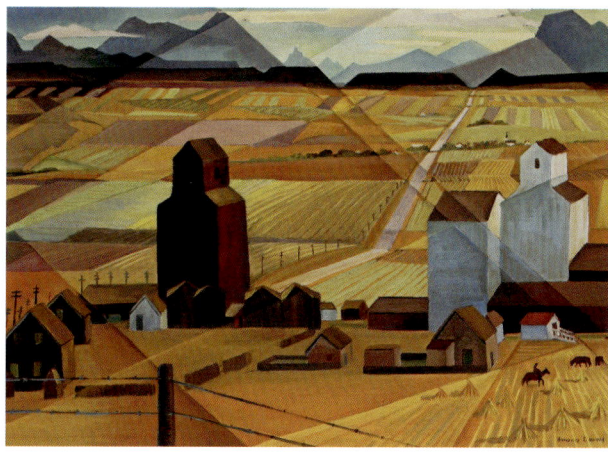

FIGURE 5.3.
Annora Brown,
Foothills Village,
c. 1955.

spatula to create three-dimensional qualities of rich and thick impasto showing the palette knife or spatula marks. Sometimes artists spray paint onto the canvas using an airbrush. The rhythm of the application of paint is essential to the whole. The actual "act of painting," as British Columbia artist Jack Shadbolt referred to it, is the personal hand of the artist. It is that action of mark making that gives visual direction in a work of art. The resulting movement of forms and directional lines within a composition becomes pathways, leading the viewer's eye through the composition into its centre and around and among its details. That visual journey, or engagement, of the viewer is an essential aspect of interaction among the artist, the viewer, and the work. The viewer is therefore encouraged to involve oneself in, and react to, the idea expressed, either positively or negatively.

Abstraction of the mid-twentieth century falls into two primary categories: geometric abstraction and abstract expressionism. The former evolved from the cubists and constructivists; the latter, from international colour theorists like Hans Hofmann and gestural painters like Jackson Pollock. The work of Canadian artists is no exception and follows a similar path. Several American painters, such as Will Barnet and Barnett Newman, had measurable impacts on the development of abstraction in Western Canada, an impact that started with their involvement with artists in Saskatchewan. Newman's spiritually powerful work based on the Book of Exodus, *Voice of Fire,* is in the National Gallery of Canada's collection. A third American whose influence was felt is New York art critic Clement Greenberg. All these influential individuals took active parts in Saskatchewan's Emma Lake Artists' Workshops run by the University of Saskatchewan. Will Barnet was the workshop's leader in 1957; Barnett Newman, in 1959; and Clement Greenberg, in 1962.

Colour theory and the influence of New York artists were very much part of the developing art scene of Western Canada at the time. International concepts were not foreign to artists in the West, despite the comparative geographical isolation from the centre of the art world and the lack of a critical mass, given the West's relatively small population. While the influences of Barnett Newman, Clement Greenberg, and Will Barnet are well known, other artists had immigrated from Europe and were conversant with the early schools of abstraction. A number of Western Canadian artists had also gone to New York's Art Students League. FitzGerald attended that prestigious, internationally acclaimed New York school over the winter of 1921–22. His instructor told him to draw a tree each morning as the first thing he did, and to draw it as if it was organically growing. The result is the human-like limbs of his subsequent painting of trees, like those in *Poplar Woods*, 1931. Other Western Canadian artists who were major forces in Canadian art and who studied at the Art Students League over the decades included Fred Varley, Jack Shadbolt, and B.C. Binning. Their introductions to the energy, the thinking, and the contemporary visual ideas in that capital of the art world were transformative for them all, and consequently to Canadian art as a whole.

In analyzing the role Western Canadian artists have had on the development of abstraction in Canadian art, one can look at work by decade from the 1920s through the 1980s and beyond; take a geographical approach, east to west, Manitoba to British Columbia; or assess the various sources of inspiration and the resulting individual forms of abstraction. In this discussion these considerations are woven together, as it is equally meaningful to understand the various sources of inspiration artists react to, as it is to when and where those reactions are expressed.

The first Canadian abstract artist, Manitoba's Bertram Brooker, painted his first abstractions in 1927. His 1928 oil on canvas *Sounds Assembling* is a truly significant painting in the annals of Canadian art. For him, music was the key influence. Born in England, Brooker moved to Portage la Prairie in 1905, and in 1913 ran the movie theatre in Neepawa, Manitoba, for several years before moving to Winnipeg. Though he moved to Toronto in 1921, while he was still in Neepawa he prophetically said, "If ever I paint, I want to paint music." He began exploring abstraction in 1924, self-described as "based on the experiences I derived from Music."[6]

Sounds Assembling is vibrant, filled with predominantly primary colours, a strong sense of movement, mathematical and geometric forms, and musical references reminiscent of organ pipes. Brooker was seeking visual language to penetrate what he called "the inner life." Recalling his time in the movie theatre, he created forms that emerge as if through a projector lens. The angularly placed organ-pipe-like rods converge, off-centre, lifting the viewer through repeated grey/blue circles. The composition spirals to the spiritual level of the cosmos, or the "fourth dimension," as its jagged, cubist-like lines reach the celestial star. The work portrays sound travelling through space. Its vivid colours and repeated contrapuntal rhythms become the intersection of music and visual art.

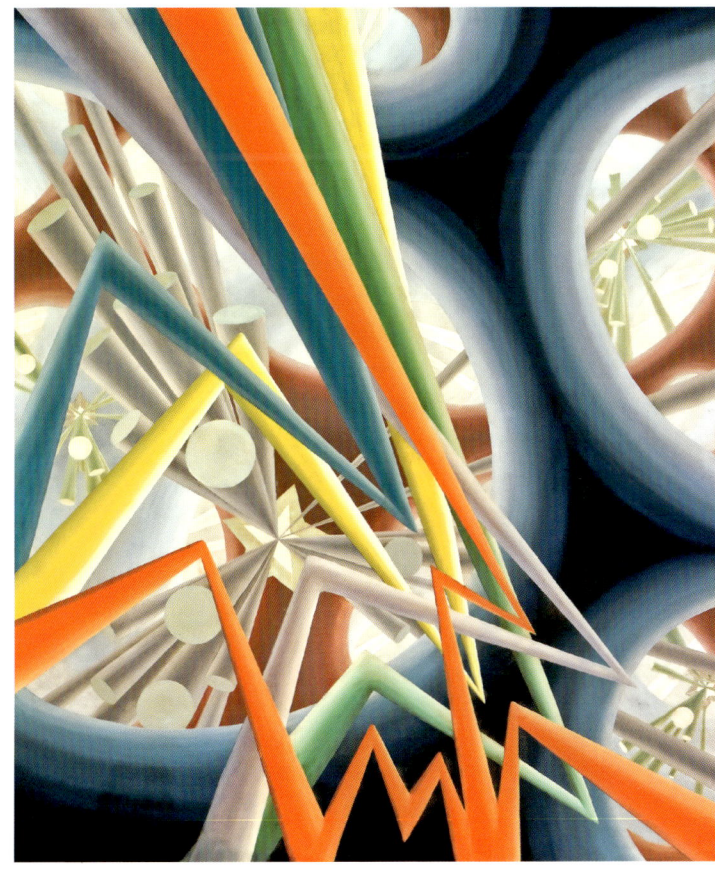

Bertram Brooker,
Sounds Assembling,
1928.

The time frame of Brooker's exploration of music and painting is especially interesting, considering the artistic experiments taking place at that time in Europe. Music and art connections were particularly strong between Russian painter and art theorist Wassily Kandinsky (1866–1944) and Austrian composer and painter Arnold Schoenberg (1874–1951). Abstraction took hold in both art and music simultaneously. Schoenberg was developing the twelve-tone scale while Kandinsky was breaking visual form to create his mid-1920s *Improvisations* and *Compositions*, among the world's early abstractions. Close friends, yet adversaries in the early twentieth century, they had a deep and passionate correspondence in which they shared, debated, and explored new ideas of form. Though Brooker had not seen Kandinsky's paintings, he seems to have been inspired by the articles about the controversies in shifting contemporary expression that surrounded the 1913 New York *Armory Show*. That international exhibition, including new leading-edge work of the cubists and those working with non-naturalistic colour, was a milestone in the presentation of early twentieth-century art. It travelled to various centres in the United States and garnered negative publicity everywhere it went. Yet, it inspired and encouraged many young artists to stretch the traditional boundaries of painting and had a significant effect on new art, including that of Bertram Brooker. Brooker likely would also have read Kandinsky's pivotal 1912 book *Concerning the Spiritual in Art* and he was knowledgeable about European cubism and fauvism, aspects of both being evident in his *Sounds Assembling*. The artist's love of contemporary music, literature, and the spiritual has also been documented, particularly his interest in English writer and artist William Blake, some of whose work Brooker illustrated. Brooker was also an author. He edited the inaugural *Yearbook of the Arts in Canada* in 1929, and in 1936 he was the first recipient of the first Governor General's Award for Fiction with his book *Think of the Earth*. This genuine multi- and interdisciplinary interest and knowledge are evident throughout his career.

Brooker's 1949 talk to the University of Toronto's Hart House, entitled "Painted Verbs," underlines his link between music and geometry:

> I shamelessly used a ruler and compass, trying to compose on the canvas some sort
> of replica of the colour, the volume and the rhythm I experienced when listening to
> music. There were shapes in some of the earlier pictures, but they were not objects
> in the ordinary sense—they were not nouns—you couldn't name them. Most of
> the shapes were floating areas of colour—they were verbs, representing action and
> movement—and when in some cases, they came close to recognition as objects,
> such as spheres and rods or peaks, these were only intended as the path or climax or
> culmination of a movement, not its finish.[7]

This insight into "painting music," with the shapes as verbs, explains the patterns of individual sounds and spiritual meanings in his painting *Sounds Assembling*. If the circles are not the lens of the projector, are they the ear canal? Are they a telescopic view of the cosmos? Are they the end of an organ pipe, or the path to spiritual being? Perhaps they represent all of these.

Brooker died in Toronto in 1955, and in the *Ontario Society of Artists Exhibition Catalogue* of the next year, Brooker's friend and colleague Lionel LeMoine FitzGerald wrote: "Intensity, precision and searching for an ever finer expression of inner compulsions, are revealed in all the drawings and paintings that Bertram Brooker has left to us and we are deeply indebted to him as an example of artistic integrity. . . . No single work was ever final, and when the emotional upsurge had subsided it was replaced by a renewal of energy to build something still better into the broad structure of his art, nothing short of perfection the ultimate goal."[8]

The longer-term impacts of Brooker's explorations in art, writing, and thought were not fully understood at the time, but this one-time Manitoban unquestionably brought a maturity to Canadian art, and the spiritual quest he expressed continues to be pursued by artists today. He is not alone in exploring the powerful union of music and visual art. Sound became a consuming subject for Pat Martin Bates, for instance. Living in Wainwright, Alberta, in the early 1960s, she was fascinated by the reverberating sound waves of the military control towers that spread across that northern landscape. She incorporated patterns of sound into her work by depicting multiple concentric circles suggesting those radiating waves. Some circles in Bates's works are pierced, allowing the light through from behind, and these pierced lines became moving tendrils symbolically carrying the sound across and beyond the work. In these pieces her colours are muted—blues and greys denoting the sky and air, the purveyors of the sounds. When mounted in light boxes and lit from behind, the colours turn to gold, as in *Signal 9: Perforated Northern Silence in an Arctic Night,* 1965. She told me, "I love the sound of silence . . . as a child I was convinced that if one listened carefully one could hear grass grow. I loved the sounds of water."[9]

The transition from music as influence for abstraction to that of the landscape as influence is not a huge step when one considers the natural rhythms of the land and the repetition of lines and forms in nature that are also reflected in music. The prairie and its horizon lines, distances, and snow-sculpted winter landscapes became critical elements in the development of abstract art. So, too, did the forms and majestic power of the mountains and the ephemeral and threatening aspects of the skies and waters. The forms and colours of the northern prairie landscape had a particular impact for abstraction in Pat Martin Bates's art, as seen in her texture-filled white-on-white and black-on-black prints. It was that Alberta landscape that eventually led to her exploration of alchemy, the turning of all to gold, as she witnessed with the ripe wheat fields and changing light at sundown.

The prairie landscape Charles Comfort painted in 1925 when he began to "abstract out" certain elements is the one that had captivated Winnipeg-born Lionel LeMoine FitzGerald. His early prairie landscapes were, of course, realistic, depicting the skies and horizons, as we have seen. However, in the late 1940s he was increasingly interested in abstraction and, as did many artists, he went back and forth between reality and abstraction. FitzGerald and Brooker met when FitzGerald visited Toronto, and they subsequently engaged in a regular and profound correspondence. In their letters they explored the visual approaches of the other. Brooker, for instance, started his artistic career as an abstract artist and only later turned to portraying reality. FitzGerald, conversely, started his artistic career depicting objects and places of reality, and later moved into abstraction. These shifts can be traced through their drawings and paintings and also in their letters. The candour with which they discussed the high points and problems of their art making is revealing. Both artists, however, ended their careers where they began: the final work by FitzGerald was realistic, and that by Brooker was an abstraction. It is clear that music fed Brooker's abstractions, and landscape and still lifes fed FitzGerald's.

The flooded Manitoba plains, resembling lakes during the 1948 and 1950 Red River floods, were major landscape inspirations for FitzGerald's abstract works. He flew over them en route to British Columbia just before his retirement when he was on leave from the University of Manitoba in 1948–49. He was captivated and stunned by their vast expanse and the reflections of the clouds. That aerial perspective resulted in particularly poignant abstract drawings, done in pencil, ink, and colour pencil. Some, like his coloured pencil drawing *Manitoba Landscape,* 1951, show cubist, geometric cloud formations. The patterned fields were executed in his unique crosshatched pencil technique. Other works are pure abstractions, the geometric forms carefully balanced and evocative of the never-ending horizons. Every line has a purpose; nothing is superfluous. His colours in these abstracted landscapes are those from the land.

Some of FitzGerald's abstractions were based on still lifes, while others were directly inspired by Russian suprematist artist Kazimir Malevich's geometric coloured pencil works. FitzGerald did a series of sensitive abstractions on coloured paper, often dark blue, on which the forms were drawn with light coloured pencils. Perhaps his best-known abstraction, however, is *Abstract in Green and Gold,* an oil on canvas done in 1954. The artist paid particular attention to the patterning of his geometric shapes and the intersections of lines and forms. Exquisitely painted soft, curvilinear forms are interlaced with straight directional lines. The flow of shapes, planes, and colours moves into and through this constructed mystical space. The repeated flowing, curved lines and forms are precise, compelling, and sensuous. He used a compass and ruler for this work, and the result is that line and colour became equal elements. Texture, built carefully with tiny brush strokes using the tip of his brush, and tone were equally paramount. The result is a balanced subtlety of colour and linear construction that enhances the rhythmic flow and receding of geometric forms into space.

FitzGerald's transition from reality to abstraction was deliberate, developed from his career-long preoccupation in form, relationship of objects, and changing perspectives in varying lights. He reflected on his shift of focus to abstraction in the late 1940s and early 1950s: "Having been experimenting pretty steadily, with a sort of abstract approach, I wanted to find out more about colour and composition and thought a good change from the object would be a refreshing thing and perhaps open a new field. Have done endless drawings in black and white as well as in colour and carried a few of these into larger spaces in oil. Will be interesting to see what will happen in the future."[10] Though he remained linked to form, FitzGerald was freed from it in many ways. Scholar Ann Davis noted, "FitzGerald was content to work with the imagination freed from the insistence of objects seen, using colours and shapes without reference to natural form."[11]

FitzGerald wrote to Canadian art writer Robert Ayre in 1954, "I am enjoying experimenting in this direction of drawing from stored-up memories and more freely playing

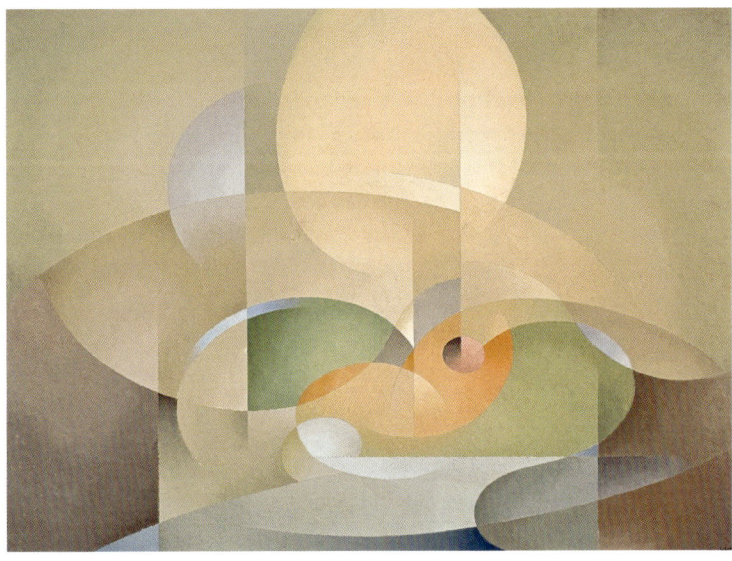

FIGURE 5.5.
Lionel LeMoine FitzGerald, *Abstract: Green and Gold*, 1954.

with forms and colours. I seem to require this freedom, for the present, from the thing seen and its restrictions. Of course, I never know when the urge will come to go back to the subject in front of me and find out what effect all this recent activity will have on the result."[12] FitzGerald did return to the "subject in front of him," still life, a source for abstraction for many artists. A neighbour of FitzGerald's gave me a photograph taken the day before FitzGerald died. It was of the artist's studio, set up for his next still life works—bottles and plants—with works in progress in the background.

Brooker also did some still life–based abstractions. They, too, exude a fluid lyricism, yet have a basis in geometric form. Brooker credited his friend FitzGerald for his artistic shift: "Your attitude toward your work and our companionship on the few days I had with you have had a very considerable effect on me. It has changed not only my own approach to things, but also my appreciation of other people's work. If I tried to put my finger on it I should say that it has made me more honest and studious and less impatient for quick results. . . . To boil it down to one word—form is the thing that obsesses me. Colour is no longer a thing that interests me for its own sake, as it did."[13]

When discussing the landscape as a root of abstraction, the work of two British Columbia artists comes to the fore—Gordon Smith of Vancouver and Takao Tanabe of Vancouver Island. The paintings of both hold seminal places in Canadian art. Both artists are recipients of Governor General's Awards in the Visual Arts: Smith in 2009 and Tanabe in 2003. They each had studied at the Winnipeg School of Art prior to its union with the University of Manitoba:

Gordon Smith from 1937 to 1940 and Tanabe from 1946 to 1949, a period when FitzGerald was head of the school. Toronto journalist Robert Fulford featured both Smith and Tanabe in his insightful and forward-looking 1961 article in *Canadian Art*: "Survey of the Work of 24 Young Canadian Artists," which covered the work of artists across Canada. He referred to Tanabe, then thirty-four years old, as a "good abstract artist." He continued: "Tanabe's paintings make their own firm, memorable impression. His abstract landscapes, unlike most of those which emerge from the studios of B.C. painters, are connected to no particular time or place. He refers to his general subject as an 'interior land.' . . . The forms themselves he has picked up in B.C., on the prairies, in his two-year tour of Europe (particularly Denmark)."[14]

Gordon Smith, in Fulford's estimation, had been influenced by the Bay Group of California painters whose work Smith saw when he was in California in 1951. Fulford said, "His work has the buoyancy and sometimes the delirious handling of light which we associate with the best California art. Like the best of British Columbia painting it also has a very intense and intimate relationship with the B.C. landscape. . . . He has been most convincing when he has abandoned the conventions of semi-realistic landscape and allowed his talent for free, spontaneous calligraphy to assert itself."[15]

Robert Fulford was prophetic about the importance of both these artists. Smith's sureness and ability with light, line, and abstraction grew from that point over the many ensuing decades of his prolific career. Takao Tanabe, too, has created powerful, evocative works linked to place, such as his *Prairie Paintings*, done between 1973 and 1980 when he was in Banff. From his early career, Tanabe travelled and studied widely, in New York and London, and Europe and Japan. When in Japan he studied sumi-e painting, a base for a number of future works. He draws simultaneously on calligraphy and the abstract expressionist theories of Hans Hofmann, which Joe Plaskett had introduced him to at the School of Art. Both approaches fuse in his *Prairie Paintings*. The structure of his hard-edge geometric abstractions of the 1960s in turn informed his 1970s prairie works, as did the precision he gained from his printmaking. Art writer Nancy Tousley describes the unique sensibility of his prairie works: "Indeed, the highly refined, thinly painted *Prairie Paintings* made by a technique that combines characteristics of Japanese sumi-e and calligraphy, portray vast, open expanses seen through an atmospheric veil, empty and timeless and placeless in their aspect. . . . As for abstraction, it sank into the structure of the prairie paintings where it became the bedrock of his landscape composition."[16]

In Tanabe's 1970 *Untitled Landscape*, the subject is the sky, light, and the land, the horizon becoming the dividing line. The sky occupies the top one-third of the canvas; the middle ground is a slim and strong horizontal, stretching across the painting; and the foreground fills the lower half of the work. The diagonal line through the foreground draws one to the dominant horizon line. His acrylic paint is smoothly applied on the wet unprimed canvas sized with glue. Working on a flat surface, Tanabe would spray the canvas with water to keep it wet while he painted. In

The Line Sketch, 1974, the subdued palette echoes the emptiness of the prairie, the sky filling more than three-quarters of the canvas. Again, a diagonal line crosses the land portion of the painting. Tousley's summation of these works is poignant: "Tanabe's minimal, abstracted realism is a metaphor for nature, and with its indeterminacy, emptiness, silence and instability, a vision more metaphysical than material, one that melds Zen and the Sublime Void. His imagery is a history of transience: times of day, the elements, the seasons, penumbras and light."[17]

Gordon Smith also experimented with colour and hard-edge abstraction through the 1960s before turning to painting the land. Of hard-edge abstraction he commented: "It could just be a temporary reaction against emotion in painting. Who knows? It's pretty painting—architecturally pleasant—and very satisfying to do. . . . I am doing it just to please myself and not to go along with the critics. I also want to see whether this latest departure fits into an over-all development of my work."[18]

FIGURE 5.6. **Takao Tanabe**, *The Line Sketch*, 1974.

In the 1970s Smith shifted to what he saw as his real interest: the natural world. *November Sea* of 1978, for example, shows a looseness of structure while still retaining reference to the abstract. The composition is divided into at least seven horizontal bands through which Smith's brushwork develops subtle patterns. His paint, applied in multiple layers, allows the inner light to glow. Vancouver critic Joan Lowndes, who kept abreast of Smith's experiments with colour and structure, admired the power of his resulting paintings, noting that his 1970s work came from "years of cumulative achievement": "In practical terms this means that as he feels his structure becoming too tight he loosens it; as he feels his colour becoming too lush he restrains it; and as he feels he is adhering too closely to reality he becomes more abstract."[19]

The artist himself recognized the struggle to achieve the balance between tension and looseness in his work: "The act of painting is the mysterious and continuous struggle with chance, hopeful that something will come. Bacon says you empty your mind, then suddenly something happens. I get excited at these times and say, 'My God, I've got something,' and finally you make it safe and that's my criticism of myself."[20] Smith produced compelling, strong works, all showing his expert ability with colour, line, and that balance of looseness and structure throughout his career into his 100th year.

Jack Shadbolt, older than Smith and Tanabe, was a friend and colleague of them both, and he, too, lived and worked in British Columbia throughout his career, earning accolades nationally and internationally. He is particularly integral to any discussion about artists and movements in Canadian art from the 1950s and 1960s, known by younger generations of British Columbia artists as "the father of BC art." Clearly affected by the horror and devastation of war that he had witnessed as an official Canadian war artist in the Second World War, torment and destruction fill his work of the immediate postwar years. His dark, restrained palette and broken angular forms reveal sombreness and devastation, and the combined power of his expression and sensibilities of form, line, and colour is simultaneously gripping and disturbing. There are interesting parallels, in my view, between Shadbolt's war and immediate postwar work and that of some major twentieth-century British artists, particularly Graham Sutherland. The impact of what Shadbolt witnessed is evident: "What I have painted since the war has in one way or another grown out of the war itself; first in the paintings of bomb ruins and in more contemplative approach to the street scenes of my familiar surroundings, then gradually as the social disruption grew too complex to be expressed in explicit terms, the need for imagery arose . . . form became correspondingly less descriptive—a more abstractly expressive vehicle for these new meanings."[21]

Shadbolt's postwar travels and his time at the Art Students League in New York fuelled his return to Vancouver with a keen sense of modernism. His work of the 1950s is realistically based and reflected the power of nature, its transformations and regrowth from apparent darkness. Elements from nature are juxtaposed with abstracted forms. In 1951 he wrote: "One would hazard a guess that the factor which puts an artist philosophically nearest in touch with

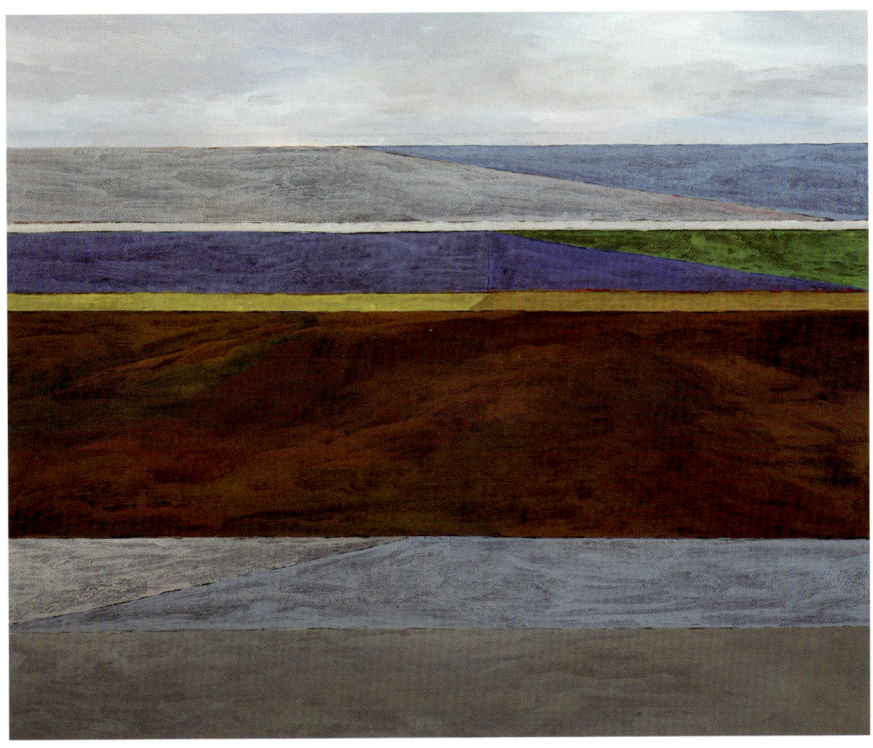

the core theme of our present period is his intuitive recognition of the picture areas as a void of solitude across which forms are reaching to touch tips in human communion. Their reaching and stretching, their gesticulating to attract one another across intervening space is the secret paraphrase of our need to commune across the vast, uncertain reaches of our spiritual insecurity, of our longing to clasp hands in reassurance of a collective belief."[22]

World Under Still Life, 1957, a watercolour on paper, is a prime example of divergent directions with the naturalistic colours and melding of forms into each other suggesting the natural. The sharper-edged, abstract forms emerge from his knowledge of cubism, and the mask-like images reflect his penchant for allegory and his interest in Indigenous cultures. These interests became a focus of his later work and foreshadow later compositions in which forms recede and move forward simultaneously. Mirrored, repeated elements build on each other in Shadbolt's unique work. He said, "My detestation of mass behavior patterns has made me shun responses that are too predictable. . . . We must leave ideas open and, as artists, we must

FIGURE 5.7. **Gordon Smith**, *West Coast #2*, 1974.

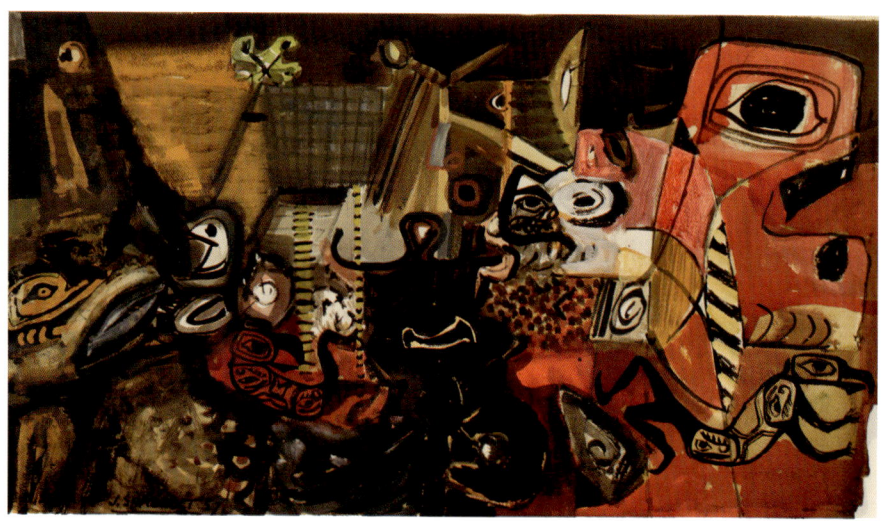

leave objects free to the give and take of reciprocal interaction with their surroundings. Thus, if the picture is to be true for us it must generate from its own plastic elements and from the associative forces that permeate the artist's consciousness."[23]

His 1960s abstractions evolved from both geometric theories and nature itself. Even while he was painting his biomorphic automatic calligraphic works, he was searching in other paintings for more formal construction and structure. This duality of approach posed a degree of inner conflict for him. Shadbolt's biographer, art historian Scott Watson, noted, "He knew he was in conflict, and in a conflict that threatened to erase his sense of identity."[24] As Shadbolt expressed it: "I have been for some long time working in two divergent directions, to the point where I have wondered on occasion which is me and whether I shouldn't try to make up my mind either one way or another and go all out in one direction."[25] These divergent explorations gave individual works a complex balance of the realistic, the abstract, and the spiritual, imbuing his oeuvre as a whole with great strength and depth.

In 1990, eight years before the artist's death, Watson summed up this artist's monumental contribution to the Canadian art scene: "His reputation as one of Canada's most important painters, established long ago with his critical triumphs of the late forties, continues to grow, and he continues to paint works that catch critics and followers off guard. For he has never fallen into formulas that his own successes might have suggested to him, but has always opened himself to the event of painting in search for truth."[26]

FIGURE 5.8. **Jack Leonard Shadbolt**, *World Under Still Life*, 1957.

A close colleague of Shadbolt's, and a founder and head of the fine arts department of the University of British Columbia, British Columbia artist B.C. Binning, was a formalist and a structural abstractionist. He became one of Canada's most noted muralists. His 1956 mosaic on the exterior of the British Columbia Electric Building gained immediate public profile and became a Vancouver landmark with its blue and green iconic diamond patterns. Binning travelled extensively, using his university study leaves to explore international visual ideas. A master of line and drawing as well as colour and form, Binning was inspired by both European and Japanese architecture and internationalism. However, his subject matter remained local. Curator Ian Thom points out, "Binning is able to subtly balance a keen interest in linear pattern with a bold use of colour, and the resultant image is an imaginative recapturing of his experience entering the inner harbour."[27]

Authors David Brunett and Marilyn Schiff noted of Binning: "The realistic elements are gone from his work after 1953," and "such rigorous abstraction was still rare in Canada in the early 1950s."[28] These comments are particularly applicable to his 1948 oil on panel painting *Ships and Tower.* The shape of the ship is dominant and the colours are naturalistic. However, other abstracted forms in the work are strong and reflect the energy and business of the harbour itself. In 1960 he painted *Black Island,* a fully abstract painting in which he showed his continued interest in architectural form. In the artist's words: "To heighten the impact, in many cases I have used other colours than those that would have appeared, and have strengthened tensions in space in order to add breadth of experience. Therefore, I have had to interpret colour and space in other than actual or representational terms. At the same time I am still interested—and suppose always will be—in the architectural discipline of the canvas."[29]

FitzGerald met Binning when he was in Vancouver during the summers of 1942 and 1943, and again at the end of the decade. Interested in his work, he spent time with Binning in 1948. FitzGerald commented on it being "semi-abstract." In some ways Binning's approach equates with FitzGerald's, with nature or still lifes as starting points for their abstractions. Binning used ships in the harbour as the basis for *Convoy Under Way* in 1948.

Toni Onley, a younger Vancouver colleague of Binning's and Shadbolt's, emigrated from the Isle of Man via Ontario, arriving in British Columbia in the late 1950s. Onley created particularly interesting abstract collage paintings from torn pieces of paper and canvas. He explained that these emerged out of his frustration with his earlier work: "I got so mad at all these paintings and began to tear them up. Then seeing them scattered on the floor, the pieces lying one on top of the other, a whole new vocabulary of shapes started to emerge. I saw in the debris things I was considering in my mind, but these were different shapes than I would have naturally painted at the time."[30]

Art historian Roald Nasgaard commented that Onley's *Coeur d'Alene,* 1959, is a key work from that period, in which "the drawing is edgy, the tearing abrupt, the colour hot, the all-over structure pulsating."[31] His *Untitled Collage 1B,* circa 1963–64, an oil on paper collage, also

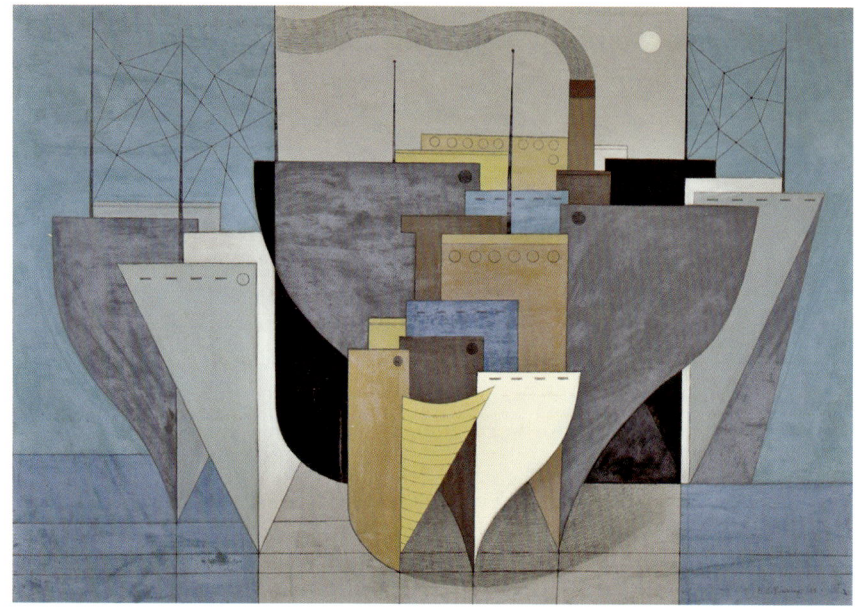

shows energy and movement, with the forms on the left poised to move across the emptiness in the centre. In my view, Onley's work of the 1950s into the 1960s is outstanding. Onley said of his abstractions: "My abstracts are landscape anyway—they are not mind paintings or urban landscapes. All my ideas come from landscape. I am always looking at it as blocks of colour, shape and spaces."[32] Onley later became a master of watercolour techniques, and painting the west coast landscape and flying into remote regions to capture the light, atmosphere, shapes, and spaces were core to his entire career.

As Shirley Thompson, former director of Canada's National Gallery, reflected of the vibrant 1950s, the decade "was one of those decisive moments in Canadian art history, and a period of radical transformation . . . penetrating voices that have transformed the conception and practice of art in this nation."[33] The decade launched pioneering directions in Canadian art. New ideas were rampant, in part because international artists, particularly from the United States and Britain, came to Canada to fill teaching positions in the newly created art schools and fine arts faculties in Canadian universities and colleges, since there was a paucity of adequately trained Canadian artists. Their international perspectives and varied experiences added to the accumulating art knowledge. Different theories were imported and integrated into the visual psyche of students, aesthetic debates deepened, and visual boundaries in art making expanded.

FIGURE 5.9. **B.C. Binning**, *Convoy Under Way*, 1948.

Further, after the Second World War, art was at the centre of many fast-paced societal changes with the explosion of new opportunities, technologies, and mass communication, including the introduction of television, less expensive and more colour reproductions of art, and new art magazines and journals. National and international air travel became more affordable and accessible, and funding from the newly founded Canada Council was another truly positive catalyst for the development of Canadian art. With that assistance artists were able to connect with colleagues and curators across the country and internationally and show their work further afield. These events had a tremendous impact on artistic vision for decades to come.

William Ashby McCloy, from Iowa, came to Winnipeg as the first principal of the Winnipeg School of Art from 1950 to 1954, after it formally joined the University of Manitoba. Under his guidance the school conferred Bachelor of Fine Arts degrees as well as diplomas. McCloy's impact on his students of the 1950s was huge, given his insistence on freedom of artistic expression and experimental approach to art making and teaching. He introduced the "push-pull spatial theories" of New York's legendary teacher and catalyst for abstract expressionism Hans Hofmann, dubbed by critic Clement Greenberg "in all probability the most important art teacher of our time."[34] That first class produced many major Canadian artists, including Ivan Eyre, Winston Leathers, Don Reichert, Bruce Head, Tony Tascona, and Frank Mikuska, to name but a few. Bruce Head, however, was perhaps the most articulate about McCloy, who told them: "All you need is desire." Head continued, "He was a godsend and one of the first intellectuals I had met. Bill McCloy told me that artists should never psychoanalyze themselves. They might lose the source of their art."[35]

American artist Will Barnet was another major inspiration, especially for Alberta's Marion Nicoll (1905–1985). She, like Gordon Smith and Takao Tanabe, created compelling abstract works based on the western landscapes in the 1960s and 1970s. In 1946 Canadian artist Jock Macdonald introduced her to abstraction and automatic painting, of which she said, "Your hand becomes fluent and ignores what the conscious mind sees."[36] In 1957 Marion Nicoll saw Will Barnet and his geometric approach to abstraction, which became important in her own art. She reflected, "I don't think I would have become an abstract painter if I had not done automatic for eleven years."[37] It seems she, like others, had read Wassily Kandinsky's book *Concerning the Spiritual in Art*. While her works of the 1960s were based in both landscape and still life, and spare in line and colour, they revealed a deep interest in the spiritual. Having embraced this mode of geometric abstract expression, Nicoll reflected: "Painting for me is all on the picture plane, the actual surface of the canvas, with the power held in the horizontal and vertical movements of the expanding colour shapes. There can be, for me, no overlapping, transparencies or fuzzy edges—all these are a hangover from romantic, naturalistic painting."[38]

Nicoll's paintings *Prairie Farm* and *Prairie Foothills,* both 1968, epitomize those comments and the importance of the picture plane and power of horizontal and vertical colour shapes

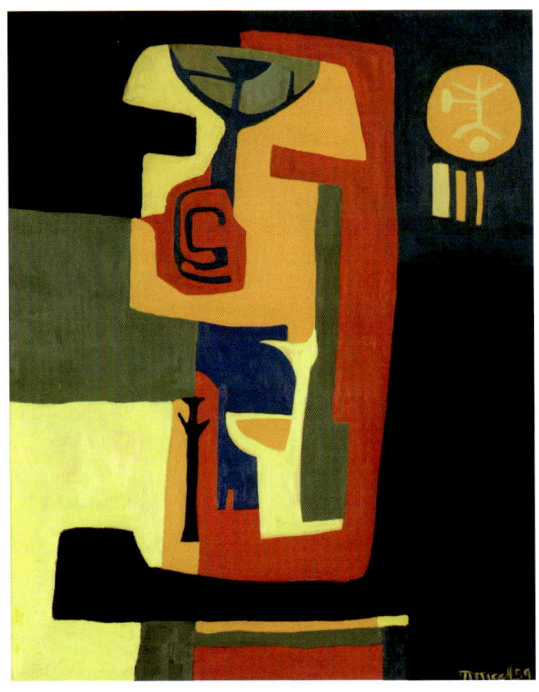

relating to the spaces and places she knew so well. *Prairie Farm*, a horizontal work, had a restricted palette of blues, greens, and black, with the colours blocked in simple geometric shapes conveying the essence of the sky, fields, buildings, doorways, and growth. There is no suggestion of romanticism or nostalgia.

Harry Kiyooka (1928–2022), husband of celebrated sculptor Katie Ohe, lived in Calgary, and his work reveals his commitment to and interest in the land and the environment around him. His rhythmic, colour-filled abstractions are redolent of the movement and undulation of the Alberta spaces and light. His brother, Roy Kiyooka (1926–1994), who lived in Vancouver, had other aspirations in creating the abstract. He began his artistic career as an abstract painter and became an acclaimed multidisciplinary artist who turned to poetry and photography, and later to performance, film, and music. Each of these disciplines informed his work in each of the others.

Doug Haynes (1936–2016), who lived and worked further north in Alberta, had a significant influence on Edmonton's artistic expressions of modernism. Colour, light, and precision were key elements in his art, with his blocks of colour evoking a strong emotional impact. As he said: "I am not a landscape painter because I don't sit down and frame the scene and just say that is the picture. I am thinking of being up there. . . . So I want the whole

FIGURE 5.11. **Roy Kiyooka**, *Untitled—Geometric Abstract*, 1963–1964.

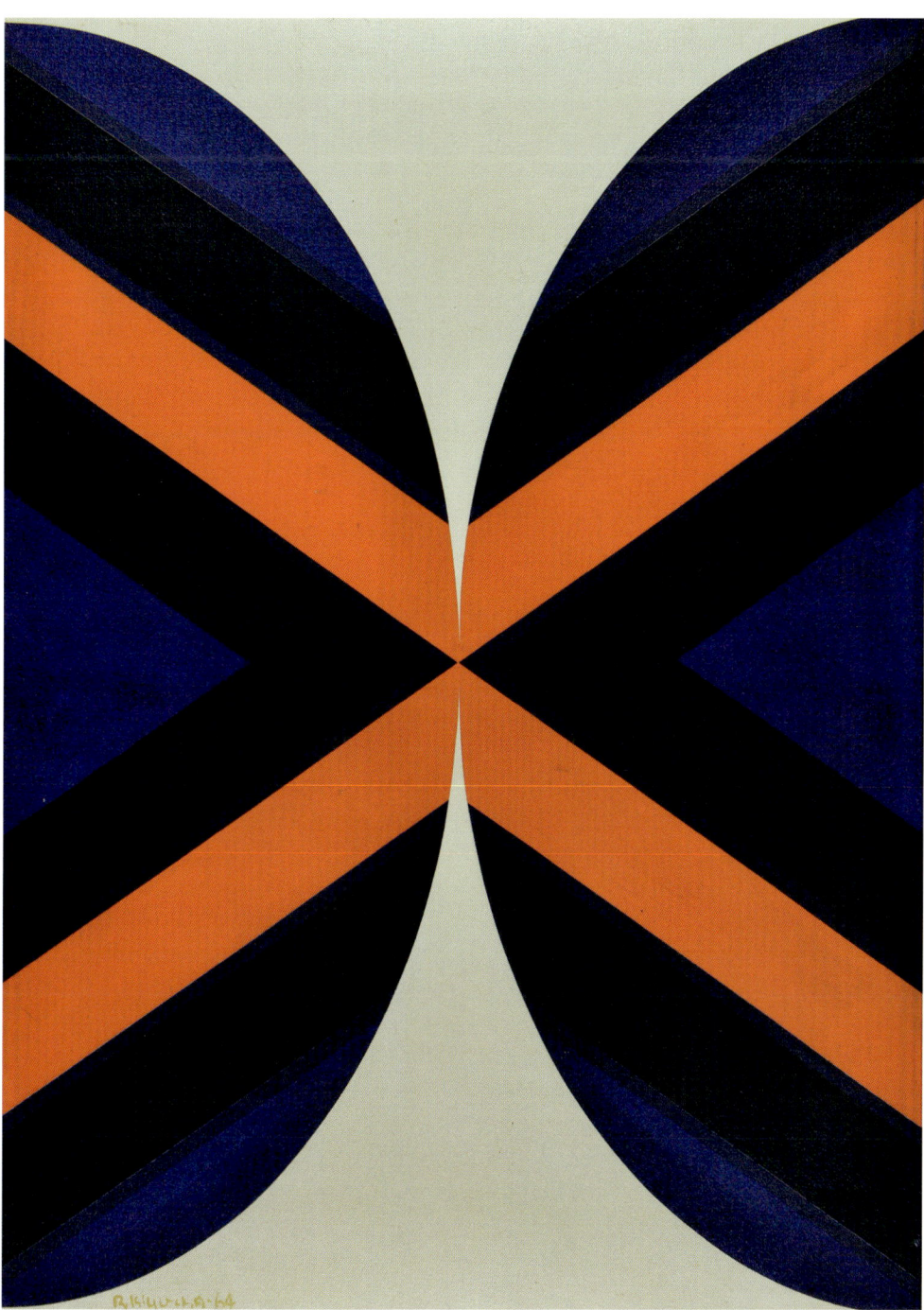

package, more the experience than the scenic look of it."[39] His reflections are evident in his 1995 artist's statement: "The paintings are about creating a presence. The central image is singular and straight forward as is a frontal portrait. It is kept simple and unobtrusive to force a dialogue across the total picture between color, surface, subtle inflection and illumination. The presence is evoked by the effect of the white canvas without relying on symbol or storyline."[40]

In 1963, the year Clement Greenberg led his session at Emma Lake Artists' Workshops, *Canadian Art* asked him to assess the state of painting and sculpture in Prairie Canada. He toured artists' studios across Manitoba, Saskatchewan, and Alberta, some having been suggested by the local gallery director and others having responded directly to the news of his impending visit. The results were electric. For some artists, they were positive as Greenberg embraced their work and opened doors for exhibitions elsewhere in Canada and the United States. For others, Greenberg's assessments of their work were devastating, never forgotten, and their bitterness continued for years.

The city of Regina, in particular, was seen by Greenberg as being truly consequential and exciting, particularly the work of five artists who were to become known as the Regina Five: Ken Lochhead, Doug Morton, Ronald Bloore, Ted Godwin, and Arthur McKay. Greenberg said:

> The vitality of art in Regina does constitute an unusual phenomenon. It may involve, immediately, only a small group of artists, but five such fired-up artists would amount to a lot in New York, let alone a city of 125,000. I am tempted to attribute it all, ultimately to the spirit of the province itself—especially since Saskatchewan has begun to show a similar vitality in art. . . .
>
> The specialness of art in Regina consists most of all in a state of mind, of awareness, and of ambition on the part of five abstract painters who live there, and whose activity is centred around the Norman Mackenzie Art Gallery.[41]

Clearly Barnett Newman's impact from his 1959 visit to Emma Lake had been significant. Greenberg said:

> The seriousness with which some among them began to take themselves as artists after Newman's visit became a main factor in the creation of the informal group of painters now known as the "Regina Five.". . . Every one of these painters is more or less what I call a "big attack" artist, by which I mean an artist of large and obvious ambition, with an aggressive and up-to-date style, and with a seriousness about himself that makes itself known in his work as much as in his demeanour. . . . the Regina Five form the only concentration of them in that region, and this, as much as anything makes Regina the art centre it is.[42]

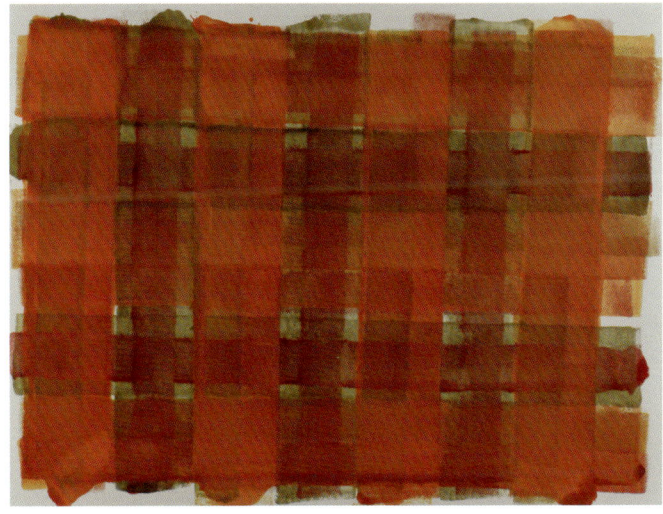

FIGURE 5.12.
Ted Godwin,
Tartan Love Float, 1968.

The 1961 *Regina Five* exhibition, first presented at the Norman MacKenzie Art Gallery in Regina and later at the National Gallery of Canada, catapulted these young artists to national and international attention. Their impression and influence were lasting.

Ted Godwin (1933–2013) used his earlier abstractions as the basis for the increased presence of landscape elements in his later work. Writer Mary-Beth Laviolette said, "Instead of looking towards the horizon as so many prairie painters do, Godwin picks up (it seems) a magnifying glass to illuminate the surface reflections of water and the kaleidoscopic textures and colours of the dense tangled shoreline. . . . there is now the organic interweave of the underbrush along the river that is also linked to his study of Celtic art, in particular its zoomorphic interlace."[43]

Ken Lochhead left Regina for a teaching position at the University of Manitoba's School of Art in 1964 and immediately became a leading figure in Manitoba's artistic landscape. He arrived with the reputation penned by Greenberg that he had "broken through to pure flat colour stated in shapes that approach 'geometry' without really touching it. This new direction relates to nothing else in contemporary Canadian painting."[44] Lochhead's large downtown loft studio became a gathering point for emerging and established artists working in all media, as well as those involved in the visual arts community as curators, dealers, writers, and critics. He was a strong advocate for artists and artists' rights. In the early 1970s Lochhead shifted from the geometric abstraction, as seen in *Sky Location,* to the fluid, large-scale colour field airbrush paintings, like *High Space Colour,* an acrylic on canvas of 1970. These airbrush paintings are sensuous, romantically rhythmic and rich, and filled with large, broad, sweeping lines, the colours merging into each other.

William Perehudoff (1918–2013), of Saskatchewan, painted compelling hard-edge abstractions of the prairie landscape. Strong in their colour, light, and simplicity, they convey the depth and space of the prairie. His work shows his understanding of place and his sense of abstracting that space to reach deeper meaning. In a CBC interview he noted that he used masking tape to achieve the hard edge and that "colour has to be tuned up; . . . you have to let colour come alive; . . . if your painting has no structure, it is not going to last; . . . to simplify . . . that is what makes art last."[45]

In Saskatoon Otto Rogers (1935–2019), Robert Christie (b. 1946), and Eli Bornstein were all leaders in abstraction. Bornstein's constructivist works with their rhythmic patterning of the colourful linear extrusions are unique in Canada. He at once engages the viewer, whose eye is taken on a journey around and through these powerful structural pieces. He and Otto Rogers were both key figures in the University of Saskatchewan's fine arts department. Rogers's works, fed by his long interest in cubism and his later Baha'i faith, are imbued with a sense of space, light, and movement. Christie, for his part, like many prairie artists, was both an attendee and leader of a number of Emma Lake Artists' Workshops. He talks of "constructing colour," and his paintings show overlapping shapes of pure colour. He states: "At the outset of painting I will have some sort of image in mind; often something related to what I've just been working on or something from my past work that I think I can re-kindle. . . . I alter, add, subtract, re-work and over-paint to the extent that the original concept is essentially non-existent. New avenues are pursued and, likewise, altered over time until something clicks with the imagery that surprises and engages me."[46] His shapes take the eye in various directions, and he constructs his works to give the perception of three-dimensional depth and, in many works, a strong sense of distance.

In Winnipeg the art scene of the early 1970s was especially vibrant. The new Winnipeg Art Gallery, designed by University of Manitoba professor and architect Gustavo da Roza, opened in the fall of 1971; CARFAC, the Canadian Artists' Representation/Le Front des artistes canadiens, was becoming truly active after its founding in 1968; and in 1972 the Professional Native Indian Artists Incorporated, which became the Indigenous Group of Seven, came together in Winnipeg at the gallery of Daphne Odjig, Indigenous artist and group member. The Grand Western Canadian Screen Shop, founded by artist Bill Lobchuk in 1968, had become one of the central meeting points for the creative community, as did the newly founded Plug In, one of the first Canadian artist-run centres. The School of Art continued to flourish and the national reputation of Winnipeg as a hotbed of the arts was strong. Artists shared studio spaces and were employed in various sectors of the community.

Bruce Head, while working as a graphic designer for CBC Winnipeg, continued a prolific art practice and was part of the growing scene of abstraction. He invented his own approach with his shaped canvases and later his torn and sewn works. Including three-dimensional shapes and heightened colour, he extended his means of conveying prairie sensibilities. He

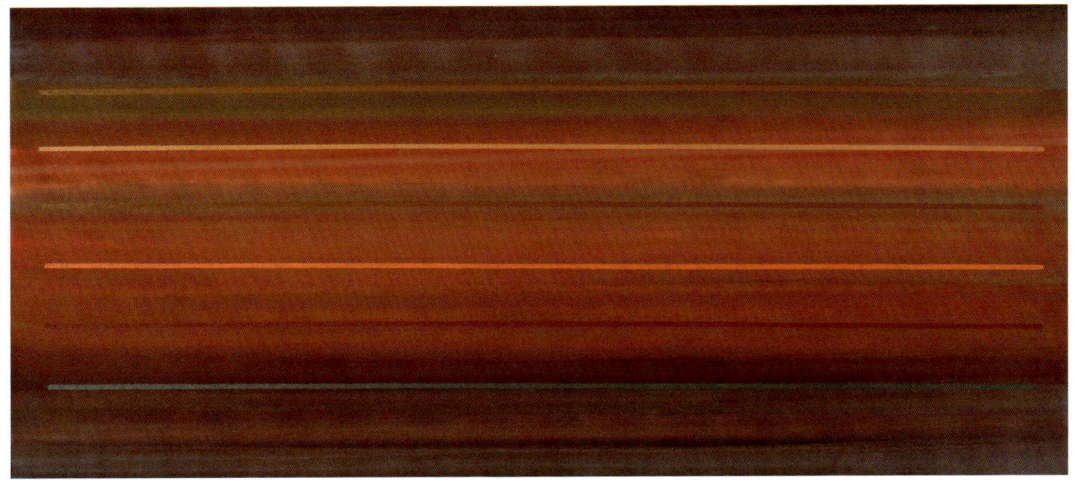

explained: "I wanted to break away from flat canvas and move to sculptured canvas. . . . In a way it combines the best of both worlds of painting and sculpture."[47] These sculpted canvases, such as the *Sky Pies* of the early 1970s or *The Forks,* 1978, began as experiments. He said, "I was bored with the flat canvas; I got some old aluminum film reels from the CBC and bent them to shape the canvas."[48] These shaped canvases allowed for the reflection and absorption of light simultaneously, thereby enhancing the sense of movement and imbuing them with magnetism. The *Sky Pies*, often two-sided, were suspended and rotated, and recalling the 1969 moon mission, they reflect the lunar surface.

By the time he was in his mid-thirties, Head had been seen, according to journalist Ralph Watkins, as "one of the finest of Winnipeg's abstract painters. His works showed complex formal relationships of considerable strength and richness. . . . Mr. Head's paintings are abstract for the legitimate painterly reason that he wants the viewer to look at his manipulation of colour and lines without being distracted by the subject of the painting. . . . They are, essentially, elegant compositions in colour, texture, mass and line."[49] Journalist Randal McIlroy said Head's 1950s and 1960s abstractions were "fusions of emotion and intellect, mediating between the two. Hot and cold images are run together, disrupting continuity, snaring attention."[50] *Transcona News* described them as "representations of a spirit. Head seems to be able to extract the life-giving force in nature and put it on canvas, sometimes in flashing colour, sometimes in warm brown and blue tones. . . . very unobtrusive, but very powerful, saying something very important as your eye moves through it."[51]

FIGURE 5.13. **William Perehudoff**, *Amyot Series #25*, 1975.

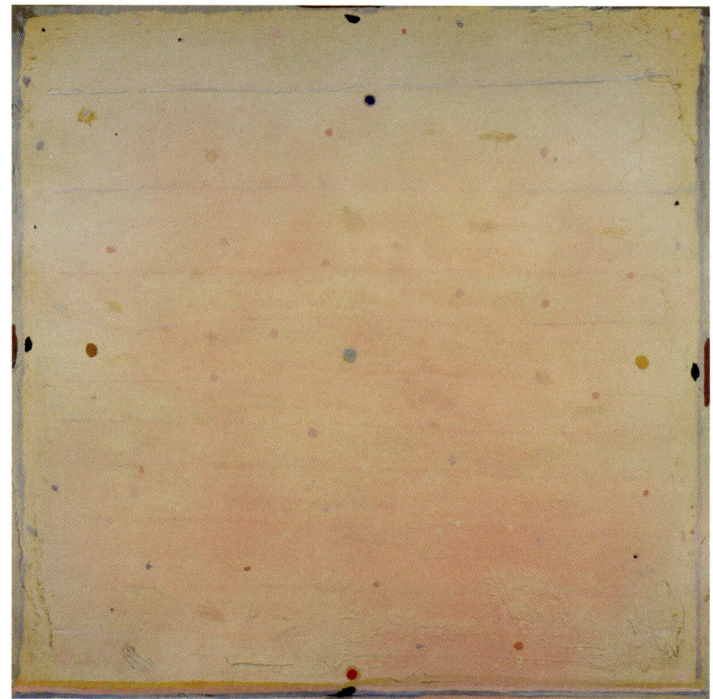

FIGURE 5.14.
Otto Rogers,
Pink Sky, 1975.

"Visual poetry" or "symphonies of colour" aptly describe Bruce Head's overall oeuvre. His large body of work was lyrical, richly textured, and vibrant, with colour as its core and the horizon and geometry of the prairie fields its foundation. His juxtapositions of pure colour, coupled with his brushwork and texture, are intense and expressive. According to *Winnipeg Free Press* writers, he said that "the landscape has become a basis . . . almost accidentally. I'm like a sponge . . . I wander around and absorb things. Then once in a while, you wring it out in a painting,"[52] and "the forms . . . of Manitoba landscapes are influenced by farm tool shapes and architecture."[53]

Don Reichert and Winston Leathers were both members of the 1956 University of Manitoba School of Art class, and both later became faculty members at the university. The space explorations in the 1960s and the 1969 moon landing affected each of them. Reichert was also one of the young artists recognized by Clement Greenberg in 1963: "Of all the abstract artists whose work I came on in Winnipeg, Donald Reichert was the one who seemed to have the most possibilities. Almost everything I saw in a show of his . . . was involved in the effort to say something."[54]

Reichert, who studied in Mexico, taught in New Brunswick for a year, and spent a year in St. Ives, Cornwall, supported by the Canada Council, where he sought as many opportunities as

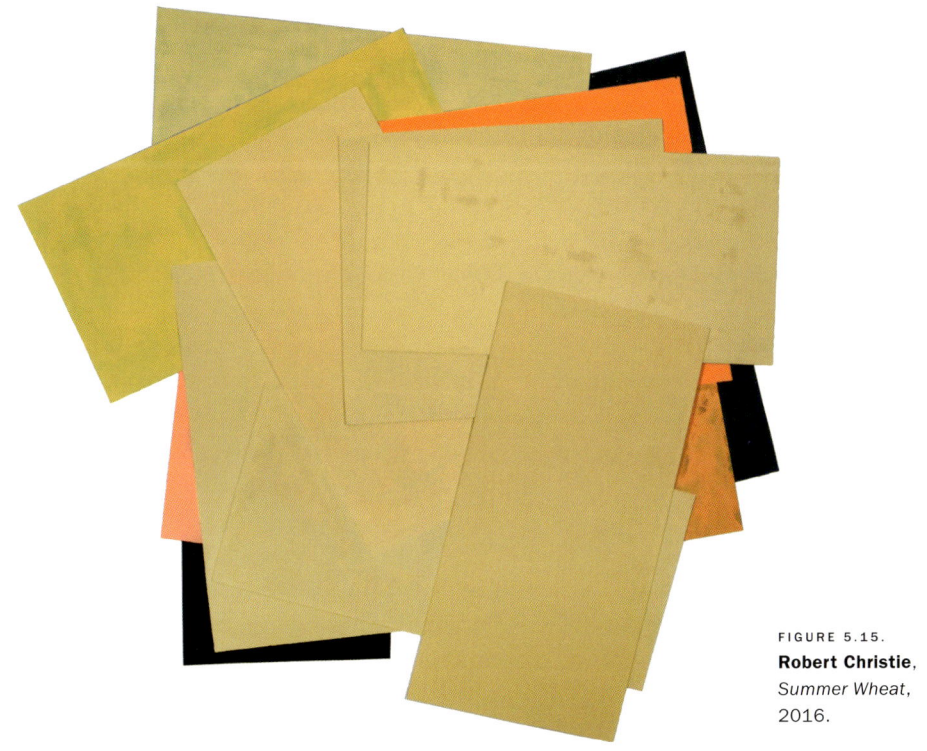

he could to meet other artists. After returning from Mexico and St. Ives, Reichert too attended the Emma Lake Artists' Workshops, doing so on three separate occasions in the mid-1960s. Connections with artists across Canada and internationally were important to him, one being Victoria's James Gordaneer, who visited Reichert in St. Ives. They later met in Mexico a number of times. Interestingly, their colour palettes and approaches to composition were affected by the Mexican light at about the same time. Reichert also connected with musicians, and meeting John Cage at Emma Lake imbued Reichert's work with an increased sense of rhythm and sound. In 1978 Reichert brought Cage to Winnipeg for a special concert presentation. Gordaneer became interested in philosophy, which was apparent in his work of the 1990s.

Reichert's early geometric abstractions, like *Superimposition I,* 1969, demonstrated his interest in structure. He balanced pure geometric elements—faceted triangles throughout the work—with suggestions of rocks and earth, and freely applied explosions of blue, evoking the fluid, vaporous effects of the water and skies in various segments of the painting. He said, "I did not want to be beholden to the hallowed surface of the canvas, but rather, beholden to the edges."[55] His patterns and forms extended beyond the work's edges. The multifaceted aspects in nature—the "jewels of nature," as he called them—and the geometric facets returned in his later digital *Redwood Bridge* series of the 2000s, where the triangles, squares, and polygons of the bridge became complex mirrored, intersecting patterns. Reichert juxtaposed the fleeting and momentary on solidity and permanence, achieving his characteristic rhythmic patterns, colour, and light. Throughout his career he developed elegant brushwork, drawing from his interest in music, Japanese calligraphy, and reflections on water, all of which enhanced his sense of natural lyricism, rhythm, and syncopation. In February 2006 Reichert reflected on the exhibition he had had in Washington: "The work can be seen to be related to Abstract Expressionism, but the most powerful experience I have had relating to the evolution of my work happened in 1963, at the Tate Gallery in London, where I saw a Japanese Zen brush drawing of such astounding strength, simplicity and delicacy that I spent most of the next year working with a Sumi brush on just about any paper I could find, trying to learn how to use a brush. I have tried to build on that experience ever since."[56]

Winston Leathers created abstractions based both on geometry and on the organic landscape and light, while he, too, explored a lifelong interest in calligraphy and Zen. His 1972 silkscreen print series, *Cosmic Variations,* often seen as his first breakthrough, was pulled at the Grand Western Canadian Screen Shop. It was a response to both the moon landing and his study of Eastern religions. His interest in and knowledge of calligraphy were extensive. Curator Ann Davis reflected that his commitment to calligraphy was spontaneous, non-rational, and intuitive, and his interest in Zen enabled "his deep and abiding commitment to nature."[57] At the same time he was experimenting with new materials, and for his *Cosmic Variations* he used the new Day-Glo and metallic inks. Regina curator Erin Gee noted of the whole series: "These bright inks pulse in fields of recurring spheres, creating landscapes of finely tuned colour. The overall impression is that of a chaotic yet balanced natural order—each composition in the exhibition is made up of circles that stand in for cells, solar systems, eggs, and supernovas. . . . Among the inspirations for these cosmic images is Zen philosophy. Leathers greatly admired the writing of Alan Watts (1915–1973), a British philosopher made famous for his role in popularizing Eastern philosophy for a Western audience."[58] The circle, dominant throughout his geometric abstractions, represents energy and the spirituality of Zen-inspired garden-raked patterns. His repetition of forms within a work generates the specific rhythms through the whole composition, each being enhanced by his use of colour.

Local and global thought in art expanded as the 1970s became the stage for exploring ideas and communication, aided by developing technologies. The art of Indigenous peoples came to the fore at this time, too, with the 1972 founding in Winnipeg and incorporation of the Professional Native Indian Artists Incorporated. This group of seven artists included its unofficial leader, Daphne Odjig, and Alex Janvier, Norval Morrisseau, Carl Ray, Eddy Cobiness, Jackson Beardy, and Joseph Sanchez. Each explored different aspects of abstraction rooted in

FIGURE 5.16. **Don Reichert**, *Superimposition I*, 1969.

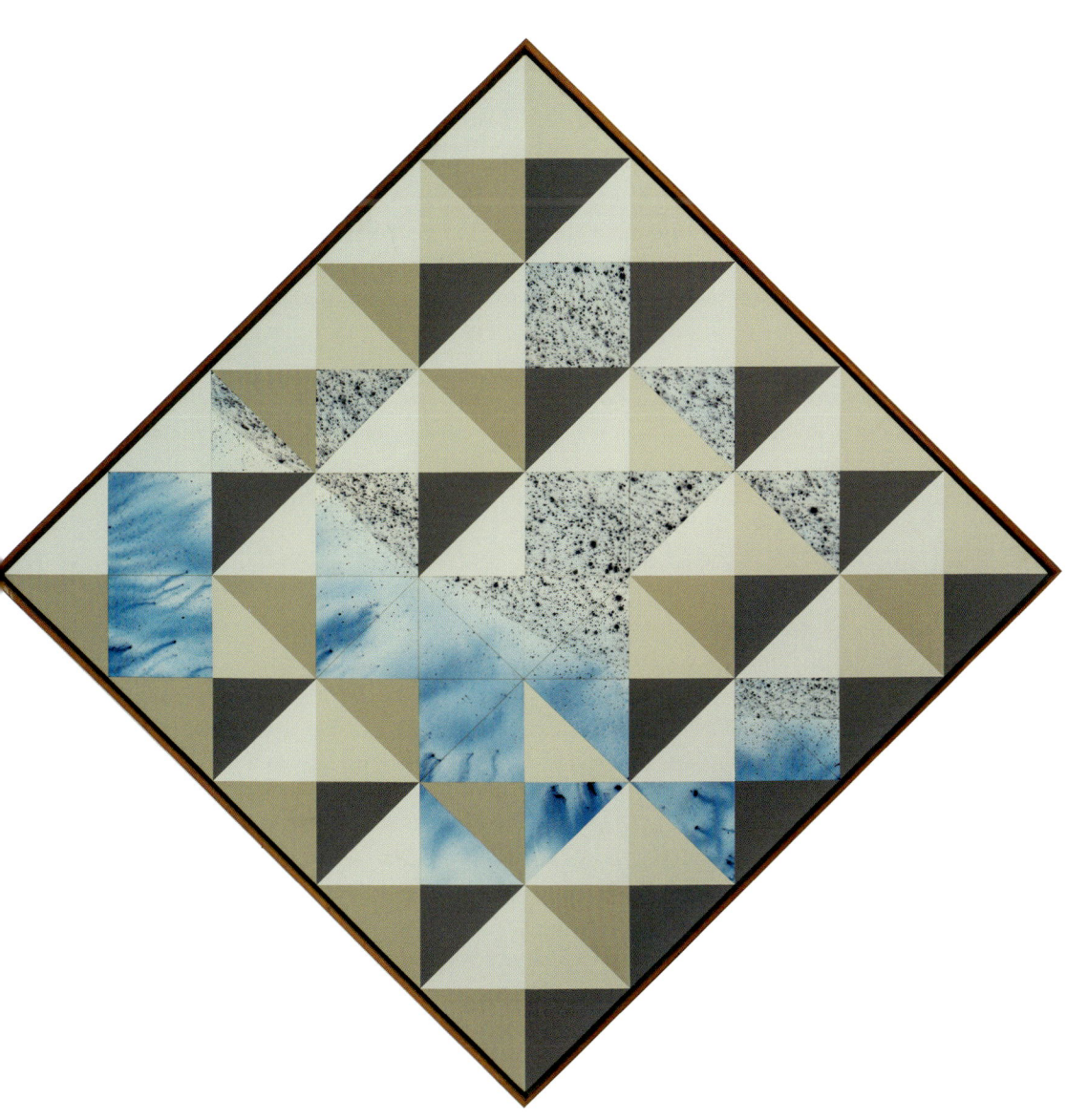

their heritage, myths, and spiritual legends. Though each had unique approaches, being a group afforded them greater publicity, and their first exhibition was at the Winnipeg Art Gallery in 1972. Breaking free from earlier long-held preconceptions of what Indigenous art should look like, they erased the idea that Indigenous work was anthropological. Alex Janvier said they "set out to change the world, the art world, for Natives of Canada."[59] They did. Their work was transformative for Indigenous and non-Indigenous artists, the art gallery community, and for wider society. Theirs was a cultural revolution that drew many issues to the forefront, including the deplorable conditions in which some Indigenous people lived, their underfunding, non-delivery of commitments made in the treaties, the residential schools, and environmental concerns. Their work also enlightened society as to the spiritual depth and meaning of the roots of Canada's Indigenous cultures. As Jackson Beardy said: "It has become my deep personal life goal to create an awareness of our culture within the public at large—thereby cementing stronger ties of mutual understanding for one country, Canada."[60] The link between the land and the spirit is strong for artists of all diversities but for Indigenous people, as many Indigenous artists have expressed to me, the land *is* culture.

Religious Philosophies and the Spirit Abstracted

> "I believe people are born searching for something in themselves; searching for certain kinds of spiritual endeavours making them feel part of something powerful."[61]

The spiritual as a source for abstraction is more complex than the inspirations derived from the land, objects, colour, or geometric theories. Spiritual abstraction emanates from a number of thoughts, places, ideas, ideologies, and philosophies, some conscious and some unconscious. "Spiritual" is defined as "of, pertaining to, consisting of spirit, incorporeal; closely akin in interests, attitude, outlook, characterized by or suggesting predominance of the spirit, ethereal, or delicately refined."[62] Some artworks examine the spiritual in the abstract overtly, as does British Columbia's Jack Wise's personal and compelling *Mandala Series*. Others are less overt, as in the multiple dimensions and layers in the work of Pat Martin Bates. In their spiritually rooted works, artists are expressing abstract thoughts and often those of religious philosophies.

George Swinton, the much-loved and -respected teacher, was deeply spiritual, as is evident in *The Birth of Spring* and in his purely religious works such as his *Crucifixion, 1968*. His friend, the English professor, art critic, and artist Arthur Adamson, wrote:

> I see George Swinton as a religious painter, although his themes are usually not overtly religious. The words "religious" and "spiritual" have been so abused over time as to have lost any precise meaning. Nevertheless, I must affirm that George, and he

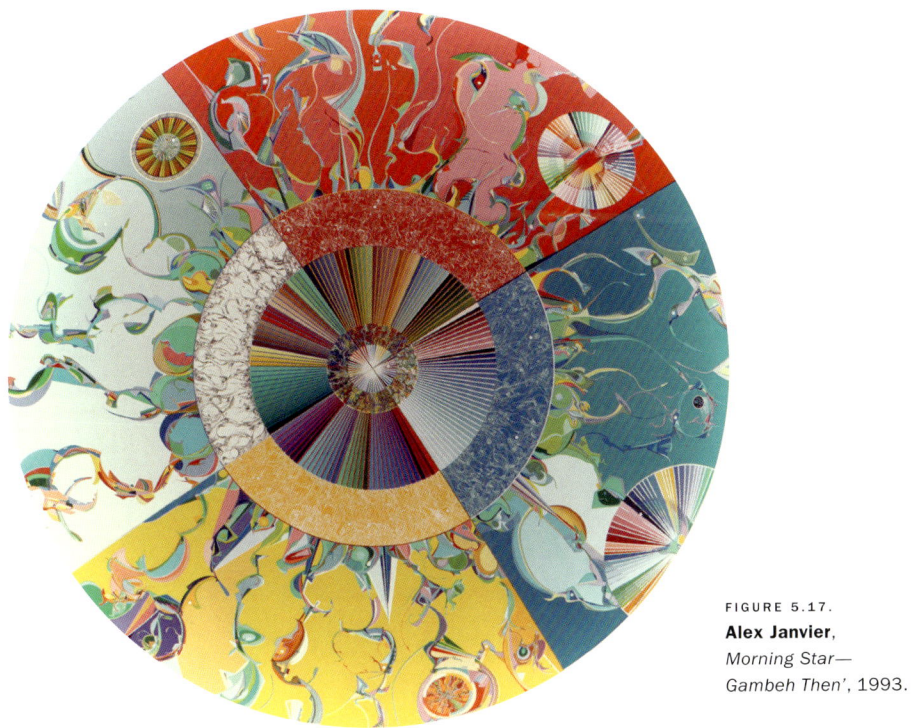

FIGURE 5.17.
Alex Janvier,
*Morning Star—
Gambeh Then'*, 1993.

is aware of this, is a religious painter in the sense that art (and indeed any avocation) must have a spiritual orientation to have any meaning or integrity. . . . The "spiritual" is simply the essentially human, in that the value of human life lies in going beyond all that rationality and science describe as reality. . . .

Both in his thought and art George attests to the awareness of the sacred in all things. . . . He has made images of specific religious iconography. . . . Lately he has done mostly landscapes. In them we find a vision of nature which is uniquely his, in which expression and communication are one.[63]

Many have noted the rich colour in Swinton's work, which at times suggests an unearthly or mythical quality. His resulting landscapes are local in sensibilities, international in spiritual essences, yet simultaneously deeply personal. In the 1960s Winnipeg Art Gallery director Ferdinand Eckhardt wrote of Swinton: "He is conservative as well as revolutionary. He likes to tackle problems whether they are new or thousands of years old. He loves to paint the great excitement of nature, the landscape, the unexplored north as well as the not yet fully recognized prairie. He tries to express it in shapes, outlines, structure, light and colour. He also tries to find

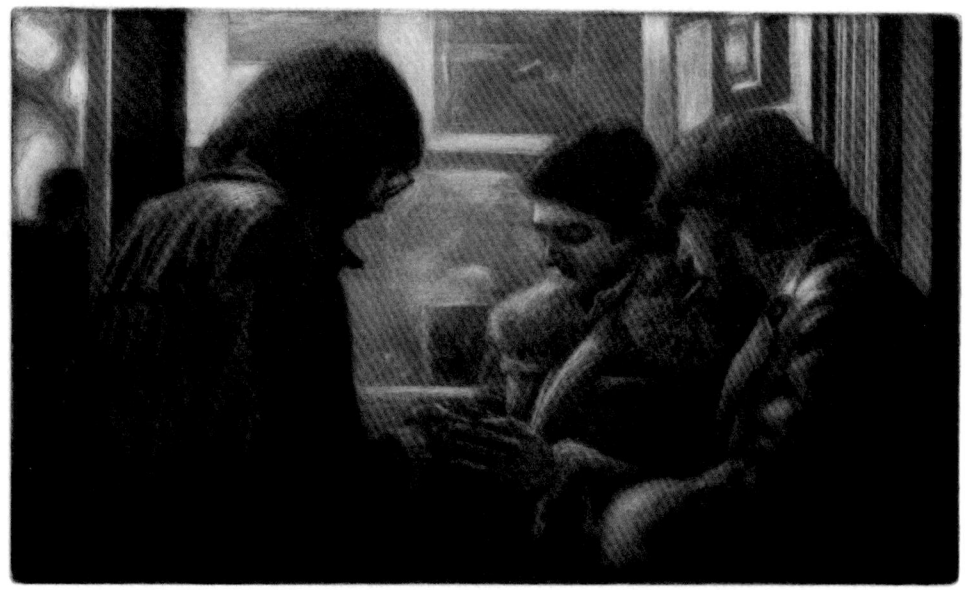

or recreate symbols for some of the immortal and imminent things; death, fear, devotion, passion and love, the threatening of the demonic or the seduction of the transcendental."[64]

Printmaking colleagues Pat Martin Bates and Winston Leathers shared Swinton's interest in Eastern philosophies. Bates and Leathers met when Bates was working at *Canadian Art* in the early 1960s. Both were experimenting with a number of printing materials at that time, and continued to experiment with materials and art-making techniques throughout their careers. In the 1960s and 1970s Leathers, for instance, tried printing on wax paper, and Bates was a pioneer of printing on Plexiglas.

Eastern philosophy inspired Leathers to invite Japanese calligraphers to Winnipeg in the late 1960s to teach the traditional elements and principles of calligraphy. The impact was transformational in his symbolism and materials, inks, papers, and brushes. The art of Chinese calligraphy had migrated to Japan, where it has been a highly esteemed art form for more than four centuries. Leathers's interest in Zen was embodied in a deep and abiding commitment to nature. For him, that was embraced in calligraphy, as he wrote: "The essence of beauty in calligraphy is movement: the brush strokes stretch and sweep, crouch and spring, strokes swell and diminish, shapes expand and contract. Line after line, gesture after gesture should have a way of giving life."[65]

FIGURE 5.18. **E.J. (Ted) Howorth**, *The Deal*, 2021.

Calligraphy affords artists a multiplicity of effects by varying the consistency and amount of ink or paint. Different brushes and parts of the brush—the tip or side—create lines of differing characteristics and meaning. The artist's arm and brush have to become one for the effect to be at its lyrical best. Curator Dawn Delbanco writes that the brush becomes "an extension of the [artist's] arm, indeed, his entire body. But the physical gestures produced by the wielding of the brush reveal much more than physical motion; they reveal much of himself—his impulsiveness, restraint, elegance, rebelliousness."[66]

Winston Leathers instinctively knew these traits and understood the power and importance of calligraphy for his own contemporary expression. Using all parts of the brush and varying the pressure and speed of his brush strokes, he created two- and three-dimensional effects imparting the various natural rhythms of the landscape. His fluid brushwork, dynamic lines, and layering of reflective and non-reflective copper, silver, and gold paints gave his later paintings the energy of nature's forces and enhanced the power of the space in his prairie landscapes. In *Autumn's Farewell Winter's Return, Window on the Landscape Series,* 2000, for instance, the energy of the sumi ink lines moves across the work from left to right, over the snowy abstract background, across the red light of the sky to the upper right corner, and extends its synergies beyond the picture plane. The repeated linear thrust from left to right magnifies the ominous feeling of the movement of the clouds and the impending storm.

Don Reichert had become interested in calligraphy when he was in St. Ives in 1963. He attended the sessions Leathers organized and, after spending time in London, he wrote George Swinton:

I came upon a folding silk screen among the recent acquisitions. It was a very simple sumi brush drawing by a Japanese artist. The beauty and expressiveness of that very spontaneous simple drawing has haunted me ever since, and has moved me to write the following little poem:

The Sumi brush leaves a different spoor
every time it moves on its magical plain:
and I, a Bushman used to tracking, read in
the marks it makes on its way a song
from the soul of its master.[67]

Leathers's personal "retreat" and the source of much of his later inspiration was his cottage at Minaki, Ontario, where he went from early spring until late fall each year. The water, light, and unspoilt natural environment were critical, and he liked to swim, with his eyes at water level, peering at the horizon line. The light dancing on the water fed his interest in luminosity and inspired his use of metallic colours. He achieved his desired textures through building layers of richly coloured paints, impasto, in varying depths, repeating parallel, linear, and rhythmic scored patterns.

American artists also had an influence on Canadian abstraction. "Each brushstroke is a decision," wrote Robert Motherwell, the well-known American abstract expressionist artist and influential voice in international art. He often spoke of the fact that he commenced a work with an idea, not an image, and that import of impulse derived from one's own experience is the case for many artists working in abstraction. Mark Tobey's influence was likewise strong in the spiritual realm of painting. A friend of Emily Carr, Tobey inspired many artists over a number of decades who were interested in Buddhism and Eastern philosophies. British Columbia artist Jack Wise was perhaps one of the first who challenged writers, me included, to explain the role calligraphy has played in Western Canadian art. Wise knew how many artists explored calligraphy and Eastern thought but was also aware that for a number of decades those interests were rarely shared beyond their own studios.[68]

A respected teacher and workshop leader, Wise frequently exhibited his spiritual pieces. They were gentle in the articulation, many based on Buddhist mandalas. In these, like his 1984 *Mandala*, the artist's innermost feelings are contained in the central circle and the feelings and connections gradually widen to broader spectrums as the concentric circles grow outwards. The outermost circle represents his relationship to the wider universe. Meticulous brushwork and colours carefully chosen for their specific meanings define the "spiritual." He was immersed in the religion and the complex iconography of mandalas when he spent considerable time at the Dalai Lama's monastery in the 1960s. Shortly before his death I had the opportunity to invite and host the Dalai Lama at the Art Gallery of Greater Victoria. Wise met him again after many years and their connection remained strong. Wise's intuition regarding the importance of calligraphy for several generations of Canadian contemporary artists was right.

Edmonton's Walter Jule has spent much time in Japanese monasteries studying and practising Zen meditation. His impact as artist, teacher, curator, and philosopher on printmaking in Canada and internationally was far-reaching. Inspired as a child by Japanese art, especially a particular woodblock print of Mount Fuji at the Seattle Art Museum, his interest, exchanges, and work with Japanese artists have been a mainstay of his art and spiritual life. The perception of time, his daily meditation, and his observation of the slightest changes in the light around him feed his art making. A quiet and stillness permeate his art. Professor Ryu Niimi of Japan's Musashino Art University describes Jule's prints as "floating stones, drapes of pinned silk or Japanese paper, like a square garden—they cause us to meditate and contemplate the time of our ancestors when they first lived as human beings. . . . Each item [in a Zen garden] is intentionally placed so as to become an external expression of inner workings. Jule's prints, like the Japanese garden, both recognize and transform nature . . . and have almost shamanistic undertones."[69] *The Logic of the Plane of Nothingness/State II,* 1997, evokes calm contemplation, and its sensitivity and feeling move across the surface with shifting rhythms. *Neither Dusk Nor Dawn,* 2008,

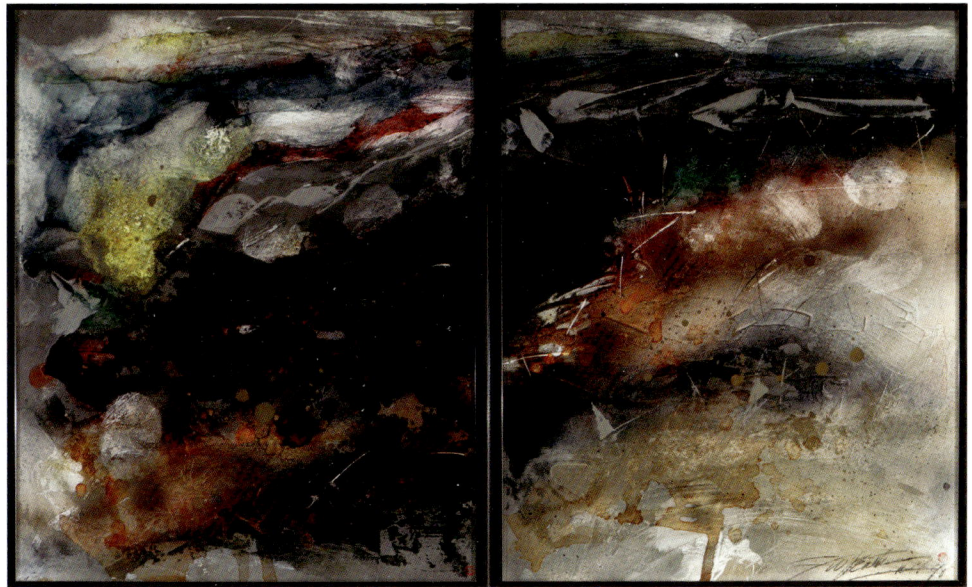

a lithograph with gampi chine collé, takes this meditative sensibility of the land, light, and space further. The real time is ambiguous, dusk or dawn, waking or sleeping. The image of the balloon, encased in gesso, moves across the work to the lower left, exuding black ink below the edge of the work. Is it a continuing dream? Does it refer to the present personally, or to society as a whole? The texture of the surface is alluring, suggesting both the physical and spiritual simultaneously.

Pat Martin Bates's religious philosophical interests led her to travel the route of Alexander the Great in 1972 to research Islamic architecture, gardens, literature, and art. Of her spiritual quest, she has commented: "We are all seeking that universal voice. Now, we are afraid of feeling ecstatic. You must have balance to be *in* this world, not just part of it."[70] Embracing Persian mystics and poets, especially Rumi, world religious philosophies, and tenets of medieval thought, she constantly juxtaposes past and present, the natural and the mystical. Poet Patricia Kathleen (P.K.) Page referred to the "three worlds" in Martin Bates's art: "Earth, Air, Heaven; three worlds, the existence of which she is constantly drawing to our attention . . . the crucial intersections of this world with eternity. The pictorial equivalent of this overlapping of the two worlds is the mandala—eye-shaped to inform us that here we arrive at a moment of vision, our blindness is cured."[71]

FIGURE 5.19. **Winston Leathers**, *Night Approaching the Island*, 1998.

For Pat Martin Bates light symbolized hope and the future. Her light box, *Chinese Night Train to the Yangtze Kiang,* 1978, is a pierced, folded, and pressed painting, and the light coming through the image is an integral part of its composition and meaning. When not lit, its surface is rich with textures and blues and golds on the black paper, and the works take on another aura. The piercings, made with her grandmother's hat pins, are flowing and rhythmic, mirroring the sensitivity of the applications of the tiny gold and silver threads and meticulous calligraphy.

Just as the numbers 2 and 5 had special meaning for John Koerner, they do, too, for Pat Martin Bates. Numerology in her work links to ancient cultures, Christian mysticism, Judaism, and Eastern philosophy, each number having a particular value in the cosmos. The mystical and esoteric relationships between numbers and objects imbue her art with a sense of ephemeral and spiritual elegance. For her, the number 7 is magical, the most celestial of all numbers, and the most perfect when combined with a circle, as in *Mandala + No. 7.* Number 2 means balance; 9 has special significance as "in many cultures it is the gateway to ten—perfection."[72]

Bertram Brooker's comment about shapes being verbs come to mind: "floating areas of colour . . . representing action and movement—. . . only intended as the path or climax or culmination of a movement." While the comment is particularly germane to the spiritual aspects of the abstract in Pat Martin Bates's work, that sense of movement was also essential for Emily Carr. Carr commented:

> A main movement must run through the picture. The transitions must be easy, not jerky.
> None must be out of step in the march. On, on, deeper and deeper, with the soul of the
> thing burrowing into its depths and intensity till that thing is a reality to us and speaks
> one grand inaudible word—God. The movement and direction of lines and planes shall
> express some attribute of God—power, peace, strength, serenity, joy. The movement shall
> be so great the picture will rock and sway together, carrying the artist and after him the
> looker with it, catching up with the soul of the thing and marching on together.[73]

While one would not call the work of Emily Carr "abstract," her approach in works such as *Grey* of 1929–30 certainly is, with the geometric formation of the trees and the triangular centre containing spiralling forms within. This movement is further developed with greater use of colour and forceful brushwork in *Juice of Life,* 1936–39. As she searched for light and in her quest for God, she wrote: "I want the BIG God, . . . a real God, not the distant mechanical theosophical one. . . . The substance is the same as my less complicated beliefs; God in all. Always looking for the face of God, always listening for the voice of God in Nature. Nature clothed in God's beauty of holiness."[74]

Carr's goal in her work and her personal aspiration was to understand the unity of spirit and nature—her spiritualism. *Juice of Life* evokes that reach with the monumental height of the forest trees and streams of light cutting through the dense greens. Her brush strokes swirl upwards, reaching for the source of light. This suggests another pertinent definition: ethereal, "light, airy, extremely delicate or refined, heavenly or celestial." In *Hundreds and Thousands: The Journals of Emily Carr,* Carr often talks about the space for the air and the movement:

> Colours you had not noticed come out, timidly or boldly. In and out, in and out your eye passes. Nothing is crowded; there is living space for all. Air moves between each leaf. Sunlight plays and dances. Nothing is still now. Life is sweeping though the spaces. Everything is alive. The air is alive. The silence is full of sound. The green is full of colour. Light and dark chase each other. Here is a picture, a complete thought, and there another and there. … There are themes everywhere, something sublime, something ridiculous, or joyous, or calm, or mysterious. Tender youthfulness laughing at gnarled oldness. Moss and ferns, and leaves and twigs, light and air, depth and colour chattering.[75]

This comment certainly reveals the sense of the "ethereal" in the work of artists and their affinity with light, air, or the "heavenly or celestial." Bertram Brooker had illustrated the spiritual writings of William Blake, as Eric Bergman did. Pat Martin Bates, drawing spiritual strength from the poems of Rumi, expressed her absorption with the spiritual through light and movement. The spiritual, philosophical, and scientific are layered with her investigations of alchemy and her combining of chemistry, physics, metallurgy, mysticism, spiritualism, and astrology. Following the evolution of thought, religious philosophies, and practice from ancient beliefs to contemporary times, she frequently juxtaposes spiritual and astrological symbols with those of mysticism within a single work. She said of her 1960s Plexiglas sculptural prints: "Every culture has an Alchemy, the bringing together of the physical and spiritual. The transmutation of colour is only a part of it. The meaning of colour is important. Moving from the black of wisdom to light is what I was seeking in *Flight Window of the Alchemy Letter from the Sun to the Moon*, 1968. The blue in this work is the hope. The last element reached is gold."[76]

Light in her complex works symbolizes flame; as she says, "The flame of light; the flame of enlightenment; the flame of fire and the rising phoenix; the light referring to wisdom, enlightenment to knowledge and the phoenix to new life."[77] To art writer Joan Lowndes, Pat Martin Bates was "a spiritual seeker, a worshipper of the mystic mandala that dwells in pure white silence."[78] In addition to the writings of Persian poet Rumi, Martin Bates said, Buddhism "appealed to me. I wanted to be in tune with the spiritual and Buddhism is in tune with nature."[79] Her personal, artistic, and spiritual quests also included traditional Persian architecture: its spaces symmetrically repeat geometric forms in serial or circular order. She also frequently uses the eight-sided star from the ancient Middle Eastern and early Hebrew sign of the "goddess" as well as the whirling dervish energy of Sufic culture, achieved through her fast-paced, circular rhythms in her piercings, echoing her drawn and painted lines.

Martin Bates's Sufic knowledge fuses with her sense of the prairie landscape. Inspired by the huge prairie skies and long horizontal distances, she turned the horizon line on its side, to form a ladder to reach the sky, the philosophical celestial place. She said, "I use ladder forms as fences turned upwards, transformed to Ladders to try the climb to a higher level of thought and being."[80] Movement from dark to light threads through all her work. Of the experience of coming from darkness to light, she says it is "physically as night turns into day; spiritually as having seen the light; and psychologically as one finding one's way out of trauma,"[81] marking the passageways toward wisdom and knowledge.

Ron (Gyo-Zo) Spickett (1926–2018) a contemporary of Pat Martin Bates, studied in Saskatchewan and taught at the Alberta College of Art. He became a Buddhist priest, but as he moved towards Buddhism, he created works with Christian themes. Critic Clement Greenberg saw Spickett's work in both Edmonton and Calgary on his 1963 prairie tour, and while he lamented the general lack of resolution in the work of Calgary artists, Ron Spickett was an exception. Greenberg wrote:

> I could, however, recognize an unmistakably "big attack" painter in Calgary. . . .
> That was Ronald Spickett. The fact that his art had a French and Franco-Oriental
> cast spoke for the case of abstract painting in general in Calgary, which showed
> surprisingly little American influence of the Tenth Street variety. I had already seen
> five or six large paintings by Spickett in Edmonton . . . and one of them, barely
> reminiscent to Mathieu, with a sparse linear motif on an empty but pregnant ground
> of saffron (or something like saffron) remained, and remains, in mind as the boldest
> abstract painting I saw in prairie Canada, and perhaps the best and most ambitious I
> saw outside Regina.[82]

A muralist as well as a painter, Spickett's relief paintings were non-objective and organic. Based on prairie themes, they are subtle and textured. He scratched his surfaces when they were wet. That allowed him to attain a calligraphic sense in the overall work.

Winnipeg's Tony Tascona, painter, sculptor, and draughtsman, drew from his spirituality in quite a different way from Spickett's. He often talked of the manner in which he "orchestrated" his work, including his paintings, prints, and drawings with their unique spirit and sensibilities, to produce works of substance and humour, rich in juxtapositions. He said, "I synthesize all the time. I abstract, search for the essence of the meaning of the work in progress while I build and construct my images in my canvases and in my drawings."[83] Tascona's abstract forms flowed and grew as he worked, his drawings being "transformations" of thoughts, ideas, and subconscious feelings into visual form. When Tascona was a mechanic with Trans-Canada Air Lines, he had

FIGURE 5.20. **Emily Carr**, *Grey*, 1929–1930.

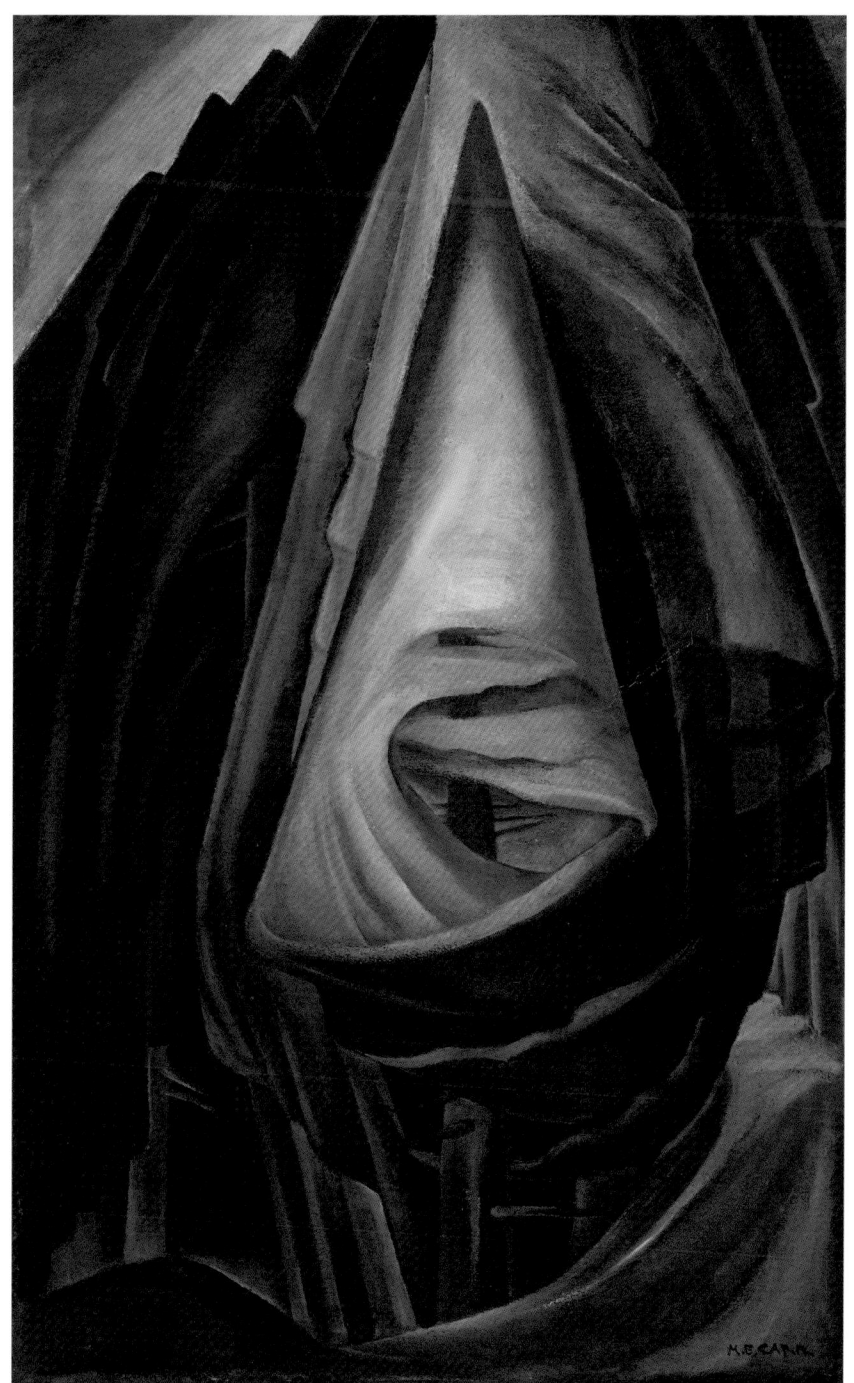

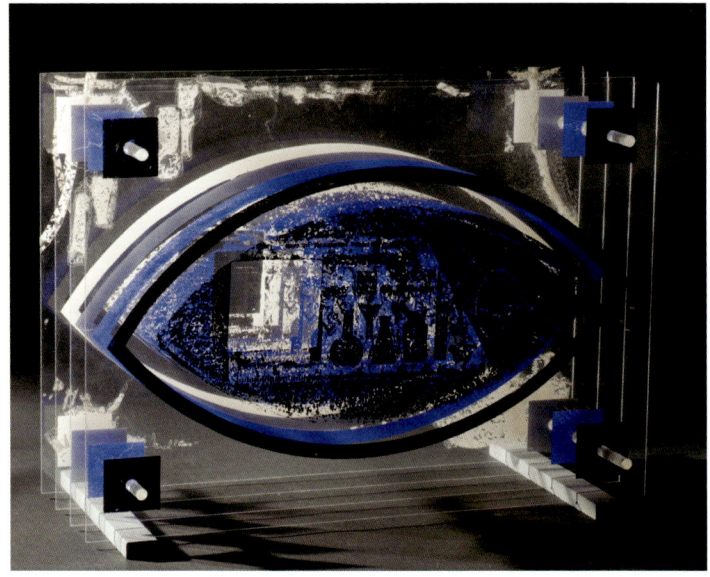

FIGURE 5.21.
Pat Martin Bates,
*Flight Window of the
Alchemy Letter from the
Sun to the Moon*, 1968.

access to machine materials not used before in making art. By layering enamels and colours, using machinist techniques, Tascona achieved a masterful balance between solid rootedness and fluidity, and between form and flight. He said, "I don't think all art has to have a message, but at least it has to have experience. There should be some kind of metaphysicality about each piece. Every time I do a piece I always feel it's an epiphany."[84] His resin pieces such as *Black Madonna I* and *Black Madonna II* reflect an ever-present spiritual quality. These were inspired on his seeing a black Madonna in a church in Sicily. Tascona's spiritual connection was never tied to any specific religious dogma, but, as evident in his work of the 1980s and 1990s, his interest in cultural and spiritual roots was central to his thinking. His self-expressed dictum, "Creative freedom is my ultimate aim,"[85] both liberated and united his work. Whether he was working in paint, coloured pencil, resin, or his unique enamel paintings, Tascona's strong rhythmic abstractions resulted in a unique visual language—powerful and reflective in conveying his mystical thoughts and ideas. The "order" Tony Tascona searched for and presents so effectively is, as he says, "the muse in flight."[86]

The work of Western Canada's Indigenous artists embodies the spiritual in myriad ways. Such themes can be seen in the totems and carvings of the West Coast artists and the paintings and prints from the coast and the plains, works created in all traditional and contemporary modes of expression. As Jane Ash Poitras (b. 1951) opined: "Only through spiritual renewal can we find out who we really are, be empowered to achieve our potential and acquire the wisdom to eliminate the influences that bring tragedy upon us and destroy us."[87]

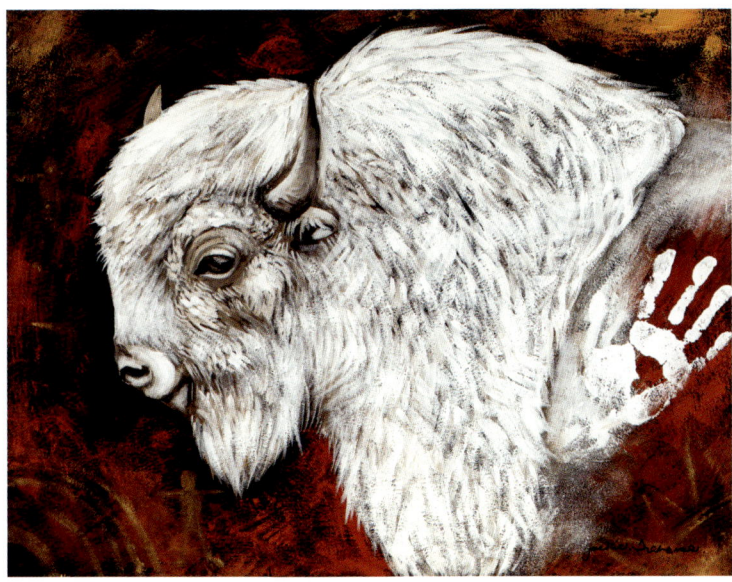

FIGURE 5.22.
Jackie Traverse,
*White Buffalo
Calf*, 2012.

Indigenous artists have been prolific, cogent, and insightful in both their art and poetry. West Coast artist Bill Reid (1920–1998) wrote *Out of the Silence* in New York and Montreal, in 1970–71. The book was first published in 1971, and the spirit within is evident:

When we look at a particular work
of Northwest Coast art
and see the shape of it,
we are only looking at its afterlife.
Its real life is the movement
by which it got to be that shape.

It's easy to become entranced
by the soft curtain of age,
seeing this
instead of what it obscures.
An ugly building
can make a beautiful ruin,
and a beautiful mask
in the dark of many years,
softened by wear,

becomes the symbol which tells us
that the cycle of life,
death, decay and rebirth
is a natural and beautiful one.[88]

These words are particularly apt in looking at his *Spirit of Haida Gwaii: The Jade Canoe,* the large bronze sculpture in the Vancouver airport, and his 1984 *Killer Whale.* Having visited Reid's studio many times as he created both these works, I can attest to his attention to the importance of every detail, his concentration on the surface qualities and patina, as well as the importance of the symbolic meanings of Haida culture and heritage they contain.

Artist, poet, and former Grand Chief Ovide Mercredi reveals the acuity between his visual and poetic works in his poem "The Earth":

The Earth is a great miracle
The author of its unique destiny
A traveler in unending space
      The designer of all its beauty
      The orchestra of all natural events
      Benign or catastrophic.[89]

The link between the sensibilities of the poems to his artwork is clear.

The work of Indigenous artists has been at the forefront of drawing society's attention to critical present-day issues. The abstract, the spirit, forms, and symbolic meanings presented in nationally heralded works are truly significant to wider reaches of the country and to the aims of reconciliation. The first group of Indigenous artists to receive national recognition was the Professional Native Indian Artists Incorporated, later known as the Indigenous Group of Seven. Three have become Governor General Laureates: Daphne Odjig, Alex Janvier, and Norval Morrisseau. Their individual distinctive styles drew from their own Indigenous backgrounds, and their art is a rich visual storytelling. As Alex Janvier said, "This is my way of speaking to the public . . . my visual language . . . to convey what's inside my spirit."[90] While not "abstract" in the conventional expectation of the word, their work stirringly conveys traditional myths, legends, and concern for nature and for their spiritual roots.

Alex Janvier's abstracted landscapes, like *Manitoba,* 2008, are powerful and lyrical, and seemingly approach *place* from an aerial perspective. They often focus on rivers, the source of life, while simultaneously commenting on the general and pervasive political blindness to the country's historical roots. His colour relates to the natural aspects of the prairie, and his work overall transmits his deep respect for the land as life and as culture. Fluidity of line and patterns evoke the interplay between the sky, rivers, land, summer growth, and winter snows. He says,

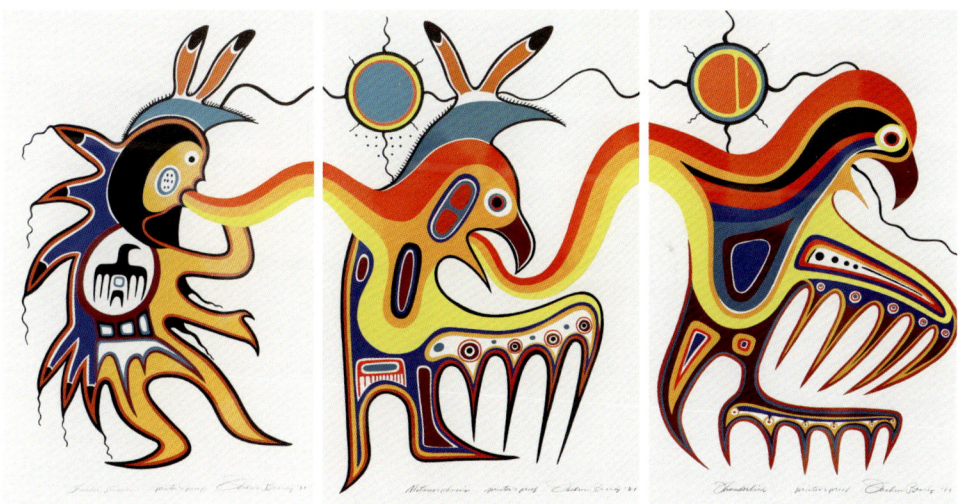

"My paintings are about who I am, where I've been, what I've seen. What I have painted is about what the hell happened to us as landlords of the land, sky and water. Painting says it all for me. It is the Redman talk in colour, in North America's language. Our Yedariye's (Creator's) voice in colour."[91]

Janvier's *The Four Seasons of '76,* 1977, using fluid lines and colours connecting the four seasons, also incorporates the plain background as part of the composition. His colour is rooted in the Indigenous Medicine Wheel and his Dene heritage, as in *Morning Star,* 1993, in the Museum of Canadian History. The star refers to its use as a direction finder. The museum records that "the four areas of colour in the outside ring represent periods in Native history: yellow, for early history in harmony with nature; blue, for the changes brought about by contact with European civilization; red for revival and optimism; and white for reconciliation and a return to harmony."[92]

The depths of the spiritual roots, their ancestral past, nature, and family are evident throughout all the work of the Indigenous Group of Seven. The life cycle, for instance, is frequently represented in Jackson Beardy's art, as seen through the flowing, ribbon-like black line connecting all the elements in *Cycle of Life,* 1972, to the sun. He used an x-ray vision to portray the inner being, birth, and overall symbiosis in nature and life. Likewise, primary colours throughout his work flow from the sun, the source of light, connecting all aspects of life. His *Thunder Dancer, Metamorphosis, Thunderbird,* 1981, a silkscreen triptych, clearly speaks of his

FIGURE 5.23. **Jackson Beardy**, *Thunder Dancer, Metamorphosis, Thunderbird*, 1981.

culture and spirit. The three sections in this work are connected by a red, orange, and yellow ribbon, which appears in much of his art.

Daphne Odjig, in her vibrant, cubist-like paintings filled with motion and emotion, heralds life and life cycles—ancestry, birth, growth, and maturity. Her *From Mother Earth Flows the River of Life,* 1973, is a strong, colourful interlocking of multiple forms with Mother Earth at its centre. Her flowing lines, colour, and rhythms fill the entire canvas and convey the spiritual depth of past and present beliefs.

The depth and significance of the spiritual in the work of Norval Morrisseau cannot be overestimated either. He said, "I used to ask my grandfather, 'Where did the Indians get these images that they put on their rock paintings?' He would say to me 'They come from the spirit world.'"[93] Curator Martin Segger commented that Morrisseau felt all "artists should devote themselves to the shamanic role in society, transforming the spiritual into the actual."[94]

Morrisseau's brilliant use of colour carried much meaning and therapeutic properties for him, and he felt that colour rid one of stress.[95] His painting *Power of the Spirit of Manitou*, 1978, shows his exploration of the connections between earthly presence and the divine, and the passageway of the soul and the place attained through meditation. Victoria artist and theatre designer Mary Kerr, who created the costumes and sets for *Copper Thunderbird,* a play based on an interpretation by playwright Marie Clements of the life of the artist, quotes Morrisseau: "By being unconditioned, we were able to travel easily on the inner highways, right to the source of all knowledge and invention. . . . Artists mediate realities and bridge worlds. The shaman lives in two or more inter-visible worlds and functions traditionally as the go-between to bring back what he sees to make art and transform the world."[96]

That expression of the connections among Indigenous artists' spiritual beliefs, their traditions, and personal experiences is poignant, and respectfully given from generation to generation, tying the verbal to the visual. As Haida artist Bill Reid wrote in 1989 about a journey to Skidegate on Haida Gwaii: "Perhaps the descriptions, rooted in myth, of the origins of this universe seem fanciful and inexact compared to the scientific logic we follow. Both give order and structure to the world and its happenings. . . . The wonderful thing about Rediscovery is that it has enabled all these different truths to exist side by side."[97]

Robert Davidson (b. 1946) has likewise created internationally acclaimed work that brings the creative strength of Indigenous peoples and specifically artists to the fore. Davidson builds on Haida traditions in his paintings, jewellery, prints, and sculpture, creating new means of expression, such as his serigraph *Two Finned Killer Whale,* or his cast silver and abalone *Happy Blowhole Pendant.* He stated, "My passion is reconnecting with my ancestors' knowledge. The philosophy is what bred the art, and now the art has become the catalyst for us to explore the philosophy. . . . What's exciting for me is to express what the art is all about from my experience. . . . When I go outside the Haida boundaries, I am challenged, too—I want the art to be recognized as a high art form."[98]

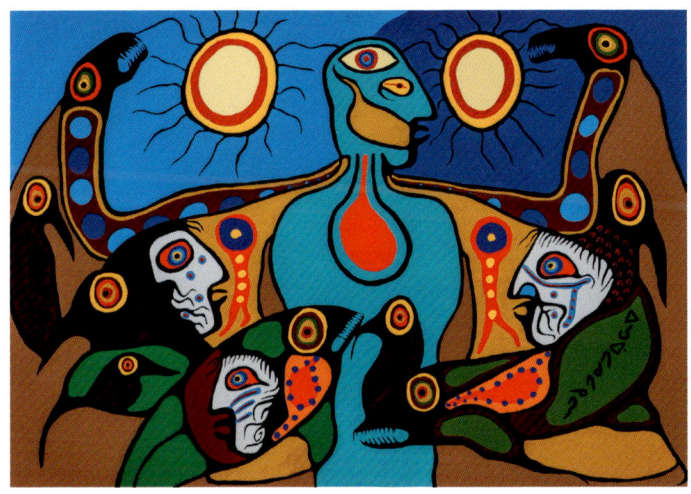

FIGURE 5.24.
Norval Morrisseau,
*Power of the Spirit
of Manitou*, 1978.

From Sandy Bay, Manitoba's Robert Houle, artist, curator, professor, and graduate of Winnipeg's School of Art, has made a seminal mark on Canadian art by posing difficult and poignant questions about cultural issues of Indigenous peoples in Canada's history, always focusing on issues of identity and spirituality. He layers the past with the present and conveys his personal reflections on political situations. He incorporates his deep understanding of both Indigenous and European spiritualities, and the intersections of Indigenous and European cultures and histories. He is well versed in the history of Western art, and his work combines artistic traditions and cultures, highlighting deep-rooted present-day concerns. His multi-panelled abstractions are complex: psychological on one hand, symbolic on the other. Through his use of colour he portrays the emotion, significance, and feeling of the particular event. Serving as documentary evidence, his work often incorporates text or collaged historic photos. His paintings are at once landscapes and history drama paintings, successfully combining many approaches within a single work through his sense of balance, proportion, and colour. His colour, sensitively applied to the canvas, is drawn both from the widely understood vernacular and from his personal perspective. He deals with the toughest of issues, the spiritual, and the contemporary, and he is able to layer the serious with humour. His pride in his ancestry creates evocative, meaningful, and, at times, uncomfortable paintings, opening new dialogues and engaging viewers in the discussions. Not presuming the answers, his works are at once compelling, disarming, and strong.

Houle incorporates the different directions of the Medicine Wheel of the Sacred Teachings of the White Buffalo Calf Woman into many of his works: east—yellow; south—red; west—black; and north—white. In 2015 Houle installed his *Seven Grandfathers*, a powerful series of seven rondels, in the Art Gallery of Ontario's Walker Court. Echoing the circular architectural

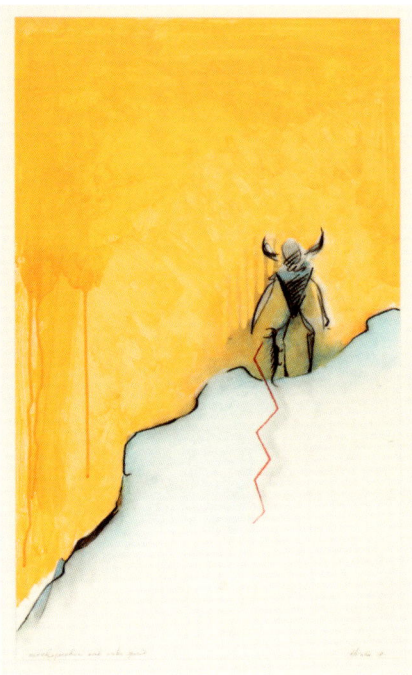

FIGURE 5.25.
Robert Houle,
*Mishipeshu and Water
Spirit*, 2018.

details within the space itself, the rondels are drums relating to the seven Indigenous teachings. Each represents one of the seven animal spirits: Humility: the wolf; Honesty: the raven; Respect: the buffalo; Courage: the bear; Wisdom: the beaver; Truth: the turtle; and Love: the eagle. Another critically major work showing Houle's spirituality is his *Parfleches for the Last Supper,* 1983, acrylic and porcupine quills on paper. Houle told me that though he was brought up Catholic, his Indigenous spirituality is strong. Comprising thirteen works, one for each of Christ's disciples and one representing Christ himself, each title bears a Biblical quote relating to the specific disciple. This series links Christian and Indigenous religious traditions. The parfleche, the bag in which Indigenous hunters carried their arrows and the porcupine quills, represent the artistic traditions and customs of his people pre-contact. The colours he has chosen are symbolic of both Christian and Indigenous traditions.

Like Houle and other Indigenous artists, Saskatchewan's Robert Boyer draws from the imagery of the dual cultures of Indigenous Plains peoples and European traditions. Boyer's art manifests spirituality, social reality, and personal and universal substance. Scholar Christian Thompson said, "His use of geometric designs reflect his personal experiences, social issues and spirituality."[99] Boyer is a colourist, and his geometric forms are informed by the earlier work

FIGURE 5.26. **Lita Fontaine**, *The Pagan*, 1996.

266

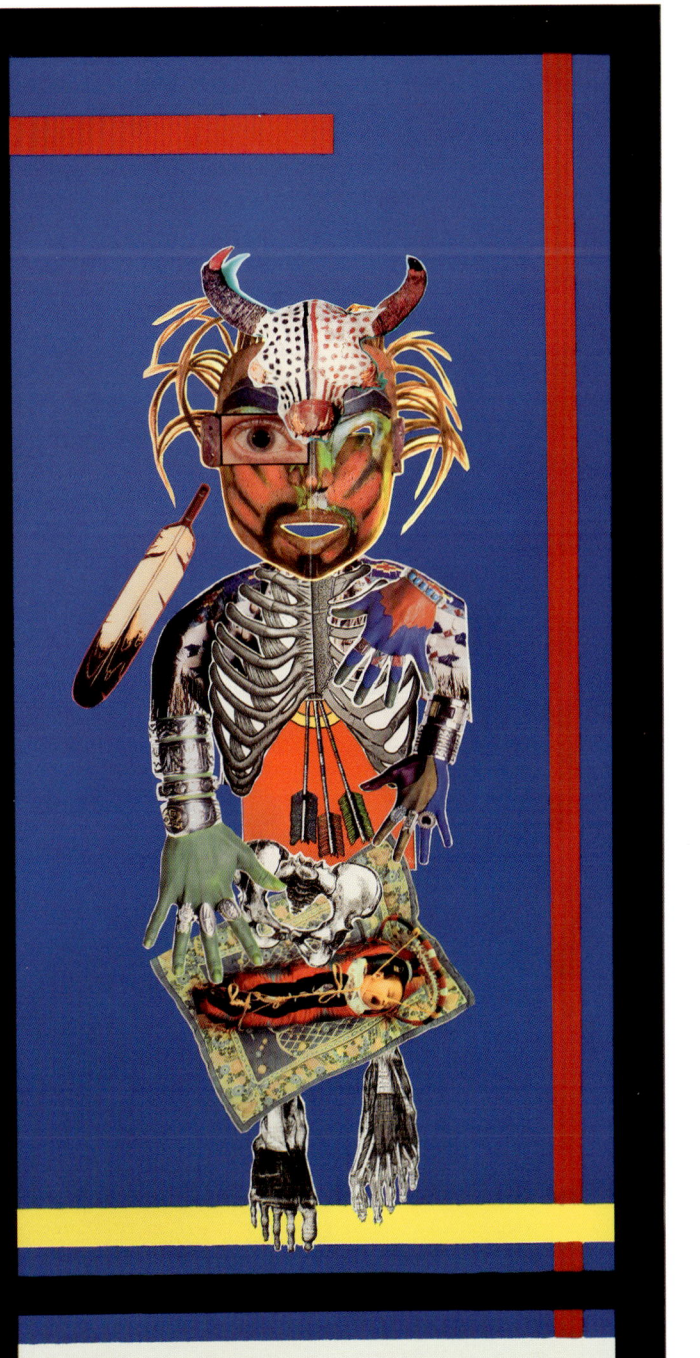

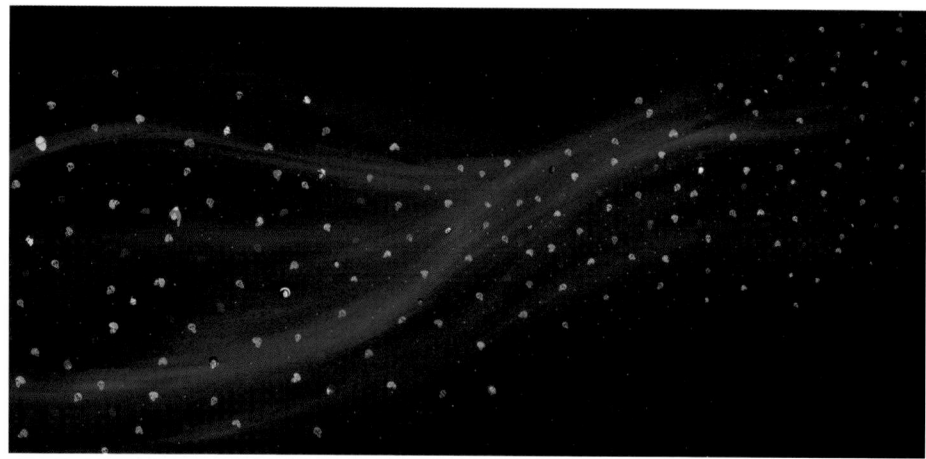

of the Regina Five. Underlining the importance of the spirit in his art, curator Janet Clark commented that his later work "is about the personal and the spiritual and his relationship with his culture on that level. The references to earlier work that remain are elements that are an inherent part of Plains Indian culture and that speak to his heritage and to time spent on the powwow circuit as a dancer. . . . His love of surface texture and colour remain, and the works, regardless of scale, are freer, elemental and immediate. They take the viewer, as the artist intends, to a place of the spirit."[100]

Indigenous artist and Brandon university teacher Colleen Cutschall is also interested in cosmology, core to her Lakota roots and teachings. Curator Shirley Madill says *House Made of Stars,* for example, is "a created environment based on Aboriginal stellar knowledge, a worldview connecting human and cosmic forces."[101] Of the sacred nature of stars and their centrality to the spirit and the universe, Cutschall wrote: "The stars are the breath of the gods. They write the message in the heavens, they tell us exactly what to do down here and that's what we follow. We've never looked at the stars as being anything but superior intelligence. Any of the cosmic forms that we see out there have always been [viewed as] primary knowledge."[102]

Cutschall's paintings *The Androgynous Landscape* and *Milky Way—Spirit Trail,* both from 1996, underline her deep sense of the spirit in, and emanating from and through, the landscape, as well as the significance of the stellar space for Indigenous peoples. *Androgynous Landscape* portrays the truly sacred place Mato Tipi Paha in Wyoming, and expresses the deep roots of the spiritual traditions. Writer Allan Ryan describes the Indigenous spiritual meanings within the painting:

FIGURE 5.27. **Colleen Cutschall**, *Milky Way, Spirit Trail*, from the series *House Made of Stars*, 1996.

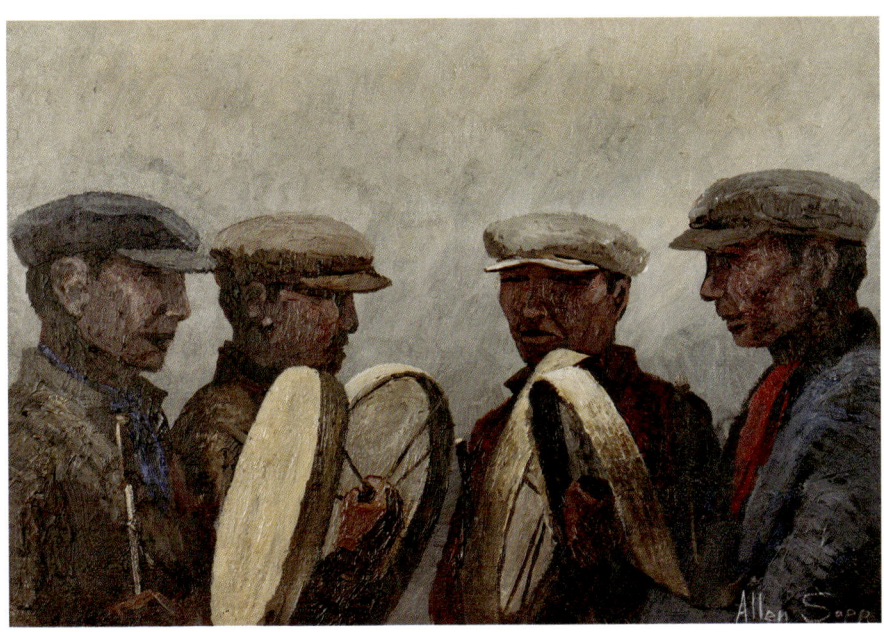

At the heart of the sacred narrative recounted in *The Androgynous Landscape* is the image of two complementary cones of light, or glowing vortices about to touch at their apexes. The resulting hourglass figure produced by this convergence is one of the most potent symbols in all of Lakota Theology. . . . It embodies the concept of cosmic reciprocity. . . . In the present context it refers to the "twist" that occurs when and where the two cones of light come together. Located midway between heaven and earth, it defines a holy place of prayer and sacred dialogue . . . whirlwind imagery—to symbolize intense cultural activity and impending changes . . . the luminous funnels of starlight are propelled across the heavens sheathed in the rainbow-wrapped whirlwinds.[103]

Milky Way—Spirit Trail, with its painterly application of the background paths of dark colour setting off the same rhythmic pathways of the stars across the work, directly honours the memory of those people close to the artist, the family and friends, who had passed into the spirit world. That trail and their influence extend beyond the edges of the painting, marking a continuum from generation to generation.

That involvement of artists' explorations of the spiritual invites viewers to delve into their own personal inner reaches of spiritual philosophy and religious beliefs.

FIGURE 5.28. **Allen Sapp**, *Indian Drums*, 1972.

Abstracting through Sculpture

> "Art is nothing if it is not a philosophy. It's an attitude to life; it's not a thing of the moment. And it must refer to the past and the present and the future; in other words, to take in the full scope, it must express something of the feeling of the span of life from birth to death. It's totemic, it's a generational thing. It refers to people yet to come, and people who have passed away."[104]

Sculptural expression in its many forms and over many centuries embodies the past, present, and future. In the nineteenth and early twentieth centuries, sculptural work was primarily that of portraits and monuments, but from the mid-twentieth century forward, the approaches, materials, and subject matter for sculptors shifted. By the 1980s old traditions were challenged and societal issues increasingly entered artists' three-dimensional vocabulary, with abstract forms being created by many.

As discussed earlier, there are essentially two methods of making sculpture: modelling and building by adding to a basic form; and carving or cutting to create a form. Victoria's Elza Mayhew primarily used the second. As she abstracted thought and form throughout her impressive oeuvre, architecture and architectural references were at the forefront of many of her monumental sculptures. Myths and creations of human cultures over centuries, involving many civilizations, are at the root of Mayhew's art. Despite its large scale, her work exudes warmth and understanding through the blending of geometric forms, richly incised surfaces, and universally symbolic motifs. All her pieces have a rectangle or circle, representing a door or a window—an opening for the viewer. She said: "My sculptures are very central. There are verticals and horizontals but few diagonals. They are highly structured and very architectural, but they always relate to the human form. Many societies found security for themselves and their towns in columns or archways. Totems give a terrific feeling of security and they also mark time. They tie people to their past and future and I feel that my works are likewise— markers in time and of a place."[105]

One might surmise correctly that First Nations' totem poles on her native Vancouver Island were an inspiration, as were classical works of ancient Greece and Rome, especially the columns in the Acropolis. In fact, her sources of inspiration were many, and she drew from them all, abstracting sensibilities to create her own sculptural vocabulary. Holes derived from architecture are important in her bronze totemic pieces. As Mayhew said, "I feel terrific things when I put a hole through a work. I am really making doorways and that is something with which I have always been fascinated. Also, when I make an opening or an archway, I always have to indicate human presence and then it is usually in a relatively minute way. It generates a sensation which is absolutely overwhelming."[106] *Princess,* 1963, exhibited at the Venice Biennale, 1964, was purchased privately in 1969 and she wrote the new owners, "*Princess* is a Janus figure, which can face either of two ways."[107] The holes, both circular and square, are evident, as is the fusion of past and present and the human and the architectural.

Mayhew cut her forms from Styrofoam blocks, a material easy to cut, to thin, and to shape. Used a curling iron to create curved edges, she worked without a mask and constantly breathed in the fumes of melting Styrofoam. That caused her affliction of styrene poisoning. She also frequently went to the foundry to oversee the process and patinas of her work. Mayhew received many public commissions for her art and exhibited widely to great acclaim, as was the case with the Victoria Limners Society's 1976 group exhibition in Toronto. As James Purdie said in the *Globe and Mail*, "The strongest images in the show are to be found in the paintings by [Maxwell] Bates and the sculptures by Mayhew."[108]

Robert de Castro (1923–1986), a friend and colleague of Mayhew's, turned to sculpture on his return from the war, deeply affected psychologically by his experiences. A sense of isolation and loneliness pervades all his art. According to Tony Gregson, "De Castro was wedded to tools—they enabled the sculptor to be, and that [his] studio seemed to speak for him perfectly—workman-like, no-nonsense, right on the harbour [Victoria] where real things happened—his things, that is. . . . De Castro's art was born of his silences and to the extent that art exists to say things we cannot say to each other, there was a tough honesty about his silence, the honesty of well-worn tools."[109]

De Castro and Elza Mayhew both studied with American Jan Zach, who operated an art school in Emily Carr's former studio on St. Andrew Street from 1951 to 1958. De Castro, who felt an important personal and creative freedom when making art, worked in wood and cement. Figures, fossil men, frequently emerge from his pieces or are contained within them. He was a perfectionist and attained a specific quality of his surface and colour. As Gregson writes, "The relationship between the finishing of the surface and the carving is integral. The polishing is a bridge between two types of surfacing, creating a unity between disparate surfaces—an unconscious reflection, perhaps, of a search for unity with himself, between the disturbed psyche that he once described as 'a disjuncture,' and a more rational self."[110]

He first stained the carefully chosen wood with black or brown shoe polish, which he rubbed well into the surface of the wood. With an eye to his desired final outcome, he then stained it with dark powdered pigment dissolved in thinners, mixed with shellac. This was, as Gregson says, "a technique that enabled him to get the full benefit of the colour. . . . Coats of varnish would be applied literally with his bare hands to avoid any brush marks, and the work would be polished to a high lustre."[111]

At times he deliberately left the imperfections of the wood visible, as he sometimes did with his chisel marks, to equate a painter's brush strokes. Writer and colleague Robin Skelton wrote of these that "the work often has a deliberate unfinished quality; the form is sometimes seen to be emerging from the wood. . . . Some pieces derive emotional power from being so clearly at a time of transition. They are caught at a moment of change, a critical point. The tension of the forms themselves add a tension of timing. . . . the work retains a powerful and authoritative presence."[112]

Indigenous artists, especially those in British Columbia, have truly strong sculptural traditions, each nation and family having their distinct iconography and symbolism referring to their cultural histories and roots. A pole rising is both a community and spiritual event, and the significance of each is palpable and an honour. Their totem poles, house fronts, and masks carry with them the past and become the foundation of the future. Richard Hunt, Robert Davidson, Tim Paul, and Arthur Vickers are all master sculptors.

Richard Hunt (b. 1951), a Kwakwaka'wakw master carver, has followed generations of his family and created totem poles, masks, carved wall pieces, bowls, and rattles, each with traditional and family iconography. His large wood carving at Victoria's Harbour Airport, *My Family,* for example, is complex, full of detail and personal meaning, best described by him:

> All the figures here are from my culture. If you came to my village in Fort Rupert, B.C. to potlatch, you would see these figures danced. The beaver and the otter, along with the bear would be used in the Dance of the Animal Kingdom and they are here because of the Harbour Air restaurants, the Flying Beaver and the Flying Otter. There is an eagle in the middle standing on a copper with its wings out-stretched. The eagle is the main crest of my people from Fort Rupert, B.C. On each side of the eagle's face are two eagles with their heads looking up. The top left corner is a moon rising. Below the eagle's wing on the left, is an eagle holding a salmon. The salmon is a staple food with our people. On the right, under the wing, is a thunderbird with a killer whale. Killer whale is the favourite food of the thunderbird. There is a moon in the blowhole of the whale, a hawk man on the tail of the whale and a raven on the inside fin of the whale.[113]

Much of Hunt's work recalls the significance of the potlatch, which had been banned by the federal government in the 1880 amendment to the Indian Act. That amendment states: "Every Indian or other person who engages in or assists in celebrating the Indian festival known as the 'Potlatch' or in the Indian dance known as the 'Tamanawas' is guilty of a misdemeanor, and shall be liable to imprisonment."[114] For seventy-one years Indigenous people were denied this right to their culture. Though potlatches continued to be held underground, it was only in 1951 that the clause was deleted and Chief Mungo Martin, Richard Hunt's honorary grandfather, held the first legal potlatch in 1952. Hunt incorporates his family history and symbols in much of his work. He recently created three bronze sculptures, one paying tribute to his father, Henry Hunt, and also to his mother, referenced with the frog depicted on his father's traditional hat. The copper on the back of the figure recalls the potlatch. His masks, like *The Chief's Wild Woman*, carved, painted, and with added horsehair, also relate to traditional teachings.

Family tradition is likewise a prime focus for Tim Paul (b. 1950), whose 1997 pole *Nas-win-is (When Night and Day Cross)* was commissioned by the Art Gallery of Greater Victoria. We had a number of discussions about what it should be, he looking for direction from us as to whether it should be traditional or contemporary, and we desiring him to create what he wanted. In the end, after consulting with the chief, the final work that represents the moon did both: one side included traditional iconography; the other was simply stained, blue, with the moon on top. As he said at the unveiling of the work: "When night & day cross it is still a deep dark blue. This is when the Maker's ear is open & you prepare for a new day."[115]

Arthur Vickers (b. 1947) is from the west coast Tsimshian village Kitkatla. His respect for Elders, particularly his grandfather, is evident in all his work and in every conversation with him. The core of his art reflects the Tsimshian and Haida traditions of his father, the stories and values of his ancestry that his grandfather taught him, and his English mother's life history. A carrier of heritage and teller of stories, Vickers pushes his art into new directions, blending culture, traditions, and new techniques and approaches. His use of gold leaf and gold powders in both his two- and three-dimensional work is compelling, in many ways evoking links between his contemporary creations and those of medieval manuscripts and gilding guilds. His mixed media and twenty-four-karat gold leaf powder in the work *Intangible Heritage* is a prime example.

Vickers is a master carver, too: his bentwood boxes, some with gold imagery, are significant in his overall oeuvre. He also carved a desk for the people of British Columbia, first installed as *The Leadership Desk,* in British Columbia's Parliament Buildings. When it was later moved to British Columbia Government House, it became *The People's Desk.* Its goal, Vickers said, was to "cause the leaders of the province to pause and consider the enormous responsibilities they have accepted on behalf of all of the people of all cultures in British Columbia."[116] Its form is a traditional bentwood box created from old-growth, edge-grained red cedar. Vickers used a special paint to ensure longevity and he hand-cut individual stencils for the symbols and iconography for the designs on each side, admitting that "creating a three-dimensional, functional piece of art is very different from sitting at your easel with your canvas angled just the way you'd like it."[117] The symbols on the desk are rich and include an eagle on the front, spreading its wings as a blanket, and, Vickers said, "representations of the male and female of this generation from the youngest to the eldest . . . their hands outstretched. . . . In the hands of the female are the salmon/trout heads as the salmon have been precious sources of nourishment that have sustained the cycle of life and the people of our province."[118]

Bill Reid is considered by many people as one who gave visual voice to Haida culture, embracing it first when he visited Haida Gwaii in 1954. Installed at both the Canadian Embassy in Washington and the Vancouver International Airport, his *Spirit of Haida Gwaii: The Jade Canoe,* 1986–1991, draws from many Haida legends and oral histories. First done in clay in 1986, it was

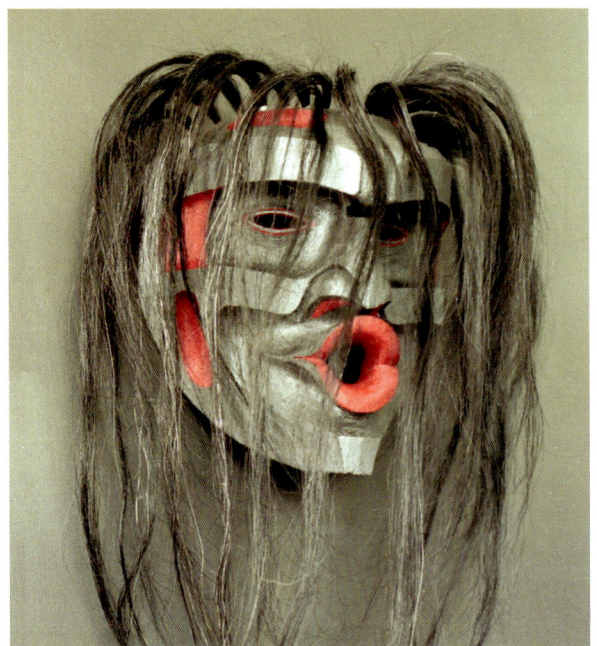

FIGURE 5.29.
Richard Hunt, *The Chief's Wild Woman*, c. 2012

cast in bronze in 1991. Reflecting on the work, Reid wrote "The Spirit of Haida Gwaii" text poem for his wife in which he recounts the symbolism of the bear, the mother bear, the beaver, the dogfish woman, the mouse woman, the raven, the wolf, the eagle, and the frog:

> Here we are at last, a long way from Haida Gwaii, not too sure where we are or where we're going, still squabbling and vying for position in the boat, but somehow managing to appear to be heading in some direction; at least the paddles are together, and the man in the middle seems to have some vision of what is to come.
>
> As for the rest, they are superficially more or less what they always were, symbols of another time when the Haidas, all ten thousand of them, knew they were the greatest of all nations. . . .
>
> So there is certainly no lack of activity in our little boat, but is there any purpose? Is the tall figure who may or may not be the Spirit of Haida Gwaii leading us, for we are all in the same boat, to a sheltered beach beyond the rim of the world as he seems to be, or is he lost in a dream of his own dreamings? The boat moves on, forever anchored in the same place.[11]

Reid was prolific in many media, and the hours I spent with him in his Granville Island studio in the 1980s were memorable. I witnessed the beginning stages of his work on *The Spirit of Haida Gwaii* and the plaster of his *Killer Whale.* Carvers including Jim Hart worked with him on both these major works, and it was clear that the surface and perfection of the forms within were paramount. Scaana, meaning "killer whale" in Haida, is the protector of the sea and, as the plaque at the Vancouver Aquarium reads, the "Chief of the Undersea world, who from his great house raises the storms of the winter and brings the calm seas of the summer. He governs the cycle of the salmon and is the keeper of all the ocean's living treasures."[120]

Robert Davidson, a true leader in Canadian visual arts, has tirelessly researched and reclaimed lost cultural traditions. He said, "There is this amazing movement now to reclaim cultural knowledge. As we reclaim that knowledge—reclaim the names, the songs, the dances, the crests, the clans, the place of chiefs in Haida villages—it's gone the whole gamut to reclaiming the land. They're all one. . . . My passion is reconnecting with my ancestors' knowledge. The philosophy is what bred the art, and now the art has become the catalyst for us to explore the philosophy."[121] His presentations, which I witnessed in the early 1980s, of Haida dances that he had reclaimed were exhilarating and movingly inspirational. In exploring his visual artistic traditions, Davidson took forms and iconography to new dimensions, and he used both traditional and new materials. A painter, printmaker, carver, and master of work in wood and silver, he has also created large cut-out abstracted sculptures, such as *Supernatural Eye,* constructed from waterjet-cut and pressure-bent aluminum. The work is fabricated in multiple pieces that are welded together over a webbed metal armature before he shapes them. These sculptures continue to draw from traditional Haida forms. Curator Karen Duffek commented: "There are contradictions in classifying Davidson's paintings and sculptures as abstract. . . . These works engage with concepts of abstraction through their formal play with isolated elements and scale. They also engage with abstract concepts—ideas specific to Haida philosophy, art and cultural practice, yet relating to modernist tradition in their break from rigid conventions of thought."[122]

In developing his personal iconography, Davidson has steadfastly maintained that he "will not create his art outside the formal language of Haida visual expression."[123] He has said:

> I know that my experiments with the art form have a lot do with my having a foot in each doorway: it means changing from hosting a potlatch to working in the studio— it means changing paths from challenging myself in the potlatch to continuing this dialogue with a new vocabulary of Haida art and with new supernatural beings. One feeds the other. The art builds on the experience of hosting a feast, it builds on the experience of going to a feast. When I start to draw an image, there's an order to it that is already established. It's very much like using the letters of the alphabet to make words: you don't just draw the letters together and think you are saying something. The art is the same way: to carve a totem pole is the same way. The art comes from experience—it's not a whim.[124]

Brian Jungen employs a truly contemporary approach in his sculpture and is always innovative in his use of everyday consumer objects as art-making materials. His *Prototypes for New Understanding,* created in the late 1990s and early 2000s, includes masks and totem poles made from Nike running shoes and other sporting goods, thus connecting traditional Indigenous forms and iconography with contemporary corporate symbols. This use of consumer goods has extended to plastic folding chairs, which he used to create the large prehistoric animals such as in *Cetology,* 2002, a large installation strung from the ceiling.

Saskatchewan Métis artist Edward Poitras, who represented Canada at the 1995 Venice Biennale, does public installations as well as creating individual sculpture works. He, too, has stretched both the visual language and the substance of art. Issues of colonialism, treaties, and urban and reservation life are redolent in his art. The coyote frequents many of his works, his *13 Coyotes* being particularly salient in its many messages. In *13 Coyotes* the artist examines transformation as the coyotes seem to come to life from various materials, including bones which are in the installation itself. Alluding to the transformation of life in general, he does so by extending space and territories as he simultaneously examines time.

Also working in Saskatchewan, Eli Bornstein is best known for his structurist reliefs, which are rooted in the tradition of early twentieth-century geometric abstraction. Bornstein's colourful reliefs explore the subtle nuances of the light falling around the work. Evoking both the prairie canola fields and industrial urban constructions, his work is built with geometrical shapes and forms to describe movement and space. "Eli's ability to translate his experience of nature into constructed reliefs is very compelling. There's something almost musical about experiencing his compositions, which are meticulously created to evoke qualities of light one experiences in nature,"[125] noted curator Sandra Fraser. Eli Bornstein's long teaching career at the University of Saskatchewan embedded him at the centre of Saskatoon's creative community while allowing him the freedom to follow his personal artistic course.

The rigour and formality of Bornstein's overlapping forms, colours, and patterns and his drawing from nature attest to Fraser's comments.[126] His *Structurist Relief in 15 Parts*, for instance, the aluminum sculpture commissioned in 1964 for the former Winnipeg International Airport, and now installed on the exterior of the University of Manitoba's Max Bell Centre, illuminates engagement of form with light and shifting shadows.

Illuminating rural life and the importance of farming and its history, Don Proch has frequently used the grain elevator as a three-dimensional form for his meticulous drawings of the Manitoba prairie landscape, many of which present foreboding environmental concerns. For him, grain elevators represent societal change and farming transformations. The iconic community wooden elevators are all but gone, and his *Elevator Series* of several decades is a nostalgic and compelling reminder of past farming. *Asessippi to Altona,* 2019, has a red elevator on one side and white on the other, the typical prairie sky surrounds the elevator itself and train tracks run through the drive-thru. It also shows wind turbines in the field, contrasting the older

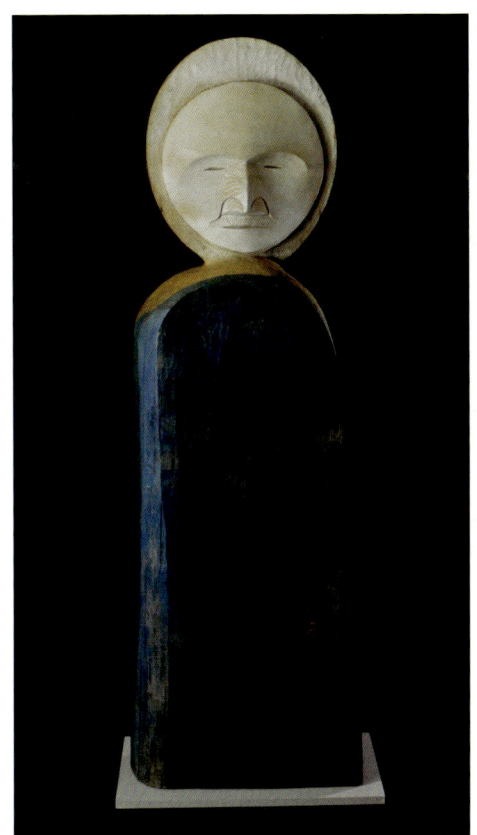
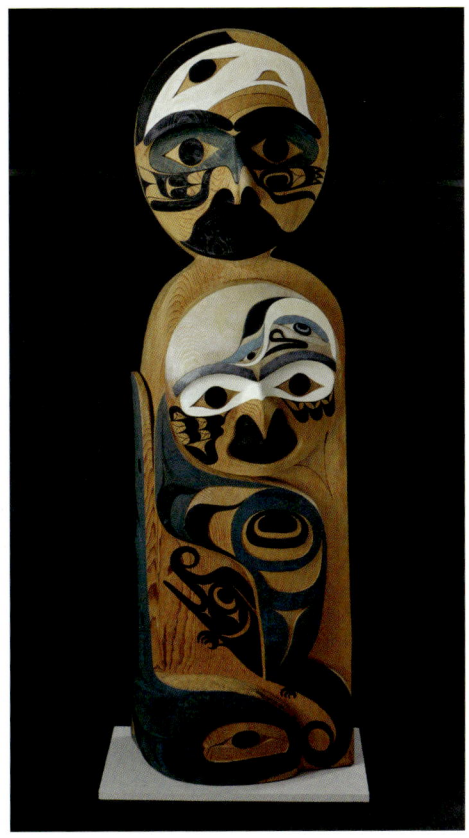

technologies. As with all his grain elevators, Proch constructed this three-dimensional sculptural form of wood and fibreglass, and the drawing is executed in pencil, coloured pencil, and silverpoint. Chromed clouds are on top and the ditch is filled with water, also in chrome, and sisal represents the grasses. In some of this series the foreboding future is highlighted by dark, ominous skies, sharp points of acid rain, and jagged edges and lightning streaks.

Proch's 2016 *Colville's Horse Races through the Prairie Drive-Thru Gallery, Brushing Past John Nugent's "No.1 Hard," Heading West to Haida Gwaii* shows the interior of the elevator with the prairie beyond. Constructed like a three-dimensional theatre stage, this piece dramatizes the passage of time from the 1930s and 1940s to today, through the heady 1960s and 1970s, which he represented with specific contemporary works of art he installed in the drive-thru. The vista

FIGURE 5.30. **Tim Paul**, *Nas-Win-Is (When Night and Day Cross)*, 1997.

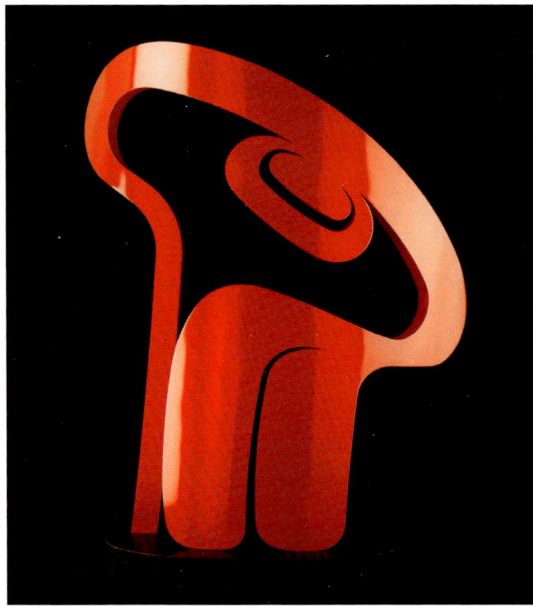

seen within, executed with his intricate and smooth pencil workings over the entire surface, is a continuation of the landscape in front of the elevator. Cloud formations follow the contours of the field, and the colour is naturalistic, showing the gold prairie grains, green grasses, and soft blues characteristic of late summer skies. A horse, its tail flying behind, gallops past the works of art Proch depicted in his gallery. It evokes speed, just as the crouched position of the figure did on the bicycle in *Asessippi Tread* of more than forty years earlier. The inclusion of paintings by colleagues effectively unites Proch's two lives—the farm boy turned environmentalist, and that of an acclaimed Canadian artist. Of his horse, reminiscent of that of Nova Scotia's Alex Colville's *Horse and Train,* 1954, Proch commented: "I was hoping that the horse had run free of the train and continued on a cross country journey where his curiosity led him through the drive-thru gallery."[127] Developmental sketches and drawings for this seminal piece, filling many pages in his sketchbooks, denote precise structural details, aesthetic decisions, materials, colours, and measurements. This pathway into Proch's personal and communal psyche begs the question: What future are we moving into? The greenish acidic quality in the grey tones he uses imparts a luminous eeriness for the future.

Saskatchewan's John Nugent, a major figure in that province's artistic scene, was known especially for his public abstract sculptures. His far-reaching stature was underlined when his studio, designed by Saskatchewan architect Clifford Wiens, was designated a provincial historic site. Nugent's controversial constructivist steel sculpture *No. 1 Hard,* 1975, referred to

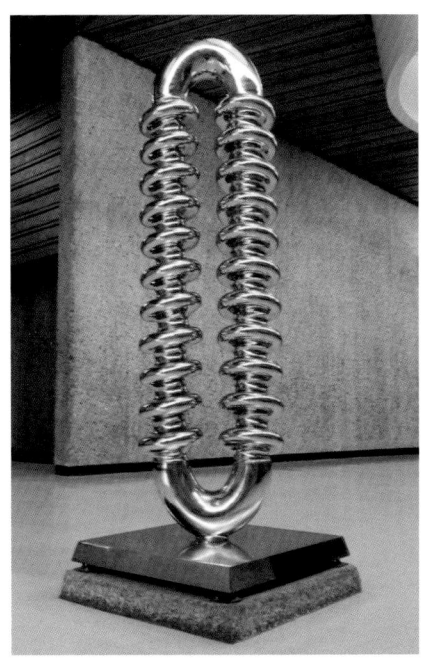

FIGURE 5.32.
Katie Ohe,
Zipper, 1975.

in Proch's sculpture and later renamed *No. 1 Northern,* is a visual metaphor for prairie wheat fields represented by the bright yellow superimposed rectangles. No. 1 Northern is, of course, a variety of wheat. His use of yellow also symbolizes the sun. About his work Timothy Long wrote: "The awkward grace of Nugent's steel sculpture, for which he is best known, results from a constructivist collage of prefabricated elements. While often incorporating identifiable parts, such as wheels, his sculpture eludes easy metaphorical readings, instead creating meaning through unexpected combinations of forms and materials."[128]

Robert Murray, another major constructivist sculptor who also worked in steel and colour, moved from his native British Columbia and youthful Saskatoon home to New York in 1960. He was a friend of Barnett Newman. His sculpture is a key part of contemporary sculptural abstraction and his public art pieces are across North America. Writer Jonathan Lippincott commented: "Murray was particularly innovative in his use of industrial fabrication methods to create his pieces and in his deep investigation of landscape as inspiration for abstract sculpture."[129]

Douglas Bentham, like John Nugent, stretches the scope and vocabulary of sculpture by setting his works within nature, creating a dialogue and interplay between the natural setting and the formal aspects of his work. By so doing he modifies and manipulates space. Linear aspects and the intersecting planes within his work take the eye along the edges and curves of the metal pieces into the surrounding space. The welded works of Peter Hide, who studied with international sculptor Anthony Caro, likewise play with the intersection of planes and geometry.

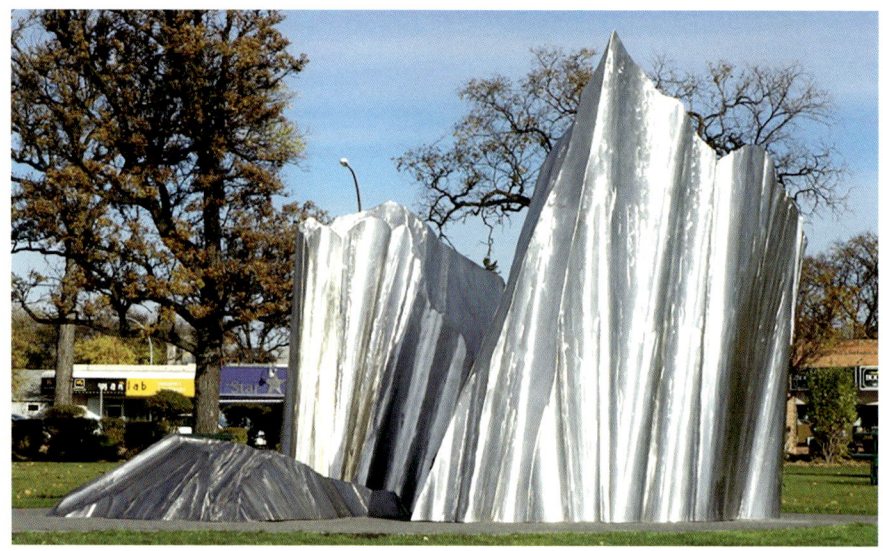

Alberta is home to a number of sculptors whose work is more than worthy of inclusion in any compendium of Canadian art. Katie Ohe (b. 1937), professor and mentor and abstract sculptor, is a key figure, with her husband, painter Harry Kiyooka, in Canada's field of abstraction. Interested in kinetic sculpture, she has used a number of materials, techniques, prefabricated objects, and industrial processes, as seen in her piece *Zipper,* 1975. Surface is a key element for her, and she uses it in a way that it is tempting for people to touch. The Esker Foundation notes of her work: "Embracing elements of reductive geometry, repetition, and visual harmony, Ohe has developed a body of work that is at once connected to Minimalism through its purity and unity of form, but is also affective, idiosyncratic, sensual, and concerned with personal experience, memory, and the perception of the natural world."[130]

Gordon Reeve (b. 1946), who taught sculpture at the University of Manitoba School of Art, has a number of pieces in public spaces, one being *Agassiz Ice,* 2008. Its three sections are seemingly "massive chunks of pristine ice floating on a sea, not of water but of grass," he said. "And like icebergs each of the Agassiz sculptures will appear to be submerged, only its tip visible above the surface. That which is hidden from our eyes need not be hidden from our mind."[131] His sculptures invite public interaction while signifying the province's geological past.

Linda Stanbridge (b. 1948) has created a body of work focused on geometric shapes, as evident in *Core 3,* a fired ceramic, with brushed steel and welded aluminum support. Although

FIGURE 5.33. **Gordon Reeve**, *Agassiz Ice*, 2008.

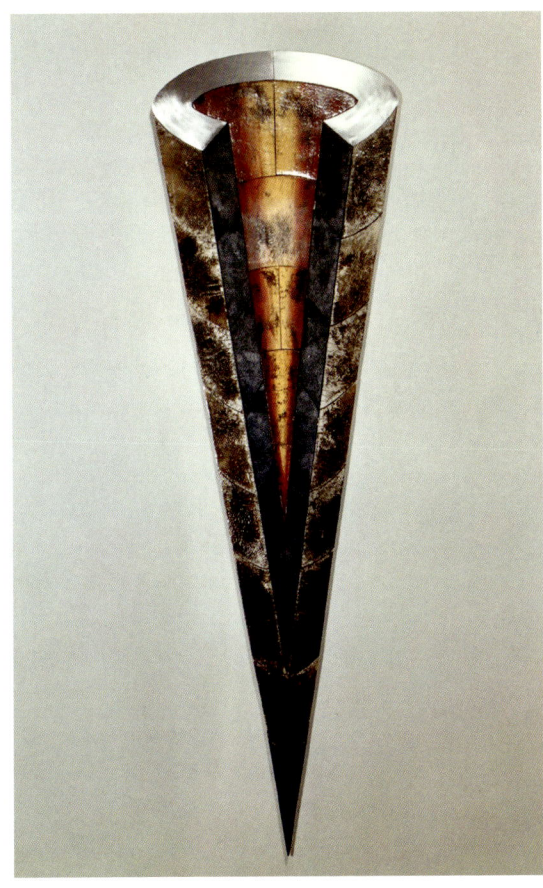

flat, the work has a strong three-dimensionality achieved through her use of repeated curved lines and colour, the interior having a golden glow which shifts with the light.

The third dimension has also always interested Ivan Eyre, primarily known for his paintings and drawings. Throughout his career he created sculptures in clay, wood, and bronze, often combining materials. In conversations with me in the 1990s and again in 2011, he talked about his long-held desire to create monumental works.[132] Drawing from themes and imagery of his earlier sculpture, paintings, and drawings, these works present perplexing enigmas that are at once both universal and personal. His balance of strength and solidity in some, and the fluid grace of others, are masterful, and his knowledge of global art history becomes the foundation for new human myths and mysteries as he builds and incorporates them into his iconography. His references to ancient Egypt, India, and medieval England are coupled with his own earlier iconography.

The kneeling male figure in *Yell,* 2010, for instance, conveys a sense of urgency. His characteristic vest, large boots, mitts, and headdress suggest unassailable power. Unlike heroic commemorative sculptures at cenotaphs across Canada or celebratory large public portrait sculptures, *Yell* looks to the future, not the past. Its northern orientation symbolically enhances that forward look. Yet, the stance of the figure itself is a profound link to tradition, the heroic bearing magnifying the warnings learned from history. *Yell* sounds a call of concern, not victory. Eyre wrote of his 1980s masked figures in his paintings: "The big-booted male has been a favourite means of depicting men. My males also typically carry some form of weapon, a spear, sword, gun or club and are, more often than not, hidden behind a mask. . . . The bird headdress . . . remains the enigmatic feature so much a part of my vocabulary of icons."[133]

Eyre's combinations of surface treatments in these monumental sculptures augment their mystery and meaning. The dotted vests and clothing are reminiscent of his pointillist brushwork, while areas of smoothness recall his careful, smooth paint application in other works. In these, as in his two-dimensional art, he presents psychological enigmas and complexities of thought.

Eva Stubbs also used traditional materials: clay and bronze. Her bronze *Structure IV,* 1992, presents multiple inspirations and its images are various. A set of stairs leads from artist Keith Oliver's built base to the lower edge of the diagonal panel with a Greco-Roman-inspired frieze. A ladder extends above the flat-plane frieze to the foot of the perilously balanced carved triangle on top. She drew over the surfaces with energetic marks, and overlapping figures in motion, monumental in feel, fill the space. Where do the stairs lead from and to? Is the ladder symbolic of a path leading from the past to the future?

Stubbs's *Memories for the Future,* 1987, carries a premonition and caution for the future. While its clay pillars are rooted in the architecture of many civilizations, projecting permanence and a time-tested strength, the wooden wedges between some of the sections suggest impermanence. The material itself—clay or earth—implies perpetuity, yet, when fired, it becomes brittle or fragile. The dichotomies of power and vulnerability and strength and fear are juxtaposed, and, though monumental, the work portrays tenderness. The seated figures in a row, their rounded backs and arms crossed in front of them, are psychologically isolated from each other. Their contrasts of lonely despair and inner strength are reminiscent of present-day society. As curator Shirley Madill commented: "Despite their initial impact of solidity and strength, the pillars, with the fragmentary nature, speak clearly of human fragility. A mysterious, spiritual energy seems to radiate from within them, transfixing the attentive viewer. . . . The ten crouching figures bear a strong relationship to the images on the pillars. In their order and balance they reflect a world of wisdom and meditation, of non-prejudice, both racial and sexual."[134]

Walter Dexter, a major figure in Canada's ceramic world, created clay pots that became figures, metaphors, and containers for and of the human condition. He is renowned for his richly and symbolically decorated raku vessels, their unique forms, colour, and texture, and his characteristically calligraphic painted surfaces. In the 1990s he began making large-scale

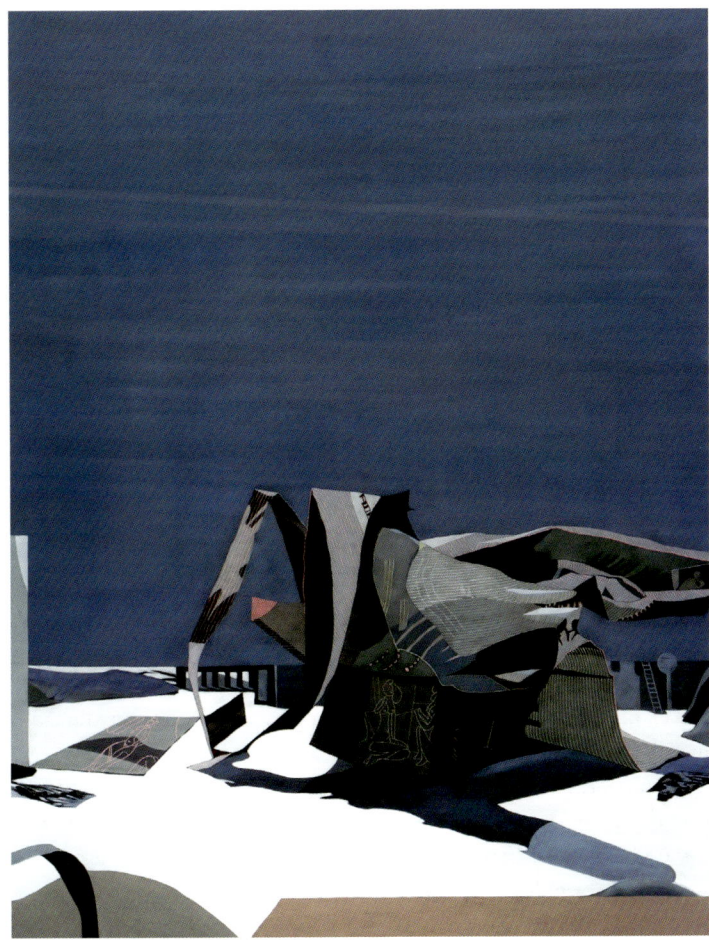

FIGURE 5.35.
Ivan Eyre,
*Stills—White
Red River,* 1971.

ceramic sculpture, with increasingly bold surfaces, rich textures, and experimental colours for ceramics, especially his reds and pinks. His hand-built slabs and coils of clay, as he told me, are painting surfaces, and have "an affinity for profound themes and a degree of personal expression increasingly imbues the expanded surfaces."[135]

Ceramic history and contemporary ceramic expression in Western Canada are significant, and it is impossible to give full justice to all those who have furthered the medium. Some have done so technically with new glazes, forms, and means of firing, and others have expanded the subject matter and international connections in the field. Many, including Robin Hopper, Robert Archambeau, Barbara Balfour, Tam Irving, Jack Sures, and John Chalke, to name just a few, have succeeded in garnering substantive international recognition.

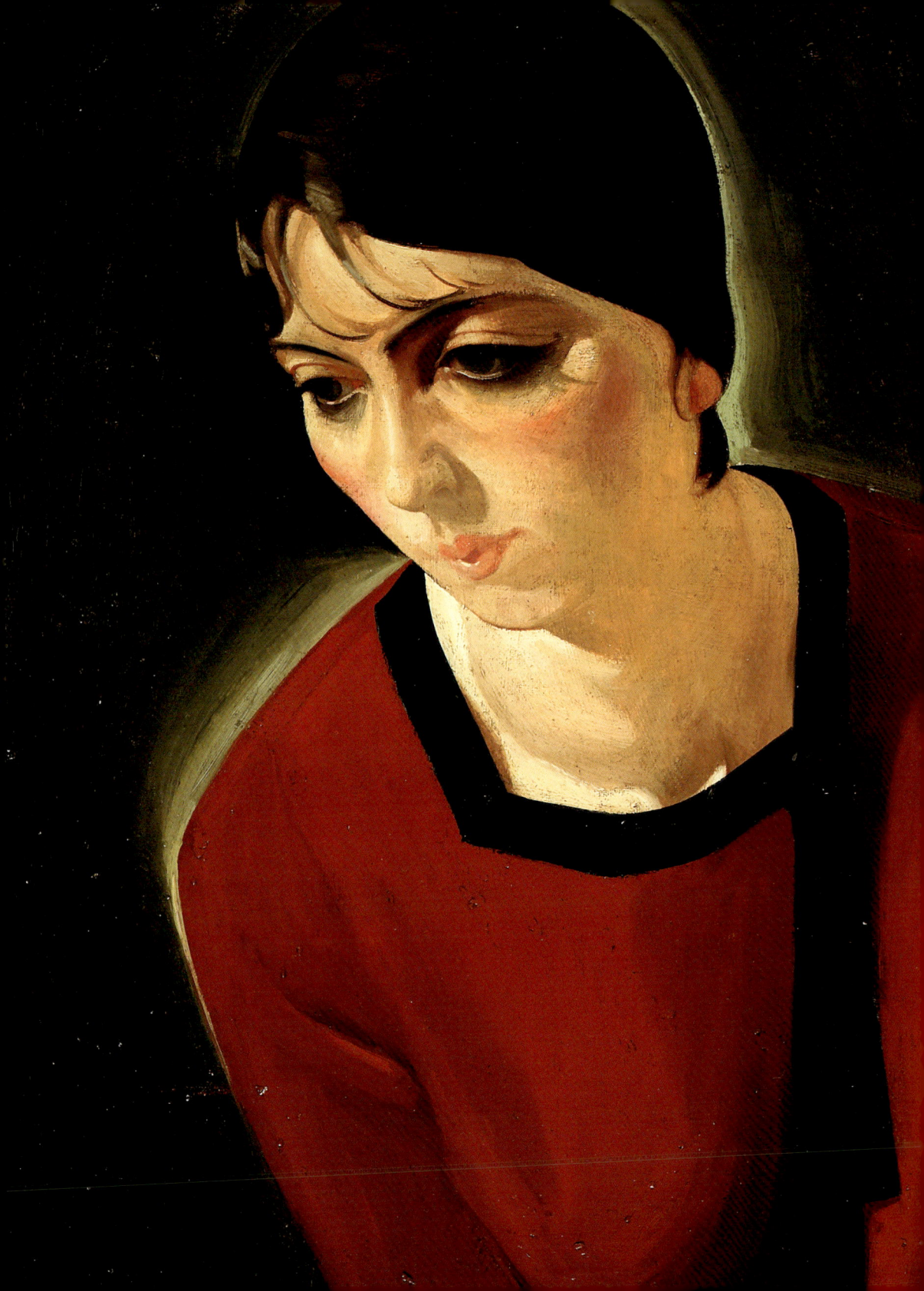

VI People: Portraits and Inscapes

Portrait: a painting, drawing, sculpture, photograph, or other likeness of an individual, especially of the face; a verbal description or picture, especially of a person's character.

Inscape: the unique essence or inner nature of a person, place, thing or event, especially depicted in poetry or a work of art.[1]

Portraiture is the art of studying people and conveying in visual form what it is to be human. When these momentary glimpses of a specific time, person, mood, gesture, or expression are committed to paper or canvas, they become permanent. Portraits are both subjective and objective, revealing the artist's feelings, connection, and perceptions with and of the sitter. Portraits are also invitations to viewers to form their impressions of the person.

As powerful forms of representation in all media of our human essence, portraits present physical and character attributes, psychological strengths and vulnerabilities, feelings and emotions. Artists also portray themselves, often in self-searching and highly personal ways, revealing their inner conflicts and feelings. Successful portraits and self-portraits are personal, insightful, and compelling. "Portraiture," says scholar Shearer West, "is about both body and soul. It represents the 'front' of a person—their gesture, expression, and manner—in such a way as to convey their distinct identity as well as to link him or her to a particular social milieu."[2]

Charles Fraser Comfort, *Louise*, 1927 (detail).

Many questions arise when discussing portraits. How do the sitter and artist relate to each other? How does the sitter want to be shown, and how does the artist want to show the sitter, and convey their moods, relationships, and state of mind? Artists generally prefer to engage directly with the sitter in order to gain a full understanding of the individual, acknowledging that the artist/sitter relationship is an integral part of the final work, rendering portraits to be about the artist as well as the subject.[3] Winnipeg's Sheila Spence, for instance, noted, "in photography it is how you as the artist feel about the subject."[4] That projection of integrity is critical.

Art historian Cynthia Freeland's comment is apt: "There is often something mysterious about portraits—they can depict people who look alive and who appear to look back at us. . . . portraits can and often do appear to us to be living and endowed with powers of animation and expression. And among a world of meaningful objects, portraits are among the most engaging of all because they reveal to us subjects in which we are all inevitably interested: persons."[5]

Over the decades artists in Western Canada have created leading-edge commissioned and non-commissioned portraits, created works as personal tributes to family and friends, and executed numerous self-portraits. They record personal histories, ceremonial occasions, and psychological inscapes. Major official commissions include Myfanwy Pavelic's portrait of former Canadian prime minister Pierre Elliott Trudeau, Andrew Valko's 2013 painting of retired Manitoba Appeal Court Chief Justice Richard Scott, and Mary Valentine's posthumous portrait of Senate Speaker Gildas Molgat. Non-commissioned personal tributes to friends include Carole Sabiston's portrait of author Carol Shields, *Connecting Threads: The Arc of Carol Shields;* Pavelic's *Yehudi Menuhin;* and Sheila Spence's portrait *Don,* portraying fellow artist Don Reichert. In another vein, group photographs like Jin-me Yoon's (b. 1960) 1996 chromogenic print *A Group of Sixty-Seven* and Michael Lexier's *David Series* explore groups as individuals—the former group connected by virtue of immigration from Korea, and the latter by merely having the same name.

Penetrating self-portraits by Western Canadian artists include Ivan Eyre's ground-breaking wrapped heads and Myfanwy Pavelic's psychological personal inscapes. For their part, Maxwell Bates and Richard Ciccimarra (1924–1973) present aspects of social and personal isolation in their figurative art. Good portraiture is the result of the ability of the artist to look within combined with their technical acuity to give a work its genuineness and poignancy.

Portraits: Commissioned and Not

"The artist must be honest about how the person looks, the position and personality. An official portrait must also be artistically posed and well painted. It must work for the public, the majority, and the artist must respect that. An official portrait is not art for self."[6]

Western Canadian portraiture gained increasing momentum at the turn of the twentieth century. Victor A. Long (1888–1938), for instance, an early Winnipeg portraitist, earned many official commissions of local leaders, including that of the city's Mayor Frank Cornish in 1901. Stark and rather static, Long's work is rooted in the nineteenth-century style and approach to portraiture, while those by his contemporary Nicholas de Grandmaison (1892–1978) took on another significance. De Grandmaison, who first came to Manitoba from Russia and spent much of his career in Alberta, is especially known for his respectful pastel portraits of First Nations leaders. The figures fill the vertical space of their respective portraits and each painting exudes the individual personality of the sitter while celebrating his position. The sitter's eyes are keen and expression sincere. Their role is clearly established through their dress and posture, and enhanced by the strength of the artist's line and colour.

Nineteenth-century photographers were portrait artists, too. Using the new technology, Humphrey Hime illustrated Henry Youle Hind's 1858 report for the "government of the territory of Canada," *Canadian Exploring Expeditions in Rupert's Land*. Hime employed innovative photographic technology with painterly sensibilities in his compositions. His images gave prominence to Red River Métis. Hime frequently positioned figures seated in front of a buffalo hide and captured them looking sideways, beyond the camera. Setting a high standard in portrait photography, Hime ably captured the countenance of his sitters and multiple textures such as clothing, buffalo robes, and beaded cradleboard. Like painters on these early expeditions, he faced difficult physical realities of constantly being on the move. The prairie terrain they crossed in ox carts and canoes and on foot was rough and wet, and they were plagued by bugs. Hime had to deal with the cumbersome weight and size of the cameras and the time it took to set up. The exposures were long and the glass plates were easily broken. Fortunately, despite the challenges, many photographs by Hime have survived and are significant works in the annals of visual expression.

Hannah Maynard, one of only two women photographers in the province of British Columbia during her time, established Victoria's first photographic studio and gallery in 1862. Her work was acclaimed and portrait sessions with her were coveted. British Columbia was prosperous at the time, and Maynard's husband, Richard, who had been involved in the gold rush, decided to keep his family in Victoria and he became active in his wife's business. While Hannah focused on portraits, Richard undertook landscapes. As Leslie Robertson writes, "It

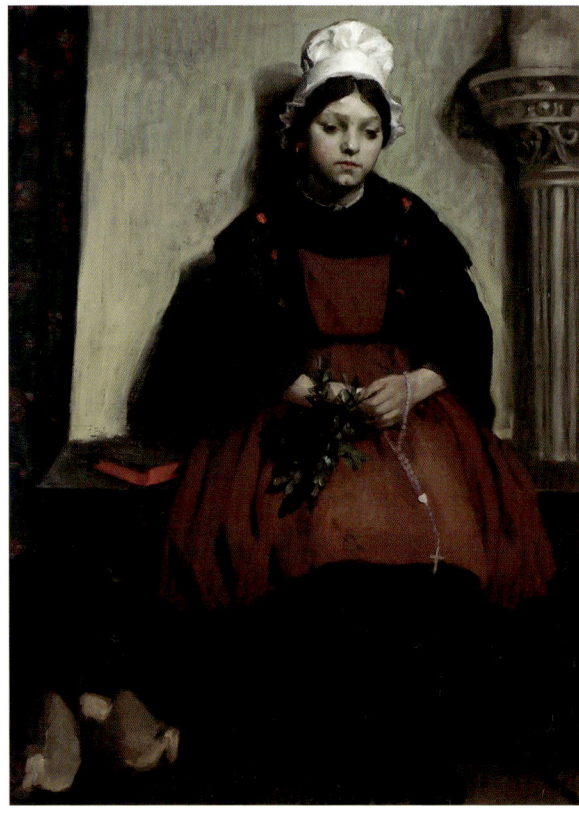

FIGURE 6.1.
Mary Riter Hamilton,
Easter Morning,
La Petite Penitente,
Brittany, c. 1900.

is Hannah's baroque artistry in her later work that attracts a great deal of attention. Her use of multiple exposures, powdering and other techniques have created very interesting and much talked about photographs."[7] Many of Hannah Maynard's portraits reveal her sitters' wealth and position, showing the latest fabrics, fashions, and furniture. Always innovative, Maynard developed "trees" of her "gems," as she called them, in which she combined multiple images of her sitters into one work.

Women painters also worked in the genre of portraiture. Vancouver Island's Paris-trained Sophie Pemberton, an artistic leader in the early twentieth century, used "modern" modes of expression and techniques. Family members partaking in their daily activities were frequent subjects, as were friends and acquaintances. Her French art training is evident in her impressionistic compositional approaches, which capture the quality of a specific moment or "slice of life." In revealing the personalities of her subjects, both adults and children, she effectively portrayed contemporary social customs and pastimes. Her 1897 oil on canvas *Portrait of a Black Lady, Seated,* for instance, shows the three-quarter view of the sitter, leaning forward

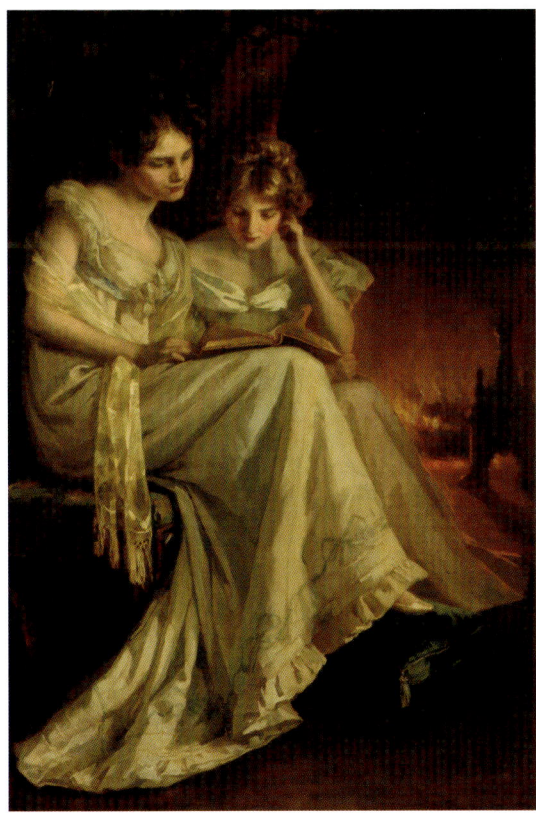

FIGURE 6.2.
Sophie Pemberton,
Un livre ouvert, 1900.

and fully engaged with the viewer. The background brushwork throughout reflects Pemberton's interest and ability. Her large painting *Un Livre Ouvert,* 1900, depicts two young Victoria society women, Ethel Vantreight and Ellie Paddon, seated by the fire, in conversation over the book; the painting underlines Pemberton's interest in portraying "the moment." Her ability in painting light is evident. The fire, as noted earlier, is the sole source of light and permeates the composition.

Emily Carr, like Pemberton, was from a prominent Victoria family. She, too, produced portraits and self-portraits, including particularly sensitive pencil drawings in 1909 of Indigenous children and adults whom she came to know almost as family. Carr's 1938 *Self-Portrait*, in the collection of the National Gallery of Canada, is a three-quarter view in which she faces sideways and looks out from the canvas. Its brushwork is free and rhythmic, and the lines, especially those in the sleeve of her dress, are repetitive, giving a sense of movement and three-dimensional volume. The technique in this work is similar to the brushwork in her trees and forest interiors.

Carr's Manitoba contemporary Marion Nelson Hooker (1866–1946) received her art training in Eastern Canada before she arrived in Selkirk as a bride in 1907. While she did many paintings of the Selkirk area, her portraits of First Nations chiefs, including *William Berens, Chief of the Saulteaux,* 1932, and that of his father, *Jacob Berens,* 1930, are particularly impressive. Hooker portrayed both chiefs with respect and dignity. In each, the sitter's head and upper torso fill the canvas. The dark backgrounds, devoid of detail, allow the sitter to take the viewer's full attention. The artist captures their sense of pride and ceremony in their medals and uniforms, which stand out against the background.

In the 1920s a number of works showed innovative departures from earlier portrait compositional approaches, particularly *Louise*, 1927, by Charles Comfort. Simple, stylized, and elegant, the figure, the artist's wife, looks downwards. She has a black band around the collar and down one side of her dress, matching her black hair and highlighted eyes. She is set against a dark background. The light around her shoulder draws the viewer to her face and neck, giving the work an ethereal sensibility. The simplicity is in contrast to the more traditional interior portrait by Alexander Musgrove, *Vera in a Green Sweater*, 1929, which is filled with details and patterns, a bookcase, and a Chinese vase in the background. The seated figure wears a lush robe and necklace.

Group of Seven member Fred Varley, who moved to Vancouver in 1926 as an instructor at the fledgling Vancouver School of Art, became a renowned portraitist following his return from war, thinking portraiture would be his strength. In his biography of his father, Peter Varley noted: "The first assignments for Varley and other war artists were to paint portraits of Canadians who received the Victoria Cross."[8] In that series of work Varley captured his sitters' psychological numbness resulting from the horrors of their wartime experiences. Shown front-on, some were particularly defiant. The backgrounds echoed the colours of the dress of the sitters and most included the acrid, disquieting green for which Varley is well known. Peter Varley noted: "He set out to experiment with the figure in the landscape" and in all his portraits sought "to empty himself of preconceived ideas about the subject . . . to find the truth emerging in a face."[9]

Varley's portrait *Vincent Massey*, 1920, was considered by Canadian art critic Fred Housser to be "the most modern piece of portraiture in the Dominion."[10] Varley positioned Massey, deep in thought, in a traditional pose against an unconventional background, reminiscent of an impressionistic, freely painted theatre scrim. In a later portrait, *Vera,* 1931, he depicted his student, Vera Weatherbie, a significant painter in her own right, and his companion from 1927 to 1937. Weatherbie featured in a number of his paintings, many of which are spiritual in feeling, portraying the essence of her thought and being. The 1931 portrait is both tender and direct. Her head and shoulders, set to the left side of the painting, fill the entire vertical space.

FIGURE 6.3. **Marion Nelson Hooker**, *William Berens, Chief of the Saulteaux*, 1932.

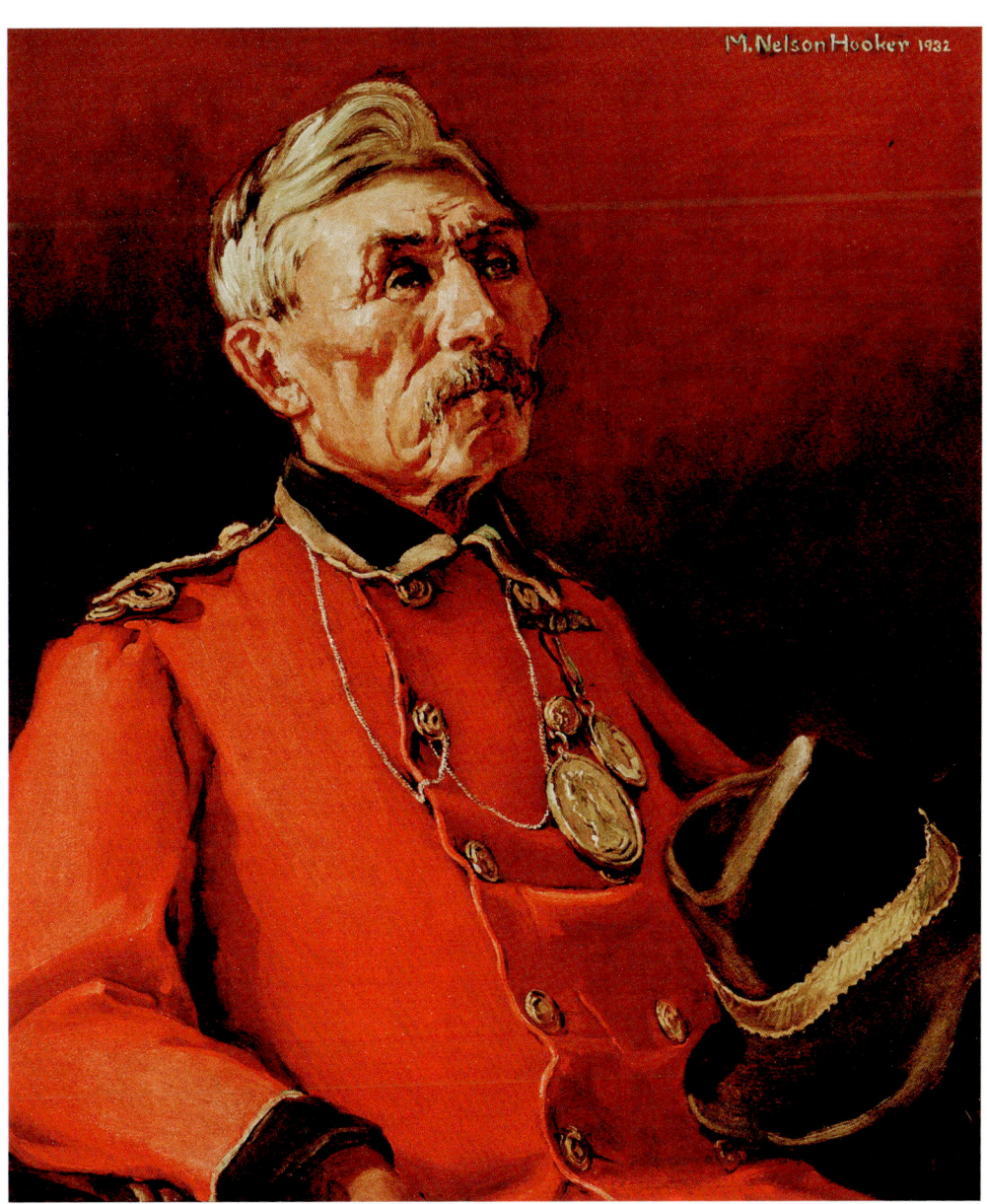

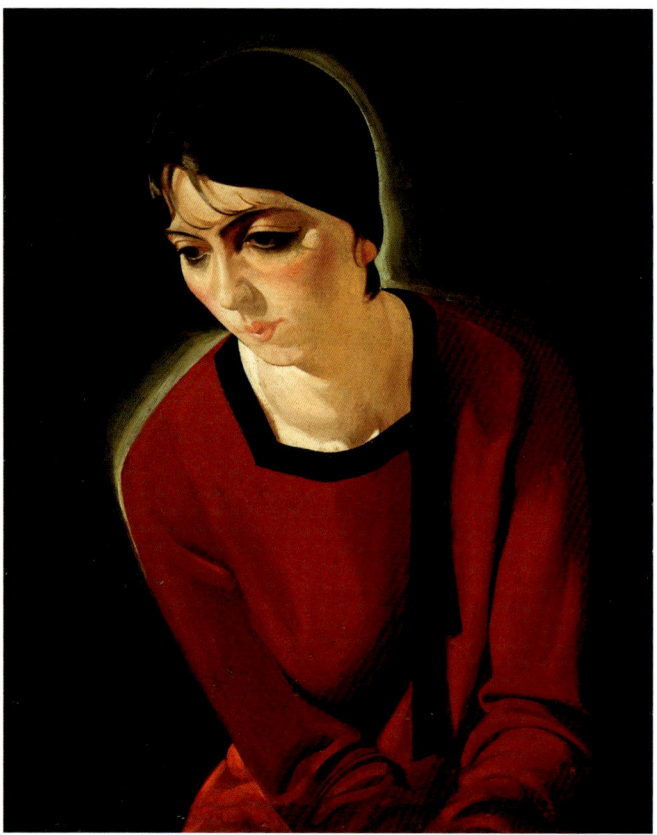

FIGURE 6.4.
Charles Fraser Comfort,
Louise, 1927.

The green, blue, and turquoise tones are repeated throughout the canvas and add a tension or edge to the whole. Free, rhythmic, and evocative brushwork permeates some parts of the work, contrasting a more solid cubist sensibility employed in others.

Varley's 1937 portrait of Weatherbie, *Dhârâna,* depicts her at her most spiritual, her eyes gazing upwards in Buddhist contemplation. Kneeling, unaware of the viewer, her ramrod back echoes the pillar behind her. The palette of greens and violets, consistent with Varley's earlier works, adds further mystery to the overall mood. Soon after he completed this painting, their ten-year relationship ended. Varley's loneliness and hurt were magnified by Weatherbie's marriage to Mortimer Lamb, acclaimed scientist and photographer and father of artist Molly Lamb Bobak.

Contrasting Varley's personal and intimate sensibilities captured in his portraits is the more formal approach of Saskatchewan artist Augustus Kenderdine. A leading artist and teacher for many decades in Saskatchewan, Kenderdine was the obvious choice to paint the 1935 official,

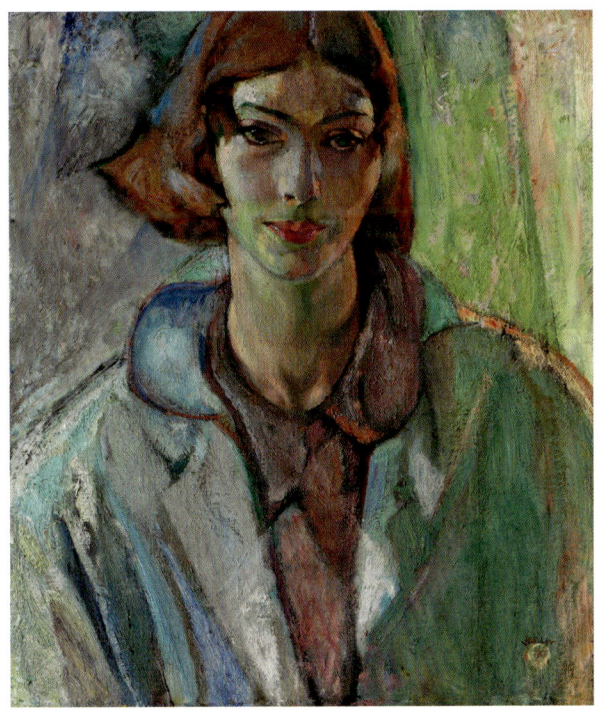

FIGURE 6.5.
**Frederick
Horsman Varley**,
Vera, 1931.

posthumous portrait of his friend and community leader Norman MacKenzie. Dark and rather stiff, its brown and green brushwork reveals the determination and firmness of this prominent lawyer, art collector, and founder of Regina's art gallery.

It is beneficial to understand artists' intentions and their sense of their own work. Though Victoria's Myfanwy Pavelic (1916–2007) painted many portraits, she disliked being categorized as a "portrait" artist. She said, "I shudder when I hear people say that I am a portrait painter. I say 'I do people. I am a painter.'"[11] Her oeuvre includes both official and personal portraits as well as many penetrating and evocative self-portraits. Robin Skelton, artist, poet, and fellow member of the Victoria Limners Society, wrote of her portraits: "They are pictures of human needs and feelings. The hands reach out with yearning and suffering or lie idle in heavy resignation; bodies hunch in concentration or gesticulate with passion. There is little distortion and the paintings may sometimes be said to be camera-true, but the camera lens is the eye of intuition, of depth perception, not that of surface observation."[12]

As a teenager Pavelic caught the attention of Emily Carr, who took the young artist under her wing, encouraged her, and admonished her to "work, work, work."[13] Pavelic lived in New York in 1943 and in 1947 for her own training, and again from 1956 to 1969, with her husband, while her daughter went to school. While there she met many international artists and witnessed the explosion of contemporary visual expression. From her youth onwards Pavelic had concentrated primarily on portraying people, and was gifted in conveying their moods, feelings, and contemplations in her drawings and paintings. Though she experimented with various modes of expression, for the most part she used oil, acrylic, watercolour, pencil, and charcoal. In the early 1970s she did a number of collages for which she selected specific papers "appropriate" for the individual sitter. She used architectural blueprints, for instance, for her 1975 portrait of Victoria architect John di Castri and sheet music for Victoria Symphony's conductor Laszlo Gati. She used soft Kleenex as a material in the collage of the portrait of her good friend and internationally acclaimed musician Yehudi Menuhin, evoking the sensibility of the violinist as if floating on music.

Pavelic was insistent that she did not "put" a person into a picture. Rather, the individual "emerged." She would start a painting by "messing up" her canvas, as she did for the official portrait of Pierre Elliott Trudeau. Writer Ted Lindberg described her beginning process as "randomly wiping brushes and using up dibs and dabs of pigment on the surface of her support—no attempt is made at drawing or composing. After the canvas or board is sufficiently covered, she begins (again intuitively) relating to the mere suggestion of volumes, colour components, light and shadows, inhabiting a 'space' which has begun to shape itself. In this instance the underpainting is the acrylic, out of which she has 'pulled' the image, adjusting the colour as she goes, although traces of the underpainting appear everywhere. This additionally has a unifying effect which melds subject and ground."[14] The resulting moods, feelings, and inner selves of the sitters evolve intact, and her colours, forms, and image are fully integrated. She insisted she always painted "what the person gave me."[15]

Pavelic expected all her sitters to come to her studio, even Prime Minister Pierre Trudeau, whose portrait was commissioned by Parliament in 1991. He recalled:

> I didn't like the idea of the invitation to "pose for a portrait." I never enjoyed posing for portraits . . . you know the artist/photographer is looking at you. There is something stiff about a portrait—an assumed position of modesty or grandeur. But when I saw how she would do my portrait I knew I'd chosen the right artist because I could see the portrait was alive not posed. She said that she tries "to draw from a blur of colours." Layer over layer it emerged. The artist spent time trying to find my soul. . . . In the portrait I am reminded of me in time . . . I am very grateful to the artist for her work of me.[16]

Trudeau stayed with Myfanwy and Niki Pavelic on several occasions for three or four days each visit during the project. Pavelic's Vancouver Island studio overlooked Patricia Bay, and Trudeau spent many hours canoeing and walking the shores. She got to know the "person" by observing him in the studio, conversing with him in her home, and walking with him in the

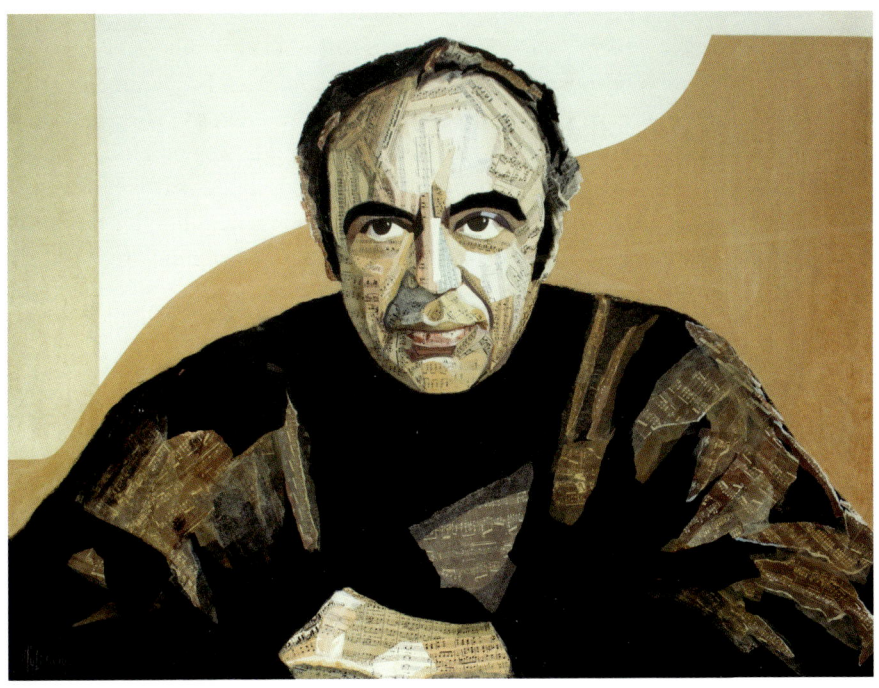

garden. She made no attempt to put anything formal on paper or canvas while he was there. She merely took in his attitudes, mannerisms, interests, beliefs, and the man himself. As Lindberg said, "Through all these quick changes, as far as she was concerned, it was still the physical and psychological presence of the man which had to be established and committed to memory in a scant time."[17] She took a few Polaroid photos and had fellow Limner and filmmaker Karl Spreitz take a number of photographs, which she used to establish the composition. Though Pavelic made a few quick sketches and washes after Trudeau retired for the night, the actual work on the portrait itself waited until he had departed. Her visual memory was keen, and with the aid of the photographs, she retained the most minute details. The resulting official portrait shows the former prime minister relaxed, and, set off by the abstracted background, she captures his "laser beam expression," as she called it, revealing the many dimensions of the man—poet, statesman, and conversationalist.

Winnipeg's Mary Valentine (1931–2016), well known for her portrait work across Canada and in the United States, also received many formal commissions. She, however, felt that her work, though it included commissioned portraits, was about more than portraits. She said,

FIGURE 6.6. **Myfanwy Spencer Pavelic**, *Laszlo Gati*, 1975.

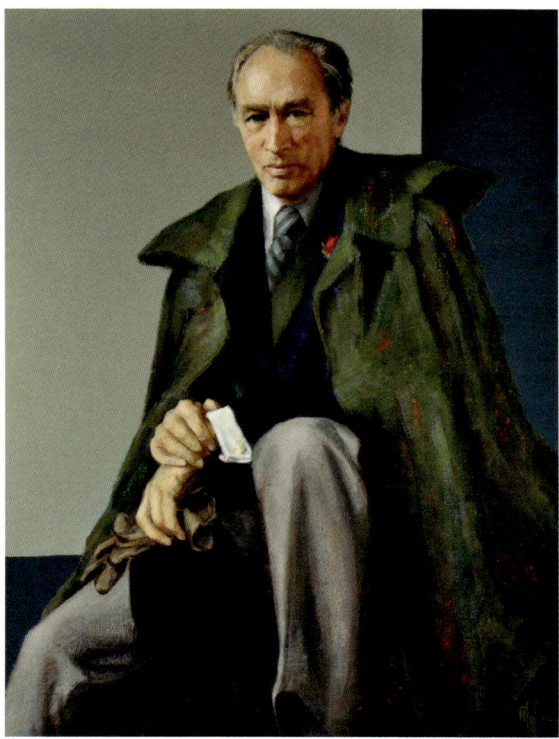

FIGURE 6.7.
Myfanwy Spencer Pavelic,
*The Right Honourable Pierre
Elliott Trudeau*, 1991.

"I never wanted to become solely a portrait painter. In spite of the very good commission fees and the people you get to meet and know, there is always the feeling that someone else is holding your brush."[18]

While still a student, Valentine, like Pavelic, did some particularly good portraits, including those of family. That of her father, *R.E. Hayes*, painted in 1947 when she was sixteen, garnered the local first prize at an Ottawa exhibition that year. Her father's gaze is intent and direct, and diagonal parallel brush strokes in the background echo the colours in the figure, highlighting his face. Her grade twelve self-portrait, *In the Studio,* foreshadows her future painting career with the portrayal of two tubes of oil paint on the mantelpiece behind her. She gazes at the viewer from a three-quarter angle, and, again, background colours are drawn from those of the subject. Her overall capable handling of paint and composition is beyond her years.

Valentine's many portrait commissions became personal histories, echoing Shearer West's statement that a portrait is "about both body and soul . . . to convey their distinct identity as well as to link him or her to a particular social milieu."[19] Valentine's 2003 portrait of Senate Speaker Gildas Molgat, a former leader of the Manitoba Liberal Party, commissioned by the

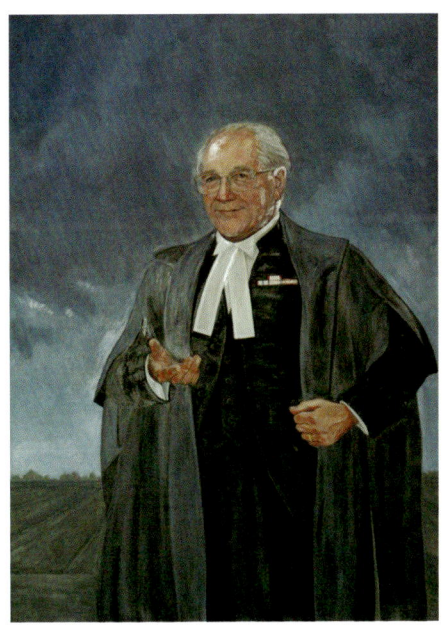

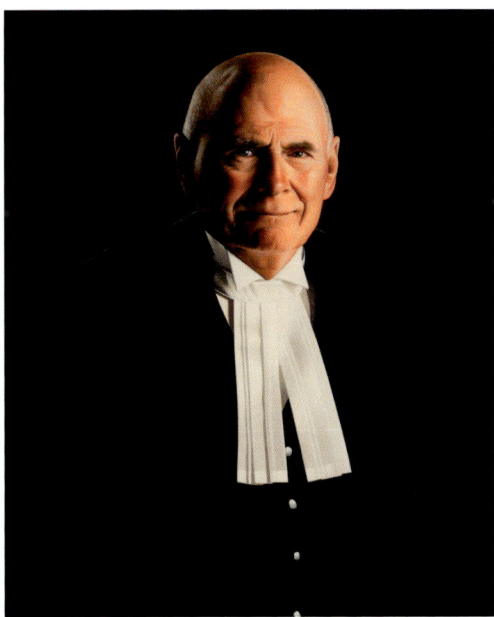

Senate after his death, is installed in the Senate of Canada Building in Ottawa. It was a distinct challenge for Valentine as she had no opportunity to observe or converse with him as she did for other commissions. She therefore worked from photographs, taped interviews, newscasts, and conversations with those who knew him well. The resulting three-quarter-length portrait shows Molgat's warmth and the importance of his position. Smiling, his hand outstretched in an inviting pose, he wears his official robes, and the expansive prairie sky and patterned fields of his native Manitoba are behind him. He is in *his* place, geographically and professionally.

Winnipeg's Andrew Valko, in addition to many socially evocative works, has painted significant portrait commissions of Manitoba's leaders including University of Manitoba chancellors Arthur Mauro and Harvey Sector; Premier Gary Doer; and, in 2013, former Chief Justice of Manitoba's Court of Appeal Richard Scott. Valko clearly enjoys engaging with the individuals he paints and always includes something personal to the sitter as well as ensures the setting is relevant to their "calling." He first takes photographs of the individual in his studio, where he controls the light. He also assesses news footage and personal photos to understand how they deport themselves and how they engage with people around them. Richard Scott is

FIGURE 6.8. **Mary Valentine**, *The Honourable Gildas L. Molgat, 1994–2001*, 2002.

FIGURE 6.9. **Andrew Valko**, *Chief Justice Richard Jamieson Scott*, 2013.

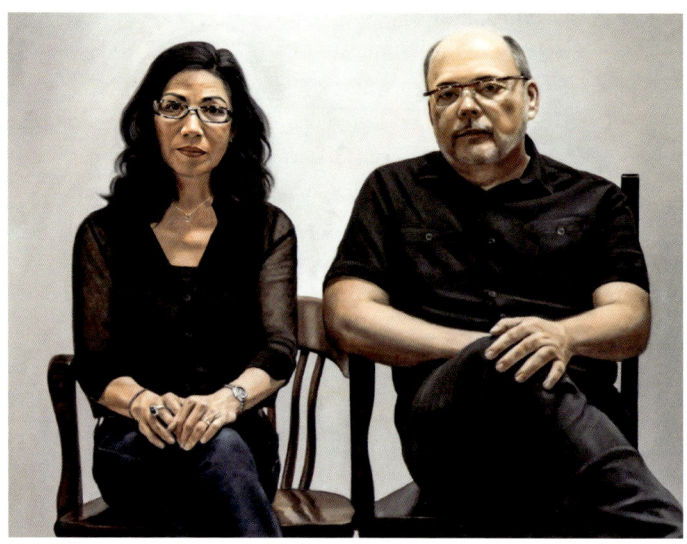

FIGURE 6.10.
David McMillan,
Julia and Andrew,
2017.

portrayed in his lawyer's robes—robes he had had for some years—which serve to convey both the length and breadth of Scott's distinguished career. Valko said of undertaking this portrait: "I was after the combination of his personality and the traits required for the position he held—the whole person—his toughness and warmth, or the two sides of his face, the happiness in repose and intensity in the courtroom."[20] Scott looks directly at the viewer, and the shadow across his face enhances the dichotomy and balance between the personal and professional. The dark curtained background pushes the face forward, bringing him closer to the public, critical for Valko in any official portrait.

David McMillan (b. 1945), who began his career as a painter doing full-sized portraits, turned to photography and left painting, as he said, "with nothing more to say." In 1977 he started the University of Manitoba's photography program and worked in photography for the next thirty-five years, returning to painting and portraits only on his retirement in 2013. His subsequent series of portraits of his former academic colleagues, artists, and art historians is compelling and insightful. The figures, set against a plain background, face the viewer directly. He wants to paint people "of the 21st century,"[21] those he knows. He, too, begins by photographing them, and squares off the canvas before priming it with a turpentine-mixed base coat. Building the image and mixing his paint with the medium, he carefully paints layer on layer. The resulting smooth surface is rather like the lustre, not sheen, surfaces of his photographic papers. Some gloss, he says "makes the black look deep."[22] Many are life-size, full-length portraits, meticulous in detail, probing the interests of the individual sitters. One is of portrait artist Andrew Valko, his wife, Julia, seated beside him.

Eva Stubbs, a long-established sculptor and official bronze portraitist, came to Canada from a very troubled Europe in 1944 as one of a group of refugees. After teaching high school art in Montreal, she settled in Winnipeg and studied sculpture at the University of Manitoba's School of Art. Unfortunately, the Winnipeg Stubbs moved to had no eye for, or interest in, sculpture at the time. Neither was it deemed appropriate for a woman, particularly a single mother as she was, to create sculpture. It was a "man's field." However, Cecil Richards, her instructor and mentor, and William McCloy, head of the School of Art, both encouraged her to persist and to take her work seriously. Stubbs's overall body of work encompasses a variety of subjects and approaches, and she found portraiture particularly rewarding. Her many head-and-shoulder bronze commissions include prominent citizens such as author Carol Shields and artist Lionel LeMoine FitzGerald.

Stubbs's 2009 portrait of business leader and philanthropist Bill Loewen, for instance, involved approximately ten weekly sittings in her studio. In-between these sessions she worked from memory and from the photographs she had taken and had blown up so she could check the smallest of details. Stubbs did not do sketches. Loewen was seated on a platform in front of her, and she continuously built, scraped, and cut the clay, and constantly looked at him, assessing his reactions, movements, and expressions. She was particularly intent on capturing the liveliness in Loewen's eyes and his lips.[23] The sculpture in progress was set on a wheeled tripod at the artist's eye level, which she turned frequently, checking the three-dimensionality of the head, the form of the neck, chin, and nose, and the jaw lines. She filled some areas in with tiny pieces of clay that she had cut from others. Her tools, on a table beside her within easy reach, were organized much as dental tools are, so she could pick up what she needed without shifting her gaze from her subject or the work on the tripod. Between studio times she covered the work with plastic to keep the clay moist, and when the clay sculpture was finished it was put in a rubber mould and shipped to the foundry in Georgetown, Ontario. For most of her career Stubbs travelled to the foundry and directed the colour and patina for each work.

Saskatchewan's Joe Fafard also did portraits in clay and bronze. He focused primarily on family and artists, including Paul Cézanne and Vincent van Gogh. Fafard studied at the University of Manitoba with fellow students Kelly Clark, Bill Lobchuk, and Don Proch. Professor George Swinton fed his curiosity, being "the most interesting person I could imagine."[24] Robert Bruce taught him the discipline of craft and technique and the ability to convey light and shadow. It was sculptor John Daniel, however, who excited his interest in three-dimensional work, and his painting instructor, Ken Lochhead, on seeing Fafard's natural ability and potential, encouraged him to spend his painting classes in the sculpture studio. Fafard excelled as an artist in many media—drawing, painting, and printmaking—ever since, but sculpture was his primary interest.

Fafard made his sculptures using both approaches in creating his forms—that of modelling and building or adding to a basic form, and that of carving or cutting. The first includes his

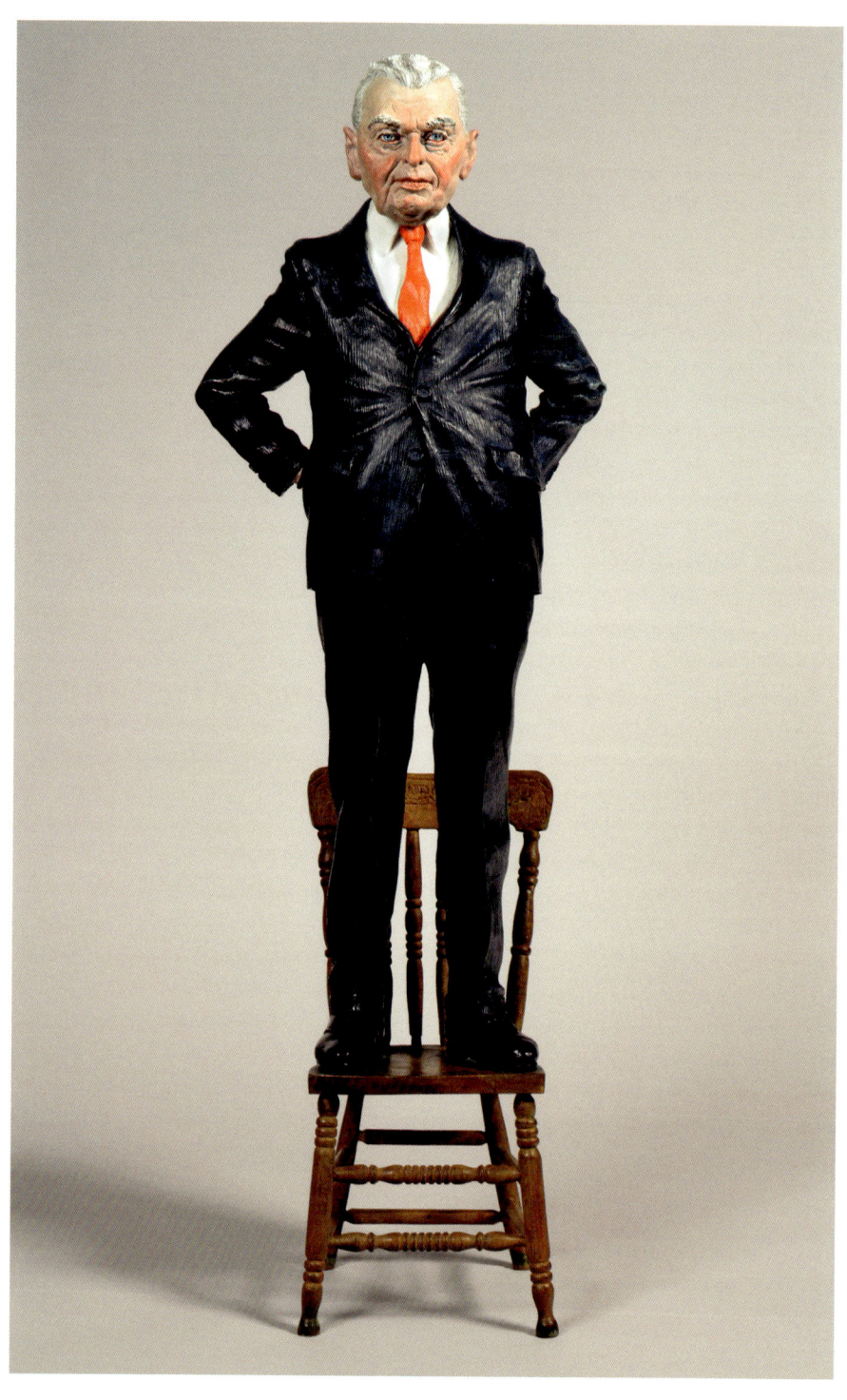

ceramic sculptures and many of his bronzes; the second included his laser-cut metal works. Curiosity fuelled Fafard's creative drive in all media: "95 percent of creativity is curiosity and discovering, essential in an artist's work," he said.[25] Fafard sought to achieve textures and realistic modulations of colour, giving richness and realism to his work. He latterly found that powder coating, by applying coloured powdered polyesters, and then baking the work gives his desired surface effects and colour and stands up better than patina to climate extremes of heat and cold, sun and snow. Fafard's sculptures include portraits of political and historical figures, former prime minister John Diefenbaker and Métis leader Gabriel Dumont, and arts celebrities such as Emily Carr, Rosa Bonheur, and Tom Connors. Family, however, is core to his work. The intimacy and care with which he conveyed his mother and father in both clay and bronze are evident.

Don Proch also created pieces honouring those whose friendship and art have special meaning for him, one being Bill Lobchuk, another Jackson Beardy. Proch's masks are three-dimensional and all include traits found in his other work: his rural roots and his nostalgic portrayals of prairie life. Proch's unique drawing surface, usually the shape of a head and shoulders, and often with externally appended elements, emphasizes the person to whom he is paying tribute, and humankind's central place in and responsibility for the land and environment. His mask metaphors allow him to explore physical representations, psychological insights, and global issues. They conceal identity while simultaneously revealing truth, identifying place, and evoking illuminating psychological inscapes. In *Wild Bill Lobchuk Back Forties Mask,* 1976, for instance, one of his few wearable masks, grass hangs down from the rim, and the furrows and cut grain are depicted over the entire surface in silverpoint and pencil. It captures Lobchuk's personality and the intensity of his quest for change in the art world. Its 360-degree landscape has a flock of geese in their characteristic "V" formation, which points to new futures and directions, underlining Lobchuk's strong, vocal advocacy for new directions in the arts scene in Winnipeg and beyond. Just as the geese fly in numbers, so did Lobchuk and his colleagues, the young artists who banded together in the late 1960s and early 1970s in protest to garner fairer remuneration and credit for their art.

Kwakwaka'wakw artist Richard Hunt's work embodies the respect and honour he has for his ancestors, his father, his mother, and Mungo Martin, the long-acclaimed carver and chief who had adopted Hunt's mother and about whom he said, "We called him Grandpa and he called us his grandkids, but we were not related."[26] In 2021 Hunt did a bronze sculpture honouring his ancestors, inspired by his father, Henry Hunt, titled *Tlingit Chief.* He describes it:

> The regalia the Chief is wearing belong to my family. Everything I do belongs to my culture. The frog on the hat represents a dance that has supernatural powers and the dance

FIGURE 6.11. **Joe Fafard**, *The Politician*, 1987.

belonged to my Mom, Helen Hunt. The neck ring belongs to me because I am a Hamatsa which is a high-ranking dance. I owned two neck rings but I gave one to my brother Alec when he passed away. The neck ring was buried with him. The smaller figure represents a child dancing. He has an eagle face. Our people believe in transformation. The hands are filler designs and could also be the hands of friendship. The copper represents wealth and has an eagle with its wings folded. A sisiutl is at the bottom of the copper. The sisiutl is the main crest of my Mother, Helen who was from Kingcome Inlet, B.C.[27]

Portraits are not restricted to painting, photography, and sculpture, as evidenced in the work of Victoria artist, and recipient of the Governor General's Award in the Visual Arts (at the time, the Bronfman Award), Carole Sabiston. Working in her own invented language of textile assemblage, she explores a variety of subjects including psychological inscapes and biographical portraits. *Connecting Threads: The Arc of Carol Shields,* 2013, is a tribute to her close friend and author Carol Shields, a personal memorial, not public commission. Sabiston commented that "this portrait inscape may be the deepest personal work I have ever done."[28] Its title mirrors the theme of the anthology *Dropped Threads,* edited by Shields and Marjorie Anderson. The ideas for this Shields tribute evolved over ten years. Bits of nascent ideas and quick coloured pencil sketches are pinned onto Sabiston's cork studio wall, which serves as her sketchbook. Ink drawings on the wall bear her rudimentary colour notes; sample strips of materials being considered for the final work are stapled to them. Descriptions of her intent, size, sundry ideas, interesting quotes, and poignant phrases from letters are there as well. Sabiston's technique is free yet detailed, expansive, deliberate, and meticulous, and each work combines the macro and micro in her juxtapositions of personal and universal meanings. Using various layers of textiles, thick and thin, rough and smooth, matte and metallic, Sabiston builds her individual pieces, superimposing translucent and opaque passages to create shifting lights and continuous shimmering effects.

In *Connecting Threads: The Arc of Carol Shields,* Sabiston creates the author's image from Shields's own clothes and buttons—her vest and jean skirt. She added other found objects and sundry bits like labels, carefully selected for symbolic reasons to enhance the layered meanings and personal reflections. Antique French silk threads and the spools, for example, are framed along the left side of *Connecting Threads: The Arc of Carol Shields,* symbolizing the Shieldses' love of France, and over the entire surface are two-inch loose thread ends casting a veil over the ghost-like figure of the author. Viewers' movements cause the thread ends to move and shimmer, connecting the audience, artist, and subject.

Winnipeg artist Ivan Eyre's prolific output includes drawings, paintings, prints, and sculptures, and comprises many subjects and approaches—unique imagined landscapes, surrealistic images of floating women, abandoned cars, wheeled horses, elements of nostalgia, and self-portraits. Acclaimed across Canada and internationally, Eyre became the first Canadian

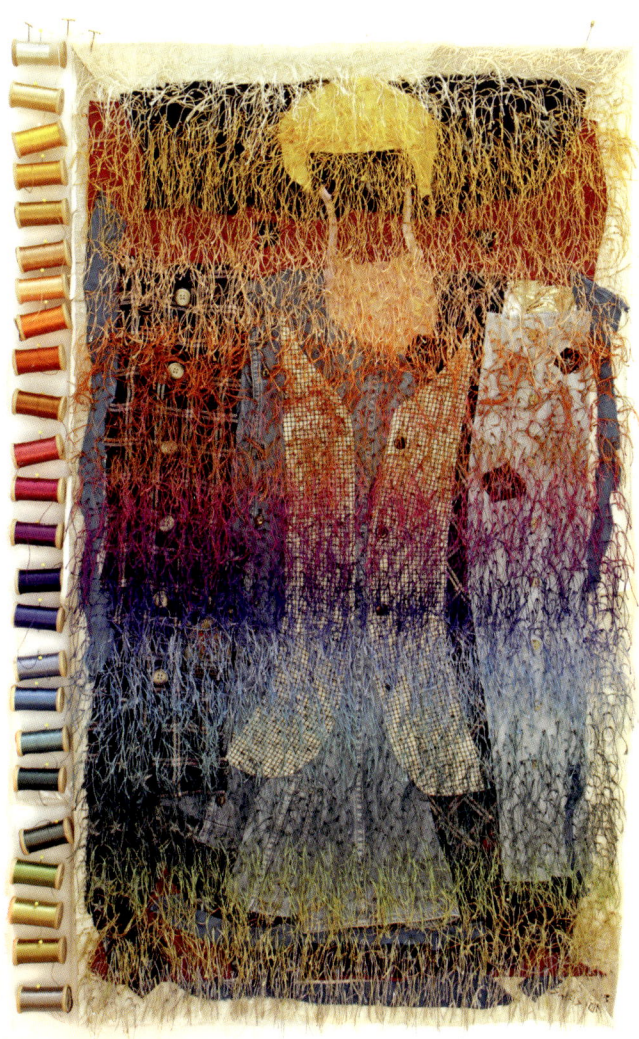

FIGURE 6.12.
Carole Sabiston,
*Connecting Threads:
The Arc of Carol
Shields*, 2013.

artist to be accorded a solo exhibition in Germany, in 1969, through an introduction from Ferdinand Eckhardt, director of the Winnipeg Art Gallery. Eyre did Eckhardt's portrait on his retirement in 1974.

Eyre's self-portraits and the portraits of his wife, Brenda, are infused with memory, metaphor, detail, and mystery, creating intense, compelling works and evoking multiple layers of meaning. He presents a synthesis of the real and imagined, weaving myth with reality to invent an autobiography. He says, "The family become stand-ins for other characters when we are not posing for single portraits."[29]

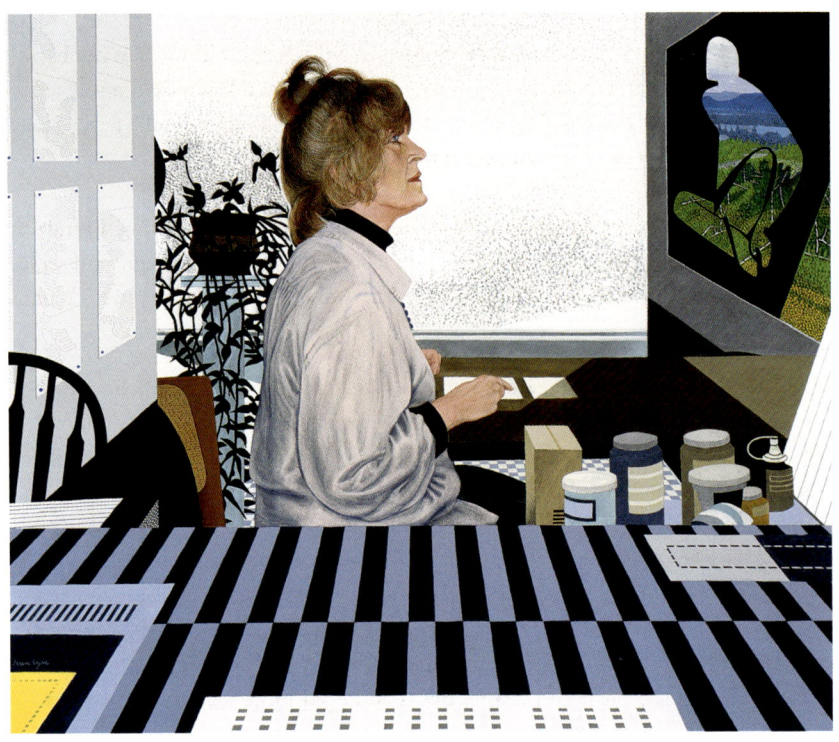

Two portraits of Brenda, whom he met at the School of Art, are particularly revealing: *Brenda Yvonne,* 1983, and *Winter Light,* 2002, both acrylics on canvas. Like his other paintings, they include multiple references superimposed in complex layered images. In *Winter Light* Brenda's profile is the primary subject, with earlier elements included. The silhouetted male figure serves here as a window with a summer landscape painted within his form. Snow, executed in Eyre's precise pointillist technique, dominates the view from the window in the centre of the work. Papers are to Brenda's left; jars are in front of her. Are the papers drawings, or blank paper ready for new works? In the composition Brenda is concentrating on something above the objects depicted, thus extending the subject beyond the picture frame. Eyre wrote:

> My wife Brenda was reluctant to sit for a frontal portrait . . . but she was willing to sit in a profile position. That suited me because I wanted the figure to be looking towards a painting on the wall. The male figure in *Summer Duo* becomes the focus of her attention. The snowy scene out the window harkens back to *Morning Snow* (1977) when Brenda

FIGURE 6.13. **Ivan Eyre**, *Winter Light*, 2002.

and I went on that eventful walk along the wintry La Salle River. The plant at her back has occupied a position in our kitchen for many years. The lines drawn on the wall are new and created just for this painting. They also assist in describing the wall's perspective. The jars of paint remind us of the studio environment.[30]

Brenda Yvonne, painted almost twenty years earlier, is also layered in meaning. Brenda sits on a stool with a drawing at her feet. Its pointillist painted snowscape in the background serves as a painting within the painting and as a window. Eyre writes of its composition and his technique:

> She chose the pose and dress and opted to sit in front of *White Mirage* (1978), one of her favourite paintings. I borrowed the stool from the University of Manitoba School of Art, where I was teaching. Brenda also selected the drawing of the masked male figure on the paint-splattered studio floor. I added the black shiny zippered bag (to echo her black boots) and placed the patterned dark mattress along the bottom of the composition.
>
> As well as functioning as a portrait, this painting demonstrates the use of simulated textures to create volume and describe space. The way in which the white moves from the wispy outdoors into her graphically active dress is indicative of the elaborate play of opposing textures throughout the painting. For example, I contrasted the stipple of her purple jacket against the fine, linear stroking in the fur wrap—setting both against her smooth skin. Brenda's hair and leather boots add even more tactile variety. These are among at least a dozen distinctive surfaces throughout the work.
>
> The figure also acts as a divide between opposing room spaces—each features unique objects and shapes. I've averted Brenda's eyes so that she directs her thoughts away from the viewer—a way of permitting her to live in the painting, rather than have her focusing on us.[31]

Extraneous details are eliminated and, with complete control, Eyre's mastery of multiple techniques within one work enhances his complex iconography and insights.

Photography artists past and present have likewise produced bodies of work that are material in the development of portraiture in Canada, expressing physical likenesses and inner thoughts and relationships. Vancouver's Jeff Wall, Saskatoon's Kathleen Pepper, and Winnipeg's Sheila Spence, for example, have each approached questions of personal histories, societal isolation, and individual relationships from different perspectives, with differing points of view.

Over his long and prestigious career, Jeff Wall has created extensive work. Craig Burnett, the curator of Wall's 2005 solo exhibition at the United Kingdom's Tate Galleries, commented: "His work is, among other things, about looking closely, about the pleasure of seeing the world in all its sensual intricacy. 'Experience and evaluation,' he has said, 'are richer responses than gesture of understanding or interpretation' . . . most of the pleasure of Wall's work lies on the

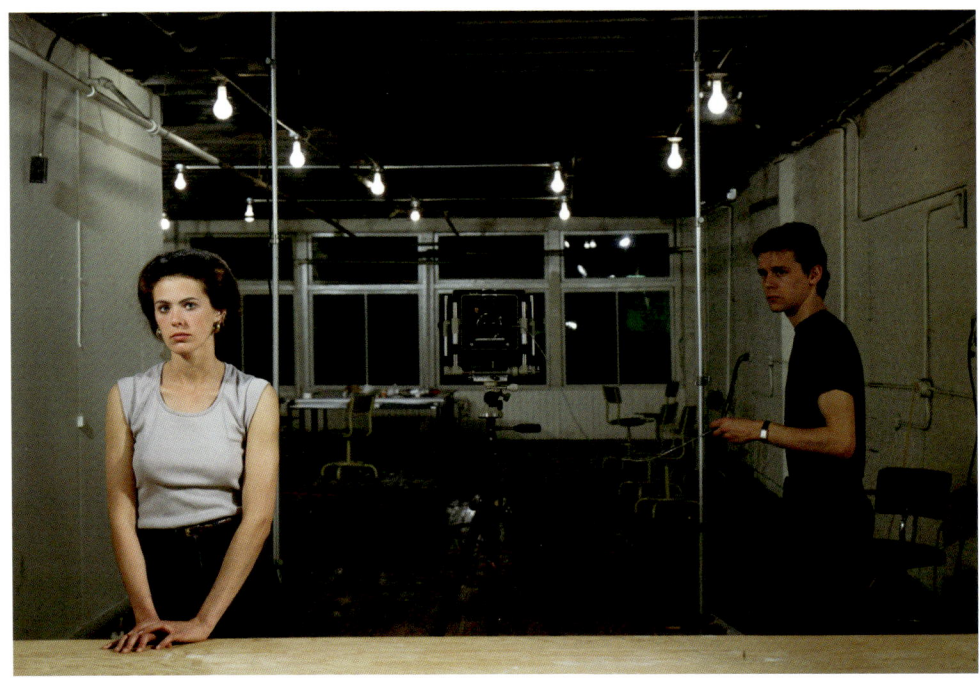

photograph's sensual surface. But it pays to look again, to examine the details and let them filter into one's experience of the picture."[32]

Wall's interests span the various themes of this book. He explores and exposes the psychological, and issues of contemporary society, war and conflict, and of self. *Picture for Women,* 1979, a transparency in a light box, has become an iconic portrait showing a woman and the artist in a relatively bare room. Wall has called it "a remake" of Edouard Manet's famous 1882 oil on canvas *A Bar at the Folies-Bergère*; "in the same way," Burnett says, "as a movie might be a remake of an older one—an update that uses new technology and a slightly inflected take on a theme."[33] Burnett's description elaborates:

> Unlike the Manet painting, set in a boisterous bar, *Picture for Women* takes place in
> an ordered studio (which is, in fact, a classroom) and is static. A man (the artist) and
> a woman (his model) are reflected in a mirror (as they are in Manet's painting), and
> the camera is a third figure, a mechanical Cyclops with an unappeasable eye, which
> acts as a kind of all-seeing chaperone to the couple. The woman is both the subject

FIGURE 6.14. **Jeff Wall**, *Picture for Women*, 1979.

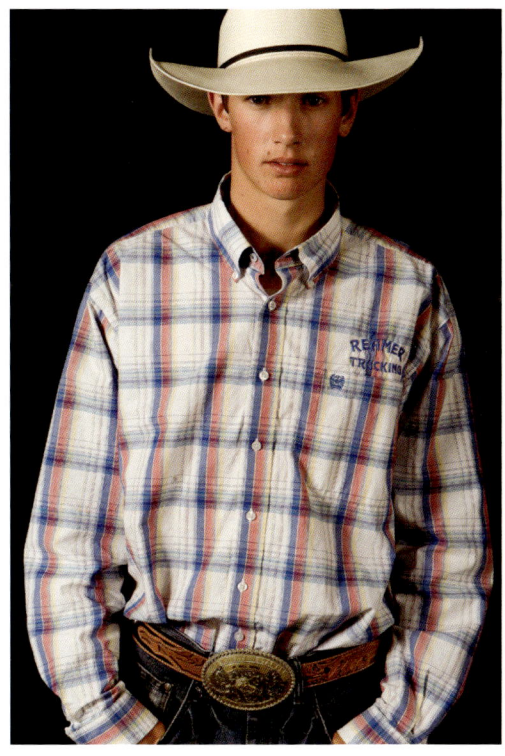

FIGURE 6.15.
Sheila Spence, *Jared Parsonage*, 2009.

of and the audience for the picture, since she looks back at herself, and the triangular structure between the artist, audience and work exists within the camera. If one looks closely at the release cable that travels from the artist's left hand to the camera, one sees that its movement is blurred, like a brushstroke. The snap of the shutter creates a kind of irretrievable moment, partly beyond the artist's control, and in this blur of cable is an uncontrollable element that distinguishes photography from painting. The artist experiences a loss of control when he releases the shutter, and at that moment he enacts an imaginary, shared desire for objectivity.[34]

The geometrical structure of the background is formed by the windows, the light grid, and the wire cables on the wall, all of which push the image of the young woman forward to the front plane of the work. The camera equipment in the room and the randomly scattered tables and chairs contrast the carefully composed foreground. The tabletop across the entire front horizontal plane recalls the bar in Manet's painting. The viewer is very much part of Wall's piece.

Winnipeg artist Sheila Spence, whose work encompasses rural and urban landscapes, is another of Canada's foremost portrait photographers. Her portraits "of" the sitter investigate place, time, and context. The dress, hairstyles, and the specific backgrounds give additional

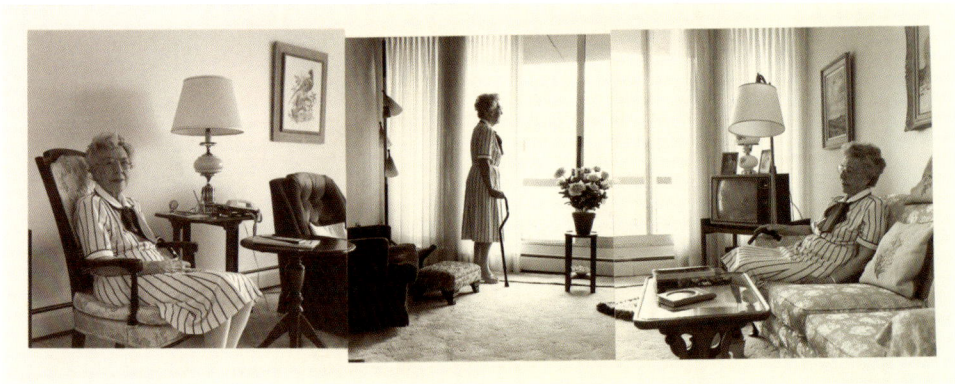

information about the individual. In some, the background is plain. In others, the backgrounds either echo or reflect light, pushing the subject closer to the viewer. Spence carefully plans her compositions and lighting, both of which are integral to the success of each work. She creates in series, such as *West Broadway Series* of the late 1990s; portraits of artists executed around 2007; and her *Rodeo Series* of 2010–11. Her printing is done to perfection in each—every nuance is exact. *Friday Night Babysitting* and *Superman,* for instance, explore the moods, the dreams, and the sense of pride in all her young subjects from Winnipeg's West Broadway area. In *Friday Night Babysitting* it is obvious from the look and stance of the young girl that she wants to be part of whatever the older two youth are doing. In *Superman* the young boy stands in front of a graffiti wall, wearing his superman necklace and proudly showing his bike. Spence respectfully captures her subject's sense of accomplishment and self-worth.

Spence has also done a number of multi-panelled, compelling portraits delving into personal relationships. *Minnie, Anna and Amy,* for example, shows Anna, Amy's daughter, in the centre panel, between her grandmother and mother. Half of Anna is also included in each of the two outer panels, that of her grandmother on the left and her mother on the right, portraying the physical and emotional connection between the three women. Spence's *Rodeo Series,* illuminating those on the rodeo circuit, explores each personality. As a series it reveals their commonalities and becomes a portrait of the profession of rodeo riding. They all—male, female, young, or mature—have a direct gaze. Each wears a colourful plaid shirt, a cowboy hat, and a significant large belt buckle, and most have their hands or thumbs in their pockets. The details of their hats and buckles and the slight variations of stance reflect the riders' individualities. Spence's expert use of lenses, lighting, and positioning and her deft control of the nuances and shadows draw the viewer intimately into the relationship between her and her subject.

FIGURE 6.16. **Thelma Pepper**, *Nellie At Home (Nellie Schnell)*, 1989.

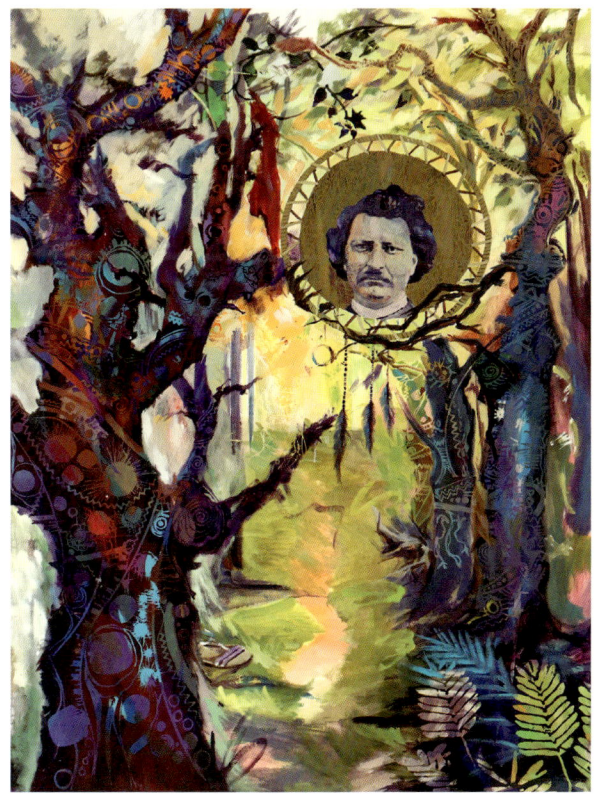

FIGURE 6.17.
Yisa Akinbolaji,
Stolen Identities, 2018.

Thelma Pepper's photographic triptych, *Nellie At Home*, 1985, depicts Nellie eagerly waiting for her family's visit in the left portion of the work; her watching them through the window as they leave in the centre, and thereafter being alone in her apartment. Pepper's son recalled her talking about *Nellie At Home*, reflecting he "could feel her understanding of what Nellie was going through. CBC's David Gutnick's opined that her work was about the power of prairie women and particularly immigrant women and she interviewed all those she depicted. His description of the artist and her work was apt:

Thelma listens so that she can see
Thelma sees so she can capture
Thelma captures so she can share
Thelma shares so we can listen
And when we listen, we too,
Thanks to Thelma, can also see.[35]

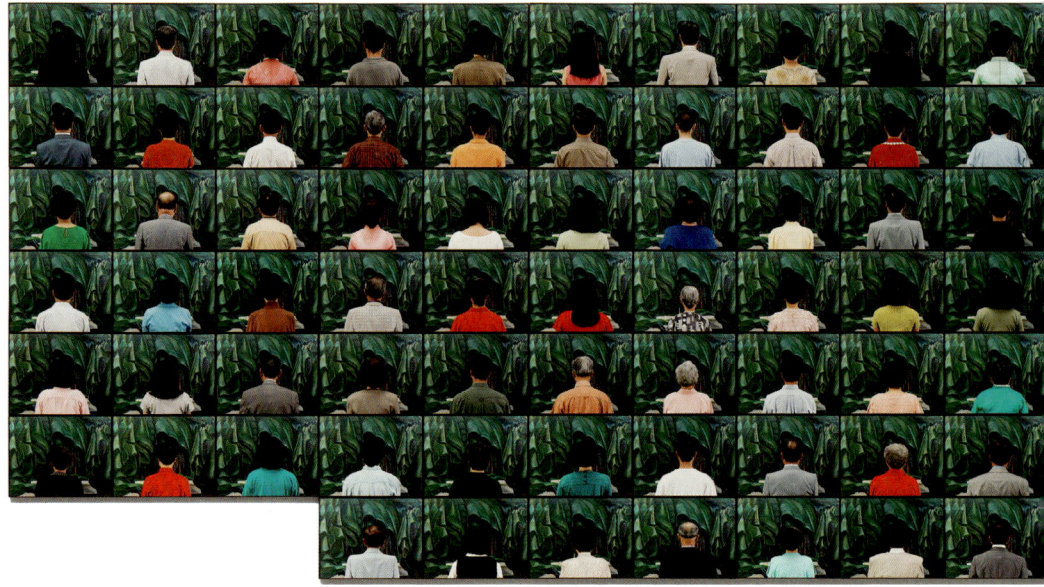

Now living in Victoria and originally from Winnipeg, Tim Gardner (b. 1973) has had a significant international career in Canada, the United States, and the United Kingdom. He uses snapshots as motifs for his investigations in his drawings, watercolours, and pastels of contemporary middle-class life. His works are realistic and technically accomplished, as evinced in his *Nick on the Prairie Facing into the Wind,* pastel on gessoed paper mounted on canvas, 2006. Curator Christopher Riopelle in his essay "To the Mountain and Back" talks about Gardner's ability to portray heroism, such as the heroism of a hockey team.[36]

Yisa Akinbolaji, who immigrated to Canada in 1997 from Nigeria, created an interesting portrait of Louis Riel, titled *Stolen Identities,* 2018. Situated in a poplar wood in Manitoba, Riel is framed by a dreamcatcher, and the background woods are filled with colours and patterns of Akinbolaji's native Nigeria. He was determined when he arrived in Canada to embrace Canadian culture and does so in much of his work by setting his adopted culture against his birth culture. He said, "My work is reflective of my experiences. . . . I do not just paint; I create using paint and forms. . . . I desire my work to engage the viewers in the upside-down thinking process and discourse relating to its creation . . . one element of composition leads to another. I use layers upon layers of paint while revealing the hidden colours and forms that lie beneath the topmost layers of my oil or acrylic paint. This interplay

FIGURE 6.18. **Jin-me Yoon**, *A Group of Sixty-Seven*, 1996.

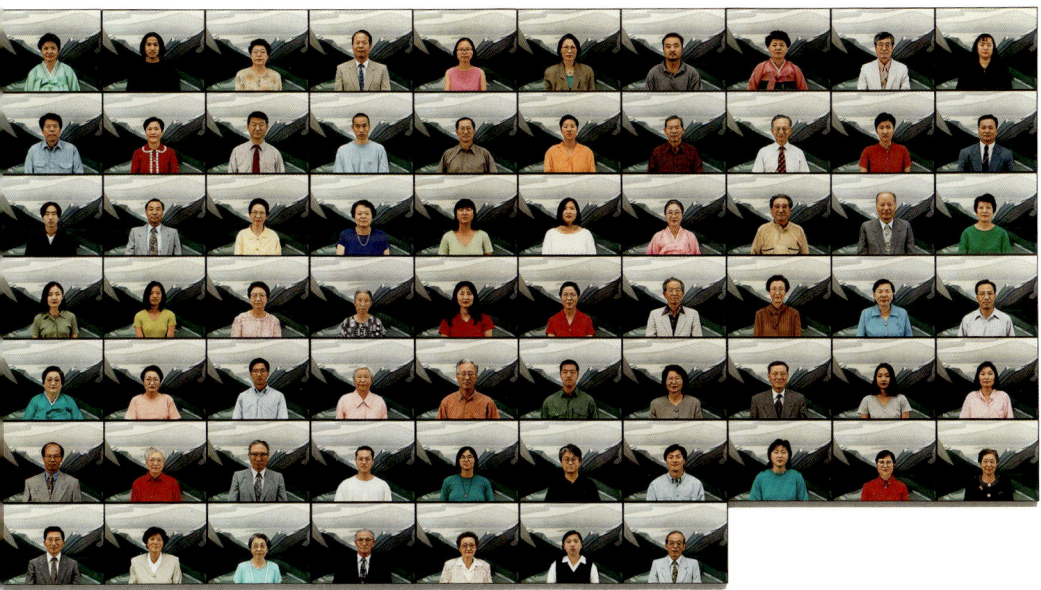

of oppositional relations between foreground forms and background ones indulges me with multiple symbolic possibilities."[37]

Group portraits are yet another facet of portraiture by Western Canadian artists. Two prime examples are Micah Lexier's two series, *A Portrait of David* and *David Then & Now,* done ten years apart, and Jin-me Yoon's *A Group of Sixty-Seven,* 1996–97, portraying Korean immigrants to Canada. Both artists explore the points of convergence between the individuals within the group while underlining their uniquenesses. In his 1994 *A Portrait of David,* Lexier (b. 1960) included seventy-five people, all named David, from ages one to seventy-five. Lexier told curator Jon Tupper, "I guess in a way a piece like *A Portrait of David* is a sort of self-portrait because it's a generalized portrait of someone growing older, something we are all going through. The reason why the piece stops with a 75-year-old David is because I am 33 years old now and according to the Canadian Global Almanac, the average 33-year-old Canadian male can expect to live for 42 more years."[38] Lexier noted at that point that this was the biggest, and simplest, work he had done, with the Davids all photographed against a blank wall. In describing the overall concept, he said, "*A Portrait of David* is from the 'circumstance' category [people who share a name, or through friendship, people you've chosen to be around]. I don't really know these people named David, but they share this commonality, and this becomes the reason for working with them.... I see these Davids as another kind of found imagery. That really excites me."[39] The exhibition *David Then & Now* was a series of diptychs with the original photograph and one from a decade later.

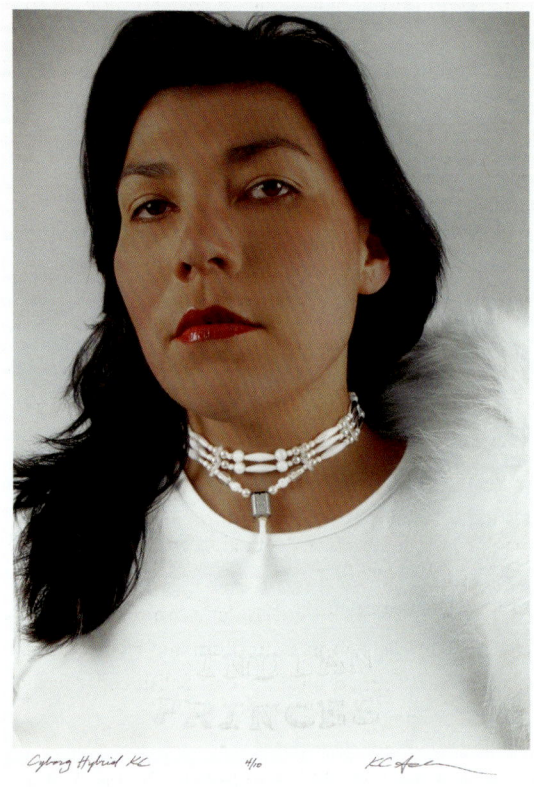

Cyborg Hybrid KC   *4/10*   *KC Adams*

Jin-me Yoon, a Korean immigrant, photographed her compatriots, each against the backdrop of the painting *Maligne Lake* by Group of Seven member Lawren Harris. She combined those individual photographs into one work, one-half of which were the frontal views; the other half were back views. The piece reveals important political relationships of sixty-seven people relating to 1967 and Canada's Confederation. There is also a strong personal element behind the work, as the 1965 federal government's changes to the Immigration Act enabled the artist's family to come to Canada.

Michael Boss (b. 1959) has approached his group portrait featuring his family past and present from another perspective. His original source materials were the family photographs and documents he inherited from his parents. These have been critically important to him, feeding his ongoing self-questioning. His rich personal ancestral background led to him to create many portraits of his ancestors, a major one being *Ancestors and Descendants,* 2015, in which five generations are portrayed together. This life-size work is done in acrylic paint and china marker on panel. He has also portrayed himself representing the duality of his cultural roots, both his pacifist Mennonite and Ukrainian Cossack sides.

Vancouver Island artist Arthur Vickers is also interested in past generations, spiritual roots, and cultural legacies. *Intangible Heritage,* 2011, his large, iconic mixed-media work explores the past of West Coast Indigenous people. Vickers explains:

> *Intangible Heritage* is about your greatest ancestor and how they invisibly touch your life. You sit in the middle with your hands resting on the children, the next generation. Through you your ancestors are passing on their wisdom, teachings and knowledge; your greatest ancestor is reaching out to the next generation. Your parents are on each side of you passing on the teachings of their parents through the touching of your spirits. Above you is your greatest grandparent, who, through the generations before you, passes down their wisdom and teachings from elder to elder invisibly touching your life, creating your Intangible Heritage. As you touch the next generation you become the teacher as you pass down your knowledge, you become the elder.[40]

His technique and imagery in this rich multi-generational visual story are unique. Created with numerous layers of clear lacquers embedded with twenty-four-karat gold powder, the imagery in *Intangible Heritage* is executed in low relief, sized, and gilded with hand-layered and hand-placed twenty-four-karat gold leaf. This work is rich in symbolism and rich in family and cultural history. Referring to a button blanket, it is topped with a Coast Salish cedar hat with three frogs depicted. Curator Nicholas Tuele explains:

> Frogs play a prominent role in First Nations lore. When the frogs stop talking at the start of winter and go to sleep, it's time for the people in the Big House to begin the ceremonial season. Frogs are able to live in two worlds, that is, on land and in the water, and by extension they live in the spirit or ancestor's world and the world that we experience through our five senses. They are the conduit between these two worlds. . . . Arthur gives us a visualization of the continuity of heritage from our ancestors through our parents to us and then to our children . . . we discern other aspects of the iconography in Arthur's work. Upper right there is Eagle, ruler of the sky, who mates for life and thus symbolizes lasting spousal dedication. Upper left we see Raven, bringer of light, and amongst other attributes, he teaches us about life and right from wrong.[41]

Every artist has his or her own process in approaching portraits. Knowledge of cultural roots, personal histories, intense observation, and decisions on the appropriate materials, composition, background, and specific symbolic or iconographic details are critical. So, too, is patience from both sitter and artist.

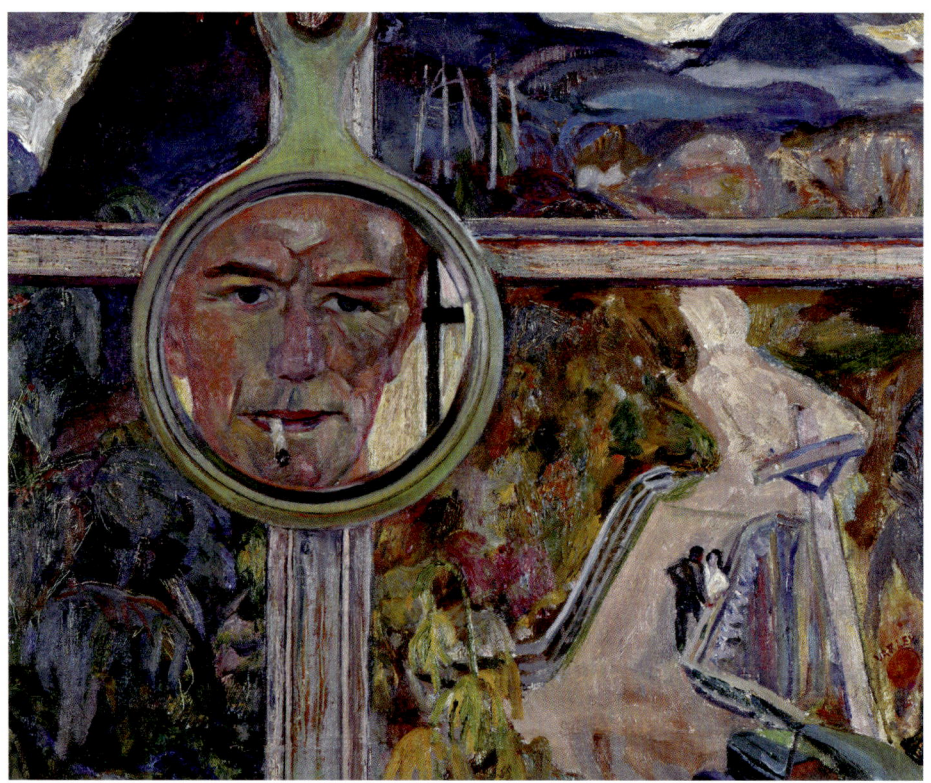

Psychological Inscapes

> "Everything happened to me in the mid-twenties. I painted seriously and after; I was given to smoking and night walking in the uninteresting streets; sat in desolate cafés; saw the dawn, the time of reality, anti-dream time."[42]

The most riveting portraits and artist's self-portraits, to me, are those that reveal the honesty of inner feelings and emotions, their unique inscape. "Inscape" is defined as "the unique essence or inner nature of a person, place, thing or event, especially depicted in poetry or a work of art."[43] While many artists depict their sitters' inner sensibilities in their portraits, artists' self-portraits are prime examples of psychological inscapes. Some, like Varley's, Kurelek's, Pavelic's, and Eyre's, are especially poignant.

FIGURE 6.20. **Frederick Horsman Varley**, *Mirror of Thought*, 1937.

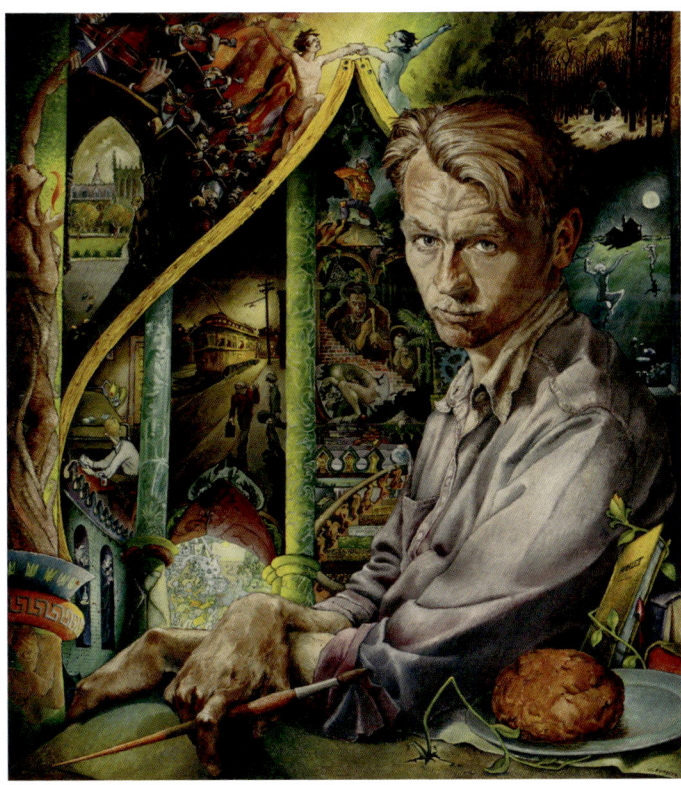

FIGURE 6.21.
William Kurelek,
*Portrait of the Artist
as a Young Man*, 1950.

Varley is a master of portraying psychological disquiet, and his self-portrait *Mirror of Thought*, 1937, is, in my view, especially important in the annals of Canadian art. Painted from the second floor of his house at the end of Lynn Valley, in North Vancouver, it shows the artist, cigarette in hand, reflected in the shaving mirror that hangs on a nail on the cross of the window frame. The window overlooks Lynn Valley, and a pair of young lovers is on the bridge below. Telephone poles in the background echo the cross formed by the window frame. Varley's son, Peter Varley, describes the painting: "Worked at in haste for submission to an exhibition in Seattle, the painting is interesting as a personal statement, within a broad spectrum of external influences. His view of the lovers on the bridge below is detached yet personal; separate at a distance, through the prison of barred window. His image is reflected as if it is hanging on a cross."[44]

The same palette as that in his portraits of Vera dominates in this self-portrait as well, once again heightening the penetrating disquiet of his stare in the mirror and adding to the foreboding sense of the scene itself. Were the young lovers his alter ego? Looking to Varley's own past, *Mirror of Thought* also reveals his present state of mind as he looks toward an unknown

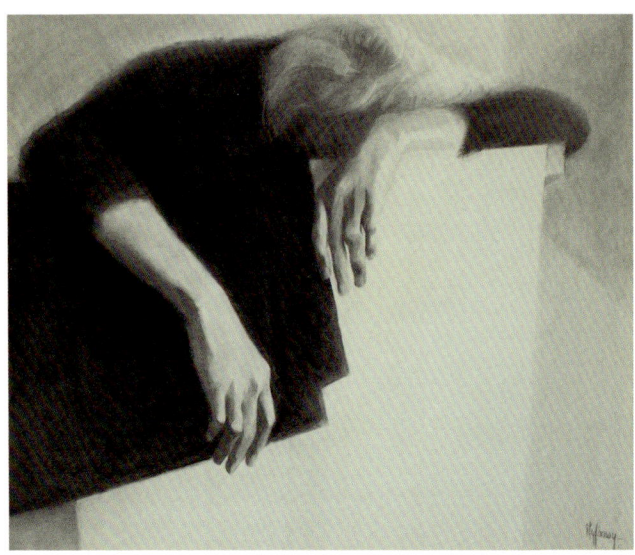

FIGURE 6.22.
Myfanwy Spencer Pavelic, *Anguish*, 1968.

future. His brush strokes are obvious and deliberate, fluid and emotive, and unite his overall colour and composition. He drew into the wet paint in the lower left quadrant of the work with the pointed end of his paintbrush. These incised lines interrupt the surrounding softer foliage, imbuing the painting with an element of sharpness. Here, too, as in his landscapes of Lynn Valley, his vibrant and rhythmic brushwork captures the moods of the weather, the clouds and winds, which seemingly echo the artist's moods, disappointments, and sorrows.

Manitoba's Lionel LeMoine FitzGerald also did a series of compelling self-portrait inscapes in watercolour. Freely drawn in monochrome, these suggestive works have nudes floating around the artist's head, which is in the centre of the image. Devoid of detail, the nudes are ephemeral, and his fluidity of drawing is evocative and compelling. One has to ask: Are we, the viewers, really voyeurs? Are these dreams or do they reflect reality? None of these paintings were seen during his lifetime. They were discovered by FitzGerald's widow in his storage locker after his death. She was dismayed, a situation that Ferdinand Eckhardt, director of the Winnipeg Art Gallery, often recounted.[45] He included the series in the *FitzGerald Memorial Retrospective* exhibition held shortly after the artist's death.

William Kurelek (1927–1977), of Ukrainian heritage, was a prolific artist who worked in various genres, including illustrations for books like *Prairie Boy's Winter*, paintings symbolic of his heritage, and his penetrating self-portraits. He suffered from serious mental health issues, and he also had a very difficult relationship with his father, who was against his becoming an artist. He set out to prove to his father that he could be, and indeed was, an artist. His 1952

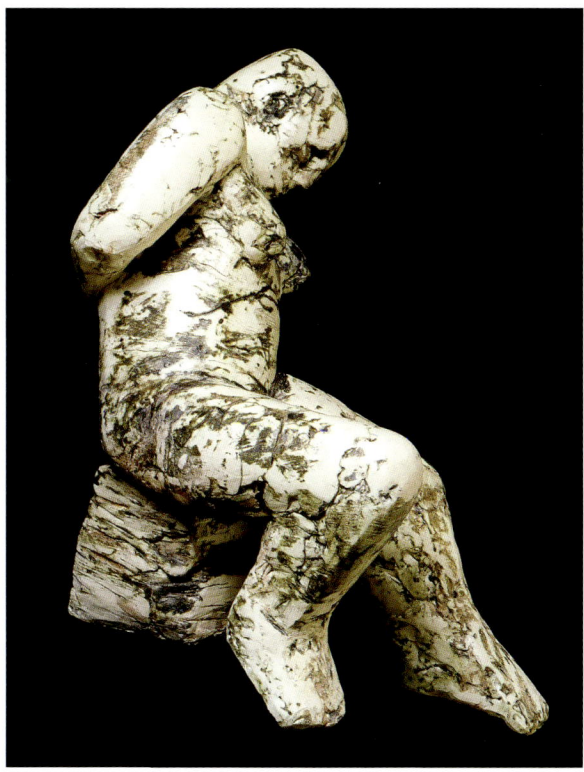

FIGURE 6.23.
Eva Stubbs,
Equilibrium, 1984.

academy piece, the oil on canvas *Zaporozhian Cossacks*, was done to sway his father's opinion. His self-portraits are filled with real and imagined images. Through his utilization of symbols, he suggests his own vulnerability and anger at being perceived as on the "fringes" of society, as is particularly apparent in his autobiographical oil on canvas *Portrait of the Artist as a Young Man,* 1950. This painting shows the artist, paintbrush in hand, looking directly at the viewer. Every centimetre of the background is filled with multiple vignettes and objects reflecting his Ukrainian heritage, his dreams, nightmares, and aspects of daily life. It was done when he was searching for his artistic and religious self. The references in the painting—a loaf of bread, a church, and two boys on the sidewalk by a trolley car—are compartmentalized, isolated from each other. Curator Mary Jo Hughes wrote:

> Later, Kurelek admitted that this painting was a blatant attempt to prove his true identity as an artist. "There were four things which I thought would prove it: if I could (1) render the appearance of bread, (2) depict living hands, (3) paint the material

of a shirt, and (4) do the likeness of my face." Holding a brush, shabbily dressed, with the starving artist's requisite loaf of bread at his elbow, Kurelek clearly communicated his identification with the role. . . . The vignettes in this self-portrait range from actual childhood experiences (Kurelek as a boy dancing naked outside in the moonlight . . .) to fantastical scenes such as the crouching figure hatching from an egg, which points to the significance of the Flemish artist Hieronymus Bosch (c. 1450–1516).[46]

Victoria's Myfanwy Pavelic's self-portraits in pencil, oil, and acrylic are sensitive and personal psychological inscapes without the angst seen in Kurelek's self-portraits, but they, too, reveal her family challenges. Pavelic was financially secure, but she suffered from serious health issues as a child and underwent surgeries on both knees in Boston when she was in her teens. Her chronically weak joints ended her dreams of being a concert pianist and thus she turned to art. Years later, her daughter Tessa needed special schooling and care. Thus, from 1956 to 1969 the family lived in New York each academic year of Tessa's education. These realities defined Pavelic's life and feelings, and her art and innate expressions are layered with aspects from within and from without. Her work exudes dignity, beauty, honesty, and depth of emotion: joy, sadness, or despair. Her acute inner perceptions render the biographical nature of her self-portraits particularly striking. Pavelic was honestly perceptive when speaking of her self-portraits: "It doesn't matter what I do to myself."[47]

During Pavelic's protracted periods of isolation, her focus often shifted from portraying others to doing self-portraits. She commented: "I do self-portraits when I run out of other people. I have done a few when I felt all tied up inside or am lonely maybe—I wanted to paint the loneliness away."[48] This ability to convey her own moods is palpable in *Despair*, 1965, *Anguish,* 1968, *Release*, 1968, and *Decision*, 1969. Her quality of line and the strength of her pencil and charcoal are powerful. Pavelic's charcoal drawing *Anguish,* for instance, is filled with emotional intensity: her head is down, and her hands and arms hang over a box. For Pavelic, hands are of great importance, and in this drawing they convey utter despair and exhaustion. As she said: "Hands are as expressive of a person as the face is . . . they can portray anything."[49] She knew the anatomy underlying the surface. Being self-taught and not having gone to art school, she worked with skeletons: "I drove myself, working with models… and bones. That was how I got my anatomy."[50] This early training stood her in very good stead.[51] She presents herself both as the objective form and as subjective emotion, as seen in her 1984 *Exercise with Head Series*. In one image of this series, she wrapped her head with a scarf; in another she set herself against a background of blue and grey blocks; and in another she focused on her glasses. All her self-portraits reveal her psychological insights—her self-reflected moods, attitudes, and expressions—and thereby become personal examples of what British world-renowned portrait artist Lucian Freud called "expressive figuration."[52]

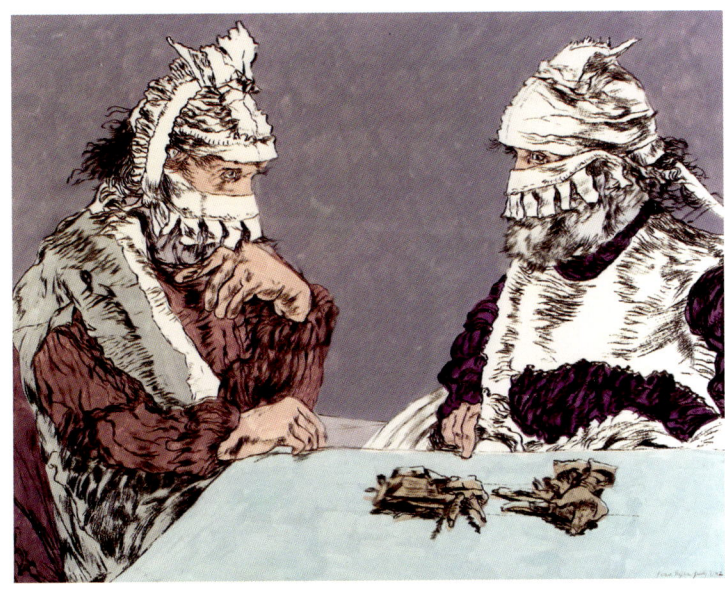

FIGURE 6.24.
Ivan Eyre, *Double Tatter Wrap*, 1992.

Winnipeg artist Eva Stubbs's substantial body of work also hearkens back to her personal circumstances of having been separated from her family during her childhood. She, however, evokes multiple vulnerabilities and emotions by portraying others and/or society as a whole. Unlike Pavelic, Stubbs does not focus on self-portraits. Combining two- and three-dimensional modes of expression, often within a single piece, she draws on society's past and looks to its future. Monumental in feel, her works are intimate in sensitivity as she probes contemporary issues affecting both the individual and society as a whole. Her sketchbook, which includes line drawings, sketches of her various concepts, and her aims for particular pieces, describes her ongoing challenge: "The actual making of art is a constant struggle. It never stops. When in the studio facing the material, whether clay, plaster, paper, the struggle goes on. One is never satisfied and the next step is difficult. . . . As it comes out of the subconscious (some of its expression speaks to the subconscious)—the conscious mind finds it hard to fully rationalize it. Unlike some artists who seem to have the solution before they start, I do not have any—the work is always a struggle to start—sometimes a long one."[53]

Family, 2003, is a monumental ceramic installation, which includes three almost life-size, seemingly solitary, figures. Although the installation embraces the family unit with the figures standing together, they are apart. Simultaneously inward and outward looking, the figures turn towards each other but gaze away. The surfaces are sensitive, painterly, textured, warm, and subtly coloured. Does this installation refer to her own childhood for the several periods she was separated from her family due to Europe's political situation? As she captures inner insecurities and traumas, Stubbs also evokes hope for humanity's future. *Silent Voices*, 1982–83, for instance, is a series of ceramic plaques, each with a female figure contained within its ten-by-eight-inch rectangular form. In some the figure emerges from the frame, and her shoulders push the confining barriers back as she steps out into apparent freedom. In others the figure is crouching, forced back into the frame by the strong, dark, diagonal brush strokes, which become a restraining barrier, and the grey-blue strips of clay suggest metal bars behind her.

Equilibrium and *Mother Waiting,* both ceramic sculptures, likewise express inner psychological contradictions. *Equilibrium,* 1984, poignantly portrays the balance, or lack thereof, in our personal contemporary lives and the line between vulnerability and strength. The solid and barely balanced figure, its broken arms reminiscent of a classical sculpture, exemplifies the figure's compromised situation. The clay is textured with the artist's characteristic drawing using oxides and colourants. The implicit precariousness shows life's emotional, psychological, and physical conundrums. In *Mother Waiting*, 1970, the figure, the artist's mother, is seated on the bench, leans on her cane, and thrusts forward in expectation. Enveloped by the curve of the arm of the bench, she is protected; but the forward lean is momentary, conveying the emotion and anxiety of waiting—for what?

Artists also depict deeply troubling and disturbing psychological works, which become portraits of situations. Some are either devoid of the human figure or have only veiled references to the figure. Steve Gouthro's *Drowned Pontiac*, 1989, for instance is a work with heightened psychological tension. The front end of the car is in the river, with no driver visible. Was he or she in the vehicle? What was the driver's state of mind? The composition and colour lend mystery to the work but no answers.

Ted Howorth also poses mysterious conundrums in some of his prints. His *Swimmer Series,* 2004, is one example, with a swimmer caught in compromised circumstances. The artist stated: "I liked portraying the calm evening by the pool, and wanted to capture the relaxed, quiet solitude—but then found I had to add an intruder. I wanted the swimmer under water, which added a fantasy, the narrative, and then I added the coral environment and the reeds. . . . I want my art to engage a viewer emotionally with my experience and memories."[54] Lush works, rich in colour, Howorth's *Swimmer Series* prints are filled with contrasting textures—fencing, reeds, and water. The prints depict a friend swimming; the light seems to cover his skin in tattoos, and the sense of the three-dimensional form of the swimmer moving through the water recalls Howorth's interest in sculpture. The reeds become a visual screen, seemingly trapping the swimmer and adding psychological tension to the work as a whole. Is this natural barrier impenetrable or not?

Drama can also be felt in Ivan Eyre's self-portraits and wrapped heads, which, like Myfanwy Pavelic's, explore the fragility and vulnerability of individual lives. Many of his conté drawings show the artist with his head wrapped or wearing headdresses and masks. Eyre reflected: "I spend a lot of time by myself by choice, and so I end up being a willing subject. I have several large mirrors around that I use during my painting. I sit there and I try drawing myself looking the same, so by wrapping my head, this makes it more interesting. But there are other connotations as well."[55] He has said that using these guises took "the boredom out of viewing my own image, as well as offering the illusions of landscape space within the contours of my head."[56] Eyre never set out to create "pretty pictures." His forms are precise, his imagery is symbolic, and his lines are strong. The final message of his works regularly transcends conventional beauty and creates mystery. The ambiguous meanings of the seemingly randomly placed unrelated objects add further unease to his unanswered conundrums.

His wrapped head portrayals develop psychological constraints, tensions, and conflicts, as Jerrold Morris opined early in Eyre's artistic career: "The bandaged heads do not conceal physical wounds, but suggest metaphorically men trapped in alienation, looking out fearfully at the world."[57] Bandages, bags, and complex headdresses enhance fear and insecurity. The bird headdresses he depicted were inspired, perhaps subconsciously, from a British Museum exhibition he saw on his Canada Council travels in 1966–67: "an exquisitely beautiful exhibition of bird skeletons—from tiny ones to very substantial ones, all in strict rows facing the same direction as if waiting for a command. It was a hauntingly beautiful visual experience. I hadn't before, nor have I since then, seen any sculpture more forceful than those delicate, white-boned creatures all standing in a line against a black background. It was difficult to pull myself away from them; I thought that if I could study them intensely enough, I might be able to steal the secret of their mysterious charm."[58]

Eyre told me that his interest in masks and wrapped heads tied together psychologically: "Hard to know why they interested me or the role they played—a different role in different drawings or paintings—sometimes friendly, sometimes not. Masks let me play with different forms—a painting within a painting. The still lifes connect with the masks—the still life constructions sometimes ended up on my head and link to the hats—mask. The fascination with the wraps evoke the landscape—the folds and lines in the cloth simulate landscape—then putting the landscape within my images and this becomes the basis for my silhouetted figures like 'Green Eve'"[59] His selected iconography consistently imbues his work with disarming overtones, penetrating well beyond the momentary appearances of things and moods: "My work projects towards that which is 'essential' in me and in you, towards our unconditioned and unpersuaded selves. It concerns itself with the passage of time and time's inversion in memory and contemplation. It is preoccupied with the unfolding of life—the contradictions, paradoxes, uncertainties, faith—all the viciousness and the beauty—as in a blizzard, its freezing winds containing within them light, drifting snowflakes."[60]

Kelly Clark (1935–1995), like FitzGerald and Eyre, did a body of work including landscapes of his favoured Delta Marsh, Manitoba, and those that can be dubbed "inscapes." Like others of his contemporaries, he studied with George Swinton, from whom he got support and inspiration. Clark graduated in 1958 and, being both a musician and a visual artist, he went to London in the early 1960s. His large, powerful crowd paintings of the 1960s show the overwhelming impact London's dense population had on him, a significant contrast to Winnipeg. These large, rich, impasto-textured canvases, recalling the angst and energy of German expressionist painter Emile Nolde, are filled with faces, covering the entire canvas, stacked on top of each other. Curator Donalda Johnson commented: "These emaciated faces appear to originate as impressionist 'snapshot' portraits of fellows, often with backdrops of generic landmark structures. Over time, they multiply obsessively until the entire surface is permeated with staring, leering faces. Evolving still, they mutate to oval abstractions representing teeming masses of humanity. Consisting of large canvases and drawings on paper, this volcanic production offers evidence of Clark's duress at the crowded population of London in the 1960s and his discomfort with the subsequent dehumanization."[61]

While in Europe, Clark spent time with Austrian expressionist painter Oskar Kokoschka in his Salzburg studio. This and his London experiences were transformative. Clark was prolific and his visual explorations continued throughout his career, but it is perhaps his *Top Hat Series,* shown in 1975 at Winnipeg's Plug In Gallery in an exhibition titled *Me and My Shadows,* that best expresses his place—the prairie—and his psyche. Reflecting his personal quest, this series was rooted in the work of Belgian artist René Magritte. As Johnson notes: "These works can be seen as cryptic self-portraits in a symbolic style. Visual puzzles, they are impeccably rendered with an impressive technical skill. . . . Clark's image of the top hat appears to be his personal signature, and one might speculate that he viewed himself as an actor on the stage of life searching for his true role, for self-understanding, or taking the form of self-psychoanalysis. . . . These . . . speak to us symbolically of yearnings, regrets and lost dreams, of the acceptance of what shapes a life, but with a humour and optimism for what is yet to be accomplished."[62]

Western Canada's link to German expressionism was forged through connections of those who moved from Europe during and after the war, and those who served in the war. Their experiences affected the art made in the West and contributed significantly to Canada's burgeoning art scene. One of the most influential of these connections was Ferdinand Eckhardt. Originally from Austria, he was director of the Winnipeg Art Gallery from 1952 to 1974, and he brought a distinct proclivity for expressionism to the prairie art scene. His German associations, for instance, were critical in making Ivan Eyre's 1960s exhibition in Germany a great success. Eckhardt knew a number of German expressionist painters and his wife's first

FIGURE 6.25. **Kelly Clark**, *Untitled,* from the series *Top Hat,* 1978.

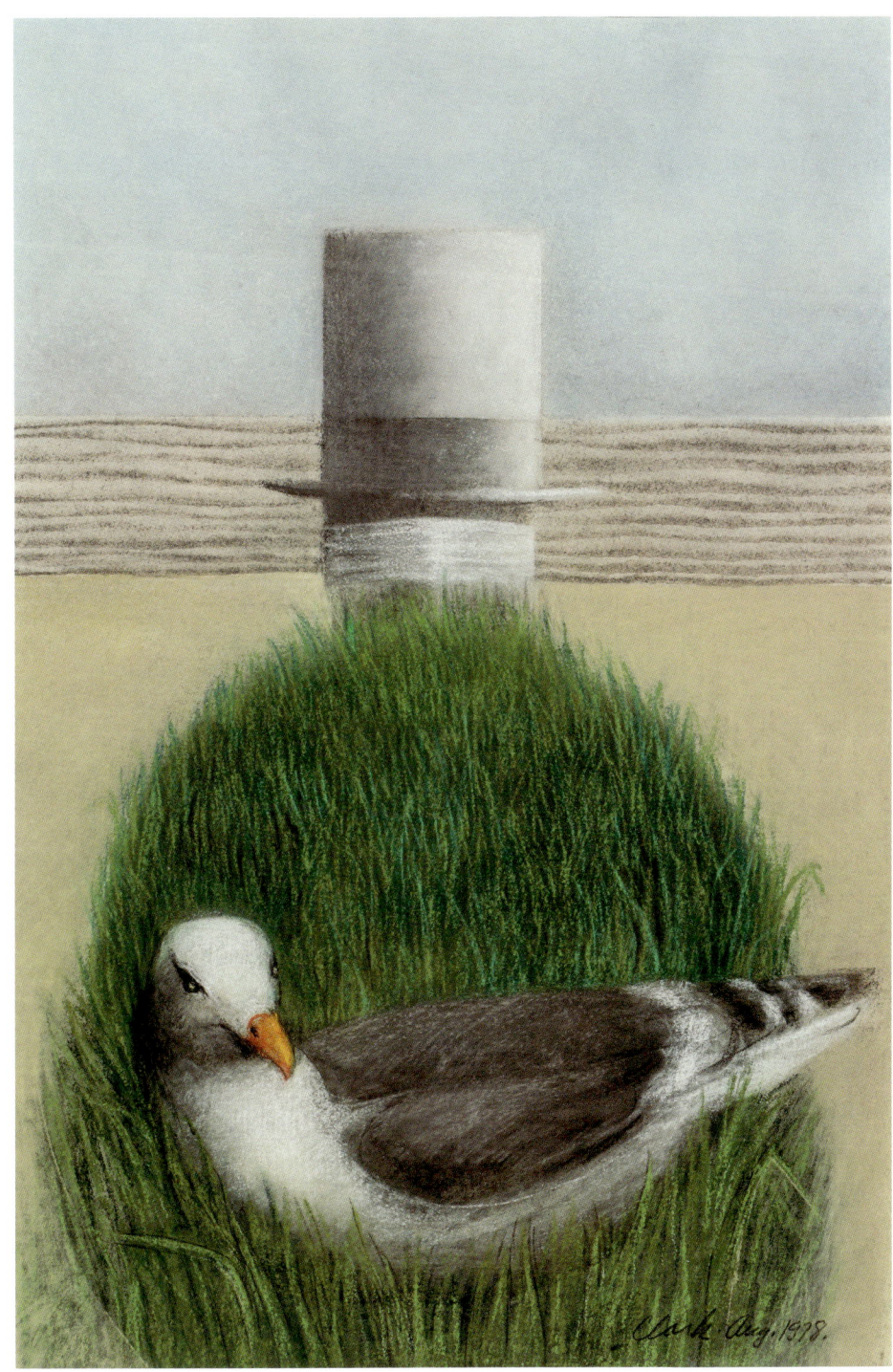

Clark Aug. 1978.

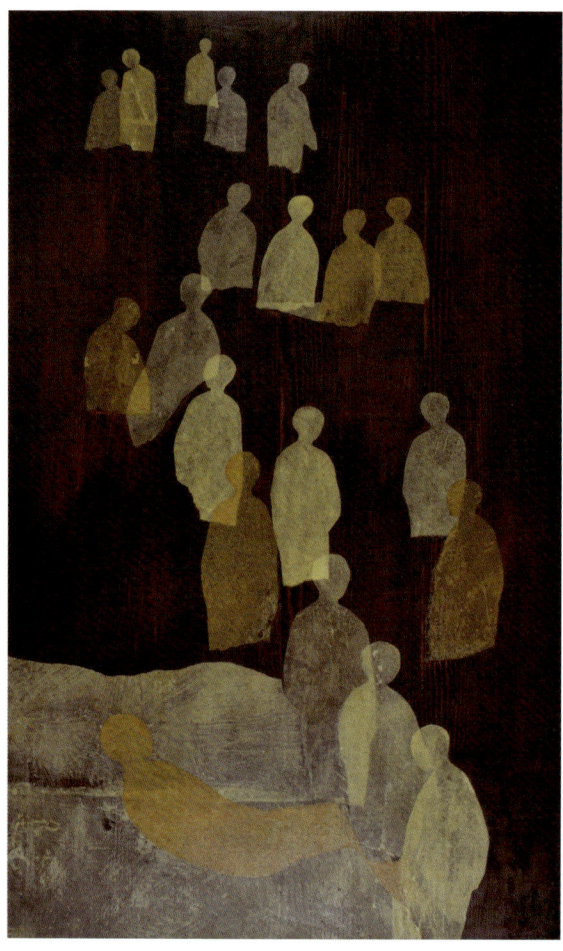

FIGURE 6.26.
Richard Ciccimarra,
Wood Collage, c. 1970.

husband, Walter Gramatté, was an expressionist artist living in Berlin at the time of his early death in 1929. Eckhardt brought work by Erich Heckel, Gramatté, Karl Schmidt-Rottluff, and other expressionist artists to Winnipeg and included their work in a number of exhibitions at the Winnipeg Art Gallery. The work also toured to other Canadian cities, drawing interest from younger artists. George Swinton had emigrated from Austria, first to Vancouver and later to Winnipeg, and he, too, furthered interest in European influences, including that of Max Beckmann, who was of particular interest to Ivan Eyre. After the Second World War, artist Herbert Siebner moved from Berlin to Victoria, and artist Richard Ciccimarra went to Victoria from Vienna. Eva Stubbs had been forced to flee Europe to Canada and Caroline Dukes (1929–

2003) likewise escaped. Their backgrounds and struggles during the upheavals and horrors in Europe certainly affected their subjects and modes of expression throughout their careers. Canadian artists who fought in the Second World War and faced the realities of Nazi Europe also brought their experiences home. Maxwell Bates's imprisonment by the Nazis for most of the war had an especially profound effect on him and on his art.

The son of an Austrian bourgeoisie family, Richard Ciccimarra is reported to have said to a friend at the outset of the Second World War, "I am going to die,"[63] when he was called to the draft at the age of seventeen. Given his artistic capabilities, he was not sent to the front but was seconded to the cartographical department of the War Ministry. Overnight his life went from one of luxury to one of serious financial concern. He immigrated to Canada in the 1950s, and in the 1960s exhibited at least twice with the Canadian Group of Painters at the National Gallery of Canada, and frequently in Victoria's public and commercial galleries. Like Kelly Clark's, however, his work received neither the attention nor acclaim it was due. He was an avid fly fisherman and a perceptive botanical painter, but it is his haunting figure paintings and wood panel collages that stand out. These particularly poignant works deal with emotional and societal isolation and the resulting psychological quandaries of loneliness and despair. Solitary figures and silhouettes recur in his art and are often seen from behind, rarely face on. His figures in his works are isolated from each other; they touch nothing or anyone, and in his compositions they are cut off from each other by strong diagonals, either a single line often in red or a deliberate shift in colour tone. Even in his crowd scenes, Ciccimarra's figures are isolated in mood, situation, and colouring, and his highly personal commentary is directed inward. His lonely, dejected figures refer to the dark side of the artist's own life. *Age*, 1963, or *The Descent*, 1968, for instance, are ominous and forbidding inscapes. Were they premonitions of his 1973 suicide? George Swinton, who had exhibited with his Viennese colleague Richard Ciccimarra at the Art Gallery of Greater Victoria in 1958, reflected thirty years later that Ciccimarra "showed a sensitive commitment to art mixed with a fear (which I share with him) of being out-of-date and of having to go his own way (of which he was not quite certain yet certain he had to do it). Ciccimarra was an artist's artist, and I am very sad indeed that he had so many psychic and physical misfortunes and disorders and so little critical recognition outside British Columbia."[64]

His *Wood Collage,* circa 1970, done on wood in gouache, tissue paper, beeswax, and varnish, is strong in image and message, yet fragile in its materials and personal in its sensibilities, enhancing the dichotomies and veils of life's emotions. His use of the wood grain in these collages further emphasizes the inner desolation. Ciccimarra's biographer, Frank Nowosad, commented:

> For the most part his paintings and drawings which depict the human figure are,
> under the surface, autobiographical. . . . This haunted and bedeviled side of his nature
> he proved with obsessive intensity in his figure paintings. . . . There are many scenes in

which several figures are in a condition of hopeless loneliness, locked away from the others in separate space cubicles; there is the theme of the single male figure in a bare room having the posture of a lost soul isolated in a condition of existential anguish; there are the paintings in which two men have turned their backs to each other in a gesture of rejection of or agreed inability to communicate.[65]

In December 1972 Colin Graham, director of the Art Gallery of Greater Victoria, wrote Ciccimarra: "Frankly, Ricky… your work looks better and better with the passing of time and it seems to me that you are beginning to stand out increasingly as one of the few genuinely original talents we are lucky enough to have in Western Canada."[66]

Myfanwy Pavelic's portraits of Ciccimarra reveal his penetrating gaze, intense eyes, strong hands, and his pervasive loneliness. Pavelic used his compositional approach and set his hands apart from his head by dividing the work with two angular diagonal lines that cut across the figure. The effect was to intensify his inner conflict, loneliness, and isolation.

Robert de Castro was another of the seventeen Victoria colleagues, including Richard Ciccimarra, Myfanwy Pavelic, and Maxwell Bates, who were members of Victoria Limners Society. Robert de Castro, like Max Bates, served overseas in the war, and his work, too, was profoundly influenced by his experiences. His psychological self-penetrations were deep. This quiet observer of life, who often assisted sculptor Elza Mayhew, did not like to talk about his own work, which was sensual, personal, and intuitive. He admitted: "My forms are psychological in origin, and I find what viewers have to say about them more interesting, opposite, and revealing than anything I have to say, which is very little."[67]

What Maxwell Bates endured as a Nazi prisoner of war for five years was life changing. Loneliness, poverty, workers, and people on the fringes of society became Bates's most frequent subjects. He captured his subjects with a directness of expression, intensity, and simplicity. Bates's "hollowmen"—the mannequins, kings, clowns, scarecrows, and whores—are symbolic, expressive skeletons of humanity's ignored inner core. As Vancouver art critic Art Perry said, "Unfeeling and isolated from the mainstream of human existence, the figures of Bates' world inhabit the marginal consciousness of us all."[68] To Bates, his scarecrows are "a symbol of the condition of man. That was the idea of the scarecrow, as a kind of despised object—a bunch of straw with a thick stick under it."[69] Perry calls Bates a "documentary realist" whose concern was the private individual and not the public person; rather, the person set apart: "He uses walls to create a private space in which we become intimate voyeurs of his figures' helpless self-isolation."[70] Artist David Blackwood recalled of Bates: "In 1968 the curator of the Memorial University Art Gallery, the artist Peter Bell, was tremendously impressed by Max's paintings. He [Bell] considered Bates one of Canada's best painters, as he expressed it, 'miles ahead of anything in Toronto.'"[71]

Bates articulated his own underlying humanistic philosophy in the section headed "Art" in his *Notebook*:[72]

Beyond the Self and Space and Times is the goal of man's spirit . . . [and] [t]he **reason** for the manifestation of art is the desire to escape from the rigid framework of space & time. The creation & appreciation of art does allow this escape to take place. . . . The means of achieving this end are rhythmic. . . . The artist finds the universe full of similarities, parallels, rhythms. He is synthetic in outlook, as opposed to the scientist who notices the differences in things & is analytic in his approach to the natural works. . . . The similarities and parallels that the artist selects and records from the great maze of phenomena and apparent chaos of the universe are rhythms and form the basis of order, the elements of artists' organization and composition . . . **the quality** of art is not a material thing but must be held in a material form to be perceived or known by each spectator.[73]

Bates's unbounded interest in figurative work, and in the contradictions of reality and appearances and of the observed and the observer, is seen in his poignant paintings such as *Workers, The Cocktail Party,* and *Prairie Figures.* The effects of his forced manual labour in the salt mines, especially the understanding he gained of the position and physical reality of workers, are interwoven in all his art. Hands and feet were of particular importance in his visual expressions. Bates recalled: "My Prisoner of War experience intensified my art . . . because I had been thinking so much about it all the time . . . I wanted to do things as simply and directly as possible and I've never changed from that idea."[74]

Bates was known for his candour, his sense of humour, his loyalty, and his commitment to better the lot of many. Colin Graham, friend, artist, and director of the Art Gallery of Greater Victoria, noted that "the harsh distortion of facial features and the sometimes apparently cruel caricature make many of the figure paintings unforgettable. . . . He has a low level of tolerance for sham and insincerity. . . . He has a perceptive wit that comes out with devastating effect."[75]

Bates honestly portrays figures, however terse and distressing. Ferdinand Eckhardt aptly wrote in 1968:

Among Canadian painters, Maxwell Bates occupies a rather unique position . . . he is one of the few who has kept his individuality over the years . . . the abrupt Germanic interpretation of life . . . the human figure in all its excitements and distortions—singly or in groups—rhythmically or better unconcerned—scattered over the background. The result therefore is harsh and dissonant, seemingly non-esthetic at first glance, stirring, provoking and disturbing. He is always true to himself. He likes to speak out rather than to be euphemistic. He is critical and sarcastic. However his painting is not only painting for the eye. It involves the whole individual. It strikes to the roots of our blood, our sense. It shakes the structure of our society and our ideals. He has a good sense for the essentials, for things which are beneath the skin, behind the human face,

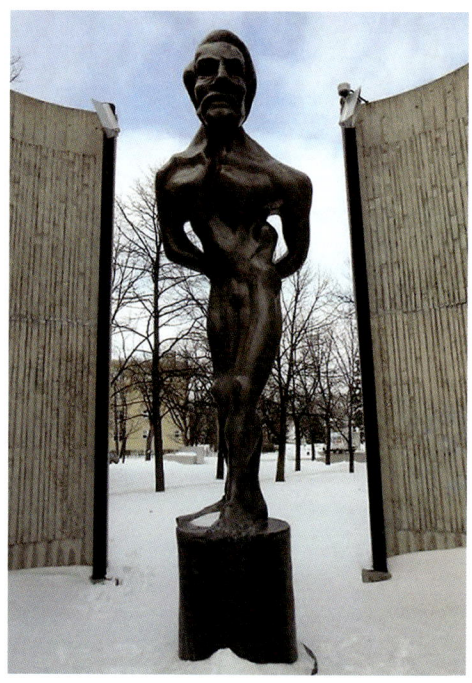

FIGURE 6.27.
**Marcien Lemay
and Étienne Gaboury**,
Louis Riel, 1971 (detail).

and behind the human behaviour. . . . Paintings like . . . *Cocktail Party* crowded with people full of arrogance, conceit and bashfulness, are like blaring fanfares in the pitch black of the night, loaded with frightening prophecy.[76]

For Bates, art was a key visceral way to understand the human dimension and human condition. His ability to dig into the depths of psychological sensibilities and tensions was significant.

Dreams are another important aspect of personal inscapes. Anishinaabe artist Scott Benesiinaabandan, based in Winnipeg and Montreal, works in photography, video, and printmaking. His work explores his interest in dreams and celebrates his sense of ancestral pride. His *Thunderbird Series* delves into his roots and futures, mapping his cultural history, depicting the roots and accomplishments of his Indigenous ancestors and peoples. He extends that exploration in *Pride (Walls, Oklahoma)*, in which their contributions to community and world events are reflected in the imagery of flags and medals in digital photographs. He also explores spiritual mapping, central in *Yellow Bird: Returned*. Benesiinaabandan does not just chart genealogy and history; he extends his explorations to memory and dream mapping, as seen in *Dreams and Knowing #3*. In this work two images are depicted one above the other, the grey tones and mist-like edges of forms conveying the fog of thought in dreams. In his *Alien*

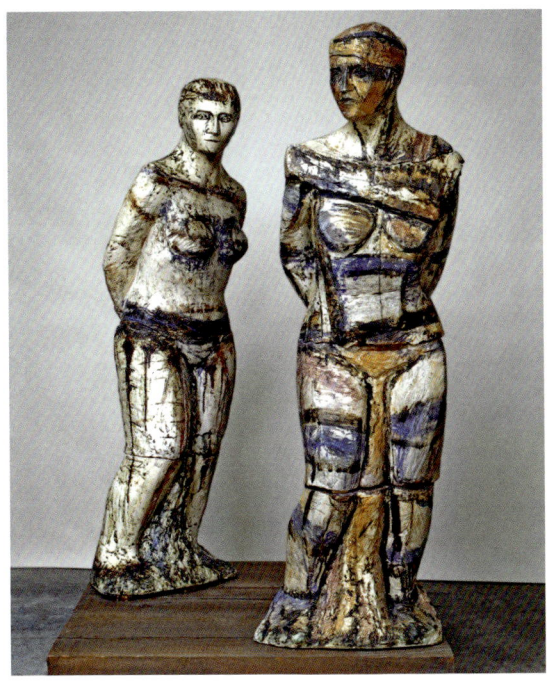

FIGURE 6.28.
Eva Stubbs, *Standing Figures*, 1983–1984.

Landscapes series he combines the known with the unknown. At times he produces his digital photograph images as silkscreened prints; at others, he adds a colourless gloss overlay, enhancing the image, heightening mystery, depth, and motion.

Victoria's Brian Grison has also explored the coming together of dreams and reality, including his incorporating into much of his work past advertising images, blackboards, and pictures of well-known figures. Memory, past experiences, and old magazines furnish him with ideas that he links with diagrams, texts, symbols, and illustrations in his psychological inscapes. As early as his 1988 Art Gallery of Greater Victoria exhibition *Dreams of Knowing,* he presented series of works developing his connections between psychological and philosophical thoughts, and he continues to explore and develop these ideas. His mixed media on paper *Artist and Model,* 2012, portrays the artist in black ink on a grey background on the left, and the model in black ink an orange-toned panel on the right. The figures, similar in form to those in 1950s advertisements, overlap in the centre. His uniting of time and imagery of the past and present fuses memory, thought, and the psychological.

The explicit candour with which artists present inner individual and societal psychological crises is visceral, deep, and at times difficult, but their messages are personal and immediate while at the same time thought-provoking and instructive.

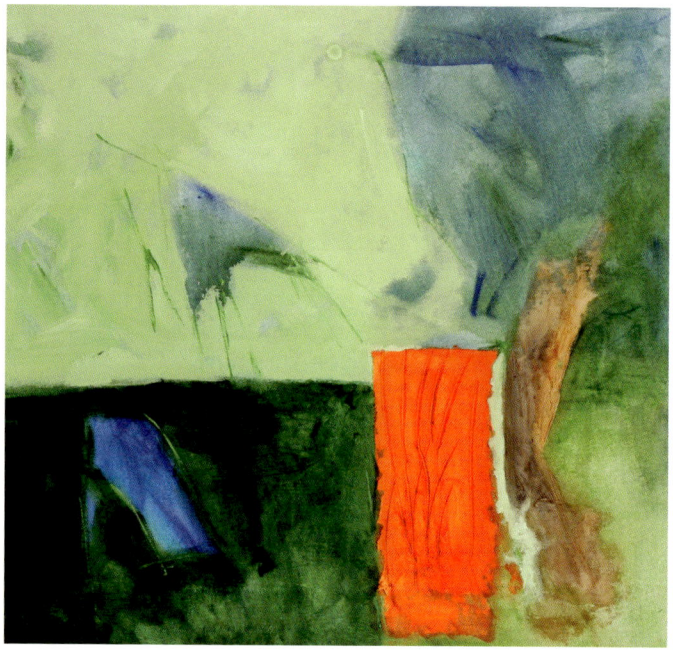

FIGURE 6.29.
Roger LaFrenière,
Melina, 2015.

Perspectives of Human Form:
The Figure and the Abstract

"If I wanted to paint a hand, I had to know what was underneath."[77]

Intensity of observation is evident in the inscapes of a number of Western Canadian artists, and leading portrait artists certainly have keen powers of observation and the ability to capture the fleeting moment of the mood or look. Those moments become windows into an individual's deeper essence. The understanding of the human figure, however, is critical to this portrayal.

Artists' figure paintings are both quick studies from models and carefully planned figure drawings and paintings. In Winnipeg work with the figure and models had been undertaken as early as the 1890s, organized by the Winnipeg Women's Art Association following the traditions of European academies. The women arranging the sessions with models allowed male artists to join them, and the association developed shared studios so they had the freedom to draw from models. Ever since then figure work has been prevalent in the collective oeuvre in Western Canadian art. Alberta's Aurora Landin is one who has been renowned in recent years for her insistence that art schools teach anatomy as an essential part of drawing curricula.

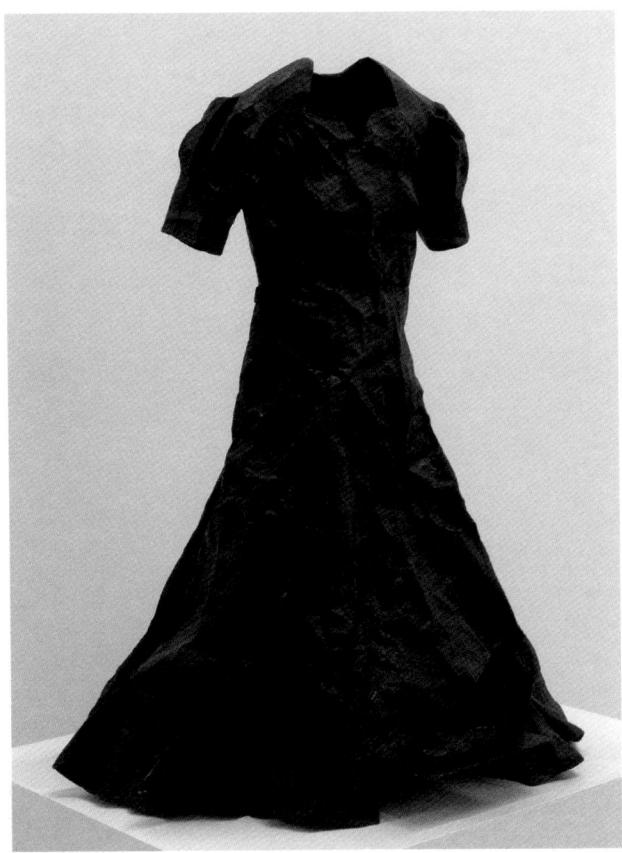

FIGURE 6.30.
Gathie Falk,
Agnes (Black Patina),
2000–2001.

Myfanwy Pavelic, who painted the figure and portraits from the time she was eight until her death in 2007, felt keenly that the knowledge of anatomy and the skeleton was essential for a portrait painter. She emphasized the need to "know what is underneath," something Pierre Trudeau realized when he was working with Pavelic. Pavelic's figure drawings show both her sensitivity and the delicacy with which she approaches her subject, and always her keen sense of form. Writer Robin Skelton noted that Pavelic "enjoyed shapes and makes use of them in her work: eggs, circles, squares, a different kind of vibrancy. She never lost her sense of form."[78] That sense of form carried through all her drawings and paintings of the figure. Her study of anatomy, which started early, continued for decades. As writer Ted Lindberg said, "To her nothing is more critical than establishing fundamental anatomy."[79]

With Limner painter and former Victoria gallery owner Nita Forrest, Pavelic often hired a model. They would do five- and ten-minute quick sketches in pencil, charcoal, or watercolour. Pavelic's were free and sure. As seen in her *Backview*, 1971, Forrest was particularly adept at doing the human figure, and, as Pat Martin Bates opined, Forrest was "a very underrated painter and her figure work is among the best anywhere."[80] Her ability to capture the three-dimensionality of the human form, movement, shade, and strength is evident in many of her paintings.

Eva Stubbs shared the same viewpoint regarding knowledge of human anatomy, and her figures show strength and purpose. The works in her *Nude Series*, executed in oil stick, reveal a strong, deliberate form, depth, and volume. Using colour and line with painterly acumen, Stubbs creates figure works that are at once universal and personal. Her sense of line is as assured as is her sense of form, and her large drawings exude the subtle palette of her fired clay sculptures. *Frieze,* 1994–95, a twenty-foot charcoal and conté drawing, relates to many of her sculptures. Its figures are solid, filling each section of the drawing. Contrasting emotions of relationship and solitude are manifest. The definition of the female figure is direct and unlaboured, and the figure often seems to be walking out of the picture frame. Stubbs worked the charcoal and oil stick into the paper. Her acuity with the human figure is equally evident in her large-scale ceramic figure sculptures like *Family.* In these group sculptures her portrayals of human psychological relationships are truly poignant, with each figure looking away from the other.

Many artists routinely draw the figure, with and without models, using quick sketches or more finished approaches. Not all figure works are realistic or a specific likeness of the model or individual. Some are metaphors. Sheila Butler (b. 1938) used the figure as a metaphor in many of her works. This is especially apparent in *Swimmer,* with its rhythmic, energetic movement, yet ambiguous setting.

Winnipeg's Roger LaFrenière did a series of forty-eight abstract colour works based on individuals' names in 2014, conveying his perception of the person's psyche. Each was done in a day and half and expressed his immediate raw feelings. They were neither planned nor belaboured. Forms, lines, and colours innately relate to his experiences, relationships, and understanding of each of the twenty-four individuals. *Melina,* for instance, is his elderly neighbour, whose cottage he often visited. This abstraction, as LaFrenière described, "shows both her softness and her dark side. She suffered from the meanness of her adult children. The colours are symbolic. Green for her was the colour of hope and the multi-shades of greens refer to her deep hopes and lesser hopes, the black in the green indicating the hurt she suffered. The orange textured rectangle refers to her garden and its many rows of carrots. That garden was her sanity, as was her lake, represented with the use of blue."[81]

From another perspective, some artists use clothes to portray the figure or life of an individual, like Gathie Falk's *Agnes*, the sculpture of a dress without the person in it; or the *Floating Coats* and *Chair* series by Aliana Au; or the ceramic works of boots and jackets by Marilyn Levine.

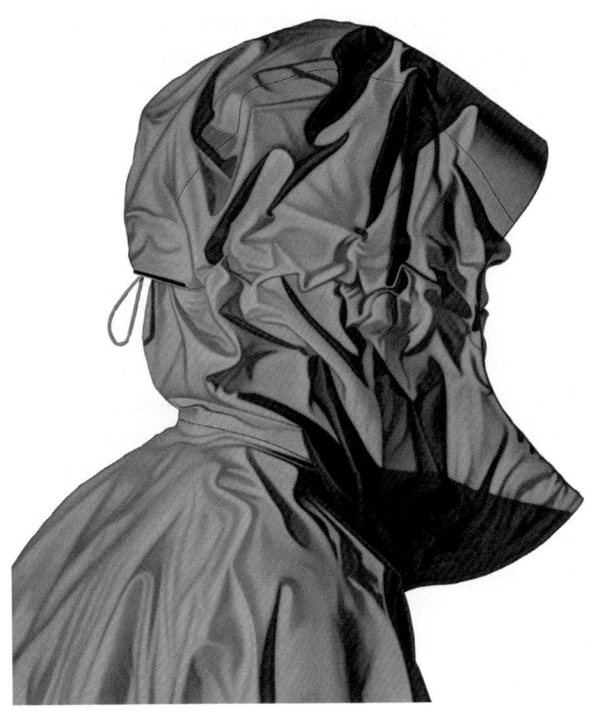

Winnipeg-born Karel Funk undertook his graduate degree at Columbia University in New York after graduating from the University of Manitoba, and stayed in New York for a few years before moving back to Winnipeg. Funk is rightfully acclaimed for his *Hood Series,* acrylic paintings on wood that are evocative and hyperrealist. They primarily depict the shoulders, backs, and hoods of jackets, and each conveys a mood, though a mood of anonymity. He chose hoodies as being the most common pieces of clothing, and paints them in different colours and of various materials: Gore-Tex, nylon, or polyester. He is particular about detail, precision, and surface, and each hoodie is silhouetted against a white background. Inspired by the portraits of Renaissance Flemish masters, Funk's work hearkens back to past painting techniques, contrasting that with the contemporary subject he depicts. He poses the jackets and crinkles them, using tape or tissue paper to retain a pose. He sets them in specific lights. He said, "I'll spend a lot of time moving the lights course around to build the right highlights and shadow. That's very important, how the shadow and highlights look. How do all the creases fold, and do they create an interesting composition? I spend a lot of time considering that when I'm photographing the model."[82]

FIGURE 6.31. **Karel Funk**, *Untitled #78*, 2016.

The result is stillness, yet radiance; distance, yet intimacy. Funk is interested in the anonymity and obscurity of personal identity and the resulting isolation in large cities. However, he points out the physical closeness of people on subways and buses, such public places where personal space disappears: "You could look over and see the earring somebody's wearing or that space behind somebody's earlobe. I use the term urban voyeur. It sounds kind of creepy, but you could look at these people, these strangers, when they're very close to you and just examine their textures and surfaces in ways that you would never do when you're socializing with friends."[83]

Of his working method, he says: "The process is very slow. I paint with very thin layers of paint, so it can slowly build up and that's why it can sometimes take a couple of months for one painting to be finished. I like to have control especially in the studio with painting—I want to really be able to think about the next step and control how the painting is developing."[84] The results are compelling and form a bridge from societies past to today. Their appeal is in their realism, but it is that realism set against the white background that creates a psychological tension. As curator Andrew Kear opined: "Karel completely contradicts the claims of portraiture. His subjects have a particular identity, and yet we still see them as anonymous. Not only is there potent psychological depth, but there is brute materiality and pure surface."[85] The artist concurred: "Tilting the head down does suggest a state of mind, and I'm very conscious of body language."[86]

Funk's portraits of contemporary life through his explorations of hoodies link to Aliana Au's *Floating Coats* series, which are equally evocative and also without the portrayal of a face. As already seen, she has consistently followed two independent artistic approaches: the traditional Chinese brush painting learned before coming to Canada, and Western painting techniques garnered when she arrived. Clothes are a central metaphor in Au's art, evoking memory and emotion and, for every viewer, they suggest multiple thoughts. Works like *My Floating Coat,* 2013, provide a connection with her father while simultaneously personalizing her Canadian experience, a heavy coat being a necessity for Manitoba's winters. She said, "The coat became the essence of the spirit without the physical being—it embodies the person. When you take the coat off it still takes the form because it is heavy with insulation and structure."[87] Au's coats, flying to regions beyond the frame of the work, exude a freedom and lightness as they hover over her landscapes, often depicted as a blue and yellow patchwork. The coats are balanced above the horizon line in her solid compositional structure. Does the patchwork portray fields of prairie canola and flax, or perhaps the floor of her Chinese classroom with patterned tiles? Merging her two cultural and artistic roots, Au told me that patchwork "is like the chessboard of life on which one plays. The subconscious influence of past experiences and memory is always there, combined with the conscious."[88] The artist wrote to me about these works:

> My family lived in the city of Canton in China for a good number of years. It was a city of very few lights at night, and the summer seasons were very hot. We spent a lot of nights lying on a canvas bed outside, with our mother sitting on a chair fanning the

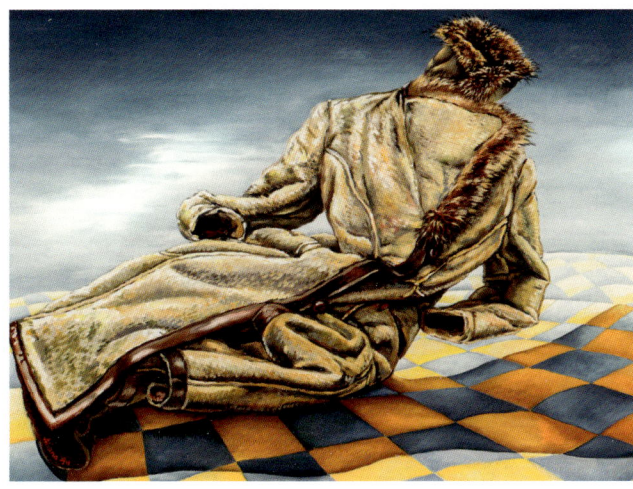

FIGURE 6.32.
Aliana Au,
My Reclining Coat, 2013.

mosquitoes away. The sky was always blue with stars, a crescent or full moon; and I remember very well my thoughts as a young child at that time.

Winters were cold there, our clothes were those from our father's childhood. He was always far away from home yet I felt a strange kind of closeness to him, perhaps from his old childhood clothes which I wore.

In my grandfather's house, I remembered observing the remnants of his existence, possessions once loved which now were left in such a way that the life force still appeared to exist in their form.[89]

Au's *Chair* series, done over a number of years, is likewise filled with many layers of personal meanings, patterns, and imagery—the upholstery on the overstuffed chairs, the tiles on the floor, or the patterns in the child's knitted sweaters, reflecting "the mosaic of life which reaches out." She returned to this theme over many years: "I wanted to capture the memory of the chair and the idea of the clothes. The chair embodies the idea of being seated; when seated one is relaxed and one's mind is elsewhere. A chair has had many people in it, sprawl in it—at formal times, informal times, in conversation, while reading, watching TV, knitting etc.—so it, the chair, has collective memories and one has favourite chairs as well."[90] Children's clothes take off into space—where are they going and why? The chair becomes a means of transport, embodying personal memories and stories. Au says, "To me, a chair is a vehicle where one's mental being expands and travels in time and space while one's physical being remains in reality. The chair series is an expression of fantasies and personal experiences, a mosaic of different elements in my life that reach out to me."[91]

Au's compositional process is fluid: "I usually have some sense, but part way through I let it go so the painting leads me. I start without necessarily knowing where it is going so it is a 'journey'. . . the colours related to my overall effect about how I feel."[92] Her past and present conjoin in these compelling works of memory and dreams. They are universal portraits, addressing critical societal issues of race, family relationships, and globalization as they connect across borders and cultures to become portraits of society as well as family.

Winnipeg's Karen Cornelius also uses clothes as her central image in her prints in the *Fabric of Belonging* and *Parka* series. As portraits of aspects of her life, they recall her personal past but are simultaneously portraits of contemporary society. Using the frilly dresses she wore as a child in the Congo and Eritrea as her focal image in her *Fabric of Belonging Series,* 2013, she highlights the morals and politics she and her parents endured during her growing-up years in the Congo. The parka she wore in the North many years later evokes the notion of needs in the Arctic. Through these personal items she questions the essence of her identity and belonging, with its multiple meanings and personal memories. In the *Parka Series,* for instance, the aperture for seeing, surrounded by the furry hood, is the key element of the work. Can one really see when fully protected from the cold? What is the impact of the environment? In both series she layers past and present realities of the diverse cultures and situations she has experienced, and poignantly voices sensibilities of place, history, and particular social concerns, being all the while autobiographical self-portraits.

Sculptors also portray portraits of personalities and times in their work without the image of a figure, as Marilyn Levine (1935–2005) did in her ceramic series of boots, bags, and jackets. She titled most of these with the name of their owner, thus providing the viewer with their personal histories and a sense of humanity. Her attention to detail, the creases, scratches, and tears through wear, achieved with her ability with trompe l'oeil, have poignancy, celebrating previous times well lived and attesting to a sense of loss.

The fictitious narratives of Esther Warkov are imaginative stories of lives and personalities past. Through her art she gives a portrait of Winnipeg's North End, initially the home of the city's Jewish population and subsequently the seat of multiethnic beginnings. Clearly connected with the growing art scene in Winnipeg, she was dubbed one of six artists to watch by university professor Kenneth Hughes in his *Manitoba Art Monographs,* along with Kelly Clark, Ted Howorth, Bill Lobchuk, Don Proch, and Tony Tascona. Hughes wrote of the six: "These artists have been involved in appropriating this place and space, rural and urban. They have created art as mirrors in which Manitobans can see themselves from a variety of angles. Of course the art is not solely of local interest. While rooted in this place and space, it has implications which extend way beyond the province and Canada as a whole. For these artists have been dealing with the big questions of our time, not simply the big artistic questions, but the human ones."[93]

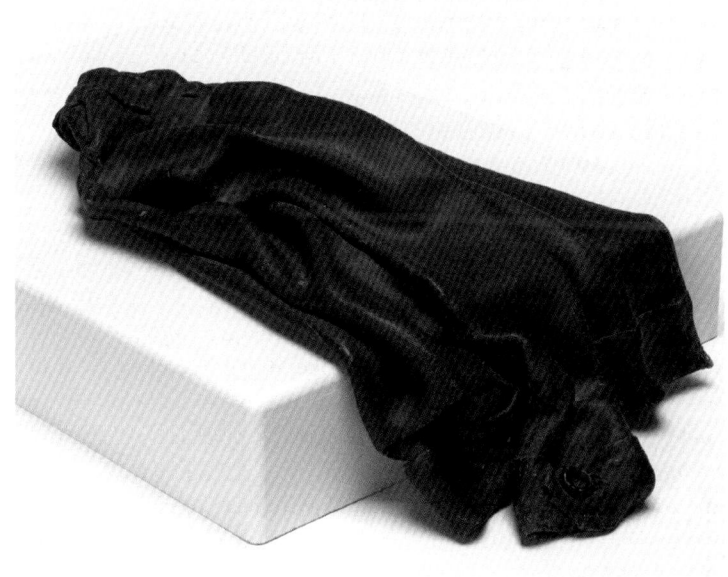

FIGURE 6.33.
Marilyn Levine,
Jacket #2, 1969.

Warkov's early works often had multiple sections, some two, some more, some rectangular, others with circular additions. They are composed with thought and filled with detail. The colours in her early works are warm and inviting, often at odds with the subject they portray. They are critical of the world and society around her, yet they have a sense of optimism.

In 1998–99 Warkov created her three-dimensional *House of Tea*. It is a masterpiece, one bought by the Winnipeg Art Gallery and toured to the National Gallery of Canada. It is a compelling commentary on upper-class society. The effigy of a young woman, a bride from Victorian times, without a head or feet, floats above a steamer trunk filled with many artifacts that collectively speak of her life. Warkov created the figure and all the objects in the trunk with her very complex technique of building her sculpture with papers, which she colours, draws, tears, rolls, and collages. Some images in the trunk, like the flowers, are elements repeated from her earlier paintings. She imbues the whole with new insights, meanings, intimacies, and textures. The detail in every aspect of this large and intricate work is rich and conveyed with sensitivity. The artist tells her imagined story:

> As a member of the upper level of society she was experienced in the rituals
> associated with the female members of her class; even in death she continues to
> pour tea from within her coffin. As well, lying on the centre edge of the coffin is

her teaspoon. . . . Her secret desire, one that was quelled by her upbringing, was to become an artist/writer, hence explaining why the handle of her teaspoon ends in the nib of a pen.

A spider is perched on her lapel, almost as if a brooch. As a member of her class never discussed death, it is fitting that a spider delicately decomposes her.

The coffin is not about death, but about memories . . . the coffin is presented as a steamer trunk—an object for storing one's life experiences. The colour of the coffin is various shades of purple and burgundy, the colour of an unused womb, symbolic of the woman's life. Her secret drawings, which she wished to be taken seriously, are found on the coffin. These include, on the outside, portraits of past lovers. The drawings on the inside depict a woman pouring tea, a boy with his cat, and the woman's version of a botanical drawing of a butterfly, the latter being another distinguishing sign of a lady. Also, within her coffin/trunk is a section of a prairie town. On the underside of the coffin lid is a mirror surrounded by a wreath. The mirror is dense and unrevealing, corresponding to her life. It is drawn in graphite to give it a slate-like feel, and to signify that the full story of her life is yet to be known.[94]

This work, to me, is one of the most inventive, compelling, and interesting works I know as it engages the audience and, as Hughes suggested years before, is a mirror that makes us look at ourselves, our society, and our customs.

Vancouver artist Gathie Falk, Manitoba-born, frequently defined her work as "veneration of the ordinary." She, like Marilyn Levine, used clay to depict multiple objects, from grapefruit to shoes to dresses, for example, *Agnes,* 2000 and 2001. As she said in a 2017 interview with the National Gallery of Canada: "It seems to me that, right from the word go, I have made the things around me—the things that I use, that everybody uses—the things that are ordinary: food, clothes, games, men's shoes, women's shoes, furniture. I saw the power of making things that are ordinary. And by making them out of clay, they wouldn't be a hard, flat surface; they would be slightly undulating—more like human flesh, so that everything that I make shows the imprint of my hands or the workings of my hands. There's always a softness to it, rather than a hardness."[95] She used papier-mâché as the medium for her *Dresses,* which were too large to be made out of clay and be fired in the kiln. Many of these were subsequently bronzed. Each has a shelf in front, on which Falk placed an object, as the candles in her 1997 *Dress with Candles.*

Well-worn, used, second-hand objects were carefully chosen by Winnipeg's Aganetha Dyck from thrift shops and bazaars for her work from the outset of her career. In the mid- and late 1970s she bought wool sweaters and dresses. She washed, rewashed, and washed them again, shrinking them in hot water and in the dryer. These became "people" or "personalities" in themselves and, when exhibited, were placed directly on the floor, giving the sense of a group of people walking. This series, *Sizes 8–46,* was done between 1976 and 1981. Some of these

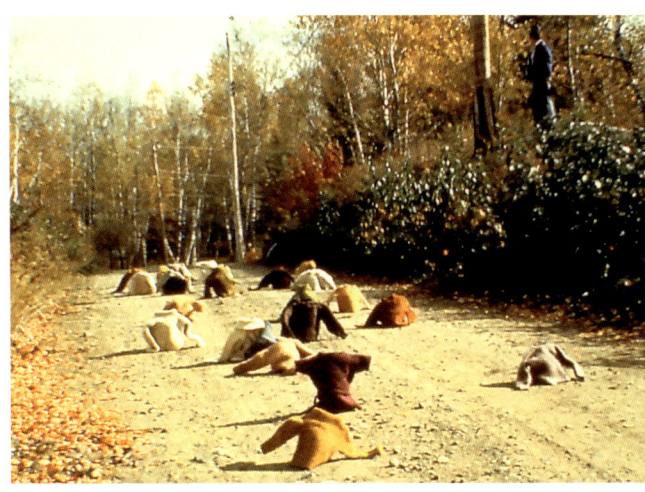

FIGURE 6.34.
Aganetha Dyck,
*Shrunken Clothing on
the Road*, 1976–1981.

articles of clothing held a personal meaning to her, like *Black Dress*, which she had originally bought for her mother and turned into a sculpture after her mother's passing. Later Dyck put objects in her beehive, and the bees became her collaborators for many years. Dyck celebrated the unique histories and the humanity of the wearers of the old shoes, bags, helmets, and skates, and the bees "added" their honeycomb elements to these well-selected ordinary objects.

After Dyck ceased working with bees due to the serious allergies that developed over her "bee-years," she created her 2012–13 sculptural woollen *Shrinks*. She crocheted long pieces of felt and wool, in various colours, and, as with her earlier *Sizes 8–46 Series,* she washed these lengths of crocheted wool many times over, shrunk them, and then transformed them into compelling sculptures, which also assumed their own individual personalities. While the beehive works were created through the addition of the honeycombs, the *Shrinks* were transformed through reduction by shrinkage. Curator Shirley Madill aptly noted that both Dyck's reduction and additive works were "chance, abstraction, expression. The domestic, the familial, the everyday."[96]

The depiction of the human figure, portraits, the complex psychological inscapes, and portrayals of lifestyles and changing societal patterns, though not always in vogue in contemporary expression, have been constant and essential aspects of Western Canadian art. Such depictions continue to be so. These perspectives of humanity throughout the decades underline the depth of the human condition and the challenges and high points of civil society. While portraying issues of humanity and society, artists also focused in large part on the political aspects of societal issues. Together, these dual perspectives on people, customs, and life and livelihoods offer insights and directions to be heeded in order to achieve equality and justice in contemporary times.

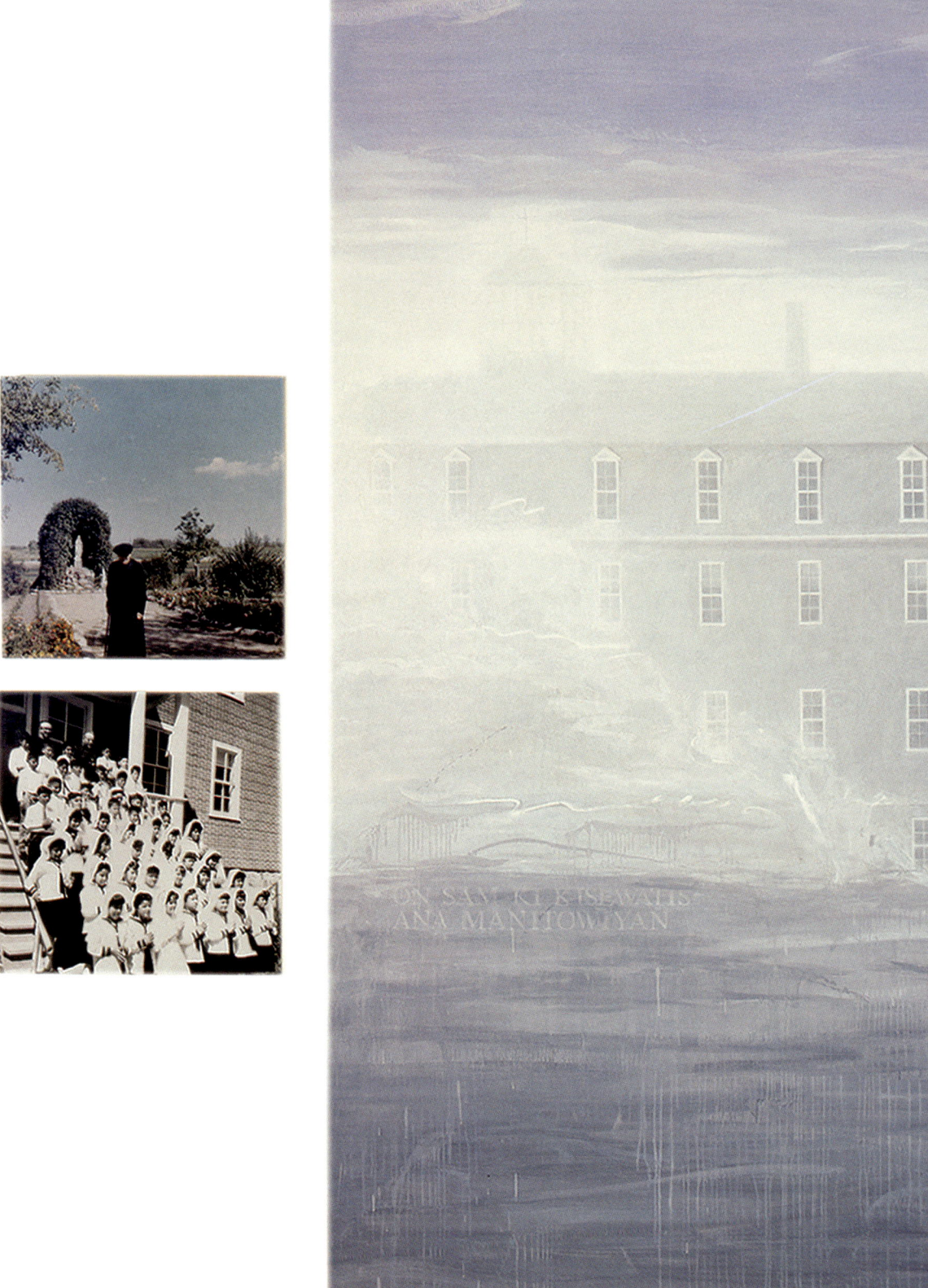

ON SAW KI KISEWATIS
ANA MANITOWIYAN

VII Visual Voices and Societal Concerns

"Only through spiritual renewal can we find out who we really are, be empowered to achieve our potential and acquire the wisdom to eliminate the influences that bring tragedy upon us and destroy us." [1]

Through history, as we have seen, the arts have always reflected society, its customs, cultures, and sense of place, frequently infusing the spiritual into the visual dialogue. The visual arts have likewise been a mirror for many crises and societal issues, and draw attention to both well-known concerns and to those not yet recognized by the community at large. The issues are wide-ranging. The year 2020, for instance, saw the impacts of the COVID-19 pandemic and the worldwide Black Lives Matter movements being added to the issues of Indigenous and minority discrimination, reconciliation, mental health, domestic violence, trauma, environmental controversies, and climate change. The subjects of Western Canadian artists also include shifting economic realities, increasing poverty, and inner-city homelessness, the lack of safe water in some northern Indigenous communities, residential schools, postcolonial injustices, and the many unresolved cases of missing and murdered Indigenous women and girls. Artists' insights into societal concerns over decades have been, and continue to be, critical. Their compelling messages and alarms, expressed in every visual medium, are calls to action for society as a whole.

The role of audiences is to see, to listen to, and to act on artists' expressions of societal alarms. The collective goal of artists is to improve societal circumstances. Artist Steve Gouthro once said to me, "One defining characteristic of art in Winnipeg in my time is a social

Robert Houle, *Sandy Bay*, 1998–1999 (detail).

conscience—art as being a purposeful way to try to improve society . . . in the 1980s a lot of art was being made to that purpose. Its root perhaps is in the Winnipeg Strike . . . the compellingness of the situation and the desire to respond to it."[2] More recently Indigenous artist KC Adams echoed that same sense. She, too, considers herself to be "a social-practice artist using the interaction of the audience."[3] Her 2015 *Perception* photos were done as a result of racist comments made by prominent citizens, and she was determined to overcome the erroneous perceptions of the city's Indigenous peoples. The series was presented on street banners, bus shelters, and billboards across Winnipeg. As she says, they "sparked conversations of racism."[4]

The preservation of human rights is central to any society's working effectively. Human needs and accomplishments must be articulated in order for rights to be acted on, and artists' visceral portrayals are critical to this articulation. Some artists express through allusion and metaphor; others, through suggestion or humour. One can only wonder what the result would be if these works of art were "heard" when they were created.

As early as the late 1930s and early 1940s, for example, Emily Carr became Canada's first, or certainly one of the earliest, environmental artists. Through her political visual–vocal protests, she drew attention to the devastation of the clear-cutting of British Columbia's primal forests. Four decades later, in the 1980s, clear-cuts remained a fundamental issue, and many artists actively protested clear-cuts in British Columbia's Carmanah Valley. Today, environmental advocacy across the country continues to be a preoccupation of artists calling for paradigm shifts in approaches to stewardship of the natural world.

The impact of postcolonial history is very much at the fore of societal issues, and vital visual expressions were created even before society took the situations emanating from the colonial era with any seriousness. The crisis of missing and murdered women, for instance, was visually and poignantly articulated in Rebecca Belmore's 2002 tour of her performance piece *The Named and the Unnamed,* presented thirteen years before the 2015 launch of the National Inquiry into Missing and Murdered Indigenous Women and Girls. Would lives have been saved if that inquiry had been established when this and other works first drew public attention to the issue? We cannot know, but as a society we must listen to the prescient concerns conveyed by artists.

Domestic violence, the gun culture, and issues of relationships and dislocation in contemporary society are other critical societal issues and these have been the focus of Winnipeg's Andrew Valko in a number of series over several years. Phyllis Serota relived her own past experiences of abuse and domestic violence in her work, as well. For instance, in her work *Kitchen,* she reveals: "On this table is only a bleeding fish. This is a painting about shame—the shame of having a violent father. I paint myself wearing a blue striped tee shirt at ten years old."[5] That composition is visceral. Its subject is far too frequent and widespread in civil society.

Space precludes a fully comprehensive discussion of the myriad social issues addressed by artists, or indeed the vast and substantive body of work advancing public concerns in civil society. As with other topics explored in this volume, the social discussions included here are based on my interactions with the artists, their work, and researches into their times. Thus, I have limited my considerations to works drawing attention to the environment and climate change; health, racism, and human rights; self-rule and postcolonialism; residential schools and reconciliation; missing and murdered Indigenous women and girls; and war and conflict.

Canada has hit truly painful "lows" at various points in our history. Racism and the residential schools are particularly dark chapters that affected the well-being and opportunities for generations of Indigenous citizens from coast to coast to coast. Yet, while plainly and honestly depicting many heart-rending situations, artists have frequently done so compassionately, in ways that are both healing and inspiring. By illuminating the searing gaps in justice and equality and the destruction of place and people, artists have provided constructive ways for communities and our nation to move to a better place.

The Environment and Climate Change

> "I am an artist interested in environmental issues and in inter-species communication, specifically interested in the power of the small."[6]

Environmental and climate concerns have been consistent themes in the work of many artists and include issues related to logging and forestry, acid rain, flooding, drought, fire, and the plight of endangered species. Some artists depict the outcomes of environmental disasters and record the consequential changes on society; others illuminate realities as they occur.

As I have noted, one of the first to depict the issues surrounding clear-cuts in British Columbia was Emily Carr, and she did so as early as the 1930s with her painting *Logged Over Country, Odds and Ends,* 1939, and *Logged-over Hillside*, circa 1940. She also addressed the issue of the spirituality and magnificence of British Columbia forests in her journal, *Hundreds and Thousands: The Journals of Emily Carr,* in which she wrote about both forest regeneration and the desecration by clear-cuts. The stumps in *Odds and Ends* are solid in form, rather like the foundations of long-ago torn-down buildings. Young trees reach skywards, interspersed between the stumps. She loved her summers spent in the woods and gravel pits in her caravan, the Elephant. She used the word "nature" in many of her writings, but one might wonder whether if she was writing today she would use the word "environment" instead. On 19 September 1935 she wrote:

> Yesterday I went into a great forest, I mean a portion of growth undisturbed for years and years. Way back, some great, grand trees had been felled, leaving their stumps with the ragged row of "screamers" in the centre, the last chords to break, chords in the

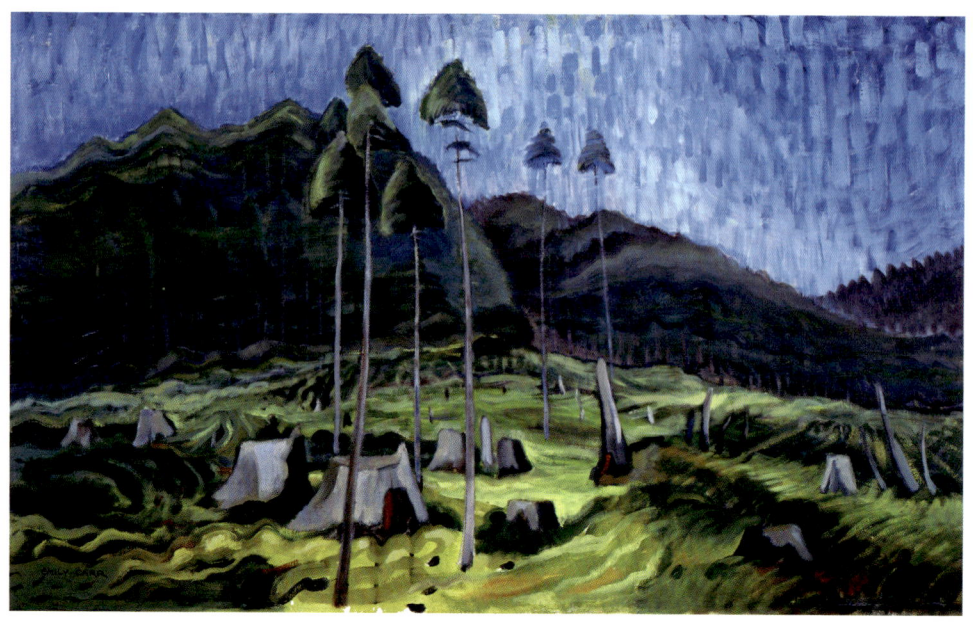

tree's very heart. Growth had repaired all the damage and hidden the scars. There were second-growth trees, lusty and fine, tall-standing bracken and sword ferns, sallal [*sic*], rose and blackberry vines, useless trees that nobody cuts, trees ill-shaped and twisty that stood at the foot of those mighty arrow-straight monarchs long since chewed by steel teeth in the mighty mills, chewed into utility, nailed into houses, churches, telephone poles, all the "woodsyness" extracted, nothing remaining but wood.[7]

Doug Morton (1926–2004), a well-known colour painter and member of the Regina Five, was also dean of fine arts at the University of Victoria and president of the Alberta College of Art. Joining many British Columbia artists in protest, he created his silkscreen print *The Big Trees,* 1989, in response to the Carmanah clear-cuts. His deep interest in and respect for nature are evident in this print. Rhythmic, curvilinear, intersecting forms and lines create depth of movement and growth. The geometric, stylized tree forms on either side of the composition have abstracted arm-like branches, seemingly holding onto and protecting the other various forms and elements. The axe shape in the middle of the foreground, above several vegetation forms, portends imminent danger to the forest. When talking about his overall oeuvre, Morton

FIGURE 7.1. **Emily Carr**, *Odds and Ends*, 1939.

said, "My primary interests are in integrating colour, form and symbols; it may be less obvious that in large part the imagery had its origin in nature, whether intentional or not."[8]

Artists have also given voice to endangered flora and fauna species. For many years, highly acclaimed British Columbia wildlife artist Robert Bateman has depicted animals of the West Coast and those from around the world. Before him award-winning artist Angus Shortt, of Winnipeg, focused his art on birdlife. Shortt's impressive career includes that as museum designer at the Manitoba Museum, the National Museum of Canada, and the American Museum of Natural History. Over a number of years he engaged in taxidermy as well as installations of bird and mammal displays. He executed naturalistic depictions of birds and ducks in flight for Ducks Unlimited, capturing their precise details of colour, proportions, flight patterns, and nesting sites. Winnipeg's Clarence Tillenius, often thought of as "the dean of wildlife painters,"[9] was likewise an environmentalist who advocated for the protection of wildlife. He realistically painted not only the wildlife but also the habitat of the myriad species he studied on his many research trips into the wilderness. His powers of observation are keenly evident in his artworks, many of which are presented at the Pavilion in Winnipeg's Assiniboine Park.

A current and particularly worrying international concern is the vastly dwindling numbers of honey bees worldwide. This was the focus of the work of Winnipeg's multimedia artist Aganetha Dyck for many years. Dyck began her career as a professional artist in 1976. With bees as her collaborators, her art has been at the forefront of international awareness highlighting the concerns about the diminishing populations of bees. Acclaimed nationally and worldwide for her bee collaborations and examinations of inter-species communication through her art, she consistently underlined the integral necessity of bees to sustain everyday life. Imaginative and otherworldly, Dyck's art has sensitized multiple audiences to the serious plight of the bees and their critical importance to human survival in food production. She has been invited to many scientific forums discussing the crisis, and her research has included residencies in the Netherlands, Britain, and France. In each she worked with bees, scientists, and beekeepers.

The way in which Dyck has linked science, art, nature, the environment, history, pop culture, and everyday objects underlines the power of the visual and the immediacy of its exchange of ideas and substance. She placed ordinary objects, such as sports helmets, skates, and purses, into beehives. The objects became part of the beehive, and when "complete," the works were either partially or fully covered in beeswax and honeycombs. As Dyck told the *Mason Journal* in her 2011 interview: "To begin a collaborative project with the honeybees, I choose a slightly broken object or damaged material from a second-hand market place. I choose damaged objects because honeybees are meticulous beings, they continuously mend anything around them and they do pay attention to detail."[10]

In 2009, in collaboration with Winnipeg's Martha Street Studio, she produced her print series *Dr. Eduard Assmuss 1865*, in which she combined past, present, and future. A rather primitive 1865 drawing of a bee in a book by nineteenth-century German bee scientist Dr.

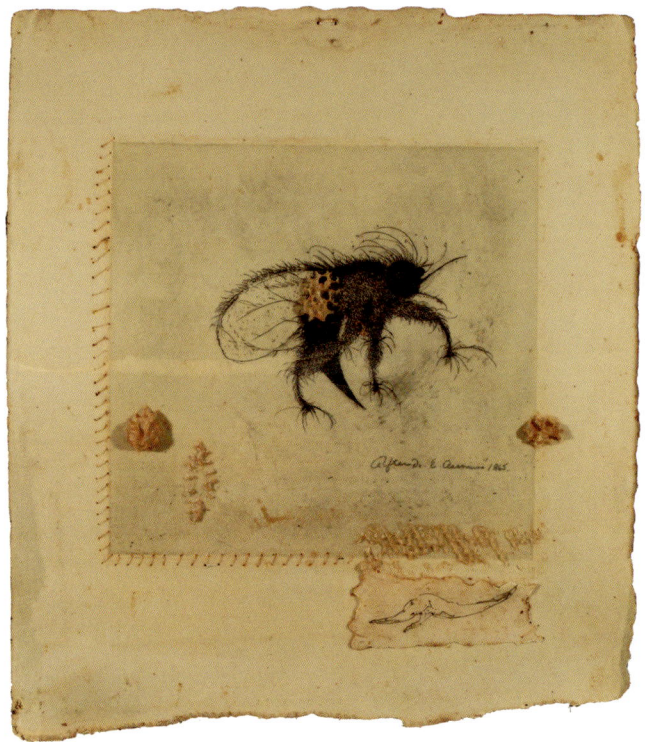

FIGURE 7.2.
**Aganetha Dyck
and Honeybees**,
*After Dr. Eduard
Assmuss 1865*, 2009.

Assmuss was her base. At the studio, she had assistance in drawing that image on a copper plate, and she placed the resulting prints in the hives for her collaborators, the bees, to add their honeycombs. The final works are sensitive and fascinating, each unique with differing placements and amounts of honeycomb. With her son, artist Richard Dyck, she created *Hive Scans,* a series of digital images of beehives. In some of these, the "hive" itself is crocheted, effectively linking this series to her more recent crocheted *Shrinks.*

The role of climate in the changing natural order around us was poignantly depicted in Manitoban Grace Nickel's porcelain memorial to Halifax's Point Pleasant Park, in the wake of Hurricane Juan that struck the region in 2003. Her ceramic installation *Devastatus Rememorari,* 2008, underlines the devastation of the trees, and her use of porcelain as a medium reflects both the preciousness and the precariousness of trees. The overall teardrop shape of the installation recalls the shape of the activity of the hurricane. The porcelain trees stand on a bed of salt, reminiscent of tears and of the ocean. Nickel balanced the surface decoration of each individual tree with the subdued palette of the work as a whole. Her artist's statement underlines her overall concept:

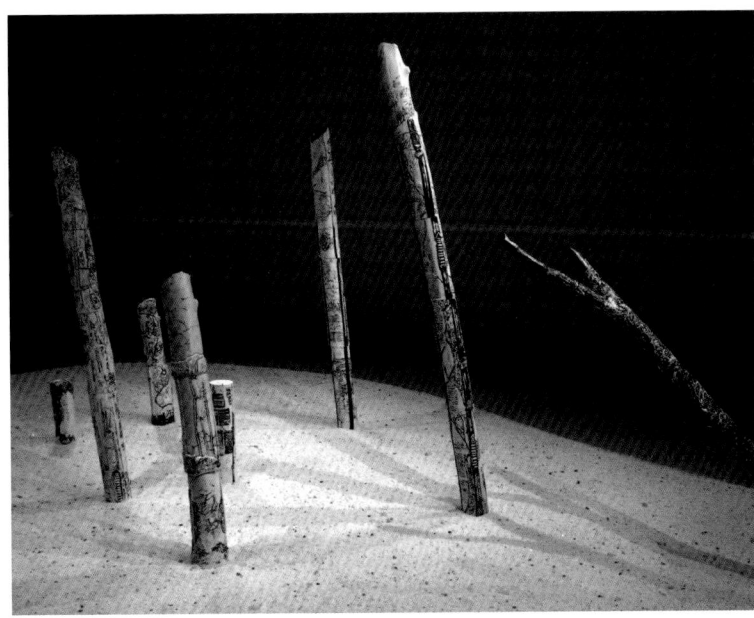

In my current work I am investigating the concept of devastated trees, damaged through natural phenomena such as floods, hurricanes, tornadoes or age, and also trees destroyed through human intervention. I have been collecting the remains of trees that have been broken, eroded, stripped of their bark, and cut. In my studio, these fragments have become metaphors for the inevitable process of decay and loss that occurs overtime. Using porcelain, I am attempting to rebuild the trees by making casts of the demolished remnants. In my reclaimed ceramic trees, organic motifs and text are embedded in the trunks or applied to the surfaces of the segments that are being pieced together in a symbolic attempt to help mend the ravaged trees. The reconfigured ceramic forms embody traces of the trees' history and stand as memorials to loss. At the same time, in my efforts to reconstruct them in clay, ... [this creates] a new textual "bark" for the trees. . . . The words *devastated* and *remembered* and their Latin counterparts *devastatus* and *rememorari*, are inscribed over and over again, imprinting a "texture of memory" on the porcelain trees. . . . I pay tribute to this cherished urban retreat.[11]

British Columbia artist Carole Sabiston's primary environmental concern is about the debris we leave in space. Various bits of debris float around the clouds and stars in many of her flying pieces, such as *Take Off: Point of Departure and Mode of Travel*, 1987–1989. This work was created only a few years after Mark Garneau became the first Canadian in space in 1984, and Sabiston was concerned about both the increasing amounts of debris from space missions and the presumption that it all would orbit the earth in perpetuity. A number of her works question what will happen to all that "stuff." As international space explorations increase and the accumulation of junk in outer space accelerates, Sabiston's textile assemblages are as relevant today as they were at the time of their creation. Given today's escalating global environmental crises, her clairvoyance in exposing these problems through her visual explorations in the 1980s and 1990s is poignant. She talks nostalgically of seeing *Sputnik*, launched in 1957, crossing the skies as she and her parents watched from their Victoria porch, sparking her ongoing interest in space, which continues these many years later. Of space debris, Sabiston has said: "The Flying Carpet, or as we fondly call it, the Magic Carpet, evoked the memory of childhood fairytales. You know, all children have ways of going on their magic carpets and finding their fantasies in the world. I've always wondered, ever since childhood, whatever happened to all those flying carpets from Persia. There must have been thousands that must have escaped, so I presume they are up there orbiting the earth along with the 7,000 pieces of space debris that the space programme has sent up."[12]

Sabiston has also voiced visual concern about our poor treatment in protecting rare species. *Flying Rufus*, 2009, her much larger-than-life hummingbird image, draws attention to the vulnerabilities of fragile species. Here she links flight in nature to her images of magical flight.

This concern for tiny fragile species continues in the work of Manitoba's Shirley Brown, a visual storyteller who throughout her art celebrates the many essences within nature around her. She uses paint, objects, and multimedia in her explorations of celebrity, power, and unforeseen disaster. Over several decades, for instance, she constructed delicate ossuaries for the remains of the twenty-nine flickers found behind the chimney in the family home in Turtle Mountain, Manitoba, after the death of her mother. "The discovery of these beautiful creatures along with personal losses compelled me to investigate the brief and precarious nature of time . . . and allowed me to explore my strong fascination with unexpected disaster."[13] Wanting to celebrate the unsung flickers' importance to our wider world, she presented these works with a museological precision and order, creating their world, where birds became individuals with histories and lives of their own. Each of the ossuaries is unique, bearing different interior and exterior fabrics and jewels and delicately drawn backgrounds. Each reflects the personalities of the particular tiny skeleton, underlining the preciousness of life for all beings, however small.

Brown fashioned a history for that imaginary ancient bird civilization with *Invasion,* the site for her mythical armies from the bird civilization and their final apocalypse. As Jack Anderson wrote, these "material traces and invented remains—artifacts such as shrines and reliquaries—coalesce into a picture of a lost fictional culture and its belief systems. While poetically pointing to cultural memory and our commemoration of the past, these elegant but somewhat creepy fragments more critically inquire into the way in which we hold and shape

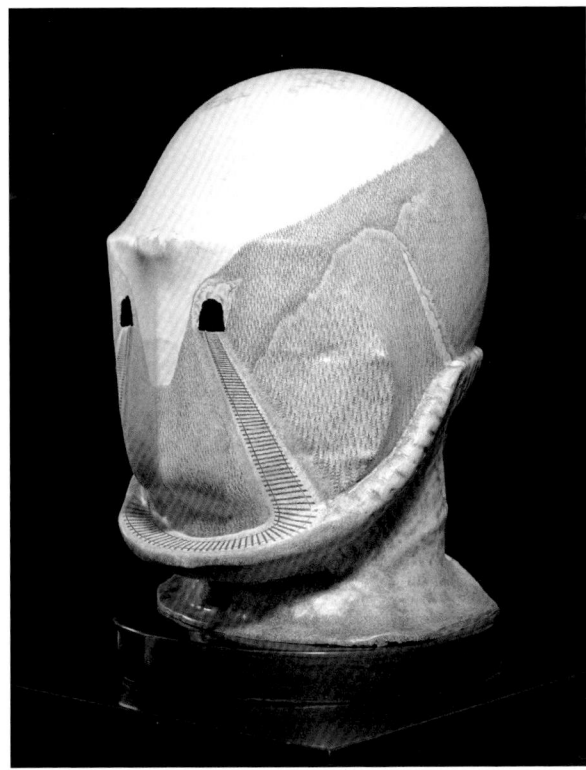

FIGURE 7.4.
Don Proch, *Rocky Mountain Mining Mask*, 1976.

memory."[14] The works are sensitive and reveal an artist who creates with the found, the known, and the unknown. Brown consistently invites her viewers to stop to think about the many delights of the world around us, yet simultaneously increase cognizance of our responsibility for the nature we share. Like Sabiston, she draws attention to the vulnerable beings in nature.

Don Proch juxtaposes critical contemporary environmental and social issues with Manitoba's geological and human history, Indigenous and non-Indigenous. His art embodies the dichotomies of rural nostalgia, intensified by present-day concerns and crises. Always sensitive to the past, he is particularly concerned for the future health of the land, knowing first-hand the devastating impacts of the increasing numbers of deserted rural towns and vanishing lifestyles. The overarching message in his sensitive and elegant oeuvre is the escalating environmental concern of acid rain. His seemingly simple, beautiful, and direct two- and three-dimensional art pieces are a clarion call for action to address today's worrisome environmental realities. He viscerally expresses the harsh consequences in the drawings on his masks and sculptures of the elevators, illuminating the interrelationship between land and humankind.

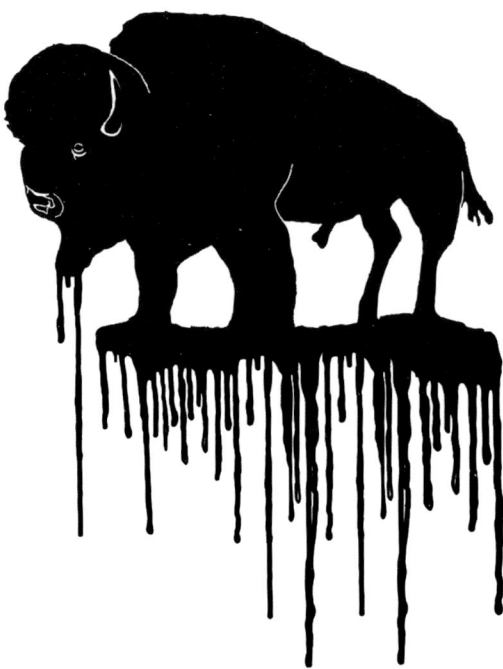

FIGURE 7.5.
Terrance Houle,
liniiwahkiimah, 2012.

Using the imagery of the place of his youth, the Asessippi Valley, and his repeated rural icons such as grain elevators, he underlines the need for humanity to secure rural sustainability. Foreboding and premonition fill these detailed portrayals of prairie skies and rolling hills. His characteristic clouds and their piercing extruding needles are sharp reminders of the dangers of acid rain and the dire consequential impacts on agriculture and the land. Proch challenges society to embrace the urgent need to stem climate change and steward the environment, and he did so long before the general society embraced the issue.

In 1976 Proch created *Rocky Mountain Mask,* a silverpoint, pencil, and coloured pencil work on a fibreglassed and inlaid silver wire construction. The black and white drawing on this mask has a rail line running in a continuous circle through the eyes as tunnels and around the chin and back. This seemingly directionless continuum imparts an ominous sensibility to the work as a whole, foreshadowing the rapidly changing technologies of transport and the perils of shipping hazardous materials by rail. The sides and back of the head of this work offer views of the forests in the mountains, executed in minute details. The cheekbones on either side of the rail lines are raised, creating a three–dimensional profile. A waterfall cascades down one side of the head and flows down the nose. Proch's use of his unique iconographical symbol, his stylized nickel waterfalls, denotes increasing environmental perils. This combination of the frontal view and a side profile in the one work gives a heightened human dimension to the sites of train accidents and derailments such as that in Hell's Gate, British Columbia, in 2017, and its resulting fuel spill in the Fraser Valley.

The effects of oil and pipelines are clearly apparent in much of the work of Alberta's Terrance Houle. He created his powerful work *Liniiwahkiimah* for the 2012 *O Kanada* exhibition in Massachusetts at the time of the first Keystone Pipeline discussions in the United States. A large vinyl decal of a buffalo dripping oil is on the wall with five car oil canisters on the floor below it. The artist told me when we talked about this work: "First Nations did not recognize boundaries and borders, provincial or that with the U.S. The buffalo gave us everything—home, spirit, and tools. The buffalo fed our people, and are still feeding our people. Colonialism killed our way of life and today we must end our dependency on oil and gas. The First Nations changed their way of life with the extinction of the buffalo; society must now change our way of life—we did it with the buffalo."[15]

Many of Wanda Koop's works over the years have included elements from her *Satellite City* images. In *The River,* 2019, there is a suggestion of those earlier compositions. Here the mood is one of melancholy. The greens and browns of the winding river and sky, with a touch of blue at the horizon, are all applied smoothly layer on layer. Two vertical drips of sharp orange-yellow flow down from the upper edge of the canvas, one stopping above the horizon line; the other falling towards the river. The tone is almost one of grief over the encroachment of climate change and the resulting impending loss of nature.

The disaster of Chernobyl's nuclear plant has absorbed Winnipeg's David McMillan since the 1994 accident. McMillan travelled to Chernobyl just several months after the devastating nuclear reactor accident, and recalls: "When I first ventured to Chernobyl in 1994, the experience was thrilling and totally absorbing. I felt I had found a subject both inexhaustible and consequential. I wanted to make photographs describing something I hadn't seen before, which had the potential to be simultaneously beautiful and unsettling."[16] As he said to me, "It was different from Winnipeg which I had explored photographically; its context was uninhabitable."[17] He returned to photograph the same places twenty-two times over the following twenty-five years, mostly in October, and when we met, he was hoping to go again. These resulting works have been acclaimed and published internationally. Their subjects are the calamitous effects of the nuclear explosion on a city, and include images of classrooms, hospital rooms, hotel rooms, machinery, gravesites, a playground, sports centres, and the landscape. In looking at the images of the same places over the years of his visits, one sees the ongoing decay and the intrusion of nature into the interior spaces with vines and trees growing like escapees from the outside attempting to get away from whatever the level of radiation might have been. His work is about the tragedy and the aftermath of the disaster, and, as he said, he brings to the fore "the proliferation of nature and the deterioration of the built environment. This is a tragic place, but one which continues to offer mystery and surprise."[18]

This series certainly portrays the end of a life and community as they had been known: the places are utterly uninhabitable. While McMillan engages in a visual discussion of energy, society, life after a catastrophe, and the changing landscape, for him it is more. The sum total of all these aspects carries with it both horror and beauty. The photographs are large, and the details are captured with perfection. In the *Music Room, Kindergarten,* for instance, over the time of his successive photographs, we see the deterioration of the classroom, which once had Soviet flags on the wall and a mural proclaiming the supremacy of the Red State. With the passing years the number of flags decreased: some were torn from the wall by looters, and others have disintegrated through natural deterioration. He found the flags metaphorically interesting, noting that "we think a civilization in its heyday can go on forever. Here we are left with vestiges of a past, remnants of Soviet culture."[19] A spot in the wall also deteriorates, and sections of peeling paint increase.

Author Claude Baillargeon wrote of McMillan's Chernobyl work:

> To grasp the full import of McMillan's work, not only its aesthetic merits, but also its unparalleled meditation on the resilience of nature, one must consider its temporal scope is unique and that its evolving subject can never be replicated. Drawing from firsthand observations gleaned in real time from twenty-five years of field experience, it might be argued that the resulting body of work lays bare nature's remarkable capacity to endure and recover from a radiological disaster as pernicious as Chernobyl. . . . McMillan's photographs confront us with compelling evidence of nature's sovereignty in the midst of unrelenting decay. . . . Nature's propensity to invade the built environment through structural openings is another recurring motif bringing forth the ostensibly incongruous symbiosis of growth and decay.[20]

McMillan likes colour. When he turned to photography he began experimenting with colour photography in 1977. He said, "Colour allowed me to escape the limitation of my palette as a painter. It seemed to transcend my limitations."[21] While much of McMillan's photographic career had been that of a landscape artist, his real interest is light. In taking the Chernobyl photographs, he used only natural light. There was no electricity. Sometimes exposures were over a minute, as he kept the lens open longer to get a brighter image. When he started the project he used two cameras, a 4-by-5-inch, and a 6-by-7-centimetre; both used film. That equipment was heavy to carry. More recently he has used a digital camera, and, for a time, all three. He was pleased with the fidelity he got digitally. Further, a digital camera is lighter to transport and the digital process is easier, as he could review and edit his images at the end of the day and was not reliant on developers.

Water has been another ongoing environmental and human rights concern that has drawn the attention of artists for decades. The issue includes more instances of flooding and of drought

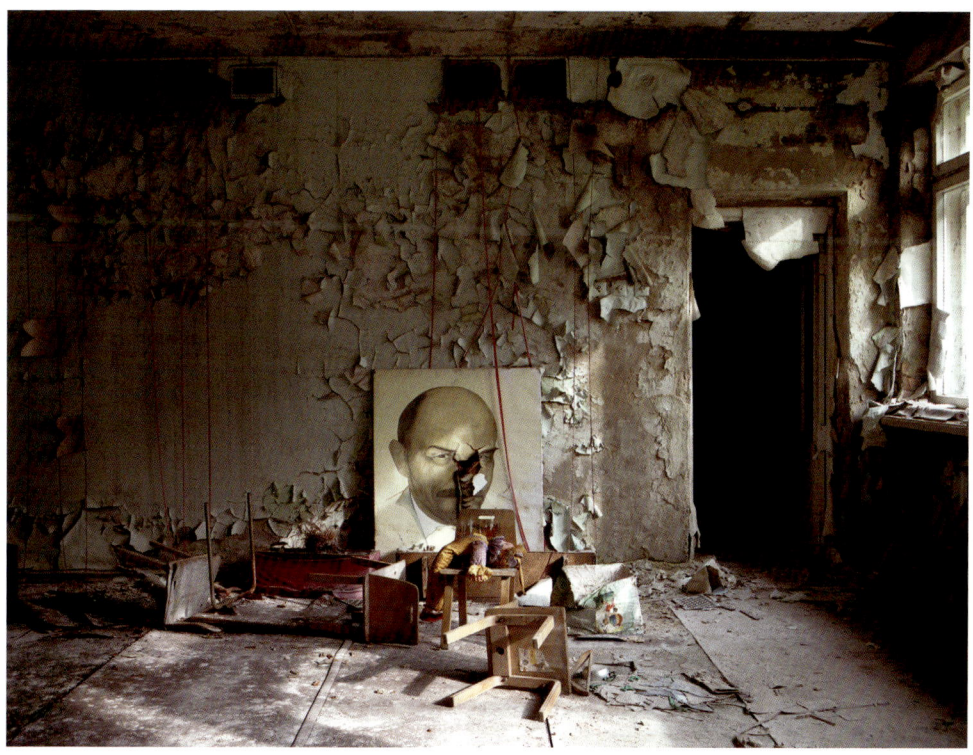

and the lack of safe drinking water in many northern communities. Recurring floods have caused both short- and long-term dislocation for many people and economic and agricultural crises. Climate change is increasing the intensity of storms and the frequency of flooding. Lionel LeMoine FitzGerald depicted the inundated southern and western Manitoba fields that he saw from the air during the 1948 and 1950 floods, and those vistas contributed to his development of abstraction.

Marianne Nicolson clearly underlines the importance of water to her Indigenous ancestry:

My ancestry comes from the Dzawada'enuxw of the Kwakwaka'wakw Nations. Our ancestral home is at Gwa'yi along the Kingcome River on the mainland coast of British Columbia. The river is our mainstay, a constant in an existence of unknowns. Our origin story describes our coming to live within this river valley in ancient times. In 2010, the Kingcome River experienced flooding of previously unknown

Figure 7.6. **David McMillan**, *Portrait of Lenin, Kindergarten, Prypiat*, from the series *Growth & Decay*, 1997.

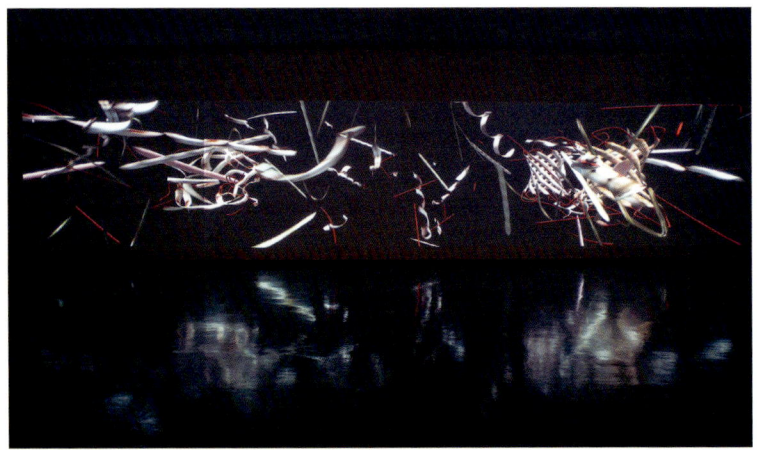

FIGURE 7.7.
Reva Stone,
Imaginal Expression, 2003.

proportions and the entire village was evacuated by helicopter. Since then the village has been rebuilt but the memory of this flood remains a tangible part of our day to day reality. In a sense the feeling of apprehension we experience at the local level seems to be also reflected in general society due to the uncertainty of global warming and the relationship between nature and industry that has influenced its birth.[22]

Her eloquent and haunting installations acknowledge the crisis of environmental concerns relating to water. Critic Robin Laurence wrote of her exhibition *Walking on Water (Thin Ice)*, 2012–13, that the dorsal fins that come out of the floor symbolize killer whales, "representing healing in Kwakwaka'wakw culture, while the blue glass represents glacial ice, . . . each fin is etched with a different figure: they're whales in human form and they emphasize the connectedness of all living things."[23]

Health and Human Rights

"Many contemporary Aboriginal artists offer their art to acknowledge and honour the ancestors and the way of life. In addition, the works have assisted with defining selfhood . . . the Aboriginal self. . . . The works portray the Aboriginal experience and imperative in all its complexities. To locate medicine through the application of art-making is an enormous undertaking. These artworks have the considerable potential to shift contemporary consciousness toward support of Aboriginal justice."[24]

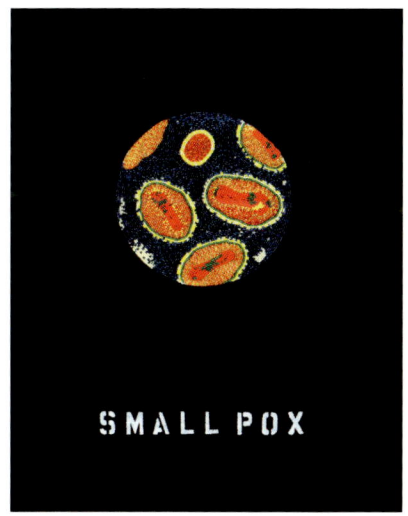
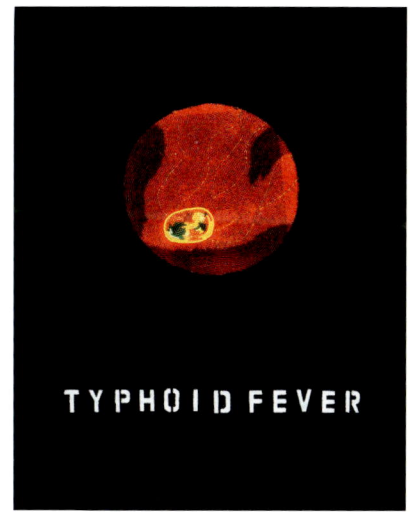

Health and human rights are overriding issues for all Canadians. The consequences of first contact of Indigenous peoples with Europeans had astronomical impacts on the health of Canada's First Peoples. Whole populations were wiped out by European diseases. Smallpox was particularly devastating to West Coast Indigenous communities, as tuberculosis has been for many people across the country. The death of large numbers of British Columbia's Haida Nation due to smallpox eradicated much of their culture. These and other historical realities, coupled with continuing human rights issues of housing, living conditions, safe drinking water, the ravages of alcohol, forced relocations, and high rates of suicide on reserves and in northern communities, are all core subjects in the art of Western Canadian artists. So, too, are the realities that refugees to Canada faced in their home countries and on their arrival in Canada. Issues of poverty, like those depicted by Maxwell Bates in 1947 in *Prairie Settlers* and *Prairie Woman,* and homelessness must be layered on top of those of racism, addictions, and mental and physical health.

The COVID-19 pandemic, causing thousands of deaths everywhere it touches, is ravaging the world as this book is in its final writing stages. The work of artists during the months of isolation across the country has given solace to the public and voice to the science, the isolation, and the psychological impacts of this virus. In her *Trading Series,* First Nations Saskatchewan artist Ruth Cuthand, recipient of the 2020 Governor General's Award in Visual Arts, brought the devastation of diseases to the fore in her beaded works portraying the microscopic cell

FIGURES 7.8 & 7.9. **Ruth Cuthand**, *Trading: Small Pox*, and *Trading: Typhoid Fever*, 2008.

355

structures of illnesses contracted by Indigenous peoples. They are both beautiful and chilling. Each work represents one disease. The images are seemingly simple—the molecule of each disease is depicted as it is seen through a microscope. One of the series, *Syphilis*, a pre-contact disease, is done in porcupine quills dyed with natural plants. The balance of the works are done with glass beads, symbolizing the impact of European contact: beads, which were traded to Indigenous people by Europeans, represent the diseases spread by Europeans. Each is done on an acrylic suedeboard black background with the name of the disease stencilled below the image itself. The images are circular, representing the petri dish used to put the microbes underneath the microscope. Installed together, the series is a powerful reminder of the past and the lasting devastating effects of European contact experienced through the generations to the present. Her series continues, the most recent subject being COVID-19, one version done on a surgical mask, representing the fact that masks were to be worn in public and that personal protective equipment (PPE) was in critically short supply at the outset of the pandemic. Many Indigenous communities did not even receive PPE.

Reva Stone addresses the human body and artificial intelligence in her *Imanginal Expression* series. For Yisa Akinbolaji, who moved to Winnipeg from his native Nigeria in 1997, the COVID-19 crisis brought back memories of his youth and the Biafran war. Those memories and COVID realities combined in his painting *Empty Playground, Silent Battlefield*, 2020. The image is rich, filled with detail, and his colour, which emanates from his cultural roots, is strong. Two doves with masks in their beaks fly towards the empty playground, symbolizing both peace in conflict and hope in the time of the virus. The playground structures and swings are painted in white, suggesting the innocence of childhood. He wrote:

> The effect of the Coronavirus pandemic on children, society and my childhood experience inspired me for the painting I title: *Empty Playground, Silent Battlefield*. I recall that when I was seven years, I forfeited playing outdoors in the evening after school to prevent injury from any bomb explosions during the Biafran civil war in Nigeria. . . . I feel that our contemporary society, workplace or the universe shouldn't be a battlefield for existence. My position with the painting is merely as a storyteller. In the painting, I provide visual footnotes of my own imagination. I also provide elements that convey with it a sense of truth about the global issue, to engage viewers and hopefully engender discussions. A focus is given a crucial timeline of human existence in the work because of the impact of the narrated circumstance on children that must not be ignored and in view of my own childhood account. I knocked out a component of my composition to suggest nonessential, yet that neutrality is my attempt to bring focus to it, recognizing that the future of a good society is determined by the attention and good foundation that is provided to its youth.[25]

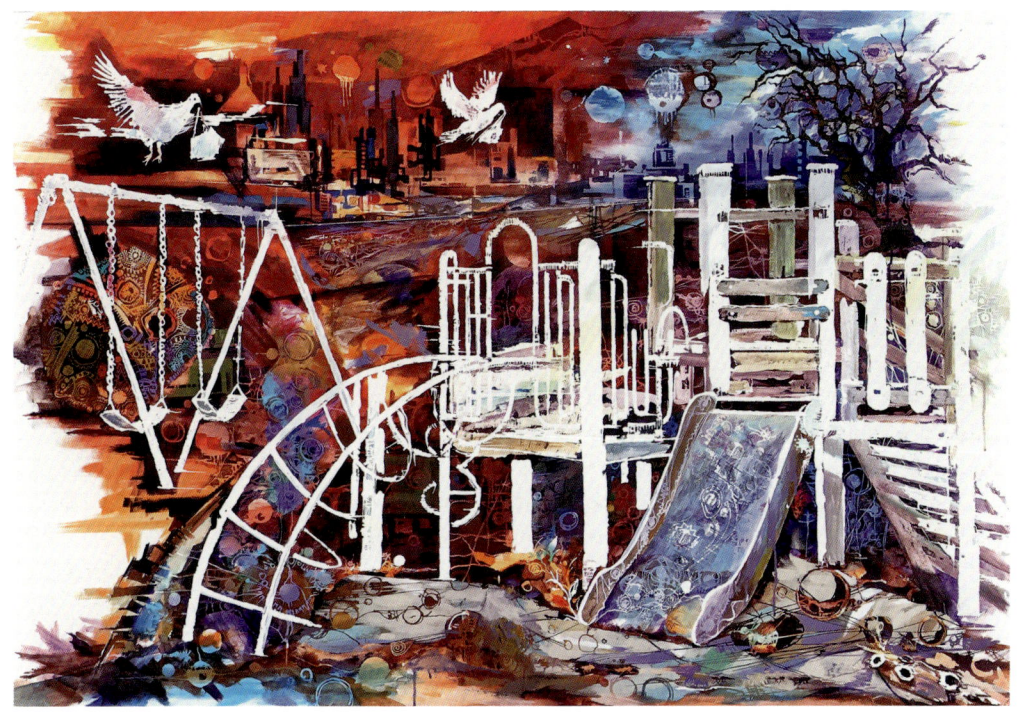

Robert Boyer, a First Nations artist from Saskatchewan and founder of the Society of Canadian Artists of Native Ancestry (SCANA), holds a significant role in Canadian art. A leader through his art and SCANA, he did much to foster an awareness of Indigenous art and changed its paradigm in the collections, exhibitions, and research of Canada's art galleries. Collectively and individually, Boyer's paintings are vivid and visceral commentaries on First Peoples' history in Canada. They address colonialism, environmental destruction, and Indigenous culture, and they call out injustice, betrayals, and cultural and political defeats. In his art Boyer overlays and intersects Indigenous and non-Indigenous visual traditions, an approach that highlights the depth and poignancy of his message, and did much to set the stage for twenty-first-century reconciliation.

Boyer's compelling series of *Blankets,* for instance, refers to both the oppression and aggression Indigenous peoples suffered at the hands of the British and to the spread of disease from contact with Europeans, the blankets themselves frequently having been tainted with infectious diseases. *A Minor Sport in Canada*, 1985, recalls the 1885 Battle of Batoche. The Union

FIGURE 7.10. **Yisa Akinbolaji**, *Empty Playground, Silent Battlefield*, 2020.

357

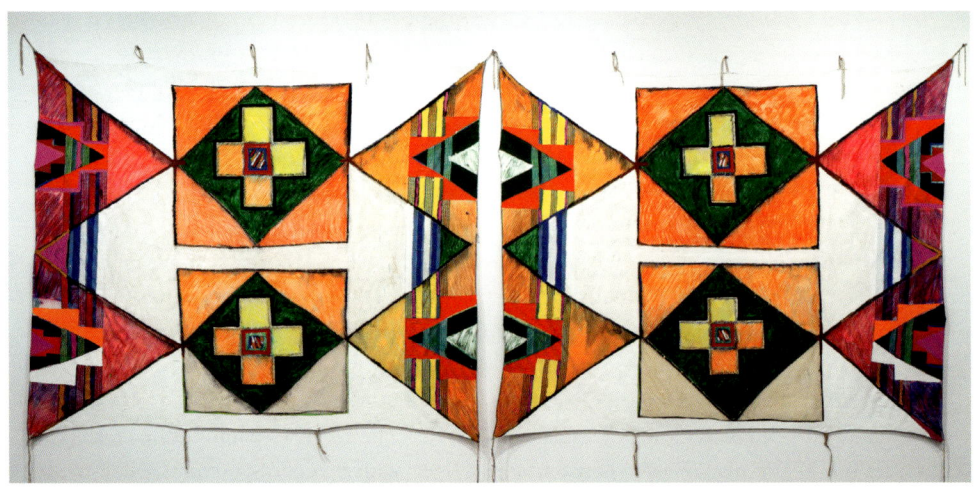

Jack morphs into traditional motifs of the Plains Indians, symbolizing the cavalier attitude of the British as they rode into Batoche and the battle that culminated in the North-West Rebellion led by Louis Riel and Gabriel Dumont. Red blotches of paint symbolize the Indigenous blood shed at that battle. Boyer's use of unstretched canvas equates to the Hudson's Bay blankets that spread the smallpox that killed large numbers of Indigenous peoples.

Christian Thompson has noted that Boyer's use of geometric designs reflects his personal experiences, social issues, and spirituality.[26] The 1980s and 1990s were a time when Plains First Nations and Indigenous peoples across Canada were actively recapturing their spiritual roots and reclaiming spiritual items from museum collections. In 1992 Boyer insisted a caption was to be posted in an exhibition; the caption read: "I don't consider myself political, I'm just very socially aware, which is different. If I were politically aware, I'd be afraid of some of the things I might do."

Through her art and through her activism, Rebecca Belmore has likewise played a truly significant role in leadership in the visual arts and in expanding the awareness, rights, and presentation of Indigenous artists' work. She was the first woman Indigenous artist to represent Canada at the Venice Biennale, doing so in 2005. She has also had residencies, teaching positions, and many solo exhibitions over her career. Her multi-story clay installation *Trace,* 2104, at the Canadian Museum for Human Rights, like the work of Boyer and Cuthand, draws attention to the post-contact spread of disease. Made of Red River clay, the beads in her installation were shaped by the public in many community workshops that involved people of

FIGURE 7.11. **Bob Boyer**, *To the End of Time*, 1986.

all ages and backgrounds. That wide engagement signifies the numbers of people who died of European disease. Hanging through four storeys, like a towel or a blanket on the back of the bathroom door, it epitomizes the extent of the reach and impact of disease and of the thousands who died. The dichotomies are clear: we wrap towels and blankets around us for warmth and coziness, yet this very symbol was the means of transmission of smallpox. Throughout her large body of work, her videos, two- and three-dimensional installations, performance pieces, and public art, Belmore points to many such injustices and realities.

Devastating illnesses past and the scourge of current ones, like cancer, affect families everywhere and permeate the work of many artists. The paintings of his self-reflection at the time of his own terminal illness consumed Winnipeg artist Kelly Clark in his last weeks of life as he was dying of throat cancer. His harsh yet truthful final series was published and exhibited posthumously in *In the Silent Hours: The Cancer Paintings of Kelly Clark*. They are insightful and very personal works. His widow, Janet Clark, reflected: "The series of paintings he created in the last six months of his life as he confronted laryngeal cancer records a remarkable journey from inner terror to serenity."[27] The images progressed in form and colour from emotional, angry, and visceral depictions to more accepting ones. Spewing volcanoes were the constant image in these works. The volcano was always dark, the lava core was red or yellow, and, in some, the letters "AEIOU" erupt into the sky. Mixed media, printers' ink, Letraset, newsprint, watercolour, and monoprints were all used to convey his pain and agony. The last, *Cancer Series #42,* was calm. Two snow-capped mountains, one red and one blue, were set before a full white moon in the night sky.

Fundamental issues of racism and human rights are also vividly expressed by artists, and their clairvoyance and insights are integral to society's ability to change. At the time of writing, racism in Canada was at the top of the public agenda among other issues including Canada's treatment of Indigenous peoples and the status of reconciliation, the recommendations of the Inquiry into Missing and Murdered Indigenous Women and Girls, and the injustices to Black Canadians and immigrants. Asian peoples have also been victims of human rights injustices and racism for decades. While difficult for many to express visually, these issues have become critical subjects throughout the bodies of work of a number of Western Canadian artists.

KC Adams's *Perception Series*, 2015, was transformational as it reverberated throughout many communities. Knowing the power of art to create, the artist's goals for this project were blunt and sincere. She was compelled to act given the systemic racist inequities across the country, past and present, but particularly after reading disparaging racist comments on Facebook and in *Maclean's* magazine made by leading Winnipeggers. At the same time, the devastating deaths of two Indigenous people, Faron Hall and Tina Fontaine, touched her and the city deeply.

Adams invited people to participate in her project through social media, and she received responses from Indigenous people from all walks of life. She had conversations with each. The image on the left of each pair of photographs shows the person's reactions to the slanderous,

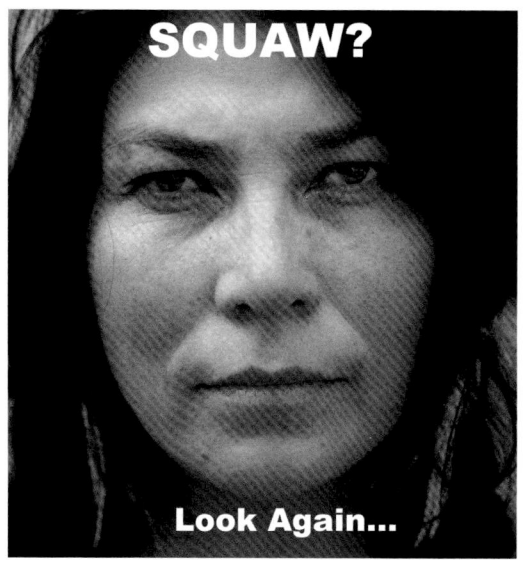
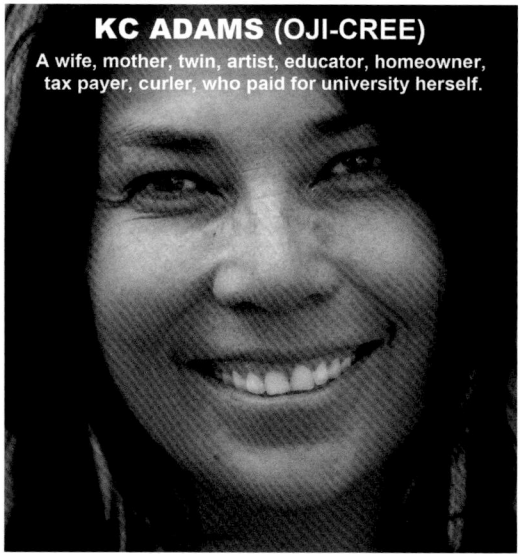

unjust, yet common slurs made about them. Those slogans are at the top of each. At the lower edge of each left-hand panel are the words "look again." The right image portrays them smiling, and the words at the top of these list their many accomplishments, reflecting their human and family dimensions.

Adams's strong series of dual black and white side-by-side portrait photographs of Indigenous people, done after the Idle No More movement, was not presented in art galleries. Rather, the works were installed outside in Winnipeg's streets, on bus shelters, billboards, walls, and posters, where gender inequality, poverty, and the effects of colonialism were being experienced by many people. The positive engagement was significant. After witnessing the public response to her work, the artist said:

> One strength of this work is that it doesn't point fingers at people—it emphasizes the injustice towards the original people of this land. The lack of confrontation allows viewers to react and ponder their own prejudices. At the same time, it gives a voice to the participants and shows the audience that they are staring into the eyes of human beings that deserve respect. . . . When I started this project, my intent was to combat racism and present First Nations, Métis, and Inuit people in the ways they see themselves. I expected some backlash, but instead got nothing but support.[28]

FIGURE 7.12. **KC Adams**, *KC Adams*, from the series *Perception*, 2014.

Human rights issues are also at the core of a number of works by Winnipeg artist Diana Thorneycroft (b. 1956). The spectacle of the Dionne quintuplets' exploitation, for instance, is but one event in Canadian history that captures her attention. The five Dionne sisters, born in 1934, became an Ontario tourist attraction, with every aspect of their childhood, including their outdoor play times and what they wore, being controlled and organized to suit public viewing. In *A People's History: Quintland,* 2010, Thorneycroft built the vignette with plastic toys, many bought on eBay. She dressed them in crocheted matching outfits of different colours. Though it is summer in the playground she depicted, the girls are wearing scarves. The doctor overseeing them is dressed in white, medical bag in hand. He has a camera around his neck, however, and thus feeds the marketing frenzy of the quintuplets. The scene turns to winter beyond the fenced play area. A tourist bus is off to the right with gawking people on the roof. Many others, voyeurs, are watching from a snowy hill, some sitting on a bench, settled in for a long stay. In the background Thorneycroft has depicted a Group of Seven northern Ontario landscape. Once her set-up for the work was completed, she photographed it, carefully adjusting the light to get the effect she desired. This thought-provoking digital photograph fascinates viewers, is seemingly fun and creative, but the tragedy and spectacle of the quintuplets' lives, which denied them any right of privacy or of living a "normal" life, is palpable.

The desperate plight of those with disabilities and crippling disfiguration is the focus of Diana Thorneycroft's installation *Herd,* 2018. She was deeply affected and outraged by the many disfigured beggars she witnessed on the streets in China, and how society callously passes these human beings by, ignoring their visible challenges. That carnival aspect of society's responses and the disregard for human rights propelled her to create *Herd,* consisting of 150 toy plastic horses. She has manipulated and disfigured half of them; many scream in agony. Each horse is unique, beautiful in detail and chilling in effect. She created unsettling disfigurations by melting the horses in her oven and adding human legs to some. She depicted the diversity of cultures by covering a few horses' backs with fabrics of varying textures and materials.[29] With meticulous precision she drew skin diseases, spots, dots, hair, and scales on them with colour pencil crayon. The seventy-seven altered horses and the seventy-seven unaltered ones are placed in procession, together, on a large, twelve-metre, wooden, ascending ramp, extending across the gallery space. The ramp is covered with snow and at its end the horses appear to be leaping through the gallery wall. Her vigorous presentations of the horrors faced by the disfigured, maimed, and tortured, contrasted by their surface beauty and delicacy, creates a sobering effect and a keen call to understanding, acting upon, and respecting of human rights.

Thorneycroft's work is tough. It is deep; it is challenging. She is a celebrated and keenly unique artist whose reach is wide. In its totality her work addresses issues of difference, alteration, and abjection. Sometimes, as in *Black Forest (dark waters),* she ties themes together as in fairy tales and mythology. Every work has truly approachable elements, plastic toys, landscape, or "heroes," but all give voice to serious societal concerns.

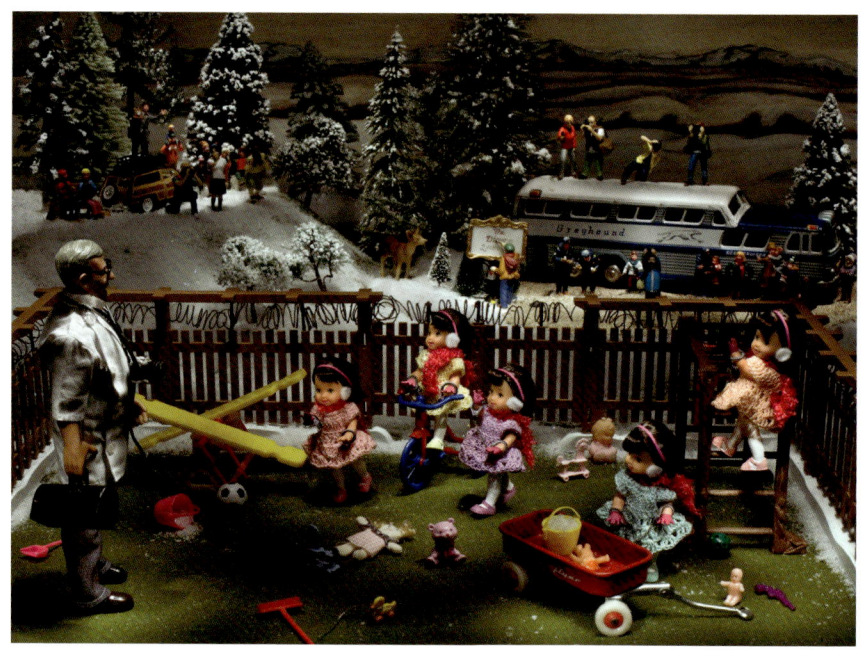

Vancouver's Simon Fraser University professor and artist Chantal Gibson, whose ancestry is Nova Scotian, examines the history of Black Canadians in her art. Her *Altered Book Series* is a demonstrative portrayal of the absence of Black history in Canada's written and taught history. She alters historical books themselves, using their covers, and either standing them up or stacking them. She replaces the pages by filling the covers with overflowing streams of braided black cotton or silk threads, themselves reminiscent of slavery. The books include *Who's Who?*, 2014, and *Braided Book, 2011,* the altered text of *A History of Canada, 1935*. At the time of my writing, Canada is facing up to the long overdue issues of Black Lives Matter, issues Gibson has been articulating for a number of years. In 2019 she created *Redacted Text,* an altered *Canadian Encyclopedia,* in which black liquid rubber flows out of the cover of the top volume in the stack and pours down those below. She says:

> My collection of altered history book sculptures is an ongoing project that explores
> the boundaries and limitations of "the book" as a bound container of fixed truths.
> Black thread is used as a rhetorical device, as a metaphor for written text and a marker
> of Otherness—and new voices.

FIGURE 7.13. **Diana Thorneycroft**, *A People's History (Quintland)*, 2010.

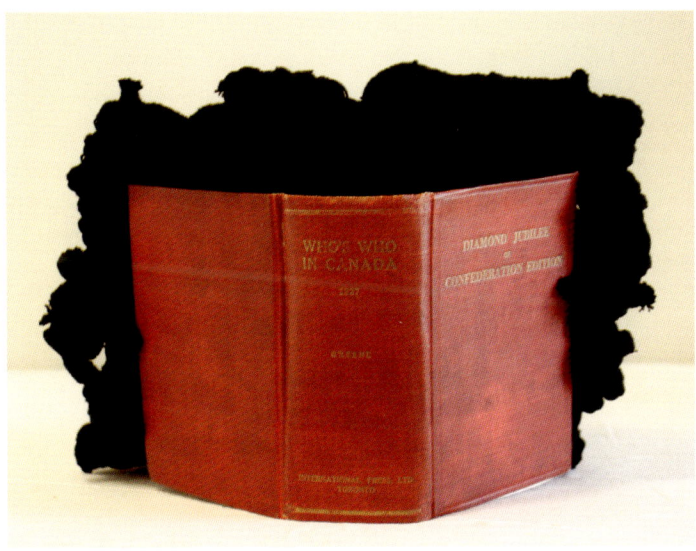

FIGURE 7.14.
Chantal Gibson,
Who's Who?, from
the series *Historical
In(ter)ventions*, 2014.

The braided, twisted, knotted material challenges what has and has not been said—erasing, redacting, editing the written content. The organic forms act as an extension of the content and make silence visible. These works challenge the ideas and ideologies embedded in the texts, reinterpret master narratives, and create new possibilities for reading and writing history.[30]

In some of the presentations of her work, she invited the public to participate by braiding the black silk for the installation and to create collages from the pages she had cut out of the book. Her call is to rewrite our history to reflect rightly on the Black history of Canada.

Karin Jones of Vancouver, a multidisciplinary artist whose background is in jewellery, is interested in examining how historical narratives shape us, and she, too, draws attention to the lack of African Canadian history in the nation's published and taught histories. Her elegant, compelling, and intricately detailed *Worn: Shaping Black Feminine Identity,* 2015, made of braided hair extensions and surrounded by cotton bolls, some stuffed with her own hair, addresses the presence/absence of Africans in Canada's historical narrative. She develops the symbolism and meaning of *Worn: Shaping Black Feminine Identity* in her artist's statement:

For me, the Victorian mourning dress is a symbol of sadness, "high" culture, the British Empire, and the constraints of feminine beauty norms. Here, I have made one out of African "hair"—actually a synthetic material created specifically for use in African-style braiding techniques. The work underlines African hairstyles as a craft as refined as any decorative art produced in Europe; it alludes to the invisible labour of the thousands of Africans who contributed to the wealth of the British Empire; and it references the story of Sarah Baartman, an African woman whose silhouette helped shape 19th Century European fashion. The dress rises from a bed of cotton bolls and African hair bolls, a mythic figure born of the cross-cultural forces of colonialism, commerce and slavery. I wear my African-Canadian identity much as a Victorian woman would have worn this type of dress: proudly, but also uncomfortably, shaped but also constrained by it.[31]

Jones began working with hair as a medium as a way to question ideas of authenticity of racial and cultural identity. A subsequent body of work, consisting of objects of adornment from 2018, furthers this theme of historical narrative. Each bears a restraint, such as chains, steel, repurposed leather from horse tack, brass, and various found objects. As she says: "I am examining the ways in which the historical narrative of slavery has shaped the identities of people of African descent living on North American soil."[32] Jones's art, like Gibson's, opens understandings as to who we are as a nation. The need to be honest about our history, and the work of both artists, are particularly poignant during the Black Lives Matter movement and in light of the 2020 protests.

Also drawing protests across Canada in the second decade of the twenty-first century is the human right to water, politically and culturally. This issue also is a prominent subject in the work of Western Canadian artists. Tanya Harnett of Saskatchewan's Carry-The-Kettle First Nation teaches at the University of Alberta, and her series *Scarred/Sacred Waters,* 2014, brings attention to contaminated water on First Nations reserves. Manitoba's Lita Fontaine highlighted critical issues around water in her photograph *Mni Wiconi, Water is Life*, drawing from multiple images in the Water is Sacred: Stop Energy East protests at Winnipeg's Forks, the meeting place for Indigenous people for many millennia at the junction of the Red and Assiniboine rivers.

Robert Houle, member of the Sandy Bay First Nation, has addressed many issues of history and culture of Canada's First Nations. The revelations about the lack of safe drinking water in a number of First Nations' reserves spurred Houle to create his 2018 Water Series including his painting *Mishipeshu and Water Spirit.* In this work, Mishipeshu divines for water, his red lightning rod penetrating the large white mountain, or cloud, in the foreground. The yellow background, with Houle's characteristic drips of paint on the left edge, forms half the composition and runs diagonally from the lower left to upper right. Yellow often symbolizes hope, light, and wisdom, and, in this work, enhances the mythical role of Mishipeshu. Depicted through millennia of Indigenous art, Mishipeshu is a figure whose form is an amalgam of a number of animals.

FIGURE 7.15. **Karin Jones**, *Worn: Shaping Black Feminine Identity*, 2014–2015.

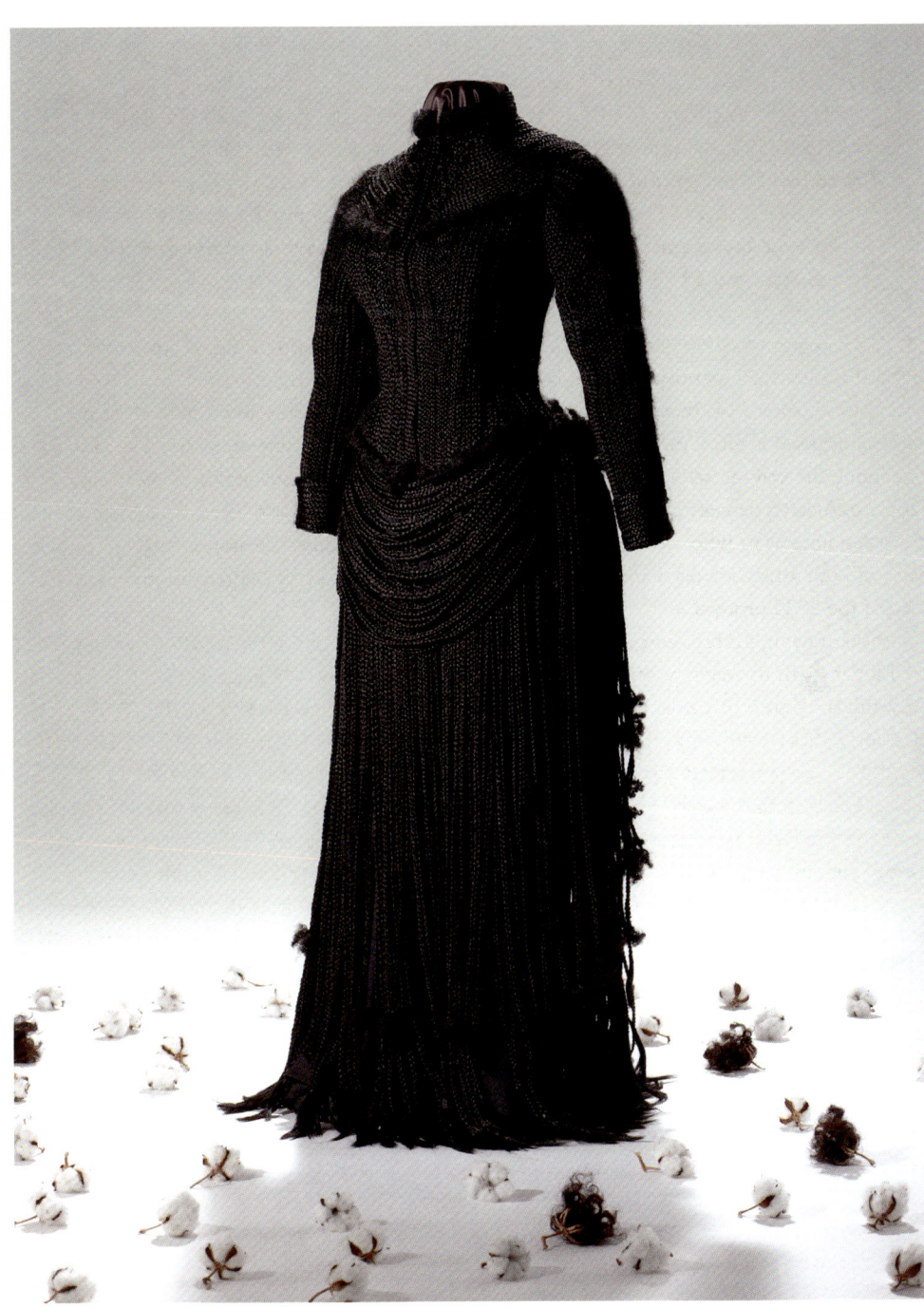

Houle has depicted him with the horns of the bison, an animal central in the lives and myths of many Indigenous cultures. Mishipeshu, the central underwater creature for the Ojibwa, is considered as the protector for some and a danger to others. In this painting Mishipeshu is the Shaman, using his healing powers to interact with the spirit world through ritual and divination. Through Houle's traditional cultural beliefs for hope and wisdom, this seemingly simple work emanates a powerful depth. It was included in his 2018 solo exhibition in Toronto, *Looking for the Shaman*. Throughout his art, teaching, and writing, Houle has consistently focused on his cultural roots and Indigenous history and is a leader in reclaiming rights and self-rule for Indigenous peoples.

Indigenous artist Jackie Traverse reveals a truly important aspect of Indigenous spirituality in her painting *White Buffalo Calf*. The importance of bison to the history and life of Canada's First Nations and Métis people is clear, and White Buffalo are considered sacred or spiritually significant in a number of Indigenous beliefs. *White Buffalo Calf* reflects that rich spirituality, and the artist has included white handprints linking the human dimension with the white buffalo's spirituality. Lita Fontaine also depicts the spiritual history in her 1996 painting *The Pagan*. The blue background and the red, yellow, black, and white stripes evoke the symbolism of the medicine wheel.

The issue of missing and murdered Indigenous women and girls is yet another devastating social matter across Canada. Grief, loss, and chilling abhorrence in response to these horrific, and largely unsolved, crimes are only some of the emotions felt by Indigenous and non-Indigenous people alike. Canada's Inquiry on the situation has been completed but its recommendations were not implemented when this book was written. Nonetheless, the issue has been poignantly expounded upon over several decades in the visual art of Western Canadian artists who have drawn attention to the catastrophic disaster.

Rebecca Belmore presented a vigil in Winnipeg at the turn of the millennium which became her video *The Named and the Unnamed*. It was performed at night in a gravel parking lot in the Exchange District. The light came from the headlights of a car, as did the music. The solemnity of the event was moving and heart-rending. Mesh had been installed on the wall of the building next to the lot. Roses and tags were distributed to those present, and we all wrote the name of a woman or girl whom we knew, or knew of, who had been murdered or was missing. The roses were then placed by the attendees into the mesh, creating the final visual— an old Winnipeg brick wall covered with red roses. This impassioned happening preceded the Inquiry by many years.

FIGURE 7.16. **Faye HeavyShield**, *Sisters*, 1993.

FIGURE 7.17. **Jaime Black**, *REDress Project*, 2014.

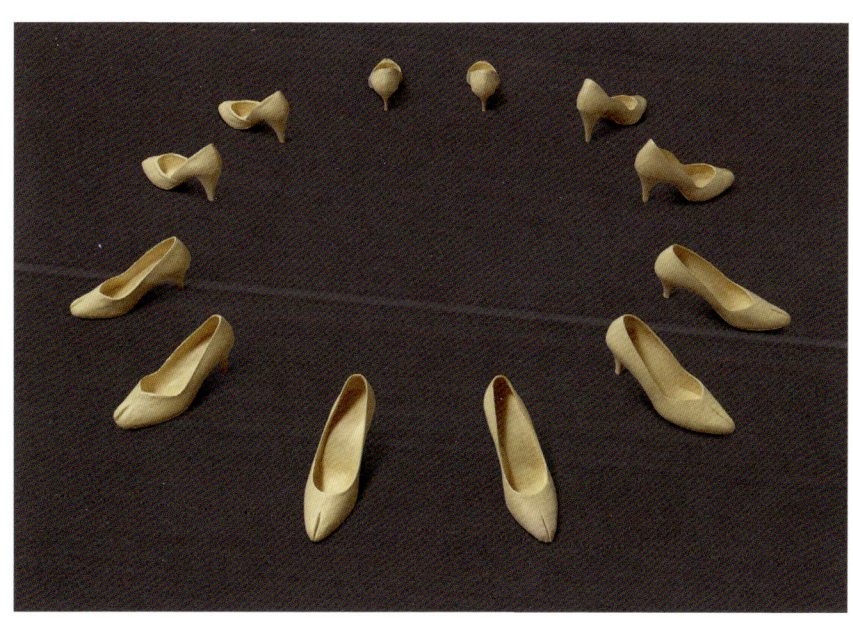

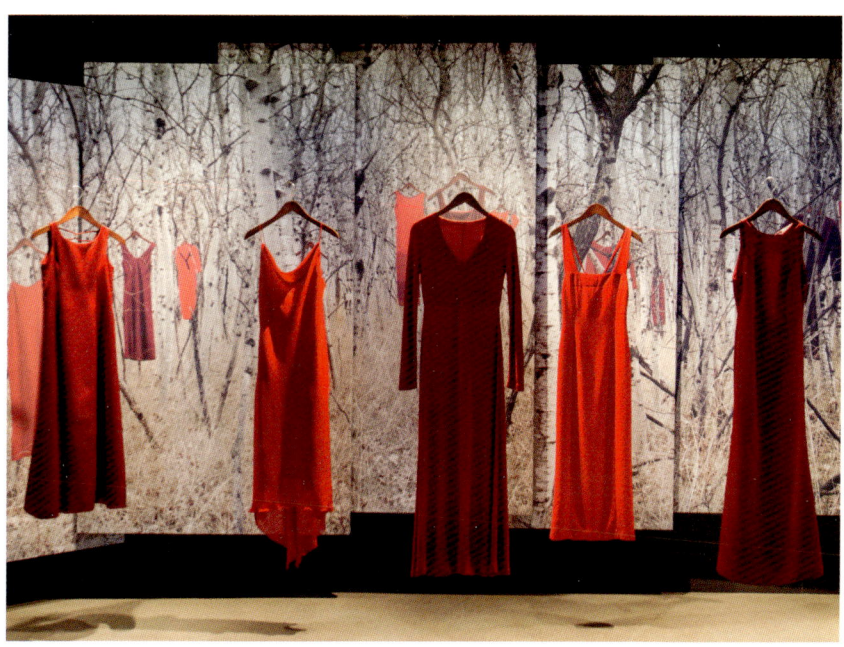

In 1985 Faye HeavyShield executed her work *Sisters*. It consists of six pairs of gold high heels, on a black circular stand, positioned in a circle with the toes pointing outwards. The six pairs represent HeavyShield and her five sisters, and symbolize the strength of women. Although the work was not done initially to call attention to the situation of missing and murdered Indigenous women and girls, it certainly emphasized the need for circles of protection for women. A circle represents the cycle of life, the spirit and the universe; the connection between family solidarity, feminism, and the societal situation of the missing and murdered women and girls cannot be ignored.

Winnipeg Métis artist Jaime Black's *REDress* project, initially presented in 2014, has become an annual installation and has grown to include sites globally in honour of the missing and murdered women. The red dresses, symbolizing the women who might have worn them, hang in windows, off trees and fences, and in public and private spaces. It began as Black's expression of her own grief and overwhelming connectedness with missing women. The artist's statement illuminates her purpose:

> The REDress Project focuses around the issue of missing or murdered Aboriginal women across Canada. It is an installation art project based on an aesthetic response to this critical national issue. The project seeks to collect 600 red dresses by community donation that will later be installed in public spaces throughout Winnipeg and across Canada as a visual reminder of the staggering number of women who are no longer with us. Through the installation I hope to draw attention to the gendered and racialized nature of violent crimes against Aboriginal women and to evoke a presence through the marking of absence.[33]

The annual installation so positively affected Alberta Indigenous artist Terry McCue that he created a visual tribute to missing and murdered Indigenous women and girls, which grew to a series of sixteen works and the exhibition *Ripples of Loss*.

Edmonton artist Tristen Jenni Sanderson has also done work to draw light to the issue, one in particular titled *Not Invisible*. Her work has likewise had international response. She elucidates her goal and ensuing works with passion:

> I'm trying to show the world this is a serious issue and a problem. I want to show the world and it's amazing that it's actually happening. The paintings feature the face of an Indigenous woman superimposed on a feather. The face is covered by a red hand print. I drew the Indigenous woman looking up and strong and proud. The hand print is red because they say a spirit can only see in red in the spirit world. So, when you put that on . . . it's calling the missing Indigenous women back home. Putting that on their face is like: "We're here and we're not going to be silent."[34]

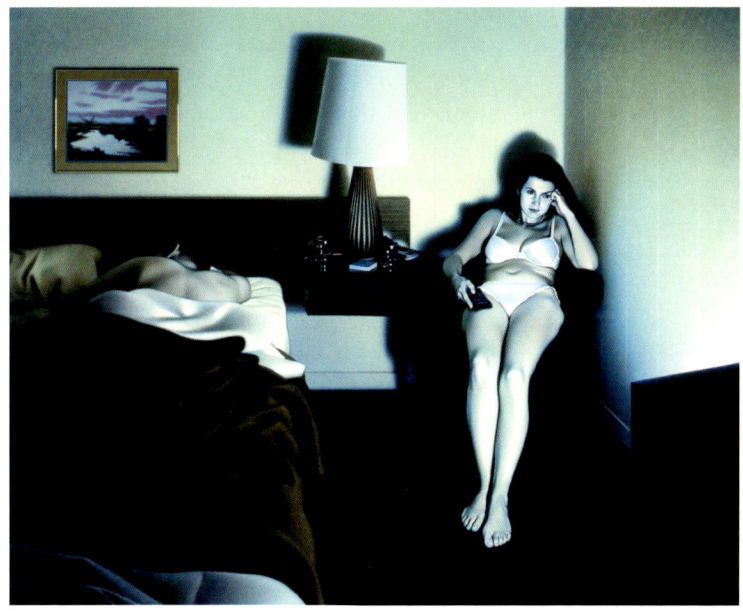

FIGURE 7.18.
Andrew Valko,
Sleepless Night,
1997.

Domestic violence is a very real scourge on contemporary society, and artists frequently draw attention to issues of relationships and vulnerabilities. In *Caressing Room*, Bev Pike draws attention to spaces of intimacy. Czechoslovakian-born Winnipeg artist Andrew Valko gives presence to these issues through his series of visual narratives in which the viewer is cast as voyeur. Valko hired models to pose for his unique commentaries on contemporary society, and he probed particularly disturbing and threatening situations in his *Motel Series*. The viewer looks into the motel rooms and witnesses ambiguous relationships and often disquieting scenes, which Valko says he purposefully sets in motels because of their nondescript character:

> I have major themes drawn from contemporary culture. . . . I'll get an idea and go around and take images. I get ideas all the time but have certain themes that appeal to me. I have sketchbooks where I do drawing. I develop the characters and story and put it together. . . . The female form, nude or semi-nude, is a reoccurring presence, often represented within the pleasure grounds of travel and escape. These sites of pleasure are fraught with danger, anxiety or detachment. A lot of my work is painted in night light, a time of melancholy and transitions. . . . Sometimes, these sites of pleasure or escape turn into scenes of unexpected loneliness and abandonments. The anticipated encounter in the get-away motel becomes a banal engagement with the television.[35]

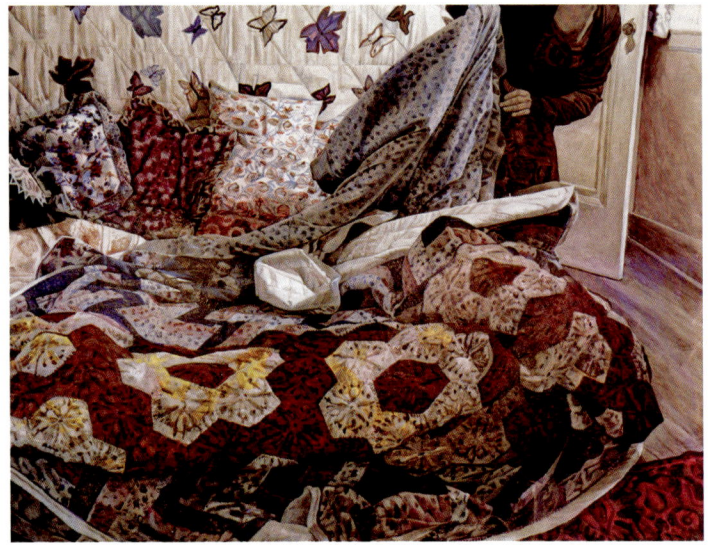

FIGURE 7.19.
Bev Pike, *Caressing Room / Frôler*, 1992.

The architecture and external and internal light of a particular motel on Kingsway in Vancouver captivated Valko. The "stuff" of the room became his props. A television, camera, and mirrors set the drama and tension as he combines objects and reflections to achieve maximum depth and apprehension. The figures are merely characters in his visual story. A semi-clad, seemingly distant woman is caught in a specific moment on the edge of a bed, or slouching in a chair. A gun might be on a table, or a male figure with his camera coolly focused on things other than her. One can but surmise the reality behind the theatre-like scene. Valko told writer Robert Enright: "I leave my paintings open-ended and in a lot of cases I don't know what the story really is. . . . You load the paintings up with clues and suggestions and little hints. I like the fact that they're multi-layered and that everybody can interpret them in a different way."[36]

Valko photographs the models in his studio, and they are unaware of the ideas he is contemplating painting. He is meticulous, and with technical perfection he applies the paint in many layers, attaining a smooth surface. His choice of colour is deliberate, specific to the mood, and the repetition of tones throughout the work increases its mystery and intensity. Valko comments: "I paint the light, not the objects. I want it all to be there but it has to have content, composition, colour use, subtlety and beauty. Beauty is very important. I want the paintings to be good on all levels."[37] Through his purposeful dichotomies and tensions, he exposes human vulnerabilities, psychological complexities, fragile individual relationships, and his own fascination with beauty. Minute details enhance the darkness of his messages. Compelling, his work simultaneously attracts and repels the viewer—the disquieted loneliness in the paintings is transferred to the viewer.

Inequality, injustice, and societal superiority fills much of Esther Warkov's early works, many set in Winnipeg's North End. She consistently used her own visual narrative to bring such social inequities to the fore in her detailed, symbol-filled paintings and unique two- and three-dimensional paper works. She emphasized: "I express myself through my work rather than through words. I am not just working automatically; the works are the presentation of ideas in progress. . . . My work is a mixture of thought and feeling. It comes from my soul, from a wordless connection to something greater. I grasp the direction of that something and through research and exploration I am able to express it visually."[38]

Warkov was a successful figurative painter who embraced surrealism and modernism early in her career, and she developed a highly personal visual vocabulary and creative methodology. People around her, her community, her Jewish heritage, the Underground Railway, and her North End Winnipeg roots continuously provided her with material, as has her vivid imagination. She combines art historical references, images from popular culture and daily life—particularly scenes from the bus window—and her highly complex, intense personal symbols. Some symbols have universal meanings; others are invented for her own purposes. Her work, whether two- or three-dimensional, has multiple qualities, combining dreamlike, enigmatic sensibilities with the harsh realities and at times the darker side of life. Her art always poses unanswerable questions, and her ability to observe what lies behind contemporary society's inequities and to invent techniques was observed early in her career in a 1968 *Time* magazine article, which described her as

> a painter with a highly personal sense of imagery and an uncommon ability to communicate a sense of the sinister. . . . Warkov's paintings are usually made up of several canvases hinged together—a device that gives free rein to her bizarre compositional sense. . . . The artist crams her canvases with observations of the passing scene—then embellishes them with a set of recurring, compulsive symbols: roses, wombs, wings, revolvers. . . . She says, "I am trying to create a mood, and anyone can make up their own story. When confronted with figurative images, people think they have to be doing something specific. But that isn't necessarily so." . . . It is Warkov's sense of irony that lifts her paintings beyond mere technical brilliance.[39]

Many of the same figures recur in her paintings, which in some ways trace the rapid development from rural to the metropolitan that has caused the problems she highlights. Professor Kenneth Hughes wrote: "Warkov, like other artist peers, sees the megalopolitan and ideological tendencies of modern technological rationality as like to cut off man from nature—external as well as his own inner potential—to produce fragmented robots who do not conform to her humanist ideals. Her works therefore address themselves to major questions at the heart of the Western European cultural and aesthetic tradition."[40]

Of her early inspirations, curator Philip Fry opined in 1972: "Some critics have said Esther's paintings are unkind, bitter, or even cruel. Others find that these works unveil meanings usually hidden from view in our everyday life. What viewers will find in Esther's work depends to a large extent on their attentiveness to the problems of the contemporary world. Her combination of images reveals the contradictions that make up the fabric of our daily experience: the struggle between birth and death, love and hate, past and present. But Esther's work only reveals this struggle; her images never force a conclusion."[41]

The performance art of Shawna Dempsey and Lorri Millan shines concerns on many social justice issues, too, including prejudice against the LGBTQ+ community. A major work of theirs that has had substantial acclaim over the years is *Lesbian National Parks and Services,* an ongoing series of performances and videos with accompanying printed matter designed and produced by the artists. This performance work was originally conceived when they were at their 1997 residency at the Banff Centre. The artists, dressed as park rangers, again set out to draw attention to several issues. First, it was "a visible homosexual presence in spaces where concepts of history and biology exclude all but a very few." Second, in their words, they sought to "*queery* . . . that icon of Canadianness by satirizing the commodification of the Banff wilderness in their site-specific performances."[42] They handed out maps of Banff, which noted both real and imaginary attractions, and they subsequently developed merchandise and published a Field Guide enhancing the project further. Less than ten years after the first presentation of *Lesbian Rangers National Parks,* same-sex marriages became legal across Canada in July 2005. Sadly, all the material they created for this performance piece was lost in the disastrous studio building fire in Winnipeg in the summer of 2019.

All these artists and many other of their peers have addressed and continue to address societal issues of health, poverty, classism, injustice, and inequality, some with harshness in their approach, and others presenting the seriousness of the realities with gentleness and surface beauty that heighten their message.

Self-Rule and Postcolonialism

"One only has to look at the dismal statistics of social, economic, political, and spiritual deprivation to see what disinheritance by colonization, marginalization, and invalidation has done to aboriginal societies."[43]

The impacts of colonialism are deep and offensive. All First Nations, Métis, and Inuit people have been affected through several generations. In order for them to begin to heal, the history, however painful, must be known. Fortunately, artists are bringing the histories to the fore, bluntly and unequivocally. Kent Monkman, Robert Houle, Dana Claxton, and Lawrence Paul

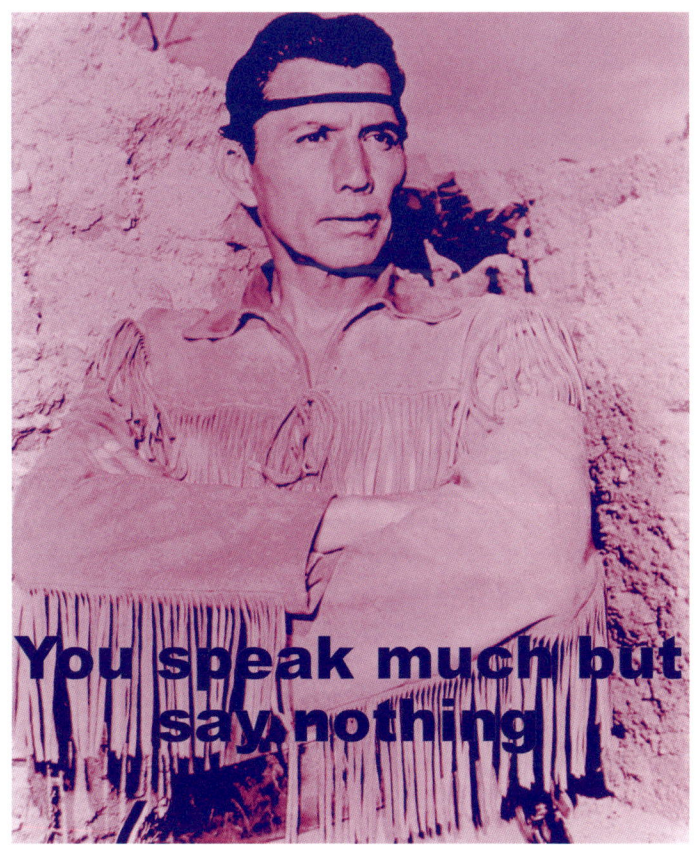

You speak much but say nothing

FIGURE 7.20.
Dana Claxton,
Tonto in Pink,
from *INDIAN
CANDY*, 2013.

Yuxweluptun are four artists whose work focuses on postcolonialism, self-rule, and sovereignty. Their art is not meant to be comfortable. Presented with passion, knowledge, and consistent values, it provides a place of discovery. Each of these artists defines the difficult unequal realities of Canadian society today while delineating pathways to a right and better future.

Dana Claxton (b. 1959) is a recipient of the 2020 Governor General's Award in Visual Arts, and a University of British Columbia visual arts professor. She expressed the situation straightforwardly: "Indigenous people have been structurally dehumanized in all facets of life in North America, whether it's through education, through the state, through the Church. In some ways my work has attempted to show us as human beings."[44] Her spiritual roots are core to her work: "My work has been about spirit-ancestors-NDN ways of knowing—Lakota teachings—generosity / wisdom / fortitude / courage / and more spirit / celebrating and honouring ourselves / and never surrendering / showing our NDN beauty."[45] Multimedia, multi-sensorial, her art includes video, installation, and performance, and the overlap of the visual and audio in her installations and videos brings the viewer into the images and dramas she presents. "I'm influenced by my own experience as a Lakota woman, a Canadian, a mixed-blood Canadian, and my own relationship to the natural and supernatural world," she said. "That whole bundle of experiences goes into the artwork, I think that's where the multi-layering comes in, because I've had a very multi-layered life."[46] Her ability to weave multiple artistic disciplines as she weaves history, the spiritual, the present and the future, her tangible and intangible ideas and inspirations, is to be celebrated. Claxton's observations are keen; her knowledge, deep. To her the sky is paramount: "I have been taught through Lakota teachings and spiritual teaching that it's all about the sky. It's all about watching and pondering, and about how the sky will show you things."[47]

Claxton's 1997 video *Buffalo Bone China* underscores the importance of the buffalo, illuminating the spiritual and physical significance of the buffalo in Indigenous Plains cultures. She smashes pieces of bone china and makes four bundles from the shards. The bundles are then arranged in a circle, which in Lakota culture is a sacred formation symbolizing the cycle of life and the sun, the moon, the earth, and universe. Her video plays in this circle. As curator/artist Tina Willard notes: "The breaking of the china refers to the exploitation and decimation of the buffalo."[48] British and Europeans had brought their bone china cups, saucers, and plates to Canada, and thus her incorporation of these in the work marks a poignant reference to colonial history. *Buffalo Bone China* is a metaphor for the destruction of Indigenous culture, and the dichotomies of the visual overlays of history, cultures, and time frames are redolent.

Winnipeg-born Cree artist Kent Monkman (b. 1965) has received significant national and international acclaim for his art, which highlights history and societal inequities to Indigenous people. He said about his work that it is "somehow related to or inspired by my Native heritage and the place that I sit between two cultures because I am of mixed blood, so I think I've always been trying to define that place in between to some degree."[49] Monkman's *Urban Rez Series*, with buildings and corners of Winnipeg's North End as their setting, is powerful and insightful. Characters in them tell the stories of loss of dignity, loss of rights, and loss of self. As he said in a CBC interview in October 2019: "The *Urban Rez Series* is about what it means to be Indigenous and the influence of the Church and Christianity, including residential schools, and the serious violence against women."[50] Throughout his oeuvre he draws from major works in Western art history as part of his means of laying bare the realities he depicts, intensifying his goal, which is "fighting for change in the culture, the art and politicians on the front lines and trying to change how the country represents Indigenous people to become the point of strong hope."[51] That is evident in *Death of the Virgin (After Caravaggio)*, 2016, his acrylic on canvas that shows the victim in bed with a blue cover and a person dressed in a blue hoodie kneeling beside. The blue of each is symbolic of the Virgin Mary. Mourners are on the far side of the bed. One is drumming. The composition itself recalls that of sixteenth-century Italian

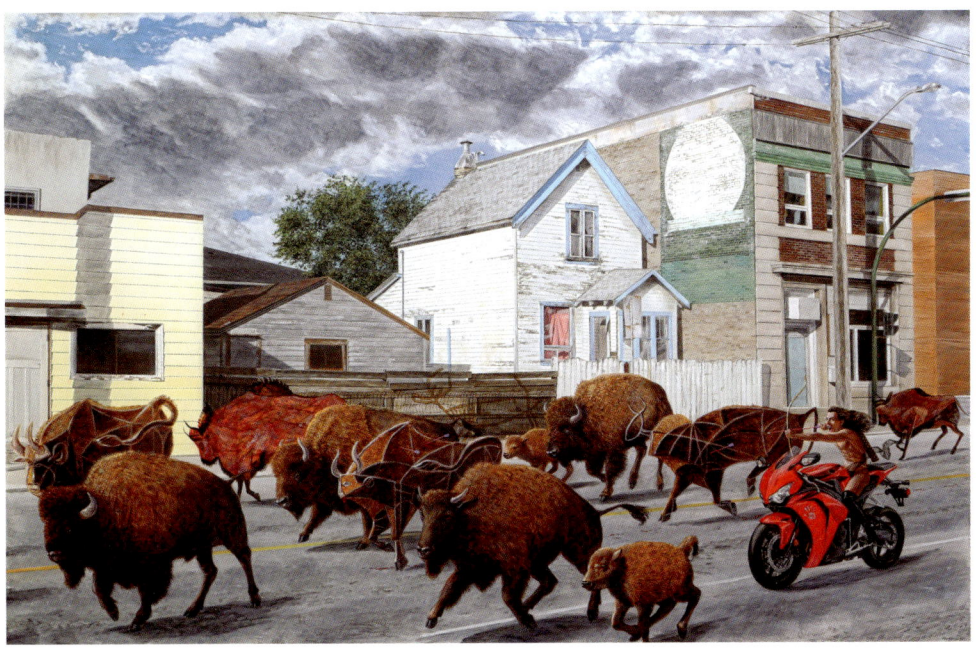

painter Caravaggio. In *Struggle for Balance,* 2013, Monkman again draws elements from art history, transforming them to recount his contemporary perspective on Indigenous realities. Set outside a dilapidated, old North End house, an eagle and angel fly over a burning car, and a youth runs away from a street fight with a hammer in his hand. The constant figure in his paintings, Miss Chief, tells the stories of abuse, violence, and dispossession. As Monkman said: "Most Canadians have no idea that their country was founded on dispossession and a genocide perpetrated against Indigenous people. There is no soft language to counter the hard language of the colonial autocrats who executed these policies. . . . I wanted to rely on the power of the painting to communicate the layers of emotion and horror and the depth of what that experience could mean to people, and I was relying on history painting itself."[52]

The vulnerability of women and Indigenous people generally across Canada as a result of colonialization and residential schools is an essential part of the history that must be told for change to ensue. It is clear that Monkman leads through his art, adding to the canon of both past and present Indigenous and world art history.

Cowichan/Syilx First Nations artist Lawrence Paul Yuxweluptun likewise elucidates the harm, lack of rights, issues of land claims, and environmental concerns in his compelling

FIGURE 7.21. **Kent Monkman**, *The Chase*, 2014.

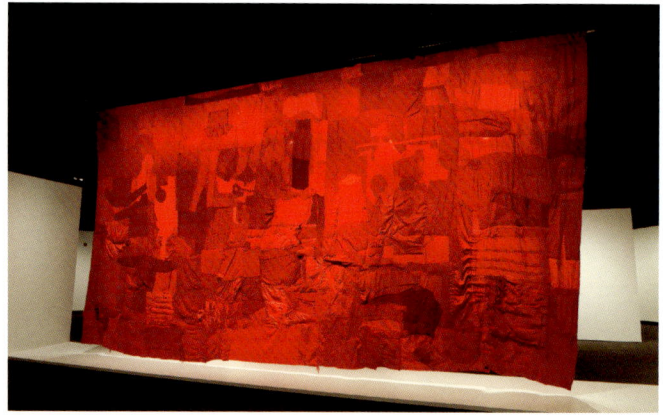

FIGURE 7.22.
Brian Jungen,
People's Flag, 2006.

paintings. In his work elements from modern art, surrealism, pop art, and abstract expressionism and his Indigenous imagery combine to portray the stark reality of the subjugation of First Nations at the hands of the Europeans, but also simultaneously underline the power and strength of Indigenous people. Yuxweluptun frequently portrays suited businessmen wearing West Coast First Nations' masks, as in his 2014 acrylic on canvas *Fish Farmers*. Some are suggestive of boardroom, corporate confrontations; others mark the importance of the environment and the spirituality and heritage of West Coast trees. *Red Man Watching White Man Trying to Fix Hole in Sky*, 1990, an acrylic on canvas, underlines the severity of the environmental issues, and the history and stature of Indigenous people. He included elements of surrealism akin to Dali's *Persistence of Memory,* though with Indigenous symbols covering the mountains and forming the Red Man figure. The power of his stylistic approaches and his symbolic imagery are gripping and transformative to the viewer. Strong colours enhance his message. His multiple stylistic aspects within his paintings are aptly discussed by art writer Karen Duffek, who notes that the artist himself dubs his approach as "visionist." Duffek continues: "Lawrence speaks of himself always as a modern artist. He stakes his territory by being First Nations and asserting that he has the right to use all art styles and forms as he wishes. . . . He uses the non-referential aspect of abstraction, that is, isolated forms on a canvas that have no cultural references but that direct back to his titles with the political points he is making."[53] Politics is at the heart of all his paintings. Writer Beverly Cramp commented: "Whether the topic is Aboriginal rights, land claims, reservations, missing and murdered women, or environmental degradation, he's got plenty to say."[54]

In 1994 Robert Houle created a series of five large, authoritative, and impressive works emphasizing unrealized self-rule and sovereignty. These include: *Premises for Self-Rule: The Royal Proclamation, 1763; Premises for Self-Rule: The British North America Act, 1967; Premises for Self-*

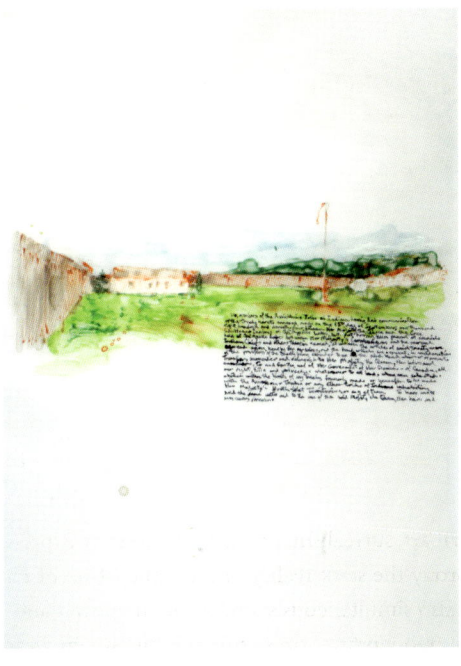

Rule: Treaty No 1, 1871; Premises for Self-Rule: Indian Act, 1886; Premises for Self-Rule: Constitution Act, 1982. Like others in his oeuvre these are multi-panelled and mixed media. The left panel of each is painted in a single colour: one is blue, two red, one green, and one last yellow. The right panel of each is text, a paragraph from the treaty or statute from the original document, each of which confirms the government's commitment to self-rule. Mounted on each text panel is a photograph taken from a postcard that in turn recalls the time and/or event of signing, one being a residential school. The colours are bold, and the brushwork is strong and evocative. The artist's message is clear—Canada has not lived up to the intent or words of the documents.

Canada's treaties with the First Nations are not First Nations treaties. Rather, they are shared treaties of, for, and by all Canadians, the promises having been made by and for *all*. Non-Indigenous Manitoba artist Tim Schouten underlines this collective responsibility in his *Treaty Suites* project. His goal was to bring attention to the long-term accountability and troubled cultural trusts that emanated from those formal agreements. He draws from history and his own sensibility for the prairie, and the landscape is his primary entry point, as seen in *To Have and to Hold the Same (Treaty 4),* 2008. Schouten visited each treaty site and researched each treaty and the subsequent impacts. He interviewed Indigenous Elders and Indigenous and non-Indigenous historians. These shared histories are philosophical archaeological digs and a foundation for dialogue towards constructive, meaningful futures, honouring the intent of the initial treaties. Like Houle, Schouten also incorporates text—clauses from letters, the treaties, or contemporary

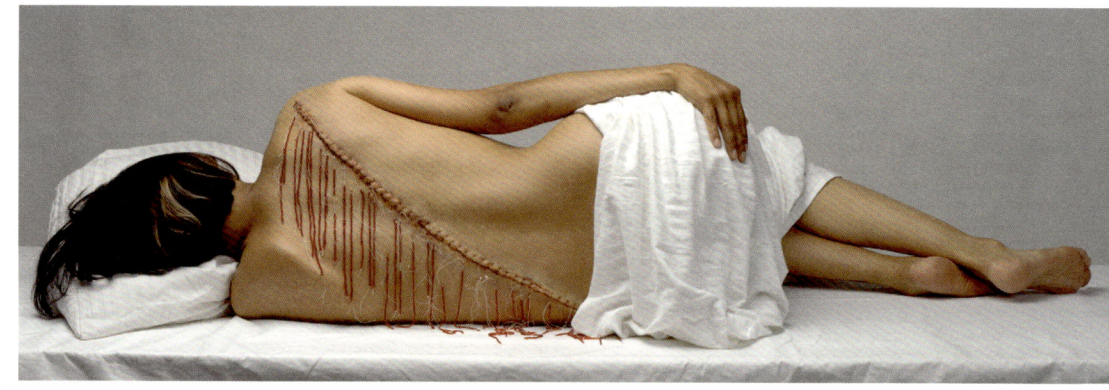

journals. His work is executed in wax on parchment or canvas, and he portrays the rough terrain, long horizons, and characteristic prairie light. His tools are brushes and hot irons; the wax is heated in old crock pots. As the series evolved Schouten's works became highly textured, layered encaustics, wax mixed with raw pigments, earth, and sand from the particular site, and as the series progressed the landscapes have become increasingly abstracted.

Rebecca Belmore's penetrating work of many media, including her performance and installation art, addresses multiple postcolonial issues and is often about survival itself. As she said: "My work often deals with the elusive equality of memory. . . . The importance of the act of remembering becomes essential in works that are often created as memorials. Current history and place become crucial elements for understanding the complexity of the terrain that we inhabit."[55] The piece for the Venice Biennale was a film, *Fountain*. Curators Jann Bailey and Scott Watson wrote that it "deals with elementals or essences: fire + water = blood. . . . The element of water is represented both as a body of water in the projection and literally as a wall of falling water. Water turns to blood. As befits our times, we do not know whether this is a metaphor for creation or an apocalyptic vision."[56] As expressed in the curators' description of this work: "*Fountain* called for a reworking of the term 'postcolonial' and addressed the trivialization of indigenous viewpoints in the contemporary global society. With the help of Winnipeg filmmaker Noam Gonick, Belmore's work is a demonstration of the preciousness of water, both as a natural resource and as a product used in the European building of monumental fountains as emblems of conquest. As a projection of water Belmore said: "I think my choice of projecting onto water itself is to acknowledge its power and our relationship to it. We are approaching a time when water could be an issue more serious than oil."[57] Belmore said the transformation of the water into blood is symbolic of "the brutal history of the relations

FIGURE 7.24. **Rebecca Belmore**, *Fringe*, 2008.

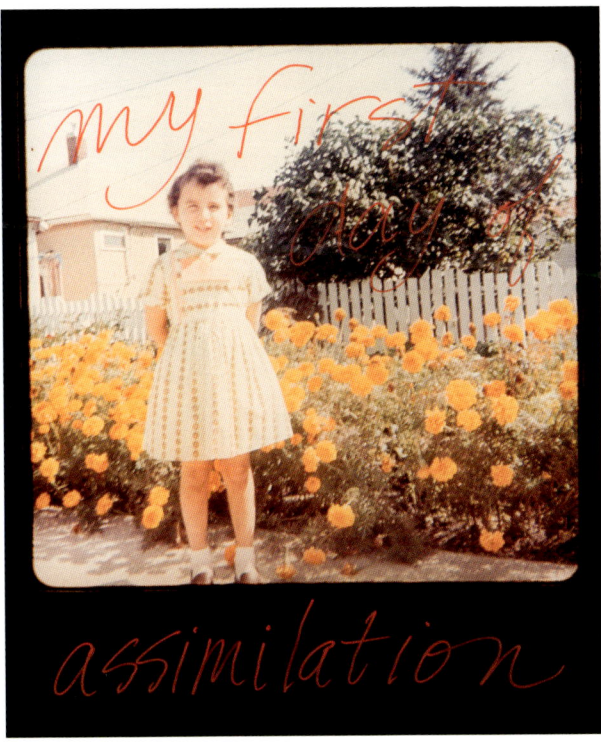

FIGURE 7.25.
Rosalie Favell,
*My First Day of
Assimilation*, from
the series *from an
early age*, 1994.

between Indigenous peoples and European society is reflected."[58] Artist Robert Houle said of Belmore that she has "emerged as one of the most polemic artists in the international contemporary art world."[59] She is also fearlessly prophetic and not afraid to deal with societal issues using new experimental and/or traditional materials.

Many of the issues arising from the decades of postcolonial attitudes, actions, and power affected Rosalie Favell (b. 1958). Winnipeg-born and of Métis and English background, Favell has done a number of visual narratives in which she searches for her place and identity in the world. Working in series, she used family photographs to delve into her personal and cultural history:

> In *Longing and Not Belonging* (1998) I explored the similarities between the family photo album and the ledger art of the plains warrior artist at the turn of the nineteenth century that acted as a record of the exploits and history of the maker. This work also explored the realization of the heroes in my life, strong women . . . my mother, my sisters, my aunts and my grandmothers. I placed images of these women with warrior women from popular culture that in turn highlighted their quiet heroism. In this work

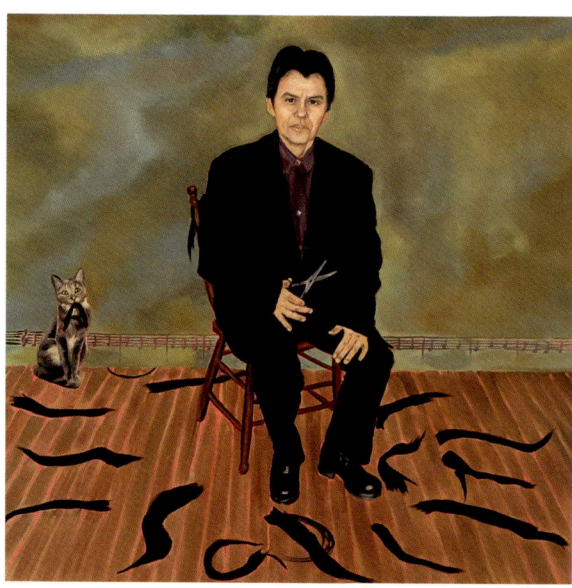

FIGURE 7.26.
Rosalie Favell,
*If only you could
love me the way
I am*, 2018.

I had turned to family snapshots in hopes that by re-visiting my early years I would discover visual evidence, clues to explain the shaping of my identity and to better situate myself as a contemporary native woman.[60]

These photo-based digital works, including self-portraiture, look to the past, convey the present, and evoke both personal and societal tensions. As curator Donna McAlear comments:

> It is the celebration of the human element that Favell seeks to communicate, especially in *Longing and Not Belonging*, and *Belonging*. Favell's ancestry and her mother's dedication to compiling family albums over decades fascinate her. Many of us first come to know our past in pictures from the family album. . . . The family photograph is a universal visual symbol of security: home, good times and connected relationships. Given past injustices and mistaken identities, it is understandable that new generations of aboriginal artists will use photographs to address past misrepresentations. Favell, like many artists who appropriate "found" familial motifs and portraits, reclaims her own past and stakes it publicly to counteract enduring stereotypes of indigenous peoples' lives.[61]

In *My First Day of Assimilation,* Favell shows the Polaroid photograph of her as a young child in a pretty dress, simply photographed standing in front of the flowerbed and picket fence of her

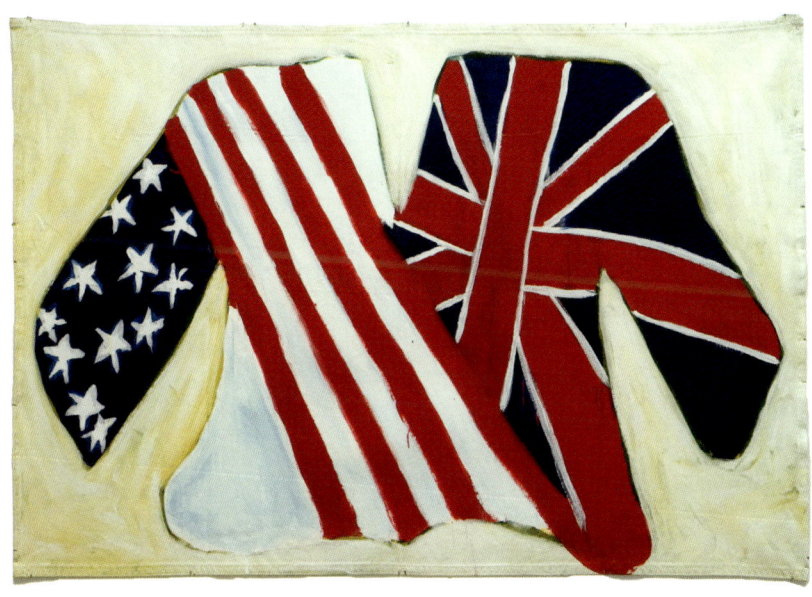

home. On the image the artist wrote "My First Day of Assimilation." It was a powerful realization, highlighting the assimilated life she was expected to lead in her adopted family away from her Indigenous roots. At that young age she realized she was "different." In her perceptive comparative analysis of Favell's penetrating self-identity examination series, McAlear continues: "If *Longing and Not Belonging* marks Favell's period of longing to be part of something bigger while feeling marginalized, and *Belonging* reflects her recent acceptance of being part of something bigger, then *Plain(s) Warrior Artist* imagines Favell's desire to be something bigger."[62] In some works she portrayed herself with the stature and dress of depictions of Napoleon, thus commenting on history while stating the place she feels Indigenous art and her own art deserves.

All these impacts of postcolonialism are seen visually in a multitude of other ways in the art of Western Indigenous artists. *Treaty Dress* by Ruth Cuthand or her *Misuse Is Abuse: Northern Tundra,* 1990, are direct statements. Her *Misuse Is Abuse Series* is biographical. The drawings are combined with text; collectively and singly they point to the devastating effect of the wrongs of governments and the pervasive societal attitudes, especially those in her small community of Cardston, Alberta. In some of the series, she incorporates poetic text from the Book of Mormon, which is particularly relevant, given that Cardston was a Mormon community. The contrast between the drawings and text in each work heightens the power of the message. The result is searing.

FIGURE 7.27. **Ruth Cuthand**, *Treaty Dress*, 1986.

Residential Schools and Reconciliation

"My people will sleep for one hundred years, but when they awake, it will be the artists who give them their spirit back."[63]

Louis Riel was prophetic in his statement above, as was Rosalie Favell with her work *I awoke to find my spirit returned,* in which Favell, covered with a Hudson's Bay blanket, the only colour in this otherwise black and white work, awakes with Louis Riel looking through the open door of the Riel House on Winnipeg's River Road.

The Sixties Scoop, during which Indigenous children were taken from their families and put into care, many being placed in middle-class Euro-Canadian families, was devastating in impact. It meant the loss of culture and family for far too many people. Whitehorse artist Joseph Tisiga (b.1984) tells a potent and personal story in his painting *With Friends,* 2011. As he said: "This painting re-imagines the moment of my mother's removal from her birth family as a child in the 'Sixties Scoop.' My mother shared her memory of this moment with me when I was a teenager. . . . Over the years I thought about her story and about all the other children who had been needlessly taken from their own families only to be haphazardly placed into another family or imprisoned within mission schools. The reality of it seemed absurd and impossible, that a man of no familiarity could go to another's house, abduct the children and escort them into an unknown and horrifying future like some perverse Pied Piper."[64] This painting shows the "man" at the door, a waiting police car outside the house, and a child in a tent made from a Hudson's Bay blanket. The story is clear.

The residential schools, spanning generations, are a truly black mark in Canada's history. The residential schools obliterated culture, language, and sense of self-worth, and in many ways destroyed generations of First Nations peoples, Inuit, and Métis, who were forced by the government to attend the schools run by the churches. In 2015 the Truth and Reconciliation Commission reported its findings at the conclusion of searing testimonies, work that began in 2008. Their ninety-four Calls to Action for reconciliation are the steps for Canada to move forward with social, educational, financial, and opportunity equality for Indigenous peoples, First Nations, Métis, and Inuit. The crisis caused by the residential schools is evident in artists' works and in my discussions with many Indigenous artists. In the 1980s, when I was director of the Art Gallery of Greater Victoria, Nuu-chah-nulth and Coast Salish artist Art Thompson (1948–2003) told me his story. It haunts me as vividly today as it did those decades ago. It was the story of his experiences as a student at the Port Alberni Residential School. Unfortunately, Art, a long-time advocate for residential school survivors, died of cancer before the Truth and Reconciliation Commission (TRC) was constituted. The circle in his art, reflecting the circle of life, of culture, of the spirit, and of humanity, recurs frequently. Thompson often depicted animals, too, each having specific meanings of family and spirituality.

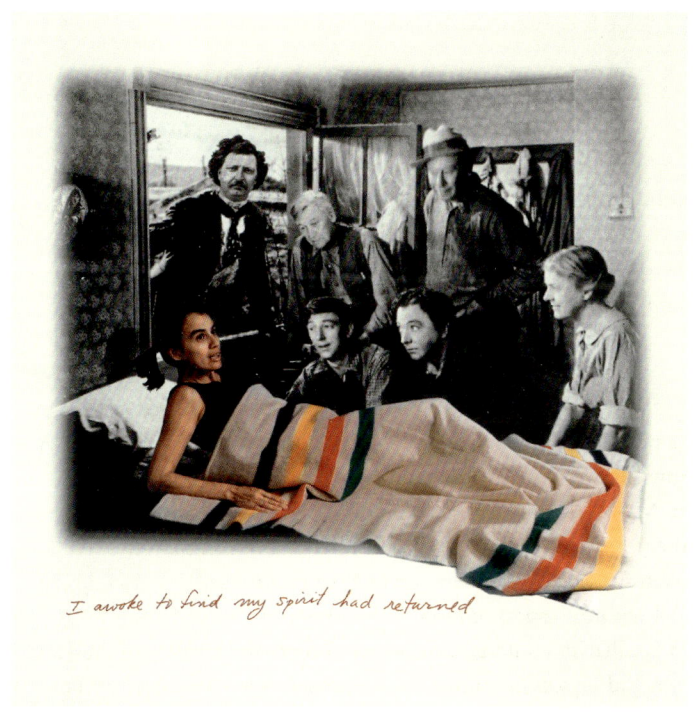

I awoke to find my spirit had returned

FIGURE 7.28.
Rosalie Favell,
*I awoke to find my
spirit had returned*,
from the series *Plain(s).
Warrior Artist*, 1999.

In raising the myriad societal issues resulting from residential schools, artists such as George Littlechild and Robert Houle used a variety of media and iconographical images to reveal their experiences in disturbing and emotional works. Alberta Indigenous artist George Littlechild, for instance, conveyed his deep-rooted pain in commenting on his 1993 painting *Red Horse Boarding School*: "the red horse is torn in half because Indian children coming to the [residential] schools were torn away from their culture, their language, their traditional ways and their families."[65] This reality was expressed by many of the more than 6,500 people who bore witness to the TRC. Author Mary-Beth Laviolette noted that, for Littlechild, "animals are often symbols of personal and social themes like family history, Canadian history, the treatment of Aboriginal cultures and the environment."[66]

The Truth and Reconciliation Commission heard hundreds of painful and intimate stories bringing to the fore memories that had been buried deeply within people's subconsciousness for years. One outcome during the hearings was Robert Houle's powerful and deeply personal 2009 *Residential School Series*. This series received the prestigious York Wilson Prize, which enabled the University of Manitoba to purchase the artworks. I was the university board chair at the time. The opening exhibition was an emotional milestone. Leah Sandals writes in *Canadian Art*:

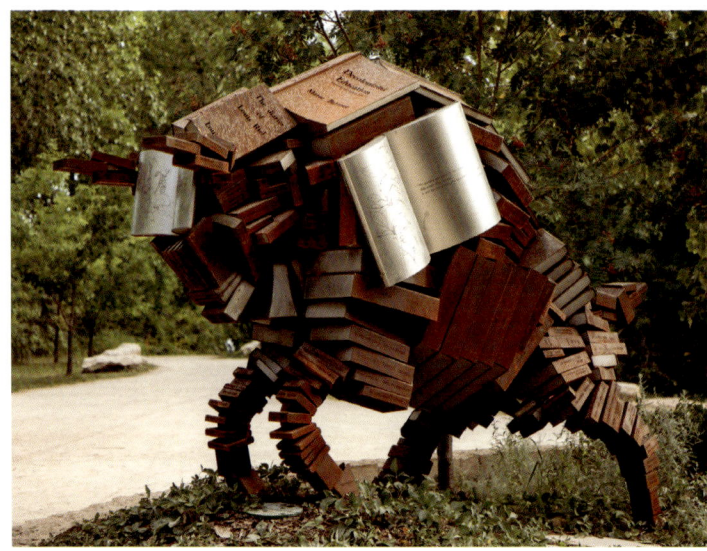

FIGURE 7.29.
Val Vint, *Education
is the New Bison
(Chi-kishkayhitamihk
si te li neu Biizon)*,
2020.

Houle tells . . . that it took him until that time [2009] to actually become conscious of the traumatic experiences he endured at the institution. Prior to that year, "I didn't know what it was, but I knew something terribly wrong had happened to me," Houle explains. Even though "shameful, dark" sentiments had come up in relation to writing about other artists' residential-school work and being involved in some official reconciliation ceremonies, it was a trip back home to Sandy Bay for a funeral that finally triggered specific memories. "I had a horrible, vivid dream about an incident that had happened to me that I had completely forgotten. . . . So I went back to Toronto two days later and decided once and for all that I was going to deal with this."[67]

This body of work was comprised of twenty-four oil stick drawings, one done every day for a month and each recalling his time in Sandy Bay Residential School. The dormitory, playground, and religious figures feature in them. Houle says: "My residential school drawings are about what happened to me, without the language of judgement and forgiveness."[68] Some of these drawings bear disturbing handwritten inscriptions such as "night predator," "I'm cornered," "outhouse abuse," "drive-in terror," "*uhnuhmeahkazooh*—pretending to pray," and "fear." He commented to me that he was exhausted at the end of each day's work, as the honesty of the recollections were devastating.

FIGURE 7.30. **George Littlechild**, *The Land Before, The Land After*, 2014.

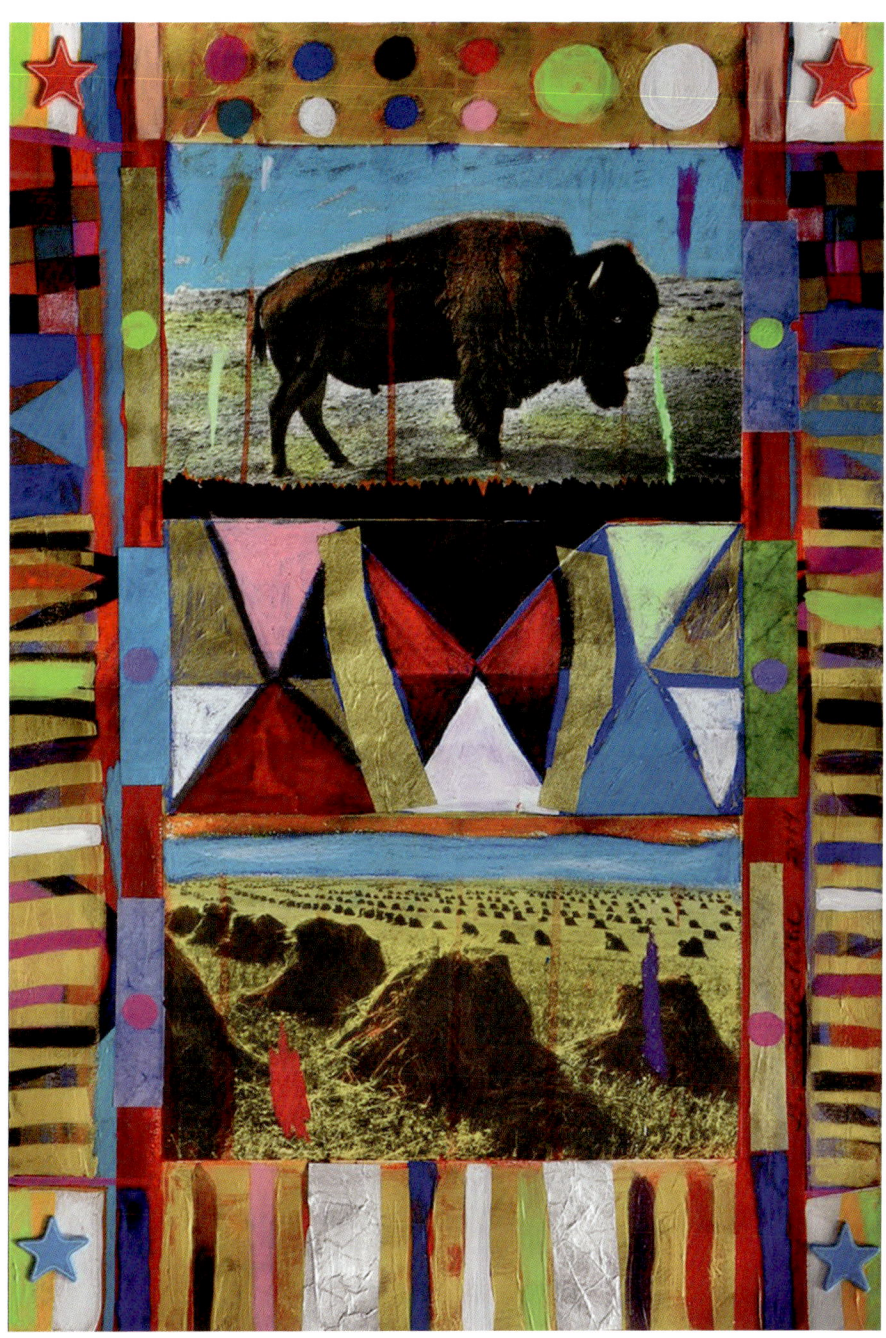

Robert Houle's large painting *Sandy Bay, 1998–99,* became for me one of the most significant works in Canadian art. In speaking to the Winnipeg Art Gallery staff in 2000, Houle told how his parents were forced to send him and his siblings to the Sandy Bay Residential School. His sisters had to go through one door; he and his brothers, another. After entering the school, the brothers were banned from seeing their sisters. Their recesses were at different times, they were in different classes, and they lived in different parts of the building.

In Houle's *Sandy Bay,* there are no doors and the windows are veiled. Two photographs, one of the priest who was buried on the reserve, and the other the communion class that included his sister, are mounted to the left of the work's two painted panels. Author Shirley Madill wrote: "Each window on the building above takes on a metaphorical reference to one of Houle's siblings. To the right are two panels: one depicts the landscape of Sandy Bay rendered in deep blue, the other a landscape in red with Houle's trademark gestural line in green. Other characteristic marks include references to traditional quillwork and the morning star."[69] Houle speaks kindly of the priest in the photograph, but he vehemently articulates that one element of kindness does not, and could not, erase the horrors of his experiences. Houle's composure struck me in 2000, but clearly the reality and impacts of his school experiences remained deeply buried within. The buried feelings are captured by the virtual veil he painted over the front of the school building. The painful and raw emotions are shown through his strength of colour and power of the gestural green line. Houle's visual revelation of his truth was expressed through the truly powerful oil stick drawings done almost ten years after the seminal painting. He told me that having shared his realities in that series, his deep anger is now past.[70] Through creating the *Residential School Series,* he built his bridge, but the scar is irreparable and neither he nor his family will ever forget what happened. Society must now build its bridge.

The Truth and Reconciliation Commission calls for reconciliation, or, for me, "reconciliaction." The raising of the *Reconciliation Pole* at the University of British Columbia on 1 April 2017, is an early and demonstrative act of reconciliation. Carved by 7idansuu (Edenshaw), James Hart, Haida Hereditary Chief and Master Carver, this pole has become one of the country's post–Truth and Reconciliation Commission landmarks. It hearkens back to traditional Northwest Coast poles, but at the same time it also breaks from artistic tradition. Carved from an 800-year-old seventeen-metre red cedar, it tells the story of before, during, and after the Indian residential school system—a system that began in Canada in the 1800s and ended in 1996 with the closure of the last school. The lower portion of the pole refers to Indigenous life pre-residential schools, and includes a salmon, bear, and raven. In the middle there is a schoolhouse, which is described by the University of British Columbia press materials as "fashioned after the residential school Hart's grandfather attended, [and] is carved with students holding hands above it. Embedded in the pole are thousands of copper nails, which represent the thousands of Indigenous children who died in the residential schools. The nails were hammered one by one by residential school survivors, affected families, school children and others."[71]

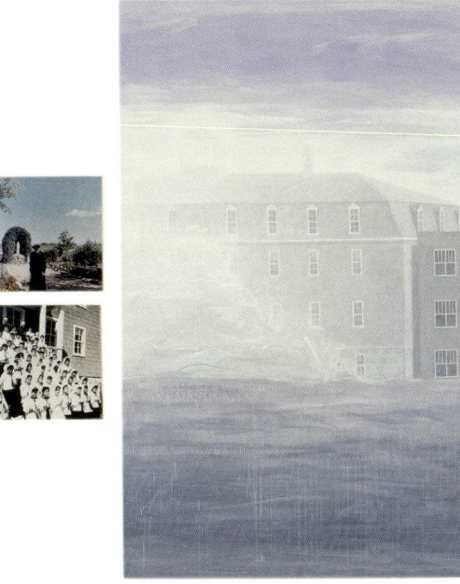

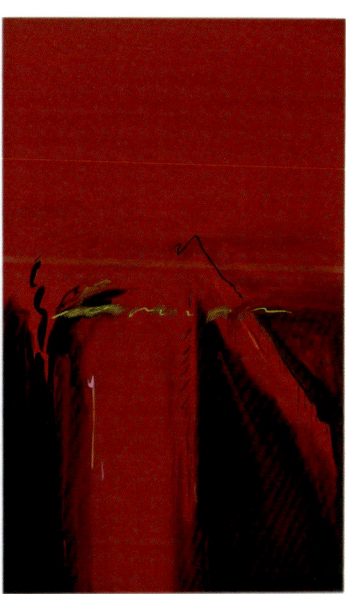

Above the school are hopeful references for the future, depicted with spiritual symbols with a family and a canoe. An eagle is on top. Commenting on his hope for the future, Hart said the eagle represents "the power and determination needed to look towards the future. . . . My hope for the pole is that it moves people to learn more about the history of residential schools and to understand their responsibility to reconciliation. The schools were terrible places. We need to pay attention to the past and work together on a brighter future."[72]

Michif artist Christi Belcourt's (b. 1966) multi-panelled Residential School Legacy Window, titled *Giniigaaniimenaaning (Looking Ahead),* was unveiled in Centre Block on Parliament Hill on 25 November 2012, creating an accessible public memorial where the legislative steps to reconciliation must be commenced. In her artist's statement she describes the meanings behind each section: "The glass design tells a story. It is a story of Indigenous people, with our ceremonies, languages, and cultural knowledge intact; through the darkness of the residential school era; to an awakening sounded by a drum; an apology that spoke to the heart; hope for reconciliation; transformation and healing through dance, ceremony, language; and resilience into the present day." Of the left-hand panel, she says:

> The broken glass also represents the shattered lives, shattered families and shattered communities that resulted from the government policy of forced assimilation.

FIGURE 7.31. **Robert Houle**, *Sandy Bay*, 1998–1999.

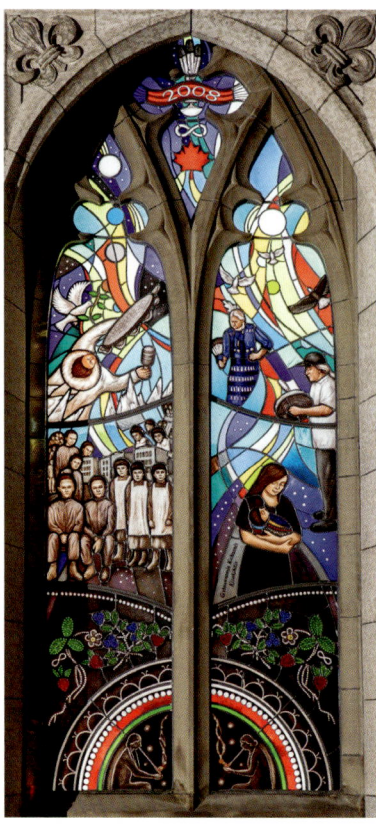

FIGURE 7.32.
Christi Belcourt,
*Giniigaaniimenaaning
(Looking Ahead)*, 2012.

The drum dancer sounds the beginning of the healing. The circles moving up and out from behind the drum represent the transformation that governments and churches made, from taking initial positions of denial, to acceptance, and finally to acknowledgement and admission, paving the way for an apology. The snow falls and the moon glows from a northern sky. The dove with the olive branch brings an offering of hope for the beginning of reconciliation and the renewal of the relationship between Aboriginal peoples and the rest of Canada.[73]

The middle section talks about the chapter when the children were taken, and the bottom section represents the time before the residential schools, when people were connected to the land. The upper portion refers to the apology of Prime Minister Harper, while the right-hand panel shows a more positive future. The overall design is complex, the symbolism rich in its references to traditional Indigenous beliefs and to the specifics of the residential schools. Her colour and the movement she achieves throughout the panels are strong.

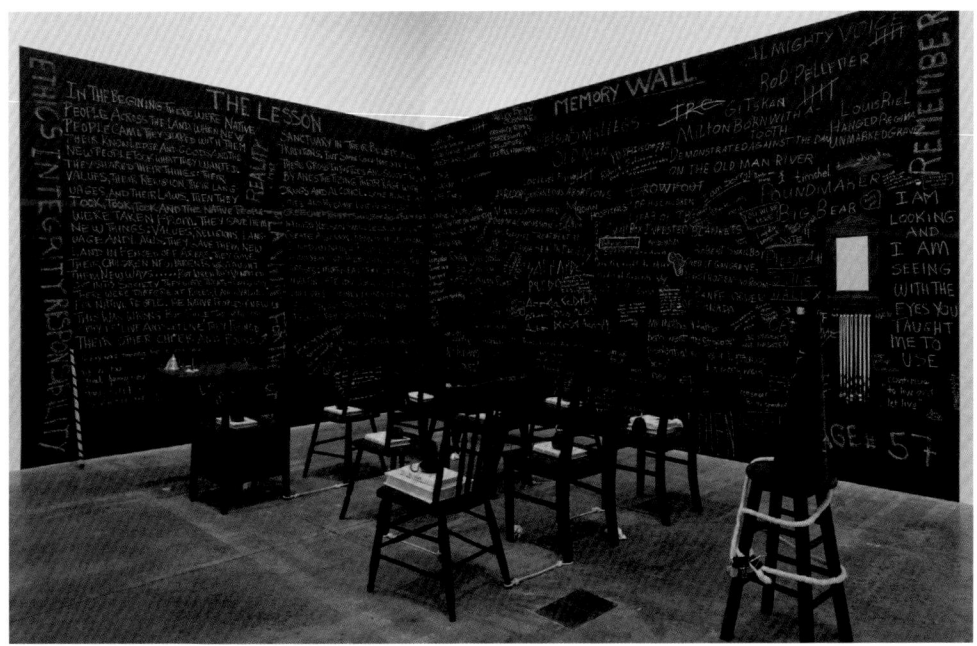

For Joane Cardinal-Schubert (1942–2009), colonialism, racism, residential schools, and destruction, as well as the environment, were the key themes throughout her work. She had the insight and vision to express societal crises emanating from the residential schools long before the rest of society did and, indeed, while residential schools were still operating. Her installation *The Lesson* depicted the attempt by the residential schools to eradicate Indigenous languages and spirituality. It is direct and unequivocal. Created in 1989, it predates the establishment of the Truth and Reconciliation Commission by nineteen years. It was a clairvoyant clarion call to understanding and redress, and its power enabled many Canadians to begin to comprehend the level of cruelty the schools inflicted on generations of Indigenous peoples, and the lasting physical and psychological havoc wreaked on them and their descendants.

The resulting effect of *The Lesson* was aptly conveyed by author Jackie Bissley: "Joane Cardinal-Schubert's work is brutally honest, evoking images and memories of a past that has often been filled with harshness and cruelty. And while embracing and exposing the truth, Cardinal-Schubert also reaffirms the power of the human spirit."[74] The work's static rows of classroom chairs, each with an apple on the seat, and the stool at the back with a dunce cap are stinging in their power and demonstrate the system's rigidity and inhumanity. The artist said of

FIGURE 7.33. **Joane Cardinal-Schubert**, *The Lesson*, 1989.

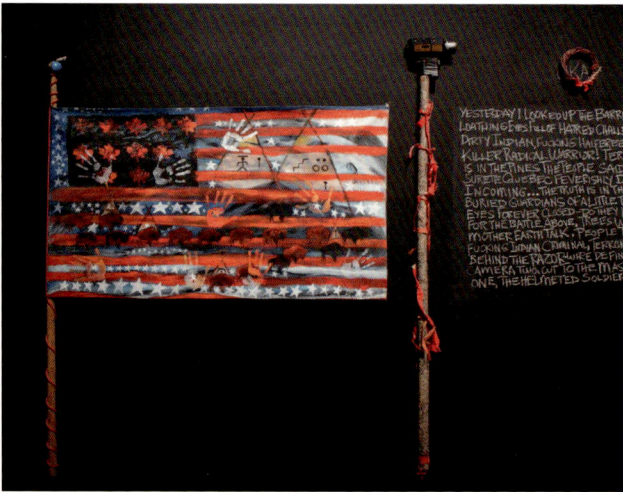

FIGURE 7.34.
Joane Cardinal-Schubert, *Where the Truth is Written— Usually*, 1991 (detail).

this work: "That classroom [*The Lesson*] for me has been kind of therapeutic. I was so sick of the rhetoric that was going on everybody talking about the effects [the assault on Native children though the education system] but I don't think non-Natives had a sense of what people actually went through. The physical state of that classroom, with its rigid little seating and the chairs together, was my attempt at trying to show just how restrictive it really was and how we were and still are looked at as if we're all the same."[75]

In the installation are two large blackboards filled with carefully selected texts highlighting the loss of their cultures and languages. Cardinal-Schubert used these in a particularly potent way with haunting memories giving voice to multiple past and present injustices to Indigenous peoples. She continued her commentary:

> My text acts as the primer. In each area people add names from their own territory, or they add a name about someone they've heard about or think about. . . . I try and create things that are going to be a mirror for people, so that when they do look at it there is something within it where their own knowledge and memory can take off, so everyone can relate to it on some level. . . . Part of my strategy is to create things that have a metaphorical jump—allow someone to understand Native issues in terms that they can relate to in their own culture so they can get it![76]

Internationally lauded Alberta Cree artist Jane Ash Poitras is a printmaker, painter, and collage artist. She, too, has depicted the history, spiritual beliefs, and individual lives of Indigenous people. Her visual directness empowers Indigenous nations while unsettling

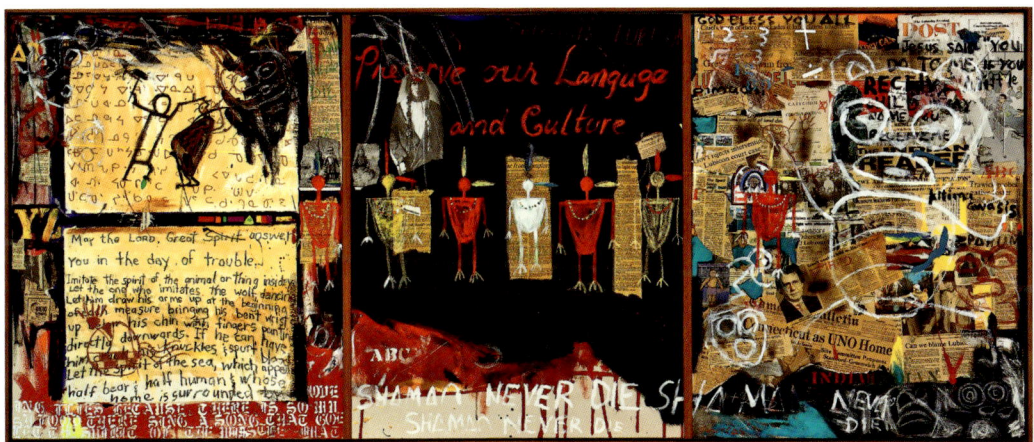

viewers who are ignorant of the history. Her work *Preservation Reservation,* 2020, commissioned by the Alberta government, refers specifically to residential schools, as have many of her earlier works. She notes that she brought back the blackboard and the "idea of the residential school and turned it into something positive for our history."[77] The composition is full of details elucidating decades of past difficult and often buried histories. She included "ephemera," as she calls it, collaged clippings, photographs, a fourteen-cent stamp of Parliament Hill, the alphabet, and reference to the Hudson's Bay Company with the characteristic stripes of the blanket running across the lower edge. She emphasized the fact that the story "has to be completely told." Further, she emphatically and rightly recognizes that "art is a healing process and a sacred act."[78] This large work becomes a ledger of all Indigenous history, residential schools, past treaties, human rights, and issues of sovereignty.

When one looks at Poitras's overall oeuvre, one sees a deep consistency in her imagery and compositional structures. Her canvases are full of rich and meaningful images, and there is not an iota of unpainted canvas. Divided into segments, her paintings tell multiple stories covering multiple time frames and situations. The whole needs time and reflection to take in. She usually uses personal photographs and always incorporates Indigenous symbols and calligraphy, and the works simultaneously relate to the past and the present while holding hope for the future. In my speaking with her after the burial findings at Western Canadian residential schools, we discussed the depth of her iconography and her overall meanings. She underlined that the fact that bodies were buried on all these sites was known for years. And, as she said, "bones are depicted in many of my works over many years."[79]

FIGURE 7.35. **Jane Ash Poitras**, *Shaman Never Die: Return to Your Ancestral Roots*, 1989.

Manitoba's Val Vint, artist and Knowledge Keeper, unveiled her major work at the Forks in Winnipeg in July 2020. *Education is the New Bison,* 2020, ties the past, present, and future together, as Poitras's art does. The work is made of steel, depicting books and films, predominantly by Indigenous authors and artists and as she says, "allies of Indigenous people." The titles on the spines show books from past decades and those recently published, and demonstrate the depth and extent of intellectual pursuits, ideas and the accomplishments by Indigenous writers. Vint quotes Louis Riel, Senator Murray Sinclair, and artist Robert Davidson in the three polished, open volumes. The bison faces across the river to the gravesite of her grandfather. She deliberately planted the same native vegetation—sage grass and berries— around the bison as she had her at her grandfather's grave. The bison looks forward. Vint wrote me: "The thing I would like to say about 'Education is the new Bison' is what happens in his presence. People begin meaningful conversations around him. Conversation is critical in any healing work. When people talk to each other usually they see each other's eyes and are no longer 'the other.' When there is no other it changes how we see each other, how we think of each other. We soon discover that nobody is the 'other'; we are all the same; we are all related."[80]

Reconciliation must happen, as is clearly expressed in these and other works of art, and, further, the "reconciliactions" must be from all individuals and communities.

War and Conflict

"On a battlefield, recently fought over, a preliminary reconnaissance includes all of these considerations, [familiarity of the subject, patterns and composition] but in addition, one must be alert for the cleverly concealed mines and traps, left lying about to catch just such unwary people as war artists. One may trip over a wire, open a door, pick up an attractive looking something, and do so for the last time, as I had witnessed in the past. Our reconnaissance therefore was a careful one."[81]

War and conflict devastate individuals, societies, and nations, in tangible, visible ways and in less outwardly discernable ones. Psychological ravages often remain well below the surface, impacting a person for the balance of their life. Victoria artist Robert de Castro was one so affected. Conflict has that same lasting effect on communities as the 1990 summer standoff at Oka still has. In addition to visible destruction, lasting physical scars of conflict include heart-rending and healing memorials. Events that were not often talked about by those who served during wars, however, were recorded by official war artists, in oil, watercolour, etching, and bronze. It is impossible to underestimate the impact of the wars on Canada's artists who served overseas with Canadian or Allied forces in both world wars and in the recent international conflicts. Effects of war in distant parts of the globe were felt at home, too. Women assumed work in factories, making supplies and

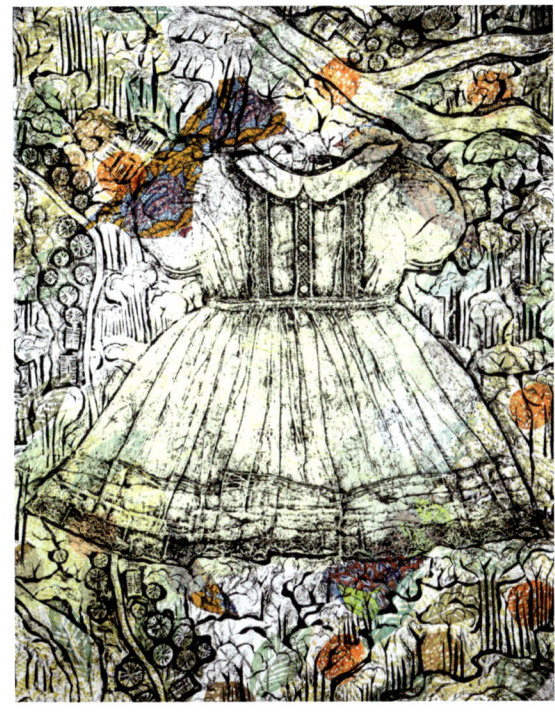

FIGURE 7.36.
Karen Cornelius,
Nylon and Lace in the Congo, from the series *Fabric of Belonging,* 2011.

equipment, labour originally done by the men who went to war. Women also had to attend to all the family responsibilities. Their work became subject matter for artists.

Some families have faced conflicting traditional cultural philosophies about peace and conflict. Winnipeg's Michael Boss's *Double Self-Portrait,* 2010, portrays that dichotomy. It reflects his dual background, pacifist Mennonite roots on his maternal side, and the more militant, warlike Ukrainian Cossack heritage on his paternal side. He commented: "My family were not Kozaks . . . as far as anyone knows. They were simply farmers from Western Ukraine. I use the Kozak to represent my Ukrainian side: The emotional, defiant aspects. The pacifist Mennonite side is represented by the black clothing, subdued, intellectual side: 'The Quiet in the Land.'"[82] This acrylic and pastel on canvas double portrait depicts the artist in guises representative of each of his bloodlines. Boss's inner strength and gentleness are coupled with his depth of personal, religious, and academic reflection. The gold background contrasts with the black and white oil pastel used for the figures. The figures are positioned almost back-to-back, apart with no connection. The work reflects the artist's boldness and his spiritual contemplation; in Boss's words, it "encapsulates the division I feel between my Mennonite and Ukrainian ancestry: warrior vs. pacifist."[83]

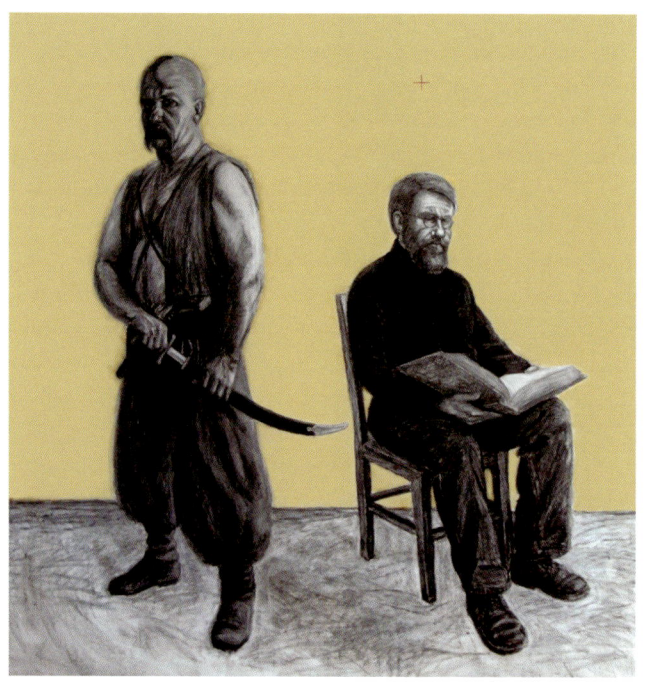

FIGURE 7.37.
Michael Boss,
*Double Self-Portrait as
Ukrainian Kozak and
Pious Mennonite*, 2010.

In 1914 the Canadian government established the Canadian War Artists program and the Department of Defence thus became the first federal department to hire artists. Artists have continued to be members of Canadian troops since, serving in the Second World War, the Korean War, many peacekeeping missions like that in Croatia, and, more recently, in Afghanistan. They have presented honest and compelling voices about the horrors and realities of war. In addition to visually documenting the events, their art is also a powerful means of healing from post-traumatic stress disorder (PTSD) and the horrors they witnessed.

Fred Varley, a member of the Group of Seven who moved to Vancouver in 1926, was a First World War artist. His works are filled with the horrors of war, and his characteristic strong brushwork and use of colour heighten those impacts. His acidic tones pervade much of his war art, including his haunting *For What?*, 1917–1919. A wagon filled with corpses is in the centre of the desolated, devasted landscape. A grave digger and multiple white crosses are just off-centre, below the clouds. A haunting yellow palette depicts the unsettling sky above the horizon. Franz Johnston, 1888–1949, principal of the Winnipeg School of Art from 1921 to 1924, was also an official war artist of the First World War. His 1918 work *Looking Up Into the Blue* depicts two aircraft, each off-centre, against the large, deep blue sky. The First World War was the first war with air attacks and, as such, portrayals of the sky, airmen, and aircraft were both documentary and innovative subject matter. Mary Riter Hamilton was upset that no women were hired as official war artists, so she went to France immediately after the war in 1919, when she had been recently widowed, and painted the battlefields where Canadian troops had served. Her watercolours, such as *Cemetery of The 7th Battalion*, circa 1919, movingly portray the devastation of postwar sites, graveyards, and destroyed buildings. They highlight both the psychological and physical costs of war.

British artists Cyril Barraud and Frank Brangwyn also played significant roles in Canada in depicting the horrors of the First World War. Barraud's etching *Entering Ypres at Dawn*, circa 1919, perhaps one of his better-known pieces of the era, captured the devastation and emotions of the troops and landscape. Brangwyn, who had been influenced by England's William Morris, and who in turn influenced Lionel LeMoine FitzGerald, was commissioned to paint the mural in the newly constructed Manitoba Legislature in 1920 to honour the contributions of Canada to the Great War. The impact of the composition, its size, the artist's handling of colour, and the manner in which he portrayed the strength of the figures and the intensity of the soldiers' faces emphasize the dual realities of death and compassion.

Artists also enlisted in the Second World War, their job once more being to document action on the front, the people, preparations for battles, and the off-duty lives of those who served and those who maintained the home fronts. This time women enlisted, including British Columbia's Molly Lamb Bobak. Women artists went overseas as part of the military but were not allowed go to the front lines. Bobak's depictions of the people and lifestyles show her artistic ability and keen powers of observation. The strength in *Private Roy, Canadian Women's Army Corps*, 1946, the camaraderie in *Gas Drill*, 1944, and the moments of leisure seen in *Canteen, Nijmegen, Holland*, 1945, collectively captured multiple aspects of life away from the front. Her career was launched as a result of her war posting. Her compositional, linear, and colourist abilities were evident in all these early works. *V–J Celebrations*, 1945, for instance, shows the same exuberance of large crowds seen in her later winter and summer scenes.

Charles Comfort, who emigrated to Winnipeg with his family in 1912 and worked in Brigdens of Winnipeg from 1914 to 1919, served as a Canadian war artist in Dieppe and on the Italian front in the Second World War. *Campobasso*, 1945, *The Hitler Line*, 1944, and *Dead German on the Hitler Line*, 1944, are dark and powerfully emotive works. He rose to the feat of painting at the line of attack in the Italian wet, cold winter weather. He conveyed the tone, destruction, and devastation around him. He wrote of Campobasso: "Then came a sudden, screaming, earsplitting CRUMP, a wall tottered outward and disintegrated as it fell into the street, enveloped in a choking pile of dust. An artificial hush fell on the scene, a sort of reflex silence following the blast."[84] In his autobiography Comfort talks of his experiences as a war artist, his reconnaissance work, and processes: "The fundamental ideal behind the selection of equipment for painting in the field was that it must be possible for the artist to handle it himself, unaided.

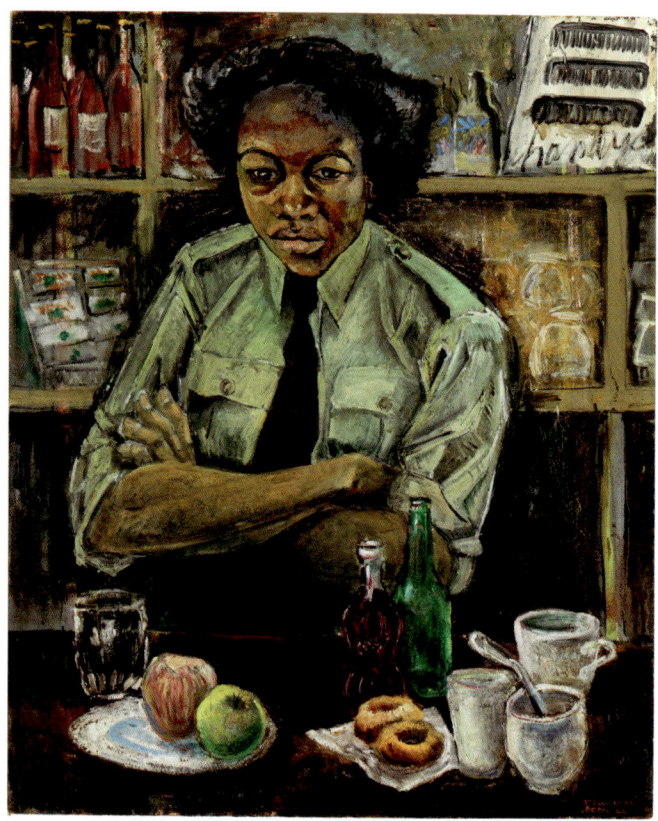

Watercolour equipment was therefore the answer. I had standardized the size of each individual painting to approximately 15" by 21", or half a sheet of standard watercolour paper. I carried a collapsible field sketching easel and a small metal stool. . . . One of the risks in our work was that one became deeply preoccupied, and danger was upon one before it was realized."[85]

A number of other Canadian Second World War artists, including Paul Goranson (1911–2002), had Western Canadian roots. His work *Marshalling of the Hallies,* 1947, is a sombre, oppressive painting. He used dark blue/black tones throughout the painting. The diagonal lines and definite brushwork highlight the monumental airplane in the foreground. Other aircraft lined up across the canvas emphasize the size of the air offence. Vancouver Island's E.J. Hughes also covered many aspects of war, its people, the action, and the deaths. Hughes approached *Canteen Queue, Kiska,* 1944, and *Signalman and RCD Armoured Car in Harbour,* 1943, with the same sense of detail and precise brushwork as he did all his pre- and postwar paintings. Caven Atkins (1907–2000), a student of Lionel LeMoine FitzGerald's at the Winnipeg School of Art,

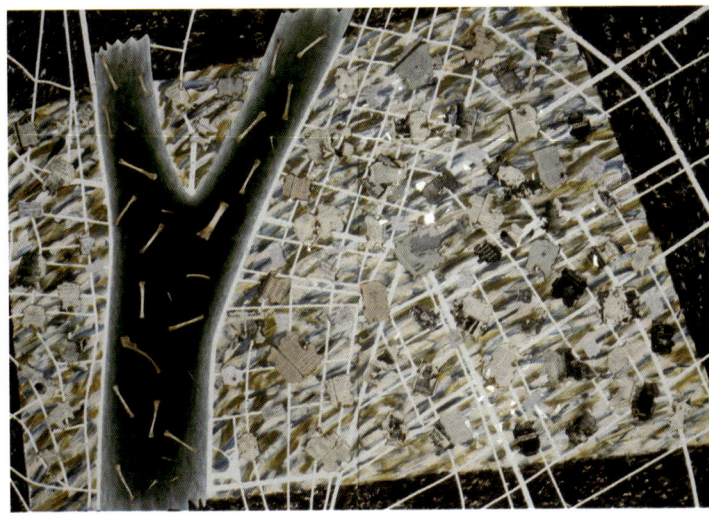

FIGURE 7.39.
Caroline Dukes,
Danube, 1996.

joined the artists' war effort, too, and many of his works, like *Arc Welder By Night,* 1942, portray the efforts in readying equipment for the front.

Calgary-born artist Maxwell Bates went to London in his twenties and had exhibited his art there before the war with some success. As soon as war was declared, however, he enlisted with the British Army, was sent to Europe, and was captured by the Nazis just a few months later. A prisoner of war for the ensuing five years, he was on forced marches, moved from place to place in open railway cars, fed starvation rations, and did forced labour in the salt mines. Throughout it all he kept a notebook, published in 1978 as *Wilderness of Days.* The impact of his experience was painful and lasting. Of Bates's incarceration, critic Nancy Townshend notes:

> In the POW camp Bates learned to veil reality with appearances . . . to unveil appearances with reality. . . . Thus his lifelong interest in appearance and reality, observer and observed, were strengthened. It was during these years that he started to include clowns in his work.
>
> Overall Bates's manual work at the salt mine greatly increased his knowledge of men at work. . . .
>
> The critical stimulus for Bates's most profound Expressionist prisoner of war–related artwork occurred during the six weeks of his second forced march in April 1945. He saw thousands of Jewish survivors of Nazi concentration camps in a "column (that) had a horrible, staggering, halting rhythm. The column was like a multitude of puppets. . . . Those moonlight ivory faces expressed courage, fear, ferocity."[86]

The war also made a strong impression on Jack Shadbolt. An administrative officer in the Canadian forces, not in the official war artists' program, he nevertheless painted throughout his 1945 posting to London. The bombed buildings and ruins became "a door to abstraction" for him. He said, "It suddenly dawned on me. . . . When the bomb blows the building apart it abstracts it, the pieces fall back together again and you get a memory image of what was there but vastly altered and psychologically made infinitely more intense than the original thing. So that was a process of extracting. . . . I started thinking of bomb ruins in terms of 'here was a building and here are the abstract elements of it.' I worked from there."[87]

Author Scott Watson quotes artist Charles Scott about Shadbolt's London work at the end of the war: "One feels that life itself has been torn and disorganized until the very heavens weep at the dumbly gaping and protesting shapes."[88] There is an interesting intersection between Shadbolt's work during the war and immediately after with that of a number of his British contemporaries, including Graham Sutherland, John Piper, and Paul Nash. Similar colour tones, forms, and mood are evident in the work of them all, and in their journals and letters they share similar senses of horror of the shattered lives resulting from the London bombing. The many photographs of sites and situations that came across Shadbolt's desk daily affected him deeply. "I found the experience devastating," he said. "For some time after this I had the need for a violent image of pathos to relieve my feelings, in my work, of this traumatic revulsion and to express my outrage."[89] *Dog Among the Ruins,* 1947, the watercolour in the collection of the Art Gallery of Greater Victoria, is perhaps one of the most poignant works, showing the bombed destruction in the background, dark ominous clouds, and the male dog howling, filling the vertical space of the work itself.

Victoria's Robert de Castro, a relatively unknown sculptor, deeply scarred, never overcame his war trauma. Writer Tony Gregson said that "a sense of emotional and physical assault became a consistent feature of de Castro's work, lending another, more agonized quality to its silence. . . . His exit interview revealed an unhappy young man who did not know what to do with himself. That he was suffering from some sort of trauma soon became apparent to his family."[90] That trauma affected his art production throughout his career, and contributed to his inability to reach out to galleries and media across Canada, which perhaps explains why his sensitive work has remained largely unrecognized. Carefully sanded and stained driftwood sculptures, executed with precision and feeling, evoke the need for compassion. His rougher-edged pieces recall the effects and scars of life. Some have seeing eyes; others suggest a person walking out from the wood itself.

Since the Second World War Canadian forces have been deployed to Korea, Croatia, Kosovo, Somalia, Afghanistan, Syria, and other peacekeeping and hot spots around the world. Artists were sent to each. As the means and modes of visual expression changed, particularly in the 1990s, artists such as Gertrude Kearns, William MacDonnell, and Allan Harding MacKay

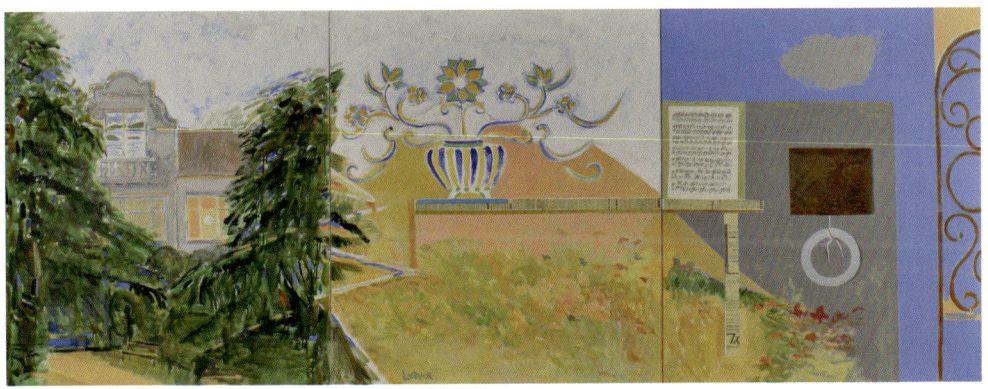

each did powerful, honest depictions of what they witnessed and the impacts on the respective societies. In March 1993 MacKay, whose artistic and art gallery careers were spent in both Western and Eastern Canada, went to Somalia as part of the Canadian Armed Forces Civilian Artists Program, and in July 2002 he went to Afghanistan to participate in the pilot launch of the Canadian Forces Artists Program. The still images and videos he took at a number of places in Somalia and at the Kandahar airfield were the bases for those works. In addition to the works done as a result of these experiences, MacKay's overall oeuvre includes portraits and landscapes, and his affinity for both is evident in the war works. Similarly, the horrific social and political events in the 1990s Yugoslavian civil war, the orphanages with large numbers of children, inspired Pat Martin Bates for her 1998 pierced oil pastel and estampille *The Angel of the Blue Sky is Crying Parallax Tears.* This light box, with her characteristic use of chine collé and silver threads, is a seminal piece of hers. The richness of the blue, which signified hope, is enhanced by the stars, the light, and the movement throughout the piece.

The coming down of the Berlin Wall on 9 November 1989 marked a new beginning for many people, especially Vancouver artist John Koerner, who had grown up in Prague. He returned to the city of his birth in 1990, and his rediscovery of his home country not only revived memories of his youth but clarified his understanding of the importance of Canadian culture for him. He found his family home intact, and it became the subject of his painting *Slavonic Dance 7 Opus 9030,* a triptych that relayed the past and the present, including the broken window from his childhood soccer ball. In the middle is a still life in a vase. It sits on a newspaper column, symbolizing past and present news. A page from Anton Dvorak's music is in the right-hand panel, as are more news clippings and a blind, pulled down, with a large ring tied with a red, blue, and white ribbon. Together, these symbols signify the years of Czech repression.

FIGURE 7.40. **John Koerner**, *Slavonic Dance 7, Opus 9030*, 1990.

The effects of war and suppression on refugees, what they were escaping, and what they were arriving to, were likewise critical subject matter for artists Caroline Dukes and Arnold Saper. Both working in Winnipeg, they dealt with the situations of war and refugees in their work. The destruction to personal lives, culture, and humanity at the hands of the Nazis, and the murdering, imprisonment, and gassing of thousands of Jews, forcing them to flee, took Dukes's attention. She suffered those ravages personally. *Music School* and *Danube,* both 1996, and her undated *Landscape #29* are examples of the lasting impacts of the war years on her. In *Landscape #29,* she shows faceless figures streaming along the road—where and why are they going and what will happen? The subdued colours and hazy background magnify the massive scale of the exodus, or their enforcement into camps. In *Music School* there is no door for escape. In *Midnight,* 1996, water flows down the halls, symbolizing the overpowering desire of the Nazis to eradicate all Jews. In her mixed-media work *Danube,* she has sewn chicken bones onto her painting of the fork of the river, representing the Jews killed by the Nazis and whose bodies were thrown into ditches. The river is shaped like a slingshot.

The Holocaust and Kristallnacht, the Night of Broken Glass, had a powerful effect on Phyllis Serota. Marking the atrocities in her 1998 series of twelve works, she delved into the horrors perpetuated on Jews. Her triptych *Order and Chaos,* a pastel, charcoal, acrylic, and oil on canvas, "was the title piece," she said in an email to me, "the final painting after my year of submersion into that most horrendous period of time, the Holocaust, . . . and includes many of the elements I explored throughout the other paintings."[91] The horror of the time is clear through her depiction of the prisoners, the train tracks into Auschwitz, the pit filled with bodies, the number on the prisoner's right shoulder, and Nazis with guns pointed at the Jewish people. The deep reds in the middle of this otherwise black and white large work enhance the horror and emotion. While conveying in detail the sense of tragedy and news past, she does so with the poignancy and currency of its long-lasting effects today.

University of Manitoba printmaking professor Arnold Saper was moved by the arrival of the Vietnamese "boat people" on the west coast of British Columbia. The idea of thousands of people fleeing from Vietnam and risking their lives on the Pacific Ocean was overwhelming to him, a fact he depicted in his small yet emotive drypoint *Refugees,* 1979.

Canada has not been spared conflict within our borders. Plans to expand a golf course on to spiritual lands of the Mohawk led to a three-month standoff between the Mohawk Nation and Canada's military in the summer of 1990. A number of Canadian artists, revolted at the way the government of Canada handled the situation, responded with compelling works of art. Saskatchewan's Bob Boyer's four-panelled mixed media work *F.U.S.Q.:Tanks for the Memories,* 1991, is but one example. Kwakwaka'wakw artist David Neel (b. 1960), from British Columbia, has created a silkscreen, *Life on the Eighteenth Hole,* 1990, that is a portrait of Ronald Cross, a Mohawk warrior active in Oka. Neel's work includes aspects of the particular situation and symbols uniting all First Nations. Four eagle feathers, two on each side of the portrait, represent

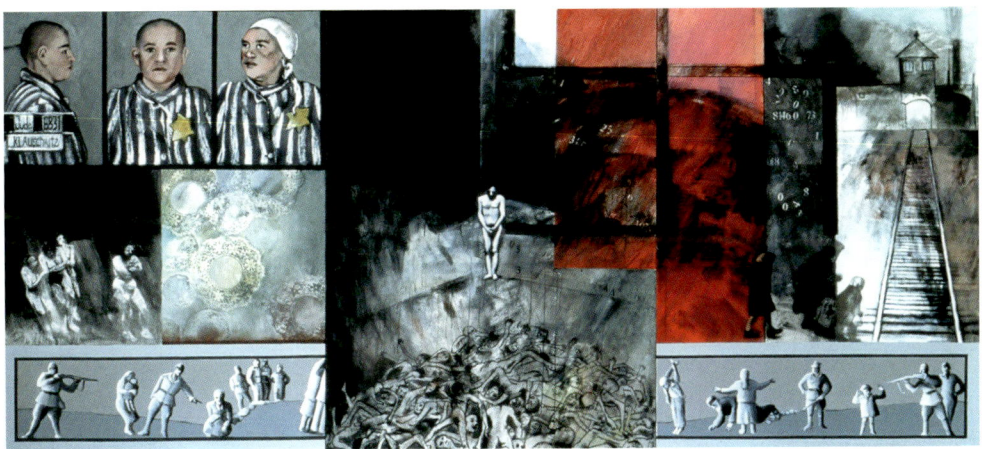

strength, bravery, and honour in Indigenous cultures. Ten Mohawk warriors frame the top and bottom edges of the portrait, recalling the nursery rhyme, "One Little, Two Little, Three Little Indians." Red sightline targets are in each corner, four arrows pointing in the four directions, representing East, West, North, and South; the four seasons; the four elements of wind, water, air, and fire; and the four races in humanity. Red represents Indigenous peoples.

The Oka struggle propelled British Columbia artist Dana Claxton into her art-making career. Throughout her oeuvre she calls for action, provoking and challenging greater communication between Indigenous and non-Indigenous communities. She frequently articulates that art has the ability to reconcile and reconfigure cultures and people. Her reflections on Oka are inspiring: "I realized there was much work to be done. Aboriginal and non-Aboriginal communities were not communicating with each other. I asked myself: how could I facilitate this huge gap, in a meaningful way."[92] Jane Ash Poitras's 1990 *Oka Spirit Power,* addresses that "gap" with her inclusion of photos of leaders past, her characteristic inclusion of symbols throughout the canvas, and the two mounted horses facing each other at the top of the composition in stand-off positions. Curator Grant Arnold wrote of the impact of Oka: "The Oka standoff corresponded roughly with a moment when contemporary Indigenous artists who were directly addressing the effects of colonialism—such as Joane Cardinal-Schubert, Robert Houle, Carl Beam and Jane Ash Poitras—were making inroads into the country's predominantly Euro-Canadian art gallery/museum system."[93]

Civil wars in international centres have also featured in work by Canadian artists, such as Yisa Akinbolaji's *Empty Playground, Silent Battlefield,* 2020, discussed earlier, where he juxtaposes

FIGURE 7.41. **Phyllis Serota**, *Order and Chaos*, 1998.

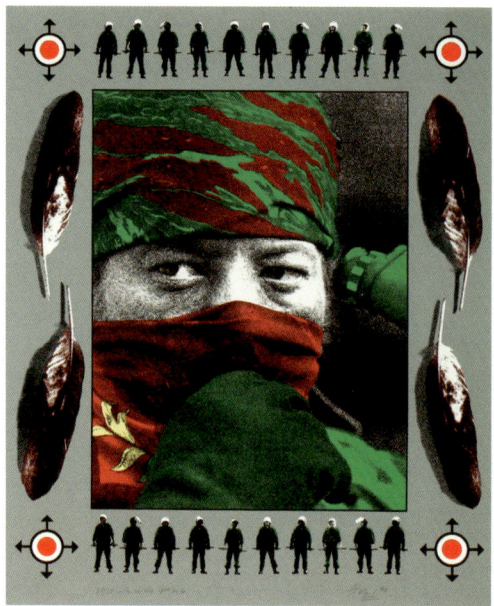

FIGURE 7.42.
David Neel, *Life on
the 18th Hole*, 1990.

the Biafran civil war in Nigeria during his childhood with COVID-19. Karen Cornelius's series, also discussed earlier, *Fabric of Belonging* likewise hearkens back to her youth growing up as a white anglophone in the Congo where her father was a medical doctor and founder of the mission clinic and hospital. First home-schooled, she later went to a mission school with both local and missionary children, and until she started university she lived in North America only for the two brief periods when the family was forced to flee from the Congo. As a young child she did not look like those around her but fully embraced their culture. Her *Fabric of Belonging Series* explores those dichotomies of cultures and peoples with its central image being a frilly dress, like the ones she wore as a child given to her by her grandmother. Through personal items she questions the essence of her own identity and belonging, weaving multiple meanings into her personal memories. In some she has included text from the letters she wrote to her grandparents; in others jungle patterns and colours are the backgrounds. She highlights both dichotomies: aesthetic cultural patterning and the personal and political dimensions. Of this series the artist says:

> This series marks the survival of me as a little girl and my escape from the Simba uprising. With the dress I work with the simplicity and innocence of childhood. With the patterning I work with the complexity of the situation, the danger, the fear, the

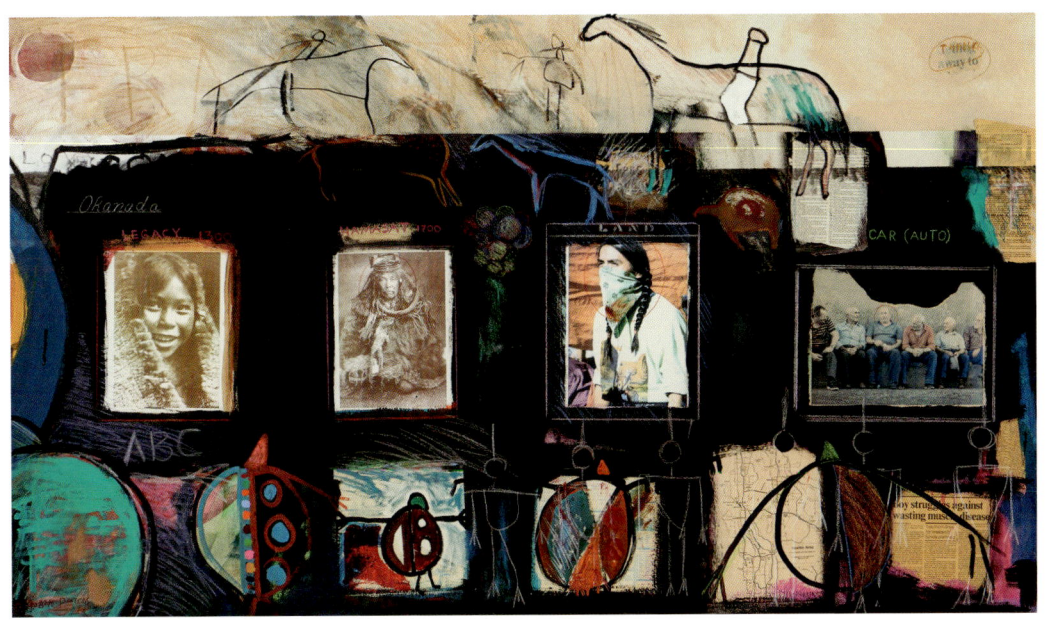

feeling of belonging to a culture and yet being an outsider. I am working with the tension of being inside and outside of a society. The translucence of the nylon fabric which is fluffy, light and fun is contrasted with a background of uncertainty and vastness represented by repetitive patterning, hard edged shapes and aerial views that evoke the endless jungle.[94]

Magnifying the unrest, the metaphor of the child's party dresses also evokes the wider fabric of society, relating to the societies' structures or frameworks. Used worldwide, fabric links peoples, situations, times, and cultures. Fabric, however, disintegrates, fades, shrinks, and tears, and holes appear. Societies do, too, particularly the ones Cornelius knew. In some of these works, the image extends beyond the paper itself, perhaps suggesting a future with better outcomes. Or do the untied bows become society's "untied ties"? Torn fabric, nostalgically looking back to places and times she remembers keenly, is Cornelius's symbol for the continuing political perils of the region today. Her experiences and subsequent understandings are reflected with gentleness and directness. Cornelius also deals with environmental and health concerns, as seen in her choice of materials and techniques, and her insistence on natural fabrics and papers, plant dyes, and water-based inks.

FIGURE 7.43. **Jane Ash Poitras**, *Oka Spirit Power*, 1990.

Wanda Koop (b. 1951), though never a "war artist," was, as gallery director Kate Davis noted, "disturbed and intrigued by scenes of conflict on television during the Gulf War."[95] Those images and her interest in light and space in her *Sightlines Series*, where she examines the beauty of place, are superimposed with the danger of fear. In *Red Dot,* 1996, with the large red dot at the centre of the work, she combines traditional landscape approaches with geometry. The dot draws the eye to her subtle and serene landscape. The word "sightlines" is primarily one used in architecture, and refers the perspective of what one can see from where they stand. Some of Koop's works in this series show the crosshairs of the sight of a gun one looks through to take aim. They are provocative paintings, with their exquisite control of colour, horizon lines, and depth conveying multiple sensibilities in the viewer. Koop's 2021 acrylic on canvas *Road to Nowhere* demonstrates her ability to convey mood, light, and danger with this almost monochrome painting. Once again, her smooth application of layer upon layer of paint gives depth and an eeriness. The two headlights peer from nowhere and raise questions of where from and where to.

Conflict in contemporary society is reflected in the gun culture, violence against women, and increasing numbers of police murders of Indigenous people. Andrew Valko tackles some of these issues, including the current gun culture, in his high realism through depicting anonymous situations. A recurring image in his work is a gun, as in his 1996 *Girl with a Gun.* The figure stands on a balcony and points a gun towards the street, contrasted by the idyllic interior in the foreground and lush garden urbanscape in the background. He continued this theme in his 1998 painting *Colt Double Eagle.* Its female figure, in her lingerie, has a revolver in her hand. *Gun* depicts a nude sitting in a chair with a gun on her lap, absorbed in looking into her hand mirror. Mystery and menace dominate places of pleasure. That danger that preoccupied Valko in the 1990s is prevalent in society in the 2020s.

At the time of writing, Russia's invasion into Ukraine is creating utter devastation and horror and Western Canadian artists are finding creative ways to support Ukrainians. Winnipeg's Michael Boss, for instance, is raising money for the Ukrainian Red Cross through the sale of his print *Ukrainian Kozaks send a letter to Putin,* 2014. The large drawing of the same title was originally done after the Russian invasion of Crimea and Eastern Europe. The artist partnered with Martha Street Studio to create the prints for the 2022 crisis. It is clear, artists will always convey the realities of conflict with the goal of truth and peace.

FIGURE 7.44. **Wanda Koop**, *Dreamland*, 2021.

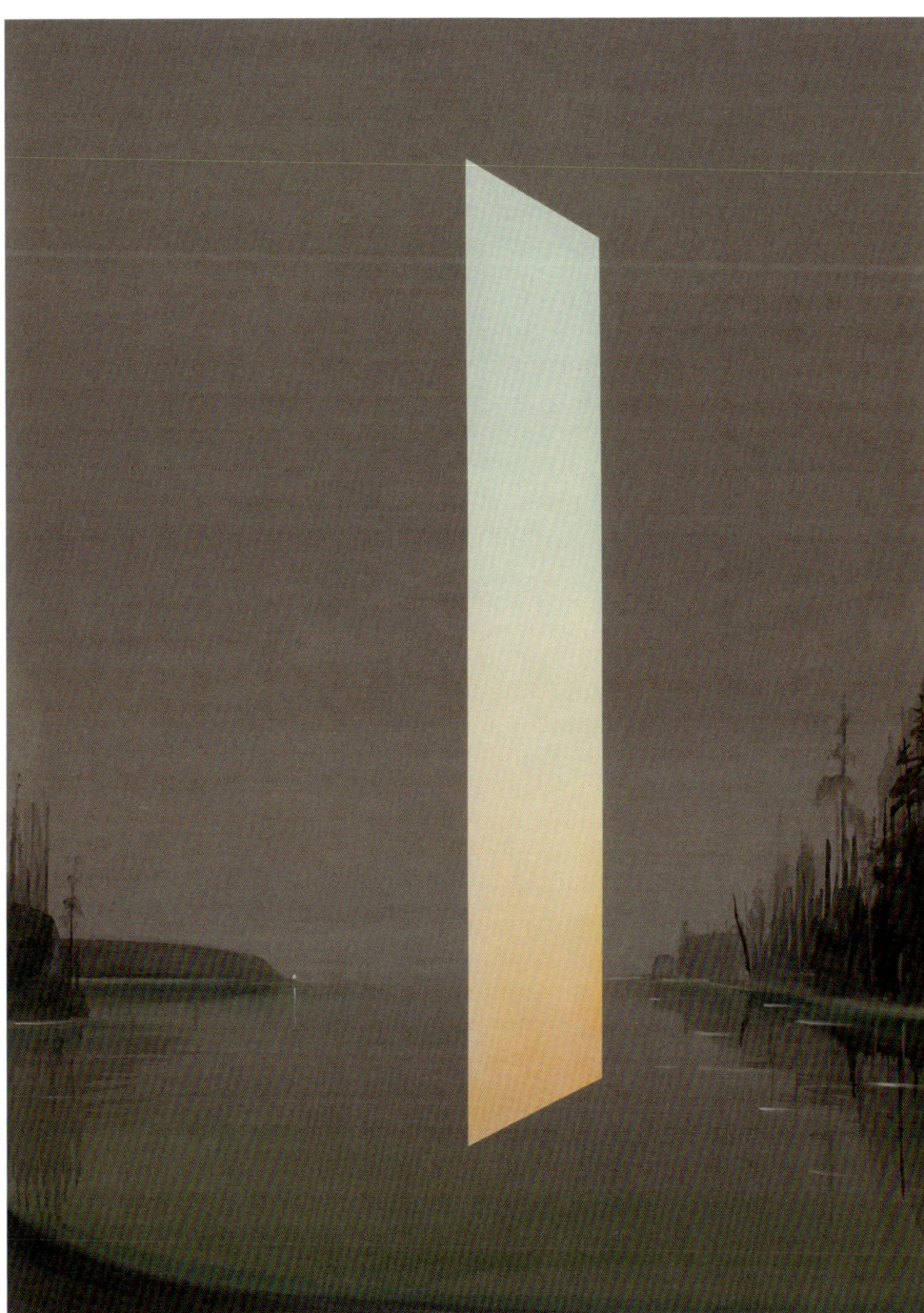

EPILOGUE

Western Canada's artists have done much in giving voice to Canadian art. Their contributions in message, innovation, insights, and substance are to be celebrated and commended. Their work from the late eighteenth century into the third decade of the twenty-first century assumes significance locally, regionally, nationally, and internationally. Their visual voices, as witnessed in the pages of this book, are an integral part of the development of Canadian art as a whole, in their subjects, materials, experimentations, and technical advances. The art of Western Canada's creators needs to be seen and heard, and their messages acted upon.

I give the final words and thoughts to the passion and commitments of the artists themselves:

> "Expression is the result of the activity of visual thought which has been a language for me."—Ivan Eyre[1]

> "I like paintings and drawings where there's room to think, where things aren't cut and dried."—Andrew Valko[2]

> "My work is a mixture of thought and feeling. It comes from my soul, from a wordless connection to something greater."—Esther Warkov[3]

> "When I make something, I am claiming the rights to it for myself, and at the same time for our children and all Kwakwaka'wakw people. They are the ones who really own it."—Richard Hunt[4]

ACKNOWLEDGEMENTS

The generosity of ideas, time and expertise from many individuals across Canada has made this book possible. I extend my sincerest gratitude to them all, especially those who have been on this journey with me from the outset. My love and highest respect for visual art, and the artists with whom I have worked for more than fifty years, inspired and drove this project. I could not have done it alone!

First and foremost, I owe a debt of gratitude to artists who have come from, and/or worked in the western regions of the country. Their creative expressions have defined who we are, our place, peoples, and issues in our world. Individually and collectively, they have added substantially to the development and annals of Canadian art. They gave me time, in person, on Zoom, on the telephone, in emails and letters. They allowed me into their studios and creative spaces, and shared their insights, goals, processes, and histories. The interviews I had with many are chronicled throughout the text and detailed in the footnotes in each part of this book. I also thank all those who gave me permission to reproduce their art in this volume. As well, my gratitude goes to the photographers of these works, and to the owners, public and private. All are noted in the List of Illustrations.

Many art galleries, archives, and art dealers across Canada assisted me with my research and in finding specific pieces, as well as allowing me to reproduce their works. They too are noted in endnotes and the image list. Having shared my professional art gallery life with many curators, directors, collections managers, conservators, educators, installers, and collectors, I know their sincere commitment to art and artists. I thank them for their careful stewardship of Canada's visual treasures. I thank all who have presented exhibitions of the art of the west, and who have written exhibition catalogues, books, articles, and videos on many visual leaders.

A number of people were on my personal book team and I thank them too. Sarah Yates joined me when the writing of this volume was in its infancy. Her expert editing skills and knowledge of the visual arts gave me truly important and critical advice in its structure and early drafting. I benefited immeasurably from her insights. Nicole Fletcher, who took on the daunting task of being my Image Editor, secured the copyright and licensing permissions and high-resolution images of all the illustrations. I could not have done that aspect of the book without her professional guidance and attention to the myriad details. Every effort has been made to secure reproduction permissions.

The University of Manitoba Press team was outstanding, supportive and encouraging at every step. Their collective and individual skills brought this book to a whole new level. My personal thanks go to David Carr, former director of the Press, for his encouragement and guidance from the outset, even when it was but an idea. David Larsen, who assumed the director position during the development of this project, took it on with similar interest and professionalism. I thank them both. Glenn Bergen was committed and active throughout the entire process. Always available, his advice, knowledge, humour, and perceptions were much appreciated. My thanks go too to Pat Sanders, who undertook the copyediting work for the Press. Her experience and attention to detail were truly important. Designer Frank Reimer has once again produced a compelling and beautiful volume, and his visual acuity was integral to its entire scope. I would like to also thank Jackie Markstrom of St. John's College for her fundraising efforts. All were, and are, a pleasure to work with and their contributions cannot be underestimated!

Others had faith in this dream of mine from the outset too. I thank the Winnipeg Arts Council for funding some of my early research. The Manitoba Arts Council provided funding to enable me to write the drafts of a number of sections. That support was truly important to me, and I thank them for their essential contributions. The Canada Council for the Arts supported the University of Manitoba Press in the actual publication. Susan Glass kindly volunteered to assist the Press in private sector financial support, and while that was not "on my plate," I thank her sincerely for helping to make this book a reality, as I do all the donors.

This project took a number of years and transited several chapters of my life. Its concept grew through my decades working in several Western Canadian art galleries, experiences which enabled me to meet artists who created in all visual disciplines, and to see tens of thousands of works of art. My serious research for this book, and the development of its basic format, began before the 2005 passing of my first husband, John Bovey. Much of the writing was done during the illness of my second husband, John Harvard. Both were active and supportive participants. My daughters Alixe and Katherine, and their families, were always on deck and interested, and their homes were some of my writing places. Friends were 'readers' as the book evolved. McNally Robinson Bookstore played a key role too, as they invited me to teach in their Community Classroom program. It was for those presentations over several years that I assembled key images and refined the themes in Part II. I very much appreciated the conversations and feedback from the participants in those classes.

Western Voices in Canadian Art has been a collaborative and collective effort in every step of its realization, from the day in 1970 when Russell Harper first challenged me to write the book, and through each stage to its final iteration.

Thank you to my family, friends, colleagues, artists, funders, photographers, and owners, and all those intimately involved in the project who cheered me on through its more challenging times, and celebrated its milestones. It has been a real pleasure and honour to examine the outstanding, leading-edge visual art, spanning more than three centuries, that has been created in Canada's four western provinces. May others follow up with more chapters!

Patricia Bovey

APPENDIX: WESTERN CANADIAN ART MILESTONES

Year	International Events	Canadian Milestones	Western Canadian Art Milestones
Pre-Contact		Indigenous Peoples develop strong visual cultures	
1731		La Verendrye organizes expeditions beyond Lake Winnipeg (1731–1743)	
1732		Fort Prince of Wales under construction (1732–1771)	
1759		Battle of the Plains of Abraham	
1771		Fort Prince of Wales completed	
1772		Cumberland House on the Lower Saskatchewan River opened by Hudson's Bay Company	
1776	American Revolution		
1778		Captain Cook's third voyage, including exploration of Nootka Sound and the Bering Strait	
1789	French Revolution		
1792		Captain George Vancouver's exploration to the Pacific Coast	
1793		Alexander McKenzie, first to cross Canada and reach Pacific Coast	

1800s

Year	International Events	Canadian Milestones	Western Canadian Art Milestones
1812	War between United States and Canada	Lord Selkirk and Selkirk Settlers arrive at Red River	
1821			Peter Rindisbacher, first European artist to settle in the West, arrives in Hudson Bay
1841		Union of Upper and Lower Canada Province of Canada formed	
1843		Fort Victoria established as British Columbia's fur-trading headquarters	
1845			Henry Warre travels west; creates drawings and water-colours from Red River to Fort Victoria

1846	Oregon Boundary Dispute resolved; Washington Treaty		Paul Kane's western travels (1846–1848)
1847			Paul Kane arrives at Fort Victoria
1848	European revolutions; Communist Manifesto published by Karl Marx and Friedrich Engels		Paul Kane exhibits western work in Toronto Henry Warre publishes *Sketches in North America and the Oregon Territory*
1858	Transatlantic telegraph cable laid		
1859			Paul Kane publishes *Wanderings of an Artist among the Indians of North America*
1861			Humphrey Hime: first photography in Western Canada (1861–1862)
1862			William Hind: first oil painting done outdoors in Canada Hannah Maynard establishes photography studio in Victoria
1864		Charlottetown Conference	
1865	American Civil War		
1867		Canadian Confederation Founding of Society of Canadian Painters	
1869		Canada purchases Rupertsland from HBC Louis Riel leads Métis in occupying Fort Garry	
1870	Franco-Prussian War	Riel Resistance Manitoba joins Confederation HBC surrenders Charter of Rupertsland	St. Boniface Hospital, founded in Manitoba; Grey Nuns recognize importance of art in healing
1871	Establishment of German Empire	British Columbia joins Confederation	Artist Emily Carr born in Victoria
1872		Founding of Ontario Society of Artists	Frederick Verner travels west
1873		Incorporation of Winnipeg	
1874	First Impressionist exhibition in Paris	Founding of RCMP	Russian Mennonites bring their traditional visual culture to Manitoba
1876	Invention of the telephone by Alexander Graham Bell		
1877		Founding of the University of Manitoba, first university in Western Canada	

1879	Thomas Edison perfects the lightbulb		
1880		Royal Canadian Academy of the Arts founded National Gallery of Canada founded CPR recruits Chinese workers to build the railway	
1884			Federal legislation bans potlatch on the Northwest Coast; Indigenous potlatch artifacts broken and confiscated
1885	First skyscraper built in Chicago	Last Spike of the CPR North-West Rebellion Battle of Batoche	
1886			Winnipeg Society for the Advancement of Painting and Drawing established
1888		Sir William Van Horne becomes president of CPR; free passes provided to artists in exchange for promotional scenic pictures	
1889	Eiffel Tower opens at the Paris World's Fair		
1890		Manitoba Schools Question	Lionel LeMoine FitzGerald born in Winnipeg
1891		First wave of Ukrainian settlements in West and arrivals of other immigrant groups	Winnipeg Industrial Exhibition includes a section devoted to art
1893			Virden Agricultural Fair presented Fine Art Section
1894			Winnipeg branch of Women's Art Association founded
1896		Gold discovered in Klondike, leading to 1898 gold rush	

1900–1910

1900	Freud's *Interpretation of Dreams* published		Frank Armington arrives in Winnipeg from Paris, establishes teaching studio
1901	First wireless communication between U.S. and U.K.		
1903	First powered flight: Wright Brothers		Founding of the Manitoba Society of Artists
1904			Carnegie Library opens in Winnipeg
1905		Saskatchewan and Alberta join Confederation	Bertram Brooker arrives in Winnipeg from Neepawa, Manitoba

1908	Ford introduces Model T— prototype of the motor car for the masses		
1909			BC Society of Artists formed Regina Society for the Advancement of Art, Literature, and Science formed Western Art Association formed in Winnipeg

1910–1919

1910			Island Arts and Crafts Society formed in Victoria Medalta Pottery established in Medicine Hat
1912	Sinking of the *Titanic*		Founding of the Winnipeg Art Gallery, first civic gallery in Canada
1913		Canadian Department of Defence becomes first government employer of artists	Founding of the Winnipeg School of Art
1914	Outbreak of the First World War	Internment of Ukrainian Canadians (1914–1918)	Establishment of Brigdens of Winnipeg to produce Eaton's catalogue Founding of the Winnipeg Sketch Club Edmonton Art Association founded University of Saskatchewan starts art collection
1916		Society of Canadian Painter-Etchers and Engravers succeeds Association of Canadian Etchers	Inglis Sheldon-Williams offers first art courses at Regina College (becomes University of Regina in 1974)
1918	End of the First World War	Women's right to vote in Canada Hutterites move to the Prairies and bring their visual culture	Calgary Art Club formed
1919		Winnipeg General Strike	Nutana Memorial Gallery, Saskatoon, starts art collection commemorating the war

1920–1929

1920		*Canadian Forum* first published	Regina and Vancouver sketch clubs formed
1921			Winnipeg Foundation established by William Alloway, first Canadian charitable foundation First meeting of British Columbia Art League, 3 February 1921 Edmonton Art Club formed

1923			Saskatoon Arts and Crafts Society formed
1924			Edmonton Art Gallery founded (becomes Art Gallery of Alberta in 2005) Group of Seven member Franz Johnston, first Canadian to head Winnipeg School of Art
1925		Canadian Society of Painters in Watercolour formed	Vancouver School of Art founded (now the Emily Carr University of Art and Design)
1926			Alberta College of Art founded Ina Uhthoff moves to Victoria from Glasgow and starts art school and studio Fred Varley appointed head of painting and drawing at Vancouver School of Art Provincial Institute of Technology and Art in Calgary offers first art courses
1927	Transatlantic telephone via radio		Emily Carr included in *Canadian West Coast Art, Native and Modern* exhibition at the National Gallery of Canada Bertram Brooker acknowledged as first abstract artist in Canada
1928		Sculptors' Society of Canada formed	
1929	Wall Street Financial Crash	Persons Decision	Lionel LeMoine FitzGerald becomes first Manitoba artist to be head of Winnipeg School of Art Women's Art Association of Saskatchewan founded
			Ina Uhthoff and Emily Carr sponsor American artist Mark Tobey to give classes in Victoria

1930–1939

1930	Dirty Thirties: Dust Bowl of the West		
1931			Vancouver Art Gallery founded Women Painters of Western Canada group formed Alberta Society of Artists formed
1932	Holodomor in Ukraine (1932–1933)	Prohibition; rum-running tunnels in Moose Jaw, Saskatchewan	
1932		Aird Commission (1932–1936) leads to founding of CBC	

1933		Canadian Society of Graphic Art succeeds Graphic Arts Club	Founding of the Mendel Art Gallery, Saskatoon Founding of Banff School of Fine Arts Fred Varley and Jock Macdonald found British Columbia College of Arts in Vancouver (closes in 1935)
1936	Spanish Civil War		Augustus Kenderdine starts Murray Point Summer Art School (later the site of Emma Lake Artists' Workshops) University of Saskatchewan opens first Western Canadian art history department Saskatoon Art Association founded
1937	Trans-Canada Air Lines begins regular flights		Founding of the Victoria School of Art Saskatoon Camera Club founded
1938			*Manitoba Arts Review* started (1938–1965)
1939	Second World War begins	Tour of King George VI and Queen Elizabeth to Canada (first sovereign to do so), including first radio broadcast from Government House in Manitoba	Founding of the National Film Board

1940–1949

1940		Rowell-Sirois Commission redefines federal-provincial relations	Lawren Harris moves to Vancouver
1941		Kingston Conference, first national meeting of Canadian artists Founding of Federation of Canadian Artists	Western artists attend Kingston Conference Emily Carr publishes *Klee Wyck* and wins Governor General's Award in Literature
1942		Internment of Japanese Canadians (1942–1945), including Takao Tanabe	
1943		*Canadian Art* starts publication	
1944		Emily Carr has first solo exhibition in a commercial gallery, Dominion Gallery in Montreal	Saskatoon Art Centre opens Western Exhibition Circuit established Regina Art Centre Association formed
1945	Second World War ends UNESCO formed with 145 member countries		Emily Carr dies in Victoria
1947	Canadian Women Artists' Exhibition in New York Cold War begins (1947–1991)		

| 1948 | | Paul-Emile Borduas publishes *Refus global* | Saskatchewan Arts Board established, first arts board in Canada |
| 1949 | | Massey Commission established to examine the state of arts and culture in Canada | |

1950–1959

1950	Korean War (1950–1953)		Ken Lochhead hired as director of newly opened School of Art at the University of Regina
1951		Massey Report calls for the establishment of the Canada Council	Union of the Winnipeg School of Art and University of Manitoba Founding of the Art Gallery of Greater Victoria as the Little Gallery
1952		Commonwealth Games in Vancouver	Emily Carr represents Canada at Venice Biennale (posthumously)
1953	Cuban Revolution (1953–1959)		Norman MacKenzie Art Gallery, Regina, founded; Richard Simmins appointed curator
1954			Vancouver artist B.C. Binning represents Canada at the Venice Biennale
1955	Vietnam War (1955–1975)		Ken Lochhead and Arthur McKay add professional artists' workshops at Emma Lake
1956	*Sputnik* launched, beginning the "Space Age" Hungarian Revolution		Lionel LeMoine FitzGerald dies in Winnipeg Vancouver's Jack Shadbolt represents Canada at Venice Biennale
1957	Establishment of the European Economic Community	Founding of the Canada Council	
1959			American artist Barnett Newman leads workshop at Emma Lake Brandon Art Club becomes Brandon Allied Arts Council

1960–1969

1960	John F. Kennedy elected U.S. president		Saskatchewan sculptor Robert Murray moves to New York
1961	Bay of Pigs Invasion	Completion of the Trans-Canada Highway	Regina Five exhibition organized by Ron Bloore Provincial Institute of Technology and Art becomes Alberta College of Art
1962			Clement Greenberg at Emma Lake

1963	Assassination of John F. Kennedy	Royal Commission on Bilingualism and Biculturalism (1963–1968)	Kenneth Noland at Emma Lake Clement Greenberg tours Prairie artists' studios
1964			Art Gallery, Saskatoon, founded University of Victoria Fine Arts Faculty started Victoria's Elza Mayhew represents Canada at Venice Biennale
1965			Manitoba Arts Council established
1966			Glenbow-Alberta Institute founded
1967		Canada's Centennial Expo 67, World's Fair in Montreal	Vancouver Art Gallery exhibition *Arts of the Raven*, first major Indigenous art exhibition
1968	Assassination of Martin Luther King	Pierre Elliott Trudeau elected prime minister National Arts Centre open in Ottawa	Bill Lobchuk founds Grand Western Canadian Screen Shop in Winnipeg
1969	First walk on the Moon	Canadian Artists' Representation/le Front des artistes (CARFAC) founded	Iain and Ingrid Baxter incorporate N.E. Thing Co.

1970–1979

1970		October Crisis in Quebec	Artist-run Photographers Gallery opens in Saskatoon Gitanmaax School of Northwest Coast Indian art opens in Ksan, BC
1971		Canadian Multiculturalism Act	New Winnipeg Art Gallery opens, Gus da Roza architect
1972		National Museums Corporation of Canada established Canada Council Art Bank established *Vanguard* magazine (1972–1989) begins publication at Vancouver Art Gallery	Artist-run gallery Shoestring opens in Saskatoon Indigenous Group of Seven founded in Winnipeg (as Professional Native Indian Artists Inc.)
1973		*Bulletin of the Canadian Conference of the Arts* begins publication	
1974		Council for Business and the Arts established Association for Native Development in the Performing and Visual Arts formed Canadian Crafts Council formed	

1975	Fall of Saigon, marking end of Vietnam War	*CARFAC News* started in Winnipeg	Art Gallery of Greater Victoria publishes *Arts Victoria* Surrey Art Gallery opens Saskatchewan Craft Council formed
1976			Saskatchewan Federated College begins programming in Regina, including Indian art program
1977			University of Calgary printmaking program starts under Bill Laing
1978			Manitoba Craft Council formed Print and Drawing Council of Canada moves headquarters to Calgary

1980–1989

1980			Vancouver's General Idea represented Canada at Venice Biennale Print and Drawing Council of Canada moves headquarters to Edmonton
1981		Canadian Society of Decorative Arts formed	Victoria Limners Society founded
1982		Applebaum-Hébert Commission on cultural policy in Canada Repatriation of Canadian Constitution and adoption of the Charter of Rights and Freedoms	
1983			Vancouver Art Gallery moved to the Vancouver Court House
1984		Roberta Bondar, first Canadian woman in space	Vancouver artists Ian Carr-Harris and Liz Magor represent Canada at Venice Biennale
1985		Parliament passes Cultural Property Export and Import Act and establishes Cultural Property Export Review Board: cultural properties designated major works of art donated to Canadian art galleries as "outstanding significance and national importance"	*Border Crossings* begins publication (succeeds *Arts Manitoba*)
1986		Bovey Taskforce on Funding of the Arts in Canada Withrow-Richard National Museums Taskforce Expo 86 in Vancouver	

1988		Amendment to the Copyright Act, extending protection to a wider range of works Calgary Olympics Reparations to Japanese Canadians interned during the Second World War	Victoria artist Roland Brenner represents Canada at Venice Biennale
1989	Fall of Berlin Wall and collapse of the Soviet Union Tiananmen Square Massacre		

1990–1999

1990		Oka Crisis	
1991	Nelson Mandela released from jail, marking end of South Africa's Apartheid		Alberta Arts Foundation established
1992	Bosnian War (1992–1995)	Charlottetown Accord Status of the Artist Act	
1993		Creation of the Department of Canadian Heritage	
1994		Commonwealth Games in Victoria	
1995			British Columbia Arts Council established First Nations Saskatchewan artist Edward Poitras represents Canada at Venice Biennale
1996		Canada Council establishes Acquisition Assistance Fund for art galleries	
1997			Vancouver artist Rodney Graham represents Canada at Venice Biennale

2000–2009

2001	9/11 Terrorist attacks on the World Trade Center, New York Afghanistan War commences (2001–2021)		Alberta artists Janet Cardiff and George Bures Miller represent Canada at Venice Biennale
2002		Canadian Voluntary Sector Accord	*Galleries West* begins publication
2005			New Alberta Art Gallery opens in Edmonton (formerly the Edmonton Art Gallery) Indigenous artist Rebecca Belmore represents Canada at Venice Biennale
2007			Buhler Gallery opens in St. Boniface Hospital, Winnipeg, first public gallery in a hospital

| 2008 | | Canadian government apologizes to survivors of residential schools | |

2010–2022

2008		Truth and Reconciliation Commission established (2008–2015)	
2010		Vancouver Winter Olympics	
2011	Syrian civil war (ongoing) Canada withdraws from Afghanistan	Occupy movement	Vancouver artist Steven Shearer represents Canada at Venice Biennale
2012		Idle No More movement	
2013			University of Manitoba School of Art receives York Wilson prize to acquire Robert Houle's *Residential School Series*
2014	Emily Carr exhibition at the Dulwich Picture Gallery, London	Canadian Museum for Human Rights opens in Winnipeg	Indigenous artist Rebecca Belmore receives "blanket" commission from Canadian Museum of Human Rights
2016		National Inquiry into Missing and Murdered Indigenous Women and Girls (2016–2019)	
2017			Vancouver artist Geoffrey Farmer represents Canada at Venice Biennale Remai Modern opens in Saskatoon
2020	Global COVID-19 pandemic and lockdowns Black Lives Matter movement	Senate of Canada inaugurates Honouring Canadian Black artists installations	
2021		Unmarked graves found at many former residential schools Marches on 1 July in honour of Indigenous children Toppling of statues and subsequent church burnings and totem pole scorching Senate of Canada unanimously endorses Parliamentary Visual Laureate	
2022	Russian invasion of Ukraine		Vancouver artist Stan Douglas represents Canada at Venice Biennale Canadian Black Artists United founded

ILLUSTRATIONS

1.1 Angelique Merasty, *Birchbark Biting*, 20th century. Birchbark, paper, 8.9 x 8.9 cm. Collection of the Manitoba Craft Museum and Library, 1331.05.

1.2 Unknown artist, *Mittens*, 1870–1880. Glass bead, copper bead, metal bead, tanned caribou hide, wool fabric, silk ribbon, 30 x 15 cm. Collection of the Manitoba Craft Museum, 62.00. Photo: Leif Norman.

1.3 Emily Carr, *Blunden Harbour*, c. 1930. Oil on canvas, 129.8 x 93.6 cm. National Gallery of Canada, Ottawa, 4285. Photo: NGC.

1.4 Lionel LeMoine FitzGerald, *Summer Afternoon, The Prairie*, 1921. Oil on canvas, 107.2 x 89.5 cm. Collection of the Winnipeg Art Gallery, L-90. Photo: Lianed Marcoleta. Courtesy of WAG-Qaumajuq.

1.5 Sophie Pemberton, *Spring*, 1902. Oil on canvas, 100.5 x 142.5 cm. Art Gallery of Greater Victoria. Bequest of the artist, 1973.210.001. Photo: Stephen Topher.

1.6 Sir George Back, *Limestone Rocks, Lake Winnipeg*, 1825. Watercolour, ink on paper, 18 x 22.7 cm. Collection of the Winnipeg Art Gallery. Gift of the Women's Committee, G-69-103. Photo: Ernest Mayer. Courtesy of WAG-Qaumajuq.

1.7 Peter Rindisbacher, *Sled Dogs Attacking a Bison*, c. 1822–1824. Watercolour on paper, 20.32 x 25.4 cm. Manitoba Museum, Hudson's Bay Collection. Image copyright Manitoba Museum, Winnipeg, MB.

1.8 William Hind, *Horse Drinking at an Ice Hole*, c. 1863. Oil on panel, 31.1 x 23.4 cm. Library and Archives Canada, 1937-282-1.

1.9 Paul Kane, *Scene in the Northwest—Portrait*, c. 1845–1846. Oil on canvas, 55.5 x 76 cm. The Thomson Collection at the Art Gallery of Ontario, 2009/507. Copyright Art Gallery of Ontario (2017). Photo: Michael Cullen.

1.10 Frederick Verner, *Buffalo in the Foothills*, 1914. Oil on canvas, 76 x 63 cm. Collection of the Art Gallery of Greater Victoria. Gift of George and Lola Kidd, 2008.003.048. Photo: Stephen Topher.

1.11 Alexander J. Musgrove, *Manitoba Farm*, n.d. Oil on canvas, 49 x 59 cm. Collection of the Winnipeg Art Gallery, gift of John P. Crabb, G-85-734. Photo: Ernest Mayer. Courtesy of WAG-Qaumajuq.

1.12 Donald MacQuarrie, *Landscape with Crescent Moon*, 1913. Oil on canvas, 50.4 x 61.3 cm. Collection of the Winnipeg Art Gallery. Gift of Mrs. Hugh Morrison, G-64-22. Courtesy of WAG-Qaumajuq.

1.13 Charles Fraser Comfort, *Prairie Road*, 1925. Oil on canvas, 116.9 x 86.4 cm. The Hart House Collection, University of Toronto. Gift of the Graduating Year of 1931, HH1931.001.

1.14 A.C. Leighton, *Molar Pass*, c. 1950. Watercolour on paper, 27.3 x 37.5 cm. The Leighton Foundation, Calgary.

1.15 Frederick Horsman Varley, *View from the Artist's Bedroom Window, Jericho Beach*, 1929. Oil on canvas, 99.4 x 83.8 cm. Collection of the Winnipeg Art Gallery. Acquired with the assistance of the Women's Committee and the Woods-Harris Trust Fund No. 1, G-72-7. Photo: Ernest Mayer. Courtesy of WAG-Qaumajuq.

1.16 Frank H. Johnston, *Serenity, Lake of the Woods*, 1922. Oil on canvas, 102.3 x 128.4 cm. Collection of the Winnipeg Art Gallery, L-102. Photo: Lianed Marcoleta. Courtesy of WAG-Qaumajuq.

1.17 Lionel LeMoine FitzGerald, *Potato Patch, Snowflake,* 1925. Oil on canvas on board, 43.4 x 52.2 cm. Collection of the Winnipeg Art Gallery. Gift of Dr. Bernhard Fast, G-98-279. Photo: Ernest Mayer. Courtesy of WAG-Qaumajuq.

1.18 Ernest Lindner, *Skeleton of the Forest*, 1966. Watercolour on paper, 75.9 x 56.1 cm. Collection of the Winnipeg Art Gallery. Acquired with the assistance of the Canada Council, G-69-27. Photo: Ernest Mayer. Courtesy of WAG-Qaumajuq.

1.19 Jock Macdonald, *Revolving Shapes*, 1950. Watercolour, wax resist on paper, 24.8 x 25.1 cm. Art Gallery of Greater Victoria. Gift of Collin and Sylvia Graham, 1981.227.001. Photo: Stephen Topher.

1.20 Jack Leonard Shadbolt, *Dog Among the Ruins*, 1947. Watercolour, carbon pencil on paper, 78.2 x 56.9 cm. Art Gallery of Greater Victoria, Colin Graham Fund/Canada Council Matching Funds, 1980.069.001. Photo: Stephen Topher. Courtesy and copyright of Simon Fraser University Galleries.

1.21 Doug Morton, *Ida Grey*, 1975. Acrylic on canvas, 108.2 x 120.6 cm. Art Gallery of Greater Victoria. Purchased with funds from the Royal Canadian Academy and the Estate of Lieutenant Commander James Denoon Laurie, R.C.N. (Retired), 1986.028.001. Photo: Stephen Topher.

1.22 William Ashby McCloy, *And Peter Followed Afar Off*, 1951. Poster paint on canvas on plaster board, 76.5 x 114.6 cm. Collection of the Winnipeg Art Gallery. Gift of the Women's Committee, G-54-13. Photo: Serge Gumenyuk. Courtesy of WAG-Qaumajuq. Photo: Ernest Mayer, courtesy WAG-Qaumajuq.

1.23 Ivan Eyre, *Director*, 1974. Acrylic on canvas, 142 x 162 cm. Collection of the Winnipeg Art Gallery. Gift of the artist on the occasion of Dr. Ferdinand Eckhardt's 90th Birthday, G-92-97. Photo: Ernest Mayer, courtesy WAG-Qaumajuq.

1.24 Myfanwy Spencer Pavelic, *Colin Graham, Director 1951–1973*, 1973. Acrylic on canvas, 111.9 x 104.3 cm. Art Gallery of Greater Victoria, Commissioned by the Women's Committee, 1985.002.001. Photo: Stephen Topher.

1.25 Kenneth Campbell Lochhead, *Sky Location*, from *L Series*, 1967. Acrylic on canvas, 346 x 206 cm. Collection of the Winnipeg Art Gallery. Gift of Gustavo and Gloria da Roza, 1999-614. Photo: Ernest Mayer. Courtesy of WAG-Qaumajuq.

1.26 Arthur McKay, *Untitled (Concentric Circles),* 1970. Enamel on Masonite, 31 x 30.5 cm. Collection of the Dunlop Art Gallery, PC89.3. Photo: Don Hall.

1.27 Maxwell Bates, *Kindergarten*, 1965. Oil on canvas, 91.2 x 121.8 cm. Art Gallery of Greater Victoria. Purchased with funds from the Mortimer-Lamb Bequest, Women's Committee and Private Donors, 1982.007.001. Photo: Stephen Topher.

1.28 Pat Martin Bates, *The Angel of the Blue Sky is Crying Parallax Tears*, 1998. Acrylic, aluminum lightbox, thread, metal grommets, feathers, 120 x 81.2 cm. Collection of the Art Gallery of Greater Victoria. Gift of the following generous donors: Oak Bay Marina Ltd.; Karin E. Koerner Robert Drurie; Ian Izard; Robert Wallace; Kathy Stole; Anne Vogel; Jayne Pullen; Terry Harper; Steve McKerrell; G.C. Aitken and Bob Brand, 1998.004.001. Photo: Stephen Topher.

1.29 Jackson Beardy, *Untitled*, 1971. Tempera, ink on birchbark, 16.2 x 18.8 cm. Collection of the Winnipeg Art Gallery. Gift of Marty Dolin in memory of the Hon. Mary Beth Dolin, G-86-116. Photo: Ernest Mayer. Courtesy of WAG-Qaumajuq.

1.30 Walter J. Phillips, *York Boat on Lake Winnipeg*, 1930. Colour woodcut on paper, 132/150, 29.4 x 38.4 cm. Collection of the Winnipeg Art Gallery, L-66-G. Photo: Ernest Mayer. Courtesy of WAG-Qaumajuq.

1.31 Bill Lobchuk, *Moo One*, 1975. Silkscreen on paper, 41.5 x 62.5 cm. Collection of the Buhler Gallery, St. Boniface Hospital. Photo: Leif Norman.

1.32 Michael Morris, *Proposed Backdrop for North Shore*, 1965. Gouache, ink on paper, 35.6 x 51 cm. Art Gallery of Greater Victoria. From the Women's Committee Cultural Fund, 1977.226.001. Photo: Stephen Topher.

1.33 Gu Xiong, *The River*, 1998. Mixed media installation, 154.9 x 914.4 x 396.2 cm. Courtesy of the artist.

1.34 Dana Claxton, *Buffalo Bone China*, 1997. Video, bone china, stanchion, rope, ribbon, 2/2. dimensions variable. Collection of the Winnipeg Art Gallery. Acquired with funds from the Winnipeg Rh Institute Foundation and with the support of the Canada Council for the Arts Acquisition Assistance Program, 1999-601. Photo: Serge Gumenyuk. Courtesy of WAG-Qaumajuq.

2.1 Terry Fenton, *GLARE, Saskatchewan*, 2016–2021. Oil on panel, 47 x 76.2 cm. Courtesy of the artist.

2.2 Reta Cowley, *Emma Lake #2*, 1963. Watercolour on paper, 56.5 x 76.8 cm. Collection of the Dunlop Art Gallery, PC83.1.8. Photo: Don Hall.

2.3 Toni Onley, *Untitled Collage 1B*, c. 1963–1964. Oil on paper collage, 30 x 40 cm. Collection of the Kelowna Art Gallery. Gift of Ron and Diane Markey, 2001, 2001-38.

2.4 Ann Kipling, *July. 31/2008*, from the series *Sky Mountain*, 2008. Colour micron pen on rag paper. Private collection. Photo: Leif Norman.

2.5 Tony Tascona, *Inverted Apex*, 1969. Acrylic lacquer on steel, 91.4 x 205.7 cm. Collection of the Great-West Life Assurance Company. Photo: Ernest Mayer. Courtesy of WAG-Qaumajuq.

2.6 Esther Warkov, *House of Tea*, 1999. Mixed media on paper, 84 x 63 cm. Private collection. Photo: Serge Gumenyuk.

2.7 Walter Jule, *Neither Dusk nor Dawn*, 2008. Etching, lithograph with gampi chine-colle on paper, 105.5 x 76 cm. Courtesy of the artist.

2.8 John Snow, *September Landscape*, 1978. Lithograph on paper, 35.6 x 50.6 cm. Art Gallery of Greater Victoria. Gift of the Women's Committee Cultural Fund and Canada Council Matching Funds, 1981.210.001. Photo: Stephen Topher.

2.9 David Thauberger, *Velvet Bunnies*, 1977. Silkscreen on white velvet, ed. 14/20, 95 x 81.5 cm. Collection of the MacKenzie Art Gallery. Gift of Veronica and David Thauberger, 1992-21.

2.10 E.J. (Ted) Howorth, *The Passion of Coquille St. Jacques*, 1985. Silkscreen on paper, 51 x 132 cm. Courtesy of the artist.

2.11 William Laing, *Walking #1*, 2020. Mixed media, 38.7 x 33 x 25.4 cm. Courtesy of Herringer Kiss Gallery.

2.12 Arthur Vickers, *Intangible Heritage*, 2011. Low relief of 24-karat gold powder, hand laid 24-karat gold leafing, mixed media, 139.7 x 123.2 cm. Courtesy of the artist.

2.13 Arthur Vickers, *Mount Baker*, 1999. Hand-pulled silkscreen on paper, 68 x 51.4 cm. Courtesy of the artist.

2.14 Ian Wallace, *Untitled (In The Street I) (Lyse)*, 1988. Diptych. Photolaminate with acrylic and ink monoprint on canvas panels, 244 x 244 cm. Photo: Stefan Altenburger Photography.

Courtesy of Catriona Jeffries, Vancouver.

2.15 Rodney Graham, *The Gifted Amateur, Nov. 10th 1962*, 2007. Dye coupler transparency in fluorescent lightbox, 286.1 x 556 x 17.8 cm installed. National Gallery of Canada, 42347.1-3. Photo: NGC.

2.16 Robert Houle, *Premises for Self-Rule: Treaty No. 1*, 1994. Acrylic, photo emulsion, vinyl lettering on canvas, Plexiglas. (a). Photographic panel: 38 x 64 x 5 cm; (b). Painting: 152 x 152 x 5 cm; (c). Plexi panel with text: 152 x 152 cm. Collection of the Winnipeg Art Gallery. Acquired with funds from the Canada Council for the Arts Acquisition Assistance Program, G-96-11 abc. Photo: Ernest Mayer. Courtesy of WAG-Qaumajuq.

2.17 Laura Vickerson, *Rose Red Curtain*, 1999. Rose petals, organza, dressmaker's pins, 243.8 x 396.2 x 640.1 cm. Courtesy of the artist. Photo: Isaac Applebaum.

2.18 Shelley Ouellet, *Johnston Falls*, 2012. Plastic beads, plastic wrapped steel wire, 548.6 x 279.4 cm. Collection of the Alberta Foundation for the Arts, 2014.030.001.

2.19 Willow Rector, *The Singing Bone* (rear view), from the series *TRAPPED*, 2013. Hand embroidery on Arctic Fox pelt, 71.1 x 36.8 x 20.3 cm. Courtesy of the artist. Photo: William Eakin.

2.20 Bruce Head, *Quartet*, 1978. Acrylic on shaped canvas, 180 x 186 cm. Collection of the Winnipeg Art Gallery. Gift of the artist, 2009-5.1 to 4. Photo: Ernest Mayer. Courtesy of WAG-Qaumajuq.

2.21 Richard Hunt, *Tlingit Chief*, c. 2000. Bronze, 45.7 x 12.7 x 12.7 cm. Courtesy of the artist. Photo: Sheila Spence.

2.22 John Nugent, *No. 1 Northern*, 1976. Steel. 1310.4 x 731.5 x 243.8 cm. Commissioned by the Canadian Grain Commission. Photo: Christian Cassidy.

2.23 Don Proch, *Colville's Horse Races Through the Prairie Drive-Thru Gallery, Brushing Past John Nugent's "No. 1 Hard," Heading West to Haida Gwaii*, 2016. Silverpoint, pencil, and coloured pencil on fibreglass, wood, welded steel, dyed sisal and cast bronze horse, 101.6 x 91.4 x 25.4 cm. Private collection. Photo: Ernest Mayer.

2.24 Douglas Bentham, *Pinnacle I: Marking Time*, 2003. Steel, rust, 373.3 x 66 x 50.8 cm.; *Pinnacle II: Relic of Memory*, 2003. Steel, rust, paint, 289.5 x 60.9 x 45.7 cm.; *Pinnacle III: Ray of Light*, 2003. Steel, rust, 345.3 x 58.4 x 40.6 cm. Collection of the Glenbow Museum. Photo: Installation in Resonance, 2004, at the Mendel Art Gallery. Courtesy of Remai Modern.

2.25 Brian Jungen, *Prototype for New Understanding #7*, 1999. Nike Air Jordans, 28 x 36 x 56 cm. Photo: Vancouver Art Gallery. Courtesy of Catriona Jeffries, Vancouver.

2.26 Warren Carther, *Aperture*, 2011. Glass, concrete, LED lighting, 371.9 x 219.5 x 103.6 cm. Winnipeg James Armstrong Richardson International Airport. Photo: Gerry Kopelow.

2.27 Ione Thorkelsson, *Incoming*, 2012. Cast glass. Installation. Winnipeg James Armstrong Richardson International Airport.

2.28 Esther Warkov, *House of Tea*, 1997–1998. Graphite, charcoal pencil, Conté crayon, pastel on hand-coloured Barrier white paper, 213.4 x 152.4 x 243.9 cm. Collection of the Winnipeg Art Gallery. Acquired with funds from the President's Appeal 2000 and with the support of the Canada Council for the Arts Acquisition Assistance Program, 2000-86. Photo: Ernest Mayer. Courtesy of WAG-Qaumajuq.

2.29 Elza Mayhew, *Princess*, 1963. Aluminum, wood, paint, 136 x 38 cm. Collection of the Art Gallery of Greater Victoria. Gift of George and Lola Kidd, 2008.003.010. Photo: Stephen Topher.

2.30 Bill Reid, *The Spirit of Haida Gwaii: The Black Canoe*, 1991. Cast bronze with black patina, 605 x 389 x 348 cm. Gift of Nabisco Brands Limited, 1991. Collection of Global Affairs Canada. Courtesy of the Canadian Embassy, Washington DC. Photo: Keegan Bursaw.

2.31 General Idea, *AIDS* (detail), 1988. Acrylic on canvas, silkscreened wallpaper. (a). Painting: 244 x 244 cm; (b). Painting: 244 x 244 cm; (c). Painting: 244 x 244 cm. Collection of the Winnipeg Art Gallery. Acquired with funds from the Eckhardt-Gramatté Foundation, G-92-191 abc. Photo: Ernest Mayer. Courtesy of WAG-Qaumajuq.

2.32 Shawna Dempsey, and Lorri Millan, *Arborite Housedress*, from *The Dress Series*, 1993. Dress: spruce plywood frame, mahogany plywood panels, Arborite laminate veneer, Velcro, chrome kitchen hardware, 107 x 76 x 50 cm. Performance: 25 minutes. Collection of the Winnipeg Art Gallery. Acquired with funds from the Canada Council for the Arts Acquisition Assistance program, 2002-43 ab. Photo: Sheila Spence.

2.33 Eric Metcalfe, *Furthermore*, 2011. Gouache on paper, 27.9 x 35.6 cm. Courtesy of the artist.

2.34 Winston Leathers, *#17 Cosmic Order/ in a line plane*, from the series *Cosmic Variations*, 1972. Screenprint 1/20, 72.5 x 57.3 cm. Courtesy of the MacKenzie Art Gallery.

2.35 IAIN BAXTER&, *Still Life*, n.d. Plastic, 81 x 95.5 x 5 cm. Collection of the Art Gallery of Greater Victoria. Gift of Colin Graham, 1980.002.002. Photo: Stephen Topher.

2.36 Rebecca Belmore, *The Named and the Unnamed* (still), 2002. Video installation. Collection of the Morris and Helen Belkin Art Gallery, University of British Columbia. Purchased with support from the Canada Council for the Arts Acquisition Assistance program and the Morris and Helen Belkin Foundation, 2005. Photo: Howard Ursuliak.

2.37 Reva Stone, *Carnevale 3.0*, 2000–2002. Computer-controlled video projections, life-size aluminum figure and robotic platform, four microcontrollers, multiple custom sensors, wireless transceivers, video camera, video projector. Collection of the Winnipeg Art Gallery. Gift of Harold Stone, 2009-36. Photo: Ernest Mayer. Courtesy of WAG-Qaumajuq.

3.1 Don Reichert, *Folds*, 1979. Acrylic on canvas, 213.4 x 274.3 cm. Private collection. Photo: Leif Norman.

3.2 George Dixon, *A View of Hippa Island, Queen Charlotte's Isles*, c. 1788. Watercolour on paper, 17.8 x 24.5 cm. Collection of National Library of Australia, Rex Nan Kivell Collection, NK7402.

3.3 Grafton Tyler Brown, *Entrance to the Harbor*, 1883. Oil on canvas, 40.6 x 66 cm. BCA, Image PDP010890 courtesy of the Royal British Columbia Museum. Purchased

through the legacy gift of Elizabeth Munro Rithet and the gift of Uno Langmann Fine Art, 2022.

3.4 Jeanette Johns, *11,500 BP, 11,100 BP, 9,900 BP*, and *9,400 BP* from the series *Retreating Agassiz*, 2009. Silkscreen, etching, gold leaf, ink on paper, 76.2 x 55.9 cm. ea. Collection of Manitoba Hydro. Photo: Jeanette Johns.

3.5 George H. Swinton, *Birth of a Prairie River*, 1959–1960. Oil on canvas, 81.5 x 122 cm. Collection of the Winnipeg Art Gallery. Gift of the Women's Committee, G-60-179. Photo: Ernest Mayer, courtesy WAG-Qaumajuq.

3.6 Humphrey Hime, *The Prairie, on the Banks of Red River, Looking South*, 1858. Photograph, 25.4 x 30.5 cm. Archives of Manitoba, Humphrey Lloyd Hime collection, Photo 23, "The Prairie, on the banks of Red River, looking south," [September–October 1858], P8290/23, N10832.

3.7 Kenneth Campbell Lochhead, *August Path*, 1964. Acrylic on canvas, 22.9 x 363 cm. Collection of the Winnipeg Art Gallery. Gift of the artist, 2000-135. Photo: Lianed Marcoleta. Courtesy of WAG-Qaumajuq.

3.8 Emily Carr, *Overhead*, 1935–1936. Oil on paper, 61 x 91 cm. Collection of the Vancouver Art Gallery, Emily Carr Trust. Photo: Vancouver Art Gallery.

3.9 Augustus Kenderdine, *Homeward Bound*, 1925. Oil on canvas, 51.3 x 76.3 cm. MacKenzie Art Gallery, University of Regina Collection. Gift of Mr. Norman MacKenzie, 1953-65.

3.10 Illingworth Kerr, *Boggy Creek Valley, Autumn [near the Qu'Appelle Valley]*, 1970. Oil on canvas board, 40.6 x 50.8 cm. Private collection. Photo: Courtesy of Hodgins Art Auctions.

3.11 James Henderson, *Qu'appelle Valley*, 1932. Oil on board, 26.9 x 30 cm. Private collection.

3.12 Luke Lindoe, *Alkali Basin*, 1947. Oil on Masonite, 59 x 83.5 cm. Collection of the Alberta Foundation of the Arts, 1981.133.001.

3.13 Dorothy Knowles, *North Saskatchewan River*, 1989. Oil on linen, 122 x 91.5 cm. MacKenzie Art Gallery. Gift of artist, 2000-27.

3.14 Norman Yates, *Landspace 241*, 2011. Acrylic on canvas, 150.5 x 537.3 cm. Collection of the Art Gallery of

Greater Victoria. Purchased with the support of David Harris Flaherty, Noel Parker-Jervis, Garry and Carol Leach, anonymous donors, and Gift of the Estate, 2016.006.001 a-c. Courtesy of the Victoria Conference Centre. Photo: Sheila Spence.

3.15 Diane Whitehouse, *Untitled*, from the series *Not Yet Quite Dark*, 2017. Acrylic, oil, mixed media on canvas. Courtesy of the artist. Photo: Lilian Bonin.

3.16 Pat Martin Bates, *Sky in Skye—The 9th Island—Darwin Night Watch on the Barque Marques*, 1985. Lightbox with screen printing, embossed perforated print with chine collé, gold threads, foils, oak leaf, needle piercing, oil pastels on handmade BFK Rives papers, 140.5 x 129.5 x 10 cm. Courtesy of the artist. Photo: John Taylor.

3.17 Don Proch, *Asessippi Tread*, 1970. Silverpoint, graphite, fiberglass, wood, steel, 42.5 x 84.5 x 197 cm. Collection of the Winnipeg Art Gallery. Gift of the Women's Committee, G-70-631. Photo: Ernest Mayer. Courtesy of WAG-Qaumajuq.

3.18 Sheila Spence, *The Creek*, 2008. Digital print. Courtesy of the artist.

3.19 Carole Sabiston, *Flying Rondels at Dawn*, 1987. Textile assemblage, diam. 151.1 cm. Courtesy of the artist.

3.20 Carole Sabiston, *Take Off: Point of Departure and Mode of Travel*, c. 1987. Textile assemblage, 365.8 x 365.8 x 365.8 cm. University of Victoria Art Acquisition Fund, U008.18.1. Photo: Jeff Barber.

3.21 Roger LaFrenière, *The Zone*, 2015. Acrylic on canvas, 167.6 x 289.6 cm. Private collection. Photo: Leif Norman.

3.22 Roger LaFrenière, *By the Lake*, 2007. Acrylic on board, 30.5 x 30.5 cm. ea. Private collection. Photo: Matt Pia.

3.23 Gathie Falk, *Pieces of Water #10—El Salvador*, 1982. Oil on canvas, 198.2 x 167.4. cm. Collection of the Art Gallery of Greater Victoria. Purchased with Women's Committee Cultural Fund and Canada Council Matching Funds, 1983.066.001. Photo: Stephen Topher.

3.24 Barbara Milne, *Nocturne Blue and Gray*, 2011. Oil on panel, 61 x 61 cm. Courtesy of the artist. Photo: Paul Kuhn.

3.25 Jane Everett, *Birch on Birch I*, 2014. Mixed media on birch panel, 106.7 x 81.2 cm. Courtesy of the artist. Photo: Yuri Akuney.

3.26 Jane Everett, *And drifted, one ear tuned to the dip of your paddle*, 2021. Oil on canvas, 152.4 x 248.9 cm. Courtesy of the artist. Photo: Yuri Akuney.

3.27 Alex Janvier, *Manitoba*, 2008. Acrylic on linen, 182.9 x 121.9 cm. Private collection. Photo: Courtesy Hambleton Gallery.

3.28 Robert Houle, *Muhnedobe uhyahyuk* [Where the gods are present], 1989. Oil on canvas, 244 x 182.4 x 5 cm. ea. National Gallery of Canada, Ottawa, 36168.1-4. Photo: NGC.

3.29 Linus Woods, *Buffalo Runner*, 2011. Mixed media on canvas, 122 x 183 cm. Manitoba Hydro Collection.

3.30 Bruce Head, *Sleeping Giant*, 2003. Acrylic on canvas, 203 x 177 cm. Collection of the Winnipeg Art Gallery. Acquired with funds from the Royal Academy Trust Fund, Mr. and Mrs. G.B. Wiswell Fund, Elizabeth Hudson, Betty Wilcox, the Honourable Mr. Justice Allen B. Sulatycky, Agnes Carrigan, the Estate of Mr. and Mrs. Bernard Naylor, funds administered by The Winnipeg Foundation, the Estate of Ann Smith, and the Estate of Dr. Jacob Isa and with funds from the Canada Council for the Arts Acquisition Assistance program, 2007-64. Photo: Ernest Mayer. Courtesy WAG-Qaumajuq.

3.31 Wanda Koop, *Road to Nowhere*, 2021. Acrylic on canvas, 101.6 x 76.2 cm. Private collection. Photo: William Eakin.

4.1 W. Frank Lynn, *The Dakota Boat*, c. 1875. Oil on canvas, 66.6 x 91.8 cm. Collection of the Winnipeg Art Gallery. Gift of Mr. and Mrs. Sam Cohen, G-71-94. Photo: Ernest Mayer. Courtesy WAG-Qaumajuq.

4.2 Ina Uhthoff, *Street in Victoria*, 1945. Oil on canvas, 58 x 41 cm. Art Gallery of Greater Victoria. Gift of Mr. John Uhthoff, 1983.076.001. Photo: Stephen Topher.

4.3 H.G. Glyde, *Rosebud, Alberta*, 1946. Watercolour on paper, 26.7 x 34.3 cm. Private collection. Photo: Courtesy of Loch Gallery.

4.4 Stanley Brunst, *Untitled (Bright Coloured Industrial Scene)*, 1935.

Watercolour on paper, 30 x 21.6 cm. Collection of the Dunlop Art Gallery, PC91.5. Photo: Don Hall.

4.5 Robert Newton Hurley, *Untitled*, 1951. Watercolour on card, 18.6 x 27.4 cm. Collection of the Dunlop Art Gallery, PC99.11. Photo: Don Hall.

4.6 Bill Lobchuk, *Grain Elevator Sentinels*, 1990. Silkscreen on paper, 53.3 x 83.8 cm. Private collection. Photo: Courtesy of Gurevich Fine Art.

4.7 Steve Gouthro, *Building*, 1990. Oil on canvas, 584.2 x 914.4 cm. Collection of the Winnipeg Art Gallery. Acquired with funds from the President's Appeal 2000, 2000-88 a-ii. Photo: Ernest Mayer. Courtesy of WAG-Qaumajuq.

4.8 Aliana Au, *Bleeding Orchid 1*, 2011. Acrylic, ink on paper, 92.7 x 61.3 cm. ea. Private collection.

4.9 David Owen Lucas, *This Sideshow's Leaving Town*, 2009. Acrylic on canvas, 274.3 x 304.8 cm. Collection of Manitoba Hydro.

4.10 David Owen Lucas, *Disraeli Undertow*, 2003. Acrylic on canvas, 152.4 x 304.8 cm. Courtesy of the artist.

4.11 Chris Flodberg, *Crowchild Trail and 17th Avenue, from the series Urban Landscapes*, 2017. Oil on wood, 121.9 x 152.4 cm. Private collection. Photo: Chris Flodberg.

4.12 E.J. (Ted) Howorth, *Spring Breakup #1*, 2008. *Spring Breakup #2*, 2009. Silkscreen on paper, 2/7, 35 x 57.5 cm. Collection of the Buhler Gallery, St. Boniface Hospital. Photo: Leif Norman.

4.13 Henry Eric Bergman, *Red River Winnipeg*, 1933. Engraving on paper, 35.8 x 28 cm. City of Burnaby Permanent Art Collection. Gift of Robert and Margaret Hucal, 2011.13.30. Photo: Harry Booth.

4.14 Jane Everett, *Race the Roaring Fraser I*, 2015. Drawing on drafting film, 91.4 x 152.4 cm. Courtesy of the artist. Photo: Yuri Akuney.

4.15 Philip Henry Surrey, *Windy Day "Street Scene,"* n.d. Charcoal, white chalk on paper, 30.5 x 46 cm. Collection of the Art Gallery of Greater Victoria. Gift of Mr. Peter Dobush, 1973.014.001. Photo: Stephen Topher. Copyright Estate of Philip Surrey/SOCAN (2022).

4.16 John Taylor, *Victoria Memorial Arena Deconstruction*, from the series *Destruction of Memory*, n.d. Photographic triptych, 200 x 300 cm. Courtesy of the artist.

4.17 Scott Benesiinaabandan, *Interland: memories no. 3*, 2014. Digital print, 61 x 40.6 cm. Courtesy of the artist.

4.18 Eleanor Bond, *Offshore Barge Draws the Beach and Sailing Communities*, 1989. Oil on canvas, 245 x 386 cm. Collection of the School of Art Gallery, University of Manitoba. Gift of the artist, 03.001. Photo: Courtesy of the artist and the University of Manitoba.

4.19 Eleanor Bond, *Departure of the Industrial Workers*, from the series *Work Station*, 1985. Oil on canvas, 239.5 x 327.5 cm. Collection of the Winnipeg Art Gallery. Acquired with funds from the Winnipeg Foundation, G-86-140. Photo: Ernest Mayer. Courtesy of WAG-Qaumajuq.

4.20 Edward John Hughes, *A Backyard in Downtown Vancouver*, c. 1936. Graphite on paper, 37.7 x 29.4 cm. Collection of the Art Gallery of Greater Victoria. Anonymous Gift, 2012.010.005. Photo: Stephen Topher.

4.21 Nan Lawson Cheney, *The Back of the House of All Sorts*, 1930. Oil on canvas, 35.4 x 30 cm. Collection of the Art Gallery of Greater Victoria. Gift of the Artist in Memory of Miss Mary Raymur Lawson MBE, 1966.020.001. Photo: Stephen Topher.

4.22 Vera Weatherbie, *Night Time*, n.d. Oil on canvas, 101.5 x 79.5 cm. Collection of the Art Gallery of Greater Victoria. Gift of Vera Weatherbie Mortimer Lamb, 1974.120.001. Photo: Stephen Topher.

4.23 Wilf Perreault, *Rebecca's Alley, Christina's Alley, Catherine's Alley*, and *Ellen's Alley*, 2019. Acrylic on canvas, 182.9 x 61 cm. ea. Private collections. Photo: Don Hall.

4.24 David Thauberger, *Bungalow*, 1989. Silkscreen on paper, 55.9 x 76.2 cm. Collection of the Glenbow Museum.

4.25 William Pura, *The Suburbs*, 2000. Oil on canvas, 61.5 x 85.1 cm. Collection of the Buhler Gallery, St. Boniface Hospital. Photo: Leif Norman.

4.26 Tad Suzuki, *Odeon Theatre, Victoria*, 2016. Acrylic on canvas, 76.2 x 101.6 cm. Collection of Kim Nayyer and Parminder Basran, Ithaca, NY. Photo: Scott Wingfield, Art Ink Print.

4.27 Andrew Valko, *Night Shift*, from the *Motel Series*, 1997. Acrylic on canvas, 63.5 x 76.2 cm. Private collection.

4.28 Ted Harrison, *Northern Sun*, 1989. Oil on canvas, 181 x 241 cm. Collection of the Art Gallery of Greater Victoria. Gift of Mr. and Mrs. J.M. Brickey, 1996.034.001. Photo: Stephen Topher.

4.29 Georgie Wilcox, *Western Industries (Steel Pour, Vulcan Iron Works, Winnipeg)*, c. 1939. Oil on Masonite, 58.6 x 71.5 cm. Collection of the Winnipeg Art Gallery. Gift of John P. Crabb, G-95-109. Photo: Ernest Mayer. Courtesy of WAG-Qaumajuq.

4.30 Steve Gouthro, *Green Rider*, 2012. Oil on canvas, 172.7 x 213.4 cm. Courtesy of the artist.

4.31 Maxwell Bates, *The Cocktail Party*, 1965. Oil on canvas, 117.4 x 153 cm. Collection of the Art Gallery of Greater Victoria, Leon and Thea Koerner Foundation, and W.C.C.F., 1967.183.001. Photo: Stephen Topher.

4.32 Joseph Plaskett, *Easter Table*, 1989–1993. Pastel on paper, 259 x 348 cm. Collection of the Art Gallery of Greater Victoria, Canada Council Purchase Fund, 1996.035.001. Photo: Stephen Topher.

4.33 Chris Flodberg, *Freakish Acts of Nature and Other Distractions*, from the series *Matters of Denial*, 2004. Oil on canvas, 121.9 x 121.9 cm. Private collection. Photo: Chris Flodberg.

4.34 Phyllis Serota, *Package of Philip Morris, Please*, 1985. Oil on canvas, 152.4 x 111.8 cm. Private collection. Photo: Trevor Mills.

4.35 Shawna Dempsey, Lorri Millan, jake moore, and Zab, *Grocery Store*, 2002. Performance installation (Ace Art Incorporated, Winnipeg, MB). Photo: Zab Design.

4.36 Molly Lamb Bobak, *Supermarket*, c. 1955. Oil on canvas, 59.8 x 74.8 cm. Collection of the Art Gallery of Greater Victoria. Gift of Dr. and Mrs. S.G. Ruskin, 1982.045.001. Photo: Stephen Topher.

4.37 Terrance Houle, *Urban Indian #7*, from the series *Urban Indian*, 2007. Digital C print, 72.4 x 92.9 cm. Collection of the Art Gallery of Greater Victoria, 2010.022.001. Photo: Jarusha Brown.

4.38 Edward John Hughes, *Steamer at the Old Wharf, Nanaimo*, 1958. Oil on canvas, 61 x 94 cm. Art Gallery of Greater Victoria. Gift of Mary

Alice Segal, Miles Keenleyside, Anne Katherine McCullum, and Sara Lynn Jackson, 1992.056.001. Photo: Stephen Topher.

4.39 Sybil Andrews, *Hauling*, 1952. Linocut on paper, 30.3 x 35.6 cm. James Y. Todd Purchase Fund. Copyright Glenbow Museum, Calgary (2009), 1977.189.001. Photo: Stephen Topher.

4.40 Sybil Andrews, *Coffee Bar*, 1952. Linocut on paper, 26.5 x 26.8 cm. Gift of the Artist. Copyright Glenbow Museum, Calgary (2009), 1991.055.003. Photo: Stephen Topher.

4.41 William Kurelek, *Lumberjack's Breakfast*, 1973. Mixed media, 59 x 82 cm. Collection of the Art Gallery of Greater Victoria, Gift of Mr. and Mrs. Freeman and Rosita Tovell, 1980.090.001. Photo: Stephen Topher.

4.42 Victor Cicansky, *Blue Pantry*, 2003. Wood, acrylic, ceramic, 195.6 x 91.4 x 22.9 cm. Private collection. Photo: Courtesy of Galerie de Bellefeuille.

4.43 Daphne Odjig, *The Indian in Transition*, 1978. Acrylic on canvas, 245 x 827 cm. Collection of the Canadian Museum of History, 1978-040-001.

5.1 Margaret Peterson, *Storm Gods*, n.d. Tempera on panel. Collection of the Art Gallery of Greater Victoria. Gift from the Estate of Margaret O'Hagan (Peterson), 1997.051.001. Photo: Stephen Topher.

5.2 George H. Swinton, *Untitled*, 1964. Oil on canvas, 87.6 x 184.8 cm. Private collection. Photo: Leif Norman.

5.3 Annora Brown, *Foothills Village*, c. 1955. Oil on canvas, 50.8 x 67.3 cm. Glenbow Museum Collection, Calgary, 57.46.1

5.4 Bertram Brooker, *Sounds Assembling*, 1928. Oil on canvas, 112.3 x 91.7 cm. Collection of the Winnipeg Art Gallery, L-80. Photo: Ernest Mayer, courtesy WAG-Qaumajuq

5.5 Lionel LeMoine FitzGerald, *Abstract: Green and Gold*, 1954. Oil on canvas, 71.7 x 92 cm. Collection of the Winnipeg Art Gallery. Gift of Mr. and Mrs. Joseph Harris, G-63-287. Photo: Ernest Mayer. Courtesy of WAG-Qaumajuq.

5.6 Takao Tanabe, *The Line Sketch*, 1974. Acrylic on canvas, 40.8 x 51.1 cm. Collection of the Winnipeg Art Gallery. Gift from the Estate of Mr. and Mrs. Bernard Naylor, G-86-454.

Photo: Ernest Mayer. Courtesy of WAG-Qaumajuq.

5.7 Gordon A. Smith, *West Coast #2*, 1974. Acrylic on canvas, 142.2 x 165.1 cm. Private collection. Photo: Courtesy of Cowley Abbott.

5.8 Jack Leonard Shadbolt, *World Under Still Life*, 1957. Watercolour on paper, 42.1 x 75.6 cm. Collection of the Winnipeg Art Gallery. Gift of Mr. Peter Dobush, G-65-132. Copyright of Simon Fraser University Galleries. Photo: Serge Gumenyuk. Courtesy WAG-Qaumajuq.

5.9 B.C. Binning, *Convoy Under Way*, 1948. Oil on canvas, 79.5 x 109 cm. Collection of the Art Gallery of Greater Victoria. Gift of Mrs. B.C. Binning, 1985.042.001. Photo: Stephen Topher.

5.10 Marion Nicoll, *Spring*, 1959. Oil on canvas, 91.8 x 71.7 cm. Collection of the Glenbow Museum.

5.11 Roy Kiyooka, *Untitled-Geometric Abstract*, 1963–1964. Acrylic on canvas, 71 x 101.5 cm. Collection of the Art Gallery of Greater Victoria. Gift of Jack Diamond, 1992.031.001. Photo: Stephen Topher.

5.12 Ted Godwin, *Tartan Love Float*, 1968. Oil on canvas, 160 x 200.7 cm. Courtesy of the Art Gallery of Greater Victoria. Gift of Toronto Dominion Bank Collection, 1994.012.004. Photo: Stephen Topher.

5.13 William Perehudoff, *Amyot Series #25*, 1975. Acrylic on canvas, 134 x 296.5 cm. MacKenzie Art Gallery, University of Regina Collection, 1976-2.

5.14 Otto Rogers, *Pink Sky*, 1975. Acrylic on canvas, 182.7 x 182.7 cm. MacKenzie Art Gallery, University of Regina Collection. Gift of the MacKenzie Art Gallery Society, 1977-2.

5.15 Robert Christie, *Summer Wheat*, 2016. Acrylic, veneer collage on canvas, 182.9 x 190.5 cm. Courtesy of the artist.

5.16 Don Reichert, *Superimposition I*, 1969. Acrylic on canvas, 180 x 180.2 cm. Collection of the Winnipeg Art Gallery. Gift of the Women's Committee, G-69-115. Photo: Ernest Mayer. Courtesy of WAG-Qaumajuq.

5.17 Alex Janvier, *Morning Star—Gambeh Then'*, 1993. Installation, 1900 cm. diam. Collection of the Canadian Museum of History, 1994-015-001.

5.18 E.J. (Ted) Howorth, *The Deal*, 2021. Mezzotint on paper, 12 x 20 cm. Courtesy of the artist.

5.19 Winston Leathers, *Night Approaching the Island*, 1998. Sumi ink, iridescent watercolour on board, 51 x 41 cm. Collection of the Buhler Gallery, St. Boniface Hospital. Photo: Leif Norman.

5.20 Emily Carr, *Grey*, 1929–1930. Oil on canvas, 106.7 x 68.9 cm. Private collection. Photo: Vancouver Art Gallery.

5.21 Pat Martin Bates, *Flight Window of the Alchemy Letter from the Sun to the Moon*, 1968. Four Plexiglas plaques: black, blue, silver, white mandorlas (lacquer paint, silkscreen on Plexiglas), 48.7 x 67.1 x 30.5 cm. Courtesy of the artist. Photo: John Taylor.

5.22 Jackie Traverse, *White Buffalo Calf*, 2012. Acrylic, mixed media on canvas, 56 x 71 cm. Collection of the Buhler Gallery, St. Boniface Hospital. Gift of the Buhler Gallery Art Advisory Committee, BGSBGH.2012.18. Photo: Leif Norman.

5.23 Jackson Beardy, *Thunder Dancer, Metamorphosis, Thunderbird*, 1981. Silkscreen on paper, 45.7 x 30.5 cm. ea. Collection of Manitoba Hydro.

5.24 Norval Morrisseau, *Power of the Spirit of Manitou*, 1978. Acrylic on canvas, 175.5 x 144.6 cm. Collection of the Winnipeg Art Gallery. Gift of DuPont Canada, 2018-88. Photo: Ernest Mayer. Courtesy of WAG-Qaumajuq.

5.25 Robert Houle, *Mishipeshu and Water Spirit*, 2017. Mixed media (graphite and acrylic paint) on mylar, 81.3 x 48.3 cm. Private collection. Photo: Leif Norman.

5.26 Lita Fontaine, *The Pagan*, 1996. Acrylic, collage on wood, 121 x 57.2 cm. Collection of the Winnipeg Art Gallery. Acquired with the support of the Canada Council for the Arts Acquisition Assistance Program and with funds from The Winnipeg Art Gallery Foundation Incorporated, G-98-337. Photo: Ernest Mayer. Courtesy of WAG-Qaumajuq.

5.27 Colleen Cutschall, *Milky Way, Spirit Trail*, from the series *House Made of Stars*, 1996. Acrylic, collage on canvas, 120 x 240 cm. Courtesy of the artist. Photo: Ernest Mayer. Courtesy of WAG-Qaumajuq.

5.28 Allen Sapp, *Indian Drums*, 1972. Acrylic on canvas, 58.4 x 73.7 cm. Courtesy of the National Capital Commission.

5.29 Richard Hunt, *The Chief's Wild Woman*, c. 2012. Red cedar, paint, horse hair, 30.5 x 27.9 x 22.9 cm. Courtesy of the artist. Photo: Richard Hunt.

5.30 Tim Paul, *Nas-Win-Is (When Night and Day Cross)*, 1997. Wood, cedar, 68 x 49.8 x 30 cm. Collection of the Art Gallery of Greater Victoria, Canada Council Funds, 1996.036.001. Photo: Stephen Topher.

5.31 Robert Davidson, *Supernatural Eye*, 2007. Epoxy powder-coated aluminum, 305.2 x 262 x 59.5 cm. Robert Davidson Gallery.

5.32 Katie Ohe, *Zipper*, 1975. Welded steel, chrome, mechanical rotary parts, 239 x 76.2 x 76.2 cm. Collection of the University of Calgary. Photo: Dave Brown, LCR Photo Services.

5.33 Gordon Reeve, *Agassiz Ice*, 2008. Stainless steel, 548.6 x 365.8 x 121.92 cm. City of Winnipeg Public Art collection. Photo: Mathias Reeve.

5.34 Linda Stanbridge, *Core 3*, 1993. Fired ceramic, brushed steel, welded aluminum support, 213 x 61 cm. Private collection. Photo: Bob Matheson.

5.35 Ivan Eyre, *Stills—White Red River*, 1971. Acrylic on canvas, 213.6 x 156.7 cm. Collection of the Winnipeg Art Gallery. Gift of the Women's Committee, G-71-103. Photo: Ernest Mayer. Courtesy of WAG-Qaumajuq.

6.1 Mary Riter Hamilton, *Easter Morning, La Petite Penitente, Brittany*, c. 1900. Oil on canvas, 117.4 x 82.2 cm. Collection of the Winnipeg Art Gallery. Gift of Mrs. Horace Crawford, G-45-152. Photo: Ernest Mayer. Courtesy of WAG-Qaumajuq.

6.2 Sophie Pemberton, *Un livre ouvert*, 1900. Oil on canvas, 166.5 x 108 cm. Collection of the Art Gallery of Greater Victoria. Gift of the artist, 1959.012.001. Photo: Stephen Topher.

6.3 Marion Nelson Hooker, *William Berens, Chief of the Saulteaux*, 1932. Oil on Masonite, 67.8 x 56 cm. Collection of the Winnipeg Art Gallery. Gift of the artist, G-36-129. Photo: Ernest Mayer. Courtesy of WAG-Qaumajuq.

6.4 Charles Fraser Comfort, *Louise*, 1927. Oil on canvas, 67.2 x 52 cm. National Gallery of Canada, Ottawa, 26541. Photo: NGC.

6.5 Frederick Horsman Varley, *Vera*, 1931. Oil on canvas, 61 x 50.6 cm. Collection of the National Gallery of Canada. Vincent Massey Bequest, 1968, 15559. Photo: NGC.

6.6 Myfanwy Spencer Pavelic, *Laszlo Gati*, 1975. Acrylic on paper on Masonite, 100 x 126 cm. University of Victoria Art Collections. Gift of Laszlo Gati, U993.23.1. Photo: University of Victoria Legacy Art Galleries.

6.7 Myfanwy Spencer Pavelic, *The Right Honourable Pierre Elliott Trudeau*, 1991. Acrylic on canvas, 122 x 91.5 cm. Collection of the House of Commons, Ottawa, O-1526.1 Copyright House of Commons Collection, Ottawa.

6.8 Mary Valentine, *The Honourable Gildas L. Molgat, 1994–2001*, 2002. Oil on canvas, 182 x 123 cm. Senate's Artwork and Heritage Collection.

6.9 Andrew Valko, *Chief Justice Richard Jamieson Scott*, 2013. Acrylic on panel, 91.4 x 76.2 cm. Collection of the Province of Manitoba. Photo: Leif Norman.

6.10 David McMillan, *Julia and Andrew*, 2017. Oil on canvas, 92 x 112 cm. Courtesy of the artist.

6.11 Joe Fafard, *The Politician*, 1987. Bronze, patina, acrylic, edition 4/12, 107 x 35 x 24 cm. MacKenzie Art Gallery, University of Regina Collection, 1987-2.

6.12 Carole Sabiston, *Connecting Threads: The Arc of Carol Shields*, 2013. Textile assemblage, 114.3 x 91.4 cm. Courtesy of the artist. Photo: John Taylor.

6.13 Ivan Eyre, *Winter Light*, 2002. Acrylic on canvas, 109.2 x 124.5 cm. Courtesy of the artist. Photo: Johansen Krause.

6.14 Jeff Wall, *Picture for Women*, 1979. Transparency in lightbox, 142.5 x 204.5 cm. Courtesy of the artist.

6.15 Sheila Spence, *Jared Parsonage*, 2009. Pigment on rag paper. Courtesy of the artist.

6.16 Thelma Pepper, *Nellie At Home (Nellie Schnell)*, 1989. Giclée print on rag paper, 20.32 x 20.32 cm. ea. Courtesy of the artist's estate.

6.17 Yisa Akinbolaji, *Stolen Identities*, 2018. Acrylic, oil on canvas, 122 x 165 cm. Courtesy of the artist. Photo: Yisa Akinbolaji.

6.18 Jin-me Yoon, *A Group of Sixty-Seven*, 1996. Installation of 134 cibachrome prints, dimensions variable. Collection of the Vancouver Art Gallery, Acquisition Fund. © Jin-me Yoon.

6.19 KC Adams, *"Indian Princess" Cyborg Hybrid KC (visual artist)*, from the series *Banff*, 2005. Digital print on paper, 4/10, 61 x 45.8 cm. Collection of the Winnipeg Art Gallery. Gift of the artist, 2009-37. Photo: Ernest Mayer. Courtesy of WAG-Qaumajuq.

6.20 Frederick Horsman Varley, *Mirror of Thought*, 1937. Oil on canvas, 66.5 x 76.8 cm. Collection of the Art Gallery of Greater Victoria. Gift of Harold Mortimer Lamb, 1978.104.001. Photo: Stephen Topher.

6.21 William Kurelek, *Portrait of the Artist as a Young Man*, 1950. Oil on Masonite, 65.5 x 59.6 cm. Private collection. Photo: Heffel Fine Art Auction House.

6.22 Myfanwy Spencer Pavelic, *Anguish*, 1968. Charcoal on paper, 66 x 76.2 cm. University of Victoria Art Collection. Gift of Dr. Myfanwy Spencer Pavelic, U993.7.137. Photo: University of Victoria Legacy Art Galleries.

6.23 Eva Stubbs, *Equilibrium*, 1984. Clay, oxides, 58.5 x 46 x 48.5 cm. Collection of Marshall and Elba Haid.

6.24 Ivan Eyre, *Double Tatter Wrap*, 1992. Grease crayon, acrylic wash on acetate, paper, 40.3 x 50.6 cm. Collection of the Winnipeg Art Gallery. Gift of the Volunteer Committee to the Winnipeg Art Gallery, G-92-509. Photo: Ernest Mayer. Courtesy WAG-Qaumajuq.

6.25 Kelly Clark, *Untitled*, from the series *Top Hat*, 1978. Pastel on paper, 94 x 70.3 cm. Collection of the Buhler Gallery, St. Boniface Hospital, from the KJ Hughes Collection. Gift of his family, BGSBH.2013.44. Photo: Leif Norman.

6.26 Richard Ciccimarra, *Wood Collage*, c. 1970. Paper, 120 x 71 cm. Collection of the Art Gallery of Greater Victoria. Harold and Vera Mortimer-Lamb Purchase Fund, 1987.013.001. Photo: Stephen Topher.

6.27 Marcien Lemay and Étienne Gaboury, *Louis Riel*, 1971. Bronze and cement installation. Photo: Joe Bryksa.

6.28 Eva Stubbs, *Standing Figures*, 1983–1984. Clay, oxides, glaze. (1) 142.0 x 46.0 x 35.5 cm. (2) 144.5 x 48.5 x 32.5 cm. Art Gallery of Burlington's Permanent Collection. Donated by Mr. George Stubbs, 1985 1985.016.0.6. Photo: Ernest Mayer. Courtesy of WAG-Qaumajuq.

6.29 Roger LaFrenière, *Melina*, 2015. Acrylic on canvas, 76.2 x 76.2 cm. Private collection. Photo: Martin LaFrenière.

6.30 Gathie Falk, *Agnes (Black Patina)*, 2000–2001. Bronze, edition of 7, 94 x 71.1 x 58.4 cm. Image courtesy of Equinox Gallery, Vancouver.

6.31 Karel Funk, *Untitled #78*, 2016. Acrylic on panel, 96.5 x 108.6 cm. Collection of the Winnipeg Art Gallery. Acquired with funds from the Estate of Mr. and Mrs. Bernard Naylor. Funds administered by the Winnipeg Foundation, and with funds from Michael Nesbitt, Susan Glass, and Arni Thorsteinson, the Price Family Foundation and with funds from the Canada Council for the Arts Acquisition Assistance Program, 2016-399. Photo: Ernest Mayer. Courtesy of WAG-Qaumajuq.

6.32 Aliana Au, *My Reclining Coat*, 2013. Oil on canvas, 59.5 x 80 cm. Private collection. Photo: Ernest Mayer.

6.33 Marilyn Levine, *Jacket #2*, 1969. Ceramic and resin, 19.5 x 58 x 32 cm. Collection of the MacKenzie Art Gallery. Gift of Vaughan McIntyre, 2002-21.

6.34 Aganetha Dyck, *Shrunken Clothing on the Road*, 1976–1981. Wool, variable dimensions. Courtesy of the artist. Photo: Peter Dyck.

7.1 Emily Carr, *Odds and Ends*, 1939. Oil on canvas, 67.4 x 109.5 cm. Collection of the Art Gallery of Greater Victoria, 1998.001.001. Formerly in the collection of the Greater Victoria Public Library. Photo: Stephen Topher.

7.2 Aganetha Dyck and Honeybees, *After Dr. Eduard Assmuss 1865*, 2009. Intaglio, pen, ink, beeswax, and honeycomb, 45.7 x 38.1 cm. Private collection. Photo: Serge Gumenyuk.

7.3 Grace Nickel, *Devastatus Rememorari*, 2008. Salt, porcelain with terra sigillata, oxide, glaze, 195 x 338 x 735 cm. Collection of the Art Gallery of Nova Scotia. Gift of the artist, Winnipeg, Manitoba, 2014, with assistance from the Jean and Lloyd Shaw Endowment Fund, 2014.15. Photo: Mary Black.

7.4 Don Proch, *Rocky Mountain Mining Mask*, 1976. Graphite, silverpoint on fiberglass with inlaid silver wire, 38 x 25 x 30 cm. Collection of the University of Calgary. Purchased with funding from the Government of Canada and Dr. William Campbell, Winnipeg, MB, NG.1988.072.002. Photo: Ernest Mayer. Courtesy of WAG-Qaumajuq.

7.5 Terrance Houle, *Iiniiwahkiimah*, 2012. Vinyl, 243.8 x 274.3 cm. Courtesy of the artist.

7.6 David McMillan, *Portrait of Lenin, Kindergarten, Prypiat*, 1997, from the series *Growth & Decay*. Digital print on paper, 40.4 x 50.7 cm. Courtesy of the artist.

7.7 Reva Stone, *Imaginal Expression*, 2003. Installation. Courtesy of the artist. Photo: Ernest Mayer. Courtesy of WAG-Qaumajuq.

7.8 Ruth Cuthand, *Trading: Small Pox*, 2008. Acrylic paint, glass seed beads on beading medium mounted on suede board, 61 x 45.7 x 3.1 cm. Collection of the MacKenzie Art Gallery. Purchased with the support of the York Wilson Endowment Award, administered by the Canada Council for the Arts, 2009-10.

7.9 Ruth Cuthand, *Trading: Typhoid Fever*, 2008. Acrylic paint, glass seed beads on beading medium mounted on suede board, 61 x 45.7 x 3.1 cm. Collection of the MacKenzie Art Gallery. Purchased with the support of the York Wilson Endowment Award, administered by the Canada Council for the Arts, 2009-7.

7.10 Yisa Akinbolaji, *Empty Playground, Silent Battlefield*, 2020. Acrylic, oil, conté on canvas, 111 x 163 cm. Courtesy of the artist. Photo: Yisa Akinbolaji.

7.11 Bob Boyer, *To the End of Time*, 1986. Acrylic, pastel, charcoal on blanket, 190.5 x 227 cm. Collection of the Winnipeg Art Gallery, G-87-295. Photo: Ernest Mayer. Courtesy of WAG-Qaumajuq.

7.12 KC Adams, *KC Adams*, from the series *Perception*, 2014. Digital image, 94 x 50.8 cm. Courtesy of the artist.

7.13 Diana Thorneycroft, *A People's History (Quintland)*, 2010. Digital photograph on paper, 101.6 x 127 cm. Courtesy of the artist. Photo: Courtesy of Gurevich Fine Art.

7.14 Chantal Gibson, *Who's Who?*, 2014, from the series *Historical In(ter)ventions*. Mixed media altered text, dimensions variable. Mixed media altered text *Who's Who in Canada*, 1927. Courtesy of the artist. Photo: C. Gibson.

7.15 Karin Jones, *Worn: Shaping Black Feminine Identity*, 2014–2015. Cotton fabric, synthetic hair extensions, cotton bolls, artist's own hair, dimensions variable. Collection of the Royal Ontario Museum. Photo: Eydis Einarsdottir.

7.16 Faye HeavyShield, *Sisters*, 1993. Shoes altered with plaster, gesso, acrylic, 105 x 105 cm. McMichael Canadian Art Collection. Purchase 1995, 1995.2 A-L.

7.17 Jaime Black, *REDress Project*, 2014. Installation, dimensions variable. Collection of the Canadian Museum of Human Rights. Photo: Ian McCausland.

7.18 Andrew Valko, *Sleepless Night*, 1997. Acrylic on panel, 121.9 x 152.4 cm. Private collection.

7.19 Bev Pike, *Caressing Room / Frôler*, 1992. Oil glazes, metallic powders, aluminium leaf, gold leaf, glimmer on canvas, 244 x 305 cm. Collection of the Winnipeg Art Gallery. Gift of the artist with support from The Winnipeg Art Gallery Foundation Incorporated, 2006-17. Photo: Ernest Mayer. Courtesy of WAG-Qaumajuq.

7.20 Dana Claxton, *Tonto in Pink*, from *INDIAN CANDY*, 2013. Aluminum mounted lightjet print, 61 x 48.3 cm. Courtesy of the artist.

7.21 Kent Monkman, *The Chase*, 2014. Acrylic on canvas, 213.4 x 320 cm. Photo: Courtesy of the artist.

7.22 Brian Jungen, *People's Flag*, 2006. Textile installation, 480 x 880 cm. Installation view, Strange Comforts, National Museum of the American Indian, 2009. Photo: Katherine Fogden. Courtesy of Catriona Jeffries, Vancouver.

7.23 Tim Schouten, *To Have and to Hold the Same (Treaty 4)*, from the suite *Treaty 4 (Adhesions-Westward into the Indian Country)*, 2008. Oil, dry pigment, beeswax, microcrystalline wax, dammer resin, on vellum, 91.4 x 61 cm. Private collection. Photo: Leif Norman.

7.24 Rebecca Belmore, *Fringe*, 2007. Digital print on archival paper, 53.3 x 160 cm. Courtesy of the artist. Photo: Henri Robideau.

7.25 Rosalie Favell, *My First Day of Assimilation*, from the series *from an early age*, 1994. Colour print on paper, 61 x 50.8 cm. Courtesy of the artist.

7.26 Rosalie Favell, *If only you could love me the way I am*, 2018. Oil on linen, 121.9 x 121.9 cm. Courtesy of the artist.

7.27 Ruth Cuthand, *Treaty Dress*, 1986. Acrylic on canvas, 121.5 x 172.9 cm. The Mendel Art Gallery Collection at Remai Modern. Purchased 1992. Photo: Remai Modern.

7.28 Rosalie Favell, *I awoke to find my spirit had returned*, from the series *Plain(s) Warrior Artist*, 1999. Giclée print on paper, 85.5 x 76 cm. Collection of the Winnipeg Art Gallery. Acquired with the Photography Endowment of The Winnipeg Art Gallery Foundation Incorporated, 2001-12. Photo: Ernest Mayer. Courtesy of WAG-Qaumajuq.

7.29 Val Vint, *Chi-kishkayhitamihk si te li neu Biizon (Education is the New Bison)*, 2020. Steel, ht. 365.8 cm. Photo: Leif Norman.

7.30 George Littlechild, *The Land Before, The Land After*, 2014. Mixed media on paper, 55.9 x 38.1 cm. Private collection.

7.31 Robert Houle, *Sandy Bay*, 1998–1999. Oil, black and white photograph, colour photograph on canvas, Masonite, 300 x 548.4 cm. Collection of the Winnipeg Art Gallery. Acquired with funds from the President's Appeal 2000 and with the support of the Canada Council for the Arts Acquisition Assistance program, 2000-87 a-e.

7.32 Christi Belcourt, *Giniigaaniimenaaning (Looking Ahead)*, 2012. Stained glass installation. Centre Block of Parliament, Ottawa, ON. Copyright House of Commons Collection, Ottawa.

7.33 Joane Cardinal-Schubert, *The Lesson*, 1989. Chairs, whistles, books, apples, rope, mirror, chalk, dimensions variable. Installation view. Witnesses: Art and Canada's Indian Residential Schools. (6 September–1 December 2013). From the Morris and Helen Belkin Art Gallery, UBC. Photo: Michael R. Barrick.

7.34 Joane Cardinal-Schubert, *Where the Truth is Written—Usually*, 1991. Oil on canvas flag with lodgepole pine, 76.2 x 152.4 cm. Estate of Joane Cardinal-Schubert. Photo by Dave Brown, LCR Photo Services, University of Calgary.

7.35 Jane Ash Poitras, *Shaman Never Die: Return to Your Ancestral Roots*, 1989. Oil, paper, plastic, silver print on canvas, 94.7 x 220.7 cm. Collection of the Winnipeg Art Gallery. Acquired with funds from The Winnipeg Art Gallery Foundation Incorporated, G-90-4. Photo: Ernest Mayer. Courtesy of WAG-Qaumajuq.

7.36 Karen Cornelius, *Nylon and Lace in the Congo*, from the series *Fabric of Belonging*, 2011. Soft-ground etching and chine collé on paper, 76.2 x 55.9 cm. Private collection.

7.37 Michael Boss, *Double Self-Portrait as Ukrainian Kozak and Pious Mennonite*, 2010. Oil pastel, acrylic on canvas, 182.9 x 182.9 cm. Courtesy of the artist.

7.38 Molly Lamb Bobak, *Private Roy, Canadian Women's Army Corps*, 1946. Oil on canvas, 76.4 x 60.8 cm. Transferred from National Gallery of Canada, 1971. Beaverbrook Collection of War Art. Canadian War Museum, 19710261-1626. Copyright Estate of Molly Lamb Bobak. Photo: Canadian War Museum.

7.39 Caroline Dukes, *Danube*, 1996. Acrylic, earth, gel, bones on gatorboard, feathers, burned/photocopied book pages, broken glass on canvas, 244 x 335 cm. Collection of the estate.

7.40 John Koerner, *Slavonic Dance 7, Opus 9030*, 1990. Acrylic on canvas, 127.0 x 106.5 cm. ea. Collection of the Art Gallery of Greater Victoria, 1993.060.001 a-c. Photo: Stephen Topher.

7.41 Phyllis Serota, *Order and Chaos*, 1998. Pastel, charcoal, acrylic, oil on canvas, 152.4 x 135.3 cm. Courtesy of the artist. Photo: Janet Dwyer.

7.42 David Neel, *Life on the 18th Hole*, 1990. Silkscreen, ink on paper, 70.7 x 56.3 cm. Collection of the Surrey Art Gallery, SAG1992.03.01. Photo: Cameron Heryet.

7.43 Jane Ash Poitras, *Oka Spirit Power*, 1990. Mixed media on canvas, 92 x 152 cm. Indigenous Art Collection, Crown-Indigenous Relations and Northern Affairs Canada. Photo: Lawrence Cook.

7.44 Wanda Koop, *Dreamland*, 2021. Acrylic on canvas, 213.4 x 152.4 cm. Private collection. Photo: William Eakin.

NOTES

Preface

1 Terrance Houle, in conversation with Patricia Bovey, November 2019.

2 The definitions of seminal, contribution, and influence are from the Shorter Oxford Dictionary, 1959.

3 Bates, *Far-Away Flags*, 57; this poem was written in Royal Oak, 1962, and the publication dedicated to his wife Charlotte.

Chapter 1. Departures: Developing Artistic Voices in Canada's West

1 Senator Murray Sinclair, in conversation with Patricia Bovey, 10 July 2020.

2 Francis, *Images of the West*.

3 J. Russell Harper, *Painting in Canada: A History* (Toronto: University of Toronto Press, 1969), vii.

4 Hatch, "Foreword."

5 Clendinning, "Exhibiting a Nation."

6 A.J. Musgrove, "An Appraisal of Canadian Painting," unpublished Radio Talk given over CKY – CKX, Wednesday, 14 February 1940, Patricia Bovey personal archives.

7 A.S. Keszthelyi, "The Value of Art to the Community," *Town Topics*, 19 June 1909, 18.

8 Angela E. Davis, "Laying the Ground: The Establishment of an Artistic Milieu in Winnipeg, 1890–1913," *Manitoba History*, 4 Number 1982, http://www.mhs.mb.ca/docs/mb_history/04/early-art.shtml (accessed 11 March 2022).

9 *Globe* [Toronto], 16 September 1859, 2, Review of the work of William Hind as quoted by Gilbert Gignac in "New Resonance form William Hind," in *Hindsight*, 48.

10 Gilbert Gignac, lecture, Winnipeg Art Gallery, 1 December 2014.

11 William Hind, Victoria, to his brother Henry Youle Hind, 31 January 1864, W.G.R. Hind Papers, RG 100, vol. 164, #15, Public Archives of Nova Scotia. Cited by Mary Jo Hughes, "William Hind's Vision of the Canadian West," in *Hindsight*, 126.

12 Kane, *Wanderings of an Artist*, 163.

13 *Manitoba Free Press*, December 1903.

14 Berry, *Taming the Frontier*, 73.

15 Ibid., 17.

16 *Manitoba Free Press*, December 1903, as cited by Berry, *Taming the Frontier*.

17 Yates, *Manitoba Society of Artists*, 7.

18 Berry, *Taming the Frontier*, 45.

19 Bovey, "The Scholar and Her Book," vii.

20 Edythe Hembroff-Schleicher, in conversation with Patricia Bovey, October 1980.

21 Correspondence to Alex J. Musgrove, Art School Glasgow, from Jas. McDiarmid, Chairman Art Section, signed Chas. A. Roland, Commissioner, Jan. 25th, 1913, Patricia Bovey's personal archives.

22 Alex Musgrove, unpublished presentation signed, 1913, Winnipeg, Patricia Bovey's personal archives.

23 Alex Musgrove, undated, unpublished talk given at the behest of Mr. Ransom, Patricia Bovey's personal archives.

24 Berry, *Taming the Frontier*, 127.

25 W.W. Thom, "Fine Arts in Vancouver, 1886–1930," MA thesis, UBC, 1969, as quoted by Lorna Farrell-Ward, "Tradition/Transition: The Keys of Change," in *Vancouver Art and Artists*, 14.

26 Lorna Farrell-Ward, "Tradition/Transition," 15.

27 Gwladys Downes, Remarks at the opening of Max Maynard exhibition at the Art Gallery of Greater Victoria, 5 May 1983, Patricia Bovey personal archives and the archives of the Art Gallery of Greater Victoria.

28 Ibid.

29 Biéler and Harrison, eds., *The Kingston Conference Proceedings*, 5.

30 Heath, *Uprooted*, 72, with quotes from President's Report, Saskatoon Art Association Minutes, 1940, Mendel Art Gallery.

31 Ibid., 70.

32 Valerie Conde, "Western Art is Winning Fame," *Windsor Star*, 9 August 1941.

33 Ibid.

34 Musgrove, "An Appraisal of Canadian Painting."

35 Shadbolt, quoted in Smith, *André Biéler*, 187.

36 Smith, *André Biéler*, 180.

37 Ibid., 191.

38 Ibid., 197.

39 Ibid., 194.

40 Heath, *Uprooted*, 76.

41 Eva Stubbs, in conversation with Patricia Bovey, 13 October 2009.

42 Massey Commission Report, 1951, Part I, Chapter I, "The Nature of the Task," *The Mandate*, online, PDF version, Library and Archives Canada, https://www.collectionscanada.gc.ca/massey/h5-406-e.html (accessed 11 March 2022).

43 Ibid.

44 Smith, *André Biéler*, 219.

45 Massey Commission Report, 1951, Library and Archives Canada, https://www.collectionscanada.gc.ca/massey/h5-400-e.html (accessed 11 March 2022). Canadian culture abroad is discussed throughout the Report, which recommends more funding and a stronger UNESCO presence by and for Canada.

46 Ibid., Chapter XXV, "A Council for the Arts, Letters, Humanities and Social Sciences," Sections 337 and 338, online, PDF version, Library and Archives Canada, https://www.collectionscanada.gc.ca/massey/h5-452-e.html (accessed 11 March 2022).

47 Heath, *Uprooted*, 125, 128.

48 Ibid., 128; Ernest Lindner to Ken Lochhead, 6 September 1955.

49 Ibid, 128; Ernest Lindner to Donald Buchanan, editor of *Canadian Art*, 17 September 1955.

50 Ibid., 130; Ernest Lindner to Ken Lochhead, 31 August 1957.

51 Dianne Scoles, "School Setting and Dedicated Staff Inspire 1950s Student Printmakers," unpublished article for 2004, Exhibition at Gallery-One-One-One at the School of Art, University of Winnipeg, 2004–2005, University of Manitoba Archives.

52 Bruce Head, in conversation with Patricia Bovey, 22 October 2004.

53 Tony Tascona, in conversation with Patricia Bovey, 1 October 2004.

54 Eyre, in conversation with Patricia Bovey, May 2010.

55 Eva Stubbs, in conversation with Patricia Bovey, 13 October 2009.

56 Laurence Wall, *Winnipeg Tribune*, 4 August 1976.

57 Bruce Head, in conversation with Patricia Bovey, 22 October 2004.

58 Ibid.

59 Woodcock, *Strange Bedfellows*, 65.

60 Heath, *Uprooted*, 126.

61 Patricia Ainslie, "Seeing Comes Before Words," in Ainslie and Laviolette, *Alberta Art and Artists*, xi.

62 Ralph Watkins, *Winnipeg Free Press*, 24 September 1966.

63 Woodcock, *Ivan Eyre*, 83–84.

64 Maxwell Bates and Pat Martin Bates are not related. From New Brunswick Pat Martin married army accountant Clive (Al) Bates; Maxwell Bates was the son of Calgary architect, William Stanley Bates. Their being colleague artists and close friends in Victoria was co-incidental.

65 Dempsey, *Live at the Centre*, 17.

66 Gu Xiong, Artist's Statement, https://www.cacnart.com/gu-xiong (accessed 10 February 2022).

67 Ted Lindberg, "John Koerner: Ways of Entry," in Bovey, *John Koerner Past/Present*, 40.

68 Reva Stone, in conversation with Patricia Bovey, January 2020.

69 Winnipeg Art Gallery, collection database.

70 Reva Stone, in conversation with Patricia Bovey, 16 January 2020.

71 Winnipeg Arts Council Public Art Website, http://winnipegarts.ca/pubart-about (accessed 11 March 2022).

72 Pat Martin Bates, in conversation with Patricia Bovey, 10 November 2007.

Chapter 2. Expanding Techniques: Creating a New Visual Language

1 Carole Sabiston, in conversation with Patricia Bovey, 23 May 2013.

2 Richard Williams, in conversation with Patricia Bovey, 30 June 2005.

3 George Swinton, *Notes on Drawings*, Winnipeg Art Gallery, 24 March 1968, Patricia Bovey's personal archives.

4 Kenneth Lochhead, in conversation with Patricia Bovey, 7 July 2005.

5 *Maxwell Bates on Painting*, reprinted courtesy National Gallery of Canada, n.d., Art Gallery of Greater Victoria Archives.

6 Emily Carr, as quoted in Shadbolt, *Emily Carr*, 170.

7 Emily Carr, as quoted in Ian Thom, *Emily Carr*, 4.

8 Richard Ciccimarra, as quoted by Frank Nowosad, *Monday Magazine*, 24 October 1977, n.p.

9 Eric Bergman, in a letter to Ainslie Loomis, the Secretary Treasurer of the Society of Canadian Painters and Engravers, undated, handwritten copy in Bergman's archives, Library and Archives Canada.

10 Bill Laing, in conversation with Patricia Bovey, 14 August 2020.

11 George Swinton, artist's statement, Upstairs Gallery, Winnipeg, 1987, Patricia Bovey's personal archives.

12 Reproduced with permission of Moira Swinton.

13 Don Proch, in conversation with Patricia Bovey, April 2016.

14 Fenton, *Reta Summers Cowley*, 30.

15 Swinton, *Notes on Drawings*.

16 Robin Laurence, "Ann Kipling: Here Now," in *The Solitudes of Place*, 11.

17 Ibid.

18 The Limners Society included seventeen Victoria artists who worked in eleven media, met, talked, argued, and partied, and despite wide differences in backgrounds and work, all focused on the human condition. They include Maxwell Bates, Pat Martin Bates, Richard Ciccimarra, Robert de Castro, Walter Dexter, Nita Forrest, Colin Graham, Helga Grove, Jan Groves, Elza Mayhew, Myfanwy Pavelic, Carole Sabiston, Herbert Siebner, Robin Skelton, Sylvia Skelton, Karl Spreitz, and Jack Wilkinson. Founded in 1971, they disbanded in 2006.

19 Tony Tascona, in conversation with Patricia Bovey, 1 October 2004.

20 Ibid.

21 Gillmor, *The Art of Tony Tascona*, n.p.

22 Tony Tascona, in conversation with Patricia Bovey, 1 October 2004.

23 Eckhardt, *Esther Warkov*, n.p.

24 Madill, *The Artists' Proof*, 1.

25 Ted Howorth, in conversation with Patricia Bovey, 3 December 2004.

26 Madill, *The Artists' Proof*, 1.

27 Coy, *FitzGerald as Printmaker*, 13.

28 Ibid.

29 Ibid.

30 Hebert, *The Art of John Snow*, 20.

31 As quoted in Hebert, *The Art of John Snow,* 23n17.

32 Richard Williams, in conversation with Patricia Bovey, 30 June 2005.

33 Kenneth Lochhead, in conversation with Patricia Bovey, 7 July 2005.

34 Citation for Kathleen Fenwick's induction as Officer of the Order of Canada, 1968, https:www.gg.ca/en/honours//recipients/146-2840 (accessed 10 February 2022).

35 Winston Leathers, in conversation with Cliff Eyland, Gallery One-One-One, April 2004, University of Manitoba Archives.

36 Cameron and Kuhl, *Art in Winnipeg 1955–1959.*

37 Davis, *The Grand Western Canadian Screen Shop*, 16.

38 Ibid.

39 Ibid.

40 David Thauberger and Bill Lobchuk, in conversation with Patricia Bovey, 11 February 2014.

41 Ibid.

42 Ibid.

43 Len Anthony, in conversation with Patricia Bovey, 13 February 2014.

44 Ibid.

45 David Thauberger and Bill Lobchuk, in conversation with Patricia Bovey, 11 February 2014.

46 Don Proch, in correspondence with Patricia Bovey, August 2017.

47 Ted Howorth, in conversation with Patricia Bovey, April 2016.

48 Ibid.

49 Pat Martin Bates, in conversation with Patricia Bovey, 17 October 2008.

50 William Laing, in conversation with Patricia Bovey, 15 August 2020.

51 William Laing, email correspondence to Patricia Bovey, 17 August 2020.

52 Pat Martin Bates, in conversation with Patricia Bovey, 17 August 2007.

53 Richard Simmins, "Critics on Air, Perforations in Silence," CBC Radio, 1972.

54 Karen Cornelius, in conversation with Patricia Bovey, September 2014.

55 Arthur Vickers, notes, Arthur Vickers archives.

56 Richard Hunt, artist's statement, https://www.richardhunt.com/about.

57 John Taylor, in conversation with Patricia Bovey, July 2020, reflecting his long-held views which formed the basis of Nicholas Tuele, "John Taylor: Geometric Progressions," *In Sight Magazine*, Spring 1991, 20–24.

58 Scott McLeod, nomination for Rodney Graham for Bank of Nova Scotia Photography Award 2014, https://www.scotiabank.com/photoaward/common/finalists/2014/statement-graham.html (accessed 11 March 2022).

59 Laura Vickerson, artist's statement, http://lauravickerson.com/?pageid=04.

60 Smith, *Celebrating the Stitch*, 10.

61 Ibid.

62 Joe Fafard, in conversation with Patricia Bovey, 20 May 2016.

63 Ibid.

64 Ibid.

65 Ibid.

66 Ione Thorkelson, video interview, "A Natural History of Utopias," Canadian Clay and Glass Gallery, Waterloo, 2016, https://www.lapaigallery.com/blogs/news/ione-thorkelson-at-the-canadian-clay-and-glass-gallery.

67 Ione Thorkelson, quoted in Boswell, *The Invention of Glass*, 57.

68 Ibid., 113.

69 William Ganis, *GLASS Quarterly*, Spring 2012, https://www.lapaigallery.com/blogs/news/ione-thorkelson-at-the-canadian-clay-and-glass-galleryhttp://www.thorkelson.com/16airport/airport.html.

70 Jill Sawyer, *Galleries West*, Spring 2004, 18.

71 Walter Dexter, in conversation with Patricia Bovey, July 2013.

72 Steggles, *MUD, Hands, Fire,* 42.

73 Esther Warkov, in conversation with Patricia Bovey, Summer 2000.

74 Esther Warkov, interview, 15 June 2000, National Gallery of Canada Archives.

75 Dempsey, *Live at the Centre*, 2.

76 LaVallee, *Thirteen Coyotes.*

77 Dempsey, *Live at the Centre*, 10.

78 Ibid., 17.

79 Ibid., 21.

80 Gathie Falk, "A Short History of Performance Art as It Influenced or Failed to Influence My Work," *artscanada*, April 1981, as reprinted in Fetherling, *Documents in Canadian Art*, 311.

81 Ibid.

82 Ibid., 313.

83 Dempsey, *Live at the Centre*, 13–14.

84 Shawna Dempsey and Lorri Millan, "Arborite Housedress," Music Gallery, Toronto, 1995, http://www.performanceart.ca/index.php?m=program&id=70.

85 Megan Gillis, "'Powerful, Captivating' Thunderhead Design Picked for LGBTQ2+ Monument," *Ottawa Sun*, 24 March 2022, https://ottawasun.com/news/local-news/powerful-captivating-thunderhead-design-picked-for-lgbtq2-monument/.

86 Winnipeg Arts Council, press release, 2009, http://winnipegarts.ca/wac/artwork/reliquary-reliquaire (accessed 11 March 2022).

87 Dempsey, *Live at the Centre*, 23.

88 Madill, *The Winnipeg Perspective 1985*, 3.

89 Joyce Zemans, "Video Activity of the N.E. Thing Co. Ltd.," *artscanada* 30, no. 4 (October 1973): 61.

90 Janet Cardiff, as quoted by John Wray, "Janet Cardiff, George Bures Miller and the Power of Sound," *New York Times Magazine*, 26 July 2012, https://www.luhringaugustine.com/press/janet-cardiff-george-bures-miller-and-the-power-of-sound-by-john-wray (accessed 11 March 2022).

91 IAIN BAXTER&, as quoted by Alexander Alberro, "Interview with Iain Baxter&," in Moos, ed., *IAIN BAXTER&*, 32.

92 Ibid.

93 Michael Darling, "Iain Baxter&'s Proto-Eco-Art Campaign," in Moos, ed, *IAIN BAXTER&*, 75.

94 IAIN BAXTER&, as quoted by Joan Lowndes, "The Message is—VSI: The Plastic World of Iain Baxter," *The Province*, Vancouver, 3 February 1967, 3.

95 Joan Lowndes, "'Easel' is a Telex," 1968, as quoted by Robert Wainstein, "Narrative Chronology," in Moos, ed., *IAIN BAXTER&*, 167.

96 Ron Basford, as quoted in the *Ottawa Journal*, 4 June 1969.

97 Don Proch, quoted in Robert Enright, "They Don't Make Horseshoe Nails Like They Used To," *Border Crossings* 9, no. 2 (1990): 10.

98 John Graham, "Asessippi Lauded," *Winnipeg Free Press*, 14 November 1975.

99 William Kirby, "Urban and Rural Relationship Explored," *Winnipeg Free Press*, 11 January 1975, 17.

Chapter 3. Landscape as Culture

1 Luke Lindoe, as quoted by Laviolette, *An Alberta Art Chronicle*, 52n1.

2 I reviewed the curricula of the Slade School from 1860 to 1940 and the documents in the Slade archives showed no evidence of landscape training.

3 Norman Yates, as quoted by Two Rivers Gallery in Convergence/Divergence, https://www.tworiversgallery.ca/.

4 Francis, *Images of the West*, 321.

5 Henry, *Early Maritime Artists*, xi.

6 Ibid.

7 Ibid., xi note 5.

8 Ibid., 75, as quoted in Beaglehole, *The Journals of Captain James Cook*, vol. 3, 367.

9 Smith, *European Vision*, 78, as quoted in Henry, *Early Maritime Artists*, 75.

10 Douglas Cole, "John Webber, A Sketch of Captain James Cook's Artist," *British Columbia Historical News* 13, no. 1 (Fall 1979): 18–19, 20, as quoted in Henry, *Early Maritime Artists*, 75.

11 As quoted in Henry, *Early Maritime Artists*, 109.

12 Ibid.

13 Dixon, *A Voyage Round the World*, 205.

14 Wilson Duff, "Contributions of Marius Barbeau to West Coast Ethnology," *Anthropologia* 6 (1964): 88.

15 Bartlett, *Remarks on Board the Ship, Massachusetts*, 34.

16 "The Boy Artist of Red River," *Winnipeg Free Press*, 29 July 1972.

17 As quoted in Lutz, *Grafton Tyler Brown*, 8.

18 Ibid., 12.

19 Mary Jo Hughes, "Preface," in Lutz, *Grafton Tyler Brown*, n.p.

20 As quoted in Lutz, *Grafton Tyler Brown*, 10.

21 Norman Yates, as quoted in *Convergence/Divergence, Landscape and Identity on the West Coast* (Victoria: Legacy Gallery, University of Victoria, 2011), n.p.

22 Francis, *Images of the West*, 231.

23 Jeanette Johns to Suzanne Pringle, as quoted in *Mapping: Martha Street Studio* (Winnipeg: Buhler Gallery, 2010).

24 George Swinton, unpublished notes regarding his 1961 exhibition at Winnipeg's Grant Gallery, 1961, as quoted in Adamson, *Eighty Years Swinton*, n.p.

25 George Swinton, unpublished notes, Vancouver, October 1960, as quoted in Adamson, *Eighty Years Swinton*, n.p.

26 Robert Ayre, "Lionel LeMoine FitzGerald," unpublished article, n.d., typescript, Ayre Papers, Queen's University Archives.

27 Ibid.

28 Lionel LeMoine FitzGerald, diary, 21 June 1930, University of Manitoba Archives.

29 L.L FitzGerald, CBC Winnipeg, Wednesday Night Talk, "Painters of the Prairies," 1 December 1954, Thomas Papers, University of Manitoba Archives.

30 Carr, *Hundreds and Thousands*, 28.

31 Heath, *Uprooted*, 92.

32 Ibid., 11.

33 Ibid., 51.

34 Ibid., 53.

35 Ibid., 63.

36 Ibid., 61.

37 Ibid., 90.

38 As quoted in Laviolette, *An Alberta Art Chronicle*, 54n37.

39 Adrian Chamberlain, "Walter Dexter: Ceramic Artist a Canadian Giant," *Victoria Times Colonist*, 20 June 2015.

40 Laviolette, *An Alberta Art Chronicle*, 54.

41 Ibid., 33.

42 Brian Brennan, "Norman Yates—Homage," *Galleries West*, 21 August 2004, https://www.gallerieswest.ca/magazine/stories/norman-yates---homage/ (accessed 11 March 2022).

43 Ibid.

44 Comments from "Norman Yates," video by Two Rivers Gallery, Prince George, Two Rivers Gallery Archives.

45 Terry Fenton, in conversation with Dorothy Knowles, c. 2008. Transcript in author's archives.

46 Reta Cowley, "Terry Fenton," in Marketa, *Biographical Dictionary of Saskatchewan Artists*, 29.

47 Terry Fenton, in conversation with Dorothy Knowles, c. 2008. Transcript in author's archives.

48 Mandy Higgins, "Dorothy Knowles Is Still Learning the Art of the Landscape Painting," *Moose Jaw Times Herald*, 28 June 2008.

49 Terry Fenton, in conversation with Dorothy Knowles, c. 2008. Transcript in author's archives.

50 Ibid.

51 Dorothy Knowles, as quoted in Reid and Klunder, *Intervention*, 38.

52 Diane Whitehouse, in conversation with Patricia Bovey, 25 August 2020.

53 Diane Whitehouse, as quoted in Reid and Klunder, *Intervention*, 68.

54 Wayne Morgan, email correspondence to Patricia Bovey, 21 November 2019.

55 Robin Laurence, "Ann Kipling: Here Now," in Burnaby Art Gallery, *The Solitudes of Place*, 10.

56 Ann Kipling, January 1994, as quoted in *Ann Kipling: The Art of Drawing* (Vancouver: Vancouver Art Gallery, 1995), n.p.

57 Pat Martin Bates, in conversation with Patricia Bovey, 9 July 2007.

58 Alma de Chantal, translated by Gwaldys Downes, "Pat Martin Bates Red, White, Black," *Vie des Arts*, Spring 1975, transcript, Pat Martin Bates personal papers.

59 Mary Kerr, review of "Pat Martin Bates, Destinations, Navigations, Illu-

minations," *Border Crossings*, November 2005, 102–3.

60 Eckhardt, as quoted in Adamson, *Eighty Years Swinton*, n.p.

61 Adamson, *Eighty Years Swinton*, n.p.

62 Patricia Bovey, "George Swinton: Myriad Talents," Manitoba Chamber Orchestra, 2014–15 season program, 15.

63 Comments made by both Winston Leathers and Bruce Head to Patricia Bovey on many occasions.

64 Bruce Head, in conversation with Patricia Bovey, April 2004.

65 Ibid.

66 Ivan Eyre, in conversation with Patricia Bovey, 27 October 2004.

67 Eyre, *Ivan on Eyre*, 322.

68 Ivan Eyre, in conversation with Patricia Bovey, 27 October 2004.

69 Sheila Spence, in discussion with Alexis Kinloch, 2010, as quoted in *Mapping*.

70 Carole Sabiston, in conversation with Patricia Bovey, May 1992.

71 Quoted in Patricia Bovey, "Carole Sabiston: The Artist's Reflections on 'Flying' and 'Take Off: Point of Departure and Mode of Travel,'" *InSight: A Magazine about Contemporary Art* (Summer 1990): 8.

72 Ibid., 33.

73 Roger LaFrenière, in conversation with Patricia Bovey, November 2016.

74 Roger LaFrenière, artist's statement, *Parcours D'un Artiste* (Winnipeg: Centre Culturel Franco-Manitobain, October 2011), n.p.

75 Barbara Milne, email correspondence to Patricia Bovey, 13 August 2020.

76 Ibid.

77 Ibid.

78 Jane Everett, as quoted in *Edmonton Journal*, 9 September 2008. Jane Everett, email to Patricia Bovey, 17 March 2022.

79 Jane Everett, in correspondence with Patricia Bovey, 17 March 2022.

80 Lubos Culen, *Watermark* (Vernon, BC: Vernon Art Gallery, 2009), n.p.

81 Bovey, *Robin Hopper*, 14.

82 Ibid., 11.

83 John Koerner, unpublished diary March 1990, 95, Patricia Bovey's personal archives.

84 National Gallery of Canada and Glenbow Institute, "Alex Janvier: Modern Indigenous Master," https://www.gallery.ca/whats-on/exhibitions-and-galleries/alex-janvier-modern-indigenous-master-0 (accessed 4 November 2022).

85 Ibid.

86 Clara Hargittay, "Robert Houle: His Creative and Spiritual Journey 1980–1990," in Houle, *Robert Houle*, 15.

87 Madill, *Robert Houle*, 42.

88 Koerner, *Unseen Dimensions*, 34.

89 These discussions took place on different occasions at my dining table in Victoria over a period of years.

90 Koerner, *Unseen Dimensions*, 67.

91 Lionel LeMoine FitzGerald to the Board of Directors at the Winnipeg School of Art, 31 October 1944, as quoted by Parke-Taylor, *In Seclusion with Nature*, 23.

92 Koerner, *Unseen Dimensions*, 110–11.

93 Ibid., 34–35.

94 Carr, *Hundreds and Thousands*, 329.

95 Shadbolt, *Emily Carr*, 64–65.

96 Emily Carr, as quoted in Shadbolt, *Emily Carr*, 170.

97 Lionel LeMoine FitzGerald, "Painters of the Prairie," CBC radio interview, 1 December 1954, University of Manitoba Archives.

98 Lionel LeMoine FitzGerald to Robert Ayre, 27 August 1954, as quoted in Parke-Taylor, *In Seclusion with Nature*, 23.

99 As quoted in Parke-Taylor, *In Seclusion with Nature*, 22.

100 Ibid.

101 Ibid., 21.

102 John Koerner, unpublished diary, March 1990, 95, Patricia Bovey's personal archives.

103 John Koerner, unpublished notes to Patricia Bovey, July 1991.

104 Bovey, *John Koerner Past/Present*, 12.

105 John Koerner, unpublished diary, 1.

106 Koerner, *Unseen Dimensions*, 60.

107 John Koerner, "My Working Process," undated note to Patricia Bovey, Summer 1991, Patricia Bovey's personal archives.

108 Bovey, *John Koerner Past/Present*, 15.

109 John Koerner, unpublished diary, March 1990, 95, Patricia Bovey's personal archives.

110 Lorne Roberts, *Winnipeg Free Press*, 20 January 2005.

Chapter 4. Urbanization and New Meanings

1 David Owen Lucas, notes to Patricia Bovey, December 2009.

2 Steve Gouthro, in conversation with Patricia Bovey, 28 October 2004.

3 Robert Epp, *Building: Artists with Their Work; Steve Gouthro* (Winnipeg: Winnipeg Art Gallery, 1992), n.p.

4 Eyre, *Ivan on Eyre*, 92.

5 Ibid., 256.

6 Ibid.

7 Ivan Eyre, in conversation with Patricia Bovey, June 2010.

8 Aliana Au, email correspondence to Patricia Bovey, 11 December 2019.

9 David Owen Lucas, notes to Patricia Bovey, December 2009.

10 David Owen Lucas, notes to Patricia Bovey, January 2010.

11 David Owen Lucas, notes to Patricia Bovey, December 2009.

12 David Owen Lucas, notes to Patricia Bovey, January 2010.

13 David Owen Lucas, email to Patricia Bovey, 10 November 2019.

14 Chris Flodberg, in conversation with Patricia Bovey, November 2019.

15 Ibid.

16 Don Reichert, in conversation with Patricia Bovey, May 2010.

17 Don Reichert, in conversation with Patricia Bovey, May 2012; Patricia Bovey, "Don Reichert: Jewels of Nature," Manitoba Chamber Orchestra, 2011–12 season program, 10.

18 Don Reichert, exhibition statement, solo exhibition, Martha Street Studio, Winnipeg, 2008.

19 Ted Howorth, in conversation with Patricia Bovey, June 2016.

20 Ibid.

21 Jane Everett, "Message and Meaning," artist's talk, c. 2016.

22 Barbara Tyner, *Jane Everett: The Unfixed Locus of Longing* (Kelowna: Kelowna Art Gallery, 2019), n.p.

23 Jane Everett, as quoted in the *Edmonton Journal*, 9 September 2008.

24 John Taylor, email to Patricia Bovey, 3 August 2021.

25 Ibid.

26 As quoted in *Bond, Dyck, Koop, Thorneycroft* (Winnipeg: Gallery One-One-One, University of Manitoba, 2006–2007), University of Manitoba Archives, n.p.

27 Shirley Madill, *Future Cities and Virtual Cities Project* (Winnipeg: Winnipeg Art Gallery, 1997).

28 David Thauberger, as quoted in Andrew Kear, "Dream Home with Some Acid Rain," in Bovey et al., *David Thauberger*, 120.

29 Lionel LeMoine FitzGerald, correspondence with Bertram Brooker, 11 January 1930, Brooker Papers, Library and Archives Canada.

30 Wilf Perreault, in conversation with Patricia Bovey, 18 November 2019.

31 Timothy Long, as quoted by Irene Seiberling, *Regina Leader-Post*, 25 November 2016.

32 Wilf Perreault, in conversation with Patricia Bovey, 18 November 2019.

33 David Thauberger, in conversation with Patricia Bovey, 15 February 2014.

34 Peter White, "David Thauberger's Saskatchewan Paintings an Historical Perspective," in Bovey et al., *David Thauberger*, 74.

35 David Thauberger, email correspondence to Patricia Bovey, 15 February 2014.

36 David Thauberger, in conversation with Patricia Bovey, 15 February 2014.

37 Bill Pura, in conversation with Patricia Bovey, 9 July 2005.

38 Hughes and Suzuki, *Honest Ed's*, 4.

39 Ibid.

40 Ibid., 7.

41 Ibid., 4.

42 Ted Harrison, as quoted in Tuele, *The World of Ted Harrison*, 6.

43 Ibid., 7.

44 Serota, *Painting My Life*, 215.

45 Henry, *Early Maritime Artists*, 169, as quoted from Archibald Menzies's Journal, 115–16 and 118–20.

46 Lord, *The History of Painting in Canada*, 100.

47 Steve Gouthro, artist's statement, in Patricia Bovey, *The Spritual from the Ordinary: Aliana Au and Steve Gouthro* (Winnipeg: Buhler Gallery, 2012), n.p.

48 Steve Gouthro, in conversation with Patricia Bovey, 20 August 2012.

49 Ibid.

50 Townshend, *Maxwell Bates*, 42.

51 As quoted in Townshend, *Maxwell Bates*, 43n118.

52 Plaskett, "Am I Contemporary?"

53 Ibid.

54 Ibid.

55 Joe Plaskett, artist's statement, solo exhibition, Winchester Gallery, Victoria, 2008. The Winchester Gallery closed in the fall of 2021.

56 Joe Plaskett, in conversation with Patricia Bovey, April 1996.

57 Joe Plaskett, as quoted in Doris Shadbolt, "An Ode to a Room," *Canadian Art*, 6 May 2008.

58 Chris Flodberg, in conversation with Patricia Bovey, November 2019.

59 Phyllis Serota, email correspondence to Patricia Bovey, 4 August 2020.

60 Ibid.

61 Shawna Dempsey and Lorri Millan, http://www.shawnadempseyandlorrimillan.net/ (accessed August 2020).

62 Terrance Houle, https://americanindian.si.edu/exhibitions/hide/terrance.html (accessed 14 March 2022).

63 Ibid.

64 E.J. Hughes, artist's statement, http://ejhughes.ca/ (accessed 11 March 2022).

65 Jacques Barbeau, *A Journey with E.J. Hughes* (Vancouver: Barbeau Foundation, 2000), as quoted in *Ottawa Citizen*, 1 July 2007, A4.

66 Timothy Long, "Cultivating Perspectives," Senate of Canada, 2021, https://sencanada.ca/en/about/art-architecture/art-heritage/cultivating-perspectives/indian-drums/ (accessed 11 March 2022).

67 Alison Mayes, *Winnipeg Free Press*, 18 June 2009, D1.

68 Andrew Valko, in conversation with Patricia Bovey, 23 September 2005.

69 Vic Cicansky, artist's statement, https://www.cicansky.ca/pantriesjars/pantries-jars.htm (accessed 11 March 2022).

Chapter 5. Abstraction into the Spiritual

1 Doug Morton, in conversation with Joan Murray, 9 September 1977, Library and Archives of Canada, Joan Murray collection, 10.

2 Elizabeth Patterson, correspondence to Don Reichert, Fredericton, NB, 6 June 1962, personal archives of the artist.

3 Chris Cran, as quoted in Nasgaard, *Abstract Painting in Canada*, 9.

4 Katherine Ylitalo, "Work of Art: Grey Green Crowd #2," *Avenue Magazine*, Calgary, 4 September 2019, https://www.avenuecalgary.com/city-life/work-of-art/grey-green-crowd-2-by-chris-cran/ (accerssed 11 March 2022).

5 Ibid.

6 Victor Brooker (Bertram Brooker's son), in conversation with Patricia Bovey, July 1974.

7 Bertram Brooker, "Painted Verbs," public lecture, Hart House, University of Toronto, 1949, Patricia Bovey's personal archives; and quoted by James King, https://www.aci-iac.ca/art-books/bertram-brooker/key-works/sounds-assembling/ (accessed 11 March 2022).

8 Lionel LeMoine FitzGerald, *84th Ontario Society of Artists*, exhibition catalogue, including Bertram Brooker Memorial Exhibition (Toronto: Art Gallery of Toronto, 1956), n.p.

9 Pat Martin Bates, in conversation with Patricia Bovey, July 2007.

10 Lionel LeMoine FitzGerald, as quoted in Bovey, Davis, and Stewart, *Lionel LeMoine FitzGerald*, 63n86.

11 Lionel LeMoine FitzGerald, "Prairie Painters," Thomas Papers, University of Manitoba Archives, 4.

12 Lionel LeMoine FitzGerald, correspondence to Robert Ayre, 27 August 1954, Patricia Bovey's personal archives.

13 Bertram Brooker to Lionel LeMoine FitzGerald, 28 December 1929, Brooker papers, Library and Archives Canada.

14 Robert Fulford, in Fetherling, *Documents in Canadian Art*, 245.

15 Ibid., 241.

16 Nancy Tousley, "Takao Tanabe: The Prairie Paintings," in Thom et al., *Takao Tanabe*, 72.

17 Ibid., 88.

18 Gordon Smith, as quoted in Thom, *Gordon Smith*, 39.

19 Joan Lowndes, as quoted in Thom, *Gordon Smith*, 42.

20 Gordon Smith, as quoted in Thom, *Gordon Smith*, 42.

21 Jack Shadbolt, as quoted in Watson, *Jack Shadbolt*, 54.

22 Ibid., 67.

23 Jack Shadbolt, as quoted in Watson, *Jack Shadbolt*, 104.

24 Watson, *Jack Shadbolt*, 104.

25 Jack Shadbolt, as quoted in Watson, *Jack Shadbolt*, 104.

26 Watson, *Jack Shadbolt*, 104.

27 Ian Thom, "Binning as a Painter," in Rogatnick, Thom, and Weder, *B.C. Binning*, 131.

28 Burnett and Schiff, *Contemporary Canadian Art*, 116.

29 B.C. Binning, as quoted in Rogatnick, Thom, and Weder, *B.C. Binning*, 146.

30 Toni Onley, as quoted in Nasgaard, *Abstract Painting in Canada*, 140.

31 Nasgaard, *Abstract Painting in Canada*, 140.

32 Toni Onley, as quoted in Nasgaard, *Abstract Painting in Canada*, 140.

33 Shirley Thompson, Foreword, in Leclerc and Barclay, *The Crisis of Abstraction in Canada*, as quoted in Bovey, *HeadSpace*, 27n8.

34 Clement Greenberg, as quoted in Irving Sandler, "Hans Hofmann: The Pedagogical Master," *Art in America*, 30 May 1973. https://www.artnews.com/art-in-america/features/archives-hans-hofmann-pedagogical-master-63547/ (accessed 11 March 2022).

35 Bovey, *HeadSpace*, 26n5.

36 Townshend, *A History of Art in Alberta*, 143.

37 Ibid., 144.

38 Ibid., 145.

39 Doug Haynes, as quoted in *Landscape as Muse*, Episode 18, "Peace Athabasca Delta with Doug Haynes." Victoria: 291 Film Company, 2005.

40 Doug Haynes, artist's statement, Willok and Sax Gallery, 1995, https://www.doughaynesfineart.com/about (accessed 11 March 2022).

41 Clement Greenberg "Painting and Sculpture in Prairie Canada," 1963, as published in Fetherling, *Documents in Canadian Art*, 271.

42 Ibid., 273.

43 Laviolette, *An Alberta Art Chronicle,* 32.

44 Clement Greenberg "Painting and Sculpture in Prairie Canada," 1963, as published in Fetherling, *Documents in Canadian Art*, 275.

45 William Perehudoff, "A Conversation with William Perehudoff," CBC, 8 February 2013, https://www.youtube.com/watch?v=AoLDMNaT418 (accessed 11 March 2022).

46 Robert Christie, artist's statement, Constructing Colour, Peter Roberson Gallery, 2016, https://www.rchristie.ca/news/.

47 Laurence Wall, *Winnipeg Tribune*, 4 August 1976.

48 Bruce Head, in conversation with Patricia Bovey, 22 October 2004.

49 Ralph Watkins, *Winnipeg Free Press*, 24 September 1966.

50 Randal McIlroy, *Winnipeg Free Press*, 22 February 1968.

51 *Transcona News* (Winnipeg), 19 April 1967.

52 Donald Campbell, *Winnipeg Free Press*, 22 January 1988.

53 Adrian Chamberlain, *Winnipeg Free Press*, 20 February 1986.

54 Clement Greenberg, "Painting and Sculpture in Prairie Canada," 1963, as published in Fetherling, *Documents in Canadian Art*, 282.

55 Don Reichert, in conversation with Patricia Bovey, August 2011.

56 Don Reichert, Nature Morph, Centre Culturel franco-manitobain, February 2006, Don Reichert personal archives.

57 Ann Davis, "Winston Leathers and Zen," December 2004, Patricia Bovey personal archives.

58 Erin Gee, curatorial assistant, MacKenzie Art Gallery, Winston Leathers, Cosmic Variations Series, exhibition, 2010.

59 LaVallee, *7: Professional Native Artists Inc.*, 23.

60 Ibid., 45.

61 Pat Martin Bates, in conversation with Patricia Bovey, August 2007.

62 Shorter Oxford English Dictionary, vol. 2, 1959, p. 1972.

63 Adamson, *Eighty Years Swinton*, n.p.

64 Ferdinand Eckhardt, "George Swinton," Winnipeg Art Gallery, c. 1960s, undated and unpublished, Patricia Bovey's personal archives.

65 Winston Leathers to Ann Davis, 9 June 1997, a note titled "Winston Leathers, RCA A Personal Calligraphy," Patricia Bovey's personal archives.

66 Dawn Delbanco, "Chinese Calligraphy," in *Heilbrunn Timeline of Art History* (New York: Metropolitan Museum of Art, 2000), as quoted by Patricia Bovey, *Caligraphic Influences: Ben Wasylyshen & John King with Winston Leathers & Aliana Au* (Winnipeg: Buhler Gallery, 2014), n.p.

67 Don Reichert to George Swinton, undated letter, 1963, Don Reichert personal archives.

68 Jack Wise, in conversation with Patricia Bovey, October 1980.

69 Ryu Niimi, "Towards the Garden of Unknown Wind: A Homage and Bioregional Reflection on the Works of Walter Jule," in Besant, *SKIN*, 7.

70 Pat Martin Bates, in conversation with Patricia Bovey, 21 January 2008.

71 Page, "Darkingbad the Brightdayler," 35–40.

72 Pat Martin Bates, in conversation with Patricia Bovey, 21 February 2007, as quoted in Bovey, *Pat Martin Bates*, 122.

73 Emily Carr, as quoted in Shadbolt, *Emily Carr*, 170.

74 Shadbolt, *Emily Carr*, 71.

75 Ibid., 180.

76 Pat Martin Bates, interview with Patricia Bovey, 10 November 2007.

77 Pat Martin Bates, interview with Patricia Bovey, 9 November 2007.

78 Joan Lowndes, "White Magic for Protection," *Vancouver Province*, 6 July 1972.

79 Pat Martin Bates, interview with Patricia Bovey, 10 November 2007.

80 Quote on the verso of the work itself.

81 Pat Martin Bates, in conversation with Patricia Bovey, July 2009.

82 Clement Greenberg, "Painting and Sculpture in Prairie Canada," 1963, as published in Fetherling, *Documents in Canadian Art*, 279.

83 Tascona et al., *Tony Tascona*, 34.

84 Tony Tascona, in conversation with Patricia Bovey, 22 June 2000.

85 Ibid.

86 Tony Tascona, in conversation with Patricia Bovey, 22 June 2000.

87 Jane Ash Poitras, as quoted in Newlands, *Canadian Paintings*, 250.

88 Bill Reid, excerpt from "Out of The Silence," 1971, as published in Bill Reid, *Solitary Raven: Selected Writings of Bill Reid*, ed. Robert Bringhurst (Vancouver, BC, and Seattle, WA: Douglas and McIntyre and University of Washington Press, 2000), 71.

89 Ovide Mercredi, "The Earth," as published in *My Silent Drum* (Winnipeg: Aboriginal Issues Press, University of Manitoba, 2015), 117.

90 Alex Janvier, as quoted in LaVallee, *7: Professional Native Artists Inc.*, 137.

91 Alex Janvier, "Yedariye's Voice in Colour," in LaVallee, *7: Professional Native Artists Inc.*, 89.

92 "Treasures Gallery: Morning Star," Canadian Museum of History, https://www.historymuseum.ca/cmc/exhibitions/tresors/treasure/283eng.html (accessed 14 March 2022).

93 Norval Morrisseau, as quoted in Martin Segger, *Copper Thunderbird: Invention, Inspiration, and Transformation* (Victoria: Legacy Art Gallery, July 2008), 3.

94 Ibid., 4.

95 Ibid.

96 Mary Kerr, in Segger, *Copper Thunderbird*, 10.

97 Bill Reid, "The Raw Material of Chaos," in Reid, *Solitary Raven*, 226.

98 Robert Davidson, in Duffek, *Robert Davidson*, 10.

99 Christian Thompson, unpublished notes, University of Regina and Canadian Plains Research Center.

100 Janet Clark, in Boyer, *Spiritual Landscapes*.

101 Shirley Madill, "Introduction," in Cutschall, *Colleen Cutschall*, 5.

102 As quoted in Allan J. Ryan, "Celestial Connections: Sacred Space, Cyberspace, Exhibition Space," in Cutschall, *Colleen Cutschall*, 9.

435

103 Ibid., 15.

104 Elza Mayhew, *Time-Markers: The Sculpture of Elza Mayhew,* film produced by Karl Spreitz and Anne Mayhew, 1985.

105 Elza Mayhew, as quoted by Frank Nowosad, *Monday Magazine,* Victoria, 8–14 December 1978.

106 Ibid.

107 Elza Mayhew, in correspondence with George and Lola Kidd, 25 November 1969.

108 James Purdie, *Globe and Mail,* 6 November 1976.

109 Tony Gregson, "Robert de Castro: A Retrospective," Maltwood Museum and Art Gallery, University of Victoria, 1996, typescript manuscript, 3.

110 Ibid., 17.

111 Ibid.

112 Skelton, "Robert de Castro," 63–64.

113 Richard Hunt, artist's statement for *My Family,* https://www.richardhunt.com/my-family-feature (accessed 4 November 2022).

114 1880 Amendment to the Indian Act, https://www.ictinc.ca/the-potlatch-ban-abolishment-of-first-nations-ceremonies.

115 Tim Paul, remarks at the unveiling of Nas-win-is, Art Gallery of Greater Victoria, 13 November 1997.

116 Arthur Vickers, email correspondence to Patricia Bovey, 1 August 2020.

117 Ibid.

118 Ibid.

119 Bill Reid, "The Spirit of Haida Gwaii," the text poem he dedicated to his wife Martine, as published by the Bill Reid Foundation.

120 Bill Reid, "Killer Whale," plaque at installation at the Vancouver Aquarium.

121 Karen Duffek, "Northwest Coast Art: At a Crossroads," *Galleries West,* 22 December 2012, https://www.gallerieswest.ca/magazine/stories/northwest-coast-art%3A-at-a-crossroads/.

122 Duffek, *Robert Davidson,* 42.

123 Ibid., 15.

124 Robert Davidson, as quoted in Duffek, *Robert Davidson,* 16.

125 Sandra Fraser, "Artist in Focus: Eli Bornstein," Remai Modern, Saskatoon, 2019, https://www.remaimodern.org/program/exhibitions/exhibition/eli-bornstein-artist-in-focus.

126 *Winnipeg Free Press,* "Eli Bornstein," 30 January 2014, 14.

127 Don Proch, in correspondence to Patricia Bovey, August 2017.

128 Timothy Long, as quoted by the Saskatchewan Arts Board, http://www.sknac.ca/index.php?page=NewsDetail&id=60 (accessed 11 March 2022).

129 Jonathan D. Lippincott, *Robert Murray: Sculpture* (Sharon, CT: Design Books, 2019).

130 "Katie Ohe," Esker Foundation exhibition, 2020, https://eskerfoundation.com/exhibition/katie-ohe/ (accessed 11 March 2022).

131 Gordon Reeve, email correspondence to Patricia Bovey, June 2008.

132 Ivan Eyre, in conversation with Patricia Bovey, June 2011.

133 Eyre, *Ivan on Eyre,* 236.

134 Shirley Madill, in Stubbs, *Eva Stubbs.*

135 Walter Dexter, as quoted in MacNayr and Dexter, *Walter Dexter,* n.p.

Chapter 6. People: Portraits and Inscapes

1 "Portrait" and "inscape," Oxford Dictionary.

2 West, *Portraiture,* 37.

3 Comments from both Sheila Spence and Arnold Saper made to the author separately in May 2014 corroborate this view.

4 Sheila Spence, in conversation with Patricia Bovey, 9 May 2014.

5 Freeland, *Portraits and Persons,* 291 and 298.

6 Andrew Valko, in conversation with Patricia Bovey, 24 February 2015.

7 Leslie Robertson, British Columbia Archives, website developed for History 481, 27 March 2003, http://web.uvic.ca/vv/student/maynard/legacy.htm (accessed 11 March 2022).

8 Varley, *Frederick H. Varley,* 86.

9 Ibid., 58.

10 Ibid., 59, as quoting, Housser, *A Canadian Art Movement,* 215.

11 Myfanwy Pavelic, interview with Eileen Leyroyd, as published in Graham, *Relationships,* n.p.

12 Skelton, *The Limners,* n.p

13 Bovey, *Myfanwy Pavelic: Inner Explorations,* 9.

14 Lindberg, *A Portrait by Myfanwy,* n.p.

15 Myfanwy Pavelic, in conversation with Patricia Bovey, 8 June 1994.

16 Comments of the Right Honourable Pierre Elliott Trudeau, video of the Trudeau Portrait Unveiling on Parliament Hill, Ottawa, Parliament Hill Communications, May 1992.

17 Lindberg, *A Portrait by Myfanwy,* n.p.

18 Mary Valentine, in conversation with Patricia Bovey, November 2011.

19 West, *Portraiture,* 37.

20 Andrew Valko, in conversation with Patricia Bovey, 24 February 2015.

21 David McMillian, in conversation with Patricia Bovey, 26 July 2020.

22 Ibid.

23 Eva Stubbs, in conversation with Patricia Bovey, February 2010.

24 Joe Fafard, in conversation with Patricia Bovey, 20 May 2016.

25 Ibid.

26 Richard Hunt, email correspondence with Patricia Bovey, 20 September 2021.

27 Ibid.

28 Carole Sabiston, in conversation with Patricia Bovey, 7 June 2013.

29 Eyre, *Ivan on Eyre,* 432.

30 Ibid.

31 Ibid., 232.

32 Burnett, *Jeff Wall,* 7.

33 Ibid., 13.

34 Ibid.

35 Ron Pepper, email correspondence to Patricia Bovey, 12 May 2022. Poem from David Gutnick used with permission.

36 Riopelle, *Tim Gardner.*

37 Yisa Akinbolaji, in conversation with Patricia Bovey, July 2020.

38 Micah Lexier, in conversation with Jon Tupper, in Lexier, *A Portrait of David,* n.p.

39 Ibid.

40 Arthur Vickers, email correspondence to Patricia Bovey, 1 August 2020.

41 Nicholas Tuele, unpublished notes for "Intangible Heritage," Royal British Columbia Museum, 2015, Arthur Vickers's archives.

42 Maxwell Bates, biographical notes, Special Collections Division, MacKimmie Library, University of Calgary, as quoted by Snow, *Maxwell Bates*, 10.

43 Oxford Dictionary. Ibid.

44 Varley, *Frederick H. Varley*, 141.

45 Ferdinand Eckhardt, in conversation with Patricia Bovey, July 1970.

46 Mary Jo Hughes, "The William Kurelek Theatre Presents William Kurelek an Epic Tragedy," in Bruce, Hughes, and Kear, *William Kurelek*, 43.

47 Myfanwy Pavelic, in conversation with Patricia Bovey, 8 June 1994.

48 Myfanwy Pavelic, film, *Portrait of Myfanwy*, produced by Karl Spreitz, University of Victoria Archives, 1980.

49 Myfanwy Pavelic, in *Art on Video: Myfanwy Pavelic* (Victoria: Art Gallery of Greater Victoria, 1991).

50 Patricia Bovey, *Myfanwy Pavelic: Mirrored Selves Within and Without* (Victoria: Legacy Art Galleries, University of Victoria, 2019), 12.

51 Ibid.

52 National Portrait Gallery, *A Guide to Twentieth Century Portraits* (London: National Portrait Gallery, 2013), 52.

53 Eva Stubbs, "Thoughts," 1 February 1984, from an unpublished notebook/sketchbook, Patricia Bovey's personal archives.

54 Ted Howorth, in conversation with Patricia Bovey, 2016.

55 Ivan Eyre, as quoted in Woodcock, *Ivan Eyre*, 159.

56 Lovatt, *Ivan Eyre Drawings*, 12.

57 Morris, *100 Years of Canadian Drawings*, 106.

58 Ivan Eyre as quoted in Woodcock, *Ivan Eyre*, 62.

59 Ivan Eyre, in conversation with Patricia Bovey, 27 October 2004.

60 Ivan Eyre, as quoted in Woodcock, *Ivan Eyre*, 112

61 Donalda Johnson, "Vigilant Observer / Vertical Invader," in Johnson and Clark, *Kelly Clark*, 52.

62 Ibid., 57.

63 Nowosad, *Cicimarra*, n.p.

64 George Swinton, in Nowosad, *Cicimarra*.

65 Frank Nowosad, in Nowosad, *Cicimarra*.

66 Colin Graham, correspondence with Richard Ciccimarra, 21 December 1972, as quoted in Nowosad, *Cicimarra*.

67 Robin Skelton, "Robert de Castro," *Malahat Review*, October 1976, 63–64.

68 Perry, "Maxwell Bates," 24.

69 Perry, "Maxwell Bates," as quoted in Vancouver Art Gallery, *Maxwell Bates in Retrospect*, 27.

70 Perry, "Maxwell Bates," 25.

71 David Blackwood, "Foreword," in Snow, *Maxwell Bates*, xiv–xv.

72 The notebook was published as Nancy Townshend, *Maxwell Bates: Canada's Premier Expressionist of the 20th Century: His Art, Life and Prisoner of War Notebook* (Calgary: Snyder Hedlin Fine Arts, 2005).

73 Maxwell Bates, as quoted in Townshend, *Maxwell Bates*, 34 (emphasis in original).

74 Townshend, *Maxwell Bates*, 36.

75 Colin Graham, "Maxwell Bates," *Arts West* 1, no. 4 (1976): 25, 27.

76 Eckhardt, *Maxwell Bates*, n.p.

77 Myfanwy Pavelic, in conversation with Patricia Bovey, 3 June 1992, as quoted in Bovey, *Myfanwy Pavelic: Inner Explorations*, 8.

78 Robin Skelton, in *Art on Video*.

79 Lindberg, *A Portrait by Myfanwy*, n.p.

80 Pat Martin Bates, in conversation with Patricia Bovey, July 2019.

81 Roger LaFrenière, in conversation with Patricia Bovey, January 2020.

82 Karel Funk, as quoted by Alan Small, "Karel Funk," *Winnipeg Free Press*, 11 June 2016, E2.

83 Marsh Lederman, "Hyperrealist artist Karel Funk's Paintings to be Shown at the Winnipeg Art Gallery," *Globe and Mail*, 5 June 2016.

84 Danielle Da Silva, "Artist's Homecoming 'Emotional,'" *The Sou'wester, Winnipeg Free Press*, digital edition, 20 June 2016.

85 Andrew Kear, as quoted by Sarah Swan, "Karel Funk: Art from the Hood," *Galleries West*, Summer 1916, 38.

86 Ibid., 38–39.

87 Aliana Au, in conversation with Patricia Bovey, as quoted in *Celebrating Manitoba Art* (Ottawa: Senate of Canada, 2017), 5.

88 Aliana Au, in conversation with Patricia Bovey, 21 August 2012.

89 Aliana Au, email correspondence to Patricia Bovey, 11 December 2019.

90 Aliana Au, in conversation with Patricia Bovey, 12 August 2012.

91 Aliana Au, email correspondence to Patricia Bovey, 11 December 2019.

92 Aliana Au, in conversation with Patricia Bovey, 12 August 2012.

93 Hughes, *Manitoba Art Monographs*, i.

94 From a conversation with Esther Warkov, as quoted in "The Winnipeg Art Gallery Guide to Selected Works: Esther Warkov Recent Drawings," Winnipeg Art Gallery, 1998–1999, Winnipeg Art Gallery Archives, n.p.

95 Gathie Falk, National Gallery of Canada interview, as quoted by Becky Rynor, *National Gallery Magazine*, 20 June 2017.

96 Madill and Dyck, *Aganetha Dyck*, 31.

Chapter 7. Visual Voices and Societal Concerns

1 Jane Ash Poitras, as quoted by Anne Newlands, in Newlands, *Canadian Paintings*, 250.

2 Steve Gouthro, in conversation with Patricia Bovey, 28 October 2004.

3 Adams, *Perception*, 10.

4 Ibid., 11.

5 Phyllis Serota, *Painting My Life*, 90.

6 Aganetha Dyck, in the *Mason Journal* Interview, 2011, http://www.mason-studio.com/journal/2011/10/interview-with-aganetha-dyck-canadian-visual-artist/ (accessed 11 March 2022).

7 Carr, *Hundreds and Thousands*, 196–96.

8 Doug Morton, as quoted in Donna Danylchuk, "A Singing of Flexibility of Colour," *The Ring*, 13 November 1980, 1.

9 Manitoba Conservancy obituary of Clarence Tillenius, 2012.

10 Aganetha Dyck, in the *Mason Journal* interview, 24 October 2011, http://www.mason-studio.com/journal/2011/10/interview-with-aganetha-dyck-canadian-visual-artist/ (accessed 11 March 2022).

11 Grace Nickel, artist's statement for her exhibition devastatus rememorari, Nova Scotia College of Art and Design, 2008, https://gracenickel.ca/

devastatus-rememorari/artists-state-ment/ (accessed 11 March 2022).

12 Patricia Bovey, "Carole Sabiston: The Artist's Reflections on 'Flying' and 'Take Off: Point of Departure and Mode of Travel,'" *Insight Magazine*, Summer 1990, 7.

13 Shirley Brown, as quoted by Patricia Bovey, "Essences of Natural Inspirations: Shirley Brown, Jane Everett, and Ann Kipling," in Bovey and Herzog, *Visual Celebrations II*, 171.

14 Jack Anderson, "Shirley Brown: Vestiges," *Galleries West*, April 2007.

15 Terrance Houle, in conversation with Patricia Bovey, 14 November 2019.

16 David McMillan, as quoted by Claude Baillargeon, "McMillan's Chernobyl: An Intimation of the Way the World Would End," in David McMillan, *Growth and Decay*, 247.

17 David McMillan, in conversation with Patricia Bovey, 26 July 2020.

18 McMillan, *Growth and Decay*, 7.

19 David McMillan, in conversation with Patricia Bovey, 26 July 2020.

20 Baillargeon, "McMillan's Chernobyl," 256–57.

21 McMillan, *Growth and Decay*, 243.

22 Marianne Nicolson, artist statement for her Waterline exhibition, 2013, https://www.kootenaygallery.com/waterline/ (accessed 11 March 2022).

23 Robin Laurence, review of "Walking on Water," Equinox Gallery, 30 April 2013, online.

24 Dana Claxton, as quoted in Layli Long Soldier, "Tribute to Dana Claxton and the Art of Generosity," in *Dana Claxton*, 10. See Figure 1. The comment is about *The Medicine Project*, 2008.

25 Yisa Akinbolaji, email correspondence to Patricia Bovey, 7 June 2020.

26 Christian Thompson, "Boyer, Bob," Indigenous Saskatchewan Encyclopedia online, https://teaching.usask.ca/indigenoussk/import/boyer_bob_1948-2004.php (accessed 17 November 2022).

27 Mulder and Clark, "In the Silent Hours," 1194.

28 KC Adams, "In The Beginning," in Adams, *Perception*, 11, 13.

29 According to Diana Thorneycroft, other materials used on the altered horses, as per 9 June 2020 email correspondence with Patricia Bovey, include "clay, gesso, acrylic, pencil crayon, graphite, water colour, glue, gel medium, clear tar gel, quake hold, flour paste, smoke, Japanese rice paper, rubber, twine, string, wire, sinew, thread, leather, fabric, lace, metal clamps, willow, doll hair, doll parts, horse hair, cat hair, rabbit fur, pubic hair, cat whiskers, badger claws, spider web, midges, mosquitoes, wasps, flies, aphids, feathers, rabbit feet, shells, cat scabs, flower stamens, pollen, lamb fur, bird claws, porcupine quills, horns, skulls, cat claw, rabbit backbone, dried onion roots, wild rice, dried carrots, lead weights, toy wheels, metal clamps, wood, artificial leech, seeds, plants, earth, sugar, rust, blood, spit, nails."

30 Chantal Gibson, artist statement for Altered Book Series, https://chantalgibson.com/altered-books (accessed 11 March 2022).

31 Karin Jones, "Worn: Shaping Black Feminine Identity," artist's statement on the artist's website, https://karinjones.ca/projects/6808738 (accessed 11 March 2022).

32 Karin Jones, artist's comments on her website confirmed in conversation with Patricia Bovey, Summer 2020.

33 Jaime Black, artist's statement, https://www.jaimeblackartist.com/exhibitions/ (accessed 14 March 2022).

34 Tristen Jenni Sanderson, as quoted by Emily Mertz in "Alberta Artist's Paintings of Missing and Murdered Indigenous Women Help Families Heal," Global News, 4 March 2020, https://globalnews.ca/news/6621401/alberta-artist-mmiw-women-not-invisible/ (accessed 15 March 2022).

35 As quoted by Amy Karlinsky, "Andrew Valko," *Galleries West*, Summer 2005, 34–35.

36 Robert Enright, "Sreentime," in *Postcard Fictions* (Toronto: Key Porter Books, 2001), 9.

37 Karlinsky, "Andrew Valko," 34.

38 Esther Warkov, unpublished notes, Winnipeg Art Gallery, 5 July 1999, Winnipeg Art Gallery Archives.

39 *Time*, 14 June 1968, as reproduced in Fry, *Esther Warkov*, n.p.

40 Hughes, *Manitoba Art Monographs*, 350.

41 Fry, *Esther Warkov*, n.p.

42 http://www.shawnadempseyandlorrimillan.net/#/alps/ (accessed 14 March 2022).

43 Robert Houle, as quoted in "The Spiritual Legacy of the Ancient Ones," in Nemiroff, Houle, and Townsend-Gault, *Land, Spirit, Power*, 60.

44 Layli Long Soldier, "Tribute to Dana Claxton and the Art of Generosity," in *Dana Claxton*, 10.

45 Dana Claxton, email to Layli Long Soldier, as quoted by Long Soldier, "Tribute to Dana Claxton," 9.

46 Dana Claxton, as quoted in Tania Willard, "Dana Claxton: Starting from Home: An Online Retrospective of Dana Claxton," Secwepemc Nation, 2015, https://www.thefreelibrary.com/Indigenous+(re)memory+and+resistance%3A+video+works+by+Dana+Claxton.-a0247034908.

47 Ibid.

48 Willard, "Dana Claxton."

49 Kent Monkman, interview with Lenard Monkman, "Kent Monkman Goes Back to the Urban Rez," CBC News, October 2019, https://www.cbc.ca/player/play/1620991555777 (accessed 15 March 2022).

50 Ibid.

51 Ibid.

52 Kent Monkman, interview with Robert Enright, "The Incredible Rightness of Mischief."

53 Karen Duffek, as quoted in Cramp, "Lawrence Paul Yuxweluptun," 35.

54 Beverly Cramp in ibid., 33.

55 Rebecca Belmore, http://ccca.concordia.ca/statements/belmore_statement.html (accessed 15 March 2022).

56 Bailey and Watson, *Rebecca Belmore*, 11.

57 Ibid., 27.

58 Rebecca Belmore, "In My Lifetime," artist's website, https://www.rebeccabelmore.com (accessed 2008).

59 Robert Houle, "Interiority as Allegory," in Augaitis and Ritter, *Rebecca Belmore*, 19.

60 Rosalie Favell, artist's statement, https://rosaliefavell.com/portfolio/longing-and-not-belonging/ (accessed 15 March 2022).

61 McAlear, "Self Possession," 14–15.

62 Ibid., 17.

63 Louis Riel, 4 July 1885, https://www.mmf.mb.ca/louis-riel-quotes (accessed 15 March 2022).

64 Joseph Tisiga, "Indigenous Arts and Stories," 2011, http://www.our-story.ca/winners/arts/3083:with-friends (accessed 15 March 2022).

65 George Littlechild, as quoted by Laviolette, *An Alberta Art Chronicle*, 63.

66 Laviolette in ibid.

67 Leah Sandals, "York Wilson Award Honours Robert Houle's Residential School Art," *Canadian Art*, 24 September 2013, https://canadianart.ca/news/robert-houle-york-wilson-prize/ (accessed 9 November 2013).

68 Robert Houle, as quoted in Mary Reid, *Robert Houle: Sandy Bay Residential School Series* (Winnipeg: School of Art Gallery, University of Manitoba, 2009), n.p.

69 Madill, *Robert Houle*, 48.

70 Robert Houle, in conversation with Patricia Bovey, March 2018.

71 "Reconciliation Pole," Indigenous Portal, University of British Columbia, https://indigenous.ubc.ca/indigenous-engagement/featured-initiatives/reconciliation-pole/ (accessed 15 March 2022).

72 Ibid.

73 See https://www.rcaanc-cirnac.gc.ca/eng/1339417945383/1571586663244#chp4 (accessed 15 March 2022).

74 Jackie Bissley, "Joane Cardinal Schubert: An Artist Setting Trap," *Windspeaker* 17, no. 2 (1999), updated 23 February 2014, https://ammsa.com/publications/windspeaker/joane-cardinal-schubert-artist-setting-traps (accessed 15 March 2022).

75 Joane Cardinal-Schubert, as quoted by Bissley, "Joane Cardinal Schubert."

76 Ibid.

77 Jane Ash Poitras, "Preservation Reservation 2020," Alberta Arts Council, https://www.youtube.com/watch?v=Y35hDvA_HEM (accessed 15 March 2022).

78 Ibid.

79 Joan Ash Poitras, in conversation with Patricia Bovey, 11 October 2021.

80 Val Vint, email correspondence to Patricia Bovey, 26 July 2020.

81 Comfort, *Artist at War*, 123.

82 Michael Boss, email correspondence to Patricia Bovey, 9 January 2015.

83 Ibid.

84 Comfort, *Artist at War*, 27.

85 Ibid., 124.

86 Townshend, *Maxwell Bates*, 36–37.

87 Jack Shadbolt, as quoted by Watson, *Jack Shadbolt,* 34n29.

88 Charles Scott, as quoted by Watson, *Jack Shadbolt,* 34n30.

89 Jack Shadbolt, as quoted by Watson, *Jack Shadbolt,* 34–35n33.

90 Tony Gregson, "Robert de Castro: A Retrospective," Maltwood Museum and Art Gallery, University of Victoria, 1996, typescript manuscript, 10.

91 Phyllis Serota, email correspondence to Patricia Bovey, 4 August 2020.

92 Dana Claxton, as quoted by Arnold, *Dana Claxton: Fringing the Cube*, 14.

93 Grant Arnold, in *Dana Claxton*, 13.

94 Karen Cornelius, as quoted in Patricia Bovey, "Karen Cornelius: Fabric of Belonging," Shenzhen University Gallery, China, 2013, n.p.

95 Kate Davis, "Foreword," in Long and Koop, *Wanda Koop*.

Epilogue

1 Ivan Eyre, in conversation with Patricia Bovey, 27 October 2004.

2 Andrew Valko, as quoted by Robert Enright, "Valko: The Summer of Our Discontents," 14.

3 Esther Warkov, in conversation with Patricia Bovey, 5 July 1999.

4 Richard Hunt, in conversation with Patricia Bovey, 20 August 2020.

Adams, KC. *Perception: A Photo Series*. Winnipeg: HighWater Press, 2019.

Adamson, Arthur. *Eighty Years Swinton*. Winnipeg: The Art Collectors Club, 1997.

Ainslie, Patricia, and Mary-Beth Laviolette. *Alberta Art and Artists: An Overview*. Calgary: Fifth House, 2007.

Augaitis, Daina, and Kathleen Ritter, eds. *Rebecca Belmore: Rising to the Occasion*. Vancouver: Vancouver Art Gallery, 2008.

Bailey, Jann, and Scott Watson. *Rebecca Belmore: Fountain*. Vancouver: Kamloops Art Gallery, The Morris and Helen Belkin Art Gallery, Canada Pavilion, Venice Biennale, 2005.

Baldissera, Lisa. *James Gordaneer: A Life in Painting*. Victoria: Art Gallery of Greater Victoria, 2010.

Bartlett, John. *Remarks on Board the Ship, Massachusetts*. Salem, Mass.: Peabody Museum, 1925.

Bates, Maxwell. *A Wilderness of Days: An Artist's Experiences as a Prisoner of War in Germany*. Victoria: Sono Nis Press, 1978.

Bates, Maxwell. *Far-Away Flags*. Victoria: Royal Oak, 1962.

Beaglehole, J.C. *The Journals of Captain James Cook*, 3 Vols. Cambridge: Cambridge University Press, 1955–1967.

Belton, Robert J. *Sights of Resistance: Approaches to Canadian Visual Culture*. Calgary: University of Calgary Press, 2001.

Berry, Virginia. *Taming the Frontier: Art and Women in the Canadian West, 1880–1920.* Calgary and Winnipeg: Bayeux Art and Winnipeg Art Gallery, 2005.

Besant, Derek. *SKIN: Walter Jule Selected Works, 1968–2008*. Edmonton: University of Alberta, 2008.

Biéler, André, and Elizabeth Harrison, eds. *The Kingston Conference Proceedings*. Kingston: Queen's University, 1941.

Boss, Michael. *Bloodlines*. Brandon, MB: Art Gallery of Southwestern Manitoba, 1998.

Boswell, John. *The Invention of Glass: The Studio Glass Movement from the Periphery*. Facsimile Publication, 2021.

Bovey, Patricia. *Carole Sabiston: Everything Below All of the Above*. Victoria: Art Gallery of Greater Victoria, 2014.

Bovey, Patricia. *Don Proch: Masking and Mapping*. Winnipeg: University of Manitoba Press, 2019.

Bovey, Patricia. *HeadSpace: Five Decades of Bruce Head*. Winnipeg: Winnipeg Art Gallery, 2008.

Bovey, Patricia. *John Koerner Past / Present*. Victoria: Art Gallery of Greater Victoria, 1991–1992.

Bovey, Patricia. "Karen Cornelius: Fabric of Belonging." Shenzhen University Gallery, China, 2013.

Bovey, Patricia. *Myfanwy Pavelic: Inner Explorations*. Victoria: Art Gallery of Greater Victoria, 1994.

Bovey, Patricia. *Pat Martin Bates: Balancing on a Thread*. Calgary: Frontenac House, 2014.

Bovey, Patricia. *Robin Hopper: Ceramic Explorations, 1957–1987*. Victoria, BC, and North York, ON: Art Gallery of Greater Victoria and Koffler Gallery Toronto, 1987.

Bovey, Patricia. "The Scholar and Her Book." In *Taming the Frontier: Art and Women in the Canadian West, 1880–1920,* edited by Virginia Berry, iii–viii. Calgary and Winnipeg: Bayeux Art and Winnipeg Art Gallery, 2005.

Bovey, Patricia. *Visual Celebrations I*. Winnipeg: Buhler Gallery, 2012.

Bovey, Patricia, Ann Davis, and Cathy Stewart. *Lionel LeMoine FitzGerald (1890–1956): The Development of an Artist*. Winnipeg: Winnipeg Art Gallery, 1978.

Bovey, Patricia, Ted Fraser, Andrew Kear, Sandra Fraser, and Timothy Long. *David Thauberger: Road Trips and Other Diversions*. Saskatoon and Regina: Mendel Art Gallery and MacKenzie Gallery, 2014.

Bovey, Patricia, and Leona Herzog. *Visual Celebrations II*. Winnipeg: Buhler Gallery, 2017.

Boyer, Bob. *Spiritual Landscapes: Recent Paintings: Thunder Bay Art Gallery April 9–May 23, 1999*. Thunder Bay: Thunder Bay Art Gallery, 1999.

Bruce, Tobi, Mary Jo Hughes, and Andrew Kear. *William Kurelek: The Messenger*. Victoria: Art Gallery of Greater Victoria, 2011.

Burnaby Art Gallery. *Aganetha Dyck Collaborations*. Burnaby Art Gallery, 2009.

Burnaby Art Gallery. *The Solitudes of Place: Recent Drawings by Ann Kipling*. Burnaby: Burnaby Art Gallery, 2011.

Burnett, Craig. *Jeff Wall*. London, UK: Tate Publishing, 2005.

Burnett, David, and Marilyn Schiff. *Contemporary Canadian Art*. Edmonton: Hurtig, 1983.

Cameron, Ann, and Daryl Kuhl. *Art in Winnipeg 1955–1959*. Winnipeg: Gallery 1.1.1., University of Manitoba, 1982.

Carr, Emily. *Hundreds and Thousands: The Journals of Emily Carr*. Toronto: Clarke, Irwin and Company, 1966.

Clendinning, Anne. "Exhibiting a Nation: Canada at the British Empire Exhibition, 1924–1925," *Social History* 39, no. 77 (2006): 79–107.

Cole, Douglas. "John Webber, A Sketch of Captain James Cook's Artist." *British Columbia Historical News* 13, no. 1 (Fall 1979): 18–19, 20.

Comfort, Charles. *Artist at War*. Toronto: Ryerson Press, 1956.

Coy, Helen. *FitzGerald as Printmaker*. Winnipeg: University of Manitoba Press, 1982.

Cramp, Beverly. "Lawrence Paul Yuxweluptun: Canada Is Not A Pretty Picture." *Galleries West*, Summer 2016, 35. https://www.gallerieswest.ca/magazine/stories/lawrence-paul-yuxweluptun-canada-is-not-a-pretty-picture/.

Cutschall, Colleen. *Colleen Cutschall: House Made of Stars*. Essays by Shirley Madill, Allan J. Ryan, and Ruth B. Phillips. Winnipeg: Winnipeg Art Gallery, 1996.

Dana Claxton: Fringing the Cube (exhibition catalogue). Edited by Grant Arnold. Vancouver: Figure 1 Publishing and Vancouver Art Gallery, 2018.

Davis, Angela. *The Grand Western Canadian Screen Shop: Printing, People and History*. Regina: MacKenzie Art Gallery, 1992.

Davis, Angela E. "Laying the Ground: The Establishment of an Artistic Milieu in Winnipeg, 1890–1913." *Manitoba History* 4 (1982): 10–15.

Davis, Ann, and Elizabeth Herbert. *Marion Nicoll: Silence and Alchemy*. Calgary: University of Calgary Press, 2013.

Dempsey, Shawna. *Live at the Centre: An Incomplete and Anecdotal History of Winnipeg Performance Art*. Winnipeg: Winnipeg Art Gallery, 2004.

Dixon, George. *A Voyage Round the World: But More Particularly to The North-West Coast of America*. London: Geo. Goulding, 1789. Republished by N. Israel / Keizersgracht 539. New York: Amsterdam and Da Capo Press, 1968.

Duff, Wilson. "Contributions of Marius Barbeau to West Coast Ethnology." *Anthropologia* 6, 1964.

Duffek, Karen. "Northwest Coast Art At a Crossroads." *Galleries West*, 22 December 2012. https://www. gallerieswest. ca/magazine/stories/northwest-coast-art%3A-at-a-crossroads/.

Duffek, Karen. *Robert Davidson: The Abstract Edge*. Vancouver: Museum of Anthropology, University of British Columbia, and the National Gallery of Canada, 2004.

Duffek, Karen, Bill McLennan, and Jordan Wilson. *Where the Power Is: Indigenous Perspectives of on Northwest Coast Art*. Vancouver: Figure 1 and the Museum of Anthropology at the University of British Columbia, 2021.

Eckhardt, Ferdinand. *Esther Warkov: Paintings and Drawings*. Winnipeg: Winnipeg Art Gallery, 1964.

Eckhardt, Ferdinand. *Maxwell Bates*. Winnipeg: Winnipeg Art Gallery, 1968.

Eckhardt, Ferdinand. *Paintings Graphics by Don Reichert*. Winnipeg: Winnipeg Art Gallery, 1960.

Enright, Robert. "The Incredible Rightness of Mischief." An Interview with Kent Monkman. *Border Crossings* 143, September 2017. https://bordercrossingsmag. com/article/the-incredible-rightnes-of-mischief.

Enright, Robert. "Valko: The Summer of Our Discontents." *Border Crossings*, Winter 1988–1989, 14.

Enright, Robert. *Wanda Koop: Green Zone*. Winnipeg: City Press, 2008.

Eyre, Ivan. *Ivan on Eyre: The Paintings*. Winnipeg: Pavilion Gallery, 2004.

Fenton, Terry. *Reta Summers Cowley*. Calgary: University of Calgary Press and Mendel Art Gallery, 2006.

Fetherling, Douglas, ed. *Documents in Canadian Art*. Peterborough, ON: Broadview Press, 1987.

Francis, R. Douglas. *Images of the West: Changing Perceptions of the Prairies 1690–1960*. Saskatoon: Western Producer Prairie Books, 1989.

Fraser, Ted. *Kenneth Lochhead: Garden of Light*. Regina: MacKenzie Art Gallery, 2005.

Freeland, Cynthia. *Portraits and Persons: A Philosophical Inquiry*. Oxford: Oxford University Press, 2010.

Fry, Philip. *Esther Warkov: The Recent Years*. Winnipeg: Winnipeg Art Gallery, 1972.

Gignac, Gilbert, and Mary Jo Hughes. *Hindsight: William Hind in the Canadian West*. Winnipeg: Winnipeg Art Gallery, 2002.

Gillmor, Alison. *The Art of Tony Tascona*. Winnipeg: University of Winnipeg, 1997.

Graham, Colin. "Maxwell Bates." *Arts West* 1, no. 4 (1976): 24–27.

Graham, Colin. *Relationships: Myfanwy Spencer Pavelic, RCA*. Victoria: Morriss Publishing, 1985.

Gregson, Tony. "Robert de Castro: A Retrospective." Victoria: Maltwood Museum and Art Gallery, University of Victoria, 1996. Typescript manuscript.

Hatch, John Davis Jr. "Foreword." In *Painting in Canada: A Selective Historical Survey*. Albany, NY: Albany Institute of History and Art, 1946.

Hebert, Elizabeth. *The Art of John Snow*. Calgary: University of Calgary Press, 2011.

Heath, Terrence. *Uprooted: The Life and Art of Ernest Lindner*. Saskatoon: Fifth House, 1983.

Henry, John Frazier. *Early Maritime Artists of the Pacific Northwest Coast, 1741–1841*. Vancouver: Douglas and McIntyre, 1984.

Hind, Henry Youle. *Report on a Topographical & Geological Exploration of the Canoe Route between Fort William, Lake Superior, and Fort Garry, Red River; and also The Valley of the Red River, North of the 49th Parallel, During the Summer of 1857; Made under the Instructions from the Provincial Secretary of Canada*. Toronto: Stewart Derbishire and George Desbarats, 1858.

Houle, Robert. *Robert Houle: Indians from A to Z*. Winnipeg: Winnipeg Art Gallery, 1990.

Housser, Fred B. *A Canadian Art Movement*. Toronto: Macmillan, 1926.

Hughes, Kenneth. *Manitoba Art Monographs: Kelly Clark, E.J. (Ted) Howorth, Bill Lobchuk, Don Proch, Tony Tascona, Esther Warkov*. Winnipeg: Manitoba Department of Cultural Affairs and Historical Resources, 1982.

Hughes, Mary Jo, and Tad Suzuki. *Honest Ed's: Lingering Lights*. Toronto: Mayberry Fine Arts, 2018.

Jackson Beardy: A Life's Work. Winnipeg: Winnipeg Art Gallery, 1995.

Johnson, Donalda, and Kelly Clark. *Kelly Clark*. Winnipeg: University of Manitoba Press, 1998.

Kane, Paul. *Wanderings of an Artist among the Indians of North America from Canada to Vancouver's Island and Oregon through the Hudson's Bay Company's Territory and Back Again*, First Edition 1859, republished. Edmonton: M.G. Hurtig, 1968.

Koerner, John. *A Brush with Life*. Vancouver: Ronsdale Press, 2005.

Koerner, John. *Unseen Dimensions: Musings on Art and Life*. Victoria: Sono Nis Press, 1997.

LaVallee, Michelle. *7: Professional Native Indian Artists Inc*. Regina: MacKenzie Art Gallery, 2014.

LaVallee, Michelle. *Thirteen Coyotes: Edward Poitras*. Regina: MacKenzie Art Gallery, 2012.

Laviolette, Mary-Beth. *An Alberta Art Chronicle: Adventures in Recent and Contemporary Art*. Canmore, AB: Attitude Publishing, 2006.

Leclerc, Denise, and Marion Barclay. *The Crisis of Abstraction in Canada: The 1950s*. Ottawa: National Gallery of Canada, 1992.

Leduc, Joanne, ed. *Overland from Canada to British Columbia By Mr. Thomas McMicking of Queenston, Canada West*. Ill., William G.R. Hind. Vancouver: University of British Columbia Press, 1981.

Lemecha, Vera, ed. *MAWA: Culture of Community*. Winnipeg: Mentoring Artists for Women's Art, 2004.

Lexier, Micah. *A Portrait of David*. Winnipeg: Winnipeg Art Gallery, 1994.

Lindberg, Ted (Theodore). *A Portrait by Myfanwy / Un Portrait par Myfanwy*. Victoria: Morriss Publishing, 1991.

Long, Timothy, and Wanda Koop. *Wanda Koop—Sightlines*. Regina: MacKenzie Art Gallery, 2002.

Lord, Barry. *The History of Painting in Canada: Toward a People's Art*. Toronto: NC Press, 1974.

Lovatt, Tom. *Ivan Eyre Drawings*. Winnipeg: Pavilion Galleries, 2003.

Lutz, John. *Grafton Tyler Brown: The Mystery of Grafton Tyler Brown: Race, Art and Landscape in 19th Century British Columbia*. Victoria: Legacy Gallery, University of Victoria, 2017.

MacNayr, Linda, and Walter Dexter. *Walter Dexter: Surface and Sculpture*. Victoria: Art Gallery of Greater Victoria, 1995.

Madill, Shirley. *The Artists' Proof: Eleanor Bond, Lew Colborne, Allan Geske, Steve Gouthro*. Winnipeg: Winnipeg Art Gallery, 1980.

Madill, Shirley. *1987: Contemporary Art in Manitoba: An Exhibition Celebrating the 75th Anniversary of the Winnipeg Art Gallery*. Winnipeg: Winnipeg Art Gallery, 1987.

Madill, Shirley. *Robert Houle: His Life and Work*. Toronto: The Canadian Art Library, Art Canada Institute, 2021.

Madill, Shirley. *The Winnipeg Perspective 1985*. Winnipeg: Winnipeg Art Gallery, 1985.

Madill, Shirley, and Aganetha Dyck. *Aganetha Dyck*. Winnipeg: Winnipeg Art Gallery, 1995.

McAlear, Donna. "Self Possession." In *Rosalie Favell: I Searched Many Worlds*. Winnipeg: Winnipeg Art Gallery, 2003.

McGill, Jean S. *Edmund Morris Frontier Artist*. Toronto: Dundurn Press, 1984.

McMaster Museum of Art and Robert McLoughlin Gallery. *Troubling Abstraction: Robert Houle*. Hamilton and Oshawa, ON: McMaster Museum of Art and Robert McLoughlin Gallery, 2007.

McMillan, David. *Growth and Decay: Prypiat and the Chernobyl Exclusion Zone*. Göttingen: Steidl Publishers, 2018.

Mercredi, Ovide. *My Silent Drum*. Winnipeg: Aboriginal Issues Press, University of Manitoba, 2015.

Moos, David, ed. *IAIN BAXTER&: Works 1958–2011*. Toronto: Art Gallery of Ontario, 2011.

Morris, Jerrold. *100 Years of Canadian Drawings*. Toronto: Methuen, 1980.

Mulder, Janice, and Janet Clark. "In the Silent Hours: The Cancer Paintings of Kelly Clark." *Canadian Association Medical Journal* 169, no. 11 (November 2003): 1194–95.

Nasgaard, Roald. *Abstract Painting in Canada*. Vancouver: Douglas and McIntyre and the Art Gallery of Nova Scotia, 2007.

Nemiroff, Diana, Robert Houle, and Charlotte Townsend-Gault. *Land, Spirit, Power: First Nations at the National Gallery of Canada*. Ottawa: National Gallery of Canada, 1992.

Newlands, Anne. *Canadian Paintings, Prints and Drawings*. Richmond Hill, ON: Firefly Books, 2007.

Newman, Marketa. *Biographical Dictionary of Saskatchewan Artists*. Saskatoon: Fifth House, 1990.

Nowosad, Frank. *Ciccimarra: Richard Ciccimarra, 1924–1973*. Victoria: Art Gallery of Greater Victoria, 1988.

O'Brian, John, ed. *The Flat Side of the Landscape: The Emma Lake Artists' Workshops*. Saskatoon: Mendel Art Gallery, 1989.

Page, P.K. "Darkingbad the Brightdayler: Transmutation Symbolism in the Work of Pat Martin Bates." *Arts Canada* 154/155 (April/May, 1971): 35–40.

Parke-Taylor, Michael. *In Seclusion with Nature: The Later Works of Lionel LeMoine Fitzgerald, 1942 To 1956*. Winnipeg: Winnipeg Art Gallery, 1988.

Perry, Art. "Maxwell Bates." *Vanguard*, May 1979.

Plaskett, Joe. "Am I Contemporary?" Unpublished Speech delivered to the Contemporary Art Society, 1995.

Plaskett, Joe. "Artist's Statement." Joseph Plaskett. Victoria: Winchester Galleries, 1998.

Public Archives of Canada. "Image of Canada: Documentary Watercolours and Drawings." From the Permanent Collection of the Public Archives of Canada, Ottawa, 1972.

Reid, Bill. *Solitary Raven: The Writings of Bill Reid*. Edited by Robert Bringhurst. Vancouver: Douglas and McIntyre, 2000.

Reid, Mary. *Sheila Spence: Pictures of Me*. Winnipeg: Winnipeg Art Gallery, 2009.

Reid, Natasha, and Harold Klunder. *Intervention: 31 Femmes Peintres / 31 Women Painters*. Montreal: McClure Gallery, 2018.

Riopelle, Christopher. *Tim Gardner: New Works*. London: National Gallery Company, 2007.

Rogatnick, Abraham, Ian M. Thom, and Adele Weder. *B.C. Binning*. Vancouver: Douglas and McIntyre, 2006.

Ruffo, Armand Garnet. *Norval Morrisseau: Man Changing into Thunderbird*. Vancouver: Douglas and McIntyre, 2014.

Sanromán, Lucía. *Embedded Conflict in the Work of James Gordaneer*. Victoria: Emdash Publishing, 2003.

Serota, Phyllis. *Painting My Life: A Memoir of Love, Art and Transformation*. Victoria: Sono Nis Press, 2011.

Shadbolt, Doris. *Emily Carr*. Vancouver: Douglas and McIntyre, 1990.

Skelton, Robin. *The Limners*. Victoria: Pharaoh Press, 1972.

Skelton, Robin. "Robert de Castro." *Malahat Review,* October 1976, 63–64.

Smith, Barbara Lee. *Celebrating the Stitch: Contemporary Embroidery of North America*. Newtown, CT: Taunton Press, 1991.

Smith, Bernard. *European Vision and the South Pacific, 1768–1850*. Oxford: Oxford University Press, 1960.

Smith, Frances K. *André Biéler: An Artist's Life and Times*. Richmond Hill: Firefly Books, 2006.

Smith, Paul Chaat. *Faye HeavyShield: Blood*. Lethbridge, AB: Southern Alberta Art Gallery, 2004.

Snow, Kathleen M. *Maxwell Bates: Biography of an Artist*. Calgary: University of Calgary Press, 1993.

Steggles, Mary Ann. *MUD, Hands, Fire*. Winnipeg: School of Art, University of Manitoba, 2015.

Stubbs, Eva. *Eva Stubbs: Memories for the Future*. Winnipeg: Winnipeg Art Gallery, 1987.

Swan, Sarah. "Karel Funk: Art from the Hood," *Galleries West*, Summer 2016, https://www.gallerieswest.ca/magazine/stories/karel-funk-art-from-the-hood/.

Tascona, Tony, Patricia Bovey, Robert Enright, and James Patten. *Tony Tascona: Resonance*. Winnipeg: Winnipeg Art Gallery, 2001.

Thom, Ian. *Emily Carr: Art and Process.* Vancouver: Vancouver Art Gallery, 1998.

Thom, Ian. *Gordon Smith: The Act of Painting.* Vancouver: Douglas and McInytre, Vancouver Art Gallery, 1997.

Thom, Ian, Roald Nasgaard, Nancy Tousely, and Jeffrey Spalding. *Takao Tanabe.* Vancouver: Douglas and McIntyre, Vancouver Art Gallery, and Art Gallery of Greater Victoria, 2005.

Townshend, Nancy. *A History of Art in Alberta, 1905–1970.* Calgary: Bayeux Arts, 2005.

Townshend, Nancy. *Maxwell Bates: Canada's Premier Expressionist of the 20th Century; His Art, Life and Prisoner of War Notebook.* Calgary: Snyder Hedlin Fine Arts, 2005.

Tuele, Nicholas. *The World of Ted Harrison.* Victoria: Art Gallery of Greater Victoria, 1996.

Tuele, Nicholas, and B.C. Binning. *B.C. Binning: A Classical Spirit.* Victoria: Art Gallery of Greater Victoria, 1986.

Valentine, Mary, and Patricia Bovey. *Experiences and Insights: My Life as Art.* Winnipeg: Patricia Bovey Incorporated, 2014.

Vancouver Art Gallery. *Emily Carr.* Vancouver: Vancouver Art Gallery, 1971.

Vancouver Art Gallery. *Maxwell Bates in Retrospect 1921–1971.* Vancouver: Vancouver Art Gallery, 1973.

Vancouver Art Gallery. *Vancouver: Art and Artists 1931–1983.* Vancouver: Vancouver Art Gallery, 1983.

Varley, Peter. *Frederick H. Varley.* Toronto: Key Porter Books, 1983.

Walker, Doreen. *Dear Nan: Letters of Emily Carr, Nan Cheney and Humphrey Thoms.* Vancouver: University of British Columbia Press, 1990.

Warre, Henry James. *Sketches in North America and the Oregon Territory.* Introduction by Archibald Hanna, Jr. Barre, Massachusetts: Imprint Society, 1970.

Watson, Scott. *Jack Shadbolt.* Vancouver: Douglas and McIntyre, 1990.

West, Shearer. *Portraiture.* Oxford: Oxford University Press, 2004.

Winnipeg Art Gallery. *Don Reichert: A Life in Work.* Winnipeg: Winnipeg Art Gallery, 1995.

Winnipeg Art Gallery. *Figure Ground: Paintings and Drawings by Ivan Eyre.* Winnipeg: Winnipeg Art Gallery, 2005.

Winnipeg Art Gallery. *Robert Houle: Sovereignty Over Subjectivity.* Winnipeg: Winnipeg Art Gallery, 1999.

Winnipeg Art Gallery. *Winston Leathers' Cosmic Variations.* Introduction by Winston Leathers. Winnipeg: Winnipeg Art Gallery, 1974.

Woodcock, George. *Ivan Eyre.* Don Mills: Fitzhenry and Whiteside, 1981.

Woodcock, George. *Strange Bedfellows: The State and the Arts in Canada.* Vancouver: Douglas and McIntyre, 1985.

Yates, Sarah. *Manitoba Society of Artists: A History.* Winnipeg: The Manitoba Society of Artists, 1992.

Ylitalo, Katherine. "Work of Art: Grey Green Crowd #2." *Avenue Magazine,* Calgary, 4 September 2019.

INDEX

A

Abbott & Cordova, 7 August 1971 (Douglas), 85

abstract art, 221–83

Abstract in Green and Gold (FitzGerald), 132, 166, 230, 231

Académie Julian, 11–12

Adams, KC, 56, 115, 213, 312, 342, 359–60

Adamson, Arthur, 250–51

Adaskin, Frances, 163

Adaskin, Harry, 163

After Dr. Eduard Assmuss 1865 (Dyck), 346

Agassiz Ice (Reeve), 280

Age (Ciccimarra), 325

Agnes (Falk), 331, 332

AIDS (General Idea), 103

Akinbolaji, Yisa, 309, 310–11, 356, 357, 402

A.L. Cole Power Plant (Hurley), 175

Albany exhibition (1946), 5

Alberta art, 25, 27, 31, 32, 50–51, 71–72, 136–40

Alberta Arts Foundation, 49

Alberta College of Art, 9, 12

Alberta Society of Artists, 27

Alien Landscapes (Benesiinaabandan), 189, 328–29

Alkali Basin (Lindoe), 137, 138

Altered Book Series (Gibson), 362

Alward, Sharon, 104

Amyot Series #25 (Perehudoff), 245

Ancestors and Descendants (Boss), 312–13

And drifted, one ear tuned to the dip of your paddle (Everett), 154–55, 158

And Peter Followed Afar Off (McCloy), 41

Andrews, Sybil, 71, 195, 213, 214–16

The Androgynous Landscape (Cutschall), 268–69

Andy's Corner (Pura), 200

The Angel of the Blue Sky is Crying Parallax Tears (Bates), 48, 399

Anguish (Pavelic), 316, 318

Anthony, Len, 50, 69, 75, 76

Aperture (Carther), 96, 97, 159–60

Arborite Housedress (Dempsey and Millan), 106

Arc Welder By Night (Atkins), 397

Archambeau, Robert, 100, 156, 283

Armington, Frank, 12

Armory Show, 227–28

Armstrong, William, 126

Arnold, Grant, 401

Art Gallery of Greater Victoria, 31

Art Students League, 226, 234

Artist and Model (Grison), 329

Asessippi Clouds (Proch), 113, 115

Asessippi to Altona (Proch), 276–77

Asessippi Tread (Proch), 146, 147–48, 278

Assiniboine Fool Society (Poitras), 86

Assiniboine Hunting Buffalo (Kane), 18

Atkins, Caven, 396

Au, Aliana, 179–81, 332, 334–36

Audio Walks (Cardiff), 108

August Path (Lochhead), 128, 130, 132–33

automatic painting, 239

B

Babysitting the Kids (Sapp), 217

Back, George, 14, 124

The Back of the House of All Sorts (Cheney), 193, 194

Backview (Forrest), 332

A Backyard in Downtown Vancouver (Hughes), 192, 193

Bagged Series (BAXTER&), 112

Bailey, Jann, 378

Balcony Series (Koerner), 168

Balfour, Barbara, 283

Banff School of Fine Arts, 9, 32

Barnet, Will, 40, 72, 141, 225, 239

Barraud, Cyril, 172, 395

Barrow, Daniel, 104

Bartlett, John, 124

Basford, Ron, 112

Bateman, Robert, 345

Bates, Maxwell, 9, 47, 60, 71, 172, 203, 204–5, 218–19, 271, 286, 325, 326–28, 355, 397

Bates, Pat Martin, 9, 13, 48, 57, 72, 73, 77, 78, 144–45, 168–69, 229, 252, 255–56, 257–58, 260, 332, 399

BAXTER&, IAIN, 109, 111–12

Beaches . . . Dieppe (Whitehouse), 142

Beardy, Jackson, 9, 49, 69, 250, 263–64

Beckmann, Max, 47, 324

Belcourt, Christi, 387–88

Bell, Alistair, 183

Bell, Peter, 326

Belmore, Rebecca, 49, 113, 115, 342, 358–59, 366, 378–79

Belonging (Favell), 381

Benesiinaabandan, Scott Stephens, 188–89, 190, 328–29

Bentham, Douglas, 92, 95, 279

Bergman, Eric, 25, 50, 61, 71, 166, 183, 186, 222, 257

Biéler, André, 34

The Big Trees (Morton), 344

Big Wig (Dempsey and Millan), 107

Binning, B.C., 163, 226, 237, 238

Birch bark biting (Merasty), 5

Birch on Birch I (Everett), 157

Birth of a Prairie River (Swinton), 130, 146

The Birth of Spring (Swinton), 250

Black, Jaime, 367, 368

Black Dress (Dyck), 338–39

Black Forest (dark waters) (Thorneycroft), 361

Black Island (Binning), 237

Black Madonna I (Tascona), 260

Black Madonna II (Tascona), 260

Blackwood, David, 326

Blankets (Boyer), 357

Bleeding Orchid I (Au), 179–80

Bloore, Ron, 44, 242

Blue Bridge Series (Taylor), 188

Blue Pantry (Cicansky), 215, 219

Blunden Harbour (Carr), 5, 7

Bobak, Molly Lamb, 36, 210, 212, 218, 292, 395, 396

Boggy Creek Valley, Autumn (Kerr), 136

Bond, Eleanor, 52, 189–92

Bonheur, Rosa, 301

Bonli, Henry, 44

Bonspiel (Lochhead), 218

Bornstein, Eli, 9, 223, 244, 276

Boss, Michael, 312–13, 393, 394, 404

Boyer, Robert "Bob," 9, 53, 266, 268, 357–58, 400

Boyle, Shary, 107

Bradford Still Life #2 (Laing), 78

Braided Book, 2011 (Gibson), 362

Brangwyn, Frank, 395

Braune, Peter, 69

Breaking a Road in Manitoba—Sioux Indians in the Background (Hind), 15

Brenda Yvonne (Eyre), 304, 305

Brenner, Roland, 48

bridges, 182–89

Bridges (Bell), 183

Brigden, Arnold, 25

Brigdens of Winnipeg Limited, 25, 70, 172

Bringing More Wood Into The House (Sapp), 217

British Columbia art, 25–29, 30–31, 214, 234

British Columbia Art League, 25

British Columbia Coast (L'Aubinière), 5

Bronson, AA, 107

Brooker, Bertram, 12–13, 28, 29, 166, 193, 221, 222, 226–29, 231, 256, 257

Brown, Annora, 223, 225

Brown, Eric, 28

Brown, Grafton Tyler, 125–26, 127

Brown, Shirley, 348–49

Bruce, Robert, 179, 299

Brunst, Stanley, 133–34, 175, 176

Buchanan, Donald, 40

Buddhism, 257

Buffalo Bone China (Claxton), 57, 374

Buffalo in the Foothills (Verner), 2, 19

Buffalo Runner (Woods), 161, 165

Building (Gouthro), 176–77, 179

Bull, Hank, 108

Bungalow (Thauberger), 76, 196, 197

Burnett, Craig, 305

Butler, Sheila, 332

By the Lake (LaFrenière), 154

C

Cage, John, 247

calligraphy, 99, 147, 232, 248, 252–53, 254, 256

Campobasso (Comfort), 395

Canada Council for the Arts, 38, 43–44, 239

Canadian Artists' Representation/ Le Front des artistes canadiens (CARFAC), 50, 244

Canadian Encyclopedia (Gibson), 362

Canadian Federation of Artists, 36

Canadian Museum of Civilization, 52

Canadian War Artists Program, 394

Cancer Series #42 (Clark), 359

Canteen Nijmegen, Holland (Bobak), 395

Canteen Queue, Kiska (Hughes), 396

Captain Bulger, Governor of Assiniboia (Rindisbacher), 202

Cardiff, Janet, 48, 108–9

Cardinal-Schubert, Joane, 9, 53, 387–89, 389, 390

Caressing Room (Pike), 64–65, 370

Carnegie Corporation, 32, 34

Carnegie Foundation, 32

Carnevale (Stone), 55, 114

Caro, Anthony, 279

Carr, Emily, 5, 7, 9, 10–11, 21, 25, 28, 29, 31, 48, 60, 62, 121, 133, 134, 142, 153, 164–65, 194, 222, 256–57, 259, 289, 293, 301, 342, 343–44

Carr-Harris, Ian, 48

Carther, Warren, 96, 97, 159–60

Cemetery of the 7th Battalion (Hamilton), 395

Centennial celebrations 1967, 49

A Century of Canadian Art (Tate exhibition), 4–5

ceramics, 62, 98–101, 121, 136–37, 156, 158–59, 215, 219, 273, 280–81, 282–83, 299–301, 317, 319–20, 329, 332, 336, 338–39, 346–47, 358–59

Cetology (Jungen), 276

Chair series (Au), 332, 335

Chalke, John, 100, 283

Cheney, Nan, 193, 194

Chernobyl, 351–52

Chief Justice Richard Jamieson Scott (Valko), 297, 298

The Chief's Wild Woman (Hunt), 273, 274

China Night and the Star That Acts in the Stillness (Bates), 169

Chinatown-Cumberland (Andrews), 195

Chinese Gold Washers on the Fraser River (Hind), 202

Chinese Night Train to the Yangtze Kiang (Bates), 256

Christie, Robert, 244, 247

Chronos Trilogy (Carther), 96

Churchill Night (King), 151

Cicansky, Victor "Vic," 86, 215, 219

Ciccimarra, Richard, 37, 286, 324, 325–26

civil wars, 402

Clark, Janet, 268, 359

Clark, Kelly, 41, 322, 323, 359

Claxton, Dana, 57, 373–74, 401

clay. *See* ceramics

Clements, Marie, 264

CNR Station (Barraud), 172

Cobiness, Eddy, 9, 250

Cochrane (Mitchell), 172

The Cocktail Party (Bates), 204, 205, 327, 328

Coeur d'Alene (Onley), 238

Coffee Bar (Andrews), 213, 215, 216

Colin Graham, Director 1951–1973 (Pavelic), 43

collage, 64, 69, 73, 104, 145, 237–38, 247, 265, 267, 268, 279, 294, 324–26, 363, 385

colonialism, 372–81

Colville, Alex, 278

Colville's Horse Races Through the Prairie Drive-Thru Gallery (Proch), 94, 277–78

Comfort, Charles, 13, 25, 26, 36–37, 223, 229, 284, 290, 292, 395

conceptual art, 102, 107–8, 109–15

Connecting Threads: The Arc of Carol Shields (Sabiston), 286, 302, 303

Connors, Tom, 301

Convoy Under Way (Binning), 237, 238

Copper Thunderbird (Clements), 264

Core 3 (Stanbridge), 280–81

Cornelius, Karen, 79–80, 336, 393, 402–4

Cosmic Variations (Leathers), 248

Country Fair (Bobak), 218

COVID-19 pandemic, 355–56

Cowley, Reta, 63, 140

Coy, Helen, 71

Cran, Chris, 224

Cranston, George, 21

The Creek (Spence), 147, 148

Cross, Ronald, 400

Crowchild Trail and 17th Avenue (Flodberg), 182, 183

Crucifixion (Swinton), 250

Culen, Lubos, 155

Cuthand, Ruth, 9, 355–356, 381

Cutshall, Colleen, 9, 268–269

Cycle of Life (Beardy), 263

D

Da Roza, Gustavo, 244

daily life, 202–19

The Dakota Boat (Lynn), 24, 171, 173

A Dance at Friendly Cove (De Suria), 202

Daniel, John, 299

Danube (Dukes), 397, 400

David Series (Lexier), 286

David Then & Now (Lexier), 311

Davidson, Robert, 9, 264, 275, 278

Davis, Ann, 248

Davis, Kate, 404

De Castro, Robert, 271, 326, 392, 398

De Suria, Tomás, 202

Dead German on the Hitler Line (Comfort), 396

The Deal (Howorth), 252

Death of the Virgin (After Caravaggio) (Monkman), 374–75

Decision (Pavelic), 318

Delbanco, Dawn, 253

Dempsey, Shawna, 50, 104, 105–7, 211, 372

Departure of the Industrial Workers (Bond), 191, 192

The Descent (Ciccimarra), 325

Devastatus Rememorari (Nickel), 346, 347

Dexter, Walter, 99, 136, 282–83

Dhârâna (Varley), 292

Di Castri, John, 294

Diefenbaker, John, 301

Dignam, Mary, 20

Dilworth, Ira, 163

Director (Eyre), 42

Disembodied Head (Dempsey and Millan), 107

Disraeli Undertow (Lucas), 182

Dixon, George, 122, 124, 125

Doc Snyder's House (FitzGerald), 5, 132, 193–94

Dog Among the Ruins (Shadbolt), 37, 398

Dogtown in July, Rosedale, Alberta (Sheldon), 172

Dolly and Bill (Thauberger), 75

domestic violence, 342, 369–70

Don (Spence), 286

The Double Crossing (Howorth), 76

Double Feature (Thauberger), 75–76

Double Self-Portrait (Boss), 393, 394

Double Tatter Wrap (Eyre), 319

Douglas, Stan, 49, 85

Downes, Gwladys, 29

Dreamland (Koop), 405

Dreams and Knowing #3 (Benesiinaabandan), 328

Dreams of Knowing (Grison), 329

Dress with Candles (Falk), 338

Dresses (Falk), 338

Drive-in series (Valko), 217–18

Drowned Pontiac (Gouthro), 320

Duffek, Karen, 275, 376

Dukes, Caroline, 324–25, 397, 400

Dumont, Gabriel, 301

Dyck, Aganetha, 86, 92, 338–39, 345–46

Dyck, Richard, 346

E

Eakin, William "Bill," 83

Easter Morning (Hamilton), 288

Easter Table (Plaskett), 206, 209

Eastern philosophies, 252–59

Echeverría, Atanasio, 202

Eckhardt, Ferdinand, 41, 42, 46, 67, 146, 252, 303, 316, 322, 324, 327–28

Edmonton Museum of Art, 25, 31

Education is the New Bison (Vint), 56, 384, 391

Elevator Series (Proch), 276

Emma Lake #2 (Cowley), 63

Emma Lake Artists Workshops, 6, 9, 31–32, 38–39, 44, 140, 141, 225, 244, 247

Empty Playground, Silent Battlefield (Akinbolaji), 356, 357, 402

Entering Ypres at Dawn (Barraud), 395

Entrance to the Harbor (Brown), 127

environmental concerns, 343–54

Equilibrium (Stubbs), 320

Erickson, Arthur, 163

Esler, John Kenneth "Ken," 72–73

Esquimalt Harbour (Brown), 126

Euphony (Carther), 96

Evening Calm (Leathers), 147

Everett, Jane, 66, 154–56, 157, 158, 170, 185–87, 188

Everything is Under Control (Fafard), 93

Exercise with Head Series (Pavelic), 318

exploring expeditions and art, 13–20, 122–25

Eyre, Brenda, 303, 304–5

Eyre, Ivan, 40, 41, 42, 46–47, 148, 177–78, 179, 239, 281–82, 283, 286, 302–5, 319, 320–21

F

Fabric of Belonging Series (Cornelius), 79, 336, 393, 402

Fafard, Joe, 50, 69, 93, 100, 299–301

Falk, Gathie, 9, 104–5, 152, 155, 331, 338

Family (Stubbs), 319–20, 332

Family Series (Serota), 210

Fanshaw, Valentine, 25

Favell, Rosalie, 379–81, 382, 383

Federation of Canadian Artists, 36

Fellows, Christine, 107

Fenton, Terry, 62, 143, 175

Fenwick, Kathleen, 72

figure painting, 330–39

Filer, Mary, 98

Firefly (Proch), 76

Firman, David, 83

First World War, 394–95

Fish Farmers (Yuxweluptun), 376

FitzGerald, Lionel LeMoine, 8, 12, 25, 29, 31, 62, 71, 130–33,

163–64, 165–66, 173, 192, 193–94, 218, 226, 228, 229–31, 237, 299, 316, 353, 395

Flight Path (Eyre), 178

Flight Window of the Alchemy Letter from the Sun to the Moon (Bates), 257, 260

Floating Coats (Au), 332

Floating Coats series (Au), 334

flocking, 75–76

Flodberg, Chris, 182, 183, 207, 210

Flying into Delos (Sabiston), 148

Flying Rondels at Dawn (Sabiston), 149

Flying Rufus (Sabiston), 348

Folds (Reichert), 120, 121

Fontaine, Lita, 220, 267, 364, 366

Foothills Village (Brown), 223, 225

For What? (Varley), 394

The Forks (Head), 245

Forrest, Nita, 331–32

Forty Part Motet (Cardiff), 108, 109

Fountain (Belmore), 378

Four Seasons of '76 (Janvier), 263

Frankenthaler, Helen, 155

Fraser, Sandra, 276

Freakish Acts of Nature and Other Distractions (Flodberg), 207, 210

Friday Night Babysitting (Spence), 308

Frieze (Stubbs), 332

Fringe (Belmore), 378

Fripp, Thomas W., 30

From an Upstairs Window (FitzGerald), 218

From Mother Earth Flows the River of Life (Odjig), 264

Fry, Philip, 372

Funk, Karel, 333–34

Furthermore (Metcalfe), 109

F.U.S.Q.: Tanks for the Memories (Boyer), 400

Future Cities and Virtual Cities Project, 190

G

Gaboury, Etienne, 328

Gabriel's Dream (Serota), 211

Gardner, Tim, 310

Gas Drill (Bobak), 396

Gati, Laszlo, 294, 295

Gee, Erin, 248

General Idea, 48, 69, 102, 103, 107–8

geology, 156–60

Geranium and Bottle (FitzGerald), 218

Gibson, Chantal, 362–63

The Gifted Amateur, Nov. 10th, 1962 (Graham), 83–84, 85

Giniigaaniimenaaning (Looking Ahead) (Belcourt), 386–87, 388

Girl with a Gun (Valko), 404

GLARE (Fenton), 62

glass, 96–98, 159–60, 218, 354, 355, 356, 387, 388, 400

Glyde, Henry (H.G.), 172–73, 175

Godwin, Ted, 44, 242, 243

Gonick, Noam, 378

Goranson, Paul, 396

Gordaneer, James "Jim," 13, 247

Gouthro, Steve, 175–76, 179, 192, 203–4, 320, 341–42

Government Street, Victoria, BC (Rice-Jones), 172

Graff, Les, 136

Graham, Colin, 42–43, 326, 327

Graham, Rodney, 9, 48, 83–84, 85

Grain Elevators Sentinels (Lobchuk), 175, 178

Gramatté, Walter, 324

Grand Western Canadian Screen Shop, 50, 69, 197, 244, 248

The Great Domes of Italy (Taylor), 83

Green Rider (Gouthro), 203, 204

Greenberg, Clement, 44, 72, 141, 225, 239, 242, 246, 258

Gregory, Ken, 104

Grey (Carr), 256, 259

Grey Green Crowd #2 (Cran), 224

Grison, Brian, 329

Grocery Store (Dempsey, Millan, moore and Zab), 209, 211

Ground and Tree (Poitras), 102

Group of Sixty-Seven (Yoon), 286, 310–11

H

Hamilton, Mary Riter, 24–25, 288, 394–95

Happy Blowhole Pendant (Davidson), 264

Harnett, Tanya, 364

Harris, Lawren, 28, 35, 36, 161, 163, 164, 166, 222, 312

Harrison, Ted, 200, 201

Hart, James "Jim," 275, 386

Harvest at Sunset (Lobchuk), 175

Harvey, Don, 121

Hatch, Jr., John Davis, 4

Haukaness, Lars, 25

Hauling (Andrews), 213, 215–16

Haynes, Doug, 240, 242

Head, Bruce, 13, 40, 41, 46, 90, 145–46, 147, 167, 169, 239, 244–46

health, 354–59

Hearne, Samuel, 14, 122

Heath, Terrence, 32, 134–35

HeavyShield, Faye, 367–368

Heckel, Erich, 324

Henderson, James, 133, 137, 142

Hepworth, Barbara, 13

Herd (Thorneycroft), 361

Hide, Peter, 92, 279

High Space Colour (Lochhead), 243

Hime, Humphrey, 16–17, 83, 128, 131, 287

Hind, William, 9–10, 13, 15–16, 17, 202

A History of Canada, 1935 (Gibson), 362

The Hitler Line (Comfort), 395

Hive Scans (Dyck), 346

Hofmann, Hans, 40, 205, 225, 232, 239

Holocaust, 400

Homeward Bound (Kenderdine), 135

Hone, MacGregor, 44

Honest Ed series (Suzuki), 200–201

The Honourable Gildas L. Molgat (Valentine), 297

Hood Series (Funk), 333

Hooker, Marion Nelson, 290, 291

Hopkins, Frances Anne, 19–20

Hopper, Robin, 13, 98, 159, 283

Horizon Detail (Proch), 76

Horse and Train (Colville), 278

Horse Drinking at an Ice Hole (Hind), 15, 17

Houle, Robert, 9, 53, 85, 86, 161, 265–66, 340, 364, 366, 376–77, 379, 383–86, 387

Houle, Terrance, 9, 211, 212–13, 350, 351

House Made of Stars (Cutschall), 268

House of Tea (Warkov), 99, 101, 337–38

Howorth, E.J. "Ted," 61, 67, 69, 76–77, 184, 185, 252, 320

Hughes, Edward J., 192, 193, 212, 214, 396

Hughes, Mary Jo, 200, 317–18

human rights, 361–66

Hunt, Eugene, 9

Hunt, Helen, 302

Hunt, Henry, 272, 301

Hunt, Richard, 9, 80, 82, 91, 272–73, 274, 301–2

Hunt, Tony, 9

Hurley, Robert, 175, 177

I

I awoke to find my spirit had returned (Favell), 382, 383

Icon (Thauberger), 75

Ida Grey (Morton), 39

Imaginal Expression (Stone), 55, 354

In the Silent Hours: The Cancer Paintings of Kelly Clark (Clark), 359

In the Studio (Valentine), 296

Incoming (Thorkelsson), 97, 98

Indian Drums (Sapp), 217, 269

The Indian in Translation (Odjig), 217

Indian Princess (Adams), 312

Indigenous Group of Seven, 50, 80, 244, 250, 262

The Industrial Bureau Doorway (Barraud), 172

inequality/injustice, 371–72

Ingram, Liz, 50

inscapes, 286, 301, 302, 314–29

Intangible Heritage (Vickers), 81, 273, 313

Interland: memories series (Benesiinaabandan), 188–89, 190

Invasion (Brown), 348

Inverted Apex (Tascona), 66

Irving, Tam, 100, 283

J

Jacket #2 (Levine), 337

Jacob Berens (Hooker), 290

Janes, Puck, 158–59

Janvier, Alex, 9, 69, 160–61, 162, 250, 251, 262–63

Jarrod Parsonage (Spence), 307

Johns, Jeanette, 127–28, 129

Johnson, Donalda, 322

Johnston, Frank H., 30

Johnston, Franz, 394

Johnston Falls (Ouellet), 87, 88

Jones, Karin, 363–64, 365

Journey into the Garden (Lochhead), 218

Juice of Life (Carr), 256–57

Jule, Walter, 50, 69, 70, 78, 254–55

Julia and Andrew (McMillan), 298, 299

July. 31/2008 (Kipling), 65

Jungen, Brian, 93, 95, 96, 276, 376

K

Kandinsky, Wassily, 227, 239

Kane, Paul, 5, 15, 17–19, 120, 126–27

Kear, Andrew, 334

Kearns, Gertrude, 398

Kenderdine, Augustus "Gus," 31, 35, 39, 133, 135, 140, 142, 292–93

Kerr, Illingworth, 133, 135, 136, 142

Kerr, Mary, 144, 264

Keszthelyi, Alexander S., 12

Killer Whale (Reid), 262, 275

Kindergarten (Bates), 47

King, John, 151

King, Mackenzie, 36

Kingston Conference, 32, 34–36

Kipling, Ann, 64, 65, 143–44

Kitchen (Serota), 342

Kiyooka, Harry, 240

Kiyooka, Roy, 240, 241

Knowles, Dorothy, 44, 136, 139, 140, 141–42

Koerner, John, 54, 163, 164, 166–68, 399

Kokoschka, Oskar, 322

Komokwa (Hunt), 82

Koop, Wanda, 64–65, 169, 351, 404, 405

Kurelek, William, 203, 214, 216, 315, 316–18

L

La Pérouse, Comte de, 123

Ladyslipper Series (Lobchuk), 74

LaFrenière, Roger, 151–52, 330, 332

Laing, William "Bill," 51, 61, 73, 77–78, 79

Lamb, Mortimer, 292

Landin, Aurora, 330

Landscape #29 (Dukes), 400

Landscape with Crescent Moon (MacQuarrie), 24

Landscape with One Tree and Three Clouds (BAXTER&), 111

Landspace #241 (Yates), 139, 140

Laszlo Gati (Pavelic), 295

Leach, Bernard, 13

Leathers, Winston, 40, 72, 73, 110, 145–46, 147, 169, 239, 246, 248, 252, 253–54, 255

Legacy (Vickers), 80

The Legend of Asessippi (Proch), 112

Leighton, Alfred C., 25–26, 27

Lemay, Marcien, 328

Lesbian National Parks and Services (Dempsey and Millan), 211, 372

The Lesson (Cardinal-Schubert), 388–89, 390

Levine, Marilyn, 332, 336, 337

Lexier, Micah, 286, 311

Life on the Eighteenth Hole (Neel), 400, 402

lifestyles, 202–19

Light Garden Series (Eakin), 83

Light Over the Island (Leathers), 147

Limestone Rocks, Lake Winnipeg (Back), 14

Lindner, Ernest, 32, 33, 34, 36, 40, 44, 63, 133, 134–36, 195

Lindoe, Luke, 99, 136–37, 138

The Line Sketch (Tanabe), 233

liniiwahkiimah (Houle), 350, 351

linocuts, 71, 213, 215

Lismer, Arthur, 31, 135

Little Boy Blue (Pemberton), 10

Little Christmas (Thauberger), 76, 197

Littlechild, George, 383

Loading Zone (Gouthro), 204

Lobchuk, Bill, 50, 52, 69, 74, 175, 178, 301

Lochhead, Ken, 39, 40, 44, 45, 60, 72, 128, 130, 132–33, 218, 223–24, 242, 243, 299

Loewen, Bill, 299

Logged Over Country, Odds and Ends (Carr), 343, 344

Logged-over Hillside (Carr), 343

The Logic of the Plane of

Nothingness/ State II (Jule), 254

Long, Timothy, 195, 217, 279

Longing and Not Belonging (Favell), 379–80, 381

Looking for the Shaman (Houle), 366

Looking Up Into the Blue (Johnston), 394

Lord, Barry, 202

Louis Riel (Lemay and Gaboury), 328

Louise (Comfort), 284, 290, 292

Lucas, David Owen, 181–82

Lum, Ken, 84

Lumberjack's Breakfast (Kurelek), 214, 216

Lynn, W. Frank, 23–24, 171, 173

M

MacDiarmid, Jasper, 22

MacDonald, D., 172

Macdonald, Jock, 27, 35, 239

MacDonnell, William, 398

MacKenzie, Norman, 32, 38, 134, 293

MacQuarrie, Donald, 24

Madill, Shirley, 67, 69–70, 108, 161, 268, 282, 339, 386

Magor, Liz, 48

Mah, Jeannie, 99

Maligne Lake (Harris), 312

Malkin, Mel, 100, 159

Mandala (Wise), 254

Mandala + No. 7 (Bates), 256

Mandala Series (Wise), 250

Manitoba (Janvier), 160, 162, 262

Manitoba Arts Council, 49

Manitoba Farm (Musgrove), 22

Manitoba Landscape (FitzGerald), 132, 230

Manitoba Party 1964 (Kurelek), 203

Manitoba Society of Artists, 21

Manning, Les, 100, 121, 143, 159

Marshalling of the Hallies (Goranson), 396

Martha Street Studio, 69, 184, 345, 404

Martin, Mungo, 9, 82, 272, 301

masks, 62, 93, 156, 272–73, 274, 276, 301, 321, 349

Massey, Vincent, 38, 290

Massey Commission, 38

Massey Report, 42

Mayer, Ernest, 76

Mayhew, Elza, 48, 100, 270–71, 326

Maynard, Hannah, 83, 287–88

Maynard, Max, 29, 195

Maynard, Richard, 287

McAlear, Donna, 380, 381

McCloy, William Ashby, 40, 41, 66, 239, 299

McCue, Terry, 368

MacKay, Allan Harding, 398, 399

McKay, Arthur "Art," 44, 46, 242

McMillan, David, 298–99, 351–52

Melina (LaFrenière), 330, 332

Melnyk, Doug, 104

Melvin, Grace, 27

Memorial Arena (Taylor), 188, 189

Memories for the Future (Stubbs), 282

Mendel Art Gallery, 31, 134

Menuhin, Yehudi, 294

Mercredi, Ovide, 262

Metcalfe, Eric, 108, 109

Midnight (Dukes), 400

Mikuska, Frank, 41, 239

Military Series (Gouthro), 203, 204

Milky Way—Spirit Trail (Cutschall), 268, 269

Millan, Lorri, 105–7, 211, 372

Miller, George Bures, 49, 108

Milne, Barbara, 143, 152–54, 156

Miners' Cottages, Canmore, Alberta (Glyde), 172

Minnie, Anna and Amy (Spence), 308

A Minor Sport in Canada (Boyer), 357

Mirror of Thought (Varley), 314, 315–16

Mishipeshu and Water Spirit (Houle), 266, 364, 366

missing and murdered Indigenous women and girls, 53, 104, 341, 342, 366–68

Misuse Is Abuse: Northern Tundra (Cuthand), 381

Misuse Is Abuse Series (Cuthand), 381

Mitchell, Janet, 172

Mittens (unknown), 6

Mni Wiconi, Water is Life (Fontaine), 364

Mocha Diffusion Series (Hopper), 159

Molar Pass (Leighton), 27

Molgat, Gildas, 296–97

Monkman, Kent, 374–75

Montreal Spring Show (exhibition), 40–41

Moo One (Lobchuk), 52

moore, jake, 209, 211

Moore, Sandee, 104

Morgan, Wayne, 143

Morning Star-Gambeh Then' (Janvier), 251, 263

Morris, Michael, 53, 102

Morrisseau, Norval, 9, 250, 262, 264, 265

Morton, Doug, 39, 44, 121, 242, 344–45

Motel Series (Valko), 201, 217, 369–70

Mother Waiting (Stubbs), 320

Motherwell, Robert, 254

Mount Baker (Vickers), 80, 82

Mudge, Zachary, 124

Muhnedobe uhyahyuk (Houle), 161, 163

Mulcaster, Nonie, 44

murals, 66, 85, 237, 258, 352, 395

Murray, Robert, 91, 222, 279

Museums Assistance Program, 50

Musgrove, Alexander J., 10, 22–23, 32, 34, 35, 290

Music Room, Kindergarten (McMillan), 352

Music School (Dukes), 400

My Family (Hunt), 272

My First Day of Assimilation (Favell), 379, 380–81

My First Pony (Fafard), 93

My Reclining Coat (Au), 335

N

N.E. Thing Co., 102, 108, 109, 111–12

The Named and the Unnamed (Belmore), 113, 115, 342, 366

Nas-win-is (When Night and Day Cross) (Paul), 273, 277

National Gallery of Canada, 25, 52, 72, 112

National Museums of Canada Corporation, 50

Neatby, Hilda, 38

Neel, David, 400, 402

Neepawa Noon I and II (Lobchuk), 74, 175

neighbourhoods, 192–201

Neither Dusk nor Dawn (Jule), 70, 254–55

Nellie At Home (Pepper), 308, 309

Newman, Barnett, 44, 141, 225, 242, 279

Newton, Allison, 203

Nick on the Prairie Facing into the Wind (Gardner), 310

Nickel, Grace, 100, 346–47

Nicoll, Marion, 9, 239–40

Nicolson, Marianne, 353–54

Night Growing Sounds (Bates), 144

Night Shift (Valko), 199

Night Sky Celebration No. 23 (Falk), 152

Night Time (Weatherbie), 194

No. 1 Hard (Nugent), 278–79

No. 1 Northern (Nugent), 92, 279

Nocturne Blue and Gray (Milne), 152, 156

Nocturne Island (Milne), 153

Noland, Kenneth, 140, 141

Norman MacKenzie Art Gallery, 31, 134, 242

North Saskatchewan River (Knowles), 139, 142

North Vancouver Ferry (Bobak), 212

Northern Sun (Harrison), 200

Northwest Triptych (Lobchuk), 74

Not Invisible (Sanderson), 368

November Sea (Smith), 234

Nude Series (Bates), 332

Nugent, John, 91, 92, 278–79

#17 Cosmic Order/in a line plane (Leathers), 111

numerology, 256

Nylon and Lace in the Congo (Cornelius), 393

O

Odds and Ends (Carr), 121

Odeon Theatre Victoria (Suzuki), 198, 201

Odjig, Daphne, 9, 50, 217, 244, 250, 262, 264

Offshore Barge Draws the Beach and Sailing Communities (Bond), 190, 191

Ohe, Katie, 240, 279, 280

Oka crisis, 400–401

Oka Spirit Power (Poitras), 401, 403

Oliver, Keith, 282

Onion Graders (Newton), 203

Onley, Toni, 63, 64, 121, 237–38

Open Space Gallery, 6, 50

Opthamalia Club, 112

Order and Chaos (Serota), 400–401

Osborne, Lyndal, 50

Ouellet, Shelley, 87, 88

Out of the Silence (Reid), 261–62

Overhead (Carr), 134

P

Pacific Gateway Series (Koerner), 166, 168

Package of Philip Morris, Please (Serota), 208, 210–11

Paddon, Ellie, 12, 289

The Pagan (Fontaine), 220, 267, 366

The Paradise Institute (Cardiff), 109

Parfleches for the Last Supper (Houle), 266

Parka series (Cornelius), 336

Parliament Buildings (Hunt), 80, 82

Partz, Felix, 107

The Passion of Coquille St. Jacques (Howorth), 76–77

Paul, Tim, 273, 277

Pavelic, Myfanwy Spencer, 43, 286, 293–95, 296, 316, 318, 326, 331–32

Pavelic, Niki, 294

Payce, Greg, 100

Pear Blues (Serota), 219

Pemberton, Sophie, 11–12, 288–89

The People's Desk (Vickers), 273

The People's Flag (Jungen), 95, 376

A People's History: Quintland (Thorneycroft), 361, 362

Pepper, Thelma, 308, 309

Perception Series (Adams), 115, 213, 342, 359–60

Perehudoff, William, 244, 245

performance art, 102–7, 209, 211, 342, 372, 378

Perreault, Wilf, 192, 195–96

Peterson, Margaret, 222

Phillips, Walter J., 13, 25, 50, 51, 70–71, 196–97

photography, 82–86, 148, 183–84, 187–88, 189, 200, 203–4, 212–13, 286, 287, 305–13, 328, 340, 342, 351–52, 364, 379–81, 384–85, 387

Picture for Women (Wall), 306–7

Pieces of Water #10— El Salvador (Falk), 155

Pike, Bev, 64, 65, 370

Pink Sky (Rogers), 246

Pinnacle I: Marking Time (Bentham), 95

Pinnacle II: Relic of Memory (Bentham), 95

Pinnacle III: Ray of Light (Bentham), 95

Plain(s) Warrior Artist (Favell), 381

Plaskett, Joseph "Joe," 163, 203, 205–9, 232

Plug In Gallery, 6, 50, 55, 244, 322

Poitras, Edward, 49, 102–4, 276

Poitras, Jane Ash, 9, 53, 85–86, 260, 390–91, 392, 401, 403

The Politician (Fafard), 300

Poplar Woods (FitzGerald), 226

Port Mann series (Everett), 186

Portrait of a Black Lady, Seated (Pemberton), 288–89

A Portrait of David (Lexier), 311

Portrait of Lenin, Kindergarten Pripiat (McMillan), 353

Portrait of the Artist as a Young Man (Kurelek), 315, 317–18

portraits, 284–313

Poruchnyk, Alex, 104

Potato Patch, Snowflake (FitzGerald), 31, 131, 132

potlatches, 272

Power of the Spirit of Manitou (Morrisseau), 264, 265

Pragnell, Bartley "Bart," 35, 173

Prairie Boy in Winter, Prairie Boy in Summer (Kurelek), 216

Prairie Boy's Dream (Carther), 96

Prairie Farm (Nicoll), 239–40

Prairie Figures (Bates), 327

Prairie Foothills (Nicoll), 239–40

The Prairie on the Banks of the Red River Looking South (Hime), 128, 131

Prairie Paintings (Tanabe), 232

Prairie Road (Comfort), 26, 223

Prairie Settlers (Bates), 355

Prairie Town (Glyde), 172

Prairie Woman (Bates), 355

Premises for Self-Rule: Constitution Act, 1982 (Houle), 377

Premises for Self-Rule: Indian Act, 1886 (Houle), 377

Premises for Self-Rule: The British North America Act, 1967 (Houle), 376

Premises for Self-Rule: Treaty No. 1, 1871 (Houle), 86, 377

Preservation Reservation (Poitras), 391

Pressure (Lochhead), 218

Pride (Walls, Oklahoma) (Benesiinaabandan), 328

Princess (Mayhew), 100, 270–71

Print and Drawing Council of Canada, 69

printmaking, 48, 50–51, 52, 61, 67–82, 103, 127, 129, 175, 178, 184, 185, 188–89, 197–99, 215, 248, 252, 254–55, 257, 260, 263–64, 328, 336, 344–45, 378, 400, 402, 404

Private Roy (Bobak), 212, 395, 396

Proch, Don, 62, 76, 94, 112–13, 115, 146, 147–48, 156, 158, 276–78, 301, 349–51

Proposed Backdrop for North Shore (Morris), 53

Prototype for New Understanding (Jungen), 93, 95, 96, 276

Provincial Institute of Technology and Art (Calgary), 25

public art, 55–56

Pura, William "Bill," 197, 199–200

Q

Qu'appelle Valley (Henderson), 137

Quartet (Head), 90

Queue (Laing), 78

R

R.E. Hayes (Valentine), 296

Race the Roaring Fraser I (Everett), 170, 187

racism, 359–60

Ray, Carl, 9, 69, 250

Rebecca's Alley, Christina's Alley, Catherine's Alley and *Ellen's*

Alley (Perreault), 195, 196

Reconciliation Pole (Hart), 386

Rector, Willow, 89

Red Angel (Falk), 105

Red Dot (Koop), 404

Red Horse Boarding School (Littlechild), 383

Red Man Watching White Man Trying to Fix Hole in Sky (Yuxweluptun), 376

Red River, Winnipeg (Bergman), 183, 186

Redacted Text (Gibson), 362

REDress Project (Black), 367, 368

Redwood Bridge Reconstruction (Reichert), 184

Redwood Bridge Series (Reichert), 248

Reeve, Gordon, 280

Reflect: Deep Magenta-Luminous Yellow (Kopp), 64

Refugees (Saper), 400

Regina Five, 6, 221, 242, 268

The Regina Five (exhibition), 44

regionalism, 30–36

Reichert, Don, 13, 41, 120–21, 183–84, 223, 239, 246–48, 249, 253, 286

Reid, Bill, 9, 101, 261–62, 264, 273–75

Reid, Mary Hiester, 20

Release (Pavelic), 318

Reliquary / Reliquaire (Fellows and Boyle), 107

Residential School Series (Houle), 383–84

residential schools, 382–91

Retreating Agassiz (Johns), 129

Revolving Shapes (Macdonald), 35

Rice-Jones, Dorothy G., 172

Richards, Cecil, 40, 299

Riel, Louis, 310, 328, 382

The Right Honourable Pierre Elliott Trudeau (Pavelic), 296

Rindisbacher, Peter, 6, 9, 10, 15, 16, 125, 202

Ripples of Loss (McCue), 368

The River (Koop), 351

The River (Xiong), 54, 56

Road to Nowhere (Koop), 169, 404

Robertson, H.J., 14, 122

Rocky Mountain Mining Mask (Proch), 349, 350–51

Rodeo Series (Spence), 308

Rogers, Otto, 244, 246

Rose Red Curtain (Vickerson), 86, 87

Rosebud, Alberta (Glyde), 173, 175

Rotterdam Pioneers New Technologies for a Subterranean Eco-suburb (Bond), 189

Royal Canadian Academy, 25

Running Horses (Fafard), 93

Ryzak, Waine, 98

S

Sabiston, Carole, 87–89, 148–51, 286, 302, 303, 347–48

Samuels, Clara, 44

Sanchez, Joseph, 9, 250

Sand Bank (Eyre), 148

Sanderson, Tristen Jenni, 368

Sandy Bay (Houle), 86, 340, 384–85, 387

Saper, Arnold, 62, 400

Sapp, Allen, 217

Saskatchewan art, 31–32, 38–40, 44, 133–36, 242–44

Saskatchewan Art Board, 38

Saskatoon Art Association, 32

Sawai, Noboru, 76

Scarred / Sacred Waters (Harnett), 364

Scene in the Northwest–Portrait (Kane), 18

Schmidt-Rottluff, Karl, 324

Schoenberg, Arnold, 227

Schouten, Tim, 66, 377–78

Scott, Charles H., 27, 35, 398

sculpture, 40, 61, 62, 77, 78, 91–95, 101–2, 115, 121, 147–48, 156, 158, 159–60, 222, 262, 270–83, 299–302, 320, 328, 332, 336–39, 349–51, 361–63, 384, 398

Second World War, 36–37, 234, 271, 322, 324, 325, 395–98

Segger, Martin, 264

Self-Portrait (Carr), 289

Selkirk, Lord, 14, 122

September Landscape (Snow), 73

Serendipity Tree (Carther), 160

Serenity, Lake of the Woods (Johnston), 30

Serota, Phyllis, 208, 210–11, 219, 342, 400, 401

Seven Grandfathers (Houle), 265–66

Shadbolt, Doris, 164

Shadbolt, Jack (Leonard), 9, 27, 29, 30, 34, 36, 37, 48, 163, 192–93, 225, 226, 234–37, 398

Shaman Never Die: Return to Your Ancestral Roots (Poitras), 392

Shared Space in the Underground City (Bond), 190, 192

Sheldon, Margaret, 172

Sheldon-Williams, Inglis, 133, 142

Shields, Carol, 286, 299, 302

Shimonek, Nicole, 104

Ships and Tower (Binning), 237

Shortt, Angus, 345

Shrinks (Dyck), 339, 346

Shrunken Clothing on the Road (Dyck), 339

Siebner, Herbert, 65–66, 324

Sightlines Series (Koop), 404

Signal 9: Perforated Northern Silence in an Arctic Night (Bates), 229

Signal Hill, 67, 69

Signalman and RCD Armoured Car in Harbour (Hughes), 396

Silent Voices (Stubbs), 320

silkscreening. *See* printmaking

Simmins, Richard, 44, 78

Sinclair, Robert, 143

The Singing Bone (Rector), 89

Sisters (HeavyShield), 367, 368

Sixties Scoop, 382

Sizes 8–46 series (Dyck), 338

Skeleton of the Forest (Lindner), 33

Skelton, Robin, 293, 331

Sky in Skye—The 9th Island—Darwin Night Watch on Barque Marques (Bates), 145

Sky Location, from the L Series (Lochhead), 45, 223–24

Sky Pies (Head), 245

Slavonic Dance 7, Opus 9030 (Koerner), 54, 399

Sled Dogs Attacking a Bison (Rindisbacher), 16.

Sleeping Giant (Head), 167, 169

Sleepless Night (Valko), 369

Smith, Gordon, 151, 163, 231, 232, 233–34, 235

Snider, Gertrude, 35

Snow, John, 9, 71–72, 73

social life as subject, 9–10

societal concerns, 341–72

Sounds Assembling (Brooker), 226–27, 228

Spalding, Jeffrey, 143

Speedway (Andrews), 215

Spence, Sheila, 147, 148, 286, 305, 307–8

Spencer, Sara, 21

Spickett, Ron "Gyo-Zo," 258

The Spirit of Haida Gwaii: The Black Canoe (Reid), 101

Spirit of Haida Gwaii: The Jade Canoe (Reid), 262, 273–74

spirituality, 160–69

spirituality in abstraction, 222–23, 239, 248, 250–69

Spreitz, Karl, 295

Spring (Nicoll), 240

Spring (Pemberton), 11, 12

Spring Breakup #1 & #2 (Howorth), 184, 185

St. Mary's Cathedral, Calgary (Bates), 172

Stafford Street (Pura), 200

Stanbridge, Linda, 280–81

Standing Figures (Stubbs), 329

Status of the Artist legislation, 52

Steady Drift Series (Johns), 127

Steamer at the Old Wharf (Hughes), 212, 214

Steel Mill Series (Gouthro), 192, 203

Still Life (Bates), 218–19

Still Life (BAXTER&), 111

Still Life with Carrot (BAXTER&), 111

Still Life with Eight Bottles (BAXTER&), 111

still lifes, 111, 218–19, 231

Stills—White Red River (Eyre), 283

Stolen Identities (Akinbolaji), 309, 310

Stone, Reva, 55, 114, 354

Storm Gods (Peterson), 222

Street in Victoria (Uhthoff), 172, 174

Structurist Relief in 15 Parts (Bornstein), 276

Structure IV (Stubbs), 282

Struggle for Balance (Monkman), 375

Stubbs, Eva, 37–38, 40, 62, 100, 282, 299, 319–20, 324, 329, 332

Suburb in Winter (Maynard), 195

The Suburbs (Pura), 197, 199–200

Sufic culture, 257–58

Summer Afternoon, The Prairie (FitzGerald), 4, 8

Summer Duo (Eyre), 304

Summer East Kildonan (FitzGerald), 131

Summer Wheat (Christie), 247

Superimposition 1 (Reichert), 184, 247, 249

Superman (Spence), 308

Supermarket (Bobak), 210, 212

Supernatural Eye (Davidson), 275, 278

Sures, Jack, 100, 283

Surrey, Philip, 187

Suzuki, Tad, 198, 200–201

Swimmer (Butler), 332

Swimmer Series (Howorth), 320

Swinton, George, 37, 40, 60, 61, 63, 118, 128, 146–47, 179, 250–52, 253, 299, 322, 324

Syphilis (Cuthand), 356

T

Take Off: Point of Departure and Mode of Travel (Sabiston), 149–51, 150, 347–48

Tanabe, Takao, 151, 163, 231–33

Tanisi keke totamak—Ka cis teneme toyak (Adams), 56

Tartan Love Float (Godwin), 243

Tascona, Tony, 40, 41, 66–67, 69, 206, 239, 258, 260

Taylor, John, 83, 187–88, 189

Ten Artists of Saskatchewan 1955 (exhibition), 44

textiles, 86–89, 95, 148–51, 221, 302, 303, 348, 376

Thauberger, David, 50, 69, 74–76, 196, 197–99

theosophy, 163, 164, 166

Think of the Earth (Brooker), 228

Thirteen Coyotes (Poitras), 102–3, 276

This Sideshow's Leaving Town (Lucas), 181, 182

Thompson, Art, 382

Thorkelsson, Ione, 96–97, 98

Thorn, Anthony, 44

Thorneycroft, Diana, 361, 362

Thunder Dancer, Metamorphosis, Thunderbird (Beardy), 263–64

Thunderbird Series (Benesiinaabandan), 328

Thunderhead (Dempsey and Millan), 107

Tiananmen Square massacre, 53, 181

Tillenius, Clarence, 345

Tisiga, Joseph, 382

Tlingit Chief (Hunt), 301–2

To the End of Time (Boyer), 358

Tobey, Mark, 28, 254

Tonto in Pink (Claxton), 373

Top Hat Series (Clark), 322

totem poles, 270, 272, 273, 276, 386

Town, Harold, 48

Trace (Belmore), 358

Trading Series (Cuthand), 355

Trading: Small Pox (Cuthand), 355

Trading: Typhoid Fever (Cuthand), 355

Traverse, Jackie, 261, 366

Treaty Dress (Cuthand), 381

Trees (Lobchuk), 74

Trudeau, Pierre Elliott, 294–95, 296, 331

Tuele, Nicholas, 313

Tulips (Atkins), 5

Tupper, Jon, 311

Turner, Evan, 41

Two Apples (FitzGerald), 218

Two Finned Killer Whale (Davidson), 264

Tyner, Barbara, 186–87

Typeface Mask (Proch), 156, 158

U

Uhthoff, Ina, 30, 172, 174

Ukrainian Kozaks send a letter to Putin (Boss), 404

Un Livre Ouvert (Pemberton), 12, 289

Untitled (Hurley), 177

Untitled (Bright Coloured Industrial Scene) (Brunst), 176

Untitled (Swinton), 224

Untitled, from the series *Not Quite Dark*, (Whitehouse), 142, 143

Untitled, from the series *Top Hat* (Clark), 323

Untitled (Concentric Circles) (McKay), 46

Untitled (In the Street I) (Lyse) (Wallace), 58, 84, 85

Untitled (Warkov), 68

Untitled #78 (Funk), 333

Untitled Collage 1B (Onley), 64, 238

Untitled—Geometric Abstract (Kiyooka), 241

Untitled Landscape (Tanabe), 232

Untitled sculpture (Hunt), 91

Urban Indian #7 (Houle), 211, 212–13

Urban Indian Series (Houle), 212–13

urban living, 189–92

Urban Rez Series (Monkman), 374

urbanization, 171–82

V

Valentine, Mary, 286, 295–97

Valko, Andrew, 199, 201, 217–18, 286, 297–98, 342, 369–70, 404

Valko, Julia, 298

Vancouver, George, 122, 124

Vancouver Art Gallery, 30

Vancouver School of Art, 9, 12, 25, 27

Vantreight, Ethel, 12, 289

Varley, Frederick "Fred" Horsman, 27, 28, 222, 226, 290, 292, 293, 314, 315–16, 394

VE Day Celebrations (Bobak), 36

Velvet Bunnies (Thauberger), 75

Vera (Varley), 290

Vera in a Green Sweater (Musgrove), 290

Verner, Frederick, 3, 18, 19, 196

Vickers, Arthur, 9, 80, 81, 82, 273, 313

Vickers, Roy, 9

Vickerson, Laura, 86, 87

Victoria Limners Society, 204, 271, 326

video art, 50, 55, 105, 106, 107, 108–9, 113–14, 328, 359, 366, 372, 374, 399

View from the Artist's Bedroom Window, Jericho Beach (Varley), 28

A View of Hippa Island, Queen Charlotte's Islands (Dixon), 125

Vincent Massey (Varley), 290

Vining Street, Victoria (Shadbolt), 193

Vint, Val, 56, 384, 392

Virden Agricultural Fair, 20

V–J Celebrations (Bobak), 395

Voice of Fire (Newman), 44, 225

W

Walking #1 (Laing), 77, 79

Walking #9 (Laing), 77

Walking on Water (Thin Ice) (Nicolson), 354

Wall, Jeff, 9, 84, 305–7

Wallace, Ian, 9, 58, 84–85

Wallace, Robert Charles, 34

war, 36–37, 234, 271, 322, 324, 325, 392–404

Warkov, Esther, 67, 68, 99, 101–2, 336–38, 371–72

Warre, Henry James, 10

Watson, Scott, 378

Watts, Alan, 248

Weatherbie, Vera, 194, 290, 292, 293

Webber, John, 123

Wembley Exhibition, 4

West Broadway Series (Spence), 308

West Coast #2 (Smith), 235

Western Canadian Art Circuit, 38, 42, 43–44

Western Industries, (Steel Pour, Vulcan Iron Works, Winnipeg) (Wilcox), 192, 203

Weston, William, 35

Where the Truth is Written—Usually (Cardinal-Schubert), 390

White Buffalo Calf (Traverse), 261, 366

White Mirage (Eyre), 305

Whitehouse, Diane, 142–43

Who's Who in Canada, 1927 (Gibson), 362, 363

Wiens, Clifford, 278

Wilcox, Georgie, 192, 203

Wild Bill Lobchuk Back Forties Mask (Proch), 301

Wilderness of Days (Bates), 397

Willard, Tina, 374

Willer, Jim, 121

William Berens, Chief of the Saulteaux (Hooker), 290, 291

Williamson's Garage (FitzGerald), 193

Willis, Dorothy, 35

Window on the Landscape Series (Leathers), 253, 255

Windy Day (Surrey), 187, 188

Winnipeg art, 20–25, 40–41, 46–47, 71, 244–46, 341–42

Winnipeg Art Gallery, 21, 49, 50, 244

Winnipeg Main Street (MacDonald), 172

Winnipeg School of Art, 12, 22–23, 40, 239, 244

Winnipeg Show (exhibition), 40–41

Winnipeg Sketch Club, 25

Winnipeg Street, Snowbound (Phillips), 196–97

Winnipeg Women's Art Association, 20–21, 23, 25, 330

Winter Light (Eyre), 304–5

Winter Lot (Eyre), 177–78

Winter Travelling with Dog Sled (Kane), 18

Wise, Jack, 222, 250, 254

With Friends (Tisiga), 382

Within the Landscape (Laing), 78

Wong, Paul, 108

Wood Collage (Ciccimarra), 324, 325

Woodcock, George, 43

Woods, Linus, 161, 163, 165

Workers (Bates), 327

Workers Series (Bates), 204

World Under Still Life
(Shadbolt), 235, 236

*Worn: Shaping Black Feminine
Identity* (Jones), 363–64, 365

Wyers, Jan, 133, 216

X

X-Changes, 69

Xiong, Gu, 53–54, 56

Y

Yates, Norman, 136, 137–40

Yehudi Menuhin (Pavelic), 286

Yell (Eyre), 282

Yellow Bird: Returned
(Benesiinaabandan), 328

Yoon, Jin-Me, 286, 310,
311, 312

York Boat on Lake Winnipeg
(Phillips), 51

Yuristy, Russell, 69

Yuxweluptun, Lawrence Paul,
375–76

Z

Zab, 209, 211

Zach, Jan, 271

Zaporozhian Cossacks
(Kurelek), 317

Zen, 248, 254

Zipper (Ohe), 279, 280

The Zone (LaFrenière),
151, 152, 153

Zontal, Jorge, 107

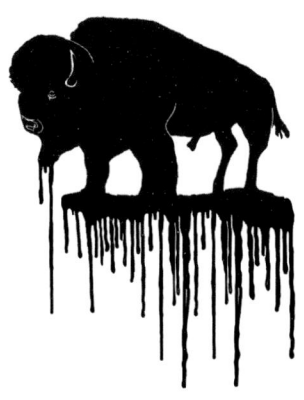

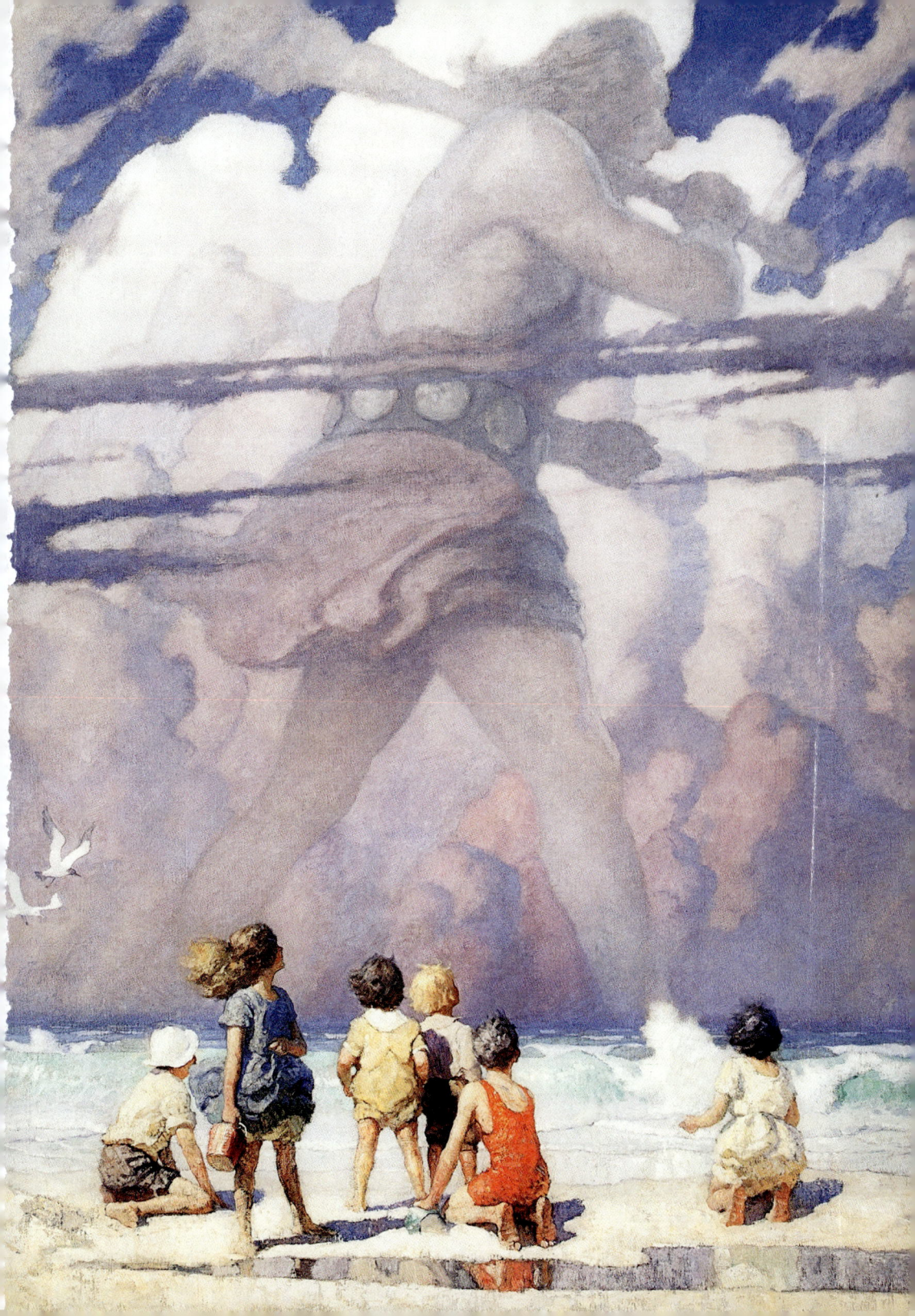